Testimonies

for the Church

Vol. 4

Ellen G. White

Copyright Notice

TABLE OF CONTENTS

Testimony 26

1. Bible Biographies

The lives recorded in the Bible are authentic histories of actual individuals. From Adam down through successive generations to the times of the apostles we have a plain, unvarnished account of what actually occurred and the genuine experience of real characters. It is a subject of wonder to many that inspired history should narrate in the lives of good men facts that tarnish their moral characters. Infidels seize upon these sins with great satisfaction and hold their perpetrators up to ridicule. The inspired writers did not testify to falsehoods to prevent the pages of sacred history being clouded by the record of human frailties and faults. The scribes of God wrote as they were dictated by the Holy Spirit, having no control of the work themselves. They penned the literal truth, and stern, forbidding facts are revealed for reasons that our finite minds cannot fully comprehend.

It is one of the best evidences of the authenticity of the Scriptures that the truth is not glossed over nor the sins of its chief characters suppressed. Many will urge that it is an easy matter to relate what has occurred in an ordinary life. But it is a proved fact that it is a human impossibility to give an impartial history of a contemporary; and it is almost as difficult to narrate, without deviating from the exact truth, the story of any person or people with whose career we have become acquainted. The human mind is so subject to prejudice that it is almost impossible for it to treat the subject impartially. Either the faults of the person under review stand out in glaring relief, or his virtues shine with undimmed luster, just as the writer is prejudiced for or against him. However impartial the historian may design to be, all critics will agree that it is a very difficult matter to be truly so.

But divine unction, lifted above the weaknesses of humanity, tells the simple, naked truth. How many biographies have been written of faultless Christians, who, in their ordinary home life and church relations, shone as examples of immaculate piety. No blemish marred the beauty of their holiness, no fault is recorded to remind us that they were common clay and subject to the ordinary temptations of humanity.

Yet had the pen of inspiration written their histories, how different would they have appeared. There would have been revealed human weaknesses, struggles with selfishness, bigotry, and pride, hidden sins perhaps, and the continual warfare between the spirit and the flesh. Even private journals do not reveal on their pages the writer's sinful deeds. Sometimes the conflicts with evil are recorded, but usually only when the right has gained the victory. But they may contain a faithful account of praiseworthy acts and noble endeavors; this, too, when the writer honestly intends to keep a faithful journal of his life. It is next to a human impossibility to lay open our faults for the possible inspection of our friends.

Had our good Bible been written by uninspired persons, it would have presented quite a different appearance and would have been a discouraging study to erring mortals, who are contending with natural frailties and the temptations of a wily foe. But as it is, we have a correct record of the religious experiences of marked characters in Bible history. Men whom God favored, and to whom He entrusted great responsibilities, were sometimes overcome by temptation and committed sins, even as we of the present day strive, waver, and frequently fall into error. But it is encouraging to our desponding hearts to know that through God's grace they could gain fresh vigor to again rise above their evil natures; and, remembering this, we are ready to renew the conflict ourselves.

The murmurings of ancient Israel and their rebellious discontent, as well as the mighty miracles wrought in their favor and the punishment of their idolatry and ingratitude, are recorded for our benefit. The example of ancient Israel is given as a warning to the people of God, that they may avoid unbelief and escape His wrath. If the iniquities of the Hebrews had been omitted from the Sacred Record, and only their virtues recounted, their history would fail to teach us the lesson that it does.

Infidels and lovers of sin excuse their crimes by citing the wickedness of men to whom God gave authority in olden times. They argue that if these holy men yielded to temptation and committed sins, it is not to be wondered at that they, too, should be guilty of wrongdoing; and intimate that they are not so bad after all, since they have such illustrious examples of iniquity before them.

The principles of justice required a faithful narration of facts for the benefit of all who should ever read the Sacred Record. Here we discern the evidences of divine wisdom. We are required to obey the law of God, and are not only instructed as to the penalty of disobedience, but we have narrated for our benefit and warning the history of Adam and Eve in Paradise, and the sad results of their disobedience of God's commands. The account is full and explicit. The law given to man in Eden is recorded, together with the penalty accruing in case of its disobedience.

Then follows the story of the temptation and fall, and the punishment inflicted upon our erring parents. Their example is given us as a warning against disobedience, that we may be sure that the wages of sin is death, that God's retributive justice never fails, and that He exacts from His creatures a strict regard for His commandments. When the law was proclaimed at Sinai, how definite was the penalty annexed, how sure was punishment to follow the transgression of that law, and how plain are the cases recorded in evidence of that fact!

The pen of inspiration, true to its task, tells us of the sins that overcame Noah, Lot, Moses, Abraham, David, and Solomon, and that even Elijah's strong spirit sank under temptation during his fearful trial. Jonah's disobedience and Israel's idolatry are faithfully recorded. Peter's denial of Christ, the sharp contention of Paul and Barnabas, the failings and infirmities of the prophets and apostles, are all laid bare by the Holy Ghost, who lifts the veil from the human heart. There before us lie the lives of the believers, with all their faults and follies, which are intended as a lesson to all the generations following them. If they had been without foible they would have been more than human, and our sinful natures would despair of ever reaching such a point of excellence. But seeing where they struggled and fell, where they took heart again and conquered through the grace of God, we are encouraged, and led to press over the obstacles that degenerate nature places in our way.

God has ever been faithful to punish crime. He sent His prophets to warn the guilty, denounce their sins, and pronounce judgment upon them. Those who question why the word of God brings out the sins of His people in so plain a manner for scoffers to deride and saints to deplore, should consider that it was all written for their instruction, that they may avoid the evils recorded and imitate only the righteousness of those who served the Lord.

We need just such lessons as the Bible gives us, for with the revelation of sin is recorded the retribution which follows. The sorrow and penitence of the guilty, and the wailing of the sin-sick soul, come to us from the past, telling us that man was then, as now, in need of the pardoning mercy of God. It teaches us that while He is a punisher of crime, He pities and forgives the repenting sinner.

In His providence the Lord has seen fit to teach and warn His people in various ways. By direct command, by the sacred writings, and by the spirit of prophecy has He made known unto them His will. My work has been to speak plainly of the faults and errors of God's people. Because the sins of certain individuals have been brought to light, it is no evidence that they are worse in the sight of the Lord than many whose failings are unrecorded. But I have been shown that it is not mine to choose my work, but humbly to obey the will of God. The errors and wrongdoings in the lives of professed Christians are recorded for the instruction of those who are liable to fall into the same temptations. The experience of one serves as a beacon light to warn others off the rocks of danger.

Thus are revealed the snares and devices of Satan, the importance of perfecting Christian character, and the means by which this result may be obtained. Thus God indicates what is necessary to secure His blessing. There is a disposition on the part of many to let rebellious feelings arise if their peculiar sins are reproved. The spirit of this generation is: "Speak unto us smooth things." But the spirit of prophecy speaks only the truth. Iniquity abounds, and the love of many who profess to follow Christ waxes cold. They are blind to the wickedness of their own hearts and do not feel their weak and helpless condition. God in mercy lifts the veil and shows them that there is an eye behind the scenes that discerns their hidden guilt and the motives of their actions.

The sins of the popular churches are whitewashed over. Many of the members indulge in the grossest vices and are steeped in iniquity. Babylon is fallen and has become the cage of every foul and hateful bird! The most revolting sins of the age find shelter beneath the cloak of Christianity. Many proclaim the law of God abolished, and surely their lives are in keeping with their faith. If there is no law, then there is no transgression, and therefore no sin; for sin is the transgression of the law.

The carnal mind is enmity against God, and it rebels against His will. Let it once throw off the yoke of obedience and it slips unconsciously into the lawlessness of crime. Iniquity abounds among those who talk grandly of pure and perfect religious liberty. Their conduct is abhorrent to the Lord, and they are co-workers with the adversary of souls. The light of revealed truth is turned from their sight, and the beauties of holiness are but as shadows to them.

It is astonishing to see upon what flimsy foundations very many build their hopes of heaven! They rail at the law of the Infinite One as though they would defy Him and make His word null. Even Satan with his knowledge of the divine law would not dare to make the speeches which some law-hating ministers make from the pulpit, yet he exults in their blasphemy.

I have been shown what man is without a knowledge of the will of God. Crimes and iniquity fill up the measure of his life. But when the Spirit of God reveals to him the full meaning of the law, what a change takes place in his heart! Like Belshazzar, he reads intelligently the handwriting of the Almighty, and conviction takes possession of his soul. The thunders of God's word startle him from his lethargy, and he calls for mercy in the name of Jesus. And to that humble plea God always listens with a willing ear. He never turns the penitent away comfortless.

The Lord has seen fit to give me a view of the needs and errors of His people. Painful though it has been to me, I have faithfully set before the offenders their faults and the means of remedying them, according to the dictates of the Spirit of God. This has, in many instances, excited the tongue of slander and embittered against me those for whom I have labored and suffered. But I have not been turned from my course because of this. God has given me my work, and, upheld by His sustaining strength, I have performed the painful duties He has set before me. Thus has the Spirit of God pronounced warnings and judgments, withholding not, however, the sweet promise of mercy.

If God's people would recognize His dealings with them and accept His teachings, they would find a straight path for their feet and a light to guide them through darkness and discouragement. David learned wisdom from God's dealings with him and bowed in humility beneath the chastisement of the Most High. The faithful portrayal of his true state by the prophet Nathan made David acquainted with his own sins and aided him to put them away. He accepted counsel meekly and humiliated himself before God. "The law of the Lord," he exclaims, "is perfect, converting the soul."

Repentant sinners have no cause to despair because they are reminded of their transgressions and warned of their danger. These very efforts in their behalf show how much God loves them and desires to save them. They have only to follow His counsel and do His will, to inherit eternal life. God sets the sins of His erring people before them, that they may behold them in all their enormity under the light of divine truth. It is then their duty to renounce them forever.

God is as powerful to save from sin today as He was in the times of the patriarchs, of David, and of the prophets and apostles. The multitude of cases recorded in sacred history where God has delivered His people from their own iniquities should make the Christian of this time eager to receive divine instruction and zealous to perfect a character that will bear the close inspection of the judgment.

Bible history stays the fainting heart with the hope of God's mercy. We need not despair when we see that others have struggled through discouragements like our own, have fallen into temptations even as we have done, and yet have recovered their ground and been blessed of God. The words of inspiration comfort and cheer the erring soul. Although the patriarchs and apostles were subject to human frailties, yet through faith they obtained a good report, fought their battles in the strength of the Lord, and conquered gloriously. Thus may we trust in the virtue of the atoning sacrifice and be overcomers in the name of Jesus. Humanity is humanity the world over from the time of Adam down to the present generation, and the love of God through all ages is without a parallel.

2. Unity of the Church

Dear Brethren: As all the different members of the human system unite to form the entire body, and each performs its office in obedience to the intelligence that governs the whole, so the members of the church of Christ should be united in one symmetrical body, subject to the sanctified intelligence of the whole.

The advancement of the church is retarded by the wrong course of its members. Uniting with the church, although an important and necessary act, does not make one a Christian nor ensure salvation. We cannot secure a title to heaven by having our names enrolled upon the church book while our hearts are alienated from Christ. We should be His faithful representatives on earth, working in unison with Him. "Beloved, now are we the sons of God." We should keep in mind this holy relationship and do nothing to bring dishonor upon our Father's cause.

Our profession is an exalted one. As Sabbathkeeping Adventists we profess to obey all God's commandments and to be looking for the coming of our Redeemer. A most solemn message of warning has been entrusted to God's faithful few. We should show by our words and works that we recognize the great responsibility laid upon us. Our light should shine so clearly that others can see that we glorify the Father in our daily lives; that we are connected with heaven and are joint heirs with Jesus Christ, that when He shall appear in power and great glory, we shall be like Him.

We should all feel our individual responsibility as members of the visible church and workers in the vineyard of the Lord. We should not wait for our brethren, who are as frail as ourselves, to help us along; for our precious Saviour has invited us to join ourselves to Him and unite our weakness with His strength, our ignorance with His wisdom, our unworthiness with His merit. None of us can occupy a neutral position; our influence will tell for or against. We are active agents for Christ or for the enemy. We either gather with Jesus or scatter abroad. True conversion is a radical change. The very drift of the mind and bent of the heart should be turned and life become new again in Christ.

God is leading out a people to stand in perfect unity upon the platform of eternal truth. Christ gave Himself to the world that He might "purify unto Himself a peculiar people, zealous of good works." This refining process is designed to purge the church from all unrighteousness and the spirit of discord and contention, that they may build up instead of tear down, and concentrate their energies on the great work before them. God designs that His people should all come into the unity of the faith. The prayer of the Christ just prior to His crucifixion was that His disciples might be one, even as He was one with the Father, that the world might believe that the Father had sent Him. This most touching and wonderful prayer reaches down the ages, even to our day; for His words were: "Neither pray I for these alone, but for them also which shall believe on Me through their word."

How earnestly should the professed followers of Christ seek to answer this prayer in their lives. Many do not realize the sacredness of church relationship and are loath to submit to restraint and discipline. Their course of action shows that they exalt their own judgment above that of the united church, and they are not careful to guard themselves lest they encourage a spirit of opposition to its voice. Those who hold responsible positions in the church may have faults in common with other people and may err in their decisions; but notwithstanding this, the church of Christ on earth has given to them an authority that cannot be lightly esteemed. Christ, after His resurrection, delegated power unto His church, saying: "Whosesoever sins ye remit, they are remitted unto them; and whosesoever sins ye retain, they are retained."

Church relationship is not to be lightly canceled; yet when the path of some professed followers of Christ is crossed, or when their voice has not the controlling influence which they think it deserves, they will threaten to leave the church. True, in leaving the church they would themselves be the greatest sufferers; for in withdrawing beyond the pale of its influence, they subject themselves to the full temptations of the world.

Every believer should be wholehearted in his attachment to the church. Its prosperity should be his first interest, and unless he feels under sacred obligations to make his connection with the church a benefit to it in preference to himself, it can do far better without him. It is in the power of all to do something for the cause of God. There are those who spend a large amount for needless luxuries; they gratify their appetites, but feel it a great tax to contribute means to sustain the church. They are willing to receive all the benefit of its privileges, but prefer to leave others to pay the bills.

Those who really feel a deep interest in the advancement of the cause will not hesitate to invest money in the enterprise whenever and wherever it is needed. They should also feel it a solemn duty to illustrate in their characters the teachings of Christ, being at peace one with another and moving in perfect harmony as an undivided whole. They should defer their individual judgment to the judgment of the body of the church. Many live for themselves alone. They look upon their lives with great complacency, flattering themselves that they are blameless, when in fact they are doing nothing for God and are living in direct opposition to His expressed word. The observance of external forms will never meet the great want of the human soul. A profession of Christ is not enough to enable one to stand the test of the day of judgment. There should be a perfect trust in God, a childlike dependence upon His promises, and an entire consecration to His will.

God has always tried His people in the furnace of affliction in order to prove them firm and true, and purge them from all unrighteousness. After Abraham and his son had borne the severest test that could be imposed upon them, God spoke through His angel unto Abraham: "Now I know that thou fearest God, seeing thou hast not withheld thy son, thine only son from Me." This great act of faith causes the character of Abraham to shine forth with remarkable luster. It forcibly illustrates his perfect confidence in the Lord, from whom he withheld nothing, not even his son by promise.

There is nothing too precious for us to give to Jesus. If we return to Him the talents of means which He has entrusted to our keeping, He will give more into our hands. Every effort we make for Christ will be rewarded by Him, and every duty we perform in His name will minister to our own happiness. God surrendered His dearly beloved Son to the agonies of the crucifixion, that all who believe on Him might become one through the name of Jesus. When Christ made so great a sacrifice to save men and bring them into unity with one another, even as He was united with the Father, what sacrifice is too great for His followers to make in order to preserve that unity?

If the world sees a perfect harmony existing in the church of God, it will be a powerful evidence to them in favor of the Christian religion. Dissensions, unhappy differences, and petty church trials dishonor our Redeemer. All these may be avoided if self is surrendered to God and the followers of Jesus obey the voice of the church. Unbelief suggests that individual independence increases our importance, that it is weak to yield our own ideas of what is right and proper to the verdict of the church; but to yield to such feelings and views is unsafe and will bring us into anarchy and confusion. Christ saw that unity and Christian fellowship were necessary to the cause of God, therefore He enjoined it upon His disciples. And the history of Christianity from that time until now proves conclusively that in union only is there strength. Let individual judgment submit to the authority of the church.

The apostles felt the necessity of strict unity, and they labored earnestly to this end. Paul exhorted his brethren in these words: "Now I beseech you, brethren, by the name of our Lord Jesus Christ, that ye all speak the same thing, and that there be no divisions among you; but that ye be perfectly joined together in the same mind and in the same judgment."

He also wrote to his Philippian brethren: "If there be there fore any consolation in Christ, if any comfort of love, if any fellowship of the Spirit, if any bowels and mercies, fulfill ye my joy, that ye be like-minded, having the same love, being of one accord, of one mind. Let nothing be done through strife or vainglory; but in lowliness of mind let each esteem other better than themselves. Look not every man on his own things, but every man also on the things of others. Let this mind be in you, which was also in Christ Jesus."

To the Romans he wrote: "Now the God of patience and consolation grant you to be like-minded one toward another according to Christ Jesus: that ye may with one mind and one mouth glorify God, even the Father of our Lord Jesus Christ. Wherefore receive ye one another, as Christ also received us to the glory of God." "Be of the same mind one toward another. Mind not high things, but condescend to men of low estate. Be not wise in your own conceits."

Peter wrote to the churches scattered abroad: "Finally, be ye all of one mind, having compassion one of another, love as brethren, be pitiful, be courteous: not rendering evil for evil, or railing for railing: but contrariwise blessing; knowing that ye are thereunto called, that ye should inherit a blessing."

And Paul, in his Epistle to the Corinthians, says: "Finally, brethren, farewell. Be perfect, be of good comfort, be of one mind, live in peace; and the God of love and peace shall be with you."

3. Go Forward

The vast armies of Israel marched in glad triumph from Egypt, the scene of their long and cruel servitude. The Egyptians would not consent to release them until they had been signally warned by the judgments of God. The avenging angel had visited every house among the Egyptians and had stricken with death the first-born of every family. None had escaped, from the heir of Pharaoh to the eldest-born of the captive in his dungeon. The first-born of the cattle also were slain according to the mandate of the Lord. But the angel of death passed over the homes of the children of Israel and did not enter there.

Pharaoh, horror-stricken at the plagues that had befallen his people, called Moses and Aaron before him in the night and bade them depart from Egypt. He was anxious that they should go without delay; for he and his people feared that unless the curse of God was removed from them, the land would become a vast burial ground.

The children of Israel were joyful to receive the tidings of their freedom and made haste to leave the scene of their bondage. But the way was toilsome, and at length their courage failed. Their journey led them over barren hills and desolate plains. The third night they found themselves walled in on each side by mountain ranges, while the Red Sea lay before them. They were perplexed and greatly deplored their condition. They blamed Moses for conducting them to this place, for they believed they had taken the wrong course. "This surely," said they, "is not the way to the wilderness of Sinai, nor to the land of Canaan promised to our fathers. We can go no farther; but must now advance into the waters of the Red Sea, or turn back toward Egypt."

Then, as if to complete their misery, behold, the Egyptian host is on their track! The imposing army is led by Pharaoh himself, who has repented that he freed the Hebrews and fears that he has sent them out to become a great nation hostile to himself. What a night of perplexity and distress was this for

Israel! What a contrast to that glorious morning when they left the bondage of Egypt and with glad rejoicings took up the line of march into the wilderness! How powerless they felt before that mighty foe! The wailing of the terror-stricken women and children, mingled with the lowing of the frightened cattle and the bleating of the sheep, added to the dismal confusion of the situation.

But had God lost all care for His people that He should leave them to destruction? Would He not warn them of their danger and deliver them from their enemies? God had no delight in the discomfiture of His people. It was He Himself who had directed Moses to encamp by the Red Sea, and He had further informed him: "Pharaoh will say of the children of Israel, They are entangled in the land, the wilderness hath shut them in. And I will harden Pharaoh's heart, that he shall follow after them; and I will be honored upon Pharaoh, and upon all his host; that the Egyptians may know that I am the Lord."

Jesus stood at the head of that vast army. The cloudy column by day and the pillar of fire by night represented their divine Leader. But the Hebrews did not patiently bear the test of the Lord. Their voices were lifted up in reproaches and denunciations against Moses, their visible leader, for bringing them into this great peril. They did not trust in the protecting power of God nor recognize His hand staying the evils that surrounded them. In their frantic terror they had forgotten the rod with which Moses had changed the water of the Nile to blood, and the calamities which God had visited upon the Egyptians for their persecution of His chosen people. They had forgotten all the miraculous interpositions of God in their behalf.

"Ah," they cried, "how much better for us had we remained in bondage! It is better to live as slaves than to die of hunger and fatigue in the desert, or be slain in war with our enemies." They turned upon Moses with bitter censure because he had not left them where they were instead of leading them out to perish in the wilderness.

Moses was greatly troubled because his people were so wanting in faith, especially as they had repeatedly witnessed the manifestations of the power of God in their favor. He felt grieved that they should charge upon him the dangers and difficulties of their position, when he had simply followed the express commands of God. But he was strong in the faith that the Lord would bring them into safety; and he met and quieted the reproaches and fears of his people, even before he could himself discern the plan of their deliverance.

True, they were in a place from which there was no possibility of release unless God Himself interposed to save them; but they were brought into this strait by obeying the divine commands, and Moses felt no fear of the consequences. He "said unto the people, Fear ye not, stand still, and see the salvation of the Lord, which He will show to you today: for the Egyptians whom ye have seen today, ye shall see them again no more forever. The Lord shall fight for you, and ye shall hold your peace."

It was not an easy thing to hold the hosts of Israel in waiting before the Lord. They were excited and full of terror. They lacked discipline and self-control. Impressed by the horrors of their situation, they became violent and unreasonable. They expected speedily to fall into the hands of their oppressors, and their wailings and recriminations were loud and deep. The wonderful pillar of cloud had accompanied them in their wanderings, and served to protect them from the fervid rays of the sun. All day it had moved grandly before them, subject neither to sunshine nor storm; and at night it had become a pillar of fire to light them on their way. They had followed it as the signal of God to go forward; but now they questioned among themselves if it might not be the shadow of some terrible calamity that was about to befall them, for had it not led them on the wrong side of the mountain into an impassable way? Thus the angel of God appeared to their deluded minds as the harbinger of disaster.

But now, as the Egyptian host approaches them, expecting to make them an easy prey, the cloudy column rises majestically into the heavens, passes over the Israelites, and descends between them and the armies of Egypt. A wall of darkness interposes between the pursued and their pursuers. The Egyptians can no longer discern the camp of the Hebrews and are forced to halt. But as the darkness of night deepens, the wall of cloud becomes a great light to the Hebrews, illuminating the whole camp with the radiance of day.

Then the hope that they might be delivered came to the hearts of Israel. And Moses lifted up his voice unto the Lord. "And the Lord said unto Moses, Wherefore criest thou unto Me? speak unto the children of Israel, that they go forward: but lift thou up thy rod, and stretch out thine hand over the sea, and divide it: and the children of Israel shall go on dry ground through the midst of the sea."

Then Moses, obeying the divine command, stretched out his rod, and the waters parted, rolling up in a wall on either side, and leaving a broad pathway across the bed of the sea for the children of Israel. The light from the pillar of fire shone upon the foam-capped billows, lighting the road that was cut like a mighty furrow through the waters of the Red Sea until it was lost in the obscurity of the farther shore.

All night long sounded the tramping of the hosts of Israel crossing the Red Sea; but the cloud hid them from the sight of their enemies. The Egyptians, weary with their hasty march, had encamped upon the shore for the night. They saw the Hebrews only a short distance before them, and as there seemed no possibility of escape, they decided to take a night's rest and make an easy capture in the morning. The night was intensely dark, the clouds seemed to encompass them like some tangible substance. Deep sleep fell upon the camp; even the sentinels slumbered at their posts.

At last a ringing blast arouses the army! The cloud is passing on! The Hebrews are moving! Voices and the sound of marching come from toward the sea. It is still so dark that they cannot discern the escaping people, but the command is given to make ready for the pursuit. The clatter of arms and the roll of chariots, the marshaling of captains and the neighing of steeds, are heard. At length the line of march is formed, and they press on through the obscurity in the direction of the escaping multitude.

In the darkness and confusion they rush on in their pursuit, not knowing that they have entered upon the bed of the sea and are hemmed in on either hand by beetling walls of water.

They long for the mist and darkness to pass away and reveal to them the Hebrews and their own whereabouts. The wheels of the chariots sink deep into the soft sand, and the horses become entangled and unruly. Confusion prevails, yet they press on, feeling sure of victory.

At last the mysterious cloud changes to a pillar of fire before their astonished eyes. The thunders roll and the lightnings flash, the waves roll about them, and fear takes possession of their hearts. Amid the terror and confusion, the lurid light reveals to the amazed Egyptians the terrible waters massed up on the right hand and on the left. They see the broad path that the Lord has made for His people across the shining sands of the sea, and behold triumphant Israel safe on the farther shore.

Confusion and dismay seize them. Amid the wrath of the elements, in which they hear the voice of an angry God, they endeavor to retrace their steps and fly to the shore they have quitted. But Moses stretches out his rod, and the piled-up waters, hissing, roaring, and eager for their prey, tumble down upon the armies of Egypt. Proud Pharaoh and his legions, gilded chariots and flashing armor, horses and riders, are engulfed beneath a stormy sea. The mighty God of Israel has delivered His people, and their songs of thanksgiving go up to heaven that God has wrought so wonderfully in their behalf.

The history of the children of Israel is written for the instruction and admonition of all Christians. When the Israelites were overtaken by dangers and difficulties, and their way seemed hedged up, their faith forsook them, and they murmured against the leader whom God had appointed for them. They blamed him for bringing them into peril, when he had only obeyed the voice of God.

The divine command was: "Go forward." They were not to wait until the way was made plain, and they could comprehend the entire plan of their deliverance. God's cause is onward, and He will open a path before His people. To hesitate and murmur is to manifest distrust in the Holy One of Israel. God in His providence brought the Hebrews into the mountain fastnesses, with the Red Sea before them, that He might work out their deliverance and forever rid them of their enemies. He might have saved them in any other way, but He chose this method in order to test their faith and strengthen their trust in Him.

We cannot charge Moses with being at fault because the people murmured against his course. It was their own rebellious, unsubdued hearts that led them to censure the man whom God had delegated to lead His people. While Moses moved in the fear of the Lord, and according to His direction, having full faith in His promises, those who should have upheld him became discouraged, and could see nothing before them but disaster, defeat, and death.

The Lord is now dealing with His people who believe present truth. He designs to bring about momentous results, and while in His providence He is working toward this end, He says to His people: "Go forward." True, the path is not yet opened; but when they move on in the strength of faith and courage, God will make the way plain before their eyes. There are ever those who will complain, as did ancient Israel, and charge the difficulties of their position upon those whom God has raised up for the special purpose of advancing His cause. They fail to see that God is testing them by bringing them into strait places, from which there is no deliverance except by His hand.

There are times when the Christian life seems beset by dangers, and duty seems hard to perform. The imagination pictures impending ruin before, and bondage or death behind. Yet the voice of God speaks clearly above all discouragements: "Go forward." We should obey this command, let the result be what it may, even though our eyes cannot penetrate the darkness and though we feel the cold waves about our feet.

The Hebrews were weary and terrified; yet if they had held back when Moses bade them advance, if they had refused to move nearer to the Red Sea, God would never have opened the path for them. In marching down to the very water, they showed that they had faith in the word of God as spoken by Moses. They did all that it was in their power to do, and then the Mighty One of Israel performed His part, and divided the waters to make a path for their feet.

The clouds that gather about our way will never disappear before a halting, doubting spirit. Unbelief says: "We can never surmount these obstructions; let us wait until they are removed, and we can see our way clearly." But faith courageously urges an advance, hoping all things, believing all things. Obedience to God is sure to bring the victory. It is only through faith that we can reach heaven.

There is great similarity between our history and that of the children of Israel. God led His people from Egypt into the wilderness, where they could keep His law and obey His voice. The Egyptians, who had no regard for the Lord, were encamped close by them; yet what was to the Israelites a great flood of light, illuminating the whole camp, and shedding brightness upon the path before them, was to the hosts of Pharaoh a wall of clouds, making blacker the darkness of night.

So, at this time, there is a people whom God has made the depositaries of His law. To those who obey them, the commandments of God are as a pillar of fire, lighting and leading the way to eternal salvation. But unto those who disregard them, they are as the clouds of night. "The fear of the Lord is the beginning of wisdom." Better than all other knowledge is an understanding of the word of God. In keeping His commandments there is great reward, and no earthly inducement should cause the Christian to waver for a moment in his allegiance. Riches, honor, and worldly pomp are but as dross that shall perish before the fire of God's wrath.

The voice of the Lord bidding His faithful ones "go forward" frequently tries their faith to the uttermost. But if they should defer obedience till every shadow of uncertainty was removed from their understanding, and there remained no risk of failure or defeat, they would never move on at all. Those who think it impossible for them to yield to the will of God and have faith in His promises until all is made clear and plain before them, will never yield at all. Faith is not certainty of knowledge; it "is the substance of things hoped for, the evidence of things not seen." To obey the commandments of God is the only way to obtain His favor. "Go forward" should be the Christian's watchword.

4. Indulgence of Appetite

Dear Brethren and Sisters:

I have been shown some things in reference to the church in ——. Individual cases were presented to me which in many respects represent the cases of many others. Among them was that of Sister A and her husband. The Lord convicted him of the truth. He was charmed with the harmony and spirit of the truth, and was blessed in confessing it. But Satan came to him with his temptations upon the point of appetite.

Brother A had long indulged his appetite for stimulants, which had had an influence to becloud the mind, weaken the intellect, and lessen the moral powers. Reason and judgment were brought into bondage to depraved, unnatural appetite, and his birthright, his God-given manhood, was sacrificed to intemperate habits. Had Brother A made the word of God his study and his guide, had he trusted in God and prayed for grace to overcome, he would have had strength in the name of Jesus to baffle the tempter.

But Brother A had never felt the high claims that God has upon him. His moral faculties had been enfeebled by his habits of eating and drinking, and by his dissipation. When he embraced the truth he had a character to form for heaven. God would test and prove him. He had a work to do for himself that no one could do for him. By his course of life he had lost many years of precious probationary time, when he might have been gaining an experience in matters of religion, and a knowledge of the life of Christ, and of the infinite sacrifice made in man's behalf to free him from the fetters that Satan had bound upon him, and enable him to glorify His name.

Christ paid a dear price for man's redemption. In the wilderness of temptation He suffered the keenest pangs of hunger; and while He was emaciated with fasting, Satan was at hand with his manifold temptations to assail the Son of God, to take advantage of His weakness and overcome Him, and thus thwart the plan of salvation. But Christ was steadfast. He overcame in behalf of the race, that He might rescue them from the degradation of the Fall. Christ's experience is for our benefit. His example in overcoming appetite points out the way for those who would be His followers and finally sit with Him on His throne.

Christ suffered hunger in the fullest sense. Mankind generally have all that is needful to sustain life. And yet, like our first parents, they desire that which God would withhold because it is not best for them. Christ suffered hunger for necessary food and resisted the temptation of Satan upon the point of appetite. Indulgence of intemperate appetite creates in fallen man unnatural desires for the things which will eventually prove his ruin.

Man came from the hand of God perfect in every faculty of mind and body; in perfect soundness, therefore in perfect health. It took more than two thousand years of indulgence of appetite and lustful passions to create such a state of things in the human organism as would lessen vital force. Through successive generations the tendency was more swiftly downward. Indulgence of appetite and passion combined led to excess and violence; debauchery and abominations of every kind weakened the energies and brought upon the race diseases of every type, until the vigor and glory of the first generations passed away, and, in the third generation from Adam, man began to show signs of decay. Successive generations after the Flood degenerated more rapidly.

All this weight of woe and accumulated suffering can be traced to the indulgence of appetite and passion. Luxurious living and the use of wine corrupt the blood, inflame the passions, and produce diseases of every kind. But the evil does not end here. Parents leave maladies as a legacy to their children. As a rule, every intemperate man who rears children transmits his inclinations and evil tendencies to his offspring; he gives them disease from his own inflamed and corrupted blood. Licentiousness, disease, and imbecility are transmitted as an inheritance of woe from father to son and from generation to generation, and this brings anguish and suffering into the world, and is no less than a repetition of the fall of man.

A continual transgression of nature's laws is a continual transgression of the law of God. The present weight of suffering and anguish which we see everywhere, the present deformity, decrepitude, disease, and imbecility now flooding the world, make it, in comparison to what it might be and what God designed it should be, a lazar house; and the present generation are feeble in mental, moral, and physical power. All this misery has accumulated from generation to generation because fallen man will break the law of God. Sins of the greatest magnitude are committed through the indulgence of perverted appetite.

The taste created for the disgusting, filthy poison, tobacco, leads to the desire for stronger stimulants; as liquor, which is taken on one plea or another for some imaginary infirmity or to prevent some possible disease. Thus an unnatural appetite is created for these hurtful and exciting stimulants; and this appetite has strengthened until the increase of intemperance in this generation is alarming. Beverage-loving, liquor-drinking men may be seen everywhere. Their intellect is enfeebled, their moral powers are weakened, their sensibilities are benumbed, and the claims of God and heaven are not realized, eternal things are not appreciated. The Bible declares that no drunkard shall inherit the kingdom of God.

Tobacco and liquor stupefy and defile the user. But the evil does not stop here. He transmits irritable tempers, polluted blood, enfeebled intellects, and weak morals to his children, and renders himself accountable for all the evil results that his wrong and dissipated course of life brings upon his family and the community. The race is groaning under a weight of accumulated woe, because of the sins of former generations. And yet with scarcely a thought or care, men and women of the present generation indulge intemperance by surfeiting and drunkenness, and thereby leave, as a legacy for the next generation, disease, enfeebled intellects, and polluted morals.

Intemperance of any kind is the worst sort of selfishness. Those who truly fear God and keep His commandments look upon these things in the light of reason and religion. How can any man or woman keep the law of God, which requires man to love his neighbor as himself, and indulge intemperate appetite, which benumbs the brain, weakens the intellect, and fills the body with disease? Intemperance inflames the passions and gives loose rein to lust. And reason and conscience are blinded by the lower passions.

We inquire: What will the husband of Sister A do? Will he, like Esau, sell his birthright for a mess of pottage? Will he sell his godlike manhood to indulge a perverted taste which only brings unhappiness and degradation? "The wages of sin is death." Has not this brother the moral courage to deny appetite? His habits have not been in harmony with the truth and with the Testimonies of reproof which God has seen fit to give His people. His conscience was not altogether dead. He knew that he could not serve God and indulge his appetite; therefore he yielded to the temptation of Satan, which was too strong for him to resist in his own strength. He was overcome. He has assigned his want of interest in the truth to other causes than the true one in order to cover his own weak purpose and the real cause of his backsliding from God, which was uncontrolled appetite.

This is where many stumble; they waver between denial of appetite and its indulgence, and finally are overcome by the enemy and yield the truth. Many who have backslidden from the truth assign as a reason for their course that they do not have faith in the Testimonies. Investigation reveals the fact that they had some sinful habit that God has condemned through the Testimonies. The question now is: Will they yield their idol which God condemns, or will they continue in their wrong course of indulgence and reject the light God has given them reproving the very things in which they delight? The question to be settled with them is: Shall I deny myself and receive as of God the Testimonies which reprove my sins, or shall I reject the Testimonies because they reprove my sins?

In many cases the Testimonies are fully received, the sin and indulgence broken off, and reformation at once commences in harmony with the light God has given. In other instances sinful indulgences are cherished, the Testimonies are rejected, and many excuses which are untrue are offered to others as the reason for refusing to receive them. The true reason is not given. It is a lack of moral courage — a will, strengthened and controlled by the Spirit of God, to renounce hurtful habits.

It is not an easy matter to overcome an established taste for narcotics and stimulants. In the name of Christ alone can this great victory be gained. He overcame in behalf of man in the long fast of nearly six weeks in the wilderness of temptation. He sympathizes with the weakness of man. His love for fallen man was so great that He made an infinite sacrifice that He might reach him in his degradation and through His divine power finally elevate him to His throne. But it rests with man whether Christ shall accomplish for him that which He is fully able to do.

Will man take hold of divine power, and with determination and perseverance resist Satan, as Christ has given him example in His conflict with the foe in the wilderness of temptation? God cannot save man against his will from the power of Satan's artifices. Man must work with his human power, aided by the divine power of Christ, to resist and to conquer at any cost to himself. In short, man must overcome as Christ overcame. And then, through the victory that it is his privilege to gain by the all-powerful name of Jesus, he may become an heir of God and joint heir with Jesus Christ. This could not be the case if Christ alone did all the overcoming. Man must do his part; he must be victor on his own account, through the strength and grace that Christ gives him. Man must be a co-worker with Christ in the labor of overcoming, and then he will be partaker with Christ of His glory.

It is a sacred work in which we are engaged. The apostle Paul exhorts his brethren: "Having therefore these promises, dearly beloved, let us cleanse ourselves from all filthiness of the flesh and spirit, perfecting holiness in the fear of God." It is a sacred duty that we owe to God to keep the spirit pure, as a temple for the Holy Ghost. If the heart and mind are devoted to the service of God, obeying all His commandments, loving Him with all the heart, might, mind, and strength, and our neighbor as ourselves, we shall be found loyal and true to the requirements of heaven.

Again the apostle says: "Let not sin therefore reign in your mortal body, that ye should obey it in the lusts thereof." He also urges his brethren to earnest diligence and steady perseverance in their efforts for purity and holiness of life, in these words: "And every man that striveth for the mastery is temperate in all things. Now they do it to obtain a corruptible crown; but we an incorruptible."

• The Christian Warfare

Paul presents before us the spiritual warfare and its reward, in contrast with the various games instituted among the heathen in honor of their gods. Young men who were trained for these games practiced close self-denial and the most severe discipline. Every indulgence which would have a tendency to weaken physical power was forbidden. Those who submitted to the training process were not allowed wine or luxurious food, for these would debilitate instead of increasing personal vigor, healthful activity, fortitude, and firmness.

Many witnesses, kings and nobles, were present on these occasions. It was considered the highest honor to gain a simple chaplet which would fade in a few short hours. But after the competitors for this perishable crown had exercised severe abstemiousness and submitted to rigid discipline in order to obtain personal vigor and activity with the hope of becoming victors, even then they were not sure of the prize. The prize could be awarded to but one. Some might labor fully as hard as others, and put forth their utmost powers to gain the crowning honor; but as they reached forth the hand to secure the prize, another, an instant before them, might grasp the coveted treasure.

This is not the case in the Christian warfare. All may run this race, and may be sure of victory and immortal honor if they submit to the conditions. Says Paul: "So run, that ye may obtain." He then explains the conditions which are necessary for them to observe in order to be successful: "And every man that striveth for the mastery is temperate in all things."

If heathen men, who were not controlled by enlightened conscience, who had not the fear of God before them, would submit to deprivation and the discipline of training, denying themselves of every weakening indulgence merely for a wreath of perishable substance and the applause of the multitude, how much more should they who are running the Christian race in the hope of immortality and the approval of High Heaven, be willing to deny themselves unhealthy stimulants and indulgences, which degrade the morals, enfeeble the intellect, and bring the higher powers into subjection to the animal appetites and passions.

Multitudes in the world are witnessing this game of life, the Christian warfare. And this is not all. The Monarch of the universe and the myriads of heavenly angels are spectators of this race; they are anxiously watching to see who will be successful overcomers and win the crown of glory that fadeth not away. With intense interest God and heavenly angels mark the self-denial, the self-sacrifice, and the agonizing efforts of those who engage to run the Christian race. The reward given to every man will be in accordance with the persevering energy and faithful earnestness with which he performs his part in the great contest.

In the games referred to, but one was sure of the prize. In the Christian race, says the apostle: "I therefore so run, not as uncertainly." We are not to be disappointed at the end of the race. To all those who fully comply with the conditions in God's word, and have a sense of their responsibility to preserve physical vigor and activity of body, that they may have well-balanced minds and healthy morals, the race is not uncertain. They all may gain the prize, and win and wear the crown of immortal glory that fadeth not away.

The apostle Paul tells us that "we are made a spectacle unto the world, and to angels, and to men." A cloud of witnesses are observing our Christian course. "Wherefore seeing we also are compassed about with so great a cloud of witnesses, let us lay aside every weight, and the sin which doth so easily beset us, and let us run with patience the race that is set before us, looking unto Jesus the Author and Finisher of our faith; who for the joy that was set before Him endured the cross, despising the shame, and is set down at the right hand of the throne of God."

The world should be no criterion for us. It is fashionable to indulge the appetite in luxurious food and unnatural stimulus, thus strengthening the animal propensities, and crippling the growth and development of the moral faculties. There is no encouragement given to any of the sons or daughters of Adam that they may become victorious overcomers in the Christian warfare unless they decide to practice temperance in all things. If they do this they will not fight as one that beateth the air.

If Christians will keep the body in subjection, and bring all their appetites and passions under the control of enlightened conscience, feeling it a duty that they owe to God and to their neighbors to obey the laws which govern health and life, they will have the blessing of physical and mental vigor.

They will have moral power to engage in the warfare against Satan, and in the name of Him who conquered appetite in their behalf they may be more than conquerors on their own account. This warfare is open to all who will engage in it.

I was shown the case of Brother B, that a cloud of darkness surrounds him. The light of heaven is not in his dwelling. Although he professes to believe the truth, he does not in his daily life exemplify its sanctifying influence upon the heart. He does not naturally possess a benevolent, kind, affectionate, courteous disposition. His temperament is very unfavorable to himself, his family, and the church where his influence is felt. He has a work to do for himself that no one can do for him. He has need of the transforming influence of the Spirit of God. We are bound by our profession as Christ's followers to test our ways and actions by comparing them with the example of our Redeemer. Our spirit and deportment must correspond with the copy that our Saviour has given us.

Brother B is not of a temperament to bring sunshine into his family. Here is a good place for him to begin to work. He is more like a cloud than a beam of light. He is too selfish to speak words of approval to the members of his family, especially to the one of all others who should have his love and tender respect. He is morose, overbearing, dictatorial; his words are frequently cutting, and leave a wound that he does not try to heal by softening his spirit, acknowledging his faults, and confessing his wrongdoings. He does not make efforts to come to the light. There is not with him a searching of heart, of motives, temper, speech, and conduct, to see if his life is like the example. He does not apply God's law to his life and character as his rule of action. The Lord would have a people honest and upright before Him.

Sister B has many trials and the weakness of her own nature to contend with, and her lot should not be made any harder than is positively necessary. Brother B should soften; he should cultivate refinement and courtesy. He should be very tender and gentle toward his wife, who is his equal in every respect; he should not utter a word that would cast a shadow upon her heart. He should begin the work of reformation at home; he should cultivate affection and overcome the coarse, harsh, unfeeling, and ungenerous traits of his disposition, for these are growing upon him. If we poor mortals reach heaven we must overcome as Christ overcame. We must be assimilated to His image; our characters must be spotless.

I was shown that Brother B has not a high sense of the perfection of character necessary to a Christian. He has not a proper sense of his duty to his fellow men. He is in danger of advancing his own interests, if an opportunity presents, irrespective of his neighbor's advantage or loss. He regards his own prosperity as exceedingly important, but is not interested in the fortunes or misfortunes of his neighbors, as a follower of Christ should be. For a trifling advantage to himself, Satan can allure him from his integrity. This darkens his own soul and brings darkness upon the church. "All this," says Satan, "shall be yours, if you will depart from strict integrity. All this will I give you if you will only please me in this, or do and say that." And too often has Brother B been deceived by the adversary to his own hurt and the darkening of other minds.

There are some others in the church who need to view things from a higher standpoint before they can be spiritually minded and in a position where they can discern the mind and will of God, and shed light instead of casting a shadow. Brother B needs to have his eyes anointed, that he may clearly discern spiritual things and also the devices of Satan. The Christian standard is high and exalted. But, alas, the professed followers of Christ lower it to the very dust!

You have need, Brother B, of constant vigilance lest you be overcome by Satan's temptations to live for yourself, to be jealous and envious, suspicious and faultfinding. If you go murmuringly along, you make not one step of progress in the heavenly road. If you stop for a moment in your earnest efforts and prayerful endeavors to subdue and control yourself, you are in danger of being overcome by some strong temptation; you may take imprudent steps; you may manifest an unchristian spirit, which will not only bring bitterness to your own soul, but sadness to the minds of others. You may bring upon them a weight of perplexity and sadness that will endanger their souls, and you will be accountable for this baneful influence. Brother B, if you would escape the pollution that is in the world through lust, you must adorn the Christian profession in all things.

You will say: This is hard work; the way is too narrow, I cannot walk in it. Is the way more strait in this letter than you find it plainly marked out in the word of God? Heaven is worth a lifelong, persevering, untiring effort. If you now draw back and become discouraged, you will certainly lose heaven—lose immortal life and the crown of glory that fadeth not away. Those who have a seat at the Saviour's side on His throne are only that class who have overcome as He overcame. Love for pure, sanctifying truth, love for the dear Redeemer, will lighten the labor of overcoming. His strength will be cheerfully granted to all who are really desirous of it. He will crown with grace and peace every persevering effort made in His name.

If your daily study is to glorify God and subdue self, He will make His strength perfect in your weakness, and you may live so that your conscience will not condemn you. You may have a good report from those who are without. A circumspect life will not only bring great profit to your own soul, but will be a bright light to shine upon the pathway of others, and will show them the way to heaven.

Brother B, how have you governed your own temper? Have you sought to overcome your hasty spirit? With the disposition and feelings you now possess, you will fail of heaven as surely as there is a heaven. For your own soul's sake, and for the sake of Christ, who has given you unmistakable evidence of His infinite love, bring yourself nearer to Him that you may be imbued with His Spirit. Cultivate a spirit of watchfulness and prayer that you may rightly represent the holy faith you profess as a follower of our dear Redeemer, who has left an example in His own life. Imitate our Saviour. Learn of Christ. Endure hardness as a good soldier of Jesus Christ, overcome the temptations of Satan as He overcame, and come off conqueror over all your defects of character.

Christ was a perfect overcomer; and we must be perfect and entire, wanting nothing, without spot or blemish. The redemption which Christ achieved for man was at infinite cost to Himself. The victory we gain over our own evil hearts and over the temptations of Satan will cost us strong effort, constant watchfulness, and persevering prayer; and we shall then not only reap the reward, which is the gift of eternal life, but shall increase our happiness on earth by a consciousness of duty performed, and by the greater respect and love of those about us.

I was shown that there is a general lack of devotion, and of sincere, earnest effort in the church. There are many who need to be converted. Brother C is not a stay and strength to the church. He does not advance in the divine life as he advances in years. He has professed the truth many years, yet has been slow to learn and live its principles; therefore he has not been sanctified through the truth. He holds himself in a position to be tempted of Satan. He is still as a child in experience. He is watching others and marking their failings, when he should be diligently searching his own heart. That readiness to question, and to see faults in his brethren and talk of them to others, is reproved by the words of Christ to one who, He saw, was more interested in the course of his brethren than careful to watch and pray lest Satan should overcome him. Said Christ to His disciples: "What is that to thee? follow thou Me."

It is all that Brother C can do, in the weakness of his nature, to guard his own soul and close every avenue whereby Satan can gain access to insinuate doubts in regard to others. He is in great danger of losing his soul by failing to perfect Christian character during probationary time. He is slow to follow Christ. His senses seem to be clouded and almost paralyzed so that he does not place a proper estimate upon sacred things. He may even now correct his errors and overcome his defects, if he will work in the strength of God.

There are several in the church at —— whose names I cannot call who have victories to gain over their appetites and passions. Some talk too much; they stand in this position: "Report, . . . and we will report it." Miserable indeed is such a position! If all these gossipers would ever bear in mind that an angel is following them, recording their words, there would be less talking and much more praying.

There are children of Sabbathkeepers who have been taught from their youth to observe the Sabbath. Some of these are very good children, faithful to duty as far as temporal matters are concerned; but they feel no deep conviction of sin and no need of repentance from sin. Such are in a dangerous condition. They are watching the deportment and efforts of professed Christians. They see some who make high professions, but who are not conscientious Christians, and they compare their own views and actions with these stumbling blocks; and as there are no outbreaking sins in their own lives, they flatter themselves that they are about right.

To these youth I am authorized to say: Repent ye and be converted, that your sins may be blotted out. There is no time for you to waste. Heaven and immortal life are valuable treasures that cannot be obtained without an effort on your part. No matter how faultless may have been your lives, as sinners you have steps to take. You are required to repent, believe, and be baptized. Christ was wholly righteous; yet He, the Saviour of the world, gave man an example by Himself taking the steps which He requires the sinner to take to become a child of God, and heir of heaven.

If Christ, the spotless and pure Redeemer of man, condescended to take the steps necessary for the sinner to take in conversion, why should any, with the light of truth shining upon their pathway, hesitate to submit their hearts to God, and in humility confess that they are sinners, and show their faith in the atonement of Christ by words and actions, identifying themselves with those who profess to be His followers? There will ever be some who do not live out their profession, whose daily lives show them to be anything but Christians; but should this be a sufficient reason for any to refuse to put on Christ by baptism into the faith of His death and resurrection?

Even when Jesus Himself was upon earth, and walked with and taught His disciples, there was one among the twelve who was a devil. Judas betrayed his Lord. Christ had a perfect knowledge of the life of Judas. He knew of the covetousness which Judas did not overcome, and in His sermons to others He gave him many lessons upon this subject. Through indulgence, Judas permitted this trait in his character to grow and take so deep a root that it crowded out the good seed of truth sown in his heart; evil predominated until, for love of money, he could sell his Lord for a few pieces of silver.

The fact that Judas was not right at heart, that he was so corrupted by selfishness and love of money that he was led to commit a great crime, is no evidence that there were not true Christians, genuine disciples of Christ, who loved their Saviour and tried to imitate His life and example, and to obey His teachings.

I was shown that the fact that Judas was numbered among the twelve, with all his faults and defects of character, is an instructive lesson, one by the study of which Christians may be profited. When Judas was chosen by our Lord, his case was not hopeless. He had some good qualities. In his association with Christ in the work, by listening to His discourses, he had a favorable opportunity to see his wrongs, to become acquainted with his defects of character if he really desired to be a true disciple. He was even placed in a position by our Lord where he could have his choice either to develop his covetous disposition or to see and correct it. He carried the little means collected for the poor and for the necessary expenses of Christ and the disciples in their work of preaching.

This little money was to Judas a continual temptation, and from time to time, when he did a little service for Christ, or devoted a little time to religious purposes, he paid himself out of the meager fund collected to advance the light of the gospel. He finally became so penurious that he made bitter complaint because the ointment poured upon the head of Jesus was expensive. He turned it over and over in his mind, and counted the money that might have been placed in his hands to expend if that ointment had been sold. His selfishness grew stronger until he felt that the treasury had really met with a great loss in not receiving the value of the ointment in money. He finally made open complaint of the extravagance of this expensive offering to Christ.

Our Saviour rebuked him for this covetousness. This rankled in the heart of Judas, until, for a small sum of money, he consented to betray his Lord. There will be those among Sabbathkeepers who are no truer at heart than was Judas; but the cases of such should be no excuse to keep others from following Christ.

God loves the children of Brother D, but they are in fearful danger of feeling whole, and in no need of a physician. Trusting in their own righteousness will never save them. They must feel the need of a Saviour. Christ came to save sinners. Said Jesus: "I came not to call the righteous, but sinners to repentance." The Pharisees, who felt that they were righteous, and who trusted in their good works, felt no need of a Saviour. They felt that they were well enough off without Christ.

The dear children of Brother D should plead with Jesus to reveal to them their sinfulness, and then ask Him to reveal Himself as their sin-pardoning Saviour. These precious children must not be deceived and miss eternal life. Except they are converted they cannot enter the kingdom of heaven. They must wash their robes of character in the blood of the Lamb. Jesus invites them to take the steps that sinners must take in order to become His children. He has given them an example in life in submitting to the ordinance of baptism. He is our example in all things.

God requires these children to give Him their hearts' best and holiest affections. He has bought them with His own blood. He claims their service. They are not their own. Jesus has made infinite sacrifice for them. A pitying, loving Saviour will receive them if they will come to Him just as they are, and depend on His righteousness and not on their own merits.

God pities and loves the youth of ——, and He wants them to find happiness in Him. He died to redeem them. He will bless them if they come to Him in meekness and sincerity. He will be found of them, if they seek Him with all the heart.

5. Choosing Earthly Treasure

I have been shown the condition of God's people. They are stupefied by the spirit of the world. They are denying their faith by their works. I was pointed back to ancient Israel. They had great light and exalted privileges; yet they did not live up to the light nor appreciate their advantages, and their light became darkness. They walked in the light of their own eyes instead of following the leadings of God. The history of the children of Israel was written for the benefit of those who live in the last days, that they may avoid following their example of unbelief.

Brother E, you were shown me enshrouded in darkness. The love of the world had taken entire control of your being. The very best of your days are past. Your vitality and power of endurance, as far as physical labor is concerned, are enfeebled; and now, when you should be able to look back on a life of noble effort in blessing others and glorifying God, you can only have regret, and realize a want of happiness and peace. You are not living a life which will meet the approval of God. Your spiritual, your eternal interests, are made secondary. Brain, bone, and muscle have been taxed to the utmost. Why all this expenditure of strength? Why this accumulation of cares and burdens for your family to bear? What is your reward? The satisfaction of laying up for yourself a treasure upon earth, which Christ has forbidden and which will prove a snare to your soul.

In Christ's Sermon on the Mount He says: "Lay not up for yourselves treasures upon earth, where moth and rust doth corrupt, and where thieves break through and steal: but lay up for yourselves treasures in heaven." If you lay up treasures in heaven, you do it for yourself, you are working for your own interest. Your treasure, my dear brother, is laid up on the earth, and your interest and affections are on your treasure. You have cultivated a love for money, for houses and lands, until it has absorbed the powers of your mind and being, and your love for worldly possessions has been greater than your love for your Creator and for the souls for whom Christ died. The god of this world has blinded your eyes so that eternal things are not valued.

In the wilderness of temptation Christ met the great leading temptations that would assail man. There He encountered, singlehanded, the wily, subtle foe, and overcame him. The first great temptation was upon appetite; the second, presumption; the third, love of the world. Satan has overcome his millions by tempting them to the indulgence of appetite. Through the gratification of the taste, the nervous system becomes excited and the brain power enfeebled, making it impossible to think calmly or rationally. The mind is unbalanced. Its higher, nobler faculties are perverted to serve animal lust, and the sacred, eternal interests are not regarded. When this object is gained, Satan can come with his two other leading temptations and find ready access. His manifold temptations grow out of these three great leading points.

Presumption is a common temptation, and as Satan assails men with this, he obtains the victory nine times out of ten. Those who profess to be followers of Christ, and claim by their faith to be enlisted in the warfare against all evil in their nature, frequently plunge without thought into temptations from which it would require a miracle to bring them forth unsullied. Meditation and prayer would have preserved them and led them to shun the critical, dangerous position in which they placed themselves when they gave Satan the advantage over them. The promises of God are not for us rashly to claim while we rush on recklessly into danger, violating the laws of nature and disregarding prudence and the judgment with which God has endowed us. This is the most flagrant presumption.

The thrones and kingdoms of the world and the glory of them were offered to Christ if He would only bow down to Satan. Never will man be tried with temptations as powerful as those which assailed Christ. Satan came with worldly honor, wealth, and the pleasures of life, and presented them in the most attractive light to allure and deceive. "All these things," said he to Christ, "will I give Thee, if Thou wilt fall down and worship me." Christ repelled the wily foe and came off victor.

Satan has better success in approaching man. All this money, this gain, this land, this power, these honors and riches, will I give thee—for what? His conditions generally are, that integrity shall be yielded, conscientiousness blunted, and selfishness indulged. Through devotion to worldly interests, Satan receives all the homage he asks. The door is left open for him to enter as he pleases, with his evil train of impatience, love of self, pride, avarice, overreaching, and his whole catalogue of evil spirits. Man is charmed and treacherously allured on to ruin. If we yield ourselves to worldliness of heart and life, Satan is satisfied.

Christ's example is before us. He overcame Satan, showing us how we may also overcome. Christ resisted Satan with scripture. He might have had recourse to His own divine power, and used His own words; but He said: "It is written, Man shall not live by bread alone, but by every word that proceedeth out of the mouth of God." To the second temptation He said: "It is written again, Thou shalt not tempt the Lord thy God." Christ's example is before us. If the Sacred Scriptures were studied and followed, the Christian would be fortified to meet the wily foe; but the word of God is neglected, and disaster and defeat follow.

Dear brother, you have neglected to heed the testimonies of warning given you years ago showing you that the enemy was upon your track to open before you the charms of this world, urging you to choose earthly treasure and sacrifice the heavenly reward. Brother E, you cannot afford to do this; there is too much at stake. "What shall it profit a man, if he shall gain the whole world, and lose his own soul? Or what shall a man give in exchange for his soul?" You are selling your soul at a cheap market. You cannot afford to make this great sacrifice. God has entrusted talents to your stewardship. They are your means and your influence. He wishes to test and prove you.

You should have lost no time, but should have commenced immediately to increase your Master's store. Had you done this, your success would have been equal to your industry, perseverance, and zeal in applying the capital placed in your hands; your talents or influence — setting aside the means which you could have called to your aid — would have turned many souls from error to truth and righteousness. These souls would have labored for others, and thus influence and means would have constantly increased and multiplied in the Master's cause; and for the faithful improvement of your talents you would have heard from the Master the most gracious words that shall ever fall upon the ear: "Well done, thou good and faithful servant: thou hast been faithful over a few things, I will make thee ruler over many things: enter thou into the joy of thy Lord."

Brother E, had you directed the powers of your intellect into the right channel, serving your heavenly Father, you would have been growing stronger in the truth, stronger in spirit and power, and would now be a pillar of the church in ——, and, by your example as well as by giving the reasons of our faith from the Scriptures, would be a successful teacher of the truth. Had the powers of mind which you have employed in getting property been used to bring souls from darkness to the light, you would have met the approval of God and been highly successful.

Those who have but small capacities, sanctified by the love of God, can do good for the Master; but those who have quick, discerning minds may employ them in His exalted work with grand results. To wrap in a napkin the talents God has entrusted to them, and hide them in the earth, thus depriving Him of their increase, is a great wrong. We are probationers. The Master is coming to investigate our course, and He will inquire what use has been made of the talents lent us.

Brother E, what use are you making of the talents God has placed in your care? Have you done what you could to enlighten the minds of men in regard to truth, or have you found no time from your business cares and perplexities to devote to this work? It is a crime to use the bounties of God as you have done, to diminish your physical strength and separate your affections from God. "Ye cannot serve God and mammon." You cannot love this world and love the truth of God. "Know ye not that the friendship of the world is enmity with God? whosoever therefore will be a friend of the world is the enemy of

God." "Love not the world, neither the things that are in the world. If any man love the world, the love of the Father is not in him."

You are not a happy man. Your family is not a happy family. Angels of God do not come in and abide with you. When the religion of Christ rules in the heart, conscience approves, and peace and happiness reign; perplexity and trouble may surround, yet there is light in the soul.

Submission, love, and gratitude to God keep sunshine in the heart, though the day may be ever so cloudy. Self-denial and the cross of Christ are before you. Will you lift the cross? Your children have been blessed by a mother's prayers. They have loved religion. They have tried to resist temptation and to live lives of prayer. Sometimes they have tried very hard; but your example before them, your love and devotion to the world, and your close application to business, have withdrawn their minds from spiritual things and turned them to earth again. Satan has been upon their track to lead them to love the world and the things of the world. They have gradually lost their confidence in God, have neglected secret prayer and religious duties, and have withdrawn their interest from holy things.

Dear Brother E, you have made a great mistake in giving this world your ambition. You are exacting and sometimes impatient, and at times require too much of your son. He has become discouraged. At your house it has been work, work, work, from early morning until night. Your large farm has brought extra cares and burdens into your house. You have talked upon business; for business was primary in your mind, and "out of the abundance of the heart the mouth speaketh." Has your example in your family exalted Christ and His salvation above your farming interest and your desire for gain? If your children fail of everlasting life, the blood of their souls will surely be found on the garments of their father.

The mother did her duty faithfully. She will hear the "Well done" as she rises in the resurrection morning. Her first inquiry will be for her children, who were the burden of her prayers during the latter portion of her life. Can you present them with beautiful characters that will give them a moral fitness for the society of angels, or will they be tarnished and sullied by the pollutions of the world? Will they be found "partakers of the divine nature, having escaped the corruption that is in the world through lust"?

Will they be as pillars polished after the similitude of a palace; or will they be found lovers of the world, cursed with the spirit of avarice, and their bright and noble qualities buried in oblivion? Your course will do much to determine the future destiny of your children. If you continue to drown your powers of mind in worldly care and scheming, you will remain a stumbling block to them. They see that, while professing Christianity, you have made no spiritual advancement, but are morally dwarfed. This is true. Your mind has been concentrated on earthly things, and, as a result, you have developed great power in this direction. You are decidedly a worldly businessman, but God designed that you should use your ability and influence in a higher calling.

You are dazzled and blinded by the god of this world. Oh, what a terrible insanity is upon you! You may gather together earthly treasure, but it will be destroyed in the great conflagration. If you now return unto the Lord, use your talents of means and influence for His glory, and send your treasure before you to heaven, you will not meet with a total loss.

The great conflagrations and the disasters by sea and land that have visited our country were the special providences of God, a warning of what is about to come upon the world. God would show man that He can kindle upon his idols a fire that water cannot quench. The great general conflagration is but just ahead, when all this wasted labor of life will be swept away in a night and day. The treasure laid up in heaven will be safe. No thief can approach nor moth corrupt it.

A young man came to Christ and said: "Good Master, what good thing shall I do, that I may have eternal life?" Jesus bade him keep the commandments. He returned answer: Lord, "All these things have I kept from my youth up: what lack I yet?" Jesus looked with love upon the young man, and faithfully pointed out to him his deficiency in keeping the commandments. He did not love his neighbor as himself. Christ showed him his true character. His selfish love of riches was a defect, which, if not removed, would debar him from heaven. "If thou wilt be perfect, go and sell that thou hast, and give to the poor, and thou shalt have treasure in heaven: and come and follow Me." Christ would have him understand that He required nothing of him more than He Himself had experienced. All He asked was that he should follow His example.

Christ left His riches and glory, and became poor, that man through His poverty might be made rich. He now requires him for the sake of these riches to yield earthly things and secure heaven. Christ knew that while the affections were upon worldly treasure, they would be withdrawn from God; therefore He said to the lawyer: "Go and sell that thou hast, and give to the poor, and thou shalt have treasure in heaven: and come and follow Me." How did he receive the words of Christ? Was he rejoiced that he could secure the heavenly treasure? He was very sorrowful, for he had great possessions. To him riches were honor and power. The great amount of his treasure made such a disposal of it seem like an impossibility.

Here is the danger of riches to the avaricious man. The more he gains, the harder it is for him to be generous. To diminish his wealth is like parting with life. Rather than do this, he turns from the attractions of the immortal reward, in order to retain and increase his earthly possessions. He accumulates and hoards. Had he kept the commandments, his worldly possessions would not have been so great. How could he, while plotting and striving for self, love God with all his heart, and with all his mind, and with all his strength, and his neighbor as himself? Had he distributed to the necessities of the poor and blessed his fellow men with a portion of his means as their wants demanded, he would have been far happier and would have had greater heavenly treasure and less of earth upon which to place his affections.

Christ assured the young man who came to Him that if he would obey His requirements, he should have treasure in heaven. This world-loving man was very sorrowful. He wanted heaven, but he desired to retain his wealth. He renounced immortal life for the love of money and power. Oh, what a miserable exchange! Yet many are doing this who profess to keep all the commandments of God. You, dear brother, are in danger of doing the same, but you do not realize it. Be not offended because I lay this matter so plainly before you. God loves you. How poorly have you returned His love!

I was shown that in your first experience your heart was all aglow with the truth; your mind was absorbed in the study of the Scriptures; you saw new beauty in every line. Then the good seed sown in your heart was springing up and bearing fruit to the glory of God. But after a time the cares of this life and the deceitfulness of riches choked the good seed of the word of God sown in your heart, and you failed to bring forth fruit. The truth struggled for supremacy in your mind, but the cares of this life and the love of other things gained the victory. Satan sought, through the attractions of this world, to enchain you and paralyze your moral powers so that you should have no sense of God's claims upon you, and he has nearly succeeded.

Now, dear brother, you must make a most earnest, persevering effort to dislodge the enemy and assert your liberty; for he has made you a slave to this world until your love of gain has become a ruling passion. Your example to others has been bad; selfish interests have been prominent. By profession you say to the world: My citizenship is not here, but above; while your works decidedly say that you are a dweller on the earth. As a snare shall the day of judgment come upon all who dwell on the face of the earth. Your profession is only a hindrance to souls. You have not corresponding works. "I know thy works" (not thy profession), says the True Witness. God is now sifting His people, testing their purposes and their motives. Many will be but as chaff—no wheat, no value in them.

Christ has committed to your trust talents of means and of influence, and He has said to you: Improve these till I come. When the Master cometh and reckoneth with His servants, and all are called to the strictest account as to how they have used the talents entrusted to them, how will you, my dear brother, bear the investigation? Will you be prepared to return to the Master His talents doubled, laying before Him both principal and interest, showing that you have been a judicious as well as faithful and persevering worker in His service? Brother E, if you follow the course that you have pursued for years, your case will be correctly represented by the servant who wrapped his talent in a napkin and buried it in the earth, that is, hid it in the world. Those to whom talents were entrusted, received reward for the labor expended in exact proportion to the fidelity, perseverance, and earnest effort made in trading with their Lord's goods.

God holds you as His debtor, and also as debtor to your fellow men who have not the light and truth. God has given you light, not to hide under a bushel, but to set on a candlestick that all in the house may be benefited. Your light should shine to others to enlighten souls for whom Christ died. The grace of God ruling in your heart, and bringing your mind and thoughts into subjection to Jesus, would make you a powerful man on the side of Christ and the truth.

Said Paul: "I am debtor both to the Greeks, and to the barbarians; both to the wise, and to the unwise." God had revealed to Paul His truth, and in so doing made him a debtor to those who were in darkness, to enlighten them. You have not had a proper sense of your accountability before God. You are handling your Lord's talents. You have powers of mind that if employed in the right direction would make you a co-worker with Christ and His angels. Had your mind been turned in the direction of doing good, of placing the truth before others, you would now be qualified to become a successful laborer for God, and as your reward you would see many souls saved that would be as stars in the crown of your rejoicing.

How can the value of your houses and lands bear comparison with that of precious souls for whom Christ died? Through your instrumentality these souls may be saved with you in the kingdom of glory, but you cannot take with you there the smallest portion of your earthly treasure. Acquire what you may, preserve it with all the jealous care you are capable of exercising, and yet the mandate may go forth from the Lord, and in a few hours a fire which no skill can quench may destroy the accumulations of your entire life and lay them a mass of smoldering ruins. This was the case with Chicago. God's word had gone forth to lay that city in ruins. This is not the only city that will realize the visible marks of God's displeasure. He has made a beginning, but not an end. The sword of His wrath is stretched out over the people who by their pride and wickedness have provoked the displeasure of a just God.

Storms, earthquakes, whirlwinds, fire, and the sword will spread desolation everywhere, until men's hearts shall fail them for fear and for looking after those things which shall come upon the earth. You know not how small a space is between you and eternity. You know not how soon your probation may close.

Make ready, my brother, for the Master to demand your talents, both principal and interest! To save souls should be the lifework of everyone who professes Christ. We are debtors to the world for the grace given us of God, for the light which has shone upon us, and for the discovered beauty and power of the truth. You may devote your entire existence to laying up treasures upon earth, but what will they advantage you when your life here closes, or when Christ makes His appearance? Not a farthing can you take with you. And just as high as your worldly honors and riches have exalted you here to the neglect of your spiritual life, just so much lower will you sink in moral worth before the great tribunal of God's judgment.

How will this wealth for which you have bartered your soul be appropriated, should you be suddenly called to close your probation, and your voice no longer control it? "What shall it profit a man, if he shall gain the whole world, and lose his own soul?" Your means are of no more value than sand, only as used to provide for the daily necessities of life and to bless others and advance the cause of God. God has given you testimonies of warning and encouragement, but you have turned from them. You have doubted the Testimonies. When you come back and gather up the rays of light, and take the position that the Testimonies are from God, then you will be settled in your belief and will not thus waver in darkness and weakness.

You can be a blessing to the church at——. You can be a pillar there even now if you will come to the light and walk in it. God calls after you again. He seeks to reach you, girded about with selfishness as you are, and covered with the cares of this life. He invites you to withdraw your affections from the world and place them upon heavenly things. In order to know the will of God, you must study it, rather than follow your inclinations and the natural bent of your own mind. "What wilt Thou have me to do?" should be the earnest, anxious inquiry of your heart.

The weight of the wrath of God will fall upon those who have misspent their time and served mammon instead of their Creator. If you live for God and heaven, pointing out the way of life to others, you will go onward and upward to higher and holier joys. You will be rewarded with the "Well done, thou good and faithful servant: . . . enter thou into the joy of thy Lord." The joy of Christ was that of seeing souls redeemed and saved in His glorious kingdom. "Who for the joy that was set before Him endured the cross, despising the shame, and is set down at the right hand of the throne of God."

To gain the treasures of this world, and use them as you have done to separate your affections from God, will be to you in the end a terrible curse. You do not take time to read, to meditate, or to pray; and you have not taken time to instruct your children, keeping before them their highest interest. God loves your children; but they have had little encouragement to live a religious life. If you destroy their faith in the Testimonies you cannot reach them. The minds of poor, fallible mortals should be disciplined and educated in spiritual things. When the training is all in reference to the world, and to making a success of acquiring property, how can spiritual growth be attained? It is an impossibility. You, my brother, and your family might have risen to the full stature of men and women in Christ Jesus had you felt one half the interest to perfect Christian character and to serve the Lord that you have had to serve the world.

God is not well pleased that His servants should be ignorant of His divine will, novices in spiritual understanding, but wise in worldly wisdom and knowledge. Your earthly interest can bear no comparison with your eternal welfare.

God has a higher work for you to do than that of acquiring property. You need a deep and thorough work accomplished for you. Your entire family need it, and may God help you all to attain perfection of Christian character. Your children can and should be a blessing to the youth of your community. By their example, by their conversation and actions, they can glorify their heavenly Father and grace the cause of religion.

6. True Benevolence

Dear Brother and Sister F:

I will now try to write what has been presented before me in regard to you; for I feel that it is time for this church to get their hearts in order and make diligent work for eternity. Both of you love the truth and want to obey it; but you are inexperienced. I was shown that you would be placed in circumstances where you would be tried and tested, and that traits of character would be revealed which you were not aware that you possessed.

Many who have never been placed in positions of trial appear to be excellent Christians, their lives seem faultless; but God sees that they have traits of character that must be revealed to them before they can perceive and correct them. Simeon prophesied under the inspiration of the Holy Ghost, and said unto Mary in reference to Jesus: "Behold, this Child is set for the fall and rising again of many in Israel; and for a sign which shall be spoken against; (yea, a sword shall pierce through thy own soul also,) that the thoughts of many hearts may be revealed."

In the providence of God we are placed in different positions to call into exercise qualities of mind calculated to develop character under a variety of circumstances. "Whosoever shall keep the whole law, and yet offend in one point, he is guilty of all." Professed Christians may live unexceptionable lives so far as outward appearance is concerned; but when a change of circumstances throws them into entirely different positions, strong traits of character are discovered, which would have remained hidden had their surroundings continued the same.

I was shown that you have selfish traits which you have need to strictly guard against. You will be in danger of regarding your prosperity and your convenience irrespective of the prosperity of others. You do not possess a spirit of self-denial that resembles the great Exemplar. You should cultivate benevolence, which will bring you more into harmony with the spirit of Christ in His disinterested benevolence. You need more human sympathy. This is a quality of our natures which God has given us to render us charitable and kind to those with whom we are brought in contact. We find it in men and women whose hearts are not in unison with Christ, and it is a sad sight indeed when His professed followers lack this great essential of Christianity. They do not copy the Pattern, and it is impossible for them to reflect the image of Jesus in their lives and deportment.

When human sympathy is blended with love and benevolence, and sanctified by the Spirit of Jesus, it is an element which can be productive of great good. Those who cultivate benevolence are not only doing a good work for others, and blessing those who receive the good action, but they are benefiting themselves by opening their hearts to the benign influence of true benevolence. Every ray of light shed upon others will be reflected upon our own hearts. Every kind and sympathizing word spoken to the sorrowful, every act to relieve the oppressed, and every gift to supply the necessities of our fellow beings, given or done with an eye to God's glory, will result in blessings to the giver. Those who are thus working are obeying a law of heaven and will receive the approval of God. The pleasure of doing good to others imparts a glow to the feelings which flashes through the nerves, quickens the circulation of the blood, and induces mental and physical health.

Jesus knew the influence of benevolence upon the heart and life of the benefactor, and He sought to impress upon the minds of His disciples the benefits to be derived from the exercise of this virtue. He says: "It is more blessed to give than to receive." He illustrates the spirit of cheerful benevolence, which should be exercised toward friends, neighbors, and strangers, by the parable of the man who journeyed from Jerusalem to Jericho, and fell among thieves, "which stripped him of his raiment, and wounded him, and departed, leaving him half dead."

Notwithstanding the exalted profession of piety made by the priest and the Levite, their hearts were not stirred with pitying tenderness for the sufferer. A Samaritan who made no such lofty pretensions to righteousness passed that way, and when he saw the stranger's need he did not regard him with mere idle curiosity, but he saw a human being in distress, and his compassion was excited. He immediately "went to him, and bound up his wounds, pouring in oil and wine, and set him on his own beast, and brought him to an inn, and took care of him." And on the morrow he left him in charge of the host, with the assurance that he would pay all charges on his return. Christ asks: "Which now of these three, thinkest thou, was neighbor unto him that fell among the thieves? And he said, He that showed mercy on him. Then said Jesus unto him, Go, and do thou likewise."

Here Jesus wished to teach His disciples the moral obligations which are binding upon man to his fellow man. Whoever neglects to carry out the principles illustrated by this lesson is not a commandment keeper, but, like the Levite, he breaks the law of God which he pretends to revere. There are some, who, like the Samaritan, make no pretensions to exalted piety, yet who have a high sense of their obligations to their fellow men and have far more charity and kindness than some who profess great love to God, but fail in good works toward His creatures.

Those truly love their neighbor as themselves who realize their responsibilities and the claims that suffering humanity has upon them, and carry out the principles of God's law in their daily lives. "And, behold, a certain lawyer stood up, and tempted Him, saying, Master, what shall I do to inherit eternal life? He said unto him, What is written in the law? how readest thou? And he answering said, Thou shalt love the Lord thy God with all thy heart, and with all thy soul, and with all thy strength, and with all thy mind; and thy neighbor as thyself. And He said unto him, Thou hast answered right: this do, and thou shalt live." Christ here shows the lawyer that to love

God with all the heart and our neighbor as ourselves is the true fruit of piety. "This do," said He, not merely believe but do, "and thou shalt live." It is not alone the professed belief in the binding claims of God's law that makes the Christian, but also the carrying out of that law.

In the parable, Christ exalts the Samaritan above the priest and the Levite, who were great sticklers for the letter of the law of Ten Commandments. The one obeyed the spirit of these commandments, while the others were content to profess an exalted faith in them; but what is faith without works? When the advocates of the law of God plant their feet firmly upon its principles, showing that they are not merely loyal in name but loyal at heart, carrying out in their daily lives the spirit of God's commandments, and exercising true benevolence to man, then will they have moral power to move the world. It is impossible for those who profess allegiance to the law of God to correctly represent the principles of that sacred Decalogue while slighting its holy injunctions to love their neighbor as themselves.

The most eloquent sermon that can be preached upon the law of Ten Commandments is to do them. Obedience should be made a personal duty. Negligence of this duty is flagrant sin. God lays us under obligations not only to secure heaven ourselves, but to feel it a binding duty to show others the way and, through our care and disinterested love, to lead toward Christ those who come within the sphere of our influence. The singular absence of principle that characterizes the lives of many professed Christians is alarming. Their disregard of God's law disheartens those who recognize its sacred claims and tends to turn those from the truth who would otherwise accept it.

In order to gain a proper knowledge of ourselves, it is necessary to look into the mirror, and there discovering our own defects, avail ourselves of the blood of Christ, the fountain opened for sin and uncleanness, in which we may wash our robes of character and remove the stains of sin. But many refuse to see their errors and correct them; they do not want a true knowledge of themselves.

If we would reach high attainments in moral and spiritual excellence we must live for it. We are under personal obligation to society to do this, in order continually to exert an influence in favor of God's law. We should let our light so shine that all may see that the sacred gospel is having an influence upon our hearts and lives, that we walk in obedience to its commandments

47

and violate none of its principles. We are in a great degree accountable to the world for the souls of those around us. Our words and deeds are constantly telling for or against Christ and that law which He came to earth to vindicate.

Let the world see that we are not selfishly narrowed up to our own exclusive interests and religious joys, but that we are liberal and desire them to share our blessings and privileges through the sanctification of the truth. Let them see that the religion which we profess does not close up nor freeze over the avenues to the soul, making us unsympathizing and exacting. Let all who profess to have found Christ, minister as He did to the benefit of man, cherishing a spirit of wise benevolence. We shall then see many souls following the light that shines from our precept and example.

We should all cultivate an amiable disposition and subject ourselves to the control of conscience. The spirit of the truth makes better men and women of those who receive it in their hearts. It works like leaven till the entire being is brought into conformity to its principles. It opens the heart that has been frozen by avarice; it opens the hand that has ever been closed to human suffering; and charity and kindness are seen as its fruits.

God requires that all of us should be self-sacrificing workers. Every part of the truth has a practical application to our daily lives. Blessed are they that hear the word of the Lord and keep it. Hearing is not enough; we must act, we must do. It is in the doing of the Commandments that there is great reward. Those who give practical demonstrations of their benevolence by their sympathy and compassionate acts toward the poor, the suffering, and the unfortunate, not only relieve the sufferers, but contribute largely to their own happiness and are in the way of securing health of soul and body. Isaiah has thus plainly described the work that God will accept and bless His people in doing:

"Is not this the fast that I have chosen? to loose the bands of wickedness, to undo the heavy burdens, and to let the oppressed go free, and that ye break every yoke? Is it not to deal thy bread to the hungry, and that thou bring the poor that are cast out to thy house? when thou seest the naked, that thou cover him; and that thou hide not thyself from thine own flesh? Then shall thy light break forth as the morning, and thine health shall spring forth speedily: and thy righteousness shall go before thee; the glory of the Lord shall be thy rearward."

"Then shalt thou call, and the Lord shall answer; thou shalt cry, and He shall say, Here I am. If thou take away from the midst of thee the yoke, the putting forth of the finger, and speaking vanity; and if thou draw out thy soul to the hungry, and satisfy the afflicted soul; then shall thy light rise in obscurity, and thy darkness be as the noonday: and the Lord shall guide thee continually, and satisfy thy soul in drought, and make fat thy bones: and thou shalt be like a watered garden, and like a spring of water, whose waters fail not."

The sympathy which exists between the mind and the body is very great. When one is affected, the other responds. The condition of the mind has much to do with the health of the physical system. If the mind is free and happy, under a consciousness of rightdoing and a sense of satisfaction in causing happiness to others, it will create a cheerfulness that will react upon the whole system, causing a freer circulation of the blood and a toning up of the entire body. The blessing of God is a healer, and those who are abundant in benefiting others will realize that wondrous blessing in their hearts and lives.

If your thoughts, dear brother and sister, were directed more in the channel of caring for others, your own souls would receive greater blessings. You both have too little human sympathy. You do not bring your feelings to the necessities of others. You hold yourselves too rigid and unsympathizing. You have become stern, exacting, and overbearing. You are in danger of making yourselves conscience for others. You have your own ideas of Christian duties and propriety, and you would gauge others by those ideas; this is overreaching the bounds of right.

Other people have opinions and marked traits of character which cannot be assimilated to your peculiar views. You have defects and faults as well as your brethren and sisters, and it is well to remember this when a difference arises. Your wrong doing is just as grievous to them as theirs is to you, and you should be as lenient to them as you desire that they should be to you. Both of you need greater love and sympathy for others, a love and sympathy like the tenderness of Jesus. In your own house you should exercise kindness, speaking gently to your child, treating him affectionately, and refraining from reproving him for every little error, lest he become hardened by continual faultfinding.

You should cultivate the charity and long-suffering of Christ. By a watchful, suspicious spirit in regard to the motives and conduct of others, you frequently counteract the good you have done. You are cherishing a feeling that is chilling in its influence, that repulses, but does not attract and win. You must be willing to become as yielding and forbearing in your disposition as you desire others to be. Selfish love of your own opinions and ways will, in a great measure, destroy your power to do the good you are desirous of doing.

Sister F, you have too great a desire to rule. You are very sensitive; if your will is crossed, you feel very much injured; self rises in arms, for you have not a meek and teachable spirit.

You need to watch closely upon this point; in short, you need a thorough conversion before your influence can be what it should be. The spirit you manifest will make you miserable if you continue to cherish it. You will see the mistakes of others, and be so eager to correct them that you will overlook your own faults, and you will have hard work to remove the mote from your brother's eye while there is a beam obstructing your own vision. God does not wish you to make your conscience a criterion for others. You have a duty to perform, which is to make yourself cheerful, and to cultivate unselfishness in your feelings until it will be your greatest pleasure to make all around you happy.

Both of you need to soften your hearts and be imbued with the Spirit of Christ, that you may, while living in an atmosphere of cheerfulness and benevolence, help those about you to be healthy and happy also. You have imagined that cheerfulness was not in accordance with the religion of Christ. This is a mistake. We may have true Christian dignity and at the same time be cheerful and pleasant in our deportment. Cheerfulness without levity is one of the Christian graces. You should guard against taking narrow views of religion, or you will limit your influence and become an unfaithful steward of God.

Forbear reprimanding and censuring. You are not adapted to reprove. Your words only wound and sadden; they do not cure and reform. You should overcome the habit of picking at little things that you think amiss. Be broad, be generous and charitable in your judgment of people and things. Open your hearts to the light. Remember that Duty has a twin sister, Love; these united can accomplish almost everything, but separated, neither is capable of good.

It is right that you should both cherish integrity and be true to your sense of right. The straight path of duty should be yours from choice. The love of property, the love of pleasure and friendship, should never influence you to sacrifice one principle of right. You should be firm in following the dictates of an enlightened conscience, and your convictions of duty; but you should guard against bigotry and prejudice. Do not run into a pharisaical spirit.

You are now sowing seed in the great field of life, and that which you now sow you will one day reap. Every thought of your mind, every emotion of your soul, every word of your tongue, every act you perform, is seed that will bear fruit for good or evil. The reaping time is not far distant. All our works are passing in review before God. All our actions and the motives which prompted them are to be open for the inspection of angels and of God.

As far as possible, you should come into harmony with your brethren and sisters. You should surrender yourselves to God and cease to manifest sternness and a disposition to find fault. You should yield your own spirit and take in its place the spirit of the dear Saviour. Reach up and grasp His hand, that the touch may electrify you and charge you with the sweet properties of His own matchless character. You may open your hearts to His love, and let His power transform you and His grace be your strength. Then will you have a powerful influence for good. Your moral strength will be equal to the closest test of character. Your integrity will be pure and sanctified. Then will your light break forth as the morning.

You both need to come more into sympathy with other minds. Christ is our example; He identified Himself with suffering humanity; He made the necessities of others a consideration of His own. When His brethren suffered, He suffered with them. Any slight or neglect of His disciples is the same as if done to Christ Himself. Thus He says: "I was an hungered, and ye gave Me no meat: I was thirsty, and ye gave Me no drink."

Dear brother and sister, you should seek for more harmonious characters. The absence of one essential qualification may render the rest almost inefficient. The principles you profess should be carried into every thought, word, and act. Self should be crucified and the entire being made subordinate to the Lord.

The church is greatly deficient in love and humanity.

Some preserve a cold, chilling reserve, an iron dignity, that repels those who are brought within their influence. This spirit is contagious; it creates an atmosphere that is withering to good impulses and good resolves; it chokes the natural current of human sympathy, cordiality, and love; and under its influence people become constrained, and their social and generous attributes are destroyed for want of exercise. Not only is the spiritual health affected, but the physical health suffers by this unnatural depression. The gloom and chill of this unsocial atmosphere is reflected upon the countenance. The faces of those who are benevolent and sympathetic will shine with the luster of true goodness, while those who do not cherish kindly thoughts and unselfish motives express in their faces the sentiments cherished in their hearts.

Sister F, your feelings toward your sister are not exactly as God would have them. She needed sisterly affection from you, and less dictating and faultfinding. Your course with her has caused a depression of spirit and an anxiety of mind injurious to her health. Be careful lest you oppress and discourage your own sister. You cannot bear anything from her; you resent anything she says that has the appearance of crossing your track.

Your sister has a positive temperament. She has a work to do for herself in this respect. She should be more yielding, but you must not expect to exert a beneficial influence over her while you are so exacting and so lacking in love and sympathy toward one who bears to you the close relationship of a sister and is also united with you in the faith. You have both erred. You have both given room to the enemy, and self has had much to do with your feelings and actions in regard to each other.

Sister F, you have an inclination to dictate to your husband, your sister, and to all around you. Your sister has suffered very much in her mind. This she could have borne had she surrendered herself to God and trusted in Him, but God is displeased with your course toward her. It is unnatural and all wrong. She is no more unyielding in her disposition than you are in yours. When two such positive temperaments come in contact with each other, it is very bad for both. You should each be converted anew and transformed into the divine likeness. You would better err, if you err at all, on the side of mercy and forbearance than that of intolerance.

Mild measures, soft answers, and pleasant words are much better fitted to reform and save, than severity and harshness. A little too much unkindness may place persons beyond your reach, while a conciliatory spirit would be the means of binding them to you, and you might then establish them in the right way. You should be actuated by a forgiving spirit also, and give due credit to every good purpose and action of those around you. Speak words of commendation to your husband, your child, your sister, and to all with whom you are associated. Continual censure blights and darkens the life of anyone.

Do not reproach the Christian religion by jealousy and intolerance toward others. This will but poorly recommend your belief to them. No one has ever been reclaimed from a wrong position by censure and reproach, but many have thus been driven from the truth and have steeled their hearts against conviction. A tender spirit, a gentle and winning deportment, may save the erring and hide a multitude of sins. God requires us to have that charity that "suffereth long, and is kind."

The religion of Christ does not require us to lose our identity of character, but merely to adapt ourselves, in some measure, to the feelings and ways of others. Many people may be brought together in a unity of religious faith whose opinions, habits, and tastes in temporal matters are not in harmony; but if they have the love of Christ glowing in their bosoms, and are looking forward to the same heaven as their eternal home, they may have the sweetest and most intelligent communion together, and a unity the most wonderful. There are scarcely two whose experience is alike in every particular. The trials of one may not be the trials of another, and our hearts should ever be open to kindly sympathy and all aglow with the love that Jesus had for all His brethren.

Conquer your disposition to be exacting with your son, lest too frequent reproof make your presence disagreeable to him and your counsels hateful. Bind him to your heart, not by foolish indulgence, but by the silken cords of love. You can be firm yet kind. Christ must be your helper. Love will be the means of drawing other hearts to yours, and your influence may establish them in the good and right way.

I have warned you against a spirit of censure, and I would again caution you in regard to that fault. Christ sometimes reproved with severity, and in some cases it may be necessary for us to do so; but we should consider that while Christ knew the exact condition of the ones He rebuked, and just the amount of reproof they could bear, and what was necessary to correct their course of wrong, He also knew just how to pity the erring, comfort the unfortunate, and encourage the weak. He knew just how to keep souls from despondency and to inspire them with hope, because He was acquainted with the exact motives and peculiar trials of every mind. He could not make a mistake.

But we may misjudge motives; we may be deceived by appearances; we may think we are doing right to reprove wrong, and go too far, censure too severely, and wound where we wished to heal; or we may exercise sympathy unwisely, and counteract, in our ignorance, reproof that is merited and timely. Our judgment may be wrong, but Jesus was too wise to err. He reproved with pity and loved with a divine love those whom He rebuked.

The Lord requires us to be submissive to His will, subdued by His Spirit, and sanctified to His service. Selfishness must be put away, and we must overcome every defect in our characters as Christ overcame. In order to accomplish this work, we must die daily to self. Said Paul: "I die daily." He had a new conversion every day, took an advance step toward heaven. To gain daily victories in the divine life is the only course that God approves. The Lord is gracious, of tender pity, and plenteous in mercy. He knows our needs and weaknesses, and He will help our infirmities if we only trust in Him and believe that He will bless us and do great things for us.

7. Co-Workers with Christ

It was an important time for —— during and after the tent meeting in 1874. Had there been a pleasant and commodious house of worship there, more than double the number that were really gained would have taken their stand for the truth. God works with our efforts. We may close the way for sinners by our negligence and selfishness. There should have been great diligence in seeking to save those who were still in error, yet interested in the truth.

Just as wise generalship is needed in the service of Christ as is needed over the battalions of an army that protects the life and liberty of the people. It is not everyone who can labor judiciously for the salvation of souls. There is much close thinking to be done. We must not enter into the Lord's work haphazard and expect success. The Lord needs men of mind, men of thought. Jesus calls for co-workers, not blunderers. God wants right-thinking and intelligent men to do the great work necessary to the salvation of souls.

Mechanics, lawyers, merchants, men of all trades and professions, educate themselves that they may become masters of their business. Should the followers of Christ be less intelligent, and while professedly engaged in His service be ignorant of the ways and means to be employed? The enterprise of gaining everlasting life is above every earthly consideration. In order to lead souls to Jesus there must be a knowledge of human nature and a study of the human mind. Much careful thought and fervent prayer are required to know how to approach men and women upon the great subject of truth.

Some rash, impulsive, yet honest souls, after a pointed discourse has been given, will accost those who are not with us in a very abrupt manner, and make the truth, which we desire them to receive, repulsive to them. "The children of this world are in their generation wiser than the children of light." Business men and politicians study courtesy. It is their policy to make themselves as attractive as possible. They study to render their address and manners such that they may have the greatest influence over the minds of those about them. They use their knowledge and abilities as skillfully as possible in order to gain this object.

There is a vast amount of rubbish brought forward by professed believers in Christ, which blocks up the way to the cross. Notwithstanding all this, there are some who are so deeply convicted that they will come through every discouragement and will surmount every obstacle in order to gain the truth. But had the believers in the truth purified their minds by obeying it, had they felt the importance of knowledge and of refinement of manners in Christ's work, where one soul has been saved there might have been twenty.

Again, after individuals have been converted to the truth, they need to be looked after. The zeal of many ministers seems to fail as soon as a measure of success attends their efforts. They do not realize that these newly converted ones need nursing—watchful attention, help, and encouragement. These should not be left alone, a prey to Satan's most powerful temptations; they need to be educated in regard to their duties, to be kindly dealt with, to be led along, and to be visited and prayed with. These souls need the meat apportioned to every man in due season.

No wonder that some become discouraged, linger by the way, and are left for wolves to devour. Satan is upon the track of all. He sends his agents forth to gather back to his ranks the souls he has lost. There should be more fathers and mothers to take these babes in the truth to their hearts, and to encourage them and pray for them, that their faith be not confused.

Preaching is a small part of the work to be done for the salvation of souls. God's Spirit convicts sinners of the truth, and He places them in the arms of the church. The ministers may do their part, but they can never perform the work that the church should do. God requires His church to nurse those who are young in faith and experience, to go to them, not for the purpose of gossiping with them, but to pray, to speak unto them words that are "like apples of gold in pictures of silver."

We all need to study character and manner that we may know how to deal judiciously with different minds, that we may use our best endeavors to help them to a correct understanding of the word of God and to a true Christian life. We should read the Bible with them, and draw their minds away from temporal things to their eternal interests. It is the duty of God's children to be missionaries for Him, to become acquainted with those who need help. If one is staggering under temptation, his case should be taken up carefully and managed wisely; for his eternal interest is at stake, and the words and acts of those laboring for him may be a savor of life unto life, or of death unto death.

Sometimes a case presents itself that should be made a prayerful study. The person must be shown his true character, understand his own peculiarities of disposition and temperament, and see his infirmities. He should be judiciously handled. If he can be reached, if his heart can be touched by this wise and patient labor, he can be bound with strong cords to Christ and led to trust in God. Oh, when a work like this is done, all the heavenly courts look and rejoice; for a precious soul has been rescued from Satan's snare and saved from death! Oh, will it not pay to work intelligently for the salvation of souls? Christ paid the price of His own life for them, and shall His followers ask: "Am I my brother's keeper?" Shall we not work in unison with the Master? Shall we not appreciate the worth of souls for whom our Saviour died?

Some efforts have been made to interest children in the cause, but not enough. Our Sabbath schools should be made more interesting. The public schools have of late years greatly improved their methods of teaching. Object lessons, pictures, and blackboards are used to make difficult lessons clear to the youthful mind. Just so may present truth be simplified and made intensely interesting to the active minds of the children.

Parents who can be approached in no other way are frequently reached through their children. Sabbath school teachers can instruct the children in the truth, and they will, in turn, take it into the home circle. But few teachers seem to understand the importance of this branch of the work. The modes of teaching which have been adopted with such success in the public schools could be employed with similar results in the Sabbath schools and be the means of bringing children to Jesus and educating them in Bible truth. This will do far more good than religious excitement of an emotional character, that passes off as rapidly as it comes.

The love of Christ should be cherished. More faith is needed in the work which we believe is to be done before the coming of Christ. There should be more self-denying, self-sacrificing labor in the right direction. There should be thoughtful, prayerful study how to work to the best advantage. Careful plans should be matured. There are minds among us that can invent and carry out if they are only put to use. Great results would follow well-directed and intelligent efforts.

The prayer meetings should be the most interesting gatherings that are held, but these are frequently poorly managed. Many attend preaching, but neglect the prayer meeting. Here, again, thought is required. Wisdom should be sought of God, and plans should be laid to conduct the meetings so that they will be interesting and attractive. The people hunger for the bread of life. If they find it at the prayer meeting they will go there to receive it.

Long, prosy talks and prayers are out of place anywhere, and especially in the social meeting. Those who are forward and ever ready to speak are allowed to crowd out the testimony of the timid and retiring. Those who are most superficial generally have the most to say. Their prayers are long and mechanical. They weary the angels and the people who listen to them. Our prayers should be short and right to the point. Let the long, tiresome petitions be left for the closet, if any have such to offer. Let the Spirit of God into your hearts, and it will sweep away all dry formality.

Music can be a great power for good, yet we do not make the most of this branch of worship. The singing is generally done from impulse or to meet special cases, and at other times those who sing are left to blunder along, and the music loses its proper effect upon the minds of those present. Music should have beauty, pathos, and power. Let the voices be lifted in songs of praise and devotion. Call to your aid, if practicable, instrumental music, and let the glorious harmony ascend to God, an acceptable offering.

But it is sometimes more difficult to discipline the singers and keep them in working order than to improve the habits of praying and exhorting. Many want to do things after their own style; they object to consultation, and are impatient under leadership. Well-matured plans are needed in the service of God. Common sense is an excellent thing in the worship of the Lord. The thinking powers should be consecrated to Christ, and ways and means should be devised to serve Him best. The church of God who are trying to do good by living out the truth and seeking to save souls, can be a power in the world if they will be disciplined by the Spirit of the Lord. They must not feel that they can work carelessly for eternity.

As a people, we lose much by lack of sympathy and sociability with one another. He who talks of independence and shuts himself up to himself is not filling the position that God designed he should. We are children of God, mutually dependent upon one another for happiness. The claims of God and of humanity are upon us. We must all act our part in this life. It is the proper cultivation of the social elements of our nature that brings us into sympathy with our brethren and affords us happiness in our efforts to bless others. The happiness of heaven will consist in the pure communion of holy beings, the harmonious social life with the blessed angels and with the redeemed who have washed their robes and made them white in the blood of the Lamb. We cannot be happy while we are wrapped up in our interest for ourselves. We should live in this world to win souls to the Saviour. If we injure others, we injure ourselves also. If we bless others, we also bless ourselves; for the influence of every good deed is reflected upon our own hearts.

We are in duty bound to help one another. It is not always that we are brought in contact with social Christians, those who are amiable and mild. Many have not received a proper education; their characters are warped, they are hard and gnarled, and seem to be crooked in every way. While we help these to see and correct their defects, we must be careful not to become impatient and irritable over our neighbor's faults. There are disagreeable ones who profess Christ; but the beauty of Christian grace will transform them if they will set diligently about the work of obtaining the meekness and gentleness of Him whom they follow, remembering that "none of us liveth to himself."

Co-workers with Christ! What an exalted position! Where are to be found the self-sacrificing missionaries in these large cities? The Lord needs workers in His vineyard. We should fear to rob Him of the time He claims from us; we should fear to spend it in idleness or in the adornment of the body, appropriating to foolish purposes the precious hours God has given us to be devoted to prayer, to becoming conversant with our Bibles, and to laboring for the good of our fellow beings, thus fitting ourselves and them for the great work devolving upon us.

Mothers spend unnecessary labor upon garments with which to beautify the persons of themselves and their children. It is our duty to dress ourselves plainly and to clothe our children neatly, without useless ornamentation, embroidery, or display, taking care not to foster in them a love of dress that will prove their ruin, but seeking rather to cultivate the Christian graces. None of us can be excused from our responsibilities, and in no case can we stand clear before the throne of God unless we do the work that the Master has left for us to do.

Missionaries for God are wanted, faithful men and women who will not shirk responsibility. Judicious labor will accomplish good results. There is real work to be done. The truth should be brought before people in a careful manner by those who unite meekness with wisdom. We should not hold ourselves aloof from our fellow men, but come close to them; for their souls are as precious as our own. We can carry the light into their homes, with a softened and subdued spirit plead with them to come up to the exalted privilege offered them, pray with them when it seems proper, and show them that there are higher attainments that they may reach, and then guardedly speak to them of the sacred truths for these last days.

There are more gatherings for singing than for prayer among our people; but even these gatherings can be conducted in so reverential yet cheerful a manner that they may exert a good influence. There is, however, too much

59

jesting, idle conversation, and gossiping to make these seasons beneficial, to elevate the thoughts and refine the manners.

• Sensational Revivals

There has been too much of a divided interest in——. When a new excitement is raised, there are some who cast their influence on the wrong side. Every man and woman should be on guard when there are deceptions abroad calculated to lead away from the truth. There are those who are ever ready to see and hear some new and strange thing; and the enemy of souls has, in these large cities, plenty to inflame the curiosity and keep the mind diverted from the great and sanctifying truths for these last days.

If every fluctuating religious excitement leads some to neglect to fully sustain, by their presence and influence, the minority who believe unpopular truth, there will be much weakness in the church where there should be strength. Satan employs various means by which to accomplish his purposes; and if, under the guise of popular religion, he can lead off vacillating and unwary ones from the path of truth, he has accomplished much in dividing the strength of the people of God. This fluctuating revival enthusiasm, that comes and goes like the tide, carries a delusive exterior that deceives many honest persons into believing it to be the true Spirit of the Lord. It multiplies converts. Those of excitable temperaments, the weak and yielding, flock to its standard; but when the wave recedes, they are found stranded on the beach. Be not deceived by false teachers, nor led by vain words. The enemy of souls is sure to have enough dishes of pleasing fables to suit the appetites of all.

There will ever be flashing meteors to arise; but the trail of light they leave immediately goes out in darkness that seems denser than it was before. These sensational religious excitements that are created by the relation of anecdotes and the exhibition of eccentricities and oddities are all surface work, and those of our faith who are charmed and infatuated by these flashes of light will never build up the cause of God. They are ready to withdraw their influence upon the slightest occasion and to induce others to attend those gatherings where they hear that which weakens the soul and brings confusion to the mind. It is this withdrawal of the interest from the work that makes the cause of God languish. We must be steadfast in the faith; we must not be movable. We have our work before us, which is to cause the light of truth, as revealed in the law of God, to shine in upon other minds and lead them out of darkness. This work requires determined, persevering energy and a fixed purpose to succeed.

There are some in the church who need to cling to the pillars of our faith, to settle down and find rock bottom, instead of drifting on the surface of excitement and moving from impulse. There are spiritual dyspeptics in the church. They are self-made invalids; their spiritual debility is the result of their own wavering course. They are tossed about here and there by the changing winds of doctrine, and are often confused and thrown into uncertainty because they move entirely by feeling. They are sensational Christians, ever hungering for something new and diverse; strange doctrines confuse their faith, and they are worthless to the cause of truth.

God calls for men and women of stability, of firm purpose, who can be relied upon in seasons of danger and trial, who are as firmly rooted and grounded in the truth as the eternal hills, who cannot be swayed to the right or to the left, but who move straight onward and are always found on the right side. There are some, who, in time of religious peril, may almost always be looked for in the ranks of the enemy; if they have any influence, it is on the wrong side. They do not feel under moral obligation to give all their strength to the truth they profess. Such will be rewarded according to their works.

Those who do little for the Saviour in the salvation of souls and in keeping themselves right before God, will gain but little spiritual muscle. We need continually to use the strength we have that it may develop and increase. As disease is the result of the violation of natural laws, so is spiritual declension the result of a continued transgression of the law of God. And yet the very transgressors may profess to keep all of God's commandments.

We must come nearer to God, place ourselves in closer connection with heaven, and carry out the principles of the law in the minutest actions of our everyday lives in order to be spiritually whole. God has given His servants ability, talents to be used for His glory, not to lie idle or be wasted. He has given them light and a knowledge of His will to be communicated to others, and in imparting to others we become living channels of light. If we do not exercise our spiritual strength we become feeble, as the limbs of the body become powerless when the invalid is compelled to remain long inactive. It is use that gives power.

Nothing will give greater spiritual strength and a greater increase of earnestness and depth of feeling than visiting and ministering to the sick and the desponding, helping them to see the light and to fasten their faith upon Jesus. There are disagreeable duties that somebody must do or souls will be left to perish. Christians will find a blessing in doing these duties, however unpleasant they may be. Christ took the disagreeable task upon Himself of coming from the abode of purity and unsurpassed glory, to dwell, a man among men, in a world seared and blackened by crime, violence, and iniquity. He did this to save souls; and shall the objects of such amazing love and unparalleled condescension excuse their lives of selfish ease? shall they choose their own pleasure, follow their own inclinations, and leave souls to perish in darkness because they will meet with disappointment and rebuffs if they labor to save them? Christ paid an infinite price for man's redemption, and shall he say: "My Lord, I will not labor in Thy vineyard; I pray Thee have me excused"?

God calls for those who are at ease in Zion to be up and doing. Will they not listen to the Master's voice? He wants prayerful, faithful workers who will sow beside all waters. Those who labor thus will be surprised to find how trials, resolutely borne in the name and strength of Jesus, will give firmness to the faith and renew the courage. In the path of humble obedience is safety and power, comfort and hope; but the reward will finally be lost by those who do nothing for Jesus. Weak hands will be unable to cling to the Mighty One, feeble knees will fail to support in the day of adversity. Bible readers and Christian workers will receive the glorious prize, and hear the "Well done, thou good and faithful servant: . . . enter thou into the joy of thy Lord."

• **Withholding Means**

The blessing of God will rest upon those in——who have the cause of Christ at heart. The freewill offerings of our brethren and sisters, made in faith and love to the crucified Redeemer, will bring back blessings to them; for God marks and remembers every act of liberality on the part of His saints.

In preparing a house of worship, there must be a great exercise of faith and trust in God. In business transactions those who venture nothing make but little advancement; why not have faith also in an enterprise for God and invest in His cause?

Some, when in poverty, are generous with their little; but as they acquire property, they become penurious. The reason they have so little faith is that they do not keep moving forward as they prosper, and give to the cause of God even at a sacrifice.

In the Jewish system it was required that beneficence should first be shown to the Lord. At the harvest and the vintage the first fruits of the field—the corn, the wine, and the oil—were to be consecrated as an offering to the Lord. The gleanings and the corners of the fields were reserved for the poor. Our gracious heavenly Father did not neglect the wants of the poor. The first fruits of the wool when the sheep were shorn, of the grain when the wheat was threshed, were to be offered to the Lord; and it was commanded that the poor, the widows, the orphans, and the strangers, be invited to their feasts. At the close of every year all were required to make solemn oath whether or not they had done according to the command of God.

This arrangement was made by the Lord to impress upon the people that in every matter He must be first. By this system of benevolence they were to bear in mind that their gracious Master was the true proprietor of their fields, their flocks, and their herds; that the God of heaven sent them sunshine and rain for their seedtime and harvest, and that everything they possessed was of His creation. All was the Lord's, and He had made them stewards of His goods.

The liberality of the Jews in the construction of the tabernacle and the erection of the temple illustrates a spirit of benevolence which has not been equaled by Christians of any later date. They had just been freed from their long bondage in Egypt and were wanderers in the wilderness; yet scarcely were they delivered from the armies of the Egyptians who pursued them in their hasty journey, when the word of the Lord came to Moses. saying: "Speak unto the children of Israel, that they bring Me an offering: of every man that giveth it willingly with his heart ye shall take My offering."

His people had small possessions and no flattering prospect of adding to them; but an object was before them—to build a tabernacle for God. The Lord had spoken, and they must obey His voice. They withheld nothing. All gave with a willing hand, not a certain amount of their increase, but a large portion of their actual possessions. They devoted it gladly and heartily to the Lord, and pleased Him by so doing. Was it not all His? Had He not given them all they possessed? If He called for it, was it not their duty to give back to the Lender His own?

No urging was needed. The people brought even more than was required, and were told to desist, for there was already more than could be appropriated. Again, in building the temple, the call for means met with a hearty response. The people did not give reluctantly. They rejoiced in the prospect of a building being erected for the worship of God, and donated more than enough for the purpose. David blessed the Lord before all the congregation, and said: "But who am I, and what is my people, that we should be able to offer so willingly after this sort? for all things come of Thee, and of Thine own have we given Thee." Again in his prayer David gave thanks in these words: "O Lord our God, all this store that we have prepared to build Thee an house for Thine holy name cometh of Thine hand, and is all Thine own."

David well understood from whom came all his bounties. Would that those of this day who rejoice in a Saviour's love could realize that their silver and gold are the Lord's and should be used to promote His glory, not grudgingly retained to enrich and gratify themselves. He has an indisputable right to all that He has lent His creatures. All that they possess is His.

There are high and holy objects that require means, and money thus invested will yield to the giver more elevated and permanent enjoyment than if it were expended in personal gratification or selfishly hoarded for greed of gain. When God calls for our treasure, whatever the amount may be, the willing response makes the gift a consecrated offering to Him and lays up for the giver a treasure in heaven that moth cannot corrupt, that fire cannot consume, nor thieves break in and steal. The investment is safe. The money is placed in bags that have no holes; it is secure.

Can Christians, who boast of a broader light than had the Hebrews, give less than they? Can Christians living near the close of time be satisfied with their offerings when not half so large as were those of the Jews? Their liberality was to benefit their own nation; the work in these last days extends to the entire world. The message of truth is to go to all nations, tongues, and people; its publications, printed in many different languages, are to be scattered abroad like the leaves of autumn.

It is written: "Forasmuch then as Christ hath suffered for us in the flesh, arm yourselves likewise with the same mind." And again: "He that saith he abideth in Him ought himself also so to walk, even as He walked." Let us inquire: What would our Saviour have done in our circumstances? what would have been His efforts for the salvation of souls? This question is answered by the example of Christ. He left His royalty, laid aside His glory, sacrificed His riches, and clothed His divinity with humanity, that He might reach men where they were. His example shows that He laid down His life for sinners.

Satan told Eve that a high state of felicity could be gained through the gratification of unlicensed appetite, but the promise of God to man is through denial of self. When upon the shameful cross Christ was suffering in agony for man's redemption, human nature was exalted. Only by the cross can the human family be elevated to connect with heaven. Self-denial and crosses meet us at every step on our heavenward journey.

The spirit of liberality is the spirit of heaven; the spirit of selfishness is the spirit of Satan. Christ's self-sacrificing love is revealed upon the cross. He gave all He had, and then gave Himself, that man might be saved. The cross of Christ appeals to the benevolence of every follower of the blessed Saviour. The principle there illustrated is to give, give. This, carried out in actual benevolence and good works, is the true fruit of the Christian life. The principle of worldlings is to get, get, and thus they expect to secure happiness; but, carried out in all its bearings, the fruit is misery and death.

To carry the truth to the inhabitants of the earth, to rescue them from their guilt and indifference, is the mission of the followers of Christ. Men must have the truth in order to be sanctified through it, and we are the channels of God's light. Our talents, our means, our knowledge, are not merely for our own benefit; they are to be used for the salvation of souls, to elevate man from his life of sin and bring him, through Christ, to the infinite God.

We should be zealous workers in this cause, seeking to lead sinners, repenting and believing, to a divine Redeemer, and to impress them with an exalted sense of God's love to man. "God so loved the world, that He gave His only-begotten Son, that whosoever believeth in Him should not perish, but have everlasting life." What an incomparable love is this! A theme for the most profound meditation! The amazing love of God for a world that did not love Him! The thought has a subduing power upon the soul and brings the mind into captivity to the will of God. Men who are crazy for gain, and are disappointed and unhappy in their pursuit of the world, need the knowledge of this truth to quiet the restless hungering and thirsting of their souls.

Missionaries for God are wanted in your large city to carry light to those who sit in the shadow of death. Experienced hands are needed, in the meekness of wisdom and the strength of faith, to lift weary souls to the bosom of a compassionate Redeemer. Oh, selfishness! What a curse! It prevents us from engaging in the service of God. It prevents us from perceiving the claims of duty, which should set our hearts aglow with fervent zeal. All our energies should be turned to the obedience of Christ. To divide our interest with the leaders of error is aiding the wrong side and giving advantage to our foes. The truth of God knows no compromise with sin, no connection with artifice, no union with transgression. Soldiers are wanted who will always answer to the roll call and be ready for immediate action, not those who, when needed, are found aiding the enemy.

Ours is a great work. Yet there are many who profess to believe these sacred truths, who are paralyzed by the sophistry of Satan, and are doing nothing for, but rather hinder, God's cause. When will they act like those who wait for the Lord? When will they show a zeal in accordance with their faith? Many people selfishly retain their means, and soothe their conscience with a plan for doing some great thing for the cause of God after their death. They make a will donating a large sum to the church and its various interests, and then settle down with a feeling that they have done all that is required of them. Wherein have they denied self by this act? They have, on the contrary, exhibited the true essence of selfishness. When they have no longer any use for their money they propose to give it to God. But they will retain it as long as they can, till they are compelled to relinquish it by a messenger that cannot be turned aside.

Such a will is often an evidence of real covetousness. God has made us all His stewards, and in no case has He authorized us to neglect our duty or leave it for others to do. The call for means to advance the cause of truth will never be more urgent than now. Our money will never do a greater amount of good than at the present time. Every day of delay in rightly appropriating it, is limiting the period in which it will do good in saving souls. If we leave others to accomplish that which God has left for us to do, we wrong ourselves and Him who gave us all we have. How can others do our work of benevolence any better than we can do it ourselves? God would have every man, during his lifetime, the executor of his own will in this matter. Adversity, accident, or intrigue may forever cut off meditated acts of benevolence, when he who has accumulated a fortune is no longer by to guard it. It is sad that so many neglect the present golden opportunity to do good, and wait to be cast out of their stewardship before giving back to the Lord the means which He has lent them to be used for His glory.

One marked feature in the teachings of Christ is the frequency and earnestness with which He rebuked the sin of covetousness and pointed out the danger of worldly acquisitions and inordinate love of gain. In the mansions of the rich, in the temple and in the streets, He warned those who inquired after salvation: "Take heed, and beware of covetousness." "Ye cannot serve God and mammon."

It is this increasing devotion to money getting, the selfishness which the desire for gain begets, that removes the favor of God from the church and deadens its spirituality. When the head and hands are constantly occupied with planning and toiling for the accumulation of riches, the claims of God and humanity are forgotten. If God has blessed us with prosperity, it is not that our time and attention should be diverted from Him and given to that which He has lent us. The giver is greater than the gift. We are not our own; we have been bought with a price. Have we forgotten that infinite price paid for our redemption? Is gratitude dead in the heart? Does not the cross of Christ put to shame a life of selfish ease and indulgence?

What if Christ, becoming weary of the ingratitude and abuse that met Him on every side, had left His work! What if He had never reached that period when He said: "It is finished." What if He had returned to heaven, discouraged by His reception! What if He had never passed through that soul agony in the garden of Gethsemane that forced from His pores great drops of blood!

Christ was influenced in His labor for the redemption of the race by a love that is without parallel, and a devotion to the Father's will. He toiled for the good of man up to the very hour of His humiliation. He spent His life in poverty and self-denial for the degraded sinner. In a world that was His own He had no place to lay His weary head. We are reaping the fruits of this infinite self-sacrifice; and yet when labor is to be done, when our money is wanted to aid the work of the Redeemer in the salvation of souls, we shrink from duty and pray to be excused. Ignoble sloth, careless indifference, and wicked selfishness seal our senses to the claims of God.

Oh, must Christ, the Majesty of heaven, the King of glory, bear the heavy cross, wear the thorny crown, and drink the bitter cup, while we recline at ease, glorifying ourselves and forgetting the souls He died to redeem by His precious blood? No; let us give while we have the power. Let us do while we have the strength. Let us work while it is day. Let us devote our time and means to the service of God, that we may have His approbation and receive His reward.

8. The Testing Process

Dear Brother G:

I feel very anxious that you should accept light and come out of darkness. You have been greatly tempted of Satan; he has used you as his instrument to hinder the work of God. He has thus far succeeded with you; but it does not follow that you should continue in the path of error. I look upon your case with great trembling. I know that God has given you great light. In your sickness last fall the providence of God was dealing with you that you might bear fruit to His glory.

Unbelief was taking possession of your soul, and the Lord afflicted you that you might gain a needed experience. He blessed us in praying for you, and He blessed you in answer to our prayers. The Lord designed to unite our hearts in love and confidence. The Holy Spirit witnessed with your spirit. The power of God in answer to prayer came upon you; but Satan came with temptations, and you did not close the door upon him. He entered and has been very busy. It is the plan of the evil one to work first upon the mind of one, and then, through him, upon others. He has thus sought to hedge up our way and hinder our labors in the very place where our influence should be most felt for the prosperity of the cause.

The Lord brought you into connection with His work at —— for a wise purpose; He designed that you should discover the defects in your character and overcome them. You know how quickly your spirit chafes when things do not move according to your mind. Would that you could understand that all this impatience and irritability must be overcome, or your life will prove an utter failure, you will lose heaven, and it would have been better had you never been born.

Our cases are pending in the court of heaven. We are rendering our accounts there day by day. Everyone will be rewarded according to his works. Burnt offerings and sacrifices were not acceptable to God in ancient times unless the spirit was right with which the gift was offered. Samuel said: "Hath the Lord as great delight in burnt offerings and sacrifices, as in obeying the voice of the Lord? Behold, to obey is better than sacrifice, and to hearken than the fat of rams." All the money on earth cannot buy the blessing of God nor ensure you a single victory.

Many would make any and every sacrifice but the very one they should make, which is to yield themselves, to submit their wills to the will of God. Said Christ to His disciples: "Except ye be converted, and become as little children, ye shall not enter into the kingdom of heaven." Here is a lesson in humility. We must all become humble as little children in order to inherit the kingdom.

Our heavenly Father sees the hearts of men, and He knows their characters better than they themselves know them. He sees that some have susceptibilities and powers, which, directed in the right channel, might be used to His glory to aid in the advancement of His work. He puts these persons on trial and in His wise providence brings them into different positions and under a variety of circumstances, testing them that they may reveal what is in their hearts and the weak points in their characters which have been concealed from their own knowledge. He gives them opportunities to correct these weaknesses, to polish off the rough corners of their natures, and to fit themselves for His service, that when He calls them to action they will be ready, and that angels of heaven may unite their labor with human effort in the work that must be done upon the earth.

To men whom God designs shall fill responsible positions, He in mercy reveals their hidden defects, that they may look within and examine critically the complicated emotions and exercises of their own hearts, and detect that which is wrong; thus they may modify their dispositions and refine their manners. The Lord in His providence brings men where He can test their moral powers and reveal their motives of action, that they may improve what is right in themselves and put away that which is wrong. God would have His servants become acquainted with the moral machinery of their own hearts. In order to bring this about, He often permits the fire of affliction to assail them that they may become purified. "But who may abide the day of His coming? and who shall stand when He appeareth? for He is like a refiner's fire, and like fullers' soap: and He shall sit as a refiner and purifier of silver: and He shall purify the sons of Levi, and purge them as gold and silver, that they may offer unto the Lord an offering in righteousness."

The purification of the people of God cannot be accomplished without their suffering. God permits the fires of affliction to consume the dross, to separate the worthless from the valuable, that the pure metal may shine forth. He passes us from one fire to another, testing our true worth. If we cannot bear these trials, what will we do in the time of trouble? If prosperity or adversity discover falseness, pride, or selfishness in our hearts, what shall we do when God tries every man's work as by fire, and lays bare the secrets of all hearts?

True grace is willing to be tried; if we are loath to be searched by the Lord, our condition is serious indeed. God is the refiner and purifier of souls; in the heat of the furnace the dross is separated forever from the true silver and gold of the Christian character. Jesus watches the test. He knows what is needed to purify the precious metal that it may reflect the radiance of His divine love.

God brings His people near Him by close, testing trials, by showing them their own weakness and inability, and by teaching them to lean upon Him as their only help and safeguard. Then His object is accomplished. They are prepared to be used in every emergency, to fill important positions of trust, and to accomplish the grand purposes for which their powers were given them. God takes men upon trial; He proves them on the right hand and on the left, and thus they are educated, trained, disciplined. Jesus, our Redeemer, man's representative and head, endured this testing process. He suffered more than we can be called upon to suffer. He bore our infirmities and was in all points tempted as we are. He did not suffer thus on His own account, but because of our sins; and now, relying on the merits of our Overcomer, we may become victors in His name.

God's work of refining and purifying must go on until His servants are so humbled, so dead to self, that, when called into active service, their eye will be single to His glory. He will then accept their efforts; they will not move rashly, from impulse; they will not rush on and imperil the Lord's cause, being slaves to temptations and passions and followers of their own carnal minds set on fire by Satan. Oh, how fearfully is the cause of God marred by man's perverse will and unsubdued temper! How much suffering he brings upon himself by following his own headstrong passions! God brings men over the ground again and again, increasing the pressure until perfect humility and a transformation of character bring them into harmony with Christ and the spirit of heaven, and they are victors over themselves.

God has called men from different states, and has been testing and proving them to see what characters they would develop, to see if they could be trusted to keep the fort at ——, and to see whether or not they would supply the deficiencies of the men already there, and, seeing the failures that these men have made, would shun the example of those who are not fit to engage in the most sacred work of God. He has followed men at —— with continual warnings, reproof, and counsel. He has poured great light about those who officiate in His cause there, that the way may be plain before them. But if they prefer to follow after their own wisdom, scorning the light, as did Saul, they will surely go astray and involve the cause in perplexity. Light and darkness have been set before them, but they have too often chosen the darkness.

The Laodicean message applies to the people of God who profess to believe present truth. The greater part are lukewarm professors, having a name but no zeal. God signified that He wanted men at the great heart of the work to correct the state of things existing there and to stand like faithful sentinels at their post of duty. He has given them light at every point, to instruct, encourage, and confirm them, as the case required. But notwithstanding all this, those who should be faithful and true, fervent in Christian zeal, of gracious temper, knowing and loving Jesus earnestly, are found aiding the enemy to weaken and discourage those whom God is using to build up the work. The term "lukewarm" is applicable to this class. They profess to love the truth, yet are deficient in Christian fervor and devotion. They dare not give up wholly and run the risk of the unbeliever, yet they are unwilling to die to self and follow out closely the principles of their faith.

The only hope for the Laodiceans is a clear view of their standing before God, a knowledge of the nature of their disease. They are neither cold nor hot; they occupy a neutral position, and at the same time flatter themselves that they are in need of nothing. The True Witness hates this lukewarmness. He loathes the indifference of this class of persons. Said He: "I would thou wert cold or hot." Like lukewarm water, they are nauseous to His taste. They are neither unconcerned nor selfishly stubborn. They do not engage thoroughly and heartily in the work of God, identifying themselves with its interests; but they hold aloof and are ready to leave their posts when their worldly personal interests demand it. The internal work of grace is wanting in their hearts; of such it is said: "Thou sayest, I am rich, and increased with goods, and have need of nothing; and knowest not that thou art wretched, and miserable, and poor, and blind, and naked."

Faith and love are the true riches, the pure gold which the True Witness counsels the lukewarm to buy. However rich we may be in earthly treasure, all our wealth will not enable us to buy the precious remedies that cure the disease of the soul called lukewarmness. Intellect and earthly riches were powerless to remove the defects of the Laodicean church, or to remedy their deplorable condition. They were blind, yet felt that they were well off. The

Spirit of God did not illumine their minds, and they did not perceive their sinfulness; therefore they did not feel the necessity of help.

To be without the graces of the Spirit of God is sad indeed; but it is a more terrible condition to be thus destitute of spirituality and of Christ, and yet try to justify ourselves by telling those who are alarmed for us that we need not their fears and pity. Fearful is the power of self-deception on the human mind! What blindness! setting light for darkness and darkness for light! The True Witness counsels us to buy of Him gold tried in the fire, white raiment, and eyesalve. The gold here recommended as having been tried in the fire is faith and love. It makes the heart rich; for it has been purged until it is pure, and the more it is tested the more brilliant is its luster.

The white raiment is purity of character, the righteousness of Christ imparted to the sinner. This is indeed a garment of heavenly texture, that can be bought only of Christ for a life of willing obedience. The eyesalve is that wisdom and grace which enables us to discern between the evil and the good, and to detect sin under any guise. God has given His church eyes which He requires them to anoint with wisdom, that they may see clearly; but many would put out the eyes of the church if they could; for they would not have their deeds come to the light, lest they should be reproved. The divine eyesalve will impart clearness to the understanding. Christ is the depositary of all graces. He says: "Buy of Me."

Some may say it is exalting our own merits to expect favor from God through our good works. True, we cannot buy one victory with our good works; yet we cannot be victors without them. The purchase which Christ recommends to us is only complying with the conditions He has given us. True grace, which is of inestimable value, and which will endure the test of trial and adversity, is only obtained through faith and humble, prayerful obedience. Graces that endure the proofs of affliction and persecution, and evidence their soundness and sincerity, are the gold which is tried in the fire and found genuine. Christ offers to sell this precious treasure to man: "Buy of Me gold tried in the fire." The dead, heartless performance of duty does not make us Christians. We must get out of a lukewarm condition and experience a true conversion, or we shall fail of heaven.

I was pointed to the providence of God among His people and was shown that every trial made by the refining, purifying process upon professed

Christians proves some to be dross. The fine gold does not always appear. In every religious crisis some fall under temptation. The shaking of God blows away multitudes like dry leaves. Prosperity multiplies a mass of professors. Adversity purges them out of the church. As a class, their spirits are not steadfast with God. They go out from us because they are not of us; for when tribulation or persecution arises because of the word, many are offended.

Let these look back a few months to the time when they were sitting on the cases of others who were in a condition similar to that which they now occupy. Let them carefully call to mind the exercise of their minds in regard to those tempted ones. Had anyone told them then that notwithstanding their zeal and labor to set others right, they would at length be found in a similar position of darkness, they would have said, as did Hazael to the prophet: "Is thy servant a dog, that he should do this great thing?"

Self-deception is upon them. During the calm, what firmness they manifest! what courageous sailors they make! But when the furious tempests of trial and temptation come, lo! their souls are shipwrecked. Men may have excellent gifts, good ability, splendid qualifications; but one defect, one secret sin indulged, will prove to the character what the worm-eaten plank does to the ship—utter disaster and ruin!

Dear brother, God in His providence brought you from your farm to — — to bear the tests and trials which you could not have where you were. He has given you some testimonies of reproof, which you professedly accepted; but your spirit was continually chafed under rebuke. You are like those who walked no more with Jesus after He brought close, practical truths to bear upon them. You have not taken hold in faith to correct the defects marked out in your character. You have not humbled your proud spirit before God. You have stood at warfare against the Spirit of God as revealed in reproof. Your carnal, unsubdued heart is not subject to control. You have not disciplined yourself. Time and again your uncontrolled temper, your spirit of insubordination, has gained complete mastery over you. How can such an impulsive, unsubdued soul live among the pure angels? It cannot be admitted into heaven, as you yourself know. If so, you cannot begin too soon to correct the evil in your nature. Be converted, and become as a little child.

Brother, you are proud-spirited, lofty in your thoughts and ideas of yourself. All this must be put away. Your relatives have learned to fear these outbreaks of temper. Your tender, God-fearing mother has done her best to soothe and indulge you, and has tried to remove every cause that would produce this self-rising, this uncontrollable disposition in her son. But coaxing, pleading, and seeking to pacify have led you to consider that this impulsive temper is incurable and that it is the duty of your friends to bear with it. All this petting and excusing has not remedied the evil, but rather given it license.

You have not fought with this wicked spirit and conquered it. When your way has been crossed you have felt the provocation sufficiently to forget your manhood and that you were created in the image of God and after His likeness. You have sadly defaced and marred that image. You have not had self-control nor power over your will. You have been headstrong, and have yielded to the power of Satan. Every time that you have given up to passion and self-rule, and let your feelings run away with your judgment, it has strengthened that set, uncontrolled will. The Lord saw that you did not know yourself, and that unless you saw yourself and the sinfulness of your course in the true light; unless you saw how aggravating in the sight of God were these outbreaks of temper which strengthened at every exhibition, you would surely fail of gaining a seat by the side of the suffering Man of Calvary.

God calls upon you, Brother G, to repent and be converted, and become as a little child. Unless the truth has a sanctifying influence upon your life to mold your character, you will fail of an inheritance in the kingdom of God. The Lord in His providence selected you to be more directly connected with His cause and work. He took you, like an undisciplined soldier, new to the army, and brought you under rules, regulations, and responsibilities, and through the drilling process. At first you did nobly and tried to be faithful at your post. You bore trial better than ever before in your life. But Satan came with his specious temptations, and you fell a prey to them. The Lord pitied you and laid His hand upon you to save you. He gave you a rich experience, which you have not profited by as you should have done. Like the children of Israel, you soon forgot the dealings of God and His great mercies. Brother G, you were raised up in answer to prayer, and God gave you a new lease of life; but you have let jealousy and envy into your soul, and have greatly displeased Him. He designed to bring you where you would develop character, where you would see and correct your defects.

There was a decided failure in your education and discipline during childhood and youth. You now have to learn the great lessons of self-control which ought to have been mastered in earlier days. God brought you where your surroundings would be changed and where you could be disciplined by His Holy Spirit, that you might acquire moral power and self-control to make you a conqueror. It will require the strongest effort, the most persevering and unfaltering determination, and the strongest energy to control self. Your spirit has long chafed under restraint, and your temper has raged like a caged lion when your will has been crossed.

The education which your parents should have assisted you to obtain must now be gained wholly by yourself. When young and small the twig might have been easily bent; but now, after it has grown gnarled and crooked and strong, how difficult the task! Your parents permitted it to be thus deformed; and now only by the grace of God, united with your own persistent efforts, can you become conqueror over your will. Through the merits of Christ you may part with that which scars and deforms the soul, and which develops a misshapen character. You must put away the old man with his errors and take the new man, Christ Jesus. Adopt His life as your guide then your talents and intellect will be devoted to God's service.

Oh, if mothers would only work with wisdom, with calmness and determination, to train and subdue the carnal tempers of their children, what an amount of sin would be nipped in the bud, and what a host of church trials would be saved! How many families that are now miserable would be happy! Many souls will be eternally lost because of the neglect of parents to properly discipline their children and to teach them submission to authority in their youth. Petting faults and soothing outbreaks is not laying the ax at the root of the evil, but proves the ruin of thousands of souls. Oh, how will parents answer to God for this fearful neglect of their duty!

Brother G, you are willing to stand at the head and dictate to others, but you will not be dictated to yourself. Your pride fires in a moment at the attempt. Self-love and a haughty spirit are unruly elements in your character, hindering spiritual advancement. Those who have this temperament must take hold of the work zealously and die to self, or they will lose heaven. God makes no compromise with this element, as do fond, mistaken parents.

In my last vision I was shown that if you refuse reproof and correction, choose your own way, and will not be disciplined, God has no further use for you in connection with His holy work. If you had commenced the work of setting your own soul right with the Lord you would have seen so great a work to be done for yourself that you would not have spent so much time over the supposed wrongs of Brother H, dwelling upon them behind his back. The work of the last thirty years should inspire confidence in the integrity of Brother H. "Honor to whom honor is due."

Men in responsible positions should improve continually. They must not anchor upon an old experience and feel that it is not necessary to become scientific workers. Man, although the most helpless of God's creatures when he comes into the world, and the most perverse in his nature, is nevertheless capable of constant advancement. He may be enlightened by science, ennobled by virtue, and may progress in mental and moral dignity, until he reaches a perfection of intelligence and a purity of character but little lower than the perfection and purity of angels. With the light of truth shining upon the minds of men, and the love of God shed abroad in their hearts, we cannot conceive what they may become nor what great work they may do.

I know that the human heart is blind to its own true condition, but I cannot leave you without making an effort to help you. We love you, and we want to see you pressing on to victory. Jesus loves you. He died for you, and He wants you to be saved. We have no disposition to hold you in ——; but we do want you to make thorough work with your own soul, to right every wrong there, and make every effort to master self, lest you miss heaven. This you cannot afford to do. For Christ's sake, resist the devil, and he will flee from you.

9. Labor Conducive to Health

Dear Brother and Sister I:

I have been shown that you have erred in the management of your children. You received ideas at —— from Dr. J, which you have spoken of before the patients and before your children. These ideas will not bear to be carried out. From Dr. J's standpoint they may not appear so objectionable;

but viewed from a Christian standpoint, they are positively dangerous. The instruction which Dr. J has given in regard to shunning physical labor have proved a great injury to many. The do-nothing system is a dangerous one. The necessity for amusements, as he teaches it and enjoins it upon his patients, is a fallacy. In order to occupy the time and engage the mind, they are made a substitute for useful, healthful exercise and physical labor. Amusements such as Dr. J recommends excite the brain more than useful employment.

Physical exercise and labor combined have a happy influence upon the mind, strengthen the muscles, improve the circulation, and give the invalid the satisfaction of knowing his own power of endurance; whereas, if he is restricted from healthful exercise and physical labor, his attention is turned to himself. He is in constant danger of thinking himself worse than he really is and of having established within him a diseased imagination which causes him to continually fear that he is overtaxing his powers of endurance. As a general thing, if he should engage in some well-directed labor, using his strength and not abusing it, he would find that physical exercise would prove a more powerful and effective agent in his recovery than even the water treatment he is receiving.

The inactivity of the mental and physical powers as far as useful labor is concerned is that which keeps many invalids in a condition of feebleness which they feel powerless to rise above. It also gives them a greater opportunity to indulge an impure imagination,—an indulgence which has brought many of them into their present condition of feebleness. They are told that they have expended too much vitality in hard labor, when, in nine cases out of ten, the labor they performed was the only redeeming thing in their lives and was the means of saving them from utter ruin. While their minds were thus engaged, they could not have as favorable an opportunity to debase their bodies and to complete the work of destroying themselves. To have all such persons cease to labor with brain and muscle is to give them ample opportunity to be taken captive by the temptations of Satan.

Dr. J has recommended that the sexes mingle together; he has taught that physical and mental health demands a closer association with one another. Such teaching has done and is doing great injury to inexperienced youth and children, and is a great satisfaction to men and women of questionable character, whose passions have never been controlled, and who for this reason are suffering from various debilitating disorders. These persons are instructed, from a health standpoint, to be much in the company of the opposite sex.

Thus a door of temptation is opened before them, passion rouses like a lion within their hearts, every consideration is overborne, and everything elevated and noble is sacrificed to lust. This is an age when the world is teeming with corruption. Were the minds and bodies of men and women in a healthy condition, were the animal passions subject to the higher intellectual powers of the mind, it might be comparatively safe to teach that boys and girls, and the youth of still more mature age, would be benefited by mingling much in the society of one another.

If the minds of the youth of this age were pure and uncorrupted, the girls might have a softening influence upon the minds and manners of the boys, and the boys, with their stronger, firmer natures, might have a tendency to ennoble and strengthen the character of the girls. But it is a painful fact that there is not one girl in a hundred who is pure-minded, and there is not one boy in a hundred whose morals are untainted. Many who are older have gone to such lengths in dissipation that they are polluted, soul and body; and corruption has taken hold of a large class who pass among men and women as polite gentlemen and beautiful ladies. It is not the time to recommend as beneficial to health the mingling of the sexes, their being as much as possible in the society of one another. The curse of this corrupt age is the absence of true virtue and modesty.

Dr. I, you have advanced these ideas in the parlor. The young have heard you, and your remarks have had as great an influence upon your own children as upon others. It would have been better to have left those ideas at——. Close application to severe labor is injurious to the growing frames of the young; but where hundreds have broken down their constitutions by overwork alone, inactivity, overeating, and delicate idleness have sown the seeds of disease in the system of thousands that are hurrying to swift and sure decay.

The reason the youth have so little strength of brain and muscle is because they do so little in the line of useful labor. "Behold, this was the iniquity of thy sister Sodom, pride, fullness of bread, and abundance of idleness was in her and in her daughters, neither did she strengthen the hand of the poor and needy. And they were haughty, and committed abomination before Me; therefore I took them away as I saw good."

There are but few of the youth of this degenerate age who can even endure the study necessary to obtain a common education. Why is this? Why do the children complain of dizziness, headache, bleeding at nose, palpitation, and a sense of lassitude and general weakness? Should this be attributed mainly to their close study? Fond and indulgent parents will sympathize with their children because they fancy their lessons are too great a task, and that their close application to study is ruining their health. True, it is not advisable to crowd the minds of the young with too many and too difficult studies. But, parents, have you looked no deeper into this matter than merely to adopt the idea suggested by your children? Have you not given too ready credence to the apparent reason for their indisposition? It becomes parents and guardians to look beneath the surface for the cause of this evil.

In ninety-nine cases out of one hundred the cause, searched out and revealed to you, would open your understanding to see that it was not the taxation of study alone that was doing the work of injury to your children, but that their own wrong habits were sapping the brain and the entire body of its vital energy. The nervous system has become shattered by being often excited, and thus has been laid the foundation for premature and certain decay. Solitary vice is killing thousands and tens of thousands.

Children should have occupation for their time. Proper mental labor and physical outdoor exercise will not break the constitutions of your boys. Useful labor and an acquaintance with the mysteries of housework will be beneficial to your girls, and some outdoor employment is positively necessary to their constitution and health. Children should be taught to labor. Industry is the greatest blessing that men, women, and children can have.

You have erred in the education of your children. You have been too indulgent. You have favored them and excused them from labor, until to some of them, it is positively distasteful. Inactivity, a lack of well-regulated employment, has injured them greatly. Temptations are on every side, ready to ruin the youth for this world and the next. The path of obedience is the only path of safety.

You have been blind to the power that the enemy had over your children. Household labor, even to weariness, would not have hurt them one-fiftieth part as much as indolent habits have done. They would have escaped many dangers had they been instructed at an earlier period to occupy their time with useful labor. They would not have contracted such a restless disposition, such a desire for change and to go into society. They would have escaped many temptations to vanity and to engage in unprofitable amusements, light reading, idle talking, and nonsense. Their time would have passed more to their satisfaction and without so great temptation to seek the society of the opposite sex and to excuse themselves in an evil way. Vanity and affectation, uselessness and positive sin, have been the result of this indolence. The parents, and especially you, the father, have flattered and indulged them to their great injury.

• Self-Conceit and Selfishness

Dear brother, you have made a sad mistake in standing before the patients in the parlor, as you have frequently done, and exalting yourself and wife. Your own children have learned lessons from these remarks that have given shape to their characters. You will now find it not an easy matter to correct the impressions that have been made. They have been proud and self-conceited. They have thought that as your children they were superior to children in general. You have felt anxious lest the people should not give you the respect due your position as a physician of the Health Institute. This has shown a vein of weakness in you which has hindered your spiritual advancement. It has also led to a jealousy of others, fearing that they would supplant you or not place the right estimate upon your position and value. You have also exalted your wife, placing her before the patients as a superior creature. You have been like a blind man; you have given her credit for qualifications which she does not possess.

You should have remembered that your moral worth is estimated by your words, your acts, your deeds. These can never be hidden, but will place you upon the right elevation before your patients. If you manifest interest for them, if you devote labor to them, they will know it, and you will have their confidence and love. But talk will never make them believe that your arduous labor for them has taxed you and exhausted your vitality, when they know that they have not had your special attention and care. The patients will have confidence and love for those who manifest a special interest in them and who labor for their recovery. If you do this work, which cannot be left undone, which the patients pay their money to have done, then you need not seek to gain esteem and respect by talking; you will as surely have it as you do the work.

You have not been free from selfishness, and therefore you have not had the blessing which God gives His unselfish workmen. Your interest has been divided. You have had such a special care for yourself and yours, that the Lord has had no reason to especially work and care for you. Your course in this respect has disqualified you for your position. I saw one year ago that you felt competent to manage the Institute yourself alone. Were it yours, and you the one to be especially benefited or injured by its losses and gains, you would see it your duty to have a special care that losses should not occur and that patients who were there upon charity should not drain the Institute of means.

You would investigate and would not have them remain a week longer than it was positively necessary. You would see many ways by which you could reduce expenses and keep up the property of the Institute. But you are merely employed, and the zeal, interest, and ability which you think you possess to carry on such an institution do not appear. The patients do not receive the attention for which they have paid and which they have a right to expect.

You were shown me as frequently turning away from invalids who were in need of your counsel and advice. You were presented before me as apparently indifferent, seeming rather impatient while scarcely listening to what they were saying, which was to them of great importance. You seemed to be in a great hurry, putting them off till some future time, when a very few appropriate words of sympathy and encouragement would have quieted a thousand fears, and given peace and assurance in the place of disquietude and distress. You appeared to dread to speak to the patients. You did not enter into their feelings, but held yourself aloof, when you should have manifested more familiarity. You were too distant and unapproachable. They look to you as children to a parent, and have a right to expect and receive attentions from you which they do not obtain. "Me and mine" comes between you and the labor your position requires you to perform. The patients and helpers need your advice frequently; but they feel an unwillingness to go to you, and do not feel free to speak with you.

You have sought to maintain an undue dignity. In the effort you have not attained the object, but have lost the confidence and love which you might have gained had you been unassuming, possessing meekness and humility of mind. True devotion and consecration to God will find a place for you in the hearts of all, and will clothe you with a dignity not assumed but genuine. You have been exalted by the words of approval which you have received. The life of Christ must be your pattern, teaching you to do good in every place that you occupy. While caring for others, God will care for you.

The Majesty of heaven did not avoid weariness. He traveled on foot from place to place to benefit the suffering and needy. Although you possess some knowledge, may have some understanding of the human system, and can trace disease to its cause,—although you may have the tongue of men and of angels,—there are yet qualifications necessary or all your gifts will be of no special value. You must have a power from God which can only be realized by those who make Him their trust and who consecrate themselves to the work that He has given them to do. Christ must be a portion of your knowledge. His wisdom instead of yours should be considered.

Then you will understand how to be a light in the rooms of the sick. You lack freedom of spirit, power, and faith. Your faith is feeble for want of exercise; it cannot be vigorous and healthful. Your efforts for those who are sick in heart and body will not be as successful as they might be, the patients will not gain in physical and spiritual strength as they might, if you do not carry Jesus with you in your visits. His words and works should accompany you. Then you will feel that those whom your prayers and words of sympathy have blessed will bless you in return.

You have not felt your whole dependence upon God and your inefficiency and weakness without His special wisdom and grace. You worry, fear, and doubt because you have worked too much in your own strength. In God you can prosper. In humility and holiness of mind you will find great peace and strength. They shine brightest who feel most their own weakness and darkness, for such make Christ their righteousness. Your strength should come from your union with Him. Be not weary in well-doing.

The Majesty of heaven has invited the weary ones: "Come unto Me, all ye that labor and are heavy-laden, and I will give you rest. Take My yoke upon you, and learn of Me; for I am meek and lowly in heart: and ye shall find rest unto your souls." The reason the burden sometimes seems so heavy and the yoke so galling is because you have got above the meekness and lowliness possessed by our divine Lord. Cease trying to gratify and exalt self; but rather let self be hidden in Jesus, and learn of Him who has invited you and promised you rest.

I saw that the Health Institute can never prosper while those who hold responsible positions connected with it have more interest for themselves than for the institution. God wants unselfish men and women as workers in His cause; and those who take charge of the Health Institute should have an oversight of every department there, practicing economy, caring for the trifles, guarding against losses. In short, they should be as careful and judicious in their management as though they themselves were the actual proprietors.

You have been troubled with a feeling that this and that was not your business. Everything connected with the Institute is your business. If certain things come under your observation that you cannot attend to properly, being called in another direction, call for the help of someone who will give these matters immediate attention. If this work is too arduous for you, someone should take your place who can perform thoroughly all the duties devolving upon one holding your responsible position.

In your parlor talks you have frequently charged the patients and helpers with bringing unnecessary burdens and cares upon you, while, at the same time, I saw that you were not performing half the duties resting upon you as a physician. You were not properly attending to the cases of the sick under your care. The patients are not blind; they perceive your neglect of them. They are away from their homes and upon expense to obtain the care and treatment that they could not receive at home. All this scolding in the parlor is injurious to the institution and displeasing to God.

It is true that you have had heavy burdens to bear, but in many cases you have blamed the patients and helpers when the trouble was in your own family. They require your constant help, but do not help you in return; there is no one in your home to stay up your hands or give you encouragement.

Had you no burden outside the Institute you could bear up much better and not lose strength and fortitude. It is your duty to care for your family, but it is not at all necessary for them to be as helpless as they are and so great a weight upon you. They could assist you if they would.

It is your duty also to preserve your health; and if your family cares are so great that the work in which you are engaged is overtaxing you, and you are unable to devote the time and attention to the patients and the Institute which is actually their due, then you should resign your position and seek to place yourself where you can do justice to your family, yourself, and to the responsibilities you assume. The position you now occupy is an important one. It requires a clear intellect, strength of brain, nerve, and muscle. Earnest devotion to the work is necessary for its success, and nothing short of this will make the institution prosperous. To be a living thing, it must have live, disinterested workers to conduct it.

Sister I, you have not been the help to your husband that you should have been. Your attention has been devoted more to yourself. You have not realized the necessity of arousing your dormant energies to encourage and strengthen your husband in his labors, or to bless your children with the right influence. Had you set yourself diligently about the duties God has enjoined upon you, had you helped to bear the burdens of your companion and united with him to properly discipline your children, the order of things in your family would have been changed.

But you have yielded to feelings of gloom and sadness, and this has brought upon your dwelling a cloud instead of sunshine. You have not encouraged hope and cheerfulness, and your influence has been depressing upon those whom you should have aided by kindly words and deeds. All this is the result of selfishness. You have required the attention and sympathy of your husband and children, and yet have not felt that it was your duty to take your mind off yourself and labor for their happiness and well-being. You have given way to impatience, and have harshly reproved your children. This has only confirmed them in their evil ways and severed the cords of affection that should bind the hearts of parents and children together.

You have lacked self-control and have censured your husband in the presence of your children; this has lessened his authority over them, and yours also. You have been very weak; when your children have come to you with complaints of others, you have immediately decided in their favor, and have unwisely censured and blamed those of whom they complained. This has cherished in the minds of your children a disposition to murmur against those who do not pay them the deference they imagine they deserve. You have indirectly encouraged this spirit instead of silencing it. You have not dealt with your children as firmly and justly as you should have done.

You have had trials. You have been oppressed in mind. You have been discouraged, but have unjustly charged this unhappiness upon others. The main cause is to be found in yourself. You have failed to make your home what it should be and what it might have been. It is yet in your power to correct the faults there. Come out of that cold and stiff reserve. Give more love, rather than exact it; cultivate cheerfulness; let the sunshine into your heart, and it will shine upon those about you; be more social in your manners; seek to gain the confidence of your children, that they may come to you for advice and counsel; encourage in them humility and unselfishness, and set before them the right example.

Awake, my dear brother and sister, to the needs of your family. Do not be blinded, but take hold of the work unitedly, calmly, prayerfully, and in faith. Set your house in order, and God will bless your efforts.

10. Influence of Social Surroundings

I was shown, December 10, 1872, the state of Brother K's family. He has been a true believer and lover of the truth, but has been drinking in the spirit of the world. Said Christ: "Where your treasure is, there will your heart be also." Brother K, your earthly treasure claims your interest and attention to such an extent that you do not afford time to serve God; yet your wife is dissatisfied that you give Him the meager pittance that you do. A worldly insanity has taken possession of her heart. Neither of you takes sufficient time for meditation and prayer. God is robbed of your daily service, and you yourselves are meeting with a greater loss than that of every earthly treasure.

Sister K, you are still farther from God than your husband is. Your conformity to the world has banished your Saviour from your heart; there is no room for Him in your affections. You have but little inclination for prayer and searching your heart. You are yielding yourself to obey the prince of the powers of darkness. "To whom ye yield yourselves servants to obey, his servants ye are to whom ye obey; whether of sin unto death, or of obedience unto righteousness."

Sister K, you know not what you are doing; you do not realize that you are warring against your Creator in drawing your husband away from the truth. Your attention is on the advantages that the world gives. You have not cultivated a love for devotion, but are better pleased with the stir and bustle of laboring to acquire wealth. You are absorbed in your desire to be like the world, that you may receive the happiness that the world gives. Your earthly ambitions and interests are greater than your desire for righteousness and for a part in the kingdom of God.

Your precious probationary time is spent in laboring for your temporal welfare, in dressing, and eating, and drinking after the manner of the world. Oh, how unsatisfying, how meager is the recompense obtained! In your worldly desires and pursuits you are carrying a heavier burden than your Saviour has ever proposed to lay upon you. Your Redeemer invites you: "Come unto Me, all ye that labor and are heavy-laden, and I will give you rest. Take My yoke upon you, and learn of Me; for I am meek and lowly in heart: and ye shall find rest unto your souls. For My yoke is easy, and My burden is light." My sister, Christ would have you lay down your heavy weight at His feet and submit your stubborn neck to His easy yoke.

What if your probation should close at this time? How would you bear the investigation of the Master? How have you employed the talents of means and influence lent you of God for wise improvement to His glory? God has given you life and its blessings, not to be devoted to your own pleasure and selfish gratification merely, but that you may benefit others and do good. The Master has entrusted you with talents that you should put out to the exchangers, that when He requires them again He may receive His own with usury.

Your influence and means have been given you to test you, to reveal what is in your heart; you should use them to win souls to Christ and thus advance the cause of your Redeemer. If you fail to do this you are making a terrible mistake. Every day that you devote to serving yourself, and to pleasing your friends by yielding to their influence in loving the world and neglecting your best Friend, who died to give you life, you are losing much.

Sister K, you have thought that it was not well for you to be different from those around you. You are in a community that has been tested on the truth and has rejected it, and you have linked your interests and affections with theirs until you are to all intents one of them. You love their society; yet you are not happy, though you flatter yourself that you are. You have said in your heart: "It is vain to serve God: and what profit is it that we have kept His ordinance, and that we have walked mournfully before the Lord of hosts?"

It is no small matter for a family to stand as representatives of Jesus, keeping God's law in an unbelieving community. We are required to be living epistles known and read of all men. This position involves fearful responsibilities. In order to live in the light, you must come where the light shines. Brother K, at any sacrifice, should feel under solemn obligation to attend, with his family, at least the yearly gatherings of those who love the truth. It would strengthen him and them, and fit them for trial and duty. It is not well for them to lose the privilege of associating with those of like faith; for the truth loses its importance in their minds, their hearts cease to be enlightened and vivified by its sanctifying influence, and they lose spirituality. They are not strengthened by the words of the living preacher. Worldly thoughts and worldly enterprises are continually exercising their minds to the exclusion of spiritual subjects.

The faith of most Christians will waver if they constantly neglect to meet together for conference and prayer. If it were impossible for them to enjoy such religious privileges, then God would send light direct from heaven by His angels, to animate, cheer, and bless His scattered people. But He does not propose to work a miracle to sustain the faith of His saints. They are required to love the truth enough to take some little pains to secure the privileges and blessings vouchsafed them of God. The least they can do is to devote a few days in the year to a united effort to advance the cause of Christ and to exchange friendly counsel and sympathy.

Many devote nearly all their time to their own temporal interests and pleasures, and grudge the few days spent and the expense involved in going a distance from their homes to meet with a company gathered together in the name of the Lord. The word of the Lord defines covetousness as idolatry;

then how many idolaters are there, even among those who profess to be the followers of Christ!

It is required that we meet together and bear testimony to the truth. The angel of God said: "Then they that feared the Lord spake often one to another: and the Lord hearkened, and heard it, and a book of remembrance was written before Him for them that feared the Lord, and that thought upon His name. And they shall be Mine, saith the Lord of hosts, in that day when I make up My jewels; and I will spare them, as a man spareth his own son that serveth him."

It will pay, then, to improve the privileges within our reach, and, even at some sacrifice, to assemble with those who fear God and speak for Him; for He is represented as hearkening to those testimonies, while angels write them in a book. God will remember those who have met together and thought upon His name, and He will spare them from the great conflagration. They will be as precious jewels in His sight, but His wrath will fall on the shelterless head of the sinner. It is not a vain thing to serve God. There is a priceless reward for those who devote their life to His service. Dear brother and sister, you have been gradually entering the darkness until almost imperceptibly it has grown to appear like the light to you. Occasionally a feeble glimmer penetrates the gloom and arouses the mind; but surrounding influences shut out the ray of light, and the darkness seems denser than before.

It would have been better for your spiritual welfare had you changed your place of residence some years ago. The light of truth tested the community in which you live. A few received the message of mercy and warning, while it was rejected by many. Still another class did not accept it because there was a cross to lift. They took a neutral position and thought that if they did not war against the truth they would be doing quite well, but the light they neglected to receive and cherish went out in darkness. They endeavored to quiet conscience by saying to the Spirit of God: "Go Thy way for this time; when I have a convenient season, I will call for Thee."

That convenient season has never come. They neglected the golden opportunity that has never again returned to them, for the world has shut out the light that they refused. The interests of this life and the charm of exciting pleasures absorb their minds and hearts, while their best Friend, the blessed Saviour, is rejected and forgotten.

Sister K, although possessing excellent natural qualities, is being drawn away from God by her unbelieving friends and relatives, who love not the truth and have no sympathy with the sacrifice and self-denial that must be made for the truth's sake. Sister K has not felt the importance of separation from the world, as the command of God enjoins. The sight of her eyes and the hearing of her ears have perverted her heart.

John the Baptist was a man filled with the Holy Ghost from his birth, and if there was anyone who could remain unaffected by the corrupting influences of the age in which he lived, it was surely he. Yet he did not venture to trust his strength; he separated himself from his friends and relatives, that his natural affections might not prove a snare to him. He would not place himself unnecessarily in the way of temptation nor where the luxuries or even the conveniences of life would lead him to indulge in ease or to gratify his appetite, and thus lessen his physical and mental strength. By such a course the important mission upon which he came would have failed of its accomplishment.

He subjected himself to privation and solitude in the wilderness, where he could preserve the sacred sense of the majesty of God by studying His great book of nature and there becoming acquainted with His character as revealed in His wonderful works. It was an atmosphere calculated to perfect moral culture and to keep the fear of the Lord continually before him. John, the forerunner of Christ, did not expose himself to evil conversation and the corrupting influences of the world. He feared the effect upon his conscience, that sin might not appear to him so exceedingly sinful. He chose rather to have his home in the wilderness, where his senses would not be perverted by his surroundings. Should we not learn something from this example of one whom Christ honored and of whom He said: "Among them that are born of women there hath not risen a greater than John the Baptist"?

The first thirty years of Christ's life were passed in retirement. Ministering angels waited upon the Lord of life as He walked side by side with the peasants and laborers among the hills of Nazareth, unrecognized and unhonored. These noble examples should teach us to avoid evil influences and to shun the society of those who do not live aright. We should not flatter ourselves that we are too strong for any such influences to affect us, but we should in humility guard ourselves from danger.

Ancient Israel were especially directed by God to be and remain a people separate from all nations. They were not to be subjected to witnessing the idolatry of those about them, lest their own hearts should be corrupted, lest familiarity with ungodly practices should make them appear less wicked in their eyes. Few realize their own weakness and that the natural sinfulness of the human heart too often paralyzes their noblest endeavors.

The baleful influence of sin poisons the life of the soul. Our only safety is in separation from those who live in its darkness. The Lord has enjoined upon us to come out from among them and be separate, and to touch not the unclean thing, and He will receive us and will be a Father unto us, and we shall be His sons and daughters. If we wish to be adopted into the family of God, to become children of the heavenly King, we must comply with His conditions; we must come out from the world and stand as a peculiar people before the Lord, obeying His precepts and serving Him.

Lot chose Sodom for his home because he saw that there were advantages to be gained there from a worldly point of view. But after he had established himself, and grown rich in earthly treasure, he was convinced that he had made a mistake in not taking into consideration the moral standing of the community in which he was to make his home.

The dwellers in Sodom were corrupt; vile conversation greeted his ears daily, and his righteous soul was vexed by the violence and crime he was powerless to prevent. His children were becoming like these wicked people, for association with them had perverted their morals. Taking all these things into consideration, the worldly riches he had gained seemed small and not worth the price he had paid for them. His family connections were extensive, his children having married among the Sodomites.

The Lord's anger was finally kindled against the wicked inhabitants of the city, and angels of God visited Sodom to bring forth Lot, that he should not perish in the overthrow of the city. They bade Lot bring his family, his wife, and the sons and daughters who married in wicked Sodom, and told him to flee from the place. "For," said the angels, "we will destroy this place, because the cry of them is waxen great before the face of the Lord; and the Lord hath sent us to destroy it."

And Lot went out and entreated his children. He repeated the words of the angel: "Up, get you out of this place; for the Lord will destroy this city."

But he seemed unto his sons-in-law as one who mocked; for they had lived so long in Sodom that they had become partakers of the sins of the people. And the daughters were influenced by their husbands to believe that their father was mad. They were well enough off where they were. They were rich and had great possessions; and they could not believe it possible that beautiful Sodom, a rich and fertile country, would be destroyed by the wrath of a sin-avenging God.

Lot returned sorrowfully to the angels and repeated the story of his failure. Then the angels commanded him to arise, and take his wife and the two daughters who were yet in his house, and leave the city. But Lot was sad; the thought of leaving his children and his wife, for she refused to go without them, almost broke his heart. They would all have perished in the terrible ruin of Sodom, had not the Lord, in His great mercy, sent His angels to the rescue.

Lot was paralyzed by the great calamity about to occur; he was stupefied with grief at the thought of leaving all he held dear on earth. But as he lingered, the angels of God laid hold upon his hand, and the hands of his wife and two daughters, and brought them out of the city, and charged them to flee for their lives, neither to look behind them nor to stay upon all the plain, but to escape to the mountains.

How reluctant was Lot to obey the angel and go as far as possible from corrupt Sodom, appointed to utter destruction! He distrusted God and pleaded to remain. Living in the wicked city had weakened his faith and confidence in the justice of the Lord. He pleaded that he could not do as he was required, lest some evil should overtake him, and he should die.

Angels were sent on a special mission to save the lives of Lot and his family; but Lot had so long been surrounded by corrupting influences that his sensibilities were blunted, and he could not discern the works of God and His purposes; he could not trust himself in His hands to do His bidding. He was continually pleading for himself, and this unbelief cost him the life of his wife. She looked back to Sodom, and, murmuring against the dealings of God, she was changed to a pillar of salt, that she might stand as a warning to all those who disregard the special mercies and providences of Heaven.

After this terrible retribution, Lot no longer dared to linger by the way, but fled into the mountains, according to the direction of the angels. The sinful conduct of his daughters after leaving Sodom was the result of wicked associations while there. The sense of right and wrong was confused in their minds, and sin did not appear as sin to them.

The case of Lot should be a warning to all those who wish to live godly lives, to separate themselves from all influences calculated to lead them away from God. Lot remained so long among the wicked that he was only able to save himself and two daughters, and even they were corrupted in morals by their sojourn in Sodom.

God means what He says, and He will not be trifled with. Oh! how many shortsighted, sinful mortals plead with God to induce Him to come to their terms, while if they would only yield themselves unreservedly into His hands He would compass their salvation and give them precious victories.

Sister K, you are in danger of making decisions that will be very injurious to you. God has a work for you to do which none can do for you, and without doing this your soul cannot be saved. God loves you and is unwilling that you should perish in the general ruin. He invites you to leave those things which hinder your spiritual advancement, and to find in Him that strength and consolation which you need. You have cares and burdens to bear in your family that often worry you; but if you do only those things necessary to your temporal comfort and happiness, you will find time to read your Bible with prayerful interest and to perfect a Christian character.

Brother K, you have had many discouragements; but you must be earnest, firm, and decided to do your duty in your family, and take them with you if possible. You should spare no effort to prevail upon them to accompany you on your heavenward journey. But if the mother and the children do not choose to accompany you, but rather seek to draw you away from your duties and religious privileges, you must go forward even if you go alone. You must live in the fear of God. You must improve your opportunities of attending the meetings and gaining all the spiritual strength you can, for you will need it in the days to come. Lot's property was all consumed. If you should meet with loss you should not be discouraged; and if you can save only a part of your family, it is much better than to lose all.

Dear brother and sister, as parents you are in a great measure accountable for the souls of your children. You have brought them into existence; and you should, by precept and example, lead them to the Lord and the courts of heaven. You should impress them with the thought that their temporal interests are of little consequence when compared with their eternal welfare.

These dear children are living among worldly people, and they are imbibing a love for the vanities of life. Your son L is a kindhearted, fine-spirited boy; but he needs the watchful care of a mother whose daily experience in the Christian life will fit her to counsel and instruct him. He is at just that age when a tender, judicious mother can mold him by her influence; but I fear, Sister K, that you seek rather to mold your children after the fashion of this world, and neglect to teach them that the important work of life is to form characters that will ensure immortality.

If L neglects to become acquainted with religious subjects and practical Christianity, his life will be a mistake. He should see that he needs an education in spiritual things, that he may use his abilities wholly for God. The Lord calls for young men to work in His vineyard. Young men should not neglect the essential branches of education. But if they turn their entire attention to secular study, and neglect to become intelligent on the great subject of religion, and do not acquire a Christian experience, they are becoming disqualified for the work of God. However favorable the educational advantage may be, something besides the knowledge of books is necessary to save the soul and lead others to repentance. Devoting a period of years to the acquisition of scientific knowledge alone is not preparing to be an efficient laborer in the service of God.

Young men should devote much time to study; but they should also unite physical labor with their mental efforts, and put in practice the knowledge they have gained, that by useful exercise all the faculties of the mind and powers of the body may be equally developed. They should not neglect the things necessary to salvation, nor consider them secondary to anything in this life.

Dear brother and sister, God loves your family, and desires to shower His special blessings upon you, that you may become instruments of righteousness in leading others toward heaven. If entirely consecrated to God, Brother K could do a great amount of good in a community where his advice and influence would be better received and appreciated. We have strong hopes that both of you will correct that which is wrong in your lives, and renew your faith and obedience to God, receiving new strength from Him who has promised to help those who call upon His name.

Young Brother L, you have made a mistake in your life. In closely pursuing your studies you have neglected the development of all your faculties. The moral growth should never be dwarfed in the effort to acquire an education, but should be cultivated in a far higher degree than is usually deemed necessary. My dear young brother, you have been ambitious to secure knowledge. This ambition is praiseworthy; but in order to gratify it, you have neglected your eternal interests and made them secondary to your studies. God and heaven have occupied a subordinate position in your affections. The claims of God's holy law have not been sacredly observed in your daily life. You have desecrated the Sabbath by bringing your studies into that holy time which was not yours to occupy for your own purposes. God has said: "In it thou shalt not do any work."

"If thou turn away thy foot from the Sabbath, from doing thy pleasure on My holy day; and call the Sabbath a delight, the holy of the Lord, honorable; and shalt honor Him, not doing thine own ways, nor finding thine own pleasure, nor speaking thine own words: then shalt thou delight thyself in the Lord; and I will cause thee to ride upon the high places of the earth, and feed thee with the heritage of Jacob thy father: for the mouth of the Lord hath spoken it." You have yielded to inclination rather than duty and made your studies paramount to the expressed command of the Most High.

Our camp meetings are arranged and held at great expense. God's ministers who advocate unpopular truth, labor excessively at these large gatherings to bear the message of mercy from a crucified Redeemer to poor fallen sinners. To neglect or treat these messages with indifference is to slight the mercy of God and His voice of warning and entreaty. Your absence from these meetings has been very detrimental to your spiritual welfare.

You have missed the strength that you might have gained there by listening to the preached word of God, and mingling with the believers of the truth. Your mind has been lulled into a fatal apathy in regard to the well-being of your soul. You have exalted your secular education above the knowledge to be gained in the school of Christ. Experience in a true religious life is necessary in order to form a character acceptable to God and to secure the pure virtues that will bear the light of heaven.

What anxiety you have manifested to discipline your mind by study, to become properly conversant with your textbooks, that you might pass a creditable examination before instructors, friends, and interested spectators! How ambitious you have been to prove that you have been a diligent student and have faithfully employed your time in storing your mind with useful knowledge! You have been as sincerely anxious to progress in your studies as you have been to secure the commendation of your friends and teachers. You have justly earned the honors you have received for scholarship.

But how has your mind been disciplined in religion? Have you not unthinkingly placed the kingdom of God and His righteousness below your advancement in the sciences? True, some of the human faculties were given more especially for the purpose of engaging in temporal matters, but the higher powers of the mind should be wholly consecrated to God. These control the man, these form his life and character. And while you should not neglect your secular studies, you have no right to give them all your attention, but should devote yourself especially to the moral and spiritual requirements of your heavenly Father.

How little anxiety you have manifested to improve the religious advantages within your reach to gain a more thorough knowledge of the laws of God, and determination to abide by them! You have made little effort to become a loyal and intelligent Christian. How, then, will you be prepared to pass the grand review, where all your deeds and words, and the inmost thoughts of your heart, will be laid open before the great Judge and the assembled saints and angels? You have had little ambition to obtain a spiritual fitness to bear this close examination in the presence of that exalted throng.

What, then, will be the final decision as to your moral and religious attainments, that decision from which there is no appeal? What will be the honors accredited to you because of your faithfulness in preserving the required harmony between religion and the pursuit of the sciences? Will you stand as one possessing unfaltering moral courage, in whom is shown excellence of human knowledge united with a holy zeal for God and the obedience of His law?

My brother, you should consider the wisdom of God as all in all. Religion must go hand in hand with science, in order to make your education a sanctified means of doing good and turning others to the truth. The more we learn in the school of Christ, the more eager we are to advance in that knowledge. All our acquirements are of little value unless the character is ennobled by religion. God has special duties for every individual to perform, and a decision will be passed upon every case as to the faithfulness with which these duties have been accomplished.

The Lord frequently places us in difficult positions to stimulate us to greater exertion. In His providence special annoyances sometimes occur to test our patience and faith. God gives us lessons of trust. He would teach us where to look for help and strength in time of need. Thus we obtain practical knowledge of His divine will, which we so much need in our life experience. Faith grows strong in earnest conflict with doubt and fear. Brother, you may be a conqueror if you take careful heed to your ways. You should devote your young life to the cause of God and pray for success.

You should not close your eyes to your danger, but should resolutely prepare for every difficulty in your Christian advancement. Take time for reflection and for humble, earnest prayer. Your talents are marked, and you are hopeful in regard to your future success; but unless you comprehend the weakness of your natural heart you will be disappointed.

You are just starting out in life; you have arrived at an age to bear responsibilities for yourself. This is a critical period in your life. Now, in your youth, you are sowing in the field of life. That which you sow you will also reap; as was the seed, so will be the harvest. If you are neglectful and indifferent concerning eternal things you will sustain a great loss yourself and, through your influence, will prevent others from fulfilling their obligations to God.

Both worlds are before you. Which will you choose? Be wise and lay hold of eternal life. Swerve not from your integrity, however unpleasant your duties may appear in the present emergency. It may seem that you are about to make great sacrifices to preserve your purity of soul, but do not hesitate; press forward in the fear of God, and He will bless your efforts and recompense you a thousandfold. Do not yield your religious claims and privileges in order to gratify the wishes of your unconsecrated friends and relatives. You are called to take your position for the truth, even if it should be in direct opposition to those who are closely connected with you. God forbid that this last trial should ever come to you, to test and prove your integrity for the right.Lay the foundation of your Christian character upon the eternal Rock of salvation, and let the structure be firm and sound.

We hope that your mother will aid you and your brothers and sisters in your efforts to perfect true characters after the pattern of Christ, that you may have a moral fitness for the society of holy angels in the kingdom of glory.

11. A Divided Interest

Dear Brethren M: In the vision given me last January I was shown some things in reference to you both. I was shown that you are not growing in spirituality as it is your duty and privilege to grow. The greatness of the work and the opening providences of God should stir your hearts. Christ designed that His believing children should be the light of the world, the salt of the earth. The holy life, the Christian example, of one good man in a community sheds a light that is reflected upon others. How great, then, would be the influence of a company of believers all walking in the commandments of God.

The preaching of the word is ordained of God to arouse and convict sinners. And when the living preacher exemplifies in his own life the self-denial and sacrifices of Christ, when his conversation and acts are in harmony with the divine Pattern, then his influence will be a powerful one upon those who listen to his voice. But all cannot be teachers of the word in the pulpit. The duties of different persons vary, and there is work for all to do.

All can aid the cause by giving unselfishly of their means to help the various branches of the work, by furnishing means for the publication of tracts and periodicals to scatter among the people and disseminate the truth. Those who give money to promote the cause are bearing a part of the burden of the work; they are colaborers with Christ; for God has furnished men with means on trust, to be used for holy and wise purposes. They are the instrumentalities which Heaven has ordained for doing good, and men are to put these talents out to the exchangers.

Dear brethren, ever bear in mind that you are the stewards of God, and that He holds you accountable for the temporal talents He has lent you to use wisely for His glory. Will you not closely search your hearts and investigate the motives which prompt you to action? I was shown that your danger is in loving your possessions. Your ears are not quick to hear the Master's call in the person of His saints and in the wants of His cause. You do not invest your treasure gladly in the enterprise of Christianity. If you desire a treasure in heaven you should be securing it while you have the opportunity. If you feel safer to apply your means toward the greater accumulation of earthly riches, and to invest sparingly in the cause of God, then you should feel satisfied to receive heavenly treasure according to your investment in heavenly stock.

You desire to see the cause of God progress, but you make little personal effort toward that end. If you, and others who profess our holy faith, could see your true position and realize your accountability to God you would become more earnest colaborers with Jesus. "Thou shalt love the Lord thy God with all thy heart, and with all thy soul, and with all thy mind, and with all thy strength." There can be no divided interest in this, for the whole heart and mind and strength comprise the entire man.

Says the apostle: "Ye are not your own; for ye are bought with a price." When the poor, condemned sinner was lying under the curse of the Father's law, Jesus so loved him that He gave Himself for the transgressor. He redeemed him by the virtue of His blood. We cannot estimate the precious ransom paid to redeem fallen man. The heart's best and holiest affections should be given in return for such wondrous love. The temporal gifts you enjoy are merely lent you to aid in the advancement of the kingdom of God.

I speak of the tithing system, yet how meager it looks to my mind! How small the estimate! How vain the endeavor to measure with mathematical rules, time, money, and love against a love and sacrifice that is measureless and incomputable! Tithes for Christ! Oh, meager pittance, shameful recompense for that which cost so much! From the cross of Calvary, Christ calls for an unconditional surrender. He promised the young ruler that if he sold all that he had and gave it to the poor, and lifted His cross and followed Him, he should have treasure in heaven. All we have should be consecrated to God. The Majesty of heaven came to the world to die a sacrifice for the sins of man. And how cold and selfish is the human heart that can turn away from such incomparable love and set itself upon the vain things of this world.

When selfishness is striving for the victory over you, bear in mind One who left the glorious courts of heaven and laid aside the robes of royalty for your sakes, becoming poor that through His poverty you might be made rich.

Will you, then, disregard this great love and boundless mercy by refusing to be inconvenienced and to deny yourselves for His dear sake? Will you cling to the treasures of this life and neglect to aid in carrying forward the great work of truth?

The children of Israel were anciently commanded to make an offering for the entire congregation to purify them from ceremonial defilement. This sacrifice was a red heifer and represented the more perfect offering that should redeem from the pollution of sin. This was an occasional sacrifice for the purification of all those who had necessarily or accidentally touched the dead. All who came in contact with death in any way were considered ceremonially unclean. This was to forcibly impress the minds of the Hebrews with the fact that death came in consequence of sin and therefore is a representative of sin. The one heifer, the one ark, the one brazen serpent, impressively point to the one great offering, the sacrifice of Christ.

This heifer was to be red, which was a symbol of blood. It must be without spot or blemish, and one that had never borne a yoke. Here, again, Christ was typified. The Son of God came voluntarily to accomplish the work of atonement. There was no obligatory yoke upon Him, for He was independent and above all law. The angels, as God's intelligent messengers, were under the yoke of obligation; no personal sacrifice of theirs could atone for the guilt of fallen man. Christ alone was free from the claims of the law to undertake the redemption of the sinful race. He had power to lay down His life and to take it up again. "Who, being in the form of God, thought it not robbery to be equal with God."

Yet this glorious Being loved the poor sinner and took upon Himself the form of a servant, that He might suffer and die in man's behalf. Jesus might have remained at His Father's right hand, wearing His kingly crown and royal robes. But He chose to exchange all the riches, honor, and glory of heaven for the poverty of humanity, and His station of high command for the horrors of Gethsemane and the humiliation and agony of Calvary. He became a man of sorrows and acquainted with grief, that by His baptism of suffering and blood He might purify and redeem a guilty world. "Lo, I come," was the joyful assent, "to do Thy will, O My God."

The sacrificial heifer was conducted without the camp and slain in the most imposing manner. Thus Christ suffered without the gates of Jerusalem, for Calvary was outside the city walls. This was to show that Christ did not die for the Hebrews alone, but for all mankind. He proclaims to a fallen world that He has come to be their Redeemer and urges them to accept the salvation He offers them. The heifer having been slain in a most solemn manner, the priest, clothed in pure white garments, took the blood in his hands as it issued from the body of the victim and cast it toward the temple seven times. "And having an high priest over the house of God; let us draw near with a true heart in full assurance of faith, having our hearts sprinkled from an evil conscience, and our bodies washed with pure water."

The body of the heifer was burned to ashes, which signified a whole and ample sacrifice. The ashes were then gathered up by a person uncontaminated by contact with the dead and placed in a vessel containing water from a running stream. This clean and pure person then took a cedar stick with scarlet cloth and a bunch of hyssop, and sprinkled the contents of the vessel upon the tent and the people assembled. This ceremony was repeated several times in order to be thorough and was done as a purification from sin.

Thus Christ, in His own spotless righteousness, after shedding His precious blood, enters into the holy place to cleanse the sanctuary. And there the crimson current is brought into the service of reconciling God to man. Some may look upon this slaying of the heifer as a meaningless ceremony, but it was done by the command of God and bears a deep significance that has not lost its application to the present time.

The priest used cedar and hyssop, dipping them into the cleansing water and sprinkling the unclean. This symbolized the blood of Christ spilled to cleanse us from moral impurities. The repeated sprinklings illustrate the thoroughness of the work that must be accomplished for the repenting sinner. All that he has must be consecrated. Not only should his own soul be washed clean and pure, but he should strive to have his family, his domestic arrangements, his property, and his entire belongings consecrated to God.

After the tent had been sprinkled with hyssop, over the door of those cleansed was written: I am not my own; Lord, I am Thine. Thus should it be with those who profess to be cleansed by the blood of Christ. God is no less exacting now than He was in olden times. The psalmist, in his prayer, refers to this symbolic ceremony when he says: "Purge me with hyssop, and I shall be clean: wash me, and I shall be whiter than snow." "Create in me a clean heart, O God; and renew a right spirit within me." "Restore unto me the joy of Thy salvation; and uphold me with Thy free spirit."

The blood of Christ is efficacious, but it needs to be applied continually. God not only wants His servants to use the means He has entrusted to them for His glory, but He desires them to make a consecration of themselves to His cause. If you, my brethren, have become selfish and are withholding from the Lord that which you should cheerfully give to His service, then you need the blood of sprinkling thoroughly applied, consecrating you and all your possessions to God.

My much-respected brethren, you have not that earnest and unselfish devotion to the work of God that He requires of you. You have given your attention to temporal matters. You have trained your minds for business in order to thereby benefit yourselves. But God calls for you to come into closer union with Him, that He may mold and train you for His work. A solemn statement was made to ancient Israel that the man who should remain unclean and refuse to purify himself should be cut off from among the congregation. This has a special meaning for us. If it was necessary in ancient times for the unclean to be purified by the blood of sprinkling, how essential for those living in the perils of the last days, and exposed to the temptations of Satan, to have the blood of Christ applied to their hearts daily. "For if the blood of bulls and of goats, and the ashes of an heifer sprinkling the unclean, sanctifieth to the purifying of the flesh: how much more shall the blood of Christ, who through the eternal Spirit offered Himself without spot to God, purge your conscience from dead works to serve the living God?"

You should both do much more than you have done toward bearing the burdens of the work of the Lord. I adjure you to arouse from your lethargy, leave the vain idolatry of worldly things, and be in earnest to secure a title to your immortal inheritance. Work while it is day. Do not imperil your souls by forfeiting present opportunities. Do not make your eternal interests of secondary importance. Do not put the world before religion, and toil day after day to acquire its riches, while the peril of eternal bankruptcy threatens you. Every day is bringing you nearer to the final reckoning. Be ready to yield up the talents lent you, with the increase gained by their wise use.

You cannot afford to sacrifice heaven or to jeopardize your safety. Do not let the deceitfulness of riches lead you to neglect the immortal treasure. Satan is a wily foe, and he is ever on your track, striving to ensnare you and compass your ruin. We are in the waiting time; let your loins be girded about and your lights shining, that you may wait for the Lord when He returns from the wedding, that when He comes and knocks you may open unto Him immediately.

Watch, brethren, the first dimming of your light, the first neglect of prayer, the first symptom of spiritual slumber. "He that endureth to the end shall be saved." It is by the constant exercise of faith and love that believers are made to shine as lights in the world. You are making but poor preparation for the Master's coming if you are serving mammon while professedly serving God. When He appears, you must then present to Him the talents that you have buried in the earth, talents neglected, abused, misused—a divided love.

Both of you have professed to be servants of Christ. How necessary that you should obey your Master's directions and be faithful to your duties. "Behold, what manner of love the Father hath bestowed upon us, that we should be called the sons of God." This love is without a parallel, giving to men the relationship of sons to God. Therefore the Father expects obedience from His children; therefore He requires a right disposition of the property He has placed in their hands. It is not their own to use for their personal gratification; but it is the capital of the Lord, for which they are responsible to Him.

Children of the Lord, how precious is the promise! How full the atonement of the Saviour for our guilt! The Redeemer, with a heart of unalterable love, still pleads His sacred blood in the sinner's behalf. The wounded hands, the pierced side, the marred feet, plead eloquently for fallen man, whose redemption is purchased at such an infinite cost. Oh, matchless condescension! Neither time nor events can lessen the efficacy of the atoning sacrifice. As the fragrant cloud of incense rose acceptably to heaven, and Aaron sprinkled the blood upon the mercy seat of ancient Israel and cleansed the people from guilt, so the merits of the slain Lamb are accepted by God today as a purifier from the defilement of sin.

"Watch and pray, that ye enter not into temptation." There are stern battles for you to fight. You should put on the whole armor of righteousness and prove yourselves strong and true in your Redeemer's service. God wants no idlers in His field, but colaborers with Christ, vigilant sentinels at their posts, valiant soldiers of the cross, ready to do and dare all things for the cause in which they are enlisted.

It is not wealth or intellect that gives happiness; it is true moral worth and a sense of duty performed. You may have the overcomer's reward and stand before the throne of Christ to sing His praises in the day when He assembles His saints; but your robes must be cleansed in the blood of the Lamb, and charity must cover you as a garment, and you be found spotless and without blemish.

John says: "After this I beheld, and, lo, a great multitude, which no man could number, of all nations, and kindreds, and people, and tongues, stood before the throne, and before the Lamb, clothed with white robes, and palms in their hands; and cried with a loud voice, saying, Salvation to our God which sitteth upon the throne, and unto the Lamb." "These are they which came out of great tribulation, and have washed their robes, and made them white in the blood of the Lamb. Therefore are they before the throne of God, and serve Him day and night in His temple: and He that sitteth on the throne shall dwell among them. They shall hunger no more, neither thirst any more; neither shall the sun light on them, nor any heat. For the Lamb which is in the midst of the throne shall feed them, and shall lead them unto living fountains of waters: and God shall wipe away all tears from their eyes."

12. Self-Exaltation

Dear Brother N:

In my last vision your case was presented before me. I was shown that there are defects in your Christian character that must be overcome before you can perfect holiness in the fear of the Lord. You love the truth, but you need to be sanctified by it. You are not selfish nor niggardly in hospitality or in sustaining the cause of truth; but there is one kind of selfishness which exists in your heart. You are wedded to your own opinion and extol your own judgment above that of others. You are in danger of exalting yourself above your brethren. You are exacting and are inclined to carry out your own ideas, independent of your brethren, because you consider your intelligence and experience superior to theirs. In this you fail to carry out the apostle's injunction: "Let nothing be done through strife or vainglory; but in lowliness of mind let each esteem other better than themselves." You have your notions, your purposes, and your plans, and you imagine they can never be incorrect.

In your household you have always taken too much of the management upon yourself. When your opinions or plans have been crossed, instead of conceding to, or compromising with, those who opposed you, considering that they as well as yourself had a right to their independent judgment, you have felt vexed and hurt. You could not endure that your family should call your plans in question or offer suggestions differing from your opinions. In consequence of this unpleasant state of affairs your family have usually submitted their wishes to yours, and allowed you to have your own way, in order to preserve harmony at home. Therefore there has been in your family much long-suffering, much patient indulgence of your whims. This appears to you only a proper observance of your legitimate authority; you consider it sound and correct management on your part.

Whenever your determination to carry out your own judgment at all hazards has driven your friends to the opposite extreme and to feel contempt for your arbitrary spirit, you have felt and intimated that all such opposition was instigated by the temptations of the enemy. This has made you more persistent in carrying out your own ideas, regardless of the wishes of others.

You are in danger of having trouble because you are unwilling to grant liberty of judgment and opinion to those connected with you. It is well for you to remember that their ways and their opinions may be as dear to them as yours are to you. We are very apt to lose sight of this fact when we censure others for not agreeing with us. You govern the members of your family too rigidly. You are very punctilious in giving them line upon line and precept upon precept; and if they venture to differ with you, it only renders you more determined to act according to your own mind, and to show that you are master in your own house, and that you are not to be interfered with.

You seem to consider that it is enough for you to say that a thing must be done in order to have it done in the very manner you indicate. In this arbitrary way you often place your mind and judgment between your family and their own good sense of what is right and proper under the circumstances. You have made a sad mistake in breaking down the will and judgment of your wife, and requiring her to unquestionably yield to your superior wisdom or bring discord into the home.

You should not seek to rule the actions of your wife, or treat her as a servile dependent. Never lift yourself above her, and excuse yourself by thinking: "She is inexperienced and inferior to me." Never seek to unreasonably bend her will to yours, for she has an individuality that can never be merged in yours. I have seen many families shipwrecked through overmanagement on the part of their head, whereas through consultation and agreement all might have moved off harmoniously and well.

My brother, you are self-conceited. You go out of your proper province in order to exercise your authority. You imagine that you understand the best way of doing the work in your kitchen. You have your own peculiar ideas of how everything should be done in the working department, and you expect all to adapt themselves like machinery to these ideas and observe the particular order that pleases you.

These efforts to bring your friends into a position where they will meekly yield every wish and inclination to your will are vain and futile. All minds are not molded alike, and it is well that it is so, for if they were exactly similar, there would be less harmony and natural adaptability to each other than now. But we are all represented as being members of the body, united in Christ. In this body there are various members, and one member cannot perform exactly the same office as another.

The eyes are made for seeing, and in no case can they perform the work of the ears, which is that of hearing; neither can the ears take the place of the mouth, nor the mouth perform the office of the nose. Yet all these organs are necessary to the perfect whole and work in beautiful harmony with one another. The hands have their office, and the feet theirs. One is not to say to the other, "You are inferior to me;" the hands are not to say to the feet, "We have no need of you;" but all are united to the body to do their specific work and should be alike respected, as they conduce to the comfort and usefulness of the perfect whole.

We cannot all have the same minds nor cherish the same ideas; but one is to be a benefit and blessing to the other, that where one lacks, another may supply what is requisite. You have certain deficiencies of character and natural biases that render it profitable for you to be brought in contact with a mind differently organized, in order to properly balance your own. Instead of superintending so exclusively, you should consult with your wife and arrive at joint decisions. You do not encourage independent effort on the part of your family; but if your specific directions are not scrupulously carried out, you too frequently find fault with the delinquents.

Were your wife and other members of your family without tact or skill, you would be more excusable in taking the reins so entirely into your own hands; but this not being the case, your course is altogether unwarrantable. After you have kindly informed them concerning your views of cooking and the management of household matters, and intimated what your desires are in this respect, go no further, but let them use your suggestions as they choose. They will be much more likely to be pleasantly influenced to please you than if you resorted to peremptory measures. And even if they do not adapt themselves to your opinions, do not persist in ruling, in having everything done in your own way. You must remember that the natural independence of others should be respected. If your wife does her work in a way convenient to herself, you have no right to interfere with her affairs and fret and burden her with your many suggestions and reflections upon her management.

You have many good and generous traits of character. You are a courteous, affable man, in general, to those outside your own family. Perhaps this is attributable, in some measure, to the fact that you dare not exhibit your natural disposition to any except those whom you consider greatly your inferiors. If your superiority is not sufficiently recognized in society, you are determined that it shall be at home, where you think that none will presume to dispute its claims.

You should go diligently about effecting a change in your self. If you are willing to sacrifice your selfishness, your exacting disposition, your pet notions and ideas, you can have a peaceful, happy home upon which angels will delight to look. Is it sweeter to have your will than to see a proper freedom of action and spirit in your household? Your home is not always just what it should be, but you are the principal cause of its discord. If you stand as a representative of Christ upon the earth, do not, I beseech you, misrepresent your blessed Redeemer, who was meek and kind, gentle and forgiving.

It is a fact well worth your consideration that it is a difficult thing for people who have sound minds and ideas of their own, to work precisely in the groove that another may lay out for them. Therefore you have no moral right to embarrass your wife and family with your whims and petulant notions concerning their employment. It will be hard for you to at once change your mode of operation, but make a firm determination that you will not enter your kitchen unless it be to encourage the efforts and praise the management of those who are laboring there. Let commendation take the place of censure.

Cultivate traits of character the opposite of those which are here reproved. Seek to develop goodness, patience, love, and all the graces which will have a transforming influence in your home and will brighten the lives of your family and your friends. Confess that you have done wrong, and then turn squarely about and strive to be just and right. Do not endeavor to make your wife a slave to your will, but by kindness and an unselfish desire to promote her comfort and happiness draw her into close sympathy with yourself. Give her an opportunity to exercise her faculties, and do not try to warp her mind and mold her judgment till she loses her mental identity.

She is a child of God and a woman of fine capabilities and good taste, one who has a humble opinion of herself at best. And you have so long dictated to her and discouraged her independent thought that it has had an influence to make her shut herself within herself and fail to develop the noble womanhood that is hers by right. While consulting with your wife upon matters that affect her interests equally with your own, you well know that if she expresses an opinion contrary to yours, a feeling of injury rises in your heart, and self takes possession of you and excludes that feeling of deference that you should naturally cherish toward the companion of your life.

The very same spirit that you exercise at home will be manifested more or less in your church relationship. Your determined will, your rigid opinions, will be urged and made a ruling power as far as possible. This will never do; you must feel the necessity of occasionally yielding your judgment to that of others, and not persist in your way to a degree that often approaches stubbornness. If you wish for the daily blessing of God you should modulate your imperious disposition and make it correspond to the divine Pattern.

You frequently grieve your wife unconsciously to yourself because you do not guard your words and acts with that tenderness that you should. You thus lessen her love for you and foster a coldness that is creeping into your home unawares.

If you will think less of yourself and more of the treasures in your household, giving due consideration to the members of your family and allowing them a proper exercise of their individual judgment, you will bring a blessing upon yourself and them, and will increase the respect they feel for you.

You have been inclined to look with a sort of contempt upon your brethren who were faulty, and who, because of their natural temperament, found it hard to overcome the evils that beset them. But Jesus pities them; He loves them and bears with their infirmities even as He does with yours. You do wrong to exalt yourself above those who are not so strong as you are. You do wrong to shut yourself up in a self-righteous spirit, thanking God that you are not like other men, but, that your faith and zeal exceed those of the poor, feeble ones striving to do right under discouragements and darkness.

Angels from a pure and holy heaven come to this polluted world to sympathize with the weakest, the most helpless and needy, while Christ Himself descended from His throne to help just such as these. You have no right to hold yourself aloof from these faltering ones, nor to assert your marked superiority over them. Come more in unison with Christ, pity the erring, lift up the hands that hang down, strengthen the feeble knees, and bid the fearful hearts be strong. Pity and help them, even as Christ has pitied you.

You have desired to do a work for the Master. Here is work for you to do that will be acceptable to Him—the very work that angels are engaged in carrying forward. You may be a colaborer with them. But you will never be called to preach the word to the people. You may have in general a correct knowledge of our faith, but you lack the qualifications of a teacher. You have not the faculty of adapting yourself to the needs and ways of others. You have not sufficient volume of voice.

Even in conference meetings you speak too low to be heard by those assembled. You are also, my dear brother, frequently in danger of being tedious. Even in small meetings, your remarks are too lengthy. Every word of what you say may be true, but in order to find its way to the soul it should be accompanied with a fervor of spiritual power. What we say should be right to the point and not of sufficient length to weary the listeners, else the subject matter will find no lodgment in their hearts.

There is plenty of work for all to do. You, my dear brother, can with all safety do good service for the Lord in helping those who most need aid. You may feel that your work in this direction is not rightly appreciated; but remember that our Savior's work was also lightly considered by those whom He benefited. He came to save those who were lost, but the very ones whom He sought to rescue refused His help and finally put Him to death.

If you fail ninety-nine times in a hundred, but succeed in saving the one soul from ruin, you have done a noble deed for the Master's cause. But to be a co-worker with Jesus, you should have all patience with those for whom you labor, not scorning the simplicity of the work, but looking to the blessed result. When those for whom you labor do not exactly meet your mind, you often say in your heart: "Let them go; they are not worth saving." What if Christ had treated poor outcasts in a similar manner? He died to save miserable sinners, and if you work in the same spirit and in the same manner indicated by the example of Him whom you follow, leaving the results with God, you can never in this life measure the amount of good you have accomplished.

You are inclined to reach for higher work than that which naturally presents itself to you. You would seek to influence only the intellectual and honorable among men. But this class will surely disappoint your expectations. If they continue long in transgression, they seldom fully feel their lost and hopeless condition. You should work, as did Christ, in all humility, and you will not lose your reward. It is as honorable to work among the humble and lowly, leading them to the Saviour, as among the rich and great. Above all, do not undertake responsibilities that you are unable to carry.

Everything possible should be done to make the meetings of our people interesting. You may be a great help in this if you take the proper course. Especially should our social meetings be properly conducted. A few pointed words in relation to your progress in the divine life, spoken in a clear, audible voice, in an earnest manner, without any effort of speech, would be edifying to others and a blessing to your own soul.

You need the softening, subduing influence of the Spirit of God upon your heart. No one should receive the idea that a correct knowledge of the truth alone will meet the demands of God. A love and good will that exists only when our ways are acknowledged by our friends as right, is of no real value, for this is natural to the unregenerate heart. Those who profess to be children of God and walking in the light should not feel annoyed or angered when their track is crossed.

You love the truth and are anxious for its advancement. You will be placed in various circumstances in order to try and prove you. You may develop a true Christian character if you will submit yourself to discipline. Your vital interests are at stake. What you most need is true holiness and a spirit of self-sacrifice. We may obtain a knowledge of the truth and read its most hidden mysteries, and even give our bodies to be burned for its sake; yet if we have not love and charity, we are as sounding brass and a tinkling cymbal.

Cultivate a disposition to esteem others better than your self. Be less self-sufficient, less confident; cherish patience, forbearance, and brotherly love. Be ready to help the erring, and have pity and tender sympathy toward those who are weak. You need not leave your business in order to glorify the Lord; but you may, from day to day, in every deed and word, while pursuing your usual avocations, honor Him whom you serve, thereby influencing for the right those with whom you are brought in contact.

Be courteous, tenderhearted, forgiving toward others. Let self sink in the love of Jesus, that you may honor your Redeemer and do the work that He has appointed for you to do. How little you know of the heart trials of poor souls who have been bound in the chains of darkness and who lack resolution and moral power. Strive to understand the weakness of others. Help the needy, crucify self, and let Jesus take possession of your soul, in order that you may carry out the principles of truth in your daily life. Then will you be, as never before, a blessing to the church and to all those with whom you come in contact.

13. Missionaries in the Home

Dear Sister:

I have been shown that you have certain faults that you should feel the importance of correcting, in order to enjoy the blessing of God. Many of your trials you have brought upon yourself by your freedom of speech. You feel that it is a virtue to talk plainly, and tell people just what you think of them and their acts. You call this frankness; but it is downright discourtesy, and arouses the combativeness of those with whom you are brought in contact. If others should pursue the same course toward you, it would be more than you could bear. Those who are accustomed to speak plainly and severely to others, are not pleased to receive the same treatment in return.

You have brought upon yourself many grievances that could have been avoided had you possessed a meek and quiet spirit. You provoke contention; for when your will is crossed, your spirit rises for conflict. Your disposition to rule is a constant source of trouble to yourself. Your nature has become jealous and distrustful. You are overbearing, and stir up strife by faultfinding and hasty condemnation. You have so long cultivated a spirit of retaliation that you continually need the grace of God to soften and subdue your nature. The dear Saviour has said: "Bless them that curse you," "and pray for them which despitefully use you, and persecute you."

Dear sister, I was shown that you bring darkness into your own soul by dwelling upon the mistakes and imperfections of others. You will never have their sins to answer for, but you have a work to do for your own soul and for your own family that no other can do for you. You need to crucify self and to check the disposition to magnify your neighbors' faults and to talk thoughtlessly. There are subjects upon which you may converse with the very best results. It is always safe to speak of Jesus, of the Christian's hope, and of the beauties of our faith. Let your tongue be sanctified to God, that your speech may be ever seasoned with grace. "Finally, brethren, whatsoever things are true, whatsoever things are honest, whatsoever things are just, whatsoever things are pure, whatsoever things are lovely, whatsoever things are of good report; if there be any virtue, and if there be any praise, think on these things."

The apostle's exhortation should be explicitly followed. There is often a great temptation to talk of things which do not profit the speaker or the hearer, but which bring evil and barrenness to both. Our probationary time is too brief to be spent in dwelling upon the shortcomings of others. We have a work before us which requires the closest diligence and the strictest watchfulness, united with unceasing prayer, or we shall be unable to overcome the defects in our characters and to copy the divine Pattern. We should all study to imitate the life of Christ. Then we shall have a sanctifying influence upon those with whom we associate. It is a wonderful thing to be a Christian, truly Christlike, peaceable, pure, and undefiled. Dear sister, God must be with us in all our efforts, or they will avail nothing. Our good works will end in self-righteousness.

In your own family there is much to correct. You have failed to give your children the attention and encouragement they need. You have not bound them to your heart by the tenderest cords of love. Your business is a great tax upon your time and energies, and causes you to neglect home duties. Yet you have become so accustomed to this burden that it would seem a great sacrifice to lay it down; still, if you could do this, it would be for your spiritual interest and for the happiness and morals of your children. It would be well for you to lay by your perplexing cares and find a retreat in the country, where there is not so strong an influence to corrupt the morals of the young.

True, you would not be entirely free from annoyances and perplexing cares in the country; but you would there avoid many evils, and close the door against a flood of temptations which threaten to overpower the minds of your children. They need employment and variety. The sameness of their home makes them uneasy and restless, and they have fallen into the habit of mingling with the vicious lads of the town, thus obtaining a street education.

You have devoted so much time to missionary work which has no connection with our faith, and been so pressed with cares and responsibilities, that you have not kept pace with the work of God for this time, and have had little leisure to make the narrow precincts of home attractive to your children. You have not studied their needs, nor understood their active, developing minds; therefore you have withheld from them simple indulgences that would have gratified them without injury. It would have been a trifling tax upon you to give your children greater attention, and it would have been of the greatest value to them.

To live in the country would be very beneficial to them; an active, out-of-door life would develop health of both mind and body. They should have a garden to cultivate, where they might find both amusement and useful employment. The training of plants and flowers tends to the improvement of taste and judgment, while an acquaintance with God's useful and beautiful creations has a refining and ennobling influence upon the mind, referring it to the Maker and Master of all.

The father of your children was harsh, relentless, and unfeeling, cold and stern in his associations with them, severe in his discipline, and unreasonable in his demands. He was a man of peculiar temperament, wrapped up in himself, thinking only of his own pleasure, and reaching out for means to gratify himself and secure the esteem of others. His indolence and his dissipated habits, together with his lack of sympathy and love for you and his children, weaned your affections from him at an early day. Your life was filled with hard and peculiar trials, while he was utterly indifferent to your cares and burdens.

These things have left their impress upon you and your children. Especially have they tended to warp your character. You have almost unconsciously developed an independent spirit. Finding that you could not depend upon your husband, you have taken that course which you thought best, without taking him into your confidence. As your best endeavors were not appreciated, you mentally braced yourself to move forward according to your best judgment, regardless of censure or approval. Conscious of being wronged and misjudged by your husband, you have cherished a feeling of bitterness against him, and when censured you have retaliated upon those who questioned your course.

But while you have fully realized your husband's faults, you have failed to mark your own. You have erred in talking of his failings to others, thus cultivating a love for dwelling upon disagreeable topics, and keeping your disappointments and trials constantly before you. You have thus fallen into the habit of making the most of your sorrows and difficulties, many of which you create by exaggeration and by talking to others.

If you should turn your attention away from outside annoyances and center them upon your family you would be happier and would become the means of doing good. The very fact that your children have missed the proper counsel and example of a father renders it more obligatory upon you to be a tender and devoted mother. Your duty is more in your home and with your family. Here is real missionary labor to perform. This responsibility cannot be shifted upon another; it is the lifework God has appointed for you.

In devoting yourself so entirely to the details of business, you are robbing yourself of time for meditation and prayer, and are robbing your children of the patient care and attention that they have a right to claim from their mother. You find that you can hurry through with many tasks yourself, easier and quicker than you can patiently teach your children to do them for you; yet it would be much better to put certain responsibilities upon them and instruct them to be useful. This would encourage and occupy them, as well as relieve you in part.

You give considerable time to those who have no special claims upon you, and in so doing you neglect the sacred duties of a mother. God has not laid upon you many of the burdens which you have assumed. You have visited and helped those who did not need your time and care half so much as your own children, who are now forming characters for heaven or perdition. God will not sustain you in ministering to many who are really suffering under the curse of God for their dissolute and wicked lives.

The first great business of your life is to be a missionary at home. Clothe yourself with humility and patience, forbearance and love, and go about the work that God has ordained you should do, which no other one can do for you. It is a work for which you will be held responsible in the day of retribution. God's blessing cannot rest upon an ill-disciplined household. Kindness and patience must rule in the home to make it happy.

From a worldly point of view, money is power; but from the Christian standpoint, love is power. Intellectual and spiritual strength are involved in this principle. Pure love has special efficacy to do good, and can do nothing but good. It prevents discord and misery, and brings the truest happiness. Wealth is often an influence to corrupt and destroy; force is strong to do hurt; but truth and goodness are the properties of pure love.

My sister, if you could see yourself as God sees you, it would be plain to your mind that without a thorough conversion you can never enter the kingdom of God. If you would bear in mind that whatever measure you mete to others it shall be meted to you again, you would be more cautious in your speech, milder and more forgiving in your disposition.

Christ came into the world to bring all resistance and authority into subjection to Himself, but He did not claim obedience through the strength of argument or the voice of command; He went about doing good and teaching His followers the things which belonged to their peace. He stirred up no strife, He resented no personal injuries, but met with meek submission the insults, the false accusations, and the cruel scourging of those who hated

Him and condemned Him to death. Christ is our example. His life is a practical illustration of His divine teachings. His character is a living exhibition of the way to do good and overcome evil.

You have nursed your resentment against your husband and others who have wronged you, but have failed to perceive wherein you have erred and made matters worse by your own wrong course. Your spirit has been bitter against those who have done you injustice, and your feelings have found vent in reproaches and censure. This would give momentary relief to your burdened heart, but it has left a lasting scar upon your soul. The tongue is a little member, but you have cultivated its improper use until it has become a consuming fire.

All these things have tended to check your spiritual advancement. But God sees how hard it is for you to be patient and forgiving, and He knows how to pity and to help. He requires you to reform your life, to correct your defects. He desires that your firm, unyielding spirit should be subdued by His grace. You should seek the help of God, for you need peace and quiet instead of storm and contention. The religion of Christ enjoins upon you to move less from impulse, and more from sanctified reason and calm judgment.

You allow your surroundings to affect you too much. Let daily watchfulness and prayer be your safeguard. Then the angels of God will be around you to shed clear and precious light upon your mind and to uphold you with their heavenly strength. Your influence over your children, and your course toward them, should be such as to attract these holy visitors to your dwelling, that they may assist you in your efforts to make your family and your home what God would have them. When you essay to independently fight your own way through, the heavenly angels are repelled, and retire from your presence in grief, leaving you to struggle on alone.

Your children have the stamp of character that their parents have given them. How careful, then, should be your treatment of them; how tenderly should you rebuke and correct their faults. You are too stern and exacting, and have frequently dealt with them when you were excited and angry. This has almost fretted away the golden cord of love that binds their hearts to yours. You should ever impress upon your children the fact that you love them; that you are laboring for their interest; that their happiness is dear to you; and that you design to do only that which is for their good.

116

You should gratify their little wants whenever you can reasonably do so. Your present location affords but little variety or amusement to their young and restless minds, and every year the difficulty increases. In the fear of God, your first consideration should be for your children. As a Christian mother, your obligations to them are neither light nor small; and in order to fill them properly, you should lay down some of your other burdens, and devote your time and energies to this work. The home of your children should be the most desirable and happy place in the world to them, and the mother's presence should be the greatest attraction.

The power of Satan over the youth of this age is fearful. Unless their minds are firmly balanced by religious principle, their morals will become corrupted by the vicious children with whom they come in contact. You think you understand these things, but you fail to fully comprehend the seducing power of evil upon youthful minds. Their greatest danger is from a lack of proper training and discipline. Indulgent parents do not teach their children self-denial. The very food they place before their children is such as to irritate the tender coats of the stomach.

This excitement is communicated to the brain through the nerves, and the result is that the animal passions are roused and control the moral powers. Reason is thus made a servant to the lower qualities of the mind. Anything which is taken into the stomach and converted into blood becomes a part of the being. Children should not be allowed to eat gross articles of food, such as pork, sausage, spices, rich cakes and pastry; for by so doing their blood becomes fevered, the nervous system unduly excited, and the morals are in danger of being affected. It is impossible for anyone to live intemperately in regard to diet and yet retain a large degree of patience. Our heavenly Father sent the light of health reform to guard against the evils resulting from a debased appetite, that those who love purity and holiness may use with discretion the good things He has provided for them, and by exercising temperance in their daily lives, may be sanctified through the truth.

You are not uniform in your treatment of your children. At times you indulge them to their injury, while at other times you refuse them some innocent gratification that would make them very happy. You turn from them with impatience and scorn their simple requests, forgetting that they can enjoy pleasures that to you seem foolish and childish. You do not stoop from the dignity of your age and station to understand and minister to the wants of your children.

In this you fail to imitate Christ. He identified Himself with the lowly, the needy, and the afflicted. He took little children in His arms, and descended to the level of the young. His large heart of love could comprehend their trials and necessities, and He enjoyed their happiness. His spirit, wearied with the bustle and confusion of the crowded city, tired of association with crafty and hypocritical men, found rest and peace in the society of innocent children. His presence never repulsed them. The Majesty of heaven condescended to answer their questions and simplified His important lessons to meet their childish understanding. He planted in their young, expanding minds the seeds of truth that would spring up and produce a plentiful harvest in their riper years.

In these children who were brought to Him that He might bless them He saw the future men and women who should be heirs of His grace and subjects of His kingdom, and some of whom would become martyrs for His name's sake. Certain unsympathizing disciples commanded that the children be taken away, lest they should trouble the Master; but as they were turning away in sadness, Christ rebuked His followers, saying: "Suffer little children to come unto Me, and forbid them not: for of such is the kingdom of God."

He knew that these children would listen to His counsel and accept Him as their Redeemer, while those who were worldly-wise and hardhearted would be less likely to follow Him and find a place in the kingdom of God. These little ones, by coming to Christ and receiving His advice and benediction, had His image and His gracious words stamped upon their plastic minds, never to be effaced. We should learn a lesson from this act of Christ, that the hearts of the young are most susceptible to the teachings of Christianity, easy to influence toward piety and virtue, and strong to retain the impressions received. But these tender, youthful ones should be approached with kindness and taught with love and patience.

My sister, bind your children to your heart by affection. Give them proper care and attention in all things. Furnish them with becoming garments, that they may not be mortified by their appearance, for this would be injurious to their self-respect. You have seen that the world is devoted to fashion and dress, neglecting the mind and morals to decorate the person; but in avoiding this evil you verge upon the opposite extreme, and do not pay sufficient attention to your own dress and that of your children. It is always right to be neat and to be clad appropriately in a manner becoming to your age and station in life.

Order and cleanliness is the law of heaven; and in order to come into harmony with the divine arrangement, it is our duty to be neat and tasty. Your ideas upon this subject are perverted. While condemning the extravagance and vanity of the world, you fall into the error of stretching economy into penuriousness. You deny yourself that which it is right and proper that you should have, and which God has furnished you means to procure. You do not suitably clothe yourself or your children. Our outward appearance should not dishonor the One we profess to follow, but should reflect credit upon His cause.

The apostle says: "Charge them that are rich in this world, that they be not high-minded, nor trust in uncertain riches, but in the living God, who giveth us richly all things to enjoy; that they do good, that they be rich in good works, ready to distribute, willing to communicate." Your means are given you to use where needed, not to hoard up for destruction in the great conflagration. You are bidden to enjoy the good gifts of the Lord, and should use them for your own comfort, for charitable purposes, and in good works to advance His cause, thereby laying up for yourself treasures in heaven.

Many of your afflictions have been visited upon you, in the wisdom of God, to bring you closer to the throne of grace. He softens and subdues His children by sorrows and trials. This world is God's workshop, where He fashions us for the courts of heaven. He uses the planing knife upon our quivering hearts until the roughness and irregularities are removed and we are fitted for our proper places in the heavenly building. Through tribulation and distress the Christian becomes purified and strengthened, and develops a character after the model that Christ has given. The influence of a true, godly life cannot be measured. It reaches beyond the immediate circle of home and friends, shedding a light that wins souls to Jesus.

Testimony 27

14. Willing Obedience

Abraham was an old man when he received the startling command from God to offer up his son Isaac for a burnt offering. Abraham was considered an old man even in his generation. The ardor of his youth had faded away. It was no longer easy for him to endure hardships and brave dangers. In the vigor of youth man may breast the storm with a proud consciousness of strength and rise above discouragements that would cause his heart to fail later in life, when his steps are faltering toward the grave.

But in His providence God reserved His last most trying test for Abraham until the burden of years was heavy upon him and he longed for rest from anxiety and toil. The Lord spoke unto him, saying: "Take now thy son, thine only son Isaac, whom thou lovest," "and offer him . . . for a burnt offering." The heart of the old man stood still with horror. The loss of such a son by disease would have been most heart-rending to the fond father, it would have bowed his whitened head with sorrow; but now he is commanded to shed the precious blood of that son with his own hand. It seemed to him a fearful impossibility.

Yet God had spoken, and His word must be obeyed. Abraham was stricken in years, but this did not excuse him from duty. He grasped the staff of faith and in dumb agony took by the hand his child, beautiful in the rosy health of youth, and went out to obey the word of God. The grand old patriarch was human; his passions and attachments were like ours, and he loved his boy, who was the solace of his old age, and to whom the promise of the Lord had been given.

But Abraham did not stop to question how God's promises could be fulfilled if Isaac were slain. He did not stay to reason with his aching heart, but carried out the divine command to the very letter, till, just as the knife was about to be plunged into the quivering flesh of the child, the word came: "Lay not thine hand upon the lad;" "for now I know that thou fearest God, seeing thou hast not withheld thy son, thine only son from Me."

This great act of faith is penciled on the pages of sacred history to shine forth upon the world as an illustrious example to the end of time. Abraham did not plead that his old age should excuse him from obeying God. He did not say: "My hairs are gray, the vigor of my manhood is gone; who will comfort my waning life when Isaac is no more? How can an aged father spill the blood of an only son?" No; God had spoken, and man must obey without questioning, murmuring, or fainting by the way.

We need the faith of Abraham in our churches today, to lighten the darkness that gathers around them, shutting out the sweet sunlight of God's love and dwarfing spiritual growth. Age will never excuse us from obeying God. Our faith should be prolific of good works, for faith without works is dead. Every duty performed, every sacrifice made in the name of Jesus, brings an exceeding great reward. In the very act of duty, God speaks and gives His blessing. But He requires of us an entire surrender of the faculties. The mind and heart, the whole being, must be given to Him, or we fall short of becoming true Christians.

God has withheld nothing from man that can secure to him eternal riches. He has clothed the earth with beauty and furnished it for his use and comfort during his temporal life. He has given His Son to die for the redemption of a world that had fallen through sin and folly. Such matchless love, such infinite sacrifice, claims our strictest obedience, our holiest love, our unbounded faith. Yet all these virtues, exercised to their fullest extent, can never be commensurate with the great sacrifice that has been offered for us.

God requires prompt and unquestioning obedience of His law; but men are asleep or paralyzed by the deceptions of Satan, who suggests excuses and subterfuges, and conquers their scruples, saying as he said to Eve in the garden: "Ye shall not surely die." Disobedience not only hardens the heart and conscience of the guilty one, but it tends to corrupt the faith of others.

That which looked very wrong to them at first, gradually loses this appearance by being constantly before them, till finally they question whether it is really sin and unconsciously fall into the same error.

Through Samuel, God commanded Saul to go and smite the Amalekites and utterly destroy all their possessions. But Saul only partially obeyed the command; he destroyed the inferior cattle, but reserved the best and spared the wicked king. The next day he met the prophet Samuel with flattering self-congratulations. Said he: "Blessed be thou of the Lord: I have performed the commandment of the Lord." But the prophet immediately answered: "What meaneth then this bleating of the sheep in mine ears, and the lowing of the oxen which I hear?"

Saul was confused and sought to shirk responsibility by answering: "They have brought them from the Amalekites: for the people spared the best of the sheep and of the oxen, to sacrifice unto the Lord thy God; and the rest we have utterly destroyed." Samuel then reproved the king, reminding him of the explicit command of God directing him to destroy all things belonging to Amalek. He pointed out his transgression and declared that he had disobeyed the Lord. But Saul refused to acknowledge that he had done wrong; he again excused his sin by pleading that he had reserved the best cattle to sacrifice unto the Lord.

Samuel was grieved to the heart by the persistency with which the king refused to see and confess his sin. He sorrowfully asked: "Hath the Lord as great delight in burnt offerings and sacrifices, as in obeying the voice of the Lord? Behold, to obey is better than sacrifice, and to hearken than the fat of rams. For rebellion is as the sin of witchcraft, and stubbornness is as iniquity and idolatry. Because thou hast rejected the word of the Lord, He hath also rejected thee from being king."

We should not look in the face of duty and delay meeting its demands. Such delay gives time for doubts; unbelief creeps in, the judgment is perverted, the understanding darkened. At length the reproofs of God's Spirit do not reach the heart of the deluded person, who has become so blinded as to think that they cannot possibly be intended for him or apply to his case.

The precious time of probation is passing, and few realize that it is given them for the purpose of preparing for eternity. The golden hours are squandered in worldly pursuits, in pleasure, in absolute sin. God's law is slighted and forgotten, yet every statute is nonetheless binding. Every transgression will bring its punishment. Love of worldly gain leads to desecration of the Sabbath, yet the claims of that holy day are not abrogated or lessened. God's command is clear and unquestionable on this point; He has peremptorily forbidden us to labor upon the seventh day. He has set it apart as a day sanctified to Himself.

Many are the hindrances that lie in the path of those who would walk in obedience to the commandments of God. There are strong and subtle influences that bind them to the ways of the world, but the power of the Lord can break these chains. He will remove every obstacle from before the feet of His faithful ones or give them strength and courage to conquer every difficulty, if they earnestly beseech His help. All hindrances will vanish before an earnest desire and persistent effort to do the will of God at any cost to self, even if life itself is sacrificed. Light from heaven will illuminate the darkness of those, who, in trial and perplexity, go forward, looking unto Jesus as the Author and Finisher of their faith.

In ancient times God spoke to men by the mouth of prophets and apostles. In these days He speaks to them by the testimonies of His Spirit. There was never a time when God instructed His people more earnestly than He instructs them now concerning His will and the course that He would have them pursue. But will they profit by His teachings? will they receive His reproofs and heed His warnings? God will accept of no partial obedience; He will sanction no compromise with self.

15. The Twelve Spies

The Lord commanded Moses to send men to search the land of Canaan, which He would give unto the children of Israel. A ruler from each tribe was to be selected for this purpose. They went; and after forty days they returned from their search, and came before Moses and Aaron, and all the congregation of Israel, and showed them the fruit of the land. All agreed that it was a good land, and they exhibited the rich fruit which they had brought as evidence. One cluster of grapes was so large that two men carried it between them on a staff. They also brought of the figs and pomegranates which grew there in abundance. After they had spoken of the fertility of the land, all but two spoke very discouragingly of their ability to possess it. They said that the people were very strong that dwelt in the land, and the cities were surrounded with great and high walls, and, more than all this, they saw the children of the giant Anak there. They then described how the people were situated around Canaan and expressed the fear that it would be impossible for them ever to possess this land.

As the people listened to this report, they gave vent to their disappointment in bitter reproaches and wailing. They did not wait to reflect and reason that God, who had brought them out thus far, would certainly give them the land. They left God out of the question. They acted as though in taking the city of Jericho, the key to the land of Canaan, they must depend solely on the power of arms. God had declared that He would give them the country, and they should have fully trusted Him to fulfill His word.

But their unsubdued hearts were not in harmony with His plans. They did not reflect how wonderfully He had wrought in their behalf, bringing them out of their Egyptian bondage, cutting a path for them through the waters of the sea, and destroying the pursuing host of Pharaoh. In their unbelief they were limiting the work of God and distrusting the hand that had hitherto safely guided them. In this instance they repeated their former error of murmuring against Moses and Aaron. "This, then, is the end of all our high hopes," said they. "This is the land we have traveled all the way from Egypt to possess." They blamed their leaders for bringing trouble upon Israel and again charged them with deceiving the people and leading them astray.

Moses and Aaron lay prostrate before God, their faces in the dust. Caleb and Joshua, the two who, of all the twelve spies, trusted in the word of God, rent their clothes in distress when they perceived that these unfavorable reports had discouraged the whole camp. They endeavored to reason with them; but the congregation were filled with madness and disappointment, and refused to listen to these two men. Finally Caleb urged his way to the front, and his clear, ringing voice was heard above all the clamor of the multitude. He opposed the cowardly views of his fellow spies, which had weakened the faith and courage of all Israel. He commanded the attention of the people, and they hushed their complaints for a moment to listen to him. He spoke of the land he had visited. Said he: "Let us go up at once, and possess it; for we are well able to overcome it." But as he spoke, the unfaithful spies interrupted him, crying: "We be not able to go up against the people; for they are stronger than we."

These men, starting upon a wrong course, set their hearts against God, against Moses and Aaron, and against Caleb and Joshua. Every step they advanced in this wrong direction made them firmer in their design to discourage every attempt to possess the land of Canaan. They distorted the truth in order to carry their baneful purpose. They represented the climate as being unhealthful and all the people of giant stature. Said they: "And there we saw the giants, the sons of Anak, which come of the giants: and we were in our own sight as grasshoppers, and so we were in their sight."

This was not only an evil report, but a lying one also. It was contradictory; for if the land was unhealthy, and had eaten up the inhabitants, how was it that they had attained to such massive proportions? When men in responsible positions yield their hearts to unbelief, there are no bounds to the advance they will make in evil. Few realize, when they start upon this dangerous course, the length that Satan will lead them.

The evil report had a terrible effect upon the people. They reproached Moses and Aaron bitterly. Some groaned and wailed, saying: "Would God that we had died in the land of Egypt! or would God we had died in this wilderness!" Then their feelings rose against the Lord; and they wept and mourned, saying: "Wherefore hath the Lord brought us unto this land, to fall by the sword, that our wives and our children should be a prey? were it not better for us to return into Egypt? And they said one to another, Let us make a captain, and let us return into Egypt."

Thus they manifested their disrespect for God and for the leaders He had appointed to conduct them. They did not ask the Lord what they should do, but said: "Let us make a captain." They took matters into their own hands, feeling themselves competent to manage their affairs without divine aid. They not only accused Moses of deception, but God also, in promising them a land which they were not able to possess. They actually went so far as to appoint one of their number as a captain to lead them back to the land of their suffering and bondage, from which God had delivered them with His strong arm of omnipotence.

Moses and Aaron still remained prostrate before God in the presence of all the assembly, silently imploring divine mercy for rebellious Israel. Their distress was too deep for words. Again Caleb and Joshua press to the front, and the voice of Caleb once more rises in sorrowful earnestness above the complaints of the congregation: "The land, which we passed through to search it, is an exceeding good land. If the Lord delight in us, then He will bring us into this land, and give it us; a land which floweth with milk and honey. Only rebel not ye against the Lord, neither fear ye the people of the land; for they are bread for us: their defense is departed from them, and the Lord is with us: fear them not."

The Canaanites had filled up the measure of their iniquity, and the Lord would no longer bear with them. His defense being removed from them, they would fall an easy prey to the Hebrews. They were not prepared for battle, for they felt so strong that they deceived themselves with the idea that no army was formidable enough to prevail against them.

Caleb reminded the people that by the covenant of God the land was ensured to Israel; but their hearts were filled with madness, and they would hear no more. If only the two men had brought the evil report, and all the ten had encouraged them to possess the land in the name of the Lord, they would still have taken the advice of the two in preference to the ten, because of their wicked unbelief. But there were only two advocating the right, while ten were in open rebellion against their leaders and against God.

The greatest excitement now rages among the people; their worst passions are aroused, and they refuse to listen to reason. The ten unfaithful spies join them in their denunciations of Caleb and Joshua, and the cry is raised to stone them. The insane mob seize missiles with which to slay these faithful men. They rush forward with yells of madness, when, lo! the stones drop from their hands, a hush falls upon them, and they shake with terror. God has interposed to check their rash design. The glory of His presence, like a flame of light, illuminates the tabernacle, and all the congregation behold the signal of the Lord. One mightier than they has revealed Himself, and not one dares continue his resistance. Every murmurer is silenced, and the spies, who have brought the evil report, crouch terror-stricken, with bated breath.

Moses arises from his humiliating position and enters the tabernacle to commune with God. Then the Lord proposes to immediately destroy this rebellious people. He desires to make of Moses a greater nation than Israel; but the meek leader of His people will not consent to this proposition. "And Moses said unto the Lord, Then the Egyptians shall hear it, (for Thou broughtest up this people in Thy might from among them;) and they will tell it to the inhabitants of this land: for they have heard that Thou Lord art among this people, that Thou Lord art seen face to face, and that Thy cloud standeth over them, and that Thou goest before them, by daytime in a pillar of a cloud, and in a pillar of fire by night. Now if Thou shalt kill all this people as one man, then the nations which have heard the fame of Thee will speak, saying, Because the Lord was not able to bring this people into the land which He sware unto them, therefore He hath slain them in the wilderness."

Moses again refuses to have Israel destroyed and himself made a mightier nation than they. This favored servant of God manifests his love for Israel and shows his zeal for the glory of his Master and the honor of His people. Thou hast forgiven this people from Egypt even until now; Thou hast been long-suffering and merciful hitherto toward this ungrateful nation; and however unworthy they may be, Thy mercy is the same. He pleads: Wilt Thou not therefore spare them this one, and add this one more instance of divine patience to the many Thou hast already given?

Moses prevailed with God to spare the people, but because of their arrogance and unbelief the Lord could not go with them to work in a miraculous manner in their behalf. Therefore in His divine mercy He bade them adopt the safest course and turn back into the wilderness toward the Red Sea. He also decreed that, as a punishment for their rebellion, all the adults who left Egypt, with the exception of Caleb and Joshua, should be forever excluded from Canaan. They had utterly failed to keep their promise of obedience to God, and this released Him from the covenant that they had so repeatedly violated. He promised that their children should possess the goodly land, but declared that their own bodies should be buried in the wilderness. And the ten unfaithful spies, whose evil report had caused Israel to murmur and rebel, were destroyed by the power of God before the eyes of the people.

When Moses made known to Israel the will of God concerning them, they seemed sincerely to repent of their sinful conduct. But the Lord knew that they sorrowed because of the result of their evil course, rather than from a deep sense of their ingratitude and disobedience. But their repentance came too late; the just anger of God was awakened, and their doom was pronounced, from which there was no reprieve. When they found that the Lord would not relent in His decree, their self-will again arose, and they declared that they would not return into the wilderness.

In commanding them to retire from the land of their enemies, God tested their apparent submission and found that it was not real. They knew that they had deeply sinned in allowing their rash feelings to control them and in seeking to slay the spies who had urged them to obey God; but they were only terrified to find that they had made a fearful mistake, the consequences of which would prove disastrous to themselves. Their hearts were unchanged, and they only needed an excuse to occasion a similar outbreak. This presented itself when Moses, by the authority of God, commanded them to go back into the wilderness.

They had rebelled against His commands when He bade them go up and take the land that He had promised them, and now, when He directed them to retreat from it, they were equally insubordinate, and declared that they would go to battle with their enemies. They arrayed themselves in warriors' dress and armor, and presented themselves before Moses, in their own estimation prepared for conflict, but sadly deficient in the sight of God and His sorrowful servant. They refused to listen to the solemn warnings of their leaders that disaster and death would be the consequence of their audacity.

When God directed them to go up and take Jericho, He promised to go with them. The ark containing His law was to be a symbol of Himself. Moses and Aaron, God's appointed leaders, were to conduct the expedition under His watchful direction. With such supervision no harm could have come to them. But now, contrary to the command of God and the solemn prohibition of their leaders, without the ark of God and without Moses, they marched out to meet the armies of the enemy.

During the time consumed by the Israelites in their wicked insubordination, the Amalekites and Canaanites had prepared for battle. The Israelites presumptuously challenged the foe that had not dared to attack them; but just as they had fairly entered the enemy's territory, the Amalekites and Canaanites met them in force and fiercely repulsed them, driving them back with great loss. The field of carnage was red with their blood, and their dead bodies strewed the ground. They were utterly routed and defeated. Destruction and death were the result of their rebellious experiment. But the faith of Caleb and Joshua was richly rewarded. According to His word, God brought these faithful ones into the land that He had promised them. The cowards and rebels perished in the wilderness, but the righteous spies ate of the grapes of Eschol.

The history of the report of the twelve spies has an application to us as a people. The scenes of cowardly complaining and drawing back from action when there are risks to be encountered are re-enacted among us today. The same unwillingness is manifested to heed faithful reports and true counsel as in the days of Caleb and Joshua. The servants of God, who bear the burden of His cause, practicing strict self-denial and suffering privation for the sake of helping His people, are seldom better appreciated now than they were then.

Ancient Israel was repeatedly tested and found wanting. Few receive the faithful warnings given them of God. Darkness and unbelief do not decrease as we near the time of the second advent of Christ. Truth becomes less and less palatable to the carnally minded; their hearts are slow to believe and tardy to repent. The servants of God might well become discouraged, were it not for the continual evidences their Master gives them of His wisdom and assistance. Long has the Lord borne with His people. He has forgiven their wanderings and waited for them to give Him room in their hearts; but false ideas, jealousy, and distrust have crowded Him out.

Few who are professedly of Israel, and whose minds have been enlightened by the revelations of divine wisdom, dare to come boldly forward, as did Caleb, and stand firmly for God and the right. Because those whom the Lord has chosen to conduct His work will not be turned from the course of integrity to gratify the selfish and unconsecrated, they become the target for hatred and malicious falsehood. Satan is wide awake and working warily in these last days, and God calls for men of spiritual nerve and stamina to resist his artifices.

Thorough conversion is necessary among those who profess to believe the truth, in order for them to follow Jesus and obey the will of God — not a submission born of circumstances, as was that of the terrified Israelites when the power of the Infinite was revealed to them, but a deep and heartfelt repentance and renunciation of sin. Those who are but half converted are as a tree whose boughs hang upon the side of truth, but whose roots, firmly bedded in the earth, strike out into the barren soil of the world. Jesus looks in vain for fruit upon its branches; He finds nothing but leaves.

Thousands would accept the truth if they could do so without denying self, but this class would never build up the cause of God. These would never march out valiantly against the enemy,—the world, the love of self, and the lusts of the flesh,—trusting their divine Leader to give them the victory.

The church needs faithful Calebs and Joshuas, who are ready to accept eternal life on God's simple condition of obedience. Our churches are suffering for laborers. The world is our field. Missionaries are wanted in cities and villages that are more certainly bound by idolatry than are the pagans of the East, who have never seen the light of truth. The true missionary spirit has deserted the churches that make so exalted a profession; their hearts are no longer aglow with love for souls and a desire to lead them into the fold of Christ. We want earnest workers. Are there none to respond to the cry that goes up from every quarter: "Come over ...and help us"?

Can those who profess to be the depositaries of God's law, and who look for the soon coming of Jesus in the clouds of heaven, stand acquitted of the blood of souls if they turn a deaf ear to the crying needs of the people who walk in shadows? There are books to be prepared and distributed, there are lessons to be given, there are self-sacrificing duties to be performed! Who will come to the rescue! Who will, for Christ's sake, deny self and extend the light to those who sit in darkness?

16. The Taking of Jericho

After the death of Moses, Joshua was appointed the leader of Israel to conduct them to the Promised Land. He was well qualified for this important office. He had been prime minister to Moses during the greater part of the time the Israelites had wandered in the wilderness. He had seen the wonderful works of God wrought by Moses and well understood the disposition of the people. He was one of the twelve spies who were sent out to search the Promised Land, and one of the two who gave a faithful account of its richness, and who encouraged the people to go up and possess it in the strength of God.

The Lord promised Joshua that He would be with him as He had been with Moses, and He would make Canaan an easy conquest to him, provided he would be faithful to observe all His commandments. Joshua had been anxious concerning the execution of his commission to lead the people into the land of Canaan; but this assurance removed his fears. He commanded the children of Israel to make ready for a three days' journey and all the men of war to prepare for battle. "And they answered Joshua, saying, All that thou commandest us we will do, and whithersoever thou sendest us, we will go. According as we hearkened unto Moses in all things, so will we hearken unto thee: only the Lord thy God be with thee, as He was with Moses. Whosoever he be that doth rebel against thy commandment, and will not hearken unto thy words in all that thou commandest him, he shall be put to death: only be strong and of a good courage."

God willed that the passage of the Israelites over Jordan should be miraculous. Joshua commanded the people to sanctify themselves, for upon the morrow the Lord would do wonders among them. At the appointed time, he directed the priests to take up the ark containing the law of God and bear it before the people. "And the Lord said unto Joshua, This day will I begin to magnify thee in the sight of all Israel, that they may know that, as I was with Moses, so I will be with thee."

The priests obeyed the commands of their leader and went before the people, carrying the ark of the covenant. The Hebrew hosts took up the line of march and followed this symbol of the divine presence. The wide column filed down the bank of Jordan, and, as the feet of the priests were dipped in the brim of the river, the water was cut off from above, and the volume below rolled on, leaving the bed of the stream dry. The priests passed on, bearing the ark of God, and Israel followed in the rear. Halfway over Jordan the priests were commanded to stand still in the channel of the river till all the Hebrew host had crossed over. This was to impress upon their minds more forcibly the fact that the power which stayed the waters of Jordan was the same that enabled their fathers to cross the Red Sea forty years before.

Many who passed through the Red Sea when they were children, now, by a similar miracle, crossed over Jordan, men of war, equipped for battle. After the host of Israel had all passed over, Joshua commanded the priests to come up out of the river. When they, bearing the ark of the covenant, stood safe upon the farther shore, God removed His mighty hand, and the accumulated waters rushed down, a mighty cataract, in the natural channel of the stream. Jordan rolled on, a resistless flood, overflowing all its banks.

But before the priests had come up out of the river, that this wonderful miracle might never be forgotten, the Lord bade Joshua select men of note from each tribe to take up stones from the spot in the river bed where the priests had stood, and bear them upon their shoulders to Gilgal, and there erect a monument in remembrance of the fact that God had caused Israel to pass over Jordan upon dry land. This would be a continual reminder of the miracle that the Lord had wrought for them. As years passed on, their children would inquire concerning the monument, and again and again they would recount to them this wonderful history, till it would be indelibly impressed upon their minds to the latest generation.

When all the kings of the Amorites and the kings of the Canaanites heard that the Lord had stayed the waters of Jordan before the children of Israel, their hearts melted with fear. The Israelites had slain two of the kings of Moab, and their miraculous passage over the swollen and impetuous Jordan filled the people with great terror. Joshua then circumcised all the people that had been born in the wilderness. After this ceremony they kept the Passover in the plains of Jericho. "And the Lord said unto Joshua, This day have I rolled away the reproach of Egypt from off you."

Heathen nations had reproached the Lord and His people because the Hebrews had failed to possess the land of Canaan, which they expected to inherit soon after leaving Egypt. Their enemies had triumphed because Israel had wandered so long in the wilderness, and they proudly lifted themselves up against God, declaring that He was not able to lead them into the land of Canaan. The Lord had now signally manifested His power and favor by leading His people over Jordan on dry land, and their enemies could no longer reproach them. The manna, which had continued up to this time, now ceased; for as the Israelites were about to possess Canaan, and eat of the fruits of that goodly land, there was no more need of it.

As Joshua withdrew from the armies of Israel to meditate and pray for God's special presence to attend him, he saw a Man of lofty stature, clad in warlike garments, with a drawn sword in His hand. Joshua did not recognize Him as one of the warriors of Israel, and yet He had no appearance of being an enemy. In his zeal he accosted Him, saying: "Art Thou for us, or for our adversaries? And He said, Nay; but as Captain of the host of the Lord am I now come. And Joshua fell on his face to the earth, and did worship, and said unto Him, What saith my Lord unto His servant? And the Captain of the Lord's host said unto Joshua, Loose thy shoe from off thy foot; for the place whereon thou standest is holy. And Joshua did so."

The glory of God hallowed the sanctuary, and for this reason the priests never entered the place sanctified by God's presence with shoes upon their feet. Particles of dust might cleave to them, which would desecrate the holy place; therefore the priests were required to leave their shoes in the court before entering the sanctuary. In the court, beside the door of the tabernacle, stood a brazen laver, wherein the priests washed their hands and their feet before entering the tabernacle, that all impurity might be removed. All who officiated in the sanctuary were required of God to make special preparation before entering the place where His glory was revealed.

It was the Son of God who stood as an armed warrior before the leader of Israel. It was the One who had conducted the Hebrews through the wilderness, enshrouded in a pillar of cloud by day and a pillar of fire by night. In order to impress the mind of Joshua that He was no less than Christ, the Exalted One, He said: "Loose thy shoe from off thy foot." He then instructed

Joshua what course to pursue in order to take Jericho. All the men of war should be commanded to compass the city once each day for six days, and on the seventh day they should march around Jericho seven times.

Accordingly Joshua gave orders to the priests and the people as the Lord directed him. He marshaled the hosts of Israel in perfect order. First was a select body of armed men, clad in their warlike dress; not now to exercise their skill in arms, but only to believe and obey the directions given them. Next followed seven priests with trumpets. Then came the ark of God, glittering with gold, a halo of glory hovering over it, borne by priests in the rich and peculiar dress denoting their sacred office. The vast army of Israel followed in perfect order, each tribe under its respective standard. Thus they compassed the city with the ark of God. No sound was heard but the tread of that mighty host, and the solemn voice of the trumpets, echoing among the hills and resounding through the streets of Jericho.

With wonder and alarm the watchmen of the doomed city marked every move and reported to those in authority. They could not imagine what all this display meant. Jericho had defied the armies of Israel and the God of heaven; but when they beheld that mighty host marching around their city once each day in all the pomp and majesty of war, with the added grandeur of the sacred ark and the attendant priests, the impressive mystery of the scene struck terror to the hearts of princes and people.

Then, again, they would inspect their strong defenses, feeling certain that they could successfully resist the most powerful attack. Many ridiculed the idea that any harm could come to them through these singular demonstrations on the part of their enemies; but others were awed as they beheld the majesty and splendor of the procession that each day wound grandly about the city. They remembered that forty years before, the Red Sea had parted before this people, and that a passage had just been opened for them through the river Jordan. They knew not what further wonders God might work for them; but they kept their gates carefully closed, and guarded them with mighty warriors.

For six days the host of Israel performed their circuit around the city. The seventh day came, and, with the first dawn of light, Joshua marshaled the armies of the Lord. Now they were directed to march seven times around

Jericho, and, at a mighty note of the trumpets, to shout with a loud voice, for God had then given them the city. The imposing army marched solemnly around the devoted walls. The resplendent ark of God lighting the early dusk of morning, the priests with their glittering breastplates and jeweled badges, and the warriors with their flashing armor presented a magnificent pageant. They were silent as the dead, save the measured tread of many feet and the occasional blare of the trumpet, cutting the blank stillness of the early morning. The massive walls of solid stone frowned darkly down, defying the siege of men.

Suddenly the vast army halts. The trumpets break forth in a blast that shakes the very earth. The united voices of all Israel rend the air with a mighty shout. The walls of solid stone, with their massive towers and battlements, totter and heave from their foundations and, with a crash like a thousand thunders, fall in shapeless ruin to the earth. The inhabitants and the army of the enemy, paralyzed with terror and amazement, offer no resistance, and Israel marches in and takes captive the mighty city of Jericho.

How easily the armies of heaven brought down the walls that had seemed so formidable to the spies who brought the false report! The word of God was the only weapon used. The Mighty One of Israel had said: "I have given into thine hand Jericho." If a single warrior had brought his strength to bear against the walls, the glory of God would have been lessened and His will frustrated. But the work was left to the Almighty; and had the foundation of the battlements been laid in the center of the earth, and their summits reached the arch of heaven, the result would have been the same when the Captain of the Lord's host led His legions of angels to the attack.

Long had God designed to give the city of Jericho to His favored people and magnify His name among the nations of the earth. Forty years before, when He led Israel out of bondage, He had proposed to give them the land of Canaan. But by their wicked murmurings and jealousy they had provoked His wrath, and He had caused them to wander for weary years in the wilderness, till all those who had insulted Him with their unbelief were no more. In the capture of Jericho God declared to the Hebrews that their fathers might have possessed the city forty years before had they trusted in Him as did their children.

The history of ancient Israel is written for our benefit. Paul says: "But with many of them God was not well pleased: for they were overthrown in the wilderness. Now these things were our examples, to the intent we should not lust after evil things, as they also lusted." "Now all these things happened unto them for ensamples: and they are written for our admonition, upon whom the ends of the world are come. Wherefore let him that thinketh he standeth take heed lest he fall."

Many who, like ancient Israel, profess to keep God's commandments have hearts of unbelief while outwardly observing the statutes of God. Although favored with great light and precious privileges, they will nevertheless lose the heavenly Canaan, even as the rebellious Israelites failed to enter the earthly Canaan that God had promised them as the reward of their obedience.

As a people we lack faith. In these days few would follow the directions given through God's chosen servant as obediently as did the armies of Israel at the taking of Jericho. The Captain of the Lord's host did not reveal Himself to all the congregation. He communicated only with Joshua, who related the story of this interview to the Hebrews. It rested with them to believe or to doubt the words of Joshua, to follow the commands given by him in the name of the Captain of the Lord's host, or to rebel against his directions and deny his authority. They could not see the host of angels, marshaled by the Son of God, who led their van; and they might have reasoned: "What unmeaning movements are these, and how ridiculous the performance of marching daily around the walls of the city, blowing trumpets of ram's horns meanwhile! This can have no effect upon those strong towering fortifications."

But the very plan of continuing this ceremony through so long a time prior to the final overthrow of the walls afforded opportunity for the increase of faith among the Israelites.

They were to become thoroughly impressed with the idea that their strength was not in the wisdom of man, nor in his might, but only in the God of their salvation. They were thus to become accustomed to putting themselves out of the question and relying wholly upon their divine Leader.

Would those who today profess to be God's people conduct themselves thus under similar circumstances? Doubtless many would wish to follow out their own plans and would suggest other ways and means of accomplishing the desired end. They would be loath to submit to so simple an arrangement and one that reflected upon themselves no glory save the merit of obedience. They would also question the possibility of a mighty city being conquered in that manner. But the law of duty is supreme. It should hold sway over human reason. Faith is the living power that presses through every barrier, overrides all obstacles, and plants its banner in the heart of the enemy's camp.

God will do marvelous things for those who trust in Him. It is because His professed people trust so much to their own wisdom, and do not give the Lord an opportunity to reveal His power in their behalf, that they have no more strength. He will help His believing children in every emergency if they will place their entire confidence in Him and implicitly obey Him.

There are deep mysteries in the word of God; there are unexplainable mysteries in His providences; there are mysteries in the plan of salvation that man cannot fathom. But the finite mind, strong in its desire to satisfy its curiosity and solve the problems of infinity, neglects to follow the plain course indicated by the revealed will of God and pries into the secrets hidden since the foundation of the world. Man builds his theories, loses the simplicity of true faith, becomes too self-important to believe the declarations of the Lord, and hedges himself in with his own conceits.

Many who profess our faith are in this position. They are weak and powerless because they trust in their own strength. God works mightily for a faithful people who obey His word without questioning or doubt. The Majesty of heaven, with His army of angels, leveled the walls of Jericho without human aid. The armed warriors of Israel had no cause to glory in their achievements. All was done through the power of God. Let the people give up self and the desire to work after their own plans, let them humbly submit to the divine will, and God will revive their strength and bring freedom and victory to His children.

17. Jeremiah Reproves Israel

The Lord gave Jeremiah a message of reproof to bear to his people, charging them with the continual rejection of God's counsel: "I have spoken unto you, rising early and speaking; but ye hearkened not unto Me. I have sent also unto you all My servants the prophets, rising up early and sending them, saying, Return ye now every man from his evil way, and amend your doings, and go not after other gods to serve them, and ye shall dwell in the land which I have given to you and to your fathers."

God pleaded with them not to provoke Him to anger with the work of their hands and their hearts, "but they hearkened not." Jeremiah then predicted the captivity of the Jews as their punishment for not heeding the word of the Lord. The Chaldeans were to be used as the instrument by which God would chastise His disobedient people. Their punishment was to be in proportion to their intelligence and to the warnings they had despised. God had long delayed His judgments because of His unwillingness to humiliate His chosen people, but now He would visit His displeasure upon them as a last effort to check them in their evil course.

In these days He has instituted no new plan to preserve the purity of His people. As of old, He entreats the erring ones who profess His name to repent and turn from their evil ways. Now, as then, by the mouth of His chosen servants He predicts the dangers before them. He sounds the note of warning and reproves sin just as faithfully as in the days of Jeremiah. But the Israel of our time have the same temptations to scorn reproof and hate counsel as had ancient Israel. They too often turn a deaf ear to the words that God has given His servants for the benefit of those who profess the truth. Though the Lord in mercy withholds for a time the retribution of their sin, as in the days of Jeremiah, He will not always stay His hand, but will visit iniquity with righteous judgment.

The Lord commanded Jeremiah to stand in the court of the Lord's house and speak unto all the people of Judah who came there to worship, those things which He would give him to speak, diminishing not a word, that they might hearken and turn from their evil ways. Then God would repent of the punishment which He had purposed to inflict upon them because of their wickedness.

The unwillingness of the Lord to chastise His erring people is here vividly shown. He stays His judgments; He pleads with them to return to their allegiance. He had brought them out of bondage that they might faithfully serve Him, the only true and living God; but they had wandered into idolatry, they had slighted the warnings given them by His prophets. Yet He defers His chastisement to give them one more opportunity to repent and avert the retribution for their sin. Through His chosen prophet he now sends them a clear and positive warning, and lays before them the only course by which they can escape the punishment which they deserve. This is a full repentance of their sin and a turning from the evil of their ways.

The Lord commanded Jeremiah to say to the people: "Thus saith the Lord; If ye will not hearken to Me, to walk in My law, which I have set before you, to hearken to the words of My servants the prophets, whom I sent unto you, both rising up early, and sending them, but ye have not hearkened; then will I make this house like Shiloh, and will make this city a curse to all the nations of the earth." They understood this reference to Shiloh and the time when the Philistines overcame Israel and the ark of God was taken.

The sin of Eli was in passing lightly over the iniquity of his sons, who were occupying sacred offices. The neglect of the father to reprove and restrain his sons brought upon Israel a fearful calamity. The sons of Eli were slain, Eli himself lost his life, the ark of God was taken from Israel, and thirty thousand of the people were slain. All this was because sin was lightly regarded and allowed to remain among them. What a lesson is this to men holding responsible positions in the church of God! It adjures them faithfully to remove the wrongs that dishonor the cause of truth.

In the days of Samuel, Israel thought that the presence of the ark containing the commandments of God would gain them the victory over the Philistines, whether or not they repented of their wicked works. Just so, in Jeremiah's time, the Jews believed that the strict observance of the divinely appointed services of the temple would preserve them from the just punishment of their evil course.

The same danger exists today among the people who profess to be the depositaries of God's law. They are too apt to flatter themselves that the regard in which they hold the commandments will preserve them from the power of divine justice. They refuse to be reproved for evil, and charge God's servants with being too zealous in putting sin out of the camp. A sin-hating God calls upon those who profess to keep His law to depart from all iniquity. Neglect to repent and obey His word will bring as serious consequences upon God's people today as did the same sin upon ancient Israel. There is a limit beyond which He will no longer delay His judgments. The desolation of Jerusalem stands as a solemn warning before the eyes of modern Israel, that the corrections given through His chosen instruments cannot be disregarded with impunity.

When the priests and the people heard the message that Jeremiah delivered to them in the name of the Lord, they were very angry and declared that he should die. They were boisterous in their denunciations of him, crying: "Why hast thou prophesied in the name of the Lord, saying, This house shall be like Shiloh, and this city shall be desolate without an inhabitant? And all the people were gathered against Jeremiah in the house of the Lord." Thus was the message of God despised and the servant with whom He entrusted it threatened with death. The priests, the unfaithful prophets, and all the people turned in wrath upon him who would not speak to them smooth things and prophesy deceit.

The unfaltering servants of God have usually suffered the bitterest persecution from false teachers of religion. But the true prophets will ever prefer reproach, and even death, rather than unfaithfulness to God. The Infinite Eye is upon the instruments of divine reproof, and they bear a heavy responsibility. But God regards the injury done to them through misrepresentation, falsehood, or abuse as though it were done unto Himself, and will punish accordingly.

The princes of Judah had heard concerning the words of Jeremiah and came up from the king's house and sat in the entry of the Lord's house. "Then spake the priests and the prophets unto the princes and to all the people, saying, This man is worthy to die; for he hath prophesied against this city, as ye have heard with your ears."

But Jeremiah stood boldly before the princes and the people, declaring: "The Lord sent me to prophesy against this house and against this city all the words that ye have heard. Therefore now amend your ways and your doings, and obey the voice of the Lord your God; and the Lord will repent Him of the evil that He hath pronounced against you. As for me, behold, I am in your hand: do with me as seemeth good and meet unto you. But know ye for certain, that if ye put me to death, ye shall surely bring innocent blood upon yourselves, and upon this city, and upon the inhabitants thereof: for of a truth the Lord hath sent me unto you to speak all these words in your ears."

Had the prophet been intimidated by the threats of those in high authority and the clamoring of the rabble, his message would have been without effect, and he would have lost his life. But the courage with which he discharged his painful duty commanded the respect of the people and turned the princes of Israel in his favor. Thus God raised up defenders for His servant. They reasoned with the priests and false prophets, showing them how unwise would be the extreme measures which they advocated.

The influence of these powerful persons produced a reaction in the minds of the people. Then the elders united in protesting against the decision of the priests regarding the fate of Jeremiah. They cited the case of Micah, who prophesied judgments upon Jerusalem, saying: "Zion shall be plowed like a field, and Jerusalem shall become heaps, and the mountain of the house as the high places of a forest." They put to them the question: "Did Hezekiah king of Judah and all Judah put him at all to death? did he not fear the Lord, and besought the Lord, and the Lord repented Him of the evil which He had pronounced against them? Thus might we procure great evil against our souls."

So, through the pleading of Ahikam and others, the prophet Jeremiah's life was spared; although many of the priests and false prophets would have been pleased had he been put to death on the plea of sedition, for they could not endure the truths that he uttered exposing their wickedness.

But Israel remained unrepentant, and the Lord saw that they must be punished for their sin; so He instructed Jeremiah to make yokes and bonds and place them upon his neck, and to send them to the kings of Edom, of Moab, of the Ammonites, and of Tyrus and Zidon, commanding the messengers to say that God had given all these lands to Nebuchadnezzar, the king of Babylon, and that all these nations should serve him and his descendants for a certain time, till God should deliver them. They were to declare that if these nations refused to serve the king of Babylon, they should be punished with famine, with the sword, and with pestilence, till they should be consumed.

"Therefore," said the Lord, "hearken not ye to your prophets, nor to your diviners, nor to your dreamers, nor to your enchanters, nor to your sorcerers, which speak unto you, saying, Ye shall not serve the king of Babylon: for they prophesy a lie unto you, to remove you far from your land; and that I should drive you out, and ye should perish. But the nations that bring their neck under the yoke of the king of Babylon, and serve him, those will I let remain still in their own land, saith the Lord; and they shall till it, and dwell therein."

Jeremiah declared that they were to wear the yoke of servitude for seventy years; and the captives that were already in the hands of the king of Babylon, and the vessels of the Lord's house which had been taken, were also to remain in Babylon till that time had elapsed. But at the end of the seventy years God would deliver them from their captivity and would punish their oppressors and bring into subjection the proud king of Babylon.

Ambassadors came from the various nations named to consult with the king of Judah as to the matter of engaging in battle with the king of Babylon. But the prophet of God, bearing the symbols of subjection, delivered the message of the Lord to these nations, commanding them to bear it to their several kings. This was the lightest punishment that a merciful God could inflict upon so rebellious a people, but if they warred against this decree of servitude they were to feel the full rigor of His chastisement. They were faithfully warned not to listen to their false teachers, who prophesied lies.

The amazement of the assembled council of nations knew no bounds when Jeremiah, carrying the yoke of subjection about his neck, made known to them the will of God. But Hananiah, one of the false prophets against whom God had warned His people through Jeremiah, lifted up his voice in opposition to the prophecy declared. Wishing to gain the favor of the king and his court, he affirmed that God had given him words of encouragement for the Jews.

Said he: "Within two full years will I bring again into this place all the vessels of the Lord's house, that Nebuchadnezzar king of Babylon took away from this place, and carried them to Babylon: and I will bring again to this place Jeconiah the son of Jehoiakim king of Judah, with all the captives of Judah, that went into Babylon, saith the Lord: for I will break the yoke of the king of Babylon."

Jeremiah, in the presence of all the priests and the people, said that it was the earnest wish of his heart that God would so favor His people that the vessels of the Lord's house might be returned and the captives brought back from Babylon; but this could only be done on condition that the people repented and turned from their evil way to the obedience of God's law. Jeremiah loved his country and ardently wished that the desolation predicted might be averted by the humiliation of the people, but he knew the wish was vain. He hoped the punishment of Israel would be as light as possible, therefore he earnestly entreated them to submit to the king of Babylon for the time that the Lord specified.

He entreated them to hear the words that he spoke. He cited them to the prophecies of Hosea, Habakkuk, Zephaniah, and others whose messages of reproof and warning had been similar to his own. He referred them to events which had transpired in their history in fulfillment of the prophecies of retribution for unrepented sins. Sometimes, as in this case, men had arisen in opposition to the message of God and had predicted peace and prosperity to quiet the fears of the people and gain the favor of those in high places.

But in every past instance the judgment of God had been visited upon Israel as the true prophets had indicated. Said he: "The prophet which prophesieth of peace, when the word of the prophet shall come to pass, then shall the prophet be known, that the Lord hath truly sent him." If Israel chose to run the risk, future developments would effectually decide which was the false prophet.

But Hananiah, incensed at this, took the yoke from Jeremiah's neck and broke it. "And Hananiah spake in the presence of all the people, saying, Thus saith the Lord; Even so will I break the yoke of Nebuchadnezzar king of Babylon from the neck of all nations within the space of two full years. And the prophet Jeremiah went his way." He had done his work; he had warned the people of their danger; he had pointed out the only course by which they could regain the favor of God. But though his only crime was that he had faithfully delivered the message of God to an unbelieving people, they had mocked his words, and men in responsible positions had denounced him and tried to arouse the people to put him to death.

But another message was given to Jeremiah: "Go and tell Hananiah, saying, Thus saith the Lord; Thou hast broken the yokes of wood; but thou shalt make for them yokes of iron. For thus saith the Lord of hosts, the God of Israel; I have put a yoke of iron upon the neck of all these nations, that they may serve Nebuchadnezzar king of Babylon; and they shall serve him: and I have given him the beasts of the field also. Then said the prophet Jeremiah unto Hananiah the prophet, Hear now, Hananiah; The Lord hath not sent thee but thou makest this people to trust in a lie. Therefore thus saith the Lord; Behold, I will cast thee from off the face of the earth: this year thou shalt die, because thou hast taught rebellion against the Lord. So Hananiah the prophet died the same year in the seventh month."

This false prophet had strengthened the unbelief of the people in Jeremiah and his message. He had wickedly declared himself to be the Lord's messenger, and he suffered death in consequence of his fearful crime. In the fifth month Jeremiah prophesied the death of Hananiah, and in the seventh month his death proved the words of the prophet true.

God had said that His people should be saved, that the yoke He would lay upon them should be light, if they submitted uncomplainingly to His plan. Their servitude was represented by a yoke of wood, which was easily borne; but resistance would be met with corresponding severity, represented by the yoke of iron. God designed to hold the king of Babylon in check, that there should be no loss of life nor galling oppression; but by scorning His warning and commands they brought upon themselves the full rigor of bondage.

It was far more agreeable to the people to receive the message of the false prophet, who predicted prosperity; therefore it was received. It wounded their pride to have their sins brought continually before their eyes; they would much rather put them out of sight. They were in such moral darkness that they did not realize the enormity of their guilt nor appreciate the messages of reproof and warning given them of God. Had they had a proper sense of their disobedience they would have acknowledged the justice of the Lord's course and recognized the authority of His prophet. God entreated them to repent, that He might spare them humiliation and that a people called by His name should not become tributary to a heathen nation; but they scoffed at His counsel and went after false prophets.

The Lord then commanded Jeremiah to write letters to the captains, elders, priests, prophets, and all the people who had been taken as captives to Babylon, bidding them not to be deluded into believing their deliverance nigh, but to quietly submit to their captors, pursue their vocations, and make for themselves peaceful homes among their conquerors. The Lord bade them not to allow their prophets or diviners to deceive them with false expectations; but He assured them by the words of Jeremiah that after seventy years of bondage they should be delivered and return to Jerusalem. He would listen to their prayers and give them His favor when they turned to Him with all their hearts. "And I will be found of you, saith the Lord: and I will turn away your captivity, and I will gather you from all the nations, and from all the places whither I have driven you, saith the Lord; and I will bring you again into the place whence I caused you to be carried away captive."

With what tender compassion did God inform His captive people in regard to His plans for Israel. He knew what suffering and disaster they would experience were they led to believe that they should speedily be delivered from bondage and brought back to Jerusalem according to the prediction of the false prophets. He knew that this belief would make their position a very difficult one. Any demonstration of insurrection upon their part would have awakened the vigilance and severity of the king, and their liberty would have been restricted in consequence. He desired them to quietly submit to their fate and make their servitude as pleasant as possible.

There were two other false prophets, Ahab and Zedekiah, who prophesied lies in the name of the Lord. These men professed to be holy teachers; but their lives were corrupt, and they were slaves to the pleasures of sin. The prophet of God had condemned the evil course of these men and warned them of their danger; but, instead of repenting and reforming, they were angry with the faithful reprover of their sins and sought to thwart his work by stirring up the people to disbelieve his words and act contrary to the counsel of God in the matter of subjecting themselves to the king of Babylon. The Lord testified through Jeremiah that these false prophets should be delivered into the hands of the king of Babylon and slain before his eyes, and in good time this prediction was fulfilled.

Other false prophets arose to sow confusion among the people by turning them away from obeying the divine commands given through Jeremiah, but God's judgments were pronounced against them in consequence of their grievous sin of bringing rebellion against Him.

Just such men arise in these days and breed confusion and rebellion among the people who profess to obey the law of God. But just as certainly as divine judgment was visited upon the false prophets, just so surely will these evil workers receive their full measure of retribution; for the Lord has not changed. Those who prophesy lies encourage men to look upon sin as a small matter. When the terrible results of their crimes are made manifest, they seek, if possible, to make the one who has faithfully warned them responsible for their difficulties, even as the Jews charged Jeremiah with their evil fortunes.

Those who pursue a course of rebellion against the Lord can always find false prophets who will justify them in their acts and flatter them to their destruction. Lying words often make many friends, as in the case of Ahab and Zedekiah. These false prophets, in their pretended zeal for God, found many more believers and followers than the true prophet, who delivered the simple message of the Lord.

• A Lesson from the Rechabites

God commanded Jeremiah to gather the Rechabites into the house of the Lord, into one of the chambers, and set wine before them and invite them to drink. Jeremiah did as the Lord commanded him. "But they said, We will drink no wine: for Jonadab the son of Rechab our father commanded us, saying, Ye shall drink no wine, neither ye, nor your sons forever."

"Then came the word of the Lord unto Jeremiah, saying, Thus saith the Lord of hosts, the God of Israel; Go and tell the men of Judah and the inhabitants of Jerusalem, Will ye not receive instruction to hearken to My words? saith the Lord. The words of Jonadab the son of Rechab, that he commanded his sons not to drink wine, are performed, for unto this day they drink none, but obey their father's commandment."

Here God contrasts the obedience of the Rechabites with the disobedience and rebellion of His people, who will not receive His words of reproof and warning. The Rechabites obeyed the commandment of their father and refused to be enticed into transgression of his requirements. But Israel refused to hearken unto the Lord. He says: "I have spoken unto you, rising early and speaking, but ye hearkened not unto Me. I have sent also unto you all My servants the prophets, rising up early and sending them, saying, Return ye now every man from his evil way, and amend your doings, and go not after other gods to serve them, and ye shall dwell in the land which I have given to you and to your fathers: but ye have not inclined your ear, nor hearkened unto Me. Because the sons of Jonadab the son of Rechab have performed the commandment of their father, which he commanded them; but this people hath not hearkened unto Me; therefore thus saith the Lord God of hosts, the God of Israel; Behold, I will bring upon Judah and upon all the inhabitants of Jerusalem all the evil that I have pronounced against them: because I have spoken unto them, but they have not heard; and I have called unto them, but they have not answered."

"And Jeremiah said unto the house of the Rechabites, Thus saith the Lord of hosts, the God of Israel; Because ye have obeyed the commandment of Jonadab your father, and kept all his precepts, and done according unto all that he hath commanded you: therefore thus saith the Lord of hosts, the God of Israel; Jonadab the son of Rechab shall not want a man to stand before Me forever."

The Rechabites were commended for their ready and willing obedience, while God's people refused to be reproved by their prophets. Because He had spoken unto them but they had not heard, because He had called unto them but they had not answered, therefore God pronounced judgment against them. Jeremiah repeated the words of commendation from the Lord to the faithful Rechabites and pronounced blessings upon them in His name. Thus God taught His people that faithfulness, and obedience to His requirements, would be reflected back upon them in blessings, as the Rechabites were blessed for their obedience to their father's command.

If the directions of a good and wise father, who took the best and most effectual means to secure his posterity against the evil of intemperance, were to be so strictly obeyed, God's authority should be held in as much greater reverence as He is holier than man. He is our Creator and commander, infinite in power and terrible in judgment. In mercy He employs a variety of means to bring men to see and repent of their sins. If they will continue to disregard the reproofs He sends them, and act contrary to His declared will, ruin must follow; for God's people are kept in prosperity only by His mercy, through the care of His heavenly messengers. He will not uphold and guard a people who disregard His counsel and despise His reproofs.

• The Warnings of God Rejected

Jeremiah was already deprived of his liberty because he would obey God and give to the king and others occupying responsible positions in Israel the words of warning which he had received from the mouth of God. The Israelites would not accept these reproofs nor allow their course to be questioned. They had manifested great anger and contempt at the words of rebuke and at the judgments which were predicted to come upon them if they continued in rebellion against the Lord. Although Israel would not hear the word of divine counsel, it did not make that word of less effect, neither did God cease to reprove and to threaten with His displeasure and His judgments those who refused to obey His requirements.

The Lord directed Jeremiah, saying: "Take thee a roll of a book, and write therein all the words that I have spoken unto thee against Israel, and against Judah, and against all the nations, from the day I spake unto thee, from the days of Josiah, even unto this day. It may be that the house of Judah will hear all the evil which I purpose to do unto them; that they may return every man from his evil way, that I may forgive their iniquity and their sin."

Here is shown the Lord's reluctance to give up His sinning people. And lest Israel had so far neglected His reproofs and warnings as to let them pass from their memory, He delays His judgments upon them and gives them a full rehearsal of their disobedience and aggravating sins from the days of Josiah down to their own time, and of the judgments He had pronounced in consequence of their transgressions. Thus they had another opportunity to see their iniquity and repent. In this we see that God does not delight in afflicting His people; but with a care that surpasses that of a pitying father for a wayward child, He entreats His wandering people to return to their own allegiance.

The prophet Jeremiah, in obedience to the commands of God, dictated the words that the Lord gave him to Baruch, his scribe, who wrote them upon a roll. See Jeremiah 36:4. This message was a reproof of the many sins of Israel and a warning of the consequences that would follow a continuance of their evil course. It was an earnest appeal for them to renounce their sins. After it was written, Jeremiah, who was a prisoner, sent his scribe to read the roll to all the people who had assembled "in the Lord's house upon the fasting day." Said the prophet: "It may be they will present their supplication before the Lord, and will return everyone from his evil way; for great is the anger and the fury that the Lord hath pronounced against this people."

The scribe obeyed the prophet, and the roll was read before all the people of Judah. But this was not all; he was summoned to read it before the princes. They listened with great interest, and fear was stamped upon their faces as they questioned Baruch concerning the mysterious writing. They promised to tell the king all they had heard in regard to him and his people, but counseled the scribe to hide himself, as they feared that the king would reject the testimony God had given through Jeremiah, and seek to slay not only the prophet, but his scribe.

When the king was told by the princes of what Baruch had read, he immediately ordered the roll brought and read to him. But instead of heeding its warnings and trembling at the danger that hung over himself and his people, in a frenzy of rage he flung it into the fire, notwithstanding certain ones who were high in his confidence had begged him not to burn it. When the wrath of this wicked monarch rose against Jeremiah and his scribe, and he forthwith sent for them to be taken; but the Lord hid them."

After the king had burned the sacred roll, the word of God came to Jeremiah, saying: "Take thee again another roll, and write in it all the former words that were in the first roll, which Jehoiakim the king of Judah hath burned. And thou shalt say to Jehoiakim king of Judah, Thus saith the Lord;

Thou hast burned this roll, saying, Why hast thou written therein, saying, The king of Babylon shall certainly come and destroy this land, and shall cause to cease from thence man and beast?"

A merciful God had graciously warned the people for their good. "It may be," said the compassionate Creator, "that the house of Judah will hear all the evil which I purpose to do unto them, that they may return every man from his evil way; that I may forgive their iniquity and their sin." God pities the blindness and perversity of man; He sends light to their darkened understanding in reproofs and threatenings which are designed to make the most exalted feel their ignorance and deplore their errors. He would cause the self-complacent to feel dissatisfied with their attainments and seek greater blessings by closer connection with heaven.

God's plan is not to send messengers who will please and flatter sinners; He delivers no messages of peace to lull the unsanctified into carnal security. But He lays heavy burdens upon the conscience of the wrongdoer, and pierces his soul with sharp arrows of conviction. The ministering angels present to him the fearful judgments of God, to deepen the sense of his great need and prompt the agonizing cry: "What shall I do to be saved?" The very hand that humbles to the dust, rebukes sin, puts pride and ambition to shame, lifts up the penitent, stricken one, and inquires with deepest sympathy: "What wilt thou that I shall do unto thee?"

When man has sinned against a holy and merciful God, he can pursue no course so noble as to sincerely repent and confess his errors in tears and bitterness of soul. This God requires of him; He will accept of nothing less than a broken heart and a contrite spirit. But the king and his lords, in their arrogance and pride, refused the invitation of God to return; they would not heed this warning and repent. This gracious opportunity was their last. God had declared that if they refused to hear His voice, He would inflict upon them fearful retribution. They did refuse to hear, and He pronounced His judgments upon Israel; He visited with special wrath the man who had proudly lifted himself up against the Almighty.

"Therefore thus saith the Lord of Jehoiakim king of Judah; He shall have none to sit upon the throne of David: and his dead body shall be cast out in the day to the heat, and in the night to the frost. And I will punish him and his seed and his servants for their iniquity; and I will bring upon them, and upon the inhabitants of Jerusalem, and upon the men of Judah, all the evil that I have pronounced against them; but they hearkened not."

The burning of the roll was not the end of the matter. The written words were more easily disposed of than the reproof and warning which they contained and the swift-coming punishment which God had pronounced against rebellious Israel. But even the written roll was reproduced at the command of the Lord. The words of the Infinite were not to be destroyed. "Then took Jeremiah another roll, and gave it to Baruch the scribe, the son of Neriah; who wrote therein from the mouth of Jeremiah all the words of the book which Jehoiakim king of Judah had burned in the fire: and there were added besides unto them many like words."

God does not send judgments upon His people without first warning them to repent. He uses every means to bring them back to obedience and does not visit their iniquity with judgments until He has given them ample opportunity to repent. The wrath of man sought to prevent the labors of the prophet of God by depriving him of his liberty; but God can speak to men through prison walls, and even increase the usefulness of His servants through the very means by which their persecutors seek to limit their influence.

Many now despise the faithful reproof given of God in testimony. I have been shown that some in these days have even gone so far as to burn the written words of rebuke and warning, as did the wicked king of Israel. But opposition to God's threatenings will not hinder their execution. To defy the words of the Lord, spoken through His chosen instruments, will only provoke His anger and eventually bring certain ruin upon the offender. Indignation often kindles in the heart of the sinner against the agent whom God chooses to deliver His reproofs. It has ever been thus, and the same spirit exists today that persecuted and imprisoned Jeremiah for obeying the word of the Lord.

While men will not heed repeated warnings, they are pleased with false teachers who flatter their vanity and strengthen their iniquity, but who will fail to help them in the day of trouble. God's chosen servants should meet with courage and patience whatever trials and sufferings befall them through reproach, neglect, or misrepresentations because they faithfully discharge the duty that God has given them to do. They should remember that the prophets of old and the Saviour of the world also endured abuse and persecution for the word's sake. They must expect to meet just such opposition as was manifested by the burning of the roll that was written by the dictation of God.

The Lord is fitting a people for heaven. The defects of character, the stubborn will, the selfish idolatry, the indulgence of faultfinding, hatred, and contention, provoke the wrath of God and must be put away from His commandment-keeping people. Those living in these sins are deceived and blinded by the wiles of Satan. They think that they are in the light when they are groping in darkness. There are murmurers among us now, even as there were murmurers among ancient Israel. Those who by unwise sympathy encourage men in rebellion when their self-love is smarting beneath merited reproof are not the friends of God, the great Reprover. God will send reproof and warning to His people as long as they continue upon earth.

Those who valiantly take their position on the right side, who encourage submission to God's revealed will and strengthen others in their efforts to put away their wrong-doings, are the true friends of the Lord, who in love is trying to correct the errors of His people, that He may wash them and, cleansing them from every defilement, fit them for His holy kingdom.

Zedekiah succeeded Jehoiakim in reigning at Jerusalem. But neither the new king nor his court nor the people of the land hearkened to the words of the Lord spoken through Jeremiah. The Chaldeans commenced the siege against Jerusalem, but were diverted for a time to turn their arms against the Egyptians. Zedekiah sent a messenger to Jeremiah, asking him to pray to the God of Israel in their behalf; but the prophet's fearful answer was that the Chaldean army would return and destroy the city. Thus the Lord showed them how impossible it is for man to avert divine judgment. "Thus saith the Lord; Deceive not yourselves, saying, The Chaldeans shall surely depart from us; for they shall not depart. For though ye had smitten the whole army of the Chaldeans that fight against you, and there remained but wounded men among them, yet should they rise up every man in his tent, and burn this city with fire."

Jeremiah considered his work done and attempted to leave the city; but he was prevented by a son of one of the false prophets, who reported that he was about to join the enemy. Jeremiah denied the lying charge, but nevertheless he was brought back. The princes were ready to believe the son of the false prophet because they hated Jeremiah. They seemed to think that he had brought upon them the calamity which he had predicted. In their wrath they smote him and imprisoned him.

After he had remained in the dungeon many days, Zedekiah the king sent for him and asked him secretly if there was any word from the Lord. Jeremiah again repeated his warning that the nation would be delivered into the hand of the king of Babylon.

"Moreover Jeremiah said unto King Zedekiah, What have I offended against thee, or against thy servants, or against this people, that ye have put me in prison? Where are now your prophets which prophesied unto you, saying, The king of Babylon shall not come against you, nor against this land? Therefore hear now, I pray thee, O my lord the king: let my supplication, I pray thee, be accepted before thee; that thou cause me not to return to the house of Jonathan the scribe, lest I die there. Then Zedekiah the king commanded that they should commit Jeremiah into the court of the prison, and that they should give him daily a piece of bread out of the bakers street, until all the bread in the city were spent. Thus Jeremiah remained in the court of the prison."

The wicked king dared not openly manifest any faith in Jeremiah, but his fear drove him to seek information of him. Yet he was too weak to brave the disapprobation of his nobles and of the people by submitting to the will of God as declared by the prophet. At last men in authority who were enraged because Jeremiah persisted in prophesying evil went to the king and told him that as long as the prophet lived he would not cease to predict calamity. They urged that he was an enemy to the nation and that his words had weakened the hands of the people and brought misfortune upon them, and they wanted him put to death.

The cowardly king knew these charges were false; but in order to propitiate those who occupied high and influential positions in the nation, he feigned to believe their falsehoods and gave Jeremiah into their hands to do with him as they pleased. Accordingly the prophet was taken and cast "into the dungeon of Malchiah the son of Hammelech, that was in the court of the prison: and they let down Jeremiah with cords. And in the dungeon there was no water, but mire: so Jeremiah sunk in the mire." But God raised up friends for him who besought the king in his behalf and had him again removed to the court of the prison.

Once more the king sent privately for Jeremiah and bade him faithfully relate the purpose of God toward Jerusalem. "Then Jeremiah said unto Zedekiah, If I declare it unto thee, wilt thou not surely put me to death? and if I give thee counsel, wilt thou not hearken unto me? So Zedekiah the king sware secretly unto Jeremiah, saying, As the Lord liveth, that made us this soul, I will not put thee to death, neither will I give thee into the hand of these men that seek thy life."

Then Jeremiah again sounded the Lord's note of warning in the ears of the king. Said he: "Thus saith the Lord, the God of hosts, the God of Israel; If thou wilt assuredly go forth unto the king of Babylon's princes, then thy soul shall live, and this city shall not be burned with fire; and thou shalt live, and thine house: but if thou wilt not go forth to the king of Babylon's princes, then shall this city be given into the hand of the Chaldeans, and they shall burn it with fire, and thou shalt not escape out of their hand. And Zedekiah the king said unto Jeremiah, I am afraid of the Jews that are fallen to the Chaldeans, lest they deliver me into their hand, and they mock me. But Jeremiah said, They shall not deliver thee. Obey, I beseech thee, the voice of the Lord, which I speak unto thee: so it shall be well unto thee, and thy soul shall live."

Here was exhibited the long-suffering mercy of God. Even at that late hour, if there were submission to His requirements, the lives of the people would be spared and the city saved from conflagration. But the king thought he had gone too far to retract. He was afraid of the Jews, afraid of becoming a subject of ridicule, afraid for his life. It was too humiliating, at that late day, to say to the people: "I accept the word of the Lord as spoken through His prophet Jeremiah. I dare not venture to war against the enemy in the face of all these warnings."

With tears Jeremiah entreated the king to save himself and his people. With anguish of spirit he assured him that he could not escape with his life, and that all his possessions would fall to the king of Babylon. He could save the city if he would. But he had started upon the wrong track and would not retrace his steps. He decided to follow the counsel of false prophets and of men whom he really despised and who ridiculed his weakness of character in yielding so readily to their wishes. He yielded the noble freedom of his manhood to become a cringing slave to public opinion. While he had no fixed purpose of evil, he also had no resolution to stand boldly for the right. While he was convicted of the truth as spoken by Jeremiah, he did not possess the moral stamina to obey his counsel, but advanced steadily in the wrong direction.

He was even too weak to be willing that his courtiers and people should know that he had held a conference with the prophet, so far had the fear of man taken possession of his soul. If this cowardly ruler had stood bravely before his people and declared that he believed the words of the prophet, already half-fulfilled, what desolation might have been averted!

He should have said: "I will obey the Lord and save the city from utter ruin. I dare not disregard the commands of God for the fear or favor of men. I love the truth, I hate sin, and I will follow the counsel of the Mighty One of Israel." Then the people would have respected his courageous spirit, and those who were wavering between faith and unbelief would have taken a firm stand for the right. The very fearlessness and justice of this course would have inspired his subjects with admiration and loyalty. He would have had ample support, and Israel would have been spared the untold woe of fire and carnage and famine.

But the weakness of Zedekiah was a crime for which he paid a fearful penalty. The enemy swept down like a resistless avalanche and devastated the city. The Hebrew armies were beaten back in confusion. The nation was conquered. Zedekiah was taken prisoner, and his sons were slain before his eyes. Then he was led away from Jerusalem a captive, hearing the shrieks of his wretched people and the roaring of the flames that were devouring their homes. His eyes were put out, and when he arrived at Babylon he perished miserably.

This was the punishment of unbelief and following ungodly counsel.

There are many false prophets in these days, to whom sin does not appear specially repulsive. They complain that the peace of the people is unnecessarily disturbed by the reproofs and warnings of God's messengers.

155

As for them, they lull the souls of sinners into a fatal ease by their smooth and deceitful teachings. Ancient Israel was thus charmed by the flattering messages of the corrupt priests. Their prediction of prosperity was more pleasing than the message of the true prophet, who counseled repentance and submission.

The servants of God should manifest a tender, compassionate spirit and show to all that they are not actuated by any personal motives in their dealings with the people, and that they do not take delight in giving messages of wrath in the name of the Lord. But they must never flinch from pointing out the sins that are corrupting the professed people of God, nor cease striving to influence them to turn from their errors and obey the Lord.

Those who seek to cloak sin and make it appear less aggravating to the mind of the offender are doing the work of the false prophets and may expect the retributive wrath of God to follow such a course. The Lord will never accommodate His ways to the wishes of corrupt men. The false prophet condemned Jeremiah for afflicting the people with his severe denunciations, and he sought to reassure them by promising them prosperity, thinking that the poor people should not be continually reminded of their sins and threatened with punishment. This course strengthened the people to resist the true prophet's counsel and intensified their enmity toward him.

God has no sympathy with the evildoer. He gives no one liberty to gloss over the sins of His people, nor to cry, "Peace, peace," when He has declared that there shall be no peace for the wicked. Those who stir up rebellion against the servants whom God sends to deliver His messages are rebelling against the word of the Lord.

18. Faithful Reproofs Necessary

The following testimony, given in my last vision, January 5, 1875, I wrote in my tent between the services of the Vermont camp meeting, August, 1875. It sets forth the condition of things at —— in January, 1875. Developments during the following summer fully justified the apparent severity of the testimony. In September I read portions of it to that church, and a great work commenced under our labors; yet, for the benefit of that church and others, I give the testimony in this humble work.

Darkness is getting the control where only the Spirit of God should rule. But few who engage in the work realize the necessity of personal effort and individual responsibility in whatever department they occupy. Few feel the sacredness of the work in which they are engaged. They regard it as upon a common level with ordinary enterprises.

Selfishness predominates with many who should know that a life of self-sacrificing love is a life of peace and liberty. Those who seek happiness by gratifying themselves and looking out mainly for their own interests are on the wrong track to secure happiness even upon earth. Whoever is unfaithful in the least of his duties is unfaithful in greater ones. If he neglects to faithfully perform the small tasks devolving upon him, he proves himself incapable of bearing weightier responsibilities; he indicates that he is not wholehearted in the work and that he does not have an eye single to the glory of God.

Some are ready to define the duties that belong to others, and realize the full importance of their responsibilities, but fail to readily perceive their own. Personal fidelity and individual responsibility are needed especially in the Health Institute [now sanitarium], and in the office, the church, and the school. If all connected with these institutions were listening eagerly to hear what Jesus directed them to do, instead of turning to ask what this man or that man shall do, we should witness a great change in every department of the work. If the language of each heart was, "I must listen to Christ's teachings, and obey His voice; no one can do my work for me; the attention of others can never repair my negligence," then we might see the cause of God advancing as it has never yet advanced.

It is this holding back, waiting for others to do, that brings spiritual feebleness. To reserve one's energies is a sure way to lessen them. Jesus requires implicit obedience and willing submission from all His servants. There must be no halting or self-indulgence in the service of Christ. There is no concord between Christ and Belial. What a lack of devotion to the work of God, what a want of caretaking, has there been at ——.

The heart of A has not been devoted to God. He has capabilities and talents for which he must render an account to the great Giver of all. His heart has been unconsecrated and his life unworthy of his profession; yet he has been closely connected with the sacred work of God for more than a score of years. What light he has had, what privileges! He has enjoyed the rarest opportunities to develop a substantial Christian character. The words of Christ when He wept over Jerusalem are applicable to him: "If thou hadst known, even thou, at least in this thy day, the things which belong unto thy peace! but now they are hid from thine eyes." A, the retribution of God hangs over you, "because thou knewest not the time of thy visitation."

B is of the same cast of mind, but not so thoroughly selfish. Both are lovers of pleasure more than lovers of God. Their course is entirely inconsistent with the Christian life. They lack stability, sobriety, and devotion to God. With B the work of grace is altogether too superficial. He desires to be a Christian, but does not strive to maintain the victory over self and act up to his convictions of right and wrong. Deeds, not idle words and empty intentions, are acceptable to God.

A, you have heard the word of God in reproofs, in counsels, in warnings, as well as in the entreaties of love. But hearing is not enough. "Be ye doers of the word, and not hearers only, deceiving your own selves." It is easy to be borne along by the current, and to cry Hosannah with the multitude; but in the calm of everyday life, when there is no special excitement or exaltation, then comes the test of true Christianity. It is then that your heart becomes cold, and your zeal abates, and religious exercises become distasteful to you.

You positively neglect to do the will of God. Says Christ: "Ye are My friends, if ye do whatsoever I command you." This is the condition imposed; this is the test that proves men's characters. Feelings are often deceiving, emotions are no sure safeguard; for they are variable and subject to external circumstances. Many are deluded by relying on sensational impressions. The test is: What are you doing for Christ? What sacrifices are you making? What victories are you gaining? A selfish spirit overcome, a temptation to neglect duty resisted, passion subdued, and willing, cheerful obedience rendered to the will of Christ are far greater evidences that you are a child of God than spasmodic piety and emotional religion.

Both of you have been averse to reproof; it has ever awakened disaffection and murmuring in your hearts against your best Friend, who has ever sought to do you good, and whom you have every reason to respect. You have separated yourselves from Him and have vexed the Spirit of God by rising up against the words He has given His servants to speak in regard to your course. You have not listened to these admonitions, and have thus rejected the Spirit of God and turned it from your hearts, and have become careless and indifferent in your deportment.

Brother A, you should have gained a valuable experience during the many years that you have been blessed with the great light God has permitted to shine upon your pathway. I heard a voice saying in reference to you: "It is an unfruitful tree; why should its fruitless branches shadow the space that a fruitful tree might occupy? Cut it down; for why cumbereth it the ground?" Then I heard the pleading tones of Mercy's sweet voice, saying: "Spare it a little longer. I will dig about its roots; I will prune it. Give it one more trial; if it fails to be fruitful then, you may cut it down." So a little longer probation is granted the unproductive tree, a little longer time for the barren life to blossom and bear fruit. Will the opportunity given be improved? Will the warnings of God's Spirit be heeded?

The words of Jesus in regard to Jerusalem after she had slighted the salvation graciously offered by her Redeemer are also, in substance, spoken unto you: "O Jerusalem, Jerusalem, . . . how often would I have gathered thy children together, even as a hen gathereth her chickens under her wings, and ye would not!" Christ pleaded, He invited; but His love was unrequited by the people He came to save. You have done no better in your day than did the poor, self-deceived and blinded Jews in theirs. You might have improved your blessed privileges and opportunities, and perfected Christian character; but your heart has been rebellious, and you "would not" humble yourself to be truly converted and live in obedience to God's requirements.

The unreconciled feelings and murmurings which have been expressed by some have also been festering in your soul, although you have not dared to speak out plainly to the same effect. It would have been better for the office and for all concerned had you been separated from it years ago. The more light you have had, the more privileges you have enjoyed, the less sincerity and righteousness have you manifested. Your heart has been carnal, and you have neglected the expressed word of God. Although you have been hedged about with warnings and counsels, and have had the strongest evidence that God was in this work and that His voice was speaking to you, yet you have slighted and rejected solemn reproofs, and gone on in your own selfish, willful way.

Sometimes your fears have been aroused, but still you have never realized your wretched spiritual condition and absolute danger. You have repeatedly fallen back again into the same state of indifference and selfishness. Your repentance has never gone deep enough to perfect a thorough reformation. You have had a surface work, but not that entire transformation which is necessary in order to bring you into acceptance with God. "He that followeth Me," says Christ, "shall not walk in darkness." But through the greater part of your professed Christian life you have walked in darkness because you have failed to connect with heaven and receive the pure light of God's Spirit.

If you were in daily communion with the Lord and cultivated a love for souls you would grow out of self and become an earnest worker in the vineyard of the Lord. You would perceive how the faithful performance of the duties of life would preserve you from self-love and self-gratification. You have not been diligent, seeking to gain an advanced experience every day. You should be at this time a trusty man in any position of responsibility, but selfishness has marked the performance of everything you have set your hand to do. You have been wise in your own conceit, but have failed to gain wisdom from the experience of many years.

B has been vain. He might have moved steadily forward, growing in grace, but the external appearance has seemed to him more important than the inward adorning, even the garment of a meek and quiet spirit, which God accounts of great value. Unbelievers who have been employed in the office, but have not had the light of present truth as you have had, have nevertheless been far more faithful and conscientious than either of you whom I am addressing. If you had been diligently gathering with Christ, some of these would now be with us in the truth. But your lives were a stumbling block to them. God looks upon these unbelievers with greater pity and favor than upon those who believe the truth, yet deny Him in their works. That belief that is laid aside when convenient, and put on and off like a garment, is not the religion of Christ, but a spurious article that will not bear the tests even of this world.

True religion is ever distinctly seen in our words and deportment, and in every act of life. With the followers of Christ, religion should never be divorced from business. They should go hand in hand, and God's commandments should be strictly regarded in all the details of worldly matters. The knowledge that we are children of God should give a high tone of character even to the everyday duties of life, making us not slothful in business, but fervent in spirit. Such a religion as this bears the scrutiny of a critical world with a grand consciousness of integrity.

Every workman in the office should consider himself God's steward and should do his work with exactness and faithful vigilance. The constant inquiry should be: "Is this in accordance with the will of God? Will this please my Redeemer?" Bible religion elevates the reason until Christ is blended with all the thoughts. Every action, every word, and every moment of our lives should bear the impress of our holy faith. The end of all things is at hand, and we have no time to be idle or to live in pleasure, at cross-purposes with God.

The Lord will not be trifled with. Those who neglect His mercies and blessings in this day of opportunities will bring impenetrable darkness upon themselves and will be candidates for the wrath of God. Sodom and Gomorrah were visited with the curse of the Almighty for their sins and iniquities. There are those in our day who have equally abused the mercies of God and slighted His warnings. It will be more tolerable for Sodom and Gomorrah in the day of judgment than for those who bear the name of Christ, yet dishonor Him by their unconsecrated lives. This class are laying up for themselves a fearful retribution when God in His wrath shall visit them with His judgments.

Sinners who have not had the light and privileges that Seventh-day Adventists have enjoyed will, in their ignorance, be in a more favorable position before God than those who have been unfaithful while in close connection with His work and professing to love and serve Him. The tears of Christ upon the mount came from an anguished, breaking heart because of His unrequited love and the ingratitude of His chosen people. He had labored untiringly to save them from the fate that they seemed determined to bring upon themselves, but they refused His mercy and knew not the time of their visitation. Their day of privilege was ending, yet they were so blinded by sin that they knew it not.

Jesus looked down through the centuries even to the close of time, and, taking in the cases of all who had repaid His love and admonitions with selfishness and neglect, and all who would thus repay Him, He addressed to them those solemn words, declaring that they knew not the time of their visitation. The Jews were gathering about themselves the dark clouds of retribution, and many today, in like manner, are drawing upon themselves the wrath of God, because of opportunities unimproved, the counsels and love of Jesus scorned, and His servants despised and hated for speaking the truth.

There is no place on the face of the earth where so great light has been granted as at ———. Even Jerusalem of old was not more highly favored with the beams of heaven's light shining upon the way that her people should tread. Yet they have failed to walk, by faithful obedience, in the full radiance of the light, serving God night and day. A sickly, dwarfed religion is the result of neglecting to follow the revealed light of the Spirit of the Lord. Energy and love increase as we exercise them, and the Christian graces can be developed only by careful cultivation.

• Necessity of Family Discipline

The state of many in ——— is truly alarming; especially is this the case with a majority of the youth. Families have moved to the place with the understanding that they were not to burden the church, but to be a help to it. With a considerable number the result has been quite the contrary. The neglect of parents to properly discipline their children has been a fruitful source of evil in many families. The youth have not been restrained as they should have been. Parents have neglected to follow the directions of the word of God in this matter, and the children have taken the reins of government into their own hands. The consequence has been that they have generally succeeded in ruling their parents instead of being under their authority.

The parents are blind to the true state of their children, who have succeeded in entirely deceiving them. But those who have lost the control of their children are not pleased when others seek to control them or to point out their defects for the purpose of correcting them. The cause of God has been retarded in —— by parents' bringing their unruly and undisciplined children into this large church. Many are living in constant neglect of their duty to bring up their children in the nurture and admonition of the Lord; yet these very ones have most to say concerning the wickedness of the youth in ——, when it is the wrong example and evil influence of their own children that have demoralized the young people with whom they have associated.

Such families have brought upon this church its heaviest burdens. They come with false ideas. They seem to expect the church to be faultless and that it will take the responsibility of making Christians of those very children whom they, as parents, are unable to control or keep within bounds. They throw themselves upon the church, a terrible and crushing weight. They might be a help if they would yield their selfishness and strive to honor God and to repair the mistakes they made in their lives. But they do no such thing; they hold themselves aloof, ready to criticize the lack of spirituality in the church, whose greatest calamity is that it numbers among its members too many like themselves—dead weights, persons whose hearts and lives are unconsecrated, and whose course is all wrong. The institutions located at —— have carried along too many diseased and lifeless bodies for their own prosperity and spiritual vitality.

• Criticizing Burden Bearers

The church is suffering for want of unselfish Christian workers. If all who are, as a rule, unable to resist temptation and are too weak to stand alone would remain away from ——, there would be a much purer spiritual atmosphere in that place. Those who live upon the husks of others' failings and deficiencies, and who gather to themselves the unwholesome miasma of their neighbors' neglects and shortcomings, making themselves church scavengers, are no advantage to the society of which they form a part, but are an actual burden to the community upon which they inflict themselves.

The church is in need, not of burdens, but of earnest workers; not of faultfinders, but of builders in Zion. Missionaries are really needed at the great heart of the work—men who will keep the fort, who will be true as steel to preserve the honor of those whom God has placed at the head of His work, and who will do their utmost to sustain the cause in all its departments, even at the sacrifice of their own interests and lives, if need be. But I was shown that there are but few who have the truth wrought into their very souls, who can bear the searching test of God. There are many who have taken hold of the truth, but the truth has not taken hold of them, to transform their hearts and cleanse them from all selfishness. There are those who come to —— to help in the work, as well as many of the old members, who have a fearful account to render to God for the hindrance they have been to the work through their self-love and unconsecrated lives.

Religion has no saving virtue if the characters of those professing it do not correspond with their profession. God has graciously given great light to His people in ——; but Satan has his work to accomplish, and he brings his power to bear most strongly at the great heart of the work. He seizes men and women who are selfish and unconsecrated, and makes of them sentinels to watch the faithful servants of God, to question their words, their actions, and their motives, and to find fault and murmur at their reproofs and warnings. Through them he creates suspicion and jealousy, and seeks to weaken the courage of the faithful, to please the unsanctified, and to bring to nought the labors of God's servants.

Satan has had great power over the minds of parents through their undisciplined children. The sin of parental neglect stands marked against many Sabbathkeeping parents.

The spirit of gossip and talebearing is one of Satan's special agencies to sow discord and strife, to separate friends, and to undermine the faith of many in the truthfulness of our positions. Brethren and sisters are too ready to talk of the faults and errors that they think exist in others, and especially in those who have borne unflinchingly the messages of reproof and warning given them of God.

The children of these complainers listen with open ears and receive the poison of disaffection. Parents are thus blindly closing the avenues through which the hearts of the children might be reached. How many families season their daily meals with doubt and questionings. They dissect the characters of their friends, and serve them up as a dainty dessert. A precious bit of slander is passed around the board to be commented upon, not only by adults, but by children. In this God is dishonored. Jesus said: "Inasmuch as ye have done it unto one of the least of these My brethren, ye have done it unto Me." Therefore Christ is slighted and abused by those who slander His servants.

The names of God's chosen servants have been handled with disrespect, and in some cases with absolute contempt, by certain persons whose duty it is to uphold them. The children have not failed to hear the disrespectful remarks of their parents in reference to the solemn reproofs and warnings of God's servants. They have understood the scornful jests and depreciatory speeches that from time to time have met their ears, and the tendency has been to bring sacred and eternal interests, in their minds, on a level with the common affairs of the world.

What a work are these parents doing in making infidels of their children even in their childhood! This is the way that children are taught to be irreverent and to rebel against Heaven's reproof of sin. Spiritual declension can but prevail where such evils exist. These very fathers and mothers, blinded by the enemy, marvel why their children are so inclined to unbelief and to doubt the truth of the Bible. They wonder that it is so difficult to reach them by moral and religious influences. Had they spiritual eyesight, they would at once discover that this deplorable condition of things is the result of their own home influence, the offspring of their jealousy and distrust. Thus many infidels are educated in the family circles of professed Christians.

There are many who find special enjoyment in discoursing and dwelling upon the defects, whether real or imaginary, of those who bear heavy responsibilities in connection with the institutions of God's cause. They overlook the good that has been accomplished, the benefits that have resulted from arduous labor and unflinching devotion to the cause, and fasten their attention upon some apparent mistake, some matter that, after it has been done and the consequences have followed, they fancy could have been done in a better manner with fairer results, when the truth is, had they been left to do the work, they would either have refused to move at all under the attending discouragements of the case, or would have managed more indiscreetly than those who did do the work, following the opening of God's providence.

But these unruly talkers will fasten upon the more disagreeable features of the work, even as the lichen clings to the roughness of the rock. These persons are spiritually dwarfed by continually dwelling upon the failings and faults of others. They are morally incapable of discerning good and noble actions, unselfish endeavors, true heroism, and self-sacrifice. They are not becoming nobler and loftier in their lives and hopes, more generous and broad in their ideas and plans. They are not cultivating that charity that should characterize the Christian's life. They are degenerating every day and are becoming narrower in their prejudices and views. Littleness is their element, and the atmosphere that surrounds them is poisonous to peace and happiness.

The great sin of —— is a neglect to cherish the light which God has given them through His servants. Said Christ to His apostles: "He that receiveth whomsoever I send receiveth Me, and he that receiveth Me receiveth Him that sent Me." Here it is made plain that those who reject the messages of God's servants reject not only the Son, but also the Father.

Again He says: "But into whatsoever city ye enter, and they receive you not, go your ways out into the streets of the same, and say, Even the very dust of your city, which cleaveth on us, we do wipe off against you: notwithstanding be ye sure of this, that the kingdom of God is come nigh unto you. But I say unto you, that it shall be more tolerable in that day for Sodom, than for that city. Woe unto thee, Chorazin! woe unto thee, Bethsaida! for if the mighty works had been done in Tyre and Sidon, which have been done in you, they had a great while ago repented, sitting in sackcloth and ashes. But it shall be more tolerable for Tyre and Sidon at the judgment, than for you. And thou, Capernaum, which art exalted to heaven, shalt be thrust down to hell. He that heareth you heareth Me; and he that despiseth you despiseth Me; and he that despiseth Me despiseth Him that sent Me."

How awfully solemn are these words! How important that we should not be found rejecting the warnings and admonitions that God delivers through His humble instruments; for in slighting the light brought by His messengers, we slight the Saviour of the world, the King of glory. Many are running this terrible risk and are thus bringing upon themselves the condemnation of God. The Almighty will not be trifled with, nor allow His voice to be disregarded with impunity.

• Evils of Lax Discipline

Brethren C and D did not bring that relief to the cause at —— that they should have brought. Had they both taken hold humbly, in the fear of God, and persevered in well-doing both in the church and the office, they would have been a great blessing to the work of God. Had they felt their accountability to God for the training and discipline of their children they would have been worthy examples to others. These children needed not only the education acquired at school, but home training also, that their mental and moral powers might be developed in due proportion, each having the requisite exercise. The physical, mental, and spiritual capabilities should be developed in order to form a properly balanced character.

Children should be watched, guarded, and disciplined in order to successfully accomplish this. It requires skill and patient effort to mold the young in the right manner. Certain evil tendencies are to be carefully restrained and tenderly rebuked; the mind is to be stimulated in favor of the right. The child should be encouraged in attempting to govern self, and all this is to be done judiciously, or the purpose desired is frustrated.

Parents may well inquire: "Who is sufficient for these things?" God alone is their sufficiency, and if they leave Him out of the question, seeking not His aid and counsel, hopeless indeed is their task. But by prayer, by study of the Bible, and by earnest zeal on their part they may succeed nobly in this important duty and be repaid a hundredfold for all their time and care. But gossiping and anxiety concerning the external appearance have taken the precious time that should have been devoted to prayer for wisdom and strength from God to fulfill their most sacred trust. Parents who are wise unto salvation will so order their surroundings that they will be favorable to the formation of correct characters in their children. This is almost always in their power. The source of wisdom is open, from which they may draw all necessary knowledge in this direction.

The Bible, a volume rich in instruction, should be their textbook. If they train their children according to its precepts they not only set their young feet in the right path, but they educate themselves in their most holy duties. Impressions made upon the minds of the young are hard to efface. How important, then, that these impressions should be of the right sort, bending the elastic faculties of youth in the right direction.

Certain parents have come to —— with their children and dropped them into the church as if they resigned from thenceforth all responsibility of their moral and religious training. Brother and Sister C and Brother and Sister D have made a decided failure in disciplining their children as well as in properly regulating themselves. Their children have gloried in their freedom to do as they pleased. They have been released from home responsibilities and have despised restraint.

A life of usefulness appears to them like a life of drudgery. Lax government at home has unfitted them for any position, and as a natural consequence they have rebelled against school discipline. Their complaints have been received and credited by their parents, who, in sympathizing with their imaginary troubles, have encouraged their children in wrong-doing. These parents have in many instances believed positive untruths that have been palmed off upon them by their deceiving children. A few such cases of unruly and dissembling children would do much toward breaking down all authority in the school and demoralizing the young people of our church.

There is perfect order in heaven, perfect concord and agreement. If parents so neglect to bring their children under proper authority here, how can they hope that they will be considered fit companions for the holy angels in a world of peace and harmony? Indulgent parents, who justify their children in their wrongdoing, are thereby creating an element that will bring discord into society and subvert the authority of both school and church.

Children need watchful care and guidance as never before; for Satan is striving to gain the control of their minds and hearts, and to drive out the Spirit of God. The fearful state of the youth of this age constitutes one of the strongest signs that we are living in the last days, but the ruin of many may be traced directly to the wrong management of the parents. The spirit of murmuring against reproof has been taking root and is bearing its fruit of insubordination. While the parents are not pleased with the characters their children are developing, they fail to see the errors that make them what they are.

Eli remonstrated with his sons, but did not act promptly in restraining them. The ease-loving, affectionate father was warned of God that retribution would follow his neglect, but even then he did not feel the importance of at once putting the disgusting evil away from Israel. He should have taken prompt measures himself; but instead of this he said, with remarkable submission: "It is the Lord: let Him do what seemeth Him good." If he had been aroused to the full guilt of his neglect, Israel might have been saved from the humiliation of defeat, and the ark of God would not have fallen into the enemy's hands.

God condemns the negligence that dallies with sin and crime, and the insensibility that is slow to detect its baleful presence in the families of professed Christians. He holds parents accountable in a great degree for the faults and follies of their offspring. God visited with His curse not only the sons of Eli, but Eli himself, and this fearful example should be a warning to the parents of this time.

As I looked upon the perilous situation of our youth, and was shown how indifferent the parents are to their welfare, my heart was sick and faint; angels were troubled and wept with grief. The youth are passing into the world, and into the hands of Satan. They are becoming less susceptible to the sweet influences of the grace of God, bolder and more defiant, and manifest increasing disregard of eternal interests. I saw Satan planting his banner in the households of those who profess to be God's chosen ones, but those who are walking in the light should be able to discern the difference between the black banner of the adversary and the bloodstained standard of Christ.

Children should be taught by precept and example. Parents should meet their grave responsibilities with fear and trembling. Fervent prayers should be offered for divine strength and guidance in this task. In many families the seeds of vanity and selfishness are sown in the hearts of the children almost during babyhood. Their cunning little sayings and doings are commented upon and praised in their presence, and repeated with exaggerations to others. The little ones take note of this and swell with self-importance; they presume to interrupt conversations, and become forward and impudent. Flattery and indulgence foster their vanity and willfulness, until the youngest not unfrequently rules the whole family, father and mother included.

The disposition formed by this sort of training cannot be laid aside as the child matures to riper judgment. It grows with his growth, and what might have appeared cunning in the baby becomes contemptible and wicked in the man or woman. They seek to rule over their associates, and if any refuse to yield to their wishes they consider themselves aggrieved and insulted. This is because they have been indulged to their injury in youth, instead of being taught the self-denial necessary to bear the hardships and toils of life.

Parents frequently pet and indulge their young children because it appears easier to manage them in that way. It is smoother work to let them have their own way than to check the unruly inclinations that rise so strongly in their breasts. Yet this course is cowardly. It is a wicked thing thus to shirk responsibility; for the time will come when these children, whose unchecked inclinations have strengthened into absolute vices, will bring reproach and disgrace upon themselves and their families. They go out into busy life unprepared for its temptations, not strong enough to endure perplexities and troubles; passionate, overbearing, undisciplined, they seek to bend others to their will, and, failing in this, consider themselves ill-used by the world and turn against it.

The lessons of childhood, good or bad, are not learned in vain. Character is developed in youth for good or evil. At home there may be praise and false flattery; in the world each stands on his own merits. The pampered ones, to whom all home authority has yielded, are there daily subjected to mortification by being obliged to yield to others. Many are even then taught their true place by these practical lessons of life. Through rebuffs, disappointments, and plain language from their superiors they often find their true level and are humbled to understand and accept their proper place. But this is a severe and unnecessary ordeal for them to pass through, and could have been prevented by proper training in their youth.

The majority of these ill-disciplined ones go through life at cross-purposes with the world, making a failure where they should have succeeded. They grow to feel that the world owes them a grudge because it does not flatter and caress them, and they take revenge by holding a grudge against the world and bidding it defiance. Circumstances sometimes oblige them to affect a humility they do not feel; but it does not fit them with a natural grace, and their true characters are sure to be exposed sooner or later.

If such persons have families of their own, they become arbitrary rulers at home and display there the selfish and unreasonable disposition they are forced to partially conceal from the outside world. Their dependents feel to the utmost all the faults of their early training. Why will parents educate their children in such a manner that they will be at war with those who are brought in contact with them?

Their religious experience is molded by the education received in childhood. The sad trials, which prove so dangerous to the prosperity of a church, and which cause the unbelieving to stumble and turn away with doubt and dissatisfaction, usually arise from an unsubdued and rebellious spirit, the offspring of parental indulgence in early youth. How many lives are wrecked, how many crimes are committed, under the influence of a quick-rising passion that might have been checked in childhood, when the mind was impressible, when the heart was easily influenced for right, and was subject to a fond mother's will. Inefficient training of children lies at the foundation of a vast amount of moral wretchedness.

Children who are allowed to have their own way are not happy. The unsubdued heart has not within itself the elements of rest and contentment. The mind and heart must be disciplined and brought under proper restraint in order for the character to harmonize with the wise laws that govern our being. Restlessness and discontent are the fruits of indulgence and selfishness. The soil of the heart, like that of a garden, will produce weeds and brambles unless the seeds of precious flowers are planted there and receive care and cultivation. As in visible nature, so is it with the human soul.

The youth of —— are in a startling condition. While some in the church have been burdened in regard to those occupying responsible positions, and have been finding fault and murmuring against reproof, insinuating their doubts, and gossiping of the affairs of others, their own souls have been enshrouded in darkness, and their children have been leavened with the spirit that was working upon their parents. This disposition is calculated to break down all restraint and authority. God holds these parents responsible for the malice and rebellion of the youth under their care.

Satan has succeeded wonderfully in his plans. Men of experience, fathers of families, who manifest a headstrong defiance when their track is crossed, show plainly that they cannot or do not control themselves. Then how can they succeed in controlling their children, who follow in their steps and rebel against their authority and all other restraint, even as they themselves rebel against the authority of the church and the institutions with which they are connected?

Some of these professed Christians have yielded themselves into the hands of Satan and have become his instruments. They influence souls against the truth by exhibiting their insubordination and restless discontent. While professing righteousness, they are flying in the face of the Almighty, and before they are aware of the enormity of their sin they have accomplished the object of the adversary. The impression has been made, the shadow of darkness has been cast, the arrows of Satan have found their mark. Verily, a little leaven has leavened the entire lump. Unbelief creeps in and fastens its grasp upon minds that would have wholly accepted the truth.

Meanwhile, these spasmodic workers for Satan look innocently upon those who have drifted into skepticism, and who stand unmoved under reproof or entreaty. While those persons who have been thus influenced have gone farther in unbelief than even they themselves had dared to venture, they flatter themselves that in comparison with them, they are virtuous and righteous. They fail to understand that those sad cases are the result of their own unbridled tongues and wicked rebellion, that the tempted ones have fallen through their evil influence. They started the difficulty; they sowed the seeds of anarchy and unbelief.

No family is justified in bringing children to —— who are not under the control of their parents. If their parents have disregarded the word of God in the matter of instructing and training their children, —— is no place for them. They will only be the means of demoralizing the young people of that place and bringing discord where peace and prosperity should reign. Let such parents take up the neglected work of restraining and disciplining their children before they venture to impose them upon the church at ——.

Many are as guilty of neglect toward their children as was Eli, and the punishment of God will as surely rest upon them as upon him. The case of Brother E was a marked one. God's hand was stretched out in the wrath of His retribution, not only over his children, but over himself also. The word of God was plain, but its admonitions had been trampled underfoot; warnings had been given him, reproofs administered, but all were unheeded, and the curse fell upon him. It is a terrible thing to neglect the education of children. Not only will they be lost in consequence, but the parents themselves, who have so far departed from God as to lose all sense of their sacred responsibility, stand in a very perilous position as regards eternal life.

Fond and indulgent parents, let me present for your instruction the directions given in the Bible for dealing with a rebellious son: "If a man have a stubborn and rebellious son, which will not obey the voice of his father, or the voice of his mother, and that, when they have chastened him, will not hearken unto them; then shall his father and his mother lay hold on him, and bring him out unto the elders of his city, and unto the gate of his place; and they shall say unto the elders of his city, This our son is stubborn and rebellious, he will not obey our voice; he is a glutton, and a drunkard. And all the men of his city shall stone him with stones, that he die; so shalt thou put evil away from among you; and all Israel shall hear, and fear."

Both the young and the old who are connected with the office should be looked after closely, lest their influence should be such as to work directly against the object designed by the office. If any are employed whose influence is of a character to lead away from God and the truth, there should not be a moment's question as to the disposal of their cases. They should be separated from the office at once, for they are scattering from Christ instead of gathering with Him. They are virtually servants of Satan.

If there are young people connected with the office who do not respect the authority of parents, and are ungovernable at home, despising counsel and restraint, the curse of God will fall upon them; and it will not only rest upon them, but upon the office, should their services be retained and they be given further opportunity to pervert the young with whom they are there brought in contact. Those who occupy responsible positions in the office are accountable for the prevailing influence there, and if they are indifferent to the course of the insubordinate and impenitent in their employ they become partakers of their sin.

There has been a covering up of iniquity in——. God calls for a different order of things. The youth connected with His work should be select, those who will be improved, refined, and ennobled by being associated with the cause of God. Faithful minutemen are needed at every post of duty, especially at the great heart of the work. Like sleepless sentinels, those who profess the truth should guard the interests of the cause at the office; they should sacredly guard themselves and one another from spiritual contamination.

Those who have imbibed the spirit of independence, and come to——as students in our school, thinking to do as they please in all matters, should be quickly undeceived and brought under proper discipline. But especially should the youth residing at——be brought under the strictest rules, to guard their integrity and morality. If they refuse to submit to these regulations they should be expelled from the school and cut off from association with those whom they are demoralizing by their wrong example.

Parents living at a distance send their children to—— to be educated, feeling perfect confidence that they will there receive the proper moral training and not be exposed to wrong influences. It is due these patrons of our school that the moral atmosphere there be purified. A lack of propriety and a disregard of strict virtue has been developing among a certain class of young men and women in——. Some of these are low in the scale of morality and are influencing the young students who have been sent there from a distance and have not the advantages of parental advice and protection. This should be attended to at once, for it is a matter of grave importance.

The influence of some youth in——is demoralizing. They seem to think it praiseworthy to appear independent and to show disrespect to the authority of their parents. Paul gives a faithful description of this class of youth in these words: "This know also, that in the last days perilous times shall come. For men shall be lovers of their own selves, covetous, boasters, proud, blasphemers, disobedient to parents, unthankful, unholy, without natural affection, trucebreakers, false accusers, incontinent, fierce, despisers of those that are good, traitors, heady, high-minded, lovers of pleasures more than lovers of God."

The influence of this class upon the youth of——is doing much harm. Their conversation and example are contemptibly low. The young whose morals are established, and whose minds are of an elevated character, would find no attraction in their society and would therefore be beyond the reach of their influence. But there are young men and women who find pleasure in the company of just such persons. Satan has marked success in benumbing the spiritual sensibilities of certain persons who have believed the truth, and in clouding their minds with false ideas until they are unable to discern right from wrong. Then suggestions are made to undermine their confidence in the chosen servants of God, and they are led into positive unbelief.

If the young would choose the company of those whose lives are an honor to their profession, they would escape many serious dangers. Satan is constantly seeking the ruin of those who are ignorant concerning his devices, yet feel no special need of the prayers and counsel of experienced and godly friends. Many of the youth who come to——with good resolutions to live Christian lives fall in with a class of young people who take them by the hand and, under the guise of friendship, lead them directly into Satan's snare. The enemy does not always come as a roaring lion; he frequently appears as an angel of light, assuming friendly airs, presenting peculiar temptations which it is difficult for the inexperienced to withstand. Sometimes he accomplishes his purpose of deluding the unwary by exciting the pity of their sympathetic natures, and presenting himself before them as a righteous being who has been persecuted without a cause.

Satan finds willing instruments to do his work. He exercises a skill in this direction that has been perfected by years of experience. He uses the accumulated knowledge of ages in executing his malicious designs. Ignorant youth play themselves into the hands of Satan for him to use as instruments to lead souls to ruin. Those who yield to Satan's power gain no happiness thereby. They are never contented or at rest. They are dissatisfied, querulous and irritable, unthankful and rebellious. Such a one is the young man now under review. But God will have mercy upon him if he sincerely repents and becomes converted. His sins may be washed away by the atoning blood of Jesus.

The Saviour of the world offers to the erring the gift of eternal life. He watches for a response to His offers of love and forgiveness with a more tender compassion than that which moves the heart of an earthly parent to forgive a wayward, repenting, suffering son. He cries after the wanderer: "Return unto Me, and I will return unto you."

If the sinner still refuses to heed the voice of mercy which calls after him with tender, pitying love, his soul will be left in darkness. If he neglects the opportunity presented him, and goes on in his evil course, the wrath of God will, in an unexpected moment, break forth upon him. "He, that being often reproved hardeneth his neck, shall suddenly be destroyed, and that without remedy." This young man has made light of his father's authority, and despised restraint. The fear of the Lord is the beginning of wisdom. It lies at the foundation of a proper education. Those who, having a favorable opportunity, have failed to learn this first great lesson, are not only disqualified for service in the cause of God, but are a positive injury to the community in which they live.

Solomon exhorts the youth: "My son, hear the instruction of thy father, and forsake not the law of thy mother: for they shall be an ornament of grace unto thy head, and chains about thy neck. My son, if sinners entice thee, consent thou not... Wisdom crieth without; she uttereth her voice in the streets: she crieth in the chief place of concourse, in the openings of the gates: in the city she uttereth her words, saying, How long, ye simple ones, will ye love simplicity? and the scorners delight in their scorning, and fools hate knowledge? Turn you at My reproof: behold, I will pour out My Spirit unto you, I will make known My words unto you."

"Because I have called, and ye refused; I have stretched out My hand, and no man regarded; but ye have set at nought all My counsel, and would none of My reproof: I also will laugh at your calamity; I will mock when your fear cometh; when your fear cometh as desolation, and your destruction cometh as a whirlwind; when distress and anguish cometh upon you. Then shall they call upon Me, but I will not answer; they shall seek Me early, but they shall not find Me: for that they hated knowledge, and did not choose the fear of the Lord: they would none of My counsel: they despised all My reproof. Therefore shall they eat of the fruit of their own way, and be filled with their own devices. For the turning away of the simple shall slay them, and the prosperity of fools shall destroy them. But whoso hearkeneth unto Me shall dwell safely, and shall be quiet from fear of evil."

Order should be maintained in our different institutions at——. Insubordination should be overruled. None should be retained in the office who have been instructed by Sabbath-keeping parents and have been privileged to hear the truth yet rebel against its teachings. No persons should be connected with the sacred work of God who speak lightly of it or treat our holy faith with disrespect. Those who have been connected with the office for quite a length of time and have had ample opportunity to become acquainted with our faith, yet manifest opposition to the truth, should no longer be retained in the office. Their influence is against the truth if they continue to neglect the light and slight salvation. This very indifference has a chilling influence upon the faith of others to draw them away from God. These impenitent, unimpressible ones should not occupy positions that might be filled by persons who will respect the truth and yield to the influence of the Spirit of God by being so closely connected with this sacred work.

The influence of our young people in the office is not what it should be. A and B have virtually worked against the cause. The influence of their conversation and deportment has been such as to disgust unbelievers and turn them from our faith and from Christ. The young who heed not the warnings of the word of God and slight the Testimonies of His Spirit can only be a living curse to the office and should be separated from it.

The youth whose influence is demoralizing should have no connection with our college. Those who are possessed of a lovesick sentimentalism, and make their attendance at school an opportunity for courting and exchanging improper attentions, should be brought under the closest restrictions. Authority must be maintained. Justice and Mercy are twin sisters, standing side by side.

If no efforts are made to correct the state of things existing at——, it will soon be a place for the encouragement of immorality and dissipation. Will parents and those in charge of our institutions sleep while Satan is taking possession of the minds of the children? God abhors the sins that are fostered and concealed by the church, cherished in the office, and sheltered under the paternal roof. Let parents, and those in authority, earnestly take hold of the work and purge this evil from among them.

We are living in the last days. John exclaims: "Woe to the inhabiters of the earth and of the sea! for the devil is come down unto you, having great wrath, because he knoweth that he hath but a short time." Christ is the only refuge in these perilous times. Satan is at work in secrecy and darkness. Cunningly he draws away the followers of Christ from the cross and brings them into self-indulgence and wickedness.

Vital interests are located at——, and Satan is opposed to everything that will strengthen the cause of Christ and weaken his own power. He is diligently laying plans to undermine the work of God. He never rests for a moment when he sees that the right is gaining the ascendancy. He has legions of evil angels that he sends to every point where light from heaven is shining upon the people. Here he stations his pickets to seize every unguarded man, woman, or child and press them into his service.

The great heart of the work is at——; and, as the human heart throws its living current of blood into all parts of the body, so does the management at this place, the headquarters of our church, affect the whole body of believers. If the physical heart is healthy, the blood that is sent from it through the system is also healthy; but if this fountain is impure, the whole organism becomes diseased by the poison of the vital fluid. So it is with us. If the heart of the work becomes corrupt, the whole church, in its various branches and interests, scattered abroad over the face of the earth, suffers in consequence.

Satan's chief work is at the headquarters of our faith. He spares no pains to corrupt men in responsible positions and to persuade them to be unfaithful to their several trusts. He insinuates his suspicions and jealousies into the minds of those whose business it is to do God's work faithfully. While God is testing and proving these helpers, and fitting them for their posts, Satan is doing his utmost to deceive and allure them, that they may not only be destroyed themselves, but may influence others to do wrong and to injure the great work. He seeks by all the means in his power to shake the confidence of God's people in the voice of warning and reproof through which God designs to purify the church and prosper His cause.

It is Satan's plan to weaken the faith of God's people in the Testimonies. Next follows skepticism in regard to the vital points of our faith, the pillars of our position, then doubt as to the Holy Scriptures, and then the downward march to perdition. When the Testimonies, which were once believed, are doubted and given up, Satan knows the deceived ones will not stop at this; and he redoubles his efforts till he launches them into open rebellion, which becomes incurable and ends in destruction.

Satan has gained marked advantage in —— because the people of God have not guarded the outposts. The very men whose labors God has signified that He would accept if they were fully consecrated have been the ones to be deceived, to fail in their duties, and to prove a terrible burden and discouragement, instead of the help and blessing that they should have been. These men who have been trusted to keep the fort have well-nigh betrayed it into the hands of the enemy. They have opened the gates to a wily foe, who has sought to destroy them.

Men of experience have seen stealthy hands slipping the bolts that Satan might enter; yet they have held their peace with apparent indifference as to the results. Some have been glad to see this, as it seemed an extenuation of their past neglect, which made it a necessity to call for others to fill the posts of responsibility that they had abused or neglected. This lack of watchfulness on the part of these newer incumbents seemed to excuse the former for their own want of faithfulness, as it showed that others were fully as derelict in duty. These persons do not realize that God holds them responsible for every advantage gained by the foe who is admitted to the fort.

The desolation and ruin following lie at the door of the unfaithful sentinels, who, by their neglect, become agents in the hands of the adversary to win souls to destruction. Men in responsible positions should seek wisdom and guidance of God, and not trust to their own judgment and knowledge. Like Solomon they should earnestly pray for faith and light, and God will give them freely of His abundant supply.

God would have His work done intelligently, not in a haphazard manner. He would have it done with faith and careful exactness, that He may place the sign of His approval upon it. Those who love Him, and walk with fear and humility before Him, He will bless and guide and connect with heaven.

If the workers rely upon Him, He will give them wisdom and correct their infirmities, so that they will be able to do the work of the Lord with perfection.

We must put on the armor and be prepared to successfully resist all the attacks of Satan. His malignity and cruel power are not sufficiently estimated. When he finds himself foiled upon one point he takes new ground and fresh tactics, and tries again, working wonders in order to deceive and destroy the children of men. The youth should be carefully warned against his power and patiently and prayerfully directed how to endure the trials sure to come upon them in this life. They should be led to cling to the word of God and give attention to counsel and advice.

Living faith in the merits of a crucified Redeemer will carry them through the fiery furnace of affliction and trial. The form of the Fourth will be with them in the fierce heat of the furnace, which will not leave even the smell of fire upon their garments. Children should be encouraged to become Bible students and to have firm religious principles that will stand the test of the perils sure to be experienced by all who live upon the earth during the last days in the closing history of the world.

19. Entire Consecration

The following testimony was written in January, 1875, and its truthfulness was acknowledged by Brother C, who said that it gave him light and hope.

Brother C, you are backslidden from God. Your views of God's requirements have never been too well defined nor too strict. It is no excuse for you to become remiss in duty and less vigilant because the course of so many professed Christians is wrong. You have not been consecrated to God. You have not felt your dependence upon Him to keep you, and therefore you have been overcome and brought into the slavery of doubt; the bondage of unbelief has chained your soul. You do not glorify God in your life. Our faith sometimes looks to you very questionable. The reason of this is in yourself. In the world, truth and falsehood are so mixed that one is not always clearly discerned from the other. But why has one who professes the truth so little strength? Because he understands not his own ignorance and his own weakness. If he knew this, if he were distrustful of himself, he would feel the importance of divine help to preserve him from the wiles of the enemy. We need to be active, working Christians, unselfish in heart and life, having an eye single to the glory of God. Oh, what wrecks we meet everywhere! what silent lips and fruitless lives! "This," said the angel, "is because of falling under temptation. Nothing mars the peace of the soul like sinful unbelief."

You should not give up in despair, thinking you must live and die in the bondage of doubt and unbelief. In the Lord we have righteousness and strength. Lean upon Him; and through His power you may quench all the fiery darts of the adversary and come off more than conqueror. You may yet become sanctified through the truth; or you may, if you choose, walk in the darkness of unbelief, lose heaven, and lose all. By walking in the light and working out the will of God, you may overcome your selfish nature.

You have been ready to give of your means, but have withheld yourself. You have not felt called upon to make sacrifices which would involve care; you have not had a willingness to do any work for Christ, be it ever so humble. God will bring you over the ground again and again until with humble heart and subdued mind you bear the test that He inflicts and are wholly sanctified to His service and work. Then you may win immortal life. You may be a fully developed man in Christ Jesus, or you may be a spiritual dwarf, gaining no victories.

My brother, which will you choose? Will you live a life of self-denial and self-sacrifice, doing your work with cheerfulness and joy, perfecting Christian character, and pressing on for the immortal reward? or will you live for yourself and lose heaven? God will not be trifled with; Christ accepts no divided service. He asks for all. It will not do to withhold anything. He has purchased you with an infinite price, and He requires that all you have shall be yielded to Him a willing offering. If you are fully consecrated to Him in heart and life, faith will take the place of doubts, and confidence the place of distrust and unbelief.

My brother, you are in positive danger through neglecting to carry out health reform more strictly in your own life and in your family. Your blood is impure, and you are still corrupting and inflaming it by the gratification of taste. Never be betrayed into indulging in the use of stimulants; for this will result not only in reaction and loss of physical strength, but in a benumbed intellect. Strictly temperate habits in eating and drinking, with firm trust in God, will improve your physical, mental, and moral health. You are of a highly excitable temperament. You have but little self-control and under excitement frequently say and do things which you afterward regret. You should call a determined will to your aid in the warfare against your own inclinations and propensities. You need to keep the avenues of your soul open to the reception of light and truth. But when something occurs to test and prove you, prejudice frequently comes in, and you rise at once against what you deem a restriction of your liberty or an infringement upon your rights.

The word of God plainly presents before us this truth, that our physical natures will be brought into warfare with the spiritual. The apostle charges us to abstain from fleshly lusts, which war against the soul. Every perverted appetite becomes a warring lust. Appetite indulged to the injury of physical strength causes disease of the soul. The lust which the apostle mentions is not confined to the violation of the seventh commandment, but every indulgence of the taste which lessens physical vigor is a warring lust. The apostle declares that he who would gain special victories and make higher attainments in righteousness must be "temperate in all things." Temperance in eating and drinking at our tables, as well as the exercise of temperance in every other respect, is essential if we would overcome as Christ overcame. God has given us light, not to be treated indifferently, but to be our guide and help.

You need to cultivate self-control. The lesson you should have learned in your youth should be mastered now. Discipline yourself to die to self, to bring your will in subjection to the will of Christ. A deep and thorough conversion is essential, or you, my dear brother, will fail of eternal life. Your service in the cause of God must be more hearty, full, and thorough. You cannot perfect a Christian character by serving God when you feel inclined to do so and neglecting it when you please. A decided change must take place in your life, and you must obtain a different experience from any you have yet had, or your service will not be accepted of God.

Our heavenly Father has been very gracious to you. He has dealt tenderly with you. Sickness and disease came upon you when you were unprepared to die, for you had not perfected a Christian character and had not a moral fitness for heaven. Satan stood by your side to afflict and destroy, that you might be numbered with the transgressors. Fervent and effectual prayer prevailed in your behalf. Angels were sent to wait and watch about you, to guard and protect you from Satan's power and preserve your life. God has, in His matchless love, granted you another trial. Not because of any goodness or virtue in you but, because of His mercy, He has answered the prayers of faith. Your probation has been lengthened that you may have an opportunity to redeem the past, overcome the defects in your character, and show in your life that devotion to God which He claims from you. You have had emotions of gratitude, but you have not experienced that heartfelt thankfulness and becoming humility that should have been kindled by His unsurpassed love.

You have not sufficiently felt your obligations to God for sparing your life. You have, for pettish reasons of your own, excused yourself time and again from religious duties which devolve upon us at all times and under all circumstances. Feelings of discouragement are no apology before God for the neglect of a single duty. You are not your own; you have been purchased by the blood of Christ. He claims all that you are capable of doing; your time and strength are not your own.

God indicated that you could be educated to act a part in His cause, but it was necessary that your mind should be trained and disciplined to work in harmony with the plan of God. You could gain the required experience if you would; you had the privilege presented before you of denying your inclination, as your Saviour had given you an example in His life. But you have not placed yourself in a position to learn all that you could and all that it was important for you to learn in order to become a correct worker in the cause of God. There were some things to reform in yourself before the Lord could use you effectually as His instrument.

Brother C, it was a sacrifice for you to leave your farm; you enjoyed your life there. You did not come to —— from choice. You had no knowledge of the work in connection with the publishing interest. But you were determined to do the best you could, and in many respects you have done well. But many things have arisen as stumbling blocks in your way. The course of Brother F was wrong in many respects; but you did not preserve your consecration to God; you united with him in spirit, and did not stand free; you displeased

God in many things and separated your soul from Him. Satan was obtaining great power over you; your steps had well-nigh slipped; you were almost gone in unbelief, when sickness arrested your course. It was in great mercy that God spared you and gave you a new lease of life. But you have not made an entire surrender to Him; your stubborn will has not been subdued and softened; you need a new conversion. You have been easily fretted and annoyed; you have braced yourself to resist everything that you thought reflected upon you; your feelings have arisen like a flash when anything has touched your pride. Now, my dear brother, this is all wrong. This you must over come, or the enemy will gain the victory over you.

You have felt sick at heart because you did not love the work in ——. You have looked back toward ——, for your heart is there, and your body should be where your heart is. God has been testing and proving you; how have you borne the test? You needed to be planed and polished, to have the rough and jagged points of your character removed, that you might become refined for the kingdom of heaven. How hard it is for human nature to deny inclination; how hard for men to leave flattering worldly inducements and, through love of their Saviour and their fellow men, to deny their own pleasure in order to engage more directly in the service of God.

Brother C, you do not enter heart and soul into the work. You have never made it a direct personal interest, and it is not agreeable to you. Had you been so disposed you could have trained your mind to better understand the work; but you have, in a measure, held aloof from it; you have not connected yourself closely with it and tried to become familiar with its various branches.

You are not as social and courteous as you should be, and your cold, unapproachable manner is not pleasing to God. You allow your feelings to be easily excited. No man can properly fill a position in connection with the work of God who is controlled by feeling and moves from impulse. Your mind must come in closer connection with God, and in sympathy and interest you must be more closely identified with those who are engaged in His work, or you can be of no use in advancing the cause in ——. You are too independent and exclusive; you need to soften and assimilate your disposition to the mind and feelings of others. You can, as a businessman and as a Christian, do much valuable service for the cause of God if you will only surrender your will and your way to the Lord. You need to be sanctified by the truth, having your mind elevated above every personal consideration and every selfish interest.

I point you to the life of Jesus as a perfect pattern. His life was characterized by disinterested benevolence. Precious Saviour! What sacrifices has He made for us that we should not perish, but have everlasting life! Heaven will be cheap enough if we resign every selfish interest to obtain it. Can we afford to have our own way, and take ourselves out of the hands of God, because it is more pleasing to the natural heart? God requires perfect submission and perfect obedience. Eternal life is worth everything to us. You may come in close connection with God if you will agonize to enter in at the strait gate.

You could never be aware of your deficiencies unless you were brought where these deficiencies were developed by circumstances. You have not felt as you should since you have come to ——. You have not entered freely and heartily into the work and made it your chief interest. You have cherished an independence that could not be maintained if you realized your true position—that you are an apprentice, learning how to work in the very best manner for the prosperity of God's cause; that you are a scholar, seeking to obtain knowledge concerning that with which you are unacquainted. You could have made much greater progress had you earnestly tried to serve God as an efficient worker.

You have been too reserved. You have not come into close relation with men engaged in the different departments of the work; you have not consulted with them as familiarly as you should to move understandingly. Had you done this you might have been a more efficient helper. You have moved too much according to your own judgment and carried out your own ideas and plans. There has been a lack of harmonious connection between the workers. Those who might have helped you have been reluctant to impart their knowledge to you on account of this lack of familiarity on your part, and also because you move so much from impulse and feeling that they have dreaded to approach you.

The Saviour of the world was the adored of angels, He was a prince in the royal courts of heaven; but He laid aside His glory and clothed His divinity with humanity. He became the meek and lowly Jesus. He left His riches and glory in heaven and became poor that we, through His poverty, might be made rich. Three years He journeyed from place to place, a homeless wanderer. But selfish men will repine and murmur if called to leave their little earthly treasure for Christ's sake, or to labor in the work of saving souls for whom He gave His precious life. Oh, what ingratitude! No one can appreciate the blessings of redemption unless he feels that he can joyfully afford to make any and every sacrifice for the love of Christ. Every sacrifice made for Christ enriches the giver, and every suffering and privation endured for His dear sake increases the overcomer's final joy in heaven.

You know but little of real sacrifice and genuine denial of self. You have had but little experience in hardships and taxation of your energies. Your burden has been light, while others have been loaded down with serious responsibilities. The young man who asked Jesus what he should do that he might have eternal life was answered: "Keep the commandments."

He confidently and proudly replied: "All these things have I kept from my youth up: what lack I yet?" Jesus looked pityingly upon the young man; He loved him, and He knew the words He spoke would forever separate the youth from Himself. Nevertheless Jesus touched the plague spot of his soul. He said to him: "Go and sell that thou hast, and give to the poor, and thou shalt have treasure in heaven: and come and follow Me."

The young man wanted heaven, but not enough to withdraw his affections from his earthly treasure. He refused to yield to the conditions required by God in order to enter into life. He was very sorrowful; for he had great possessions, which he thought were too valuable to exchange for eternal rewards. He had asked what he must do to be saved, and the answer had been given; but his worldly heart could not make the sacrifice of his wealth to become Christ's disciple. His decision was to give up heaven and to cling to his earthly treasure. How many are now making the very same decision which fixed the destiny of this young man?

Have any of us an opportunity of doing something for Christ, how eagerly should we seize it and with the greatest earnestness do all we can to be co-workers with Him. The very trials that test our faith most severely, and make it seem that God has forsaken us, are designed to lead us more closely to Christ, that we may lay all our burdens at His feet and experience the peace

He will give us in exchange. You need a new conversion; you need to be sanctified through the truth and to become in spirit like a little child, meek and humble, relying wholly upon Christ as your Redeemer. Your pride and independence are closing your heart to the blessed influences of the Spirit of God and rendering it as unimpressible as the hard-beaten highway. You have yet to learn the great lesson of faith.

When you surrender yourself entirely to God, when you fall all broken upon Jesus, you will be rewarded by a victory the joy of which you have never yet experienced. As you review the past with a clear vision, you will see that at the very time when life seemed to you only a perplexity and a burden, Jesus Himself was near you, seeking to lead you into the light. Your Father was by your side, bending over you with unutterable love, afflicting you for your good, as the refiner purifies the precious ore. When you have thought yourself forsaken, He has been near you to comfort and sustain. We seldom view Jesus as He is, and are never so ready to receive His help as He is to help us.

What a victory you will gain when you learn to follow the opening providences of God with a grateful heart and a determination to live with an eye single to His glory, in sickness or health, in abundance or want. Self is alive and quivering at every touch. Self must be crucified before you can overcome in the name of Jesus and receive the reward of the faithful.

20. Necessity of Harmony

The Spirit of God will not abide where there is disunion and contention among believers in the truth. Even if these feelings are unexpressed, they take possession of the heart, and drive out the peace and love that should characterize the Christian church. They are the result of selfishness in its fullest sense. This evil may take the form of inordinate self-esteem, or of an undue longing for the approbation of others, even if that approbation is obtained undeservedly. Self-exaltation must be renounced by those who profess to love God and keep His commandments, or they need not expect to be blessed by His divine favor.

The moral and religious influence at the Health Institute must be elevated in order to meet the approbation of heaven. The indulgence of selfishness will surely grieve the Spirit of God from the place. Physicians, superintendent, and helpers should work harmoniously in the spirit of Christ, each esteeming others better than himself.

The apostle Jude says: "Of some have compassion, making a difference." This difference is not to be exercised in a spirit of favoritism. No countenance should be given to a spirit that implies: "If you favor me, I will favor you." This is unsanctified, worldly policy, which displeases God. It is paying favors and admiration for the sake of gain. It is showing a partiality for certain ones, expecting to secure advantages through them. It is seeking their good will by indulgence, that we may be held in greater estimation than others fully as worthy as ourselves. It is a hard thing to see one's own errors, but everyone should realize how cruel is the spirit of envy, rivalry, distrust, faultfinding, and dissension.

We call God our Father; we claim to be children of one family, and when there is a disposition to lessen the respect and influence of another to build up ourselves, we please the enemy and grieve Him whom we profess to follow. The tenderness and mercy that Jesus has revealed in His own precious life should be an example to us of the manner in which we should treat our fellow beings and especially those who are our brethren in Christ.

God is continually benefiting us, but we are too indifferent to His favors. We have been loved with an infinite tenderness, and yet many of us have little love for one another. We are too severe upon those we suppose to be in error, and are very sensitive to the least blame or question in regard to our own course.

Hints are thrown out and sharp criticisms of one another, but at the same time the very ones who throw out these hints and criticisms are blind to their own failings. Others can see their errors, but they cannot see their own mistakes. We are daily recipients of the bounties of heaven and should have loving gratitude springing up in our hearts to God, which should cause us to sympathize with our neighbors and make their interests our own. Thoughts and meditations upon the goodness of God to us would close the avenues of the soul to Satan's suggestions.

God's love for us is proved daily; yet we are thoughtless of His favors and indifferent to His entreaties. He seeks to impress us with His Spirit of tenderness, His love and forbearance; but we scarcely recognize the marks of His kindness and have little sense of the lesson of love He desires us to learn. Some, like Haman, forget all God's favors, because Mordecai is before them and is not disgraced; because their hearts are filled with enmity and hatred rather than love, the spirit of our dear Redeemer, who gave His precious life for His enemies. We profess to have the same Father, to be bound for the same immortal home, to enjoy the same solemn faith, and to believe the same testing message; and yet many are at strife with one another like quarrelsome children. Some who are engaged in the same branch of the work are at variance with one another and therefore at variance with the Spirit of Christ.

The love of praise has corrupted many hearts. Those who have been connected with the Health Institute have at times manifested a spirit of finding fault with the plans laid, and Satan has given them a hold upon the minds of others there who have accepted these persons as blameless while innocent persons have been charged with wrong. It is a wicked pride that delights in the vanity of one's own works, that boasts of one's excellent qualities, seeking to make others seem inferior in order to exalt self, claiming more glory than the cold heart is willing to give to God. The disciples of Christ will heed the Master's instruction. He has bidden us love one another even as He has loved us. Religion is founded upon love to God, which also leads us to love one another. It is full of gratitude, humility, long-suffering. It is self-sacrificing, forbearing, merciful, and forgiving. It sanctifies the whole life and extends its influence over others.

Those who love God cannot harbor hatred or envy. When the heavenly principle of eternal love fills the heart, it will flow out to others, not merely because favors are received of them, but because love is the principle of action and modifies the character, governs the impulses, controls the passions, subdues enmity, and elevates and ennobles the affections. This love is not contracted so as merely to include "me and mine," but is as broad as the world and as high as heaven, and is in harmony with that of the angel workers. This love cherished in the soul sweetens the entire life and sheds a refining influence on all around. Possessing it, we cannot but be happy, let fortune smile or frown. If we love God with all the heart, we must love His children also. This love is the spirit of God. It is the heavenly adorning that gives true nobility and dignity to the soul and assimilates our lives to that of the Master. No matter how many good qualities we may have, however honorable and refined we may consider ourselves, if the soul is not baptized with the heavenly grace of love to God and one another, we are deficient in true goodness and unfit for heaven, where all is love and unity.

Some who have formerly loved God and lived in the daily enjoyment of His favor are now in continual unrest. They wander in darkness and despairing gloom because they are nourishing self. They are seeking so hard to favor themselves that all other considerations are swallowed up in this. God in His providence has willed that no one can secure happiness by living for himself alone. The joy of our Lord consisted in enduring toil and shame for others, that they might be benefited thereby. We are capable of being happy in following His example and living to bless our fellow men.

We are invited by our Lord to take His yoke and bear His burden. In doing this we may be happy. In bearing our own self-imposed yoke and carrying our own burdens, we find no rest; but in bearing the yoke of Christ there is rest to the soul. Those who want some great work to do for the Master can find it just where they are, in doing good and in being self-forgetful and self-sacrificing, remembering others and carrying sunshine wherever they go.

There is great need that the pitying tenderness of Christ should be manifested at all times and in all places—not that blind sympathy which would gloss over sin and allow God's cause to be reproached by ill-doing, but that love which is a controlling principle of the life, which flows out naturally to others in good works, remembering that Christ has said: "Inasmuch as ye have done it unto one of the least of these My brethren, ye have done it unto Me."

Those at the Health Institute are engaged in a great work. During the life of Christ the sick and afflicted were objects of His special care. When He sent out His disciples He commissioned them to heal the sick as well as to preach the gospel. When He sent forth the seventy He commanded them to heal the sick, and next to preach that the kingdom of God had come nigh unto them. Their physical health was to be first cared for, in order that the way might be prepared for their minds to be reached by those truths which the apostles were to preach.

The Saviour of the world devoted more time and labor to healing the afflicted of their maladies than to preaching. His last injunction to His apostles, His representatives upon the earth, was to lay hands on the sick that they might recover. When the Master shall come, He will commend those who have visited the sick and relieved the necessities of the afflicted.

We are slow to learn the mighty influence of trifles and their bearing upon the salvation of souls. At the Health Institute those who desire to be missionaries have a large field in which to work. God does not mean that any of us shall constitute a privileged few, who shall be looked upon with great deference while others are neglected. Jesus was the Majesty of heaven; yet He stooped to minister to the humblest, having no respect to persons or station.

Those who have their whole hearts in the work will find at the Health Institute enough to do for the Master in relieving the suffering ones placed under their care. Our Lord, after performing the most humiliating office for His disciples, recommended them to follow His example. This was to keep constantly before them the thought that they must not feel superior to the lowliest saint.

Those who profess our exalted faith, who are keeping God's commandments and expecting the soon coming of our Lord, should be distinct and separate from the world around them, a peculiar people, zealous of good works. Among the peculiarities which should distinguish God's people from the world in these last days, is their humility and meekness. "Learn of Me," says Christ, "for I am meek and lowly in heart: and ye shall find rest unto your souls." Here is the repose which so many crave and in vain spend time and money to obtain. Instead of being ambitious to be equal to another in honor and position, or perhaps even higher, we should seek to be the humble, faithful servants of Christ. This spirit of self-aggrandizement made contention among the apostles even while Christ was with them. They disputed who should be greatest among them. Jesus sat down and, calling the twelve, said unto them: "If any man desire to be first, the same shall be last of all, and servant of all."

When the mother of two sons made a request that her sons should be especially favored, one sitting on the right hand and the other on the left in His kingdom, Jesus impressed upon them that the honor and glory of His kingdom was to be the reverse of the honor and glory of this world. Whoever would be great must be a humble minister unto others, and whoever would be chief must be a servant, even as the Son of God was a minister and servant unto the children of men.

Again, our Saviour taught His disciples not to be anxious for position and name. "Be not ye called Rabbi... Neither be ye called masters... But he that is greatest among you shall be your servant. And whosoever shall exalt himself shall be abased." Jesus cited the lawyer to the sacred law code given from Sinai: "Thou shalt love the Lord thy God with all thy heart, and with all thy soul, and with all thy strength, and with all thy mind, and thy neighbor as thyself." He told him that if he did this he should enter into life.

"Thy neighbor as thyself." The question arises: "Who is my neighbor?" His reply is the parable of the good Samaritan, which teaches us that any human being who needs our sympathy and our kind offices is our neighbor. The suffering and destitute of all classes are our neighbors, and when their wants are brought to our knowledge, it is our duty to relieve them as far as possible. A principle is brought out in this parable that it would be well for the followers of Christ to adopt. First meet the temporal necessities of the needy and relieve their physical wants and sufferings, and you will then find an open avenue to the heart, where you may plant the good seeds of virtue and religion.

In order to be happy, we must strive to attain to that character which Christ exhibited. One marked peculiarity of Christ was His self-denial and benevolence. He came not to seek His own. He went about doing good, and this was His meat and drink. We may, by following the example of the Saviour, be in holy communion with Him, and by daily seeking to imitate His character and follow His example, we shall be a blessing to the world and shall secure for ourselves contentment here and an eternal reward hereafter.

21. Opposition to Faithful Warnings

January 3, 1875, I was shown that there is a great work to be done for those who profess to believe the truth in California, before God can work for them. Many are flattering themselves that they are right with God, when they have not the principles of the truth in their hearts. This class can be brought into working order only by seeking with diligent, persevering earnestness to heed the counsel of the True Witness. They are in a cold, formal, backslidden state.

These are addressed by the True Witness: "I know thy works, that thou art neither cold nor hot: I would thou wert cold or hot. So then because thou art lukewarm, and neither cold nor hot, I will spew thee out of My mouth. Because thou sayest, I am rich, and increased with goods, and have need of nothing; and knowest not that thou art wretched, and miserable, and poor, and blind, and naked: I counsel thee to buy of Me gold tried in the fire, that thou mayest be rich, and white raiment, that thou mayest be clothed, and that the shame of thy nakedness do not appear; and anoint thine eyes with eyesalve, that thou mayest see. As many as I love, I rebuke and chasten: be zealous therefore, and repent."

Brother G, God has claims upon you to which you do not respond. Your spiritual strength and growth in grace will be proportionate to the labor of love and good works which you do cheerfully for your Saviour, who has withheld nothing, not even His own life, that He might save you. You have the injunction of the apostle: "Bear ye one another's burdens, and so fulfill the law of Christ."

It is not enough to merely profess faith in the commandments of God; you must be a doer of the work. You are a transgressor of His law. You do not love God with all your heart, might, mind, and strength; neither do you live in obedience to the last six commandments and love your neighbor as yourself. You love yourself more than you love God or your neighbor. Keeping the commandments of God requires more of us than you are willing to perform. God requires of you good works, self-denial, self-sacrifice, and devotion to the good of others, that through your instrumentality souls may be brought to the truth.

Our good works alone will not save any of us, but we cannot be saved without good works. And after we have done all that we can do, in the name and strength of Jesus we are to say: "We are unprofitable servants." We are not to think that we have made great sacrifices and that we should receive great reward for our feeble services.

Self-righteousness and carnal security have closed you about as with bands of iron. You need to be zealous and repent. You have been unfortunate in sympathizing with the disaffected, whose course has been in opposition to the work that the Lord through His servants was doing upon this coast. The wrong men have had your sympathy. Because your heart was not right with God, you did not receive the light He sent to you. You set up your stubborn will to resist the reproof which the Lord gave to you in love. You knew these things were true, but tried to close your eyes to the true state of your case.

Whether you heed the voice of reproof and warning God has sent to you or not; whether you reform, or retain your defects of character, you will one day realize what you have lost by placing yourself in a defiant position, warring in spirit against the servants of God. Your bitterness of feeling toward Elder H is astonishing. He has endured and sacrificed and toiled on this coast to do the work of God. But in your blindness, while unconsecrated in heart and life, you have ventured, in connection with I and J, to handle the servant of God in a cruel manner. "Touch not Mine anointed," saith God, "and do My prophets no harm." It is not a small matter for you to array yourself, as you have done, against men whom God has sent with light and truth for the people. Beware how your influence turns souls from the truth which God has sent His servants to declare, for a heavy woe hangs over you.

Satan has been using you as his agent to insinuate doubts and to reiterate insinuations and misrepresentations which have originated in an unsanctified heart, which God would have cleansed from its pollution. But you refused to be instructed, refused correction, rejected reproof, and followed your own will and way. Souls are defiled by this root of bitterness and are, through these questioning, murmuring ones, placed where the testimony of reproof which God sends will not reach them. The blood of these souls will be chargeable to you and to the spirits with whom you are in harmony.

God has given us, as His servants, our work. He has given us a message to bear to His people. For thirty years we have been receiving the words of God and speaking them to His people. We have trembled at the responsibility, which we have accepted with much prayer and meditation. We have stood as God's ambassadors, in Christ's stead beseeching souls to be reconciled to God. We have warned of danger as God has presented before us the perils of His people. Our work has been given us of God. What, then, will be the condition of those who refuse to hear the words which God has sent them, because they cross their track or reprove their wrongs? If you are thoroughly convinced that God has not spoken by us, why not act in accordance with your faith and have no more to do with a people who are under so great a deception as this people are?

If you have been moving according to the dictates of the Spirit of God you are right and we are wrong. God is either teaching His church, reproving their wrongs and strengthening their faith, or He is not. This work is of God, or it is not. God does nothing in partnership with Satan. My work for the past thirty years bears the stamp of God or the stamp of the enemy. There is no halfway work in the matter. The Testimonies are of the Spirit of God, or of the devil. In arraying yourself against the servants of God you are doing a work either for God or for the devil. "By their fruits ye shall know them." What stamp does your work bear? It will pay to look critically at the result of your course.

It is not a new thing for a man to be deluded by the arch-deceiver and array himself against God. Consider your course critically before you venture to go any further in the path you are traveling. The Jews were self-deceived. They rejected the teachings of Christ because He exposed the secrets of their hearts and reproved their sins. They would not come to the light, fearing that their deeds would be reproved. They chose darkness rather than light. "This is the condemnation," said Christ, "that light is come into the world, and men loved darkness rather than light, because their deeds were evil."

The Jews pursued their course of rejecting Christ until, in their self-deceived, deluded state, they thought that in crucifying Him they were doing God service. This was the result of their refusing light. You are in danger of similar deception. It will be profitable for your soul, Brother G, to consider where the path which you are now traveling will end. God can do without you, but you cannot afford to do without God. He does not compel any man to believe. He sets light before men, and Satan presents his darkness.

While the deceiver is constantly crying, "Light is here; truth is here," Jesus is saying: "I am the truth; I have the words of eternal life. If any man follow Me, he shall not walk in darkness." God gives to us all evidence sufficient to balance our faith on the side of truth. If we surrender to God we shall choose the light and reject the darkness. If we desire to maintain the independence of the natural heart, and refuse the correction of God, we shall, as did the Jews, stubbornly carry out our purposes and our ideas in the face of the plainest evidence, and shall be in danger of as great deception as came upon them; and in our blind infatuation we may go to as great lengths as they did, and yet flatter ourselves that we are doing work for God.

Brother G, you will not long stand where you now are. The path you have started upon is diverging from the true path and separating you from the people whom God is testing in order to purify them for the final victory. You will either come into union with this body, and labor earnestly to answer the prayer of Christ, or you will become more and more unbelieving. You will question point after point of the established faith of the body, become more self-willed in your opinion, and grow darker and darker in regard to the work of God for this time, until you set light for darkness and darkness for light.

Satan has great power to entangle souls by confusing the minds of those who do not cherish the light and the privileges which Providence sends them. Minds which are submitted to Satan's control are led continually from the light of truth into error and darkness. If you give Satan the least advantage, he will claim more and will watch the outposts to make the most of any circumstance to advantage his cause and ruin your soul.

Brother and Sister G, you are neither of you in a safe position. You despise reproof. Had smooth words been spoken to you rather than words of reproof, had you been praised and flattered, you would now occupy a very different position from what you do in regard to your belief in the Testimonies.

There are some in these last days who will cry: "Speak unto us smooth things, prophesy deceits." But this is not my work. God has set me as a reprover of His people; and just so surely as He has laid upon me the heavy burden, He will make those to whom this message is given responsible for the manner in which they treat it. God will not be trifled with, and those who despise His work will receive according to their deeds. I have not chosen this unpleasant labor for myself. It is not a work which will bring to me the favor or praise of men. It is a work which but few will appreciate. But those who seek to make my labor doubly hard by their misrepresentations, jealous suspicions, and unbelief, thus creating prejudice in the minds of others against the Testimonies God has given me, and limiting my work, have the matter to settle with God, while I shall go forward as Providence and my brethren may open the way before me. In the name and strength of my Redeemer I shall do what I can. I shall warn and counsel and reprove and encourage as the Spirit of God dictates, whether men will hear or whether they will forbear. My duty is not to please myself, but to do the will of my heavenly Father, who has given me my work.

Christ warned His disciples: "Beware of false prophets, which come to you in sheep's clothing, but inwardly they are ravening wolves. Ye shall know them by their fruits. Do men gather grapes of thorns, or figs of thistles? Even so every good tree bringeth forth good fruit; but a corrupt tree bringeth forth evil fruit. A good tree cannot bring forth evil fruit, neither can a corrupt tree bring forth good fruit. Every tree that bringeth not forth good fruit is hewn down, and cast into the fire. Wherefore by their fruits ye shall know them."

Here is a test, and, Brother G, you can apply it if you will. You need not go in uncertainty and doubt. Satan is at hand to suggest a variety of doubts, but if you will open your eyes in faith you will find sufficient evidence for belief. But God will never remove from any man all causes for doubts. Those who love to dwell in the atmosphere of doubt and questioning unbelief can have the unenviable privilege. God gives sufficient evidence for the candid mind to believe; but he who turns from the weight of evidence because there are a few things which he cannot make plain to his finite understanding will be left in the cold, chilling atmosphere of unbelief and questioning doubts, and will make shipwreck of faith.

You have seemed to consider it a virtue to be on the side of the doubting rather than on the side of the believing. Jesus never praised unbelief; He never commended doubts. He gave to His nation evidences of His Messiahship in the miracles He wrought, but there were some who considered it a virtue to doubt and who would reason these evidences away and find something in every good work to question and censure.

The centurion who desired Christ to come and heal his servant felt unworthy to have Jesus come under his roof; his faith was so strong in the power of Christ that he entreated Him just to say the word and the work would be done. "When Jesus heard it, He marveled, and said to them that followed, Verily I say unto you, I have not found so great faith, no, not in Israel. And I say unto you, That many shall come from the east and west, and shall sit down with Abraham, and Isaac, and Jacob, in the kingdom of heaven. But the children of the kingdom shall be cast out into outer darkness: there shall be weeping and gnashing of teeth. And Jesus said unto the centurion, Go thy way; and as thou hast believed, so be it done unto thee. And his servant was healed in the selfsame hour."

Here Jesus exalted faith in contrast with doubt. He showed that the children of Israel would stumble because of their unbelief, which would lead to the rejection of great light and would result in their condemnation and overthrow. Thomas declared that he would not believe unless he put his finger into the prints of the nails and thrust his hand into the side of his Lord. Christ gave him the evidence he desired and then reproved his unbelief: "Because thou hast seen Me, thou hast believed: blessed are they that have not seen, and yet have believed."

In this age of darkness and error, men who profess to be followers of Christ seem to think that they are at liberty to receive or reject the servants of the Lord at pleasure and that they will not be called to an account for so doing. Unbelief and darkness lead them to this. Their sensibilities are blunted by their unbelief. They violate their consciences and become untrue to their own convictions and weaken themselves in moral power. They view others in the same light with themselves.

When Christ sent out the twelve, He commanded them: "And into whatsoever city or town ye shall enter, inquire who in it is worthy, and there abide till ye go thence. And when ye come into an house, salute it. And if the house be worthy, let your peace come upon it: but if it be not worthy, let your peace return to you. And whosoever shall not receive you, nor hear your words, when ye depart out of that house or city, shake off the dust of your feet. Verily I say unto you, It shall be more tolerable for the land of Sodom and Gomorrah in the day of judgment, than for that city." They were warned to beware of men, for they should be delivered up to the councils and scourged in the synagogues.

Men's hearts are no softer today than when Christ was upon the earth. They will do all in their power to aid the great adversary in making it as hard as possible for the servants of Christ, just as the people did with Christ when He was upon the earth. They will scourge with the tongue of slander and falsehood. They will criticize, and turn against the servant of God the very efforts he is leading them to make. They will, with their evil surmisings, see fraud and dishonesty where all is right and where perfect integrity exists. They lay selfish motives to the charge of God's servants, when He Himself is leading them, and when they would give even their lives if God required, if by so doing they could advance His cause. They who have done the least, and made the least investment in the cause of truth, are the most forward to express lack of faith in the integrity of the servants of God who are placed in a position to bear financial responsibilities in the great work. They who have confidence in the work of God are willing to venture something for its advancement, and their spiritual prosperity will be in proportion to their works of faith. God's word is our standard, but how few follow it!

Our religion will be of but little worth to our fellow men if it is only theoretical and not practical. The influence of the world and of selfishness is carried about by many who profess to be following the Bible. They are like a cloud, chilling the atmosphere in which others move.

• Obstinacy Not Independence

Brother G, it will be uphill work for you to cultivate pure, unselfish love and disinterested benevolence. You have not much experience in yielding your opinions and ideas, and in sometimes giving up your own judgment and being guided by the counsel of others. Brother and Sister G, you both need to have less of self and more of the grace of God. You both need to acquire a habit of self-government, that your thoughts may be brought into subjection to the Spirit of Christ. It is the grace of God that you need in order that your thoughts may be disciplined to flow in the right channel, that the words you utter may be right words, and that your passions and appetites may be subject to the control of reason, and the tongue be bridled against levity and unhallowed censure and faultfinding. "If any man offend not in word, the same is a perfect man, and able also to bridle the whole body." The greatest triumph given us by the religion of Christ is control over ourselves. Our natural propensities must be controlled, or we can never overcome as Christ overcame.

There are some among the professed followers of Christ who are spiritual dyspeptics. They are self-made invalids, and their spiritual debility is the direct result of their own shortcomings. They do not obey the laws of God nor carry out the principles of His commandments. They are indolent in His cause and work, accomplishing nothing themselves; but when they think they see something with which they can find fault, then they are active and zealous.

A Christian who does not work cannot be healthy. Spiritual disease is the result of neglected duty. In order for a man's faith to be strong, he must be much with God in secret prayer. How can a man's benevolence be a blessing to him if he never exercises it? How can we ask God to help in the conversion of souls unless we are doing all in our power to bring them to the knowledge of the truth? You have brought upon yourself a debility which has made you useless to yourself and to the church, and the remedy is repentance, confession, and reform. You need moral power and the real nourishment of the grace of God. Nothing will give bone and sinew to your piety like working to advance the cause you profess to love, instead of binding it.

There is but one genuine cure for spiritual laziness, and that is work—working for souls who need your help. Instead of strengthening souls, you have been discouraging and weakening the hearts and hands of those who would see the cause of God advance.

God has given you abilities which you can use to good account, or abuse to your own injury and to the injury of others. You have not realized the claims that God has upon you. It should be ever borne in mind that we are living in this world to form characters for the next. And all our associations with our fellow mortals should be with reference to their eternal interest and to our own; but if our interviews with them are devoted only to pleasure and to our own selfish gratification, if we are light and trifling, if we indulge in wrong acts, we are not co-workers with God, but are decidedly working against Him. The precious lives God has given us are not to be molded by unbelieving relatives in a way to please the carnal mind, but to be spent in a manner which God can approve.

If Brother J enjoyed the love of God, he would be a channel of light. He has too little moral power, with strong tendencies to unbelief. He is pitied by the heavenly angels, for he is surrounded with darkness. His ears hear words of unbelief and darkness almost continually. He has doubts and questionings constantly thrown before him. The tongue is a world of iniquity. "The tongue can no man tame; it is an unruly evil, full of deadly poison." If Brother J would cling to God more firmly and feel that he should preserve his integrity before God even at the cost of his natural life, he would receive strength from above. If he allows his faith to be affected by the darkness and unbelief that surrounds him—the doubts and questioning and much talk—he will soon be all darkness and doubt and unbelief, and will have no light or strength in the truth.

He need not think that by seeking to compromise with his friends, who are embittered against our faith, he will make it easier for himself. If he stands with the single purpose to obey God at any cost he will have help and strength. God loves and pities Brother J. He knows every perplexity, every discouragement, every bitter speech. He is acquainted with it all. If he will lay aside his unbelief and stand in God unmoved, his faith will be strengthened by exercise. "Now the just shall live by faith: but if any man draw back, My soul shall have no pleasure in him."

I saw Brethren J and G in special danger of losing eternal life. They did not see that they were standing directly in the way of the advancement of the work of God in _____. When the tent meeting was held there the first time we were upon this coast, hundreds were convicted of the truth; but God knew the material of which that church was composed. If souls came out into the truth, there were none to nourish and cherish them, and to lead them along to an elevated life. Brother I was of an envious, faultfinding, jealous spirit.

Unless he could be first, he would not do anything. He esteemed himself far more highly than God esteemed him.

A man of his temperament will not, long at a time, be in agreement with anyone; for it is his element to contend, and to array himself in opposition to anything that does not suit his ideas. The Lord left him to take his own course and to manifest what manner of spirit he was of. He brought into the church, and sought to carry out there, the very same spirit that he carried out in his family. His bitterness and his cruel speeches against the servants of God are written in the book. He will meet them again. He went out from us because he was not of us. And in no case should the church encourage him to unite with them again; for, with the spirit he now has, he would quarrel even with the angels of God. He would wish to rule and dictate the work of the angels.

No such spirit can enter heaven. I and J, whom God frowns upon, have dared to withstand the servants of God, to malign them, and to impute to them evil motives. They have tried to destroy the confidence of the brethren in these workers as well as in the Testimonies. But if the work is of God, they cannot overthrow it. Their efforts will lie in vain. Brother G, you were in such darkness that you thought these men were right. You have repeated their words and talked of the one-man power. Oh, how little you knew what you were talking about!

Some have been ready to say anything, to prefer any charge, against the servants of God, and to be jealous and faultfinding. And if they can find any instance where, in their zeal for the cause of God, they think ministers have spoken decidedly, and perhaps severely, they have been willing to make the most of their words, and have felt at liberty to cherish the most bitter, wicked spirit, and to charge the Lord's servants with wrong motives. Let these faultfinders ask what they would have done under similar circumstances, bearing similar burdens.

Let them look and search and condemn their own wrong, overbearing course and their own impatience and fretfulness; and when without sin themselves, let them cast the first stone of censure at the brethren who are trying to get them into working order. A holy God will not bring out souls to the truth to come under such an influence as has existed in the church. Our heavenly Father is too wise to bring souls into the truth to be molded by the influence of these men who are unconsecrated in heart and life. These men are not in harmony with the truth. They are not in union with the body, but are drawing off from the church. They are working at cross purposes with those whom God is using to bring souls into the truth.

Who would nourish those who should take their stand to obey all of God's commandments? Who would be nursing fathers and nursing mothers to those who need help and strength? Do these brethren know what they are doing? They are standing directly in the way of sinners. They are blocking up the way by their own wrong course. The blood of souls will be on their garments unless they repent and entirely change their course. Do these disaffected ones think that they are right and the body of Sabbathkeepers deluded? By their fruits ye shall know them. Whom is God blessing? Whom is He leading? Who are at work for Him? Who are doing good in laboring to get the truth before other minds? Do these men think that the body will come to them and give up their experience and views to follow the judgment of these unconsecrated ones? or will they come into harmony with the body?

Brother G boasts of his independence of mind and judgment, while he is blocking up the way of sinners by his unconsecrated life and his opposition to the work in blindly warring against Christ in the persons of His servants; but he is deceived in the quality of true independence. Independence is not obstinacy, although obstinacy is often confounded with independence.

When Brother G has formed an opinion, and expressed it in his family or in the church with considerable confidence and with some publicity, he is then inclined to make it appear that he is right by every argument he can produce. He is in danger, great danger, of closing his eyes and violating his conscience by his persistency; for the temptation of the enemy is strong upon him. His pride of opinion is hard to yield, even in the face of light and evidence sufficient to convince him if he would be convinced. He thinks that if he should admit that he was wrong, it would be a reflection on his judgment and discernment.

Brother G, you are in great danger of losing your soul. You want to have the pre-eminence. At times you feel deeply if you think you are slighted. You are not a happy man. You will not be happy if you leave the people of God, taking offense at plain words and facts, as did many of the followers of Christ, because the truth spoken was too close. You will not be a happy man, for you will take yourself with you. You are not right; you make trouble for yourself. Your temperament is your enemy, and go where you will you will take yourself with your burden of unhappiness. It is an honor to confess a wrong as soon as it is discerned.

There are many matters in connection with the work of God with which you find fault, because it is natural for you to do so. And since you have turned your face against the light God revealed to you in regard to yourself, you are fast losing your discernment and are more than ever ready to find fault with everything. You give your opinion with dictatorial confidence and treat the queries of others in regard to your opinion as personal abuse. True, refined independence never disdains to seek counsel of the experienced and of the wise, and it treats the counsel of others with respect.

• Religion in the Family

Brother G, you must be a converted man or you will lose eternal life. You cannot be a happy man until you obtain the meekness of wisdom. You and your wife have too long worked at cross purposes. You must lay down this faultfinding, these suspicions, jealousies, and unhappy bickerings. The spirit which is developed in your family is carried into your religious experience. Be careful how you speak of each other's faults in the presence of your children; and be careful how you let your spirit control you. You see only the bad and evil in your oldest son; you give him no credit for the good qualities, which, should he die, you would suddenly become convinced that he had possessed. Neither of you pursues a consistent course toward your son. You dwell upon his faults in the presence of others and show that you have no confidence in his good traits of character.

In each of you there is a disposition to see the faults of the other, and of all others; but you are each blind to your own faults and many errors. You are both nervous, easily excited and irritated. You need the meekness of wisdom. You cling tenaciously to your own frailties, passions, and prejudices as though if you let them go you would no more have happiness in this life, when they are thorns, pricking, bruising thorns. Jesus invites you to lay down the yoke you have been bearing, which has been galling your neck, and take His yoke, which is easy, and His burden, which is light. How wearisome is the load of self-love, covetousness, pride, passion, jealousy, and evil surmising. Yet how closely do men clasp these curses, and how loath are they to give them up. Christ understands how grievous are these self-imposed burdens, and He invites us to lay them down. The heavy-laden and weary souls He invites to come to Him, and take His burden, which is light, in exchange for the burdens which they bind upon themselves. He says: "Ye shall find rest unto your souls. For My yoke is easy, and My burden is light." The requirements of our Saviour are all consistent and harmonious, and if cheerfully borne will bring peace and rest to the soul.

When Brother G once takes a position on the wrong side, it is not easy for him to confess that he has erred; but if he can let his wrong course pass out of his mind and pass from the memory of others, and he can make some changes for the better without an open acknowledgment of his wrong, he will do so. But all these errors and unconfessed sins stand registered in heaven and will not be blotted out until he complies with the directions given in the word of God: "Confess your faults one to another, and pray one for another, that ye may be healed." If Brother G has found another plan besides that given us by our Lord, it is not a safe way and will prove his ruin at last. This other way is ruinous to the church, and ruinous to the prosperity and happiness of his family. He needs to soften his heart and to let tenderness, humility, and love into his soul. He needs to cultivate unselfish qualities.

Brother and Sister G, you should cultivate qualities of mind which will make you pure, forgetful of self, and more interested in those with whom you are brought in contact. There is a vein of self-love and care for self which does not increase your happiness, but brings to you grief and sorrow. You have a conflict with yourself in which you alone can act a part. Both of you should control the tongue and keep back many things to which you give utterance. The first evil is in thinking wrong; then come the words which are wrong. But you leave undone the work of cultivating love, deference, and respect for each other. Be kindly considerate of each other's feelings, and seek to sacredly guard each other's happiness. You can do this only in the strength and name of Jesus.

Sister G has made strong efforts to gain victories, but she has not had much encouragement from her husband. Instead of seeking God in earnest prayer for strength to overcome the defects in their characters, they have been watching each other's course and weakening themselves by finding fault with the course of others. The garden of the heart has not had attention.

If Brother G had received the light that the Lord sent him months ago and had frankly conversed with his wife, if both had broken their hard hearts before the Lord, how different would be their present state. They both slighted the words of reproof and entreaty of the Spirit of God, and did not reform their lives.

But closing their eyes to the light God had sent them did not make one of their faults less grievous in the sight of God nor lessen their accountability. They have hated the reproof which the Lord in pitying tenderness gave them. Brother G has naturally a kind and tender heart, but it is crusted over with self-love, vanity, and evil surmising. His heart is not callous, but he lacks moral power. He is a coward as soon as the necessity of self-denial and self-sacrifice is brought before him, for he loves himself. To control self, to put a watch upon his words, to acknowledge that he has done wrong or spoken wrongly, is a cross which he feels is too humiliating to lift; and yet if he is ever saved this cross must be lifted.

Brother and Sister G, both of you need to watch your words; for just as surely as there is not a sentinel placed over your thoughts and actions, you will discourage each other and make it a sure case that neither of you can be saved. Both of you need to guard against a hasty spirit, which prompts hasty words and actions. Resentment, which is indulged because you think you have been misused, is the spirit of Satan and leads to great moral evil.

When you are controlled by a hasty spirit you deprive your reason, for the time, of the power of regulating your words and your conduct, while you make yourselves responsible for all the evil consequences. That which is done in haste and anger is not excusable. The action is bad. You may, by a single word spoken in haste and passion, leave a sting in the hearts of friends which may never be forgotten. Unless you exercise self-control you will be a most unhappy couple. You each ascribe your unhappy life to the faults of the other;

but do this no more. Make it a rule never to speak a word of censure to each other, but commend and praise whenever you can.

Some think it is a virtue to be unrestrained, and they will speak in praise of their outspoken habit of talking out disagreeable things which are in the heart. They let an angry spirit exhaust itself in a torrent of reproach and faultfinding. The more they talk, the more excited they become, and Satan stands by to help on the work, for it suits him.

The words irritate the one to whom they are spoken, and they will be thrown back, giving provocation for still harder words, until a little matter has blazed into a great flame. Both of you feel that you have all the trials that you can possibly endure and that your lives are most unhappy. Resolutely commence the work of controlling your thoughts, your words, your actions. When either of you feels the rising of resentment, make it a rule to go by yourself and humbly pray to God, who will hearken to the prayer which goeth not forth from feigned lips.

Every passion must be under the control of enlightened conscience. "Put on therefore, as the elect of God, holy and beloved, bowels of mercies, kindness, humbleness of mind, meekness, long-suffering; forbearing one another, and forgiving one another, if any man have a quarrel against any: even as Christ forgave you, so also do ye. And above all these things put on charity, which is the bond of perfectness. And let the peace of God rule in your hearts, to the which also ye are called in one body; and be ye thankful."

If you live upon the plan of addition, adding grace to grace, God will multiply unto you His grace. While you add, God multiplies. If you cherish a habitual impression that God sees and hears all that you do and say, and keeps a faithful record of all your words and actions, and that you must meet it all, then in all you do and say you will seek to follow the dictates of an enlightened and wakeful conscience. Your tongue will be used to the glory of God and will be a source of blessing to yourself and to others. But if you separate from God, as you have been doing, take heed lest your tongue shall prove a world of iniquity and bring upon you fearful condemnation; for souls will be lost through you.

• Duty of Self-Control

The appetites of our animal natures ought to be kept in rigid subjection. These appetites were given us for important purposes, for good, and not to become the ministers of death by being perverted and becoming warring lusts. The appetite for tobacco, which you, Brother G, strengthen by indulgence, is becoming a warring lust against your soul. An intemperate man cannot be a patient man. The almost imperceptible indulgence of the taste will create an appetite for stronger stimulants. If the thoughts, passions, and appetites are kept in due subjection, the tongue will be controlled.

Call to your aid moral power, and abandon the use of tobacco forever. You have tried to hide from others the fact that you used tobacco, but you did not hide the matter from God. "Cleanse your hands, ye sinners; and purify your hearts, ye double-minded. Be afflicted, and mourn, and weep: let your laughter be turned to mourning, and your joy to heaviness. Humble yourselves in the sight of the Lord, and He shall lift you up." I commend these words to you in the name of Jesus, who has given me my commission. Do not reject them.

You would never have rejected the Testimonies as you have, had your wrongdoings not been reproved. You thought it would be easier to sacrifice the Testimonies and close your eyes to the light God has given you than to give up your tobacco and cease your life of levity and joking with unbelievers. The cleansing process involves denial and restraint which you have not moral power to endure; therefore you think to excuse your sins by your unbelief of the light God has sent you. Remember, you must meet all these things again; for they are written in the book, with all the warnings and reproofs that God has committed to me to give to you.

Brother J is to be pitied, for he has naturally a defective organization. His hope is small. His unbelief and doubts control his judgment. It is in his nature to place himself on the side of doubting and questioning. The only way to overcome this great evil is to cultivate opposite traits of character. He should repress unbelief, and not cultivate it. He should not express his doubts. He has no right to thrust the defects of his character before others, to cause them sadness and discouragement. If he must be affected with this sad evil, he should not embitter the happiness of others by introducing his unbelief to chill the faith of his brethren. He is inclined to pass over almost everything in every discourse and exhortation from which he might draw comfort and encouragement, and pick up something which he thinks will afford an excuse for his questioning and criticism. The avenues of his soul are thrown open and left unguarded for Satan to come in and mold his mind to his purposes.

I was shown that your meetings are losing interest because God's Spirit does not attend them. The brethren and sisters are in complete bondage because of these two men. They dare not exercise their freedom and speak out their faith in the simplicity of their souls, for here is Brother J, with his cool, severe, critical eye, watching and ready to catch at any word which will give him a chance to exercise the faculties of his unbelieving mind. Between these two, the Spirit of God is grieved away from the meetings.

When brethren manifest the spirit of the dragon, to make war upon those who believe that God has communicated light and comfort to them through the Testimonies, it is time for the brethren and sisters to assert their liberty and perfect freedom of conscience. God has given them light, and it is their privilege to cherish the light and to speak of it to strengthen and encourage one another. Brother J would confuse the mind by seeking to make it appear that the light God has given through the Testimonies is an addition to the word of God, but in this he presents the matter in a false light. God has seen fit in this manner to bring the minds of His people to His word, to give them a clearer understanding of it.

The church of —— are growing weaker and weaker because of the influence which has been exerted over them—not an influence to help them advance, but to clog the wheels. It is the privilege of Brother J to cast aside his unbelief and to advance with the light, if he will. If he refuses to do this, the cause of God will advance all the same without his aid. But God designs that a change shall be made in the church at ——. They will either advance or retrograde. God can do more with six souls who are united and of the same mind and judgment, than with scores of men who do as Brother J and G have been doing. They have brought with them into the meeting, not angels of light, but angels of darkness. The meetings have been unprofitable and sometimes a positive injury. God calls for these men to come over on the

Lord's side and to be united with the body, or to cease hindering those who would be wholly for the Lord.

The great reason why so many professed disciples of Christ fall into grievous temptation and make work for repentance is that they are deficient in a knowledge of themselves. Here is where Peter was so thoroughly sifted by the enemy. Here is where thousands will make shipwreck of faith. You do not take your wrongs and errors to heart, and afflict your souls over them. I entreat you to purify your souls by obeying the truth. Connect yourselves with heaven. And may the Lord save you from self-deception.

22. Sacredness of God's Commandments

Much-respected Brother K:

In January, 1875, I was shown that there are hindrances in the way of the spiritual prosperity of the church. The Spirit of God is grieved because many are not right in heart and life; their professed faith does not harmonize with their works. The sacred rest day of Jehovah is not observed as it should be. Every week God is robbed by some infringement upon the borders of His holy time; and the hours that should be devoted to prayer and meditation are given to worldly employments.

God has given us His commandments, not only to be believed in, but to be obeyed. The great Jehovah, when He had laid the foundations of the earth, had dressed the whole world in the garb of beauty, and had filled it with things useful to man,—when He had created all the wonders of the land and the sea,—instituted the Sabbath day and made it holy. God blessed and sanctified the seventh day, because He rested upon it from all His wondrous work of creation. The Sabbath was made for man, and God would have him put by his labor on that day, as He Himself rested after His six days' work of creation.

Those who reverence the commandments of Jehovah will, after light has been given them in reference to the fourth precept of the Decalogue, obey it without questioning the feasibility or convenience of such obedience. God made man in His own image and then gave him an example of observing the seventh day, which He sanctified and made holy. He designed that upon that day man should worship Him and engage in no secular pursuits. No one who disregards the fourth commandment, after becoming enlightened concerning the claims of the Sabbath, can be held guiltless in the sight of God.

Brother K, you acknowledge the requirements of God to keep the Sabbath, but your works do not harmonize with your declared faith. You give your influence to the side of the unbeliever, insofar as you transgress the law of God.

When your temporal circumstances seem to require attention, you violate the fourth commandment without compunction. You make the keeping of God's law a matter of convenience, obeying or disobeying as your business or inclination indicates. This is not honoring the Sabbath as a sacred institution. You grieve the Spirit of God and dishonor your Redeemer by pursuing this reckless course.

A partial observance of the Sabbath law is not accepted by the Lord and has a worse effect upon the minds of sinners than if you made no profession of being a Sabbathkeeper. They perceive that your life contradicts your belief, and lose faith in Christianity. The Lord means what He says, and man cannot set aside His commands with impunity. The example of Adam and Eve in the garden should sufficiently warn us against any disobedience of the divine law. The sin of our first parents in listening to the specious temptations of the enemy brought guilt and sorrow upon the world, and led the Son of God to leave the royal courts of heaven and take a humble place on earth. He was subjected to insult, rejection, and crucifixion by the very ones He came to bless. What infinite expense attended that disobedience in the Garden of Eden! The Majesty of heaven was sacrificed to save man from the penalty of his crime.

God will not pass over any transgression of His law more lightly now than in the day when He pronounced judgment against Adam. The Saviour of the world raises His voice in protest against those who regard the divine commandments with carelessness and indifference. Said He: "Whosoever therefore shall break one of these least commandments, and shall teach men so, He shall be called the least in the kingdom of heaven: but whosoever shall do and teach them, the same shall be called great in the kingdom of heaven." The teaching of our lives is wholly for or against the truth. If your works seem to justify the transgressor in his sin, if your influence makes light of breaking the commandments of God, then you are not only guilty yourself, but you are to a certain extent responsible for the consequent errors of others.

At the very beginning of the fourth precept, God said, "Remember," knowing that man, in the multitude of his cares and perplexities, would be tempted to excuse himself from meeting the full requirements of the law or, in the press of worldly business, would forget its sacred importance. "Six days shalt thou labor, and do all thy work," the usual business of life, for worldly profit or pleasure. These words are very explicit; there can be no mistake. Brother K, how dare you venture to transgress a commandment so solemn and important? Has the Lord made an exception by which you are absolved from the law He has given to the world?

Are your transgressions omitted from the book of record? Has He agreed to excuse your disobedience when the nations come before Him for judgment? Do not for a moment deceive yourself with the thought that your sin will not bring its merited punishment. Your transgressions will be visited with the rod, because you have had the light, yet have walked directly contrary to it. "That servant, which knew his Lord's will, and prepared not himself, neither did according to His will, shall be beaten with many stripes."

God has given man six days in which to do his own work and carry on the usual business of life; but He claims one day, which He has set apart and sanctified. He gives it to man as a day in which he may rest from labor and devote himself to worship and the improvement of his spiritual condition. What a flagrant outrage it is for man to steal the one sanctified day of Jehovah and appropriate it to his own selfish purposes!

It is the grossest presumption for mortal man to venture upon a compromise with the Almighty in order to secure his own petty, temporal interests. It is as ruthless a violation of the law to occasionally use the Sabbath for secular business as to entirely reject it; for it is making the Lord's commandments a matter of convenience. "I the Lord thy God am a jealous God," is thundered from Sinai. No partial obedience, no divided interest, is accepted by Him who declares that the iniquities of the fathers shall be visited upon the children to the third and fourth generation of them that hate Him, and that He will show mercy unto thousands of them that love Him and keep

His commandments. It is not a small matter to rob a neighbor, and great is the stigma attached to one who is found guilty of such an act; yet he who would scorn to defraud his fellow man will without shame rob his heavenly Father of the time that He has blessed and set apart for a special purpose.

My dear brother, your works are at variance with your professed faith, and your only excuse is the poor plea of convenience. The servants of God in past times have been called upon to lay down their lives in vindication of their faith. Your course illy harmonizes with that of the Christian martyrs, who suffered hunger and thirst, torture and death, rather than renounce their religion or yield the principles of truth.

It is written: "What doth it profit, my brethren, though a man say he hath faith, and have not works? can faith save him?" Every time you put your hands to labor on the Sabbath day, you virtually deny your faith. The Holy Scriptures teach us that faith without works is dead, and that the testimony of one's life proclaims to the world whether or not he is true to the faith he professes. Your conduct lessens God's law in the estimation of your worldly friends. It says to them: "You may or may not obey the commandments. I believe that the law of God is, in a manner, binding upon men; but, after all, the Lord is not very particular as to a strict observance of its precepts, and an occasional transgression is not visited with severity on His part."

Many excuse themselves for violating the Sabbath by referring to your example. They argue that if so good a man, who believes the seventh day is the Sabbath, can engage in worldly employments on that day when circumstances seem to require it, surely they can do the same without condemnation. Many souls will face you in the judgment, making your influence an excuse for their disobedience of God's law. Although this will be no apology for their sin, yet it will tell fearfully against you.

God has spoken, and He means that man shall obey.

He does not inquire if it is convenient for him to do so. The Lord of life and glory did not consult His convenience or pleasure when He left His station of high command to become a man of sorrows and acquainted with grief, accepting ignominy and death in order to deliver man from the consequence of his disobedience. Jesus died, not to save man in his sins, but from his sins. Man is to leave the error of his ways, to follow the example of

Christ, to take up his cross and follow Him, denying self, and obeying God at any cost.

Said Jesus: "No man can serve two masters: for either he will hate the one, and love the other; or else he will hold to the one, and despise the other. Ye cannot serve God and mammon." If we are true servants of God, there should be no question in our minds as to whether we will obey His commandments or consult our own temporal interests. If the believers in the truth are not sustained by their faith in these comparatively peaceful days, what will uphold them when the grand test comes and the decree goes forth against all those who will not worship the image of the beast and receive his mark in their foreheads or in their hands? This solemn period is not far off. Instead of becoming weak and irresolute, the people of God should be gathering strength and courage for the time of trouble.

Jesus, our great Exemplar, in His life and death taught the strictest obedience. He died, the just for the unjust, the innocent for the guilty, that the honor of God's law might be preserved and yet man not utterly perish. Sin is the transgression of the law. If the sin of Adam brought such inexpressible wretchedness, requiring the sacrifice of God's dear Son, what will be the punishment of those, who, seeing the light of truth, set at nought the fourth commandment of the Lord?

Circumstances will not justify anyone in working upon the Sabbath for the sake of worldly profit. If God excuses one man, He may excuse all. Why may not Brother L, who is a poor man, work upon the Sabbath to earn means for a livelihood when he might by so doing be better able to support his family? Why may not other brethren, or all of us, keep the Sabbath only when it is convenient to do so? The voice from Sinai makes answer: "Six days shalt thou labor, and do all thy work: but the seventh day is the Sabbath of the Lord thy God."

Wrongs perpetrated by believers in the truth bring great weakness upon the church. They are stumbling blocks in the way of sinners and prevent them from coming to the light. Brother, God calls you to come out fully upon His side and let your works show that you regard His precepts and keep inviolate the Sabbath. He bids you wake up to your duty and be true to the responsibilities that devolve upon you. These solemn words are addressed to you: "If thou turn away thy foot from the Sabbath, from doing thy pleasure on My holy day; and call the Sabbath a delight, the holy of the Lord, honorable; and shalt honor Him, not doing thine own ways, nor finding thine own pleasure, nor speaking thine own words: then shalt thou delight thyself in the Lord; and I will cause thee to ride upon the high places of the earth, and feed thee with the heritage of Jacob thy father: for the mouth of the Lord hath spoken it."

Like many of our brethren, you are becoming entangled with the transgressors of God's law, viewing matters in their light and falling into their errors. God will visit with His judgments those who are professedly serving Him, yet really serving mammon. Those who disregard the Lord's express injunction for their personal advantage are heaping future woe upon themselves. The church in —— should inquire closely if they have not, like the Jews, made the temple of God a place of merchandise. Christ said: "It is written, My house shall be called the house of prayer; but ye have made it a den of thieves."

Are not many of our people falling into the sin of sacrificing their religion for the sake of worldly gain; preserving a form of piety, yet giving all the mind to temporal pursuits? God's law must be considered first of all and obeyed in spirit and in letter. If God's word, spoken in awful solemnity from the holy mountain, is lightly regarded, how will the Testimonies of His Spirit be received? Minds that are so darkened as not to recognize the authority of the Lord's commandments given directly to man can receive little good from a feeble instrument whom He has chosen to instruct His people.

Your age does not excuse you from obeying the divine commands. Abraham was sorely tested in his old age. The words of the Lord seemed terrible and uncalled-for to the stricken old man, yet he never questioned their justice or hesitated in his obedience. He might have pleaded that he was old and feeble, and could not sacrifice the son who was the joy of his life. He might have reminded the Lord that this command conflicted with the promises that had been given in regard to this son. But the obedience of Abraham was without a murmur or a reproach. His trust in God was implicit.

The faith of Abraham should be our example, yet how few will patiently endure a simple test of reproof for the sins which imperil their eternal welfare.

How few receive reproof with humility, and profit by it. God's claim upon our faith, our services, our affections, should meet with a cheerful response. We are infinite debtors to the Lord and should unhesitatingly comply with the least of His requirements. In order to be a commandment breaker it is not necessary that we should trample upon the whole moral code. If one precept is disregarded, we are transgressors of the sacred law. But if we would be true commandment keepers we should strictly observe every requirement that God has enjoined upon us.

God allowed His own Son to be put to death in order to answer the penalty of the transgression of the law; then how will He deal with those who, in the face of all this evidence, dare venture upon the path of disobedience, after having received the light of truth? Man has no right to urge his convenience or wants in this matter. God will provide; He who fed Elijah by the brook, making a raven His messenger, will not suffer His faithful ones to want for food.

The Saviour asked His disciples, who were pressed with poverty, why they were anxious and troubled in regard to what they should eat or how they should be clothed. Said He: "Behold the fowls of the air: for they sow not, neither do they reap, nor gather into barns; yet your heavenly Father feedeth them. Are ye not much better than they?" He pointed to the lovely flowers, formed and tinted by a divine hand, saying: "And why take ye thought for raiment? Consider the lilies of the field, how they grow; they toil not, neither do they spin: and yet I say unto you, That even Solomon in all his glory was not arrayed like one of these. Wherefore, if God so clothe the grass of the field, which today is, and tomorrow is cast into the oven, shall He not much more clothe you, O ye of little faith?"

Where is the faith of God's people? Why are they so unbelieving and distrustful of Him who provides for their wants and upholds them by His strength? The Lord will test the faith of His people; He will send rebukes, which will be followed by afflictions if these warnings are not heeded. He will break the fatal lethargy of sin at any cost to those who have departed from their allegiance to Him, and awaken them to their sense of duty.

My brother, your soul must be quickened and your faith enlarged. You have so long excused yourself in your disobedience on one plea or another that your conscience has been lulled to rest and ceases to remind you of your errors. You have so long followed your own convenience in regard to keeping the Sabbath that your mind has been rendered unimpressible as to your course of disobedience; yet you are none the less responsible, for you have brought yourself into this condition. Begin at once to obey the divine commandments, and trust in God. Provoke not His wrath, lest He visit you with terrible punishment. Return to Him before it is too late, and find pardon for your transgressions. He is rich and abundant in mercies; He will give you His peace and approbation if you come to Him in humble faith.

23. Selfishness in the Church and in the Family

Dear Brother M:

I have been shown in vision that you have defects in your character which must be remedied. You are not right in your views and feelings in regard to your wife. You do not appreciate her. She has not received the words of sympathy and love from you that you should have given her. It would not lessen the dignity of your manhood to praise her for the care she takes and the burdens she bears in the family.

You are selfish and exacting. You mark little things and talk of small errors in your wife and children. In short, you seek to gauge their consciences by your own; you try to be conscience for them. Your wife has an identity of her own, which can never be merged in that of her husband. She has an individuality which she should preserve, for she is accountable before God for herself. You cannot, Brother M, be responsible before God for the character your wife forms. She alone will bear this responsibility. God is just as willing to impress the conscience of your God-fearing wife as He is to impress your conscience for her.

You expect too much of your wife and children. You censure too much. If you would encourage a cheerful, happy temper yourself, and speak kindly and tenderly to them, you would bring sunlight into your dwelling instead of clouds, sorrow, and unhappiness. You think too much of your opinion; you have taken extreme positions and have not been willing that your wife's judgment should have the weight it should in your family. You have not encouraged respect for your wife yourself nor educated your children to respect her judgment. You have not made her your equal, but have rather taken the reins of government and control into your own hands and held them with a firm grasp. You have not an affectionate, sympathetic disposition. These traits of character you need to cultivate if you want to be an overcomer and if you want the blessing of God in your family.

You are very set and unyielding in your opinion, which makes it very hard for your family. You need to have your heart softened by the grace of God. You need such love in your heart as characterized the works of Christ. Love proceeds from God. It is a plant of heavenly growth, and it cannot live and flourish in the natural heart. Where it exists, there is truth and life and power. But it cannot live without action, and whenever it is exercised it increases and extends. It will not observe little mistakes and be quick to mark little errors. It will prevail when argument, when any amount of words, will prove vain and useless. The very best way to reform the character and regulate the conduct of your family is through the principle of love. It is indeed a power and will accomplish that which neither money nor might ever can.

My brother, your words that are harsh and unsympathizing cut and wound. It is very easy for you to censure and find fault, but this is only productive of unhappiness. You would quickly resent the words you address to others, were they spoken to you. You have looked upon it as a weakness to be kind, tender, and sympathetic, and have thought it beneath your dignity to speak tenderly, gently, and lovingly to your wife. Here you mistake in what true manliness and dignity consist. The disposition to leave deeds of kindness undone is a manifest weakness and defect in your character. That which you would look upon as weakness, God regards as true Christian courtesy, that should be exercised by every Christian; for this was the spirit which Christ manifested.

You have a very selfish disposition and think more highly of yourself than you ought to think. You frequently take extremely singular and fanciful views of the Scriptures, and often cling to these as zealously as did the Jews to their traditions. Not possessing a teachable spirit, you will be in constant danger of making trouble in the church unless you set yourself at the work of correcting these wrongs in the strength of the mighty Conqueror. That which makes your case alarming is that you think you know these things better than your brethren, and you are very difficult to be approached. You have a self-righteous, pharisaical spirit, which would say: "Stand off, come not near me; for I am holier than thou."

You have not seen the corruptions of your own heart and that you have made life almost a failure. Your opinions cannot and must not rule in the church of God. You need to be cultivating all the Christian graces, but especially charity, which suffereth long and is kind, envieth not, vaunteth not itself, is not puffed up, "doth not behave itself unseemly, seeketh not her own, is not easily provoked, thinketh no evil; rejoiceth not in iniquity, but rejoiceth in the truth; beareth all things, believeth all things, hopeth all things, endureth all things."

"Put on therefore, as the elect of God, holy and beloved, bowels of mercies, kindness, humbleness of mind, meekness, long-suffering; forbearing one another, and forgiving one another, if any man have a quarrel against any: even as Christ forgave you, so also do ye. And above all these things put on charity [love], which is the bond of perfectness. And let the peace of God rule in your hearts, to the which also ye are called in one body; and be ye thankful."

You mark little deviations from what you think is right, and you sternly seek to correct them. While you are thus overbearing and dictatorial, quick to observe a brother's faults, you do not closely search your own heart to see the evils existing in your life. You show great moral weakness in the indulgence of your appetite and passions. The slavery of appetite for tobacco has such control over you that although you resolve and re-resolve to overcome the habit, you do not accomplish it. This wrong habit has perverted your senses. My brother, where is your self-denial? Where is your moral power to overcome? Christ overcame the power of appetite in the wilderness of temptation on your account, making it possible for you to overcome on your own account. Now the battle is yours. In the name of the Conqueror you have an opportunity to deny your appetite and gain a victory for yourself.

You require much of others; what are you willing to do to get the victory over a disgusting, health-destroying, soul-polluting indulgence? The battle is yours. No one can fight it for you. Others can pray for you, but the work must be wholly your own.

God calls upon you to no longer dally with the tempter, but to cleanse yourself from all filthiness of the flesh and of the spirit, perfecting holiness in His fear. You need to work fast to remove the defects from your character. You are in God's workshop. If you will submit to the process of hewing and squaring and planing, that the rough edges may be removed, the knots and uneven surface smoothed and fitted by the planing knife of God, you will be fitted by His grace for the heavenly building. But if you cling to self, and are not willing to endure the trying process of fitting for the heavenly building, you will have no place in that structure which will come together without the sound of ax or hammer. If your nature is not transformed, if you are not refined and elevated by the sanctifying truth for these last days, you will be found unworthy of a place among the pure and holy angels.

Can you afford to cling to your defiling habits and at last be found among the unbelieving and the unsanctified? Can you afford to run any risk in this matter? There is too much at stake for you to venture to pursue the course of self-indulgence that you have followed. You have been forward to talk the truth to unbelievers in a very positive, objectionable manner, which has had a very bad influence upon their minds. When there is one inconsistent advocate of the truth, Satan uses him to special advantage to disgust those who, under a proper influence, would have been favorably impressed. You should soften your manners, and when you advocate the truth, let it be with a spirit of meekness.

"Be ready always to give an answer to every man that asketh you a reason of the hope that is in you with meekness and fear." The fear here spoken of does not mean distrust or indecision, but with due caution, guarding every point, lest an unwise word be spoken, or excitement of feeling get the advantage, and thus leave unfavorable impressions upon minds, and balance them in the wrong direction. Godly fear, humility, and meekness are greatly needed by all in order to correctly represent the truth of God.

One of your greatest dangers is a spirit of self-confidence and pride. The great unhappiness which exists with you and in your family results immediately from the operation of pride. The usefulness of a man who has this pride must be greatly limited, for his pride and self-love keep him in a narrow sphere. His spirit is not generous. His efforts are not extended, but contracted. By his conversation and deportment this pride will be discovered if it exists.

Dear brother, the influence under which your character has been formed has given you a haughty, overbearing spirit. This spirit you act out in your family and among your neighbors and all with whom you associate. In order to overcome these wrong habits, you must watch unto prayer. You should now be thoroughly in earnest, for you have little time in which to work. Do not feel that you are sufficient in your own strength. Only in the name of the mighty Conqueror can you gain the victory. In conversation with others dwell upon the mercy, goodness, and love of God instead of upon His strict judgment and justice. Cling fast to His promises. You can do nothing in your own strength, but in the strength of Jesus you can do all things. If you are in Christ, and Christ is in you, you will be transformed, renewed, and sanctified.

"If ye abide in Me, and My words abide in you, ye shall ask what ye will, and it shall be done unto you." Be sure that Christ is in you, that your heart is broken and submissive and humble. God will accept only the humble and contrite. Heaven is worth a lifelong, persevering effort; yes, it is worth everything. God will help you in your efforts if you strive only in Him. There is a work to be done in your family which God will help you to perform if you take hold of it aright. I entreat of you to set your own heart in order and then seek patiently to work for the salvation of your family, that the angels of God may come into your house and abide with you.

24. Appeal to Ministers

We are living in a most solemn time. All have a work to do requiring diligence. Especially is this true of the pastor, who is to care for and feed the flock of God. The one whose special work it is to lead the people into the path of truth, should be an able expositor of the word, capable of adapting his teachings to the wants of the people. He should be so closely connected with heaven as to become a living channel of light, a mouthpiece for God.

A pastor should have a correct understanding of the word and also of the human character. Our faith is unpopular. The people are unwilling to be convinced that they are so deeply in error; a great work is to be done, and at present there are but few to do it. One man usually performs the labor which should be shared by two; for the work of the evangelist is necessarily combined with that of the pastor, bringing a double burden upon the worker in the field.

The minister of Christ should be a Bible student, that his mind may be stored with Bible evidence; for a minister is strong only when he is fortified with Scripture truth. Argument is good in its place, but far more can be reached by simple explanations of the word of God. The lessons of Christ were illustrated so clearly that the lowest and most simple-minded could readily comprehend them. Jesus did not employ long and difficult words in His discourses, but used plain language, adapted to the minds of the common people. He ventured no further into the subject He was expounding than they were able to follow Him.

There are many men of good minds, who are intelligent in regard to the Scriptures, whose usefulness is greatly hindered by their defective method of labor. Some ministers who engage in the work of saving souls fail to secure the best results because they do not carry through with thoroughness the work that they commenced with so much enthusiasm. Others are not acceptable because they cling tenaciously to preconceived notions, making these prominent, and thereby failing to conform their teachings to the actual needs of the people. Many have no idea of the necessity of adapting themselves to circumstances and meeting the people where they are. They do not identify themselves with those whom they wish to help and elevate to the true Bible standard of Christianity.

In order to be a truly successful minister, one must wholly consecrate himself to the work of saving souls. It is highly essential that he should be closely united with Christ, seeking continual counsel from Him and depending upon His aid. Some fail of success because they trust to the strength of argument alone and do not cry earnestly to God for His wisdom to direct them and His grace to sanctify their efforts. Long discourses and tedious prayers are positively injurious to a religious interest and fail to carry conviction to the consciences of the people. This propensity for speechmaking frequently dampens a religious interest that might have produced great results.

The true ambassador of Christ is in perfect union with Him whom he represents, and his engrossing object is the salvation of souls. The wealth of earth dwindles into insignificance when compared with the worth of a single soul for whom our Lord and Master died. He who weigheth the hills in scales and the mountains in a balance regards a human soul as of infinite value.

In the work of the ministry there are battles to fight and victories to gain. "Think not that I am come to send peace on earth," said Christ, "I came not to send peace, but a sword." The opening labors of the Christian church were attended with hardships and bitter griefs, and the successors of the early apostles find that they must meet with trials similar to theirs; privations, calumny, and every species of opposition meet them in their labors. They must be men of stanch moral courage, and of spiritual muscle.

Great moral darkness prevails, and only the power of truth can drive away the shadows from a single mind. We are battling with giant errors and the strongest prejudices, and without the special help of God our efforts will fail either to convert souls or to elevate our own moral natures. Human skill and the very best natural abilities and acquisitions are powerless to quicken the soul to discern the enormity of sin and to banish it from the heart.

Ministers should be careful not to expect too much from persons who are still groping in the darkness of error. They should do their work well, relying upon God to impart to inquiring souls the mysterious, quickening influence of His Holy Spirit knowing that without this their labors will be unsuccessful. They should be patient and wise in dealing with minds, remembering how manifold are the circumstances that have developed such different traits in individuals. They should strictly guard themselves also lest self should get the supremacy and Jesus should be left out of the question.

Some ministers fail of success because they do not give their undivided interest to the work when very much depends upon persistent and well-directed labor. Many are not laborers; they do not pursue their business outside of the pulpit. They shirk the duty of going from house to house and laboring wisely in the home circle. They need to cultivate that rare Christian courtesy which would render them kind and considerate toward the souls under their care, working for them with true earnestness and faith, teaching them the way of life.

Ministers can do much toward molding the characters of those with whom they are associated. If they are sharp, critical, and exacting, they will be sure to meet these unhappy elements in the people upon whom their influence is strongest; though the result is not, perhaps, of the nature which they desire, yet it is nonetheless the effect of their own example.

It cannot be expected that the people will enjoy peace and harmony unless their religious teachers, whose footsteps they follow, have these principles largely developed and manifest them in their lives. The minister of Christ has great responsibilities to bear if he would become an example for his people and a correct exponent of his Master's doctrine. Men were awed by the purity and moral dignity of our Saviour, while His unselfish love and gentle benignity won their hearts. He was the embodiment of perfection. If His representatives would see fruits attending their labors similar to those that crowned the ministry of Christ, they should earnestly strive to imitate His virtues and cultivate those traits of character which would make them like Him.

It requires much forethought and wisdom from God to labor successfully for the salvation of sinners. If the soul of the laborer is filled with the grace of God, his teaching will not irritate his hearers, but melt its way to their hearts and open them for the reception of the truth.

The workers in the field should not allow themselves to be discouraged; but whatever their surroundings, they should exercise hope and faith. The minister's work is but just begun when he has presented the truth from the pulpit. He is then to become acquainted with his hearers. Many greatly fail in not coming in close sympathy with those who most need their help. With the Bible in their hand they should seek in a courteous manner to learn the objections which exist in the minds of those who are beginning to inquire: "What is truth?"

They should be carefully and tenderly led and educated as pupils in school. Many have to unlearn theories which have been engrafted into their lives. As they become convinced that they have been in error concerning Bible subjects, they are thrown into perplexity and doubt. They need the tenderest sympathy and the most judicious help; they should be carefully instructed; they should be prayed for and prayed with, watched and guarded with the kindest solicitude. Those who have fallen under temptation and have backslidden from God need help. This class is represented in the lessons of Christ by the lost sheep. The shepherd left the ninety and nine in the wilderness, and hunted for the one lost sheep until he found it; he then returned with rejoicing, bearing it on his shoulder.

Also by the illustration of the woman who searched for the lost piece of silver until she found it, and called together her neighbors to rejoice with her that the lost was found. The connection of heavenly angels with the Christian's work is here brought clearly to light. There is more joy in the presence of the angels in heaven over one sinner that repents than over ninety and nine just persons who need no repentance. There is joy with the Father and with Christ. All heaven is interested in the salvation of man. He who is instrumental in saving a soul is at liberty to rejoice; for angels of God have witnessed his efforts with the most intense interest, and rejoice with him in his success.

How thorough, then, should be the labor, and how deep the sympathy, of man for his fellow man. It is a great privilege to be a co-worker with Jesus Christ in the salvation of souls. He with patient, unselfish efforts sought to reach man in his fallen condition and to rescue him from the consequences of sin; therefore His disciples, who are the teachers of His word, should closely imitate their great Exemplar.

It is necessary, in order to pursue this great and arduous work, that the ministers of Christ should possess physical health. To attain this end they must become regular in their habits and adopt a healthful system of living. Many are continually complaining and suffering from various indispositions. This is almost always because they do not labor wisely nor observe the laws of health. They frequently remain too much indoors, occupying heated rooms filled with impure air. There they apply themselves closely to study or writing, taking little physical exercise, and having little change of employment. As a consequence, the blood becomes sluggish, and the powers of the mind are enfeebled.

The whole system needs the invigorating influence of exercise in the open air. A few hours of manual labor each day would tend to renew the bodily vigor and rest and relax the mind. In this way the general health would be promoted, and a greater amount of pastoral labor could be performed. The incessant reading and writing of many ministers unfit them for pastoral work. They consume valuable time in abstract study, which should be expended in helping the needy at the right moment.

Some ministers have given themselves to the work of writing during a period of decided religious interest, and it has frequently been the case that their writings have had no special connection with the work in hand. This is a glaring error, for at such times it is the duty of the minister to use his entire strength in pushing forward the cause of God. His mind should be clear and centered upon the one object of saving souls. Should his thoughts be preoccupied with other subjects, many might be lost to the cause who could have been saved by timely instruction. Some ministers are easily diverted from their work. They become discouraged, or are attracted to their homes, and leave a growing interest to die for want of attention.

The harm done to the cause in this way can scarcely be estimated. When an effort to promulgate the truth is started, the minister in charge should feel responsible to carry it through successfully. If his labors appear to be without result, he should seek by earnest prayer to discover if they are what they should be. He should humble his soul before God in self-examination and by faith cling to the divine promises, humbly continuing his efforts till he is satisfied that he has faithfully discharged his duty and done everything in his power to gain the desired result.

Ministers frequently report that they left the best of interest at one point to enter a new field. This is wrong; they should have finished the work they began; for in leaving it incomplete, they do more harm than good by spoiling the field for the next laborer. No field is so unpromising as that which has been cultivated just enough to give the weeds a more luxuriant growth.

Much prayer and wise labor are needed in new fields. Men of God are wanted, not merely men who can talk, but those who have an experimental knowledge of the mystery of godliness and who can meet the urgent wants of the people, those who solemnly realize the importance of their position as servants of Jesus and will cheerfully take up the cross that He has taught them how to bear.

When the temptation comes to seclude themselves and indulge in reading and writing at a time when other duties claim their immediate attention, they should be strong enough to deny self and devote themselves to the work that lies directly before them. This is undoubtedly one of the most trying tests that a studious mind is called to undergo.

The duties of a pastor are often shamefully neglected because the minister lacks strength to sacrifice his personal inclinations for seclusion and study. The pastor should visit from house to house among his flock, teaching, conversing, and praying with each family, and looking out for the welfare of their souls. Those who have manifested a desire to become acquainted with the principles of our faith should not be neglected, but thoroughly instructed in the truth. No opportunity to do good should be lost by the watchful and zealous minister of God.

Certain ministers who have been invited to houses by the heads of families have spent the few hours of their visit in secluding themselves in an unoccupied room to indulge their inclination for reading and writing. The family that entertained them derived no benefit from the visit. The ministers accepted the hospitality extended them without giving an equivalent in the labor that was so much needed.

People are easily reached through the avenues of the social circle. But many ministers dread the task of visiting; they have not cultivated social qualities, have not acquired that genial spirit that wins its way to the hearts of the people. It is highly important that a pastor should mingle much with his people, that he may become acquainted with the different phases of human nature, readily understand the workings of the mind, adapt his teachings to the intellect of his people, and learn that grand charity possessed only by those who closely study the nature and needs of men.

Those who seclude themselves from the people are in no condition to help them. A skillful physician must understand the nature of various diseases and must have a thorough knowledge of the human structure. He must be prompt in attending to the patients. He knows that delays are dangerous. When his experienced hand is laid upon the pulse of the sufferer, and he carefully notes the peculiar indication of the malady, his previous knowledge enables him to determine concerning the nature of the disease and the treatment necessary to arrest its progress. As the physician deals with physical disease, so does the pastor minister to the sin-sick soul. And his work is as much more important than that of the former as eternal life is more valuable than temporal existence. The pastor meets with an endless variety of temperaments; and it is his duty to become acquainted with the members of families that listen to his teachings, in order to determine what means will best influence them in the right direction.

In view of these grave responsibilities, the question will arise: "Who is sufficient for these things?" The heart of the laborer will almost faint as he considers the various arduous duties devolving upon him; but the words of Christ strengthen the soul with the comforting assurance: "Lo, I am with you alway, even unto the end of the world." The difficulties and dangers that threaten the safety of those he loves should make him cautious and circumspect in his manner of dealing with them, and watchful of them as one who must give an account. He should judiciously employ his influence in winning souls to Christ and impressing the truth upon inquiring minds. He should take care that the world, by its delusive attractions, does not lead them away from God and steel their hearts to the influence of His grace.

The minister is not to rule imperiously over the flock entrusted to his care, but to be their ensample, and to show them the way to heaven. Following the example of Christ, he should intercede with God for the people of his care till he sees that his prayers are answered. Jesus exercised human and divine sympathy toward man. He is our example in all things. God is our Father and Governor, and the Christian minister is the representative of His Son on earth. The principles which rule in heaven should rule upon earth; the same love that animates the angels, the same purity and holiness that reign in heaven, should, as far as possible, be reproduced upon earth. God holds the minister responsible for the power he exercises, but does not justify His servants in perverting that power into despotism over the flock of their care.

God has given to His servants precious knowledge of His truth, and He desires that they shall closely connect themselves with Jesus and, through sympathy, draw near to their brethren, that they may do them all the good that lies in their power. The Redeemer of the world did not consult His own pleasure, but went about doing good. He bound Himself closely to the

Father, that He might bring Their united strength to bear upon the souls of men to save them from eternal ruin. In like manner should His servants cultivate spirituality if they expect to succeed in their work.

Jesus pitied poor sinners so much that He left the courts of heaven and laid aside the robes of royalty, humiliating Himself to humanity, that He might become acquainted with the needs of man and help him to rise above the degradation of the Fall. When He has given to man such unquestionable evidence of His love and tenderest sympathy, how important that His representatives should imitate His example in coming close to their fellow men and helping them to form a true Christian character. But some have been too ready to engage in church trials, and have borne sharp and unsympathizing testimony against the erring. In thus acting, they have yielded to a natural propensity that should have been firmly subdued.

This is not the calm justice of the Christian executive, but the harsh criticism of a hasty temperament.

The churches need education more than censure. Instead of blaming them too severely for their want of spirituality and neglect of duty, the minister should, by precept and example, teach them to grow in grace and in the knowledge of the truth. "Whereof I am made a minister, according to the dispensation of God which is given to me for you, to fulfill the word of God; even the mystery which hath been hid from ages and from generations, but now is made manifest to His saints; to whom God would make known what is the riches of the glory of this mystery among the Gentiles; which is Christ in you, the hope of glory: whom we preach, warning every man, and teaching every man in all wisdom; that we may present every man perfect in Christ Jesus: whereunto I also labor, striving according to His working, which worketh in me mightily."

Our ministers who have reached the age of forty or fifty years should not feel that their labor is less efficient than formerly. Men of years and experience are just the ones to put forth strong and well-directed efforts. They are specially needed at this time; the churches cannot afford to part with them. Such ones should not talk of physical and mental feebleness nor feel that their day of usefulness is over.

Many of them have suffered from severe mental taxation, unrelieved by physical exercise. The result is a deterioration of their powers and a tendency to shirk responsibilities. What they need is more active labor. This is not alone confined to those whose heads are white with the frost of time, but men young in years have fallen into the same state and have become mentally feeble. They have a list of set discourses, but if they get beyond the boundaries of these they lose their soundings.

The old-fashioned pastor, who traveled on horseback and spent much time in visiting his flock, enjoyed much better health, notwithstanding his hardships and exposures, than our ministers of today, who avoid all physical exertion as far as possible and confine themselves to their books.

Ministers of age and experience should feel it their duty, as God's hired servants, to go forward, progressing every day, continually becoming more efficient in their work, and constantly gathering fresh matter to set before the people. Each effort to expound the gospel should be an improvement upon that which preceded it. Each year they should develop a deeper piety, a tenderer spirit, a greater spirituality, and a more thorough knowledge of Bible truth. The greater their age and experience, the nearer should they be able to approach the hearts of the people, having a more perfect knowledge of them.

Men are needed for this time who are not afraid to lift their voices for the right, whoever may oppose them. They should be of strong integrity and tried courage. The church calls for them, and God will work with their efforts to uphold all branches of the gospel ministry.

Testimony 28

25. Experience and Labors

My reason for sending out another Testimony to my dear brethren and sisters at this time is that the Lord has graciously manifested Himself to me and has again revealed matters of very great importance to those who profess to be keeping the commandments of God and waiting for the coming of the Son of man. More than three years elapsed between the vision given me January 3, 1875, and the recent manifestation of God's love and power. But before entering upon the views recently shown me, I will give a brief sketch of my experience for a year or two past.

May 11, 1877, we left Oakland, California, for Battle Creek, Michigan. I had been afflicted with pain in my heart for several months and suffered much with oppressed breathing on my journey across the plains. The difficulty did not leave me when we reached Michigan. Others occupied our home at Battle Creek, and we had no relatives there to care for us, our children all being in California. However, kind friends did what they could for me; but I did not feel free to burden them when they had all the care they should have with their own families.

A telegram had been sent to my husband, requesting his presence at Battle Creek to give attention to important business relative to the cause, but more especially to take the supervision of planning the large sanitarium building. In answer to this summons he came and engaged earnestly in preaching, writing, and holding board meetings at the Review office, the college, and the sanitarium, nearly always working into the night. This wore him fearfully. He felt the importance of these institutions, but especially of the sanitarium building, in which more than fifty thousand dollars was being invested. His constant mental anxiety was preparing the way for a sudden breakdown. We both felt our danger and decided to go to Colorado to enjoy retirement and rest. While planning for the journey, a voice seemed to say to me: "Put the armor on. I have work for you to do in Battle Creek." The voice seemed so plain that I involuntarily turned to see who was speaking. I saw no one, and at the sense of the presence of God my heart was broken in tenderness before Him. When my husband entered the room, I told him the exercises of my mind. We wept and prayed together. Our arrangements had been made to leave in three days, but now all our plans were changed.

May 30, the patients and faculty of the sanitarium having planned to spend the day two miles from Battle Creek in a beautiful grove that bordered Goguac Lake, I was urged to be present and speak to the patients. Had I consulted my feelings I should not have ventured, but I thought perhaps this might be a part of the work I was to do in Battle Creek. At the usual hour, tables were spread with hygienic food, which was partaken of with a keen relish. At three o'clock the exercises were opened with prayer and singing.

I had great freedom in speaking to the people. All listened with the deepest interest. After I had ceased speaking, Judge Graham of Wisconsin, a patient at the sanitarium, arose and proposed that the lecture be printed and circulated among the patients and others for their moral and physical benefit, that the words spoken that day might never be forgotten or disregarded. The proposition was approved by a unanimous vote, and the address was published in a small pamphlet entitled: The Sanitarium Patients at Goguac Lake.

The close of the school year of the Battle Creek College was now at hand. I had felt very anxious for the students, many of whom were either unconverted or backslidden from God. I had desired to speak to them and make an effort for their salvation before they should scatter to their homes, but I had been too feeble to engage in labor for them. After the experience I have related I had all the evidence I could ask that God would sustain me in laboring for the salvation of the students.

Meetings were appointed in our house of worship for the benefit of the students. I spent a week laboring for them, holding meetings every evening and on the Sabbath and first day. My heart was touched to see the house of worship nearly filled with the students of our school. I tried to impress upon them that a life of purity and prayer would not be a hindrance to them in obtaining a thorough knowledge of the sciences, but that it would remove many hindrances to their progress in knowledge. By becoming connected with the Saviour, they are brought into the school of Christ; and if they are diligent students in this school, vice and immorality will be expelled from the midst of them. These being crowded out, increased knowledge will be the result. All who become learners in the school of Christ excel both in the quality and the extent of their education. I presented Christ before them as the great teacher, the source of all wisdom, the greatest educator the world has ever known.

"The fear of the Lord is the beginning of wisdom." A knowledge of God and His requirements will open the understanding of the student to realize his responsibilities to God and to the world. To this end he will feel that his talents must be developed in that way which will produce the very best results. This cannot be done unless all the precepts and principles of religion are connected with his school education. In no case should he disconnect God from his studies. In the pursuit of knowledge he is searching for truth; and all truth comes from God, the source of truth. Students who are virtuous and are imbued with the Spirit of Christ will grasp knowledge with all their faculties.

The college at Battle Creek was established for the purpose of teaching the sciences and at the same time leading the students to the Saviour, whence all true knowledge flows. Education acquired without Bible religion is disrobed of its true brightness and glory. I sought to impress upon the students the fact that our school is to take a higher position in an educational point of view than any other institution of learning, by opening before the young nobler views, aims, and objects in life, and educating them to have a correct knowledge of human duty and eternal interests. The great object in the establishment of our college was to give correct views, showing the harmony of science and Bible religion.

The Lord strengthened me and blessed our efforts. A large number came forward for prayers. Some of these through lack of watchfulness and prayer had lost their faith and the evidence of their connection with God. Many testified that in taking this step they received the blessing of God. As the result of the meetings quite a number presented themselves for baptism.

As the closing exercises of the college year were to be held at Goguac Lake, it was decided that the baptism be administered there. The services of the occasion were of deep interest to the large congregation assembled, and were conducted with due solemnity, being appropriately closed with this sacred ordinance. I spoke at the commencement and close of the exercises. My husband led fourteen of the precious youth down into the water of the beautiful lake, and buried them with their Lord in baptism. Several of those who presented themselves as subjects for baptism chose to receive this ordinance at their homes. Thus closed the memorable services of this college year of our beloved school.

• Temperance Meetings

But my work was not yet done in Battle Creek. Immediately on our return from the lake we were earnestly solicited to take part in a temperance mass meeting, a very praise-worthy effort in progress among the better portion of the citizens of Battle Creek. This movement embraced the Battle Creek Reform Club, six hundred strong, and the Woman's Christian Temperance Union, two hundred and sixty strong. God, Christ, the Holy Spirit, and the Bible were familiar words with these earnest workers. Much good had already been accomplished, and the activity of the workers, the system by which they labored, and the spirit of their meetings, promised greater good in time to come.

It was on the occasion of the visit of Barnum's great menagerie to this city on the 28th of June that the ladies of the Woman's Christian Temperance Union struck a telling blow for temperance and reform by organizing an immense temperance restaurant to accommodate the crowds of people who gathered in from the country to visit the menagerie, thus preventing them from visiting the saloons and groggeries, where they would be exposed to temptation. The mammoth tent, capable of holding five thousand people, used by the Michigan Conference for camp meeting purposes, was tendered for the occasion. Beneath this immense canvas temple were erected fifteen or twenty tables for the accommodation of guests.

By invitation the sanitarium set a large table in the center of the great pavilion, bountifully supplied with delicious fruits, grains, and vegetables. This table formed the chief attraction, and was more largely patronized than any other. Although it was more than thirty feet long, it became so crowded that it was necessary to set another about two thirds as long, which was also thronged.

By invitation of the committee of arrangements, Mayor Austin, W. H. Skinner, cashier of the First National Bank, and C. C. Peavey, I spoke in the mammoth tent, Sunday evening, July 1, upon the subject of Christian Temperance. God helped me that evening, and although I spoke ninety minutes, the crowd of fully five thousand persons listened in almost breathless silence.

• Visit to Indiana

August 9-14 I attended the camp meeting in Indiana, accompanied by my daughter, Mary K. White. My husband found it was impossible for him to leave Battle Creek. At this meeting the Lord strengthened me to labor most earnestly. He gave me clearness and power to appeal to the people. As I looked upon the men and women assembled here, noble in appearance and commanding in influence, and compared them with the little company assembled six years before, who were mostly poor and uneducated, I could but exclaim: "What hath the Lord wrought!"

Monday I suffered much with my lungs, having taken a severe cold, but I pleaded with the Lord to strengthen me to make one more effort for the salvation of souls. I was raised above my infirmity and was blessed with great freedom and power. I appealed to the people to give their hearts to God. About fifty came forward for prayers. The deepest interest was manifested. Fifteen were buried with Christ in baptism as the result of the meeting.

We had planned to attend the Ohio and Eastern camp meetings; but as our friends thought that in my present state of health it would be presumptuous, we decided to remain at Battle Creek. My throat and lungs pained me much, and my heart was still affected. Being much of the time a great sufferer, I placed myself under treatment at the sanitarium.

• **Effects of Overwork**

My husband labored incessantly to advance the interests of the cause of God in the various departments of the work centering in Battle Creek. His friends were astonished at the amount of labor he accomplished. Sabbath morning, August 18, he spoke in our house of worship. In the afternoon his mind was closely and critically exercised for four consecutive hours, while he listened to the reading of manuscript for Spirit of Prophecy, volume 3. The matter was intensely interesting and calculated to stir the soul to its very depths, being a relation of the trial, crucifixion, resurrection, and ascension of Christ. Before we were aware of it, he was very weary. He commenced labor on Sunday at five o'clock in the morning and continued working until twelve at night.

The next morning, at about half past six, he was attacked with giddiness and was threatened with paralysis. We greatly feared this dreadful disease, but the Lord was merciful and spared us the affliction. However, his attack was followed by great physical and mental prostration; and now, indeed, it seemed impossible for us to attend the Eastern camp meetings, or for me to attend them and leave my husband, depressed in spirits and in feeble health.

When my husband was thus prostrated, I said: "This is the work of the enemy. We must not submit to his power. God will work in our behalf." On Wednesday we had a special season of prayer that the blessing of God might rest upon him and restore him to health. We also asked for wisdom that we might know our duty in regard to attending the camp meetings.

The Lord had many times strengthened our faith to go forth and work for Him under discouragements and infirmities; and at such times He had wonderfully preserved and upheld us. But our friends pleaded that we ought to rest and that it appeared inconsistent and unreasonable for us to attempt such a journey and incur the fatigue and exposure of camp life. We ourselves tried to think that the cause of God would go forward the same if we were set aside and had no part to act in it. God would raise up others to do His work.

I could not, however, find rest and freedom in the thought of remaining away from the field of labor. It seemed to me that Satan was striving to hedge up my way to prevent me from bearing my testimony and from doing the work that God had given me to do. I had about decided to go alone and do my part, trusting in God to give me the needful strength, when we received a letter from Brother Haskell, in which he expressed gratitude to God that Brother and Sister White would attend the New England camp meeting.

Elder Canright had written that he could not be present, as he would be unable to leave the interest in Danvers, and also that none of the company could be spared from the tent. Elder Haskell stated in his letter that all preparations had been made for a large meeting at Groveland; and he had decided to hold the meeting, with the help of God, even if he had to carry it through alone.

We again took the matter to the Lord in prayer. We knew that the mighty Healer could restore both my husband and me to health, if it was for His glory so to do. It seemed hard to move out, weary, sick, and discouraged; but at times I felt that God would make the journey a blessing to us both if we went trusting in Him. The thought would frequently arise in my mind: "Where is your faith? God has promised, 'As thy days, so shall thy strength be.'"

I sought to encourage my husband; he thought that if I felt able to undergo the fatigue and labor of camp meeting, it would be best for me to go; but he could not endure the thought of accompanying me in his state of feebleness, unable to labor, his mind clouded with despondency, and himself a subject of pity to his brethren. He had been able to sit up but little since his sudden attack and seemed to grow no stronger.

We sought the Lord again and again, hoping that there would be a rift in the cloud, but no special light came. While the carriage was waiting to take us to the depot, we again went before the Lord in prayer and pleaded with Him to sustain us on our journey. We both decided to walk out by faith and to venture all on the promises of God. This movement upon our part required considerable faith; but upon taking our seats in the cars, we felt that we were in the path of duty. We rested in traveling and slept well at night.

• Camp Meetings

About eight o'clock on Friday evening we reached Boston. The next morning we took the first train to Groveland. When we arrived at the camp ground, the rain was literally pouring.

Elder Haskell had labored constantly up to this time, and excellent meetings were reported. There were forty-seven tents on the ground, besides three large tents, the one for the congregation being 80 x 125 feet in dimensions. The meetings on the Sabbath were of the deepest interest. The church was revived and strengthened, while sinners and backsliders were aroused to a sense of their danger.

Sunday morning the weather was still cloudy; but before it was time for the people to assemble, the sun shone forth. Boats and trains poured their living freight upon the ground in thousands. Elder Smith spoke in the morning upon the Eastern Question. The subject was of special interest, and the people listened with the most earnest attention. In the afternoon it was difficult to make my way to the desk through the standing crowd. Upon reaching it, a sea of heads was before me. The mammoth tent was full, and thousands stood outside, making a living wall several feet deep.

My lungs and throat pained me very much, yet I believed that God would help me upon this important occasion. While speaking, my weariness and pain were forgotten as I realized that I was speaking to a people that did not regard my words as idle tales. The discourse occupied over an hour, and the very best attention was given throughout. As the closing hymn was being sung, the officers of the Temperance Reform Club of Haverhill solicited me, as on the previous year, to speak before their association on Monday evening. Having an appointment to speak at Danvers, I was obliged to decline the invitation.

Monday morning we had a season of prayer in our tent in behalf of my husband. We presented his case to the Great Physician. It was a precious season; the peace of heaven rested upon us. These words came forcibly to my mind: "This is the victory that overcometh the world, even our faith." We all felt the blessing of God resting upon us. We then assembled in the large tent; my husband met with us and spoke for a short time, uttering precious words from a heart softened and aglow with a deep sense of the mercy and goodness of God. He endeavored to make the believers in the truth realize that it is their privilege to receive the assurance of the grace of God in their hearts, and that the great truths we believe should sanctify the life, ennoble the character, and have a saving influence upon the world. The tearful eyes of the people showed that their hearts were touched and melted by these remarks.

We then took up the work where we had left it on the Sabbath, and the morning was spent in special labor for sinners and backsliders, of whom two hundred came forward for prayers, ranging in years from the child of ten to gray-headed men and women. More than a score of these were setting their feet in the way of life for the first time. In the afternoon thirty-eight persons were baptized, and quite a number delayed baptism until they should return to their homes.

Monday evening, in company with Elder Canright and several others, I took the cars for Danvers. My husband was not able to accompany me. When released from the immediate pressure of the camp meeting, I realized that I was sick and had but little strength; yet the cars were fast bearing us on to my appointment in Danvers. Here I must stand before entire strangers, whose minds had been prejudiced by false reports and wicked slander.

I thought that if I could have strength of lungs, clearness of voice, and freedom from pain of heart, I would be very grateful to God. These thoughts and feelings were kept to myself, and in great distress I silently called upon God. I was too weary to arrange my thoughts in connected words; but I felt that I must have help, and asked for it with my whole heart. Physical and mental strength I must have if I spoke that night. I said over and over again in my silent prayer: "I hang my helpless soul on Thee, O God, my Deliverer. Forsake me not in this the hour of my need."

As the time for the meeting drew on, my spirit wrestled in an agony of prayer for strength and power from God. While the last hymn was being sung, I went to the stand. I stood up in great weakness, knowing that if any degree of success attended my labors it would be through the strength of the Mighty One. The Spirit of the Lord rested upon me as I attempted to speak. Like a shock of electricity I felt it upon my heart, and all pain was instantly removed. I had suffered great pain in the nerves centering in the brain; this also was entirely removed. My irritated throat and sore lungs were relieved.

My left arm and hand had become nearly useless in consequence of pain in my heart, but natural feeling was now restored. My mind was clear; my soul was full of the light and love of God. Angels of God seemed to be on every side, like a wall of fire.

The tent was full, and about two hundred persons stood outside the canvas, unable to find room inside. I spoke from the words of Christ in answer to the question of the learned scribe as to which was the great commandment in the law: "Thou shalt love the Lord thy God with all thy heart, and with all thy soul, and with all thy mind." Matthew 22:37. The blessing of God rested upon me, and my pain and feebleness left me. Before me were a people whom I might not meet again until the judgment; and the desire for their salvation led me to speak earnestly and in the fear of God, that I might be free from their blood. Great freedom attended my effort, which occupied one hour and ten minutes. Jesus was my helper, and His name shall have all the glory. The audience was very attentive.

We returned to Groveland on Tuesday to find the camp breaking up, tents being struck, our brethren saying farewell and ready to step on board the cars to return to their homes. This was one of the best camp meetings I ever attended. Before leaving the ground, Elders Canright and Haskell, my husband, Sister Ings, and I sought a retired place in the grove and united in prayer for the blessing of health and the grace of God to rest more abundantly upon my husband. We all deeply felt the need of my husband's help, when so many urgent calls for preaching were coming in from every direction. This season of prayer was a very precious one, and the sweet peace and joy that settled upon us was our assurance that God heard our petitions. In the afternoon Elder Haskell took us in his carriage, and we started for South Lancaster to rest at his home for a time. We preferred this way of traveling, thinking it would benefit our health.

We had daily conflicts with the powers of darkness, but we did not yield our faith or become in the least discouraged. My husband, because of disease, was desponding, and Satan's temptations seemed to greatly disturb his mind. But we had no thought of being overcome by the enemy. No less than three times a day we presented his case to the Great Physician, who can heal both soul and body. Every season of prayer was to us very precious; on every occasion we had special manifestations of the light and love of God. While pleading with God in my husband's behalf one evening at Brother Haskell's, the Lord seemed to be among us in very deed. It was a season never to be forgotten. The room seemed to be lighted up with the presence of angels. We praised the Lord with our hearts and voices. One blind sister present said: "Is this a vision? is this heaven?" Our hearts were in such close communion with God that we felt the hallowed hours too sacred to be slept away. We retired to rest; but nearly the entire night was passed in talking and meditating upon the goodness and love of God, and in glorifying Him with rejoicing.

We decided to travel by private conveyance a part of the way to the Vermont camp meeting, as we thought this would be beneficial to my husband. At noon we would stop by the roadside, kindle a fire, prepare our lunch, and have a season of prayer. These precious hours spent in company with Brother and Sister Haskell, Sister Ings, and Sister Huntley will never be forgotten. Our prayers went up to God all the way from South Lancaster to Vermont. After traveling three days, we took the cars and thus completed our journey.

This meeting was of especial benefit to the cause in Vermont. The Lord gave me strength to speak to the people as often as once each day. I give the following from Elder Uriah Smith's account of the meeting, published in the Review and Herald: "Brother and Sister White and Brother Haskell were at this meeting, to the great joy of the brethren. Sabbath, September 8, the day appointed as a fast day with especial reference to Brother White's state of health, was observed on the camp ground. It was a good day. There was freedom in prayer, and good tokens that these prayers were not in vain. The blessing of the Lord was with His people in large measure. Sabbath afternoon Sister White spoke with great freedom and effect. About one hundred came forward for prayers, manifesting deep feeling and an earnest purpose to seek the Lord."

We went directly from Vermont to the New York camp meeting. The Lord gave me great freedom in speaking to the people. But some were not prepared to be benefited by the meeting. They failed to realize their condition and did not seek the Lord earnestly, confessing their backslidings and putting away their sins. One of the great objects of holding camp meetings is that our brethren may feel their danger of being overcharged with the cares of this life. A great loss is sustained when these privileges are not improved.

We returned to Michigan, and after a few days went to Lansing to attend the camp meeting there, which continued two weeks. Here I labored very earnestly, and was sustained by the Spirit of the Lord. I was greatly blessed in speaking to the students and in laboring for their salvation. This was a remarkable meeting. The Spirit of God was present from the beginning to the close. As the result of the meeting, one hundred and thirty were baptized. A large part of these were students from our college. We were rejoiced to see the salvation of God in this meeting. After spending a few weeks in Battle Creek, we decided to cross the plains to California.

• Labors in California

My husband labored but little in California. His restoration seemed to be deferred. Our prayers ascended to heaven no less than three, and sometimes five, times a day; and the peace of God often rested upon us. I was not in the least discouraged. Not being able to sleep much nights, a large share of the time was spent in prayer and grateful praise to God for His mercies. I felt the peace of God ruling in my heart constantly, and could indeed say that my peace was as a river. Unforeseen and unexpected trials came upon me, which, in addition to my husband's sickness, nearly overwhelmed me. But my trust and confidence in God were unshaken. He was truly a present help in every time of need.

We visited Healdsburg, St. Helena, Vacaville, and Pacheco. My husband accompanied me when the weather was favorable. The winter was rather a trying one to us; and as my husband had improved in health, and the weather in Michigan had become mild, he returned to be treated at the sanitarium. Here he received great benefit, and resumed writing for our papers with his usual clearness and force.

I dared not accompany my husband across the plains; for constant care and anxiety, and inability to sleep, had brought upon me heart difficulties which were alarming. We felt keenly as the hour of separation drew on. It was impossible to restrain our tears; for we knew not that we should meet again in this world. My husband was returning to Michigan, and we had decided that it was advisable for me to visit Oregon and bear my testimony to those who had never heard me.

I left Healdsburg for Oakland the 7th of June and met with the Oakland and San Francisco churches under the large tent in San Francisco, where Brother Healey had been laboring. I felt the burden of testimony and the great need of persevering personal efforts on the part of these churches to bring others to the knowledge of the truth. I had been shown that San Francisco and Oakland were missionary fields and ever would be. Their increase of numbers would be slow; but if all in these churches were living members and would do what they might do in getting the light before others, many more would be brought into the ranks and obey the truth.

The present believers in the truth were not interested for the salvation of others as they should be. Inactivity and indolence in the cause of God would result in backsliding from God themselves, and by their example they would hinder others from going forward. Unselfish, persevering, active exertion would be productive of the very best results. I tried to impress upon them that which the Lord had presented before me, that He would have the truth presented to others by earnest, active laborers, not those who merely profess to believe it. They should not present the truth in words merely, but by a circumspect life, by being living representatives of the truth.

I was shown that those who compose these churches should be Bible students, studying the will of God most earnestly that they may learn to be laborers in the cause of God. They should sow the seeds of truth wherever they may be, at home, in the workshop, in the market, as well as in the meetinghouse. In order to become familiar with the Bible, they should read it carefully and prayerfully. In order to cast themselves and their burden on Christ, they must begin at once to study to realize the value of the cross of Christ and learn to bear it. If they would live holy lives they must now have the fear of God before them.

It is trial that leads us to see what we are. It is the reason of temptation that gives a glimpse of one's real character and shows the necessity for the cultivation of good traits. Trusting in the blessing of God, the Christian is safe anywhere. In the city he will not be corrupted. In the counting room he will be marked for his habits of strict integrity. In the mechanic's shop every portion of his work will be done with fidelity, with an eye single to the glory of God. When this course is pursued by its individual members, a church will be successful. Prosperity will never attend these churches until the individual members shall be closely connected with God, having an unselfish interest in the salvation of their fellow men. Ministers may preach pleasing and forcible discourses, and much labor may be put forth to build up and make the church prosperous; but unless its individual members shall act their part as servants of Jesus Christ, the church will ever be in darkness and without strength. Hard and dark as the world is, the influence of a really consistent example will be a power for good.

A person might as well expect a harvest where he has never sown, or knowledge where he has never sought for it, as to expect to be saved in indolence. An idler and a sluggard will never make a success in breaking down pride and overcoming the power of temptation to sinful indulgences which keep him from his Saviour. The light of truth, sanctifying the life, will discover to the receiver the sinful passions in his heart, which are striving for the mastery, making it necessary for him to stretch every nerve and exert all his powers to resist Satan, that he may conquer through the merits of Christ. When surrounded by influences calculated to lead away from God, his petitions must be unwearied for help and strength from Jesus that he may overcome the devices of Satan.

Some in these churches are in constant danger because the cares of this life and worldly thoughts so occupy the mind that they do not think upon God or heaven and the needs of their own souls. They rouse from their stupor now and then, but fall back again in deeper slumber. Unless they shall fully rouse from their slumbers, God will remove the light and blessings He has given them. He will in His anger remove the candlestick out of its place. He has made these churches the depositary of His law. If they reject sin, and by active, earnest piety show stability and submission to the precepts of God's word, and are faithful in the discharge of religious duty, they will help to establish the candlestick in its place, and will have the evidence that the Lord of hosts is with them and the God of Jacob is their refuge.

• Visit to Oregon

Sunday, June 10, the day we were to start for Oregon, I was prostrated with heart disease. My friends thought it almost presumption for me to take the steamer, but I thought I should rest if I could get on board the boat. I arranged to do considerable writing during the passage.

In company with a lady friend and Elder J. N. Loughborough I left San Francisco on the afternoon of the 10th upon the steamer "Oregon." Captain Conner, who had charge of this splendid steamer, was very attentive to his passengers. As we passed through the Golden Gate into the broad ocean, it was very rough. The wind was against us, and the steamer pitched fearfully, while the ocean was lashed into fury by the wind. I watched the clouded sky, the rushing waves leaping mountain high, and the spray reflecting the colors of the rainbow.

The sight was fearfully grand, and I was filled with awe while contemplating the mysteries of the deep. It is terrible in its wrath. There is a fearful beauty in the lifting up of its proud waves with roaring, and then falling back in mournful sobs. I could see the exhibition of God's power in the movements of the restless waters, groaning beneath the action of the merciless winds, which tossed the waves up on high as if in convulsions of agony.

We were in a beautiful boat, tossed at the mercy of the ever-restless waves; but there was an unseen power holding a steady grasp upon the waters. God alone has power to keep them within their appointed boundaries. He can hold the waters as in the hollow of His hand. The deep will obey the voice of its Creator: "Hitherto shalt thou come, but no further: and here shall thy proud waves be stayed."

What a subject for thought was the broad, grand Pacific Ocean! In appearance it was the very opposite of pacific; it was madness and fury. As we take a surface view of the water, nothing seems so utterly unmanageable, so completely without law or order, as the great deep. But God's law is obeyed by the ocean. He balances the waters and marks their bed. As I looked at the heavens above and the waters beneath, I inquired: "Where am I? Where am I going? Nothing but the boundless waters around me. How many have thus embarked upon the waters and never again seen the green fields or their happy homes! They were dropped into the deep as a grain of sand, and thus ended their lives."

As I looked upon the white-capped, roaring billows, I was reminded of that scene in the life of Christ, when the disciples, in obedience to the command of their Master, went in their boats to the farther side of the sea. A terrible tempest broke upon them. Their vessels would not obey their will, and they were driven hither and thither, until they laid down their oars in despair. They expected to perish there; but while the tempest and the billows talked with death, Christ, whom they had left upon the other side, appeared to them, walking calmly upon the boisterous, white-capped waves. They had been bewildered by the uselessness of their efforts and the apparent hopelessness of their case and had given up all for lost.

When they saw Jesus before them upon the water, it increased their terror; they interpreted it as a sure precursor of their immediate death. They cried out in great fear. But, instead of His appearance heralding the presence of death,. He came as the messenger of life. His voice was heard above the roar of the elements: "It is I; be not afraid." How quickly the scene now changed from the horror of despair to the joy of faith and hope in the presence of the beloved Master! The disciples felt no more anxiety nor dread of death, for Christ was with them.

Shall we refuse obedience to the Source of all power, whose law even the sea and the waves obey? Shall I fear to trust myself to the protection of Him who has said that not a sparrow falleth to the ground without the notice of our heavenly Father?

When nearly all had left for their staterooms, I continued on deck. The captain had provided me a reclining cane chair, and blankets to serve as a protection from the chilly air. I knew that if I went into the cabin I should be sick. Night came on, darkness covered the sea, and the plunging waves were pitching our ship fearfully. This great vessel was as a mere chip upon the merciless waters; but she was guarded and protected on her course by the heavenly angels, commissioned of God to do His bidding. Had it not been for this, we might have been swallowed up in a moment, leaving not a trace of that splendid ship. But that God who feeds the ravens, who numbers the hairs of our heads, will not forget us.

The captain thought it was too cool for me to remain on deck. I told him that so far as my safety was concerned, I would rather remain there all night than go into my stateroom, where two ladies were seasick, and where I should be deprived of pure air. Said he: "You will not be required to occupy your stateroom. I will see that you have a good place to sleep." I was assisted by the stewardess into the upper saloon, and a hair mattress was laid upon the floor. Although this was accomplished in the quickest time possible, I had become very sick. I lay down upon my bed, and did not arise from it until the next Thursday morning. During that time I ate only once, a few spoonfuls of beef tea and crackers.

During that four days' voyage, one and another would occasionally venture to leave their rooms, pale, feeble, and tottering, and make their way on deck. Wretchedness was written on every countenance. Life itself did not seem desirable. We all longed for the rest we could not find, and to see something that would stand still. Personal importance was not much regarded then. We may here learn a lesson on the littleness of man.

Our passage continued to be very rough until we passed the bar and entered the Columbia River, which was as smooth as glass. I was assisted to go upon the deck. It was a beautiful morning, and the passengers poured out on deck like a swarm of bees. They were a very sorry-looking company at first; but the invigorating air and the glad sunshine, after the wind and storm, soon awakened cheerfulness and mirth.

The last night we were on the boat I felt most grateful to my heavenly Father. I there learned a lesson I shall never forget. God had spoken to my heart in the storm and in the waves and in the calm following. And shall we not worship Him? Shall man set up his will against the will of God? Shall we be disobedient to the commands of so mighty a Ruler? Shall we contend with the Most High, who is the source of all power, and from whose heart flows infinite love and blessing to the creatures of His care?

My visit to Oregon was one of special interest. I here met, after a separation of four years, my dear friends, Brother and Sister Van Horn, whom we claim as our children. Brother Van Horn has not furnished as full and favorable reports of his work as he might justly have done. I was accordingly somewhat surprised, and very much pleased, to find the cause of God in so prosperous a condition in Oregon. Through the untiring efforts of these faithful missionaries, a conference of Seventh-day Adventists has been raised up, also several ministers to labor in that broad field.

Tuesday evening, June 18, I met a goodly number of the Sabbathkeepers in this state. My heart was softened by the Spirit of God. I gave my testimony for Jesus and expressed my gratitude for the sweet privilege that is ours of trusting in His love and of claiming His power to unite with our efforts to save sinners from perdition. If we would see the work of God prosper we must have Christ dwelling in us; in short, we must work the works of Christ. Wherever we look, the whitening harvest appears; but the laborers are so few. I felt my heart filled with the peace of God and drawn out in love for His dear people with whom I was worshiping for the first time.

On Sunday, June 23, I spoke in the Methodist church of Salem on the subject of temperance. The attendance was unusually good, and I had freedom in treating this, my favorite subject. I was requested to speak again in the same place on the Sunday following the camp meeting, but was prevented by hoarseness. On the next Tuesday evening, however, I again spoke in this church. Many invitations were tendered me to speak on temperance in various cities and towns of Oregon, but the state of my health forbade my complying with these requests. Constant speaking, and the change of climate, had brought upon me a temporary but severe hoarseness.

We entered upon the camp meeting with feelings of the deepest interest. The Lord gave me strength and grace as I stood before the people. As I looked upon the intelligent audience, my heart was broken before God. This was the first camp meeting held by our people in the state. I tried to speak, but my utterance was broken because of weeping.

I had felt very anxious about my husband on account of his poor health. While speaking, a meeting in the church at Battle Creek came vividly before my mind's eye, my husband being in the midst, with the mellow light of the Lord resting upon and surrounding him. His face bore the marks of health, and he was apparently very happy.

I tried to present before the people the gratitude we should feel for the tender compassion and great love of God. His goodness and glory impressed my mind in a remarkable manner. I was overwhelmed with a sense of His unparalleled mercies and of the work He was doing, not only in Oregon, and in California and Michigan, where our important institutions are located, but also in foreign countries. I can never represent to others the picture that vividly impressed my mind on that occasion. For a moment the extent of the work came before me, and I lost sight of my surroundings. The occasion and the people I was addressing passed from my mind. The light, the precious light from heaven, was shining in great brilliancy upon those institutions which are engaged in the solemn and elevated work of reflecting the rays of light that heaven has let shine upon them.

All through this camp meeting the Lord seemed very near me. When it closed, I was exceedingly weary, but free in the Lord. It was a season of profitable labor and strengthened the church to go on in their warfare for the truth. Just before the camp meeting commenced, in the night season, many things were opened to me in vision; but silence was enjoined upon me that I should not mention the matter to anyone at that time. After the meeting closed, I had in the night season another remarkable manifestation of God's power.

On the Sunday following the camp meeting I spoke in the afternoon in the public square. The love of God was in my heart, and I dwelt upon the simplicity of gospel religion. My own heart was melted and overflowing with the love of Jesus, and I longed to present Him in such a manner that all might be charmed with the loveliness of His character.

During my stay in Oregon I visited the prison in Salem, in company with Brother and Sister Carter and Sister Jordan. When the time arrived for service, we were conducted to the chapel, which was made cheerful by an abundance of light and pure, fresh air. At a signal from the bell, two men opened the great iron gates, and the prisoners came flocking in. The doors were securely closed behind them, and for the first time in my life I was immured in prison walls.

I had expected to see a set of repulsive-looking men, but was disappointed; many of them seemed to be intelligent, and some to be men of ability. They were dressed in the coarse but neat prison uniform, their hair smooth, and their boots brushed. As I looked upon the varied physiognomies before me, I thought: "To each of these men have been committed peculiar gifts, or talents, to be used for the glory of God and the benefit of the world; but they have despised these gifts of heaven, abused, and misapplied them." As I looked upon young men from eighteen to twenty and thirty years of age, I thought of their unhappy mothers and of the grief and remorse which was their bitter portion. Many of these mothers' hearts had been broken by the ungodly course pursued by their children. But had they done their duty by these children? Had they not indulged them in their own will and way, and neglected to teach them the statutes of God and His claims upon them?

When all the company were assembled, Brother Carter read a hymn. All had books and joined heartily in singing. One, who was an accomplished musician, played the organ. I then opened the meeting by prayer, and again all joined in singing. I spoke from the words of John: "Behold, what manner of love the Father hath bestowed upon us, that we should be called the sons of God: therefore the world knoweth us not, because it knew Him not. Beloved, now are we the sons of God, and it doth not yet appear what we shall be: but we know that, when He shall appear, we shall be like Him; for we shall see Him as he is."

I exalted before them the infinite sacrifice made by the Father in giving His beloved Son for fallen men, that they might through obedience be transformed and become the acknowledged sons of God. The church and the world are called upon to behold and admire a love which thus expressed is beyond human comprehension, and which amazed even the angels of heaven. This love is so deep, so broad, and so high that the inspired apostle, failing to find language in which to describe it, calls upon the church and the world to behold it —to make it a theme of contemplation and admiration.

I presented before my hearers the sin of Adam in the transgression of the Father's express commands. God made man upright, perfectly holy and happy; but he lost the divine favor and destroyed his own happiness by disobedience to the Father's law. The sin of Adam plunged the race in hopeless misery and despair. But God, in His wonderful, pitying love, did not leave men to perish in their hopeless, fallen condition. He gave His well-beloved Son for their salvation. Christ entered the world, His divinity clothed in humanity; He passed over the ground where Adam fell; He bore the test which Adam failed to endure; He overcame every temptation of Satan, and thus redeemed Adam's disgraceful failure and fall.

I then referred to the long fast of Christ in the wilderness. The sin of the indulgence of appetite, and its power over human nature, can never be fully realized, except as that long fast of Christ when contending single-handed with the prince of the powers of darkness is studied and understood. Man's salvation was at stake. Would Satan or the Redeemer of the world come off conqueror? It is impossible for us to conceive with what intense interest angels of God watched the trial of their loved Commander.

Jesus was tempted in all points like as we are, that He might know how to succor those who should be tempted. His life is our example. He shows by His willing obedience that man may keep the law of God and that transgression of the law, not obedience to it, brings him into bondage. The Saviour was full of compassion and love; He never spurned the truly penitent, however great their guilt; but He severely denounced hypocrisy of every sort.

He is acquainted with the sins of men, He knows all their acts and reads their secret motives; yet He does not turn away from them in their iniquity. He pleads and reasons with the sinner, and in one sense—that of having Himself borne the weakness of humanity—He puts Himself on a level with him. "Come now, and let us reason together, saith the Lord: though your sins be as scarlet, they shall be as white as snow; though they be red like crimson, they shall be as wool."

Man, who has defaced the image of God in his soul by a corrupt life, cannot, by mere human effort, effect a radical change in himself. He must accept the provisions of the gospel; he must be reconciled to God through obedience to His law and faith in Jesus Christ. His life from thenceforth must be governed by a new principle. Through repentance, faith, and good works he may perfect a righteous character, and claim, through the merits of Christ, the privileges of the sons of God. The principles of divine truth, received and cherished in the heart, will carry us to a height of moral excellence that we had not deemed it possible for us to reach. "And it doth not yet appear what we shall be: but we know that, when He shall appear, we shall be like Him; for we shall see Him as He is. And every man that hath this hope in Him purifieth himself, even as He is pure."

Here is a work for man to do. He must face the mirror, God's law, discern the defects in his moral character, and put away his sins, washing his robe of character in the blood of the Lamb. Envy, pride, malice, deceit, strife, and crime will be cleansed from the heart that is a recipient of the love of Christ and that cherishes the hope of being made like Him when we shall see Him as He is. The religion of Christ refines and dignifies its possessor, whatever his associations or station in life may be. Men who become enlightened Christians rise above the level of their former character into greater mental and moral strength. Those fallen and degraded by sin and crime may, through the merits of the Saviour, be exalted to a position but little lower than that of the angels.

But the influence of a gospel hope will not lead the sinner to look upon the salvation of Christ as a matter of free grace, while he continues to live in transgression of the law of God. When the light of truth dawns upon his mind and he fully understands the requirements of God and realizes the extent of his transgressions, he will reform his ways, become loyal to God through the strength obtained from his Saviour, and lead a new and purer life.

While in Salem I formed the acquaintance of Brother and Sister Donaldson, who desired that their daughter should return to Battle Creek with us and attend the college. Her health was poor, and it was quite a struggle for them to part with her, their only daughter, but the spiritual advantages she would there receive induced them to make the sacrifice. And we are happy to here state that at the recent camp meeting in Battle Creek this dear child was buried with Christ in baptism. Here is another proof of the importance of Seventh-day Adventists' sending their children to our school, where they can be brought directly under a saving influence.

Our voyage from Oregon was rough, but I was not so sick as on my former passage. This boat, the "Idaho," did not pitch, but rolled. We were treated very kindly on the boat. We made many pleasant acquaintances and distributed our publications to different ones, which led to profitable conversation. When we arrived at Oakland we found that the tent was pitched there and that quite a number had embraced the truth under the labors of Brother Healey. We spoke several times under the tent. Sabbath and first day the churches on San Francisco and Oakland met together, and we had interesting and profitable meetings.

I was very anxious to attend the camp meeting in California, but there were urgent calls for me to attend the Eastern camp meetings. As the condition of things in the East had been presented before me, I knew that I had a testimony to bear especially to our brethren in the New England Conference, and I could not feel at liberty to remain longer in California.

• Eastward Bound

July 28, accompanied by our daughter, Mrs. Emma White, and Edith Donaldson, we left Oakland for the East. We arrived in Sacramento the same day and were met by Brother and Sister Wilkinson, who gave us a hearty welcome and took us to their home, where we were kindly entertained during our stay. According to appointment, I spoke Sunday. The house was well filled with an attentive congregation, and the Lord gave me freedom in speaking to them from His word. Monday we again took the cars, stopping at Reno, Nevada, where we had an appointment to speak Tuesday evening in the tent in which Elder Loughborough was giving a course of lectures. I spoke with freedom to about four hundred attentive hearers, on the words of John: "Behold, what manner of love the Father hath bestowed upon us, that we should be called the sons of God."

As we passed over the great American desert in the heat and alkali dust, we became very weary of the barren scenery, though we were furnished with every convenience and glided swiftly and smoothly over the rails, drawn by our iron steed. I was reminded of the ancient Hebrews, who traveled over rocks and arid deserts for forty years. The heat, dust, and roughness of the way drew complaints and sighs of fatigue from many who trod that weary path. I thought that if we were obliged to travel on foot across the barren desert, often suffering from thirst, heat, and fatigue, very many of us would murmur more than did the Israelites.

The peculiar features of mountain scenery on the overland route have often been sketched by pen and pencil. All who are delighted with the grandeur and beauty of nature must feel a thrill of joy as they behold these grand old mountains, beautiful hills, and the wild and rocky canyons. This is especially true of the Christian. He sees in the granite rocks and babbling streams the work of God's all-powerful hand. He longs to climb the lofty hills; for its seems that he would then be nearer heaven, though he knows that God hears the prayers of His children in the lowly valley as well as on the mountaintop.

• **Colorado**

On the way from Denver to Walling's Mills, the mountain retreat where my husband was spending the summer months, we stopped in Boulder City and beheld with joy our canvas meetinghouse, where Elder Cornell was holding a series of meetings. We found a quiet retreat in the comfortable home of Sister Dartt. The tent had been lent to hold temperance meetings in, and, by special invitation, I spoke to a tent full of attentive hearers. Though wearied by my journey, the Lord helped me to successfully present before the people the necessity of practicing strict temperance in all things.

Monday, August 8, I met my husband and found him much improved in health, cheerful and active, for which I felt thankful to God. Elder Canright, who had spent some time with my husband in the mountains, was about this time called home to his afflicted wife; and on Sunday, husband and I accompanied him to Boulder City to take the cars. In the evening I spoke in the tent, and the next morning we returned to our temporary home at Walling's Mills. The next Sabbath I again spoke to those assembled in the tent. Following my remarks we had a conference meeting. Some excellent testimonies were borne. Several were keeping their first Sabbath. I spoke to the people evening after the Sabbath and also Sunday evening.

Our family were all present in the mountains but our son Edson. My husband and children thought that as I was much worn, having labored almost constantly since the Oregon camp meeting, it was my privilege to rest; but my mind was impressed to attend the Eastern camp meetings, especially the one in Massachusetts. My prayer was that if it was the will of God for me to attend these meetings, my husband would consent to have me go.

When we returned from Boulder City, I found a letter from Brother Haskell urging us both to attend the camp meeting; but if my husband could not come, he wished me to come if possible. I read the letter to my husband and waited to see what he would say. After a few moments' silence, he said: "Ellen, you will have to attend the New England camp meeting." The next day our trunks were packed. At two o'clock in the morning, favored with the light of the moon, we started for the cars, and at half past six we stepped on board the train. The journey was anything but pleasant; for the heat was intense, and I was much worn.

• Eastern Meetings

Upon arriving at Battle Creek, we learned that an appointment had been made for me to speak Sunday evening in the mammoth tent pitched on the college grounds. The tent was filled to overflowing, and my heart was drawn out in earnest appeals to the people.

I tarried at home but a very short period, and then, accompanied by Sister Mary Smith Abbey and Brother Farnsworth, I was again on the wing, bound for the East. When we arrived at Boston, I was much exhausted. Brethren Wood and Haskell met us at the depot and accompanied us to Ballard Vale, the place of meeting. We were welcomed by our old friends with a heartiness that, for the time being, seemed to rest me. The weather was excessively warm, and the change from the bracing climate of Colorado to the oppressive heat of Massachusetts made the latter seem almost unendurable.

I tried to speak to the people, notwithstanding my great weariness, and was strengthened to bear my testimony. The words seemed to go straight home to the heart. Much labor was required at this meeting. New churches had been raised up since our last camp meeting. Precious souls had accepted the truth, and these needed to be carried forward to a deeper and more thorough knowledge of practical godliness. The Lord gave me freedom in bearing my testimony.

On one occasion during this meeting I made some remarks upon the necessity of economy in dress and in the expenditure of means. There is danger of becoming careless and reckless in the use of the Lord's money. Young men who engage in tent labor should be careful not to indulge in unnecessary expense. As tents are entering new fields, and as the missionary work is enlarging, the wants of the cause are many, and, without stinginess, the most rigid economy should be used in this matter. It is easier to run up a bill than to settle it.

There are many things that would be convenient and enjoyable that are not needful, and that can be dispensed with without actual suffering. It is very easy to multiply hotel bills and railroad fares, expenses that might be avoided or very much lessened. We have passed over the road to and from California twelve times, and have not expended one dollar for meals at the restaurants or in the attached dining car. We eat our meals from our lunch baskets. After being three days out, the food becomes quite stale, but a little milk or warm gruel supplies our lack.

On another occasion I spoke in reference to genuine sanctification, which is nothing less than a daily dying to self and daily conformity to the will of God. While in Oregon I was shown that some of the young churches of the New England Conference were in danger through the blighting influence of what is called sanctification. Some would become deceived by this doctrine, while others, knowing its deceptive influence, would realize their danger and turn from it. Paul's sanctification was a constant conflict with self. Said he: "I die daily." His will and his desires every day conflicted with duty and the will of God. Instead of following inclination, he did the will of God, however unpleasant and crucifying to his nature.

We called on those who desired to be baptized, and those who were keeping the Sabbath for the first time, to come forward. Twenty-five responded. These bore excellent testimonies, and before the close of the camp meeting twenty-two received baptism.

We were pleased to meet here our old friends of the cause whose acquaintance we made thirty years ago. Our much-esteemed Brother Hastings is as deeply interested in the truth today as he was then. We were pleased to meet Sister Temple, and Sister Collins of Dartmouth, Massachusetts, and Brother and Sister Wilkinson, at whose house we were entertained more than thirty years ago. The pilgrimage of some of these dear ones may close erelong; but if faithful unto the end, they will receive a crown of life.

We were interested in Brother Kimbal, who is a mute and has been a missionary among the mutes. Through his persevering labors quite a little company have accepted the truth. We meet this faithful brother at our yearly camp meetings, surrounded by several of his mute converts. Someone who can hear writes out as much as possible of the discourse, and he sits surrounded by his mute friends, reading and actively preaching it over again to them with his hands. He has freely used his means to advance the missionary work, thus honoring God with his substance.

We left Ballard Vale Tuesday morning, September 3, to attend the Maine camp meeting. We enjoyed a quiet rest at the home of young Brother

Morton, near Portland. He and his good wife made our tarry with them very pleasant. We were upon the Maine camp ground before the Sabbath, and were happy to meet here some of the tried friends of the cause. There are some who are ever at their post of duty, come sunshine or come storm. There is also a class of sunshine Christians. When everything goes well and is agreeable to their feelings, they are fervent and zealous; but when there are clouds and disagreeable things to meet, these will have nothing to say or do.

The blessing of God rested upon the active workers, while those who did nothing were not benefited by the meeting as they might have been. The Lord was with His ministers, who labor faithfully in presenting both doctrinal and practical subjects. We greatly desired to see many benefited by that meeting who gave no evidence that they had been blessed of God. I long to see this dear people coming up to their exalted privileges.

We left the camp ground on Monday, feeling much exhausted. We designed to attend the Iowa and Kansas camp meetings. My husband had written that he would meet me in Iowa. Being unable to attend the Vermont meeting, we went directly from Maine to South Lancaster. I had much difficulty in breathing, and my heart pained me continually. I rested at the quiet home of Sister Harris, who did all in her power to help me. Thursday evening we ventured to resume our journey to Battle Creek. I dared not trust myself on the cars any length of time in my state of health; so we stopped at Rome, New York, and spoke to our people on the Sabbath. There was a good attendance.

Monday morning I visited Brother and Sister Ira Abbey at Brookfield. We had a profitable interview with this family. We felt interested, and anxious that they should finally be victorious in the Christian warfare and win eternal life. We felt deeply anxious that Brother Abbey should overcome his discouragements, cast himself unreservedly upon the merits of Christ, make a success of overcoming, and at last wear the victor's crown.

Tuesday we took the cars for Battle Creek, and the next day arrived at home, where I was glad to rest once more and take treatment at the sanitarium. I felt that I was indeed favored in having the advantages of this institution. The helpers were kind and attentive, and ready at any time of day or night to do their utmost to relieve me of my infirmities.

- ## At Battle Creek

The national camp meeting was held at Battle Creek, October 2-14. This was the largest gathering of Seventh-day Adventists ever held. More than forty ministers were present.

We were all happy to here meet Elders Andrews and Bourdeau from Europe, and Elder Loughborough from California. At this meeting was represented the cause in Europe, California, Texas, Alabama, Virginia, Dakota, Colorado, and in all of the Northern States from Maine to Nebraska.

Here I was happy to join my husband in labor. And although much worn, and suffering with heart difficulty, the Lord gave me strength to speak to the people nearly every day, and sometimes twice a day. My husband labored very hard. He was present at nearly all the business meetings, and preached almost every day in his usual plain, pointed style. I did not think I should have strength to speak more than twice or three times during the meeting; but as the meeting progressed, my strength increased. Upon several occasions I stood on my feet four hours, inviting the people forward for prayers. I never felt the special help of God more sensibly than during this meeting. Notwithstanding these labors, I steadily increased in strength. And to the praise of God I here record the fact that I was far better in health at the close of that meeting than I had been for six months.

On Wednesday of the second week of the meeting a few of us united in prayer for a sister who was afflicted with despondency. While praying I was greatly blessed. The Lord seemed very near. I was taken off in a vision of God's glory and shown many things. I then went to meeting, and with a solemn sense of the condition of our people I made brief statements of the things which had been shown me. I have since written out some of these in testimonies to individuals, appeals to ministers, and in various other articles given in this book.

These were meetings of solemn power and of the deepest interest. Several connected with our office of publication were convicted, and converted to the truth, and bore clear, intelligent testimonies. Infidels were convicted and took their stand under the banner of Prince Immanuel. This meeting was a decided victory. One hundred and twelve were baptized before its close.

The week following the camp meeting my labors in speaking, praying, and writing testimonies were more taxing than during the meeting. Two or three meetings were held each day in behalf of our ministers. These were of intense interest and of great importance. Those who bear this message to the world should have a daily experience in the things of God and be in every sense converted men, sanctified through the truth which they present to others, representing in their lives Jesus Christ.

Then, and not till then, will they be successful in their work. Most earnest efforts were made to draw nigh to God by confession, humiliation, and prayer. Many said that they saw and felt the importance of their work as ministers of Christ as they had never seen and felt it before. Some felt deeply the magnitude of the work and their responsibility before God, but we longed to see a greater manifestation of the Spirit of God. I knew that when the way was cleared the Spirit of God would come in, as on the Day of Pentecost. But there were so many at such a distance from God that they did not seem to know how to exercise faith.

The appeals to ministers, found elsewhere in this number, more fully express what God has shown me relative to their sad condition and their high privileges.

• Kansas Camp Meetings

Accompanied by my daughter Emma, we left Battle Creek, October 23, for the Kansas camp meeting. At Topeka, Kansas, we left the cars and rode by private conveyance twelve miles to Richland, the place of meeting. We found the settlement of tents in a grove. It being late in the season for camp meetings, every preparation was made for cold weather that could be made. There were seventeen tents on the ground besides the large tent, which accommodated several families; and every tent had a stove.

Sabbath morning it commenced snowing, but not one meeting was suspended. About an inch of snow fell, and the air was piercing cold. Women with little children clustered about the stoves. It was touching to see one hundred and fifty people, assembled for a convocation, meeting under these circumstances. Some came two hundred miles by private conveyance. All seemed hungry for the bread of life and thirsty for the water of salvation.

Elder Haskell spoke Friday afternoon and evening. Sabbath morning I felt called upon to speak encouraging words to those who had made so great an effort to attend the meeting. Sunday afternoon there was quite a large outside attendance, considering that the meeting was located so far from the thoroughfares of travel.

Monday morning I spoke to the brethren from the third chapter of Malachi. We then called for those to come forward who wanted to be Christians and who had not the evidence of their acceptance with God. About thirty responded. Some were seeking the Lord for the first time, and some who were members of other churches were taking their position upon the Sabbath. We gave all an opportunity to speak, and the free Spirit of the Lord was in our meeting. After prayer had been offered for those who had come forward, candidates for baptism were examined. Six were baptized.

I was glad to hear Elder Haskell present before the people the necessity of placing reading matter in private families, especially the three volumes of Spirit of Prophecy and the four volumes of Testimonies. These could be read aloud during the long winter evenings by some member of the family, so that all the family might be instructed. I then spoke of the necessity of parents' properly educating and disciplining their children. The greatest evidence of the power of Christianity that can be presented to the world is a well-ordered, well-disciplined family. This will recommend the truth as nothing else can, for it is a living witness of its practical power upon the heart.

Tuesday morning the meeting closed, and with my daughter Emma, Elder Haskell, and Brother Stover, we went to Topeka and took the cars for Sherman, Kansas, where another camp meeting had been appointed. This meeting was interesting and profitable. It appeared small when compared with our camp meetings in other states, as there were only about one hundred brethren and sisters present. It was designed for a general gathering of the scattered ones. Some were present from southern Kansas, Arkansas, Kentucky, Missouri, Nebraska, and Tennessee. At this meeting my husband joined me, and from here, with Elder Haskell and our daughter, we went to Dallas, Texas.

• Visit to Texas

Thursday we went to Brother McDearman's at Grand Prairie. Here our daughter met her parents, brother, and sister, who had all been brought near to the door of death by the fever which prevailed in the state during the past season. We took great pleasure in ministering to the wants of this afflicted family, who had in years past liberally assisted us in our affliction.

We left them, somewhat improved in health, to attend the Plano camp meeting. This meeting was held November 12-19. The weather was fine at the commencement; but it soon began to rain, and this, with high winds, prevented a general attendance from the surrounding country. Here we were happy to meet our old friends, Elder R. M. Kilgore and wife. And we were highly pleased to find a large and intelligent body of brethren on the ground. Whatever prejudices have existed here against people from the North, nothing of the kind appeared among these dear brethren and sisters.

My testimony was never received more readily and heartily than by this people. I became deeply interested in the work in the great State of Texas. It has ever been Satan's object to preoccupy every important field; and probably he has never been more busily employed at the introduction of the truth in any state than he has been in Texas. This is the best evidence to my mind that there is a great work to be done here.

26. Preparation for Christ's Coming

In the late vision given me at Battle Creek during our general camp meeting, I was shown our danger, as a people, of becoming assimilated to the world rather than to the image of Christ. We are now upon the very borders of the eternal world, but it is the purpose of the adversary of souls to lead us to put far off the close of time. Satan will in every conceivable manner assail those who profess to be the commandment-keeping people of God and to be waiting for the second appearing of our Saviour in the clouds of heaven with power and great glory. He will lead as many as possible to put off the evil day and become in spirit like the world, imitating its customs. I felt alarmed as I saw that the spirit of the world was controlling the hearts and minds of many who make a high profession of the truth. Selfishness and self-indulgence are cherished by them, but true godliness and sterling integrity are not cultivated.

The angel of God pointed to those who profess the truth, and in a solemn voice repeated these words: "And take heed to yourselves, lest at any time your hearts be overcharged with surfeiting, and drunkenness, and cares of this life, and so that day come upon you unawares. For as a snare shall it come on all them that dwell on the face of the whole earth. Watch ye therefore, and pray always, that ye may be accounted worthy to escape all these things that shall come to pass, and to stand before the Son of man."

In consideration of the shortness of time we as a people should watch and pray, and in no case allow ourselves to be diverted from the solemn work of preparation for the great event before us. Because the time is apparently extended, many have become careless and indifferent in regard to their words and actions. They do not realize their danger and do not see and understand the mercy of our God in lengthening their probation, that they may have time to form characters for the future, immortal life.

Every moment is of the highest value. Time is granted them, not to be employed in studying their own ease and becoming dwellers on the earth, but to be used in the work of overcoming every defect in their own characters and in helping others, by example and personal effort, to see the beauty of holiness. God has a people upon the earth who in faith and holy hope are tracing down the roll of fast-fulfilling prophecy and are seeking to purify their souls by obeying the truth, that they may not be found without the wedding garment when Christ shall appear.

Many who have called themselves Adventists have been time setters. Time after time has been set for Christ to come, but repeated failures have been the result. The definite time of our Lord's coming is declared to be beyond the ken of mortals. Even the angels who minister unto those who shall be heirs of salvation know not the day nor the hour. "But of that day and hour knoweth no man, no, not the angels of heaven, but My Father only." Because the times repeatedly set have passed, the world is in a more decided state of unbelief than before in regard to the near advent of Christ. They look upon the failures of the time setters with disgust; and because men have been so deceived, they turn from the truth substantiated by the word of God that the end of all things is at hand.

Those who so presumptuously preach definite time, in so doing gratify the adversary of souls; for they are advancing infidelity rather than Christianity. They produce Scripture and by false interpretation show a chain of argument which apparently proves their position. But their failures show that they are false prophets, that they do not rightly interpret the language of inspiration. The word of God is truth and verity, but men have perverted its meaning. These errors have brought the truth of God for these last days into disrepute. Adventists are derided by ministers of all denominations, yet God's servants must not hold their peace. The signs foretold in prophecy are fast fulfilling around us. This should arouse every true follower of Christ to zealous action.

Those who think they must preach definite time in order to make an impression upon the people do not work from the right standpoint. The feelings of the people may be stirred and their fears aroused, but they do not move from principle. An excitement is created; but when the time passes, as it has done repeatedly, those who moved out upon time fall back into coldness, darkness, and sin, and it is almost impossible to arouse their consciences without some great excitement.

In Noah's day the inhabitants of the old world laughed to scorn what they termed the superstitious fears and forebodings of the preacher of righteousness. He was denounced as a visionary character, a fanatic, an alarmist. "As it was in the days of Noah, so shall it be also in the days of the Son of man." Men will reject the solemn message of warning in our day, as they did in Noah's time. They will refer to those false teachers who have predicted the event and set the definite time, and will say that they have no more faith in our warning than in theirs. This is the attitude of the world today. Unbelief is widespread, and the preaching of Christ's coming is mocked at and derided. This makes it all the more essential that those who believe present truth should show their faith by their works. They should be sanctified through the truth which they profess to believe; for they are a savor of life unto life or of death unto death.

Noah preached to the people of his time that God would give them one hundred and twenty years in which to repent of their sins and find refuge in the ark, but they refused the gracious invitation. Abundant time was given them to turn from their sins, overcome their bad habits, and develop righteous characters. But inclination to sin, though weak at first with many, strengthened through repeated indulgence and hurried them on to irretrievable ruin. The merciful warning of God was rejected with sneers, with mockery and derision; and they were left in darkness to follow the course that their sinful hearts had chosen. But their unbelief did not hinder the predicted event. It came, and great was the wrath of God which was seen in the general ruin.

These words of Christ should sink into the hearts of all who believe present truth: "And take heed to yourselves, lest at any time your hearts be overcharged with surfeiting, and drunkenness, and cares of this life, and so that day come upon you unawares." Our danger is presented before us by Christ Himself. He knew the perils we should meet in these last days, and would have us prepare for them. "As it was in the days of Noah, so shall it be also in the days of the Son of man." They were eating and drinking, planting and building, marrying and giving in marriage, and knew not until the day that Noah entered into the ark, and the Flood came and swept them all away.

The day of God will find men absorbed in like manner in the business and pleasures of the world, in feasting and gluttony, and in indulging perverted appetite in the defiling use of liquor and the narcotic tobacco. This is already the condition of our world, and these indulgences are found even among God's professed people, some of whom are following the customs and partaking of the sins of the world. Lawyers, mechanics, farmers, traders, and even ministers from the pulpit are crying, "Peace and safety," when destruction is fast coming upon them.

Belief in the near coming of the Son of man in the clouds of heaven will not cause the true Christian to become neglectful and careless of the ordinary business of life. The waiting ones who look for the soon appearing of Christ will not be idle, but diligent in business. Their work will not be done carelessly and dishonestly, but with fidelity, promptness, and thoroughness. Those who flatter themselves that careless inattention to the things of this life is an evidence of their spirituality and of their separation from the world are under a great deception. Their veracity, faithfulness, and integrity are tested and proved in temporal things. If they are faithful in that which is least they will be faithful in much.

I have been shown that here is where many will fail to bear the test. They develop their true character in the management of temporal concerns. They manifest unfaithfulness, scheming, dishonesty, in dealing with their fellow men. They do not consider that their hold upon the future, immortal life depends upon how they conduct themselves in the concerns of this life, and that the strictest integrity is indispensable to the formation of a righteous character. Dishonesty is practiced all through our ranks, and this is the cause of lukewarmness on the part of many who profess to believe the truth. They are not connected with Christ and are deceiving their own souls. I am pained to make the statement that there is an alarming lack of honesty even among Sabbathkeepers.

I was referred to Christ's Sermon on the Mount. Here we have the injunction of the Great Teacher: "All things whatsoever ye would that men should do to you, do ye even so to them: for this is the law and the prophets." This command of Christ is of the highest importance and should be strictly obeyed. It is like apples of gold in pictures of silver. How many carry out in their lives the principle Christ has here enjoined, and deal with others just as they would wish to be dealt with under similar circumstances? Reader, please answer.

An honest man, according to Christ's measurement, is one who will manifest unbending integrity. Deceitful weights and false balances, with which many seek to advance their interests in the world, are abomination in the sight of God. Yet many who profess to keep the commandments of God are dealing with false weights and false balances. When a man is indeed connected with God, and is keeping His law in truth, his life will reveal the fact; for all his actions will be in harmony with the teachings of Christ. He will not sell his honor for gain. His principles are built upon the sure foundation, and his conduct in worldly matters is a transcript of his principles.

Firm integrity shines forth as gold amid the dross and rubbish of the world. Deceit, falsehood, and unfaithfulness may be glossed over and hidden from the eyes of man, but not from the eyes of God. The angels of God, who watch the development of character and weigh moral worth, record in the books of heaven these minor transactions which reveal character. If a workman in the daily vocations of life is unfaithful and slights his work, the world will not judge incorrectly if they estimate his standard in religion according to his standard in business.

"He that is faithful in that which is least is faithful also in much: and he that is unjust in the least is unjust also in much." It is not the magnitude of the matter that makes it fair or unfair. As a man deals with his fellow men, so will he deal with God. He that is unfaithful in the mammon of unrighteousness, will never be entrusted with the true riches. The children of God should not fail to remember that in all their business transactions they are being proved, weighed in the balances of the sanctuary.

Christ has said: "A good tree cannot bring forth evil fruit, neither can a corrupt tree bring forth good fruit." "Wherefore by their fruits ye shall know them." The deeds of a man's life are the fruit he bears. If he is unfaithful and dishonest in temporal matters he is bringing forth briers and thorns; he will be unfaithful in the religious life and will rob God in tithes and offerings.

The Bible condemns in the strongest terms all falsehood, false dealing, and dishonesty. Right and wrong are plainly stated. But I was shown that God's people have placed themselves on the enemy's ground; they have yielded to his temptations and followed his devices until their sensibilities have become fearfully blunted. A slight deviation from truth, a little variation from the requirements of God, is thought to be, after all, not so very sinful, when pecuniary gain or loss is involved. But sin is sin, whether committed by the possessor of millions or by the beggar in the streets. Those who secure property by false representations are bringing condemnation on their souls. All that is obtained by deceit and fraud will be only a curse to the receiver.

Adam and Eve suffered the terrible consequences of disobeying the express command of God. They might have reasoned: This is a very small sin, and will never be taken into account. But God treated the matter as a fearful evil, and the woe of their transgression will be felt through all time. In the times in which we live, sins of far greater magnitude are often committed by those who profess to be God's children. In the transaction of business, falsehoods are uttered and acted by God's professed people that bring His frown upon them and a reproach upon His cause.

The least departure from truthfulness and rectitude is a transgression of the law of God. Continual indulgence in sin accustoms the person to a habit of wrongdoing, but does not lessen the aggravated character of the sin. God has established immutable principles, which He cannot change without a revision of His whole nature. If the word of God were faithfully studied by all who profess to believe the truth, they would not be dwarfs in spiritual things. Those who disregard the requirements of God in this life would not respect His authority were they in heaven.

Every species of immorality is plainly delineated in the word of God and its result spread before us. The indulgence of the lower passions is presented before us in its most revolting character. No one, however dark may be his understanding, need to err. But I have been shown that this sin is cherished by many who profess to be walking in all the commandments of God. God will judge every man by His word.

Said Christ: "Search the Scriptures; for in them ye think ye have eternal life: and they are they which testify of Me." The Bible is an unerring guide. It demands perfect purity in word, in thought, and in action. Only virtuous and spotless characters will be permitted to enter the presence of a pure and holy God. The word of God, if studied and obeyed, would lead the children of men, as the Israelites were led by a pillar of fire by night and a pillar of cloud by day. The Bible is God's will expressed to man. It is the only perfect standard of character, and marks out the duty of man in every circumstance of life. There are many responsibilities resting upon us in this life, a neglect of which will not only cause suffering to ourselves, but others will sustain loss in consequence.

Men and women professing to revere the Bible and follow its teachings fail in many respects to perform its requirements. In the training of children they follow their own perverse natures rather than the revealed will of God. This neglect of duty involves the loss of thousands of souls. The Bible lays down rules for the correct discipline of children. Were these requirements of God heeded by parents, we should today see a different class of youth coming upon the stage of action. But parents who profess to be Bible readers and Bible followers are going directly contrary to its teachings. We hear the cry of sorrow and anguish from fathers and mothers who bewail the conduct of their children, little realizing that they are bringing this sorrow and anguish upon themselves, and ruining their children, by their mistaken affection. They do not realize their God-given responsibilities to train their children to right habits from their babyhood.

Parents, you are in a great degree responsible for the souls of your children. Many neglect their duty during the first years of their children's lives, thinking that when they get older they will then be very careful to repress wrong and educate them in the right. But the very time for them to do this work is when the children are babes in their arms. It is not right for parents to pet and humor their children; neither is it right for them to abuse them. A firm, decided straightforward course of action will be productive of the best results.

27. Address to Ministers

A great and solemn truth has been entrusted to us, for which we are responsible. Too often this truth is presented in cold theory. Sermon after sermon upon doctrinal points is delivered to people who come and go, some of whom will never have another as favorable opportunity of being convicted and converted to Christ. Golden opportunities are lost by delivering elaborate discourses, which display self, but do not magnify Christ. A theory of the truth without vital godliness cannot remove the moral darkness which envelops the soul.

Most precious gems of truth are often rendered powerless by the wisdom of words in which they are clothed, while the power of the Spirit of God is lacking. Christ presented the truth in its simplicity; and He reached not only the most elevated, but the lowliest men of earth. The minister who is God's ambassador and Christ's representative on the earth, who humbles himself that God may be exalted, will possess the genuine quality of eloquence. True piety, a close connection with God, and a daily, living experience in the knowledge of Christ, will make eloquent even the stammering tongue.

As I see the wants in young churches, as I see and realize their great need of vital godliness and their deficiency in true religious experience, my heart is sad. I know that those who bear the message of truth to them do not properly instruct them on all points essential to the perfection of a symmetrical character in Christ Jesus. These things may be neglected too long by the teachers of the truth. Speaking of the gospel, Paul says: "Whereof I am made a minister, according to the dispensation of God which is given to me for you, to fulfill the word of God, even the mystery which hath been hid from ages and from generations, but now is made manifest to His saints: to whom

God would make known what is the riches of the glory of this mystery among the Gentiles [mark the explanation of the mystery]; which is Christ in you, the hope of glory: whom we preach, warning every man and teaching every man in all wisdom; that we may present every man perfect in Christ Jesus: whereunto I also labor, striving according to His working, which worketh in me mightily."

Here the ministers of Christ have their work, their qualifications, and the power of God's grace working in them, clearly defined. God has been pleased recently to show me a great deficiency in many who profess to be representatives of Christ. In short, if they are deficient in faith and in a knowledge of vital godliness they are not only deceiving their own souls, but are making a failure in the work of presenting every man perfect in Christ. Many whom they bring into the truth are destitute of true godliness. They may have a theory of the truth, but they are not thoroughly converted. Their hearts are carnal; they do not abide in Christ and He in them. It is the duty of the minister to present the theory of the truth; but he should not rest with having done this merely. He should adopt the language of Paul: "I also labor, striving according to His working, which worketh in me mightily."

A vital connection with the Chief Shepherd will make the undershepherd a living representative of Christ, a light indeed to the world. An understanding of all points of our faith is indeed essential, but it is of greater importance that the minister be sanctified through the truth which he presents for the purpose of enlightening the consciences of his hearers. In a series of meetings not one discourse should be given consisting of theory alone, nor should one long, tedious prayer be made. Such prayers God does not hear.

I have listened to many prosy, sermonizing prayers that were uncalled for and out of place. A prayer with one half the number of words, offered in fervor and faith, would have softened the hearts of the hearers; but, instead of this, I have seen them wait impatiently, as though wishing that every word would end the prayer. Had the minister wrestled with God in his chamber until he felt that his faith could grasp the eternal promise, "Ask, and ye shall receive," he would have come to the point at once, asking with earnestness and faith for what he needed.

We need a converted ministry; otherwise the churches raised up through their labors, having no root in themselves, will not be able to stand alone. The faithful minister of Christ will take the burden upon his soul. He will not hunger after popularity. The Christian minister should never enter the desk until he has first sought God in his closet and has come into close connection with Him. He may, with humility, lift his thirsty soul to God and be refreshed with the dew of grace before he shall speak to the people. With an unction of the Holy Spirit upon him, giving him a burden for souls he will not dismiss a congregation without presenting before them Jesus Christ, the sinner's only refuge, making earnest appeals that will reach their hearts. He should feel that he may never meet these hearers again until the great day of God.

The Master who has chosen him, who knows the hearts of all men, will give him tongue and utterance, that he may speak the words he ought to speak at the right time and with power. And those who become truly convicted of sin, and charmed with the Way, the Truth, and the Life, will find sufficient to do without praising and extolling the ability of the minister. Christ and His love will be exalted above any human instrument. The man will be lost sight of because Christ is magnified and is the theme of thought. Many are converted to the minister who are not really converted to Christ. We marvel at the stupor that benumbs the spiritual senses. There is a lack of vital power. Lifeless prayers are offered, and testimonies are borne which fail to edify or strengthen the hearers. It becomes every minister of Christ to inquire the cause of this.

Paul writes to his Colossian brethren: "As ye also learned of Epaphras our dear fellow servant, who is for you a faithful minister of Christ; who also declared unto us your love in the Spirit. [Not an unsanctified love of the smartness, ability, or oratory of the preacher, but a love born of the Spirit of God, which His servant represented in his words and character.] For this cause we also, since the day we heard it, do not cease to pray for you, and to desire that ye might be filled with the knowledge of His will in all wisdom and spiritual understanding; that ye might walk worthy of the Lord unto all pleasing, being fruitful in every good work, and increasing in the knowledge of God; strengthened with all might, according to His glorious power, unto all patience and long-suffering with joyfulness; giving thanks unto the Father, which hath made us meet to be partakers of the inheritance of the saints in light."

Ministers who labor in towns and cities to present the truth should not feel content, nor that their work is ended, until those who have accepted the theory of the truth realize indeed the effect of its sanctifying power and are truly converted to God. God would be better pleased to have six truly converted to the truth as the result of their labors than to have sixty make a nominal profession and yet not be thoroughly converted. These ministers should devote less time to preaching sermons and reserve a portion of their strength to visit and pray with those who are interested, giving them godly instruction, to the end that they may "present every man perfect in Christ Jesus."

The love of God must be living in the heart of the teacher of the truth. His own heart must be imbued with that deep and fervent love which Christ possessed; then it will flow out to others. Ministers should teach that all who accept the truth should bring forth fruit to the glory of God. They should teach that self-sacrifice must be practiced every day; that many things which have been cherished must be yielded; and that many duties, disagreeable though they may appear, must be performed.

Business interests, social endearments, ease, honor, reputation, — in short, everything, must be held in subjection to the superior and ever-paramount claims of Christ. Ministers who are not men of vital piety, who stir up an interest among the people, but leave the work in the rough, leave an exceedingly difficult field for others to enter and finish the work they failed to complete. These men will be proved; and if they do not do their work more faithfully, they will, after a still further test, be laid aside as cumberers of the ground, unfaithful watchmen.

God would not have men go forth as teachers who have not studiously learned their lessons and who will not continue to study that they may present every point of present truth in an intelligent, acceptable manner. With a knowledge of the theory they should continually be obtaining a more thorough knowledge of Jesus Christ. Rules and studies are necessary; but with them the minister should combine earnest prayer that he may be faithful, not building upon the foundation wood, hay, or stubble, which will be consumed by the fires of the last day. Prayer and study should go hand in hand. The fact that a minister is applauded and praised is no evidence that he has spoken under the influence of the Spirit.

It is too frequently the case that young converts, unless guarded, will set their affections more upon their minister than upon their Redeemer. They consider that they have been greatly benefited by their minister's labors. They conceive that he possesses the most exalted gifts and graces, and that no other can do equally as well as he; therefore they attach undue importance to the man and his labors. This is a confidence that disposes them to idolize the man and look to him more than to God, and in doing this they do not please God nor grow in grace. They do great harm to the minister, especially if he is young and developing into a promising gospel laborer.

These teachers, if they are really men of God, receive their words from God. Their manner of address may be faulty and need much improvement, yet if God breathes through them words of inspiration, the power is not of man, but of God. The Giver should have the glory and the heart's affections, while the minister should be esteemed, loved, and respected for his work's sake, because he is God's servant to bear the message of mercy to sinners. The Son of God is often eclipsed by the man standing between Him and the people. The man is praised, petted, and exalted, and the people scarcely get a glimpse of Jesus, who, by the precious beams of light reflected from Him, should eclipse everything besides.

The minister of Christ who is imbued with the Spirit and love of his Master will so labor that the character of God and of His dear Son may be made manifest in the fullest and clearest manner. He will strive to have his hearers become intelligent in their conceptions of the character of God, that His glory may be acknowledged on the earth. A man is no sooner converted than in his heart is born a desire to make known to others what a precious friend he has found in Jesus; the saving and sanctifying truth cannot be shut up in his heart. The Spirit of Christ illuminating the soul is represented by the light, which dispels all darkness; it is compared to salt, because of its preserving qualities; and to leaven, which secretly exerts its transforming power.

Those whom Christ has connected with Himself will, as far as in them lies, labor diligently and perseveringly, as He labored, to save souls who are perishing around them. They will reach the people by prayer, earnest, fervent prayer, and personal effort. It is impossible for those who are thoroughly converted to God, enjoying communion with Him, to be negligent of the vital interests of those who are perishing outside of Christ.

The minister should not do all the work himself, but he should unite with him those who have taken hold of the truth. He will thus teach others to work after he shall leave. A working church will ever be a growing church. They will ever find a stimulus and a tonic in trying to help others, and in doing it they will be strengthened and encouraged.

I have read of a man who, journeying on a winter's day through the deep, drifted snow, became benumbed by the cold, which was almost imperceptibly stealing away his vital powers. And as he was nearly chilled to death by the embrace of the frost king, and about to give up the struggle for life, he heard the moans of a brother traveler, who was perishing with cold as he was about to perish. His humanity was aroused to rescue him. He chafed the ice-clad limbs of the unfortunate man, and, after considerable effort, raised him to his feet; and as he could not stand, he bore him in sympathizing arms through the very drifts he had thought he could never succeed in getting through alone.

And when he had borne his fellow traveler to a place of safety, the truth flashed home to him that in saving his neighbor he had saved himself also. His earnest efforts to save another quickened the blood which was freezing in his own veins, and created a healthful warmth in the extremities of the body.

These lessons must be forced upon young believers continually, not only by precept, but by example, that in their Christian experience they may realize similar results. Let the desponding ones, those disposed to think the way to life is very trying and difficult, go to work and seek to help others. In such efforts, mingled with prayer for divine light, their own hearts will throb with the quickening influence of the grace of God; their own affections will glow with more divine fervor, and their whole Christian life will be more of a reality, more earnest, more prayerful.

The minister of Christ should be a man of prayer, a man of piety; cheerful, but never coarse and rough, jesting or frivolous. A spirit of frivolity may be in keeping with the profession of clowns and theatrical actors, but it is altogether beneath the dignity of a man who is chosen to stand between the living and the dead, and to be mouthpiece for God.

Every day's labor is faithfully chronicled in the books of God. As men claiming spiritual illumination, you will give moral tone to the character of all with whom you are connected. As faithful ministers of the gospel, you should bend all the energies of the mind and all the opportunities of your life to make your work wholly successful, and present every man perfect in Christ Jesus. In order to do this, you must pray earnestly. Ministers of the gospel must be in possession of that power which wrought such wonders for the humble fishermen of Galilee.

Moral and intellectual powers are needed in order to discharge with fidelity the important duties devolving upon you; but these may be possessed, and yet there may be a great lack of godliness. The endowment of the Holy Spirit is indispensably essential to success in your great work. Said Christ: "Without Me ye can do nothing." But through Christ strengthening you, you can do all things.

28. Sympathy for the Erring

Dear Brother A:

I have risen early to write to you. Additional light has been given me of late, for which I am responsible. Twice while in this state has the Lord revealed Himself to me. While pleading with Him in the night season, I was shown in vision many things connected with the cause of God. The state of things in the church, the college, the sanitarium, and the publishing houses located at Battle Creek, and the work of God in Europe and England, in Oregon and Texas, and in other new fields, was presented before me. There is the greatest need of the work in new fields starting right, bearing the impress of the divine.

Many in these new fields will be in danger of accepting the truth or assenting to it, who have not a genuine conversion of heart. When tested by storm and tempest, it will be found that their house is not built upon a rock but upon sliding sand. Practical godliness must be possessed by the minister and developed in his daily life and character. His discourses should not be exclusively theoretical.

I was shown some things not favorable to the prosperity of the cause of truth in Texas. The Brethren B and their families have not heretofore been a blessing or help to the cause of God in any place. Their influence has been shown me before this as not being a sweet-smelling savor. They cannot build up the cause of God because they have not the elements within them which make them capable of exerting a healthful influence on the side of God and the truth. If you had had the mind of God you would not have been so void of discernment, especially after you had been faithfully warned by those in whom you should have had confidence.

Smooth words and fair speeches have deceived you. These brothers are not all alike, but all have defective characters. By constant watchfulness over themselves, and by earnest prayer to God in faith, they may make a success of keeping self in its proper position. Through Jesus Christ they may be transformed in character and obtain a moral fitness to meet the Lord when He shall come, but God will not lay any important responsibility upon them, for souls would thus be imperiled. These men are unfitted to lead the flock of God. At the very time when their words should be few and well chosen, modest and unassuming, their natural traits of character are woven into all they do and say, and the work of God is marred.

You and Brother C have not had true discernment. You have had too great confidence in the ability of these men. A ship may be sound in nearly every respect; but if there is one defect,—a bit of timber worm-eaten,—the lives of all on board are imperiled. Nearly all the links of a chain may be sound, but one defective link destroys its worth. Individuals who possess excellent qualities may have some marked traits of character which unfit them to be entrusted with the solemn, sacred work of God. But these men are deficient in nearly everything that pertains to Christian character. Their example is not worthy of imitation.

You need to have much done for you, my brother, before your labors can be what they might and should be. Your understanding has been darkened. Sympathy and union with those whose characters have been cast in an inferior mold will not elevate and ennoble you, but will rust and corrode your spirit, and will mar your usefulness and disconnect you from God. You are of an impulsive nature. Burdens of domestic life and of the cause do not rest very heavily upon you, and unless you are constantly under the refining influence of the Spirit of God you will be in danger of becoming coarse in your manners. In order to rightly represent the character of Christ, you need to be spiritualized and brought into a closer connection with God in the great work in which you are engaged. Your own thoughts must be elevated, your own heart sanctified, in order for you to be a co-worker with Jesus Christ. "Be ye clean, that bear the vessels of the Lord."

The work of God in Texas would stand higher today if the B brothers had no connection with it. I might mention more particular reasons why this is so, but will not at this time. Suffice it to say that these men are not right with God. Feeling self-sufficient and competent for almost any calling, they have not made efforts to correct the objectionable traits of character which were transmitted to them as a birthright, but which by education, culture, and training might have been overcome. They have made some improvements in this direction; but if weighed in the balances, they would still be found wanting.

The word of God abounds in general principles for the formation of correct habits of living, and the testimonies, general and personal, have been calculated to call their attention more especially to these principles; but all these have not made a sufficient impression upon their hearts and minds to cause them to realize the necessity of decided reform. If they had correct views of themselves in contrast with the perfect Pattern, they would cherish that faith that works by love and purifies the soul. These brothers, A B excepted, are naturally arbitrary, dictatorial, and self-sufficient. They do not consider others better than themselves. They are envious and jealous of any member of the church who, they think, will be esteemed more highly than themselves. They profess conscientiousness; but they strain at a gnat and swallow a camel in their dealings with their brethren, who, they fear, will be considered superior to themselves. They seize upon little things, and talk over particulars, putting their own construction upon words and acts. This is particularly true of two of these brothers.

These men, especially A B, are free, easy speakers. Their smooth manner of relating things has such an appearance of honesty and genuine interest for the cause of God that it has a tendency to deceive and becloud the minds of those who hear them. My heart aches with sadness as I write, because I know the influence of this family wherever it is felt. I did not design to speak in regard to these persons again, but the solemn opening of these matters before me compels me to write once more. If the ministers of the word, who profess to be connected with God, cannot discern the influence of such men, they are unfit to stand as teachers of the truth of God. If these persons would only keep their proper position and never attempt to teach or to lead, I would be silent; but when I see that the cause of God is in danger of suffering I can hold my peace no longer.

These brothers should not be allowed to all locate in one place and compose the leading element in the church. They are wanting in natural affection. They do not manifest sympathy, love, and refined feeling toward one another, but indulge in envy, jealousy, bickerings, and strife among themselves. Their consciences are not tender. The love, gentleness, and meekness of Christ does not help to compose their experience. God forbid that such an element should exist in the church. Unless these persons are converted, they cannot see the kingdom of heaven. It is much more congenial to their feelings to be tearing down, picking flaws, and seeking spot and stain in others, than to be washing their own robes of character from the defilement of sin and making them white in the blood of the Lamb.

But I now come to the most painful part of this history, that concerning Brother D. The Lord caused me to pass through an investigation in which you and Brother C figured largely. God was grieved with you both. I saw and heard that which caused me pain and regret. Such an unreasonable, godless course as was pursued in this investigation was just what might have been looked for from the Brethren B; but my greatest surprise and grief was that such men as Brother C and yourself should bear an active part in this shameful, one-sided investigation.

To Brother C, who acted the lawyer, to question and bring out the minutiae in the strongest light, I would say: I would not have that work laid to my charge for the riches of the world. You were simply deceived and deluded by a strange spirit that should have had no semblance of quarter, no grain of respect. Envy, jealousy, evil surmisings, and doubtful disputations held a carnival on that occasion.

You may think me too severe, but I cannot be more severe than the transaction deserves. Did you all think, when you condemned the guiltless, that God was altogether such a one as yourselves? The subsequent condition of Brother D was the result of the position taken by you on that occasion. Had you shown fairness and sympathy, he would stand today where his influence would tell on the side of truth with the power that a meek and quiet spirit exerts.

Brother D was not a ready speaker, and the smooth words and fair speeches of A B, uttered with apparent coolness and candor, had effect. The poor, sightless man should have been regarded with pity and tenderness; but, instead of this, he was placed in the worst possible light. God saw and will not hold one of you guiltless who acted a part in that unfair investigation. Brother A, it will not then appear so amusing to you as when you were sitting in judgment against a blind brother. You should learn a lesson from this experience; namely, to close your ears to those who would prejudice you against the very ones whom God would have you sustain, pity, and strengthen.

Brother C and you could not see the defects in the Brethren B; neither could you discern the opposite traits of character in Brother D. But his influence, sanctified by the Spirit of God, would tell upon the cause of God with tenfold greater power than that of the Brethren B. You have done much to injure Brother D; and I advise you to repent of this wrong as heartily as you committed it. In the name of the Master, I entreat you to shake yourself from human influences and close your ears to gossiping reports. Let no person put a testimony in your mouth; but let God, rather than men who are unconsecrated at home and abroad, give you a burden for His cause.

Brother C needs the softening, refining Spirit of God in his heart. He needs to exercise it in his home. "Let love be without dissimulation." Let the arbitrary, dictatorial, censorious spirit be put away from his home, with all malice.

The same overbearing, judging spirit will be carried out in the church. If his feelings are somewhat softened for the time being, he will act in a more kindly manner; but if they happen to be the opposite, he will act accordingly. Self-control and self-discipline he has not exercised. Where Brother D has one defect, his judges and those who condemned him have ten.

Brother A, why did you not fully take the part of the oppressed? Why did you not compromise this matter? Why did you not lift your voice, as did your Saviour, and say: "He that is without sin among you, let him first cast a stone"? You have made a fearful mistake, which may result in the loss of more souls than one, notwithstanding you did it ignorantly. Had one word of tender, genuine pity been expressed by you to Brother D, it would have been registered to your account in heaven.

But you had no more sense of the work you were doing for time and for eternity than had those who condemned Christ; and you have judged and condemned your Saviour in the person of His saint. "Inasmuch as ye have done it unto one of the least of these My brethren, ye have done it unto Me." Hypocrisy always met the severest rebuke from Jesus; while the veriest sinners who came to Him in sincere repentance were received, pardoned, and comforted.

Did you think Brother D could be made to believe that wrong was right and right was wrong, because his brethren would have him believe it? He was diseased and nervous. Everything looked dark and uncertain to him. His confidence in you and Brother C was gone, and to whom should he look? He was censured for one thing and then for another, until he became confused, distracted, and desperate. Those who drove him to this state have committed the greater sin.

Where was compassion, even on the ground of common humanity? Worldlings would not, as a general rule, have been so careless, so devoid of mercy and courtesy; and they would have exercised more compassion toward a man on account of his very infirmity, considering him entitled to the tenderest consideration and neighborly love. But here was a blind man, a brother in Christ, and several of his brethren were sitting as judges upon his case.

More than once during the progress of the trial, while a brother was being hunted like a rabbit to his death, you would break out into a loud laugh. There sat Brother C, naturally so kind and sympathetic that he censured his brethren for cruelty in killing game to subsist upon, yet here was a poor blind man, of as much more value than birds as man formed in the image of God is above the dumb creatures of His care. Ye "strain at a gnat, and swallow a camel" would have been the verdict of Him who spake as never man spake, had His voice been heard in your assembly.

He who had such tender compassion for the birds might have exercised a praiseworthy compassion and love for Christ in the person of His afflicted saint. But you were as men blindfolded. Brother B presented a smooth, able speech. Brother D was not a ready speaker. His thoughts could not be clothed in language that would make a case, and he was altogether too much surprised to make the best of the situation. His sharp, criticizing brethren turned lawyers and placed the blind man at great disadvantage.

God saw and marked the transactions of that day. These men, adepts in casting mist and making out a case, apparently obtained a triumph, while the blind brother, misused and abused, felt that everything was sinking beneath his feet. His confidence in those whom he had believed were the representatives of Christ was terribly shaken. The moral shock he received has nearly proved his ruin, spiritually and physically. Everyone who was engaged in this work should feel the deepest remorse and repentance before God.

Brother D has made a mistake in sinking under this load of reproach and undeserved criticism, which should have fallen on other heads than his. He has loved the cause of God with his whole soul. God has shown His care for the blind in giving him prosperity, but even this has been turned against him by his envious brethren. God has put it into the hearts of unbelievers to be kind and sympathetic to him because he is a blind man. Brother D has been a Christian gentleman, and has made even his worldly enemies to be at peace with him.

God has been to him a tender father and has smoothed his pathway. He should have been true to his knowledge of truth, and served God with singleness of heart, irrespective of censure, envy, and false accusations. It was the position you took, Brother A, that was the finishing stroke to Brother D. But he should not have let go his hold on God, though ministers and people did take a course in which he could see no justice. Riveted to the eternal Rock, he should have stood firm to principle and carried out his faith and the truth at all hazards. Oh, what necessity for Brother D to cling more closely to the Arm that is mighty to save.

All the worth and greatness of this life is derived from its connection with heaven and the future, immortal life. God's everlasting arm encircles the soul that turns to Him for aid, however feeble that soul may be. The precious things of the hills shall perish; but the soul that lives for God, unmoved by censure, unperverted by applause, shall abide forever with Him. The city of God will open its golden gates to receive him who learned while on earth to lean on God for guidance and wisdom, for comfort and hope amid loss and affliction. The songs of angels will welcome him there, and for him the tree of life will yield its fruits.

Brother D has failed where he should have been victorious. But the pitying eye of God is upon him. Although the compassion of man may fail, still God loves and pities, and reaches out His helping hand. If he will only be humble, meek, and lowly of heart, He will yet lift up his head and plant his feet firmly upon the Rock of Ages. "The mountains shall depart, and the hills be removed; but My kindness shall not depart from thee, neither shall the covenant of My peace be removed, saith the Lord that hath mercy on thee."

Not one of us is excusable, under any form of trial, for letting our hold upon God become loosened. He is our source of strength, our stronghold in every trial. When we cry unto Him for help, his hand will be stretched forth mightily to save. Brother D should have felt that, having God for his father, he could hope and rejoice, though every human friend should forsake him. I entreat him not to rob God of his service because frail man has misjudged him, but make haste and consecrate himself to God and serve Him with all the powers of his being.

God loves him, and he loves God; and his works must be in accordance with his faith, whatever course men may pursue toward him. His enemies may point to his present position as an evidence that they were right in their judgment of him. Brother D's course has been hasty and without due thought. His soul has been disgusted, and he thinks it has been too thoroughly wounded for recovery. Those who have pursued him so relentlessly have been in life and character far from blameless. If God had dealt with their crooked ways and imperfect characters as they have dealt with Brother D, they would have perished long ago. But a compassionate God has borne with them and not dealt with them according to their sins.

God has been true to Brother D, and he should respond to His merciful dealings, notwithstanding man has shown so little of tenderness and the feelings of common humanity. It is Brother D's privilege to hide in Christ from the strife of tongues, and to feel that exhaustless sources of gratitude, contentment, and peace are open to him and accessible every moment. Had he earthly treasures without limit, he would not be as rich as he may now be in the privilege of being on the side of right and of drinking to the full of the streams of salvation.

What has not God done for Brother D in giving His Son to die for him? and will He not with Him freely give him all things? Why should he be unfaithful to God because man has proved unfaithful to him? How much stronger than death is the love that binds the mother's heart to her afflicted child; "yet God declares that even a mother may forget her child, yet will I not forget thee." No; not a single soul who puts his trust in Him will be forgotten. God thinks of His children with the tenderest solicitude and keeps a book of remembrance before Him, that He may never forget the children of His care.

Every human tie may perish,
  Friend to friend unfaithful prove,
Mothers cease their own to cherish,
  Heaven and earth at last remove;
    But no changes
  Can attend Jehovah's love.

Brother and Sister D might have been a precious help to the church in bringing them up to a position of better understanding had the church accepted their efforts. But envy, evil surmisings, and jealousy have driven them away from the church. Had they left the scenes of their trial sooner than they did, it would have been better for them.

Salem, Oregon
July 8, 1878

29. The Cause in Texas

God has shown me much in regard to the work of Satan in Texas and the unchristian conduct of some who have moved there from Michigan. I was shown that the Brethren B have not in heart accepted the testimony which has been given them. They have more confidence in themselves than in the spirit of prophecy. They have felt that the light given was not of heaven, but that it originated from reports made to me in regard to them. This is not correct. But let me ask: Was there not foundation for reports? Does not their very life history condemn their course?

Not one of this family has had a religious experience that would qualify him to take any leading position in teaching the truth to others. "Be ye clean, that bear the vessels of the Lord," were the words spoken by the angel of God. "Ye are not chosen vessels of God to do any part of His most sacred work. Ye mar and corrode, but do not purify and bless." You have, Brethren B, ever held a low standard of Christianity. For a time, where you are not fully known, you have influence.

This once gained, you become less guarded and act out the natural propensities of the heart, until the lovers of the truth feel that you are a great hindrance to the advancement of the work of God. This is no evil surmising, but the actual facts in the case.

If you would always manifest kindness, respect, noble love and generosity, toward even wicked men, you might render effectual service to Christ. If the spirit of Christ dwelt in you, you would represent Him in your words, in your actions, and even in the expression of your countenance. Your conversation would be expressive of meekness, not proud and boastful. You would not seek to exalt and glorify self. Humility is a Christian grace with which you are unacquainted. You have aspired for the supremacy and have tried to cause your power and superiority to be felt in ruling and dictating to others.

Especially has this been the case with A B. He and his wife cannot advance the moral and spiritual standing of the cause of God by their influence. The more limited their sphere in connection with the cause of God the better will it be for the cause. Their words and acts in matters of deal are not reliable. This is the case with A B and his brothers generally. The world and the church have a right to say that their religion is vain. They are worldly and scheming, and watch their opportunity to make a close bargain. They are harsh and severe with those who are connected with them. They are envious, jealous, puffed up.

Those who thus represent the truth rear a mighty barrier to the salvation of others. Unless they become transformed, it would be better had they never embraced the truth. Their minds are controlled more by Satan than by the Spirit of God. Brother A B's wife naturally possesses a kind heart, but she has been molded by her husband. She is a careless talker. Her tongue is frequently set on fire of hell; it is untamable. "In the multitude of words," says Solomon, "there wanteth not sin." This is certainly true in her case. She exaggerates and bears false witness and is thus constantly transgressing the commandment of God, while she professes to be a commandment keeper. She does not mean to do wrong, but her heart is not sanctified by the truth.

While you, Brethren B, have been forward to engage in controversy with others upon points of our faith, without an exception you have been asleep in reference to those things which pertain to Christianity. You are not even dreaming of the perilous position you occupy. This apathy extends over the church and over everyone who, professing Christ as you have done, denies Him by his works. You are leading others in the same path of recklessness in which you are treading. God's word declares that without holiness no man shall see God. Jesus died to redeem us from all iniquity and to purify unto Himself a peculiar people, zealous of good works.

"The grace of God that bringeth salvation hath appeared to all men, teaching us that, denying ungodliness and worldly lusts, we should live soberly, righteously, and godly, in this present world." Christ says: "Be ye therefore perfect, even as your Father which is in heaven is perfect." What do your prayers amount to while you regard iniquity in your hearts? Unless you make a thorough change, you will, not far hence, become weary of reproof, as did the children of Israel; and, like them, you will apostatize from God. Some of you in words acknowledge reproof, but you do not in heart accept it. You go on the same as before, only being less susceptible to the influence of the Spirit of God, becoming more and more blinded, having less wisdom, less self-control, less moral power, and less zeal and relish for religious exercises; and, unless converted, you will finally yield your hold upon God entirely. You have not made decided changes in your life when reproof has come, because you have not seen and realized your defects of character and the great contrast between your life and the life of Christ. It has been your policy to place yourselves in a position where you would not entirely lose the confidence of your brethren.

I was shown that the condition of the —— church is deplorable. Your influence, Brother A B, and that of your wife, has resulted, as you and all may see, in discord and strife, and will prove utter ruin to the church unless you either change your location or become converted. You rust and corrode those connected with you. You have sympathizers, because all do not see you as God sees. Their perception is perverted by your multiplicity of words and fair speeches. This is a sad, discouraging state of things.

I was shown that so far as talk is concerned, A B is qualified to lead the meetings; but when moral fitness is weighed, he is found wanting. His heart is not right with God. When others are placed in a leading position, they have the opposing spirit of himself and his wife to meet. This unsanctified spirit is not manifested openly, but works secretly to hinder, perplex, and discourage those who are trying to do the very best they can. God sees this, and it will in due time receive its just reward. Rule or ruin is the policy of this brother, and his wife is now in no better condition herself. Her senses are perverted. She is not right with God.

Brother A B, a record of the sad history you are making is kept in heaven. In heart you are at war with the testimonies of reproof. The E family have been, and are still, deceived in you. Others are more or less perplexed because you can talk well on present truth. Harmony and unity do not exist in the church at ——. You have not received and acted upon the light given you. Had you heeded the words of Solomon you would not today be found standing in such a slippery path. He says: "Trust in the Lord with all thine heart; and lean not unto thine own understanding." Entire submission to the will and ways of God, united with deep distrust of your own wisdom, would have led you in a safer path.

Your self-confidence has been very great. No sooner has a brother been suggested to lead the meetings, or to take a position of trust in preference to yourself, than you have resolved that he should not succeed if you could help it, and with the might of your perverse will you have set your spirit to oppose.

Your course toward Brother D was abusive. His heart was stirred with the deepest sympathy for you. He had been your friend, but the fact that he disconnected from you was sufficient to create in you a spirit of jealousy which was as cruel as the grave. And this spirit was exercised against a blind man, one who should have had the kindest care and the deepest sympathy from all. It was your perverse and deceptive spirit which led others to sympathize with you rather than with him. When he saw that the clear light of the case could not be brought before the brethren, and was fully convinced that wrong was triumphing over right, his spirit was so wounded that he became desperate. It was then that he let go his hold upon God. A partial shock of paralysis came upon him. He was nearly ruined, mentally and physically. In the church meetings, matters of no special account were talked over, dwelt upon, and made the most of; and wrong, cruelly wrong impressions were made upon the minds of those present.

To thus seek to injure a man who is in full possession of all his faculties is a great sin; but such a course toward a man who is blind, and who should be treated in such a manner as to cause him to feel his loss of sight as little as possible, is a sin of far greater magnitude. Had you been a man of fine feelings, or a Christian, as you profess to be, you could not have abused him as you did. But Brother D has a Friend in heaven who has pleaded his cause for him and strengthened him to grasp God's promises anew. When Brother D was crazed with his great grief and the treatment he had received, he acted like an insane man. This was used against him as evidence that he had a wrong spirit. But the all-seeing Judge weighs motives, and He will reward as the works have been.

You, Brother A B, have been puffed up with vain conceit and have felt yourself competent for any task. You have renounced the Testimonies of the Spirit of God; and if you had your own way, would cast everything in a new mold. How hard it is for you to see things in a just light when duty leads in one direction and inclination in another. Your ideas of the character of Christ, and of the necessary preparation for the life to come, are narrow and perverted.

I was shown that the brothers B and their families are descending lower and lower. "Clouds they are without water, carried about of winds; trees whose fruit withereth, without fruit;" and if they continue in the course they have been pursuing, they will finally be "twice dead, plucked up by the roots." In leaning to their own understanding, they have gone down to the point where they have no practical godliness, no heaven, no God as theirs.

If God's people were all connected with Him, they would discern the limited capacities of these men, their prejudices, envy, jealousy, and self-confidence. The objections which their wicked hearts may raise against the Testimonies of the Spirit of God, will not, in the providence of God, be removed. They may stumble and fall upon questions of their own originating. But God's people should see that their proud hearts have never been humbled, and their high looks have never been brought low. The Bible is clear upon all points which relate to Christian duty. All who do the will of God shall know of the doctrine. But these persons are seeking light from their own tapers and not from the Sun of Righteousness.

No man who does not utter the real sentiment of his heart can be called a truthful man. Falsehood virtually consists in an intention to deceive; and this may be shown by a look or a word. Even facts may be so arranged and stated as to constitute falsehoods. Some are adepts at this business, and they will seek to justify themselves for departing from strict veracity. There are some who, in order to tear down or injure the reputation of another, will, from sheer malice, fabricate falsehoods concerning them. Lies of self-interest are uttered in buying and selling goods, cattle, or any kind of merchandise. Lies of vanity are uttered by men who love to appear what they are not. A story cannot pass through their hands without embellishment. Oh, how much is done in the world which the doers will one day wish to undo! But the record of words and deeds in the books of heaven will tell the sad story of falsehoods spoken and acted.

Falsehood and deception of every cast is sin against the God of truth and verity. The word of God is plain upon these points. Ye shall not "deal falsely, neither lie one to another." "All liars shall have their part in the lake which burneth with fire and brimstone: which is the second death." God is a God of sincerity and truth. The word of God is a book of truth. Jesus is a faithful and true witness. The church is the witness and ground of the truth. All the precepts of the Most High are true and righteous altogether. How, then, must prevarication and any exaggeration or deception appear in His sight? For the falsehood he uttered because he coveted the gifts which the prophet refused, the servant of Elisha was struck with leprosy, which ended only with death.

Even life itself should not be purchased with the price of falsehood. By a word or a nod the martyrs might have denied the truth and saved their lives. By consenting to cast a single grain of incense upon the idol altar they might have been saved from the rack, the scaffold, or the cross. But they refused to be false in word or deed, though life was the boon they would receive by so doing. Imprisonment, torture, and death, with a clear conscience, were welcomed by them, rather than deliverance on condition of deception, falsehood, and apostasy. By fidelity and faith in Christ they earned spotless robes and jeweled crowns. Their lives were ennobled and elevated in the sight of God because they stood firmly for the truth under the most aggravated circumstances.

Men are mortals. They may be sincerely pious and yet have many errors of understanding and many defects of character, but they cannot be Christ's followers and yet be in league with him who "loveth and maketh a lie." Such a life is a fraud, a perpetual falsehood, a fatal deception. It is a close test upon the courage of men and women to be brought to face their own sins and to frankly acknowledge them. To say, "That mistake must be charged to my account," requires a strength of inward principle that the world possesses in but a limited degree. But he who has the courage to say this in sincerity gains a decided victory over self and effectually closes the door against the enemy.

An adherence to the strictest principles of truth will frequently cause present inconvenience and may even involve temporal loss, but it will increase the reward in the future life. Religion does not consist merely in a system of dry doctrines, but in practical faith, which sanctifies the life and corrects the conduct in the family circle and in the church. Many may tithe mint and rue, but neglect the weightier matters, mercy and the love of God. To walk humbly with God is essential to the perfection of Christian character. God requires undeviating principle in the minutest details of the transactions of life. Said Christ: "He that is faithful in that which is least is faithful also in much."

It is neither the magnitude nor the seeming insignificance of a business transaction that makes it fair or unfair, honest or dishonest. By the least departure from rectitude we place ourselves on the enemy's ground, and may go on, step by step, to any length of injustice. A large proportion of the Christian world divorce religion from their business. Thousands of little tricks and petty dishonesties are practiced in dealing with their fellow men, which reveal the true state of the heart, showing its corruption.

You, Brother A B, do not honor the cause of truth. The fountain needs to be cleansed, that the streams may be pure. Your wife is engaged too much in seeking spot and stain upon the characters of her brethren and sisters. While seeking to weed the gardens of her neighbors, she has neglected her own. She must make most diligent efforts in order to build up a spotless character. There is the most fearful danger that she will fail here. If she loses heaven, she loses everything. Both of you should cleanse the soul-temple, which has become terribly polluted. Your minds have become sadly perverted. "The fear of the Lord is the beginning of wisdom." Be very jealous and distrustful of self, but never let your tongues be used to express the jealousy of your hearts in regard to another.

A great work remains for both of you to do, to so humble yourselves before God that He will accept your repentance. Hitherto you have been hearers but not persevering doers of the word. You have admitted again and again that you were wrong, but the carnal mind has remained unchanged. You have made a little change under the influence of feeling, but there has not been a reformation of principle. I saw that the time has now fully come when action must be taken in your cases unless a thorough change is wrought in your lives. The church of God must not compromise with your coarse ways and low standard of Christianity.

One of you brothers is enough in a place. You are continually at strife and war among yourselves, hateful, and hating one another. But although you are a byword to those of the world with whom you associate, yet you are so far distant from God that you cannot see but that you are about right. You each need a nearer view of the character of Christ, that you may discern more clearly what it is to be like Him. Unless you all change your deportment, and entirely overcome your pompous, dictatorial, uncourteous course of conduct, you will dishonor the cause wherever you are; and it would have been better had you never been born.

The time has come for you to turn to the right or to the left. "If the Lord be God, follow Him: but if Baal, then follow him." The deformed character developed in you is a disgrace to the Christian name. No church will prosper under your rule or guidance, for you are not connected with God. You are boastful, proud, and self-important, and would mold others after the same pattern as yourselves.

The church of God has long been burdened with your unchristian acts and deportment. God help you to see and feel that your eternal interests demand an entire transformation. By your example others are led astray from the pure, elevated path of holiness. Truly great men are invariably modest. Humility is a grace which sits naturally upon them as a garment.

Those who have stored their minds with useful knowledge, and who possess genuine attainments and refinement, are the ones who will be most willing to admit the weakness of their own understanding. They are not self-confident nor boastful; but in view of the higher attainments to which they might rise in intellectual greatness, they seem to themselves to have but just begun the ascent. It is the superficial thinker, the one who has but a beginning or smattering of knowledge, who deems himself wise and who takes on disgusting airs of importance.

You might today be men of honor and of trust, but you have all been so well satisfied with yourselves that you have not improved the light and privileges which have been graciously granted you. Your minds have not been expanded by the Christian graces, neither have your affections been sanctified by communion with the Life-giver. There is a littleness, an earthliness, which stamps the outer character and reveals the fact beyond doubt that you have been walking in the way of your own heart and in the sight of your own eyes and that you are filled with your own devices.

When connected with God and sincerely seeking His approval, man becomes elevated, ennobled, and sanctified. The work of elevation is one that man must perform for himself through Jesus Christ. Heaven may give him every advantage so far as temporal and spiritual things are concerned, but it is all in vain unless he is willing to appropriate these blessings and to help himself. His own powers must be put to use, or he will finally be weighed in the balances and pronounced wanting; he will be a failure so far as this life is concerned, and will lose the future life.

All who will with determined effort seek help from above, and subdue and crucify self, may be successful in this world, and may gain the future, immortal life. This world is the field of man's labor. His preparation for the future world depends upon the way he discharges his duties in this world. He is designed of God to be a blessing to society; and he cannot, if he would, live and die to himself. God has bound us together as members of one family, and this relationship everyone is bound to cherish. There are services due to others which we cannot ignore and yet keep the commandments of God. To live, think, and act for self only is to become useless as servants of God. High-sounding titles and great talents are not essential in order to be good citizens or exemplary Christians.

We have in our ranks too many who are restless, talkative, self-commending, and who take the liberty to put themselves forward, having no reverence for age, experience, or office. The church is suffering today for help of an opposite character —modest, quiet, God-fearing men, who will bear disagreeable burdens when laid upon them, not for the name, but to render service to their Master, who died for them. Persons of this character do not think it detracts from their dignity to rise up before the ancient and to treat gray hairs with respect. Our churches need weeding out. Too much self-exaltation and self-sufficiency exists among the members.

Those who fear and reverence God, He will delight to honor. Man may be so elevated as to form the connecting link between heaven and earth. He came from the hand of his Creator with a symmetrical character, endowed with such capacities for improvement that, combining divine influence with human effort, he might elevate himself almost to an angel's sphere. Yet, when thus elevated, he will be unconscious of his goodness and greatness.

God has given man intellectual faculties capable of the highest cultivation. Had the Brethren B seen the natural coarseness and roughness of their characters, and with assiduous care cultivated and trained the mind, strengthening their weak points of character and overcoming their glaring defects, some of them would have been accepted as Christ's messengers. But as they now are, God cannot accept any one of them as His representative. They have not sufficiently realized the need of improvement to cause them to seek for it. Their minds have not been trained by study, observation, reflection, and a constant effort to thoroughly discipline themselves for the duties of life. The means of improvement are within the reach of all. None are so poor or so busy but that with Jesus to help them they can make improvements in their life and character.

30. Self-Caring Ministers

Brother and Sister F:

I have been shown the great mercy and infinite love of God in giving you another trial. There will be a positive necessity of your holding fast to the mighty Healer, that you may have physical and spiritual strength. You have poor health, but you are in danger of thinking that you are in a worse condition than you really are. You have not had power of endurance, because you have not cherished a patient, hopeful, courageous spirit. You yield to infirmities instead of rising above them.

Temptations will assail you on the right hand and on the left, but by patient continuance in well-doing you may overcome the defects in your characters. I was shown that your feet had indeed taken hold on perdition, but God did not wholly forsake either of you. His matchless mercy in giving you another opportunity to prove your loyalty to Him calls upon you to walk with great humility and to guard self. You have petted and indulged yourselves so much that you need now to work in an opposite direction.

You, Brother F, have been very selfish, and this has been contemptible in the sight of God. You and your wife have stumbled again and again over this evil. Your powers have been greatly dwarfed by self-gratification and self-indulgence. Neither of you is deficient in natural reason and judgment; but you have followed inclination rather than the path of duty, and have failed to repress the wrong traits of character and to strengthen weak moral power.

Brother F, you are naturally an impatient, fretful, exacting man at home; and after a short acquaintance you show this out in new places. You frequently talk in an impatient, overbearing manner. This must all be repented of. You may now begin anew. God has in His boundless mercy given you another chance. Your wife has much in herself to contend against, and you should be on your guard that you do not throw her upon Satan's ground. Fretting, faultfinding, and making strong statements must be given up. What time have you set to gain the victory over your perverse will and the defects in your character? With the advancement you now make, your probation may close before you have made the determined efforts essential to give you the victory over self. You will, in the providence of God, be placed in positions where your peculiarities, if existing, will be tried and revealed. You neither see nor realize the effect of your thoughtless, impatient, complaining, whining words.

You and your wife have another golden opportunity to suffer for Christ's sake. If you do this complainingly you will have no reward; if willingly, gladly, having the same spirit which Peter possessed after his apostasy, you will be victors. He felt a sense of his cowardly denial of Christ throughout his lifetime; and when called to suffer martyrdom for his faith, this humiliating fact was ever before him, and he begged that he might not be crucified in the exact manner in which his Lord suffered, fearing that it would be too great an honor after his apostasy. His request was that he might be crucified with his head downward. What a sense did Peter have of his sin in denying his Lord! What a conversion he experienced! His life ever after was a life of repentance and humiliation.

You may have cause to tremble when you see God through His law. When Moses thus saw the majesty of God, he exclaimed: "I exceedingly fear and quake." The law pronounced death upon the transgressor; then the atoning sacrifice was presented before Moses. The cleansing blood of Christ was revealed to purify the sinner, and his fears were swept away, as the morning fog before the beams of the rising sun. Thus he saw it might be with the sinner.

Through repentance toward God and faith toward our Lord Jesus Christ, pardon is written, and the Sun of Righteousness sheds His bright, healing beams upon him, dispelling the doubt and fear that befog the soul. Moses came down from the mount where he had been in converse with God, his face shining with a heavenly luster which was reflected upon the people. He appeared to them like an angel direct from glory. That divine brightness was painful to those sinners; they fled from Moses and begged that the bright glory might be covered from their sight lest it slay them if they came near him.

Moses had been a student. He was well educated in all the learning of the Egyptians, but this was not the only qualification which he needed to prepare him for his work. He was, in the providence of God, to learn patience, to temper his passions. In a school of self-denial and hardships he was to receive an education which would be of the utmost importance to him. These trials would prepare him to exercise a fatherly care over all who needed his help.

No knowledge, no study, no eloquence, could be a substitute for this experience in trials to one who was to watch for souls as they that must give an account. In doing the work of a humble shepherd, in being forgetful of self and interested for the flock given to his charge, he was to become fitted for the most exalted work ever entrusted to mortals, that of being a shepherd of the sheep of the Lord's pasture. Those who fear God in the world must be connected with Him. Christ is the most perfect educator the world ever knew. To receive wisdom and knowledge from Him was more valuable to Moses than all the learning of the Egyptians.

Brother and Sister F, I entreat you to be in earnest and come to God through Jesus Christ. "Be not deceived; God is not mocked: for whatsoever a man soweth, that shall he also reap." He who spends his talents and his means in self-indulgence, in gratification of the lower passions, will reap corruption. His harvest is sure. His mind will lose its susceptibility and power. His intellect will be shattered and his life shortened. God requires you to make more thorough efforts to subdue and control self. I was shown that God and angels are ready and waiting to help you in this important work. If you delay, if you are even dilatory, it may be too late. Your probation is lengthened, your character is now forming, and soon, my dear brother and sister, it will be stereotyped forever. Halfway work with you will not advance you one step toward heaven. Indecision soon becomes decision in the wrong direction.

Many decide to serve themselves and Satan by not making determined efforts to overcome their defects of character. While many are petting sinful propensities, expecting to be overcomers sometime, they are deciding for perdition. Brother and Sister F, in the name of Jesus Christ you may be victorious even now "in this thy day." Do not plan and study for self. You cannot be wholly the Lord's while encouraging any degree of selfishness. Such great love as the Redeemer has shown you should be received with great humility and continual rejoicing. In order to be happy, you must control your thoughts and words. It will require a masterly effort on your part; nevertheless it must be done if you are to be the acknowledged children of God. Be not weary in your efforts. Satan is battling for your souls, and he must be disappointed.

When you, Brother F, first commence to labor in a place, you generally have the confidence of the people; but after a more thorough acquaintance your defects of character become so apparent that many lose confidence in your piety. Reflections are thus cast upon all the ministers of the denomination. A short stay in a place would not injure your reputation. While engaged in earnest labor, pressed by opposing influences, your mind is absorbed in the work in which you are engaged, and you have neither time nor opportunity to think and reflect upon yourself.

But when the work is over, and you begin to think upon self, as it is natural for you to do, you pet yourself, become babyish, sharp, and cross in temper, and thus greatly mar the work of God. You manifest the same spirit in the church, and thus your influence is greatly injured in the community, in some cases beyond remedy. You have frequently exhibited childish contention, even while laboring to convert souls to the truth; and the impressions made have been terrible upon those who were witnesses. Now, one of two things must be done; you must either be a consecrated man at home, in your family, and in the church, at all times tender and patient, or you must not settle down in a church; for your defects will be made apparent, and the Redeemer you profess to love and serve will be dishonored.

The faith of Moses led him to look at the things which are unseen, which are eternal. He left the splendid attractions of court life because sin was there. He gave up present and seeming good that flattered only to ruin and destroy. The real attractions, the eternal, were of value to him. The sacrifices made by Moses were really no sacrifices. With him it was letting go a present, apparent, flattering good for a sure, high, immortal good.

Moses endured the reproach of Christ, considering reproach greater riches than all the treasures of Egypt. He believed what God had said and was not influenced to swerve from his integrity by any of the world's reproaches. He walked the earth as God's free man. He had the love of Christ in his soul, which not only made him a man of dignity, but added the luster of the true Christian graces to the dignity of the man. Moses walked a rough and perilous path, but he looked to the things unseen and faltered not. The recompense of reward was attractive to him, and it may be also to us. He was familiar with God.

The work is before you to improve the remnant of your life in reforming and elevating the character. A new life begins in the renewed soul. Christ is the indwelling Saviour. That which may be regarded as hard to give up must be yielded. The overbearing, dictatorial word must be left unspoken; then a precious victory will be gained. True happiness will be the result of every self-denial, every crucifixion of self. One victory won, the next is more easily gained. Had Moses neglected the opportunities and privileges granted him of God, he would have neglected the light from heaven and would have been a disappointed, miserable man.

Sin is from beneath; and when it is indulged, Satan is enshrined in the soul, there to kindle the very fires of hell. God has not given His law to prevent the salvation of souls, but He wants all to be saved. Man has light and opportunities, and if he will improve them he may overcome. You may show by your life the power of the grace of God in overcoming. Satan is trying to set up his throne in the soul-temple. When he reigns he makes himself heard and felt in angry passions, in words of bitterness that grieve and wound; but as light has no communion with darkness, and Christ no union with Belial, the man must be wholly for one or the other. In yielding to self-indulgence, avarice, deception, fraud, or sin of any kind, he encourages the principles of Satan in his soul and closes the door of heaven to himself. Because of sin, Satan was thrust out of heaven; and no man indulging and fostering sin can go to heaven, for then Satan would again have a foothold there.

When a man is earnestly engaged day by day in overcoming the defects in his character, he is cherishing Christ in his soul-temple; the light of Christ is in him. Under the bright beams of the light of Christ's countenance his entire being becomes elevated and ennobled. He has the peace of heaven in his soul. Many give loose rein to passion, avarice, selfishness, and deception, and all the time excuse themselves and lay the blame on the circumstances which brought around the trial to themselves. This has been your case. God permitted your surroundings to exist to develop character. But you could have made your surroundings; for by resisting or enduring temptation, circumstances are controlled by the might of the will in the name of Jesus.

This is overcoming as Christ overcame. "This is the victory that overcometh the world, even our faith."

Brother F, God is merciful to you. Your life has been a mistake, nothing like what it might and should have been. There has not been in you genuine manliness, true elevation and purity of feeling. You have not had proper self-respect, and therefore have not had proper respect for others. You have not magnified Christ and the power of His grace. You have needed guardians all the way along through life.

The same frivolity and fickleness, the same inconsideration and lack of self-control, the same selfishness and impatience, which were seen in your conduct at an early period of your life, are developed in a marked manner now that you are past the meridian. This need not have been, had you put away childish feelings and childish temper, and put on the firmness of the man. You have favored yourself altogether to your injury. Your pains and infirmities have been magnified. You look at them and talk complainingly of them, but do not look away to Jesus. Think how little you suffer, how little you endure, in comparison with the sufferings of Christ; and He was sinless—the Just suffering for the unjust.

A good tree will not produce corrupt fruit. Good conversation will accompany a good conscience, as surely as good fruit will be produced by a good tree. If a man is unkind and churlish in his family and to others connected with him, no one need to inquire how he will manage in the church. He will exhibit the same petulant, overbearing disposition which he shows at home. No man can have the spirit and the mind of Christ without being rendered better by it in all the relations and duties of life. Murmuring, complaining, and fretful passion are not the fruit of good principles. You will need to be instant in prayer, because you have not strengthened the high, noble, moral traits of character. This is to be done now by you. The work will be difficult, but it is positively essential.

While in Texas you were hopeless and felt yourself forsaken of God and man; but now that you again make a start, let the work of reformation be thorough, your repentance such as needeth not to be repented of. The best of your days, so far as health and vigor are concerned, are in the past; but with proper habits, a cheerful mind, and a clear conscience in reference to your present deportment, you may turn your defeat into victory. You have no time to lose. Your wife can help you in all your efforts in the harvest field. If she is sanctified through the truth she can be a blessing to you and to the cause of God by conversing with others and being social.

Many falter and fall because of the indulgence of a perverse temper. Alexander and Caesar found it much easier to subdue a kingdom than to rule their own spirits. After conquering nations, the world's so-called great men fell, one of them through the indulgence of appetite, a victim of intemperance, the other through presumption and mad ambition.

God calls upon you to yield pride and stubbornness, and to let His peace rule in your hearts. A meek and quiet spirit must be cherished. Carry Christ's meekness with you in all your labors. An excited temper and cutting censure will not impress the people or gain their sympathy. If we have the truth, we can afford to be calm and unexcited. Our language should be modest and elevated. The spirit you have cherished within has left its impression upon the countenance. Christ, enthroned in the soul-temple, will efface that fretful, peevish, unhappy look; and as the cloud of witnesses look upon a man reflecting the image of Christ, they will realize that he is surrounded by a pleasant atmosphere. The world will see that amid storms of abuse he stands unmoved, like the lofty cedar. That man is one of God's heroes. He has overcome himself.

The largest share of the annoyances of life, its daily corroding cares, its heartaches, its irritation, is the result of a temper uncontrolled. The harmony of the domestic circle is often broken by a hasty word and abusive language. How much better were it left unsaid. One smile of pleasure, one peaceful, approving word spoken in the spirit of meekness, would be a power to soothe, to comfort, and to bless. The government of self is the best government in the world. By putting on the ornament of a meek and quiet spirit, ninety-nine out of a hundred of the troubles which so terribly embitter life might be saved. Many excuse their hasty words and passionate tempers by saying: "I am sensitive; I have a hasty temper." This will never heal the wounds made by hasty, passionate words. Some, indeed, are naturally more passionate than others; but this spirit can never harmonize with the Spirit of God. The natural man must die, and the new man,

Christ Jesus, take possession of the soul, so that the follower of Jesus may say in verity and truth: "I live; yet not I, but Christ liveth in me."

Self is difficult to conquer. Human depravity in every form is not easily brought into subjection to the Spirit of Christ. But all should be impressed with the fact that unless this victory is gained through Christ, there is no hope for them. The victory can be gained; for nothing is impossible with God. By His assisting grace, all evil temper, all human depravity, may be overcome. Every Christian must learn of Christ, "who, when He was reviled, reviled not again."

The work before you is no light task, no child's play. You have failed to go forward to perfection, but now you may begin anew. You may show by your life what the power and grace of God can do in transforming the natural man into a spiritual man in Christ Jesus. You may be overcomers if you will, in the name of Christ, take hold of the work decidedly.

There is one solemn statement that I wish you to write upon your hearts: When persons have yielded to Satan's devices, and have thus placed themselves upon his ground, if they would then recover themselves from his snares through the mercy of God, they must come into close connection with Him, daily crucify self, and be thoroughly transformed, in order to gain the victory and win eternal life. You both went a long distance from God. You have brought great reproach upon His cause. Now you must be most zealously in earnest to overcome every defect in your characters and lead a life of humiliation and trusting, pleading prayer; in faith ask God for Christ's sake to cancel the past, so that the seeds of evil that you have sown may not be extended and be treasured up as wrath against the day of wrath.

Now to go on in the same course, fractious in spirit, petting yourselves, babyishly talking of your infirmities, expatiating upon your feelings, and dwelling upon the dark side, will make you weak and spiritless. It was these things that made you easy subjects to Satan's devices. If you begin the same course you were pursuing when your feet began to slip, your cases will be hopeless. If you break off your sins by repentance, and avoid the fearful consequences by taking refuge in a Saviour's intercession, pleading with God earnestly for His Spirit that you may be led and taught and quickened, you may reap life everlasting. Do not fail to unitedly, humbly, cast your helpless souls in faith upon the merits of Christ.

31. Uprightness in Deal

Brother G:

In my last vision your case was shown me. I saw that you love the truth which you profess, but you are not sanctified through it. Your affections have been divided between the service of God and of mammon. This division of affection stands as a barrier in the way of your being a missionary for God. While professedly serving the cause of God, self-interest has marred your work and greatly injured your influence. God could not work with you, because your heart was not right with Him.

So far as words go, you have been deeply interested in the truth; but when it comes to showing your faith by works, there has been a great lack. You have not correctly represented our faith. You have injured the cause of God by your manifest love of gain; and your love to trade and bicker has not been for your good, nor for the spiritual health of those with whom you are brought in contact. You are a sharp man in trade, and you often overreach. You have peculiar tact for looking out for the best end of the bargain, watching for your own good rather than that of others. If a man would cheat himself, and you were to be advantaged thereby, you have let him do it. This is not following the golden rule, doing unto others as you would wish them to do by you.

While engaged in the missionary work, you have at the same time manifested your scheming propensities in buying and selling. This makes a poor combination. You should be one thing or the other. "If the Lord be God, follow Him: but if Baal, then follow him." "Choose you this day whom ye will serve." God will not accept your labors in the tract and missionary work while you are scheming to advantage yourself. You are in danger of counting gain as godliness. The tempter will present flattering inducements before you to fascinate you and allure you on to indulge a spirit of scheming which will kill your spirituality.

The world, angels, and men look upon you as a sharper, as a man who is studying his own interest and securing advantages to himself without looking carefully and conscientiously after the interest of those with whom he deals. In your business life there is a vein of dishonesty that tarnishes the soul and dwarfs religious experience and growth in grace. You are watching with keen business eye the best chance to secure a bargain. This scheming propensity has become second nature with you, and you do not see and realize the evil of encouraging it.

Business which you may engage in fairly and squarely, advantaging others as well as yourself, would be all right so far as dealing honorably is concerned; but the Lord would have accepted your service and used your powers, your keen perceptions, in securing the salvation of souls, had you been sanctified through the truth. The desire of the eye in the love of gain has warred against the Spirit. The habits and culture of years have left their deforming impress upon your character, and have been disqualifying you for God's work. You have a constant, longing desire to traffic. If sanctified to the service of God, this would make you an earnest, persevering laborer for the Master; but, abused as it has been, it has endangered your own soul, and others also are in danger of being lost through your influence.

At times reason and conscience remonstrate, and you feel rebuked because of your course; your soul longs after holiness and the surety of heaven; the din of the world looks repulsive to you, and you put it aside and cherish the Spirit of God. Then, again, your worldly propensity comes in, and overrules everything. You will surely have to meet the assaults of Satan, and you should prepare for them by firmly resisting your inclination.

While the apostle Paul was immured in prison walls that were reeking with dampness, himself a sufferer from infirmities, he greatly desired to see Timothy, his son in the gospel, and leave him his dying charge. He had no hope of release from his bondage until his life should be yielded up. The wicked Nero's heart was thoroughly satanic, and at a word or a nod from him the apostle's life would be cut short. Paul urged the immediate presence of Timothy, and yet feared he would not come soon enough to receive the last testimony from his lips. He therefore repeated the words he would speak to Timothy, to one of his fellow laborers, who was allowed to be his companion in bonds. This faithful attendant wrote the dying charge of Paul, a small portion of which we here quote:

"They that will be rich fall into temptation and a snare, and into many foolish and hurtful lusts, which drown men in destruction and perdition. For the love of money is the root of all evil: which while some coveted after, they have erred from the faith, and pierced themselves through with many sorrows. But thou, O man of God, flee these things; and follow after righteousness, godliness, faith, love, patience, meekness. Fight the good fight of faith, lay hold on eternal life, whereunto thou art also called, and hast professed a good profession before many witnesses." "Charge them that are rich in this world, that they be not high-minded, nor trust in uncertain riches, but in the living God, who giveth us richly all things to enjoy; that they do good, that they be rich in good works, ready to distribute, willing to communicate; laying up in store for themselves a good foundation against the time to come, that they may lay hold on eternal life."

"And the things that thou hast heard of me among many witnesses, the same commit thou to faithful men, who shall be able to teach others also. Thou therefore endure hardness as a good soldier of Jesus Christ. No man that warreth entangleth himself with the affairs of this life; that he may please him who hath chosen him to be a soldier. And if a man also strive for masteries, yet is he not crowned, except he strive lawfully." A man may be avaricious, and yet excuse himself by saying that he is working for the cause of God; but he obtains no reward, for God does not want money that is obtained by overreaching or by any semblance of dishonesty.

Paul further urges Timothy: "Do thy diligence to come shortly unto me: for Demas hath forsaken me, having loved this present world, and is departed unto Thessalonica." These words, dictated by Paul just prior to his death, were written by Luke for our profit and warning.

Christ, in teaching His disciples, said: "I am the True Vine, and My Father is the Husbandman. Every branch in Me that beareth not fruit He taketh away: and every branch that beareth fruit, He purgeth it [pruneth it], that it may bring forth more fruit." He who is united to Christ, partaking of the sap and nourishment of the Vine, will work the works of Christ. The love of Christ must be in him or he cannot be in the Vine. Supreme love to God, and love to your neighbor equal to that which you bear to yourself, is the basis of true religion.

Christ inquires of everyone professing His name: "Lovest thou Me?" If you love Jesus you will love the souls for whom He died. A man may not bear the most pleasant exterior, he may be deficient in many respects; but if he has a reputation for straightforward honesty, he will gain the confidence of others. The love of truth, the dependence and confidence which men can place in him, will remove or overbear objectionable features in his character. Trustworthiness in your place and calling, a willingness to deny self for the purpose of benefiting others, will bring peace of mind and the favor of God.

Those who will walk closely in the footsteps of their self-sacrificing, self-denying Redeemer will have the mind of Christ reflected in their minds. Purity and the love of Christ will shine forth in their daily lives and characters, while meekness and truth will guide their way. Every fruitful branch is pruned, that it may bring forth more fruit. Even fruitful branches may display too much foliage and appear what they really are not. The followers of Christ may be doing some work for the Master and yet not be doing half what they might do. He then prunes them, because worldliness, self-indulgence, and pride are cropping out in their lives. Husbandmen clip off the surplus tendrils of the vines that are grasping the rubbish of earth, thus making them more fruitful. These hindering causes must be removed and the defective overgrowth cut away, to give room for the healing beams of the Sun of Righteousness.

God purposed through Christ that fallen man should have another trial. Many misunderstand the object for which they were created. It was to bless humanity and glorify God, rather than to enjoy and glorify self. God is constantly pruning His people, cutting off profuse, spreading branches, that they may bear fruit to His glory and not produce leaves only. God prunes us with sorrow, with disappointment and affliction, that the outgrowth of strong, perverse traits of character may be weakened and that the better traits may have a chance to develop. Idols must be given up, the conscience must become more tender, the meditations of the heart must be spiritual, and the entire character must become symmetrical. Those who really desire to glorify God will be thankful for the exposure of every idol and every sin, that they may see these evils and put them away; but the divided heart will plead for indulgence rather than denial.

The apparently dry branch, by being connected with the living vine, becomes a part of it. Fiber by fiber, and vein by vein, it adheres to the vine till it derives its life and nourishment from the parent stock. The graft buds, blossoms, and produces fruit. The soul, dead in trespasses and sins, must experience a similar process in order to be reconciled to God and to become a partaker of Christ's life and joy. As the graft receives life when united to the vine, so the sinner partakes of the divine nature when connected with Christ. Finite man is united with the infinite God. When thus united, the words of Christ abide in us, and we are not actuated by a spasmodic feeling, but by a living, abiding principle. The words of Christ must be meditated upon and cherished and enshrined in the heart. They should not be repeated, parrot-like, finding no place in the memory and having no influence over the heart and life.

As the branch must abide in the vine to obtain the vital sap which causes it to flourish, so those who love God and keep all His sayings must abide in His love. Without Christ we cannot subdue a single sin or overcome the smallest temptation. Many need the Spirit of Christ and His power to enlighten their understanding, as much as blind Bartimaeus needed his natural sight. "As the branch cannot bear fruit of itself, except it abide in the vine; no more can ye, except ye abide in Me." All who are really in Christ will experience the benefit of this union. The Father accepts them in the Beloved, and they become objects of His solicitude and tender, loving care. This connection with Christ will result in the purification of the heart and in a circumspect life and faultless character. The fruit borne upon the Christian tree is "love, joy, peace, long-suffering, gentleness, goodness, faith, meekness, temperance."

My brother, you need a close connection with God. You have traits of character for which you are responsible. Your powers have been put to a wrong use. God cannot approve your course. Your standard is that of the worldling, and not that which Christ has given us in His life. You have looked through the eyes of the world and discerned with their unsanctified judgment. Your soul must be cleansed from the polluting influence of the world. You have repeatedly deviated from strict integrity for that which you flattered yourself was gain, but which was really loss. Every act of overreaching in deal will detract from your reward in heaven, should you gain that home. Every man will receive his reward as his works have been.

You have no time to lose, but should make diligent efforts to overcome the marked traits in your character, which, if indulged, will close the doors of glory against you. You cannot afford to lose heaven. You now need to make a decided change in your words and deeds, to overcome your avaricious spirit, and to turn your thoughts into the channel of sanctified truth. In short, you need to be transformed. Then God will accept your labors in His cause. You should be a man of such undeviating veracity that the love of gain will not seduce you and no temptation overcome you. The Lord requires of all who profess His name a strict adherence to truth. This will be as salt which has not lost its savor, as a light amid the moral darkness and deception of the world.

"Ye are the light of the world," says Christ. Those who are truly connected with God, by reflecting the light of heaven will have a saving power in the church and also in the world; for the perfume of good deeds and truthful acts will make them of good repute, even among those who are not of our faith. Those who fear God will respect and honor such a character; and even the enemies of our faith, as they see the spirit and life of Christ exhibited in their daily works, will glorify God, the source of their strength and honor.

You, my brother, should have been truly converted to the truth and wholly given to the work of God years ago. Precious years, which should have been rich with experience in the things of God and in practical labor in His cause, have been lost. Whereas you should now be able to teach others, you have failed to come to the full knowledge of the truth yourself. You ought now to have an experimental knowledge of the truth and be qualified to bear the message of warning to the world. Your services have been nearly lost to the cause of God because your mind has been divided; you have been planning and scheming, buying and selling, serving tables.

The mildew of the world has clouded your perception and perverted your intellect, so that your feeble efforts have not been acceptable offerings to God. Had you divorced yourself from your speculating propensities, and worked in the opposite direction, you would now be enriched with divine knowledge and would be a gainer in spiritual things generally, whereas you have been losing spiritual power and dwarfing your religious experience.

To have fellowship with the Father and His Son Jesus Christ is to be ennobled and elevated, and made a partaker of joys unspeakable and full of glory. Food, clothing, station, and wealth may have their value; but to have a connection with God and to be a partaker of His divine nature is of priceless value. Our lives should be hid with Christ in God; and although it "doth not yet appear what we shall be," "when Christ, who is our life, shall appear," "we shall be like Him; for we shall see Him as He is." The princely dignity of the

Christian character will shine forth as the sun, and the beams of light from the face of Christ will be reflected upon those who have purified themselves even as He is pure. The privilege of becoming sons of God is cheaply purchased, even at the sacrifice of everything we possess, be it life itself.

My dear brother, you should set your face to be a man after God's own heart. What others may venture to do or say that is not strictly in accordance with the Christian standard should be no excuse for you. You must stand before the Judge of all the earth, not to answer for another, but for yourself. We have an individual responsibility, and no man's defects of character will be the least excuse for our guilt; for Christ has given us in His character a perfect pattern, a faultless life.

The most persistent attacks of the enemy of souls are made upon the truth we profess, and any deviation from the right reflects dishonor upon it. Our chief danger is in having the mind diverted from Christ. The name of Jesus has power to drive back the temptations of Satan and lift up for us a standard against him. So long as the soul rests with unshaken confidence in the virtue and power of the atonement, it will stand firm as a rock to principle, and all the powers of Satan and his angels cannot sway it from its integrity. The truth as it is in Jesus is a wall of fire around the soul that clings to Him. Temptations will pour in upon us, for by them we are to be tried during our probation upon earth. This is the proving of God, a revelation of our own hearts. There is no sin in having temptations; but sin comes in when temptation is yielded to.

If your aptness and skill had been as much exercised in saving souls, and in disseminating the truth to those who are in darkness, as it has been to get gain and to increase your earthly possessions, you would have many stars in the crown of your rejoicing in the kingdom of glory. There are but few who are as faithful in the service of God as they are in serving their own temporal interests. A resolute purpose is sure to accomplish the desired end. Many do not feel that it is essential to be as discriminating, apt, and accomplished in the work of God as in their own temporal business. The mind and heart of those who profess to believe the truth should be elevated, refined, ennobled, and spiritualized. The work of educating the mind for this great and important matter is fearfully neglected. The work of God is done negligently, slothfully, and in a most bungling manner, because so often left to the caprice of feeling, rather than to sanctified principle and holy purpose.

There is the greatest necessity that men and women who have a knowledge of the will of God should learn to become successful workers in His cause. They should be persons of polish, of understanding, not having the deceptive outside gloss and simpering affectation of the worldling, but that refinement and true courteousness which savors of heaven, and which every Christian will have if he is a partaker of the divine nature. The lack of true dignity and Christian refinement in the ranks of Sabbathkeepers is against us as a people and makes the truth which we profess unsavory. The work of educating the mind and manners may be carried forward to perfection. If those who profess the truth do not now improve their privileges and opportunities to grow up to the full stature of men and women in Christ Jesus, they will be no honor to the cause of truth, no honor to Christ.

If you, my brother, had studied the Holy Scriptures as faithfully as you have watched to get gain, you would now be an able man in the word of God and able also to teach others. It is your own fault that you are not qualified to teach the truth to others. You have not been cultivating that set of faculties which will make you an intelligent, successful, spiritual worker for your Master. Such traits of character as acquisitiveness and shrewdness in worldly dealing have been exercised so much that your mind has been largely developed in the direction of buying and selling, and getting the best end of the bargain.

Instead of establishing yourself in the confidence of your brethren and sisters and friends as a man who possesses true nobility of character, elevating you above all smallness and avariciousness, you make them afraid of you. Your religious faith has been used to secure the confidence of your brethren that you might practice your sharp dealing and make a saving. This has been done so much by you that it has become second nature, and you do not realize how your course appears to others. True godliness must mark all your future life and course of action if you would counteract the influence you have exerted to scatter from Christ and the truth.

Your relation to God and your fellow men demands a change in your life. In the Sermon on the Mount the injunction of the world's redeemer was: "All things whatsoever ye would that men should do to you, do ye even so to them:

for this is the law and the prophets." These words are of the highest value to us, a golden rule given us by which to measure our conduct. This is the true rule of honesty. Very much is comprehended in these words. We are here required to deal with our neighbors as we would wish them to deal with us were we in their circumstances.

Plano, Texas
Nov. 24, 1878

32. Religion in the Daily Life

Brother H:

I was shown that you really love the truth, but that you are not sanctified through it. You have a great work before you to do. "Every man that hath this hope in Him purifieth himself, even as He is pure." You have this work to do, and you have no time to lose. I was shown that your life has been a stormy one. You have not been right yourself; but you have been deeply wronged, and your motives have been misjudged. But your disappointments and pecuniary losses have, in the providence of God, been overruled for your good.

It has been difficult for you to feel that your heavenly Father is still your kind benefactor. Your troubles and perplexities have had a tendency to discourage, and you have felt that death would be preferable to life. But at a certain time, could your eyes have been opened, you would have seen angels of God seeking to save you from yourself. The angels of God led you where you could receive the truth and plant your feet upon a foundation that would be more firm than the everlasting hills. Here you saw light and cherished it. New faith, new life, sprang up in your pathway. God in His providence connected you with His work in the office of the Pacific Press. He has been at work for you, and you should see His guiding hand.

Sorrow has been your portion; but you have brought much of it upon yourself because you have not had self-control. You have been very severe at times. You have a quick temper, which must be overcome. In your life you have been in danger, either of indulging in self-confidence or else of throwing yourself away and becoming despondent. A continual dependence upon the word and providence of God will qualify you to exert your powers wholly for your Redeemer, who has called you, saying: "Follow Me." You should cultivate a spirit of entire submission to the will of God, earnestly, humbly seeking to know His ways and to follow the leadings of His Spirit. You must not lean to your own understanding. You should have deep distrust of your own wisdom and supposed prudence. Your condition demands these cautions. It is unsafe for man to confide in his own judgment. He has limited capacities at best, and many have received, as their birthright, both strong and weak points of character, which are positive defects. These peculiarities color the entire life.

The wisdom which God gives will lead men to self-examination. The truth will convict them of their errors and existing wrongs. The heart must be open to see, realize, and acknowledge these wrongs, and then, through the help of Jesus, each must earnestly engage in the work of overcoming them. The knowledge gained by the wise of the world, however diligent they may be in acquiring it, is, after all, limited and comparatively inferior. But few comprehend the ways and works of God in the mysteries of His providence. They advance a few steps, and then are unable to touch bottom or shore. It is the superficial thinker who deems himself wise. Men of solid worth, of high attainments, are the most ready to admit the weakness of their own understanding. God wants everyone who claims to be His disciple to be a learner, to be more inclined to learn than to teach.

How many men in this age of the world fail to go deep enough. They only skim the surface. They will not think closely enough to see difficulties and grapple with them, and will not examine every important subject which comes before them with thoughtful, prayerful study and with sufficient caution and interest to see the real point at issue. They talk of matters which they have not fully and carefully weighed. Frequently persons of mind and candor have opinions of their own which need to be firmly resisted, or these of less mental strength will be in danger of being misled. Through the mental bias, habits are formed, and customs, feelings, and wishes have a greater or less influence. Sometimes a course of conduct is pursued every day, and persisted in, because it is a habit, and not because the judgment approves. In these cases, feeling, rather than duty, bears sway.

If we could understand our own weakness, and see the sharp traits in our character which need repressing, we should see so much to do for ourselves that we would humble our hearts under the mighty hand of God. Hanging our helpless souls upon Christ, we should supplement our ignorance with His wisdom, our weakness with His strength, our frailty with His enduring might, and, connected with God, we should indeed be lights in the world.

Dear brother, God loves you, and is very patient toward you, notwithstanding your many errors and mistakes. In view of the tender, pitying love of God exercised in your behalf, should you not be more kind, forbearing, patient, and forgiving to your children? Your harshness and severity is weaning their hearts from you. You cannot give them lessons in regard to patience, forbearance, long-suffering, and gentleness, when you are overbearing and manifest temper in dealing with them. They have the stamp of character which their parents have given them; and if you wish to counsel and direct them, and turn them from following any wrong course, the object cannot be gained by harshness and that which looks to them like tyranny.

When in the fear of God you can advise and counsel them with all the solicitude and tender love which a father should manifest toward an erring child, then you will have demonstrated to them that there is power in the truth to transform those who receive it. When your children do not act according to your ideas, instead of manifesting sorrow for their wrongs, and earnestly pleading with and praying for them, you fly into a passion and pursue a course that will do them no good, but will only wean their affections and finally separate them from you.

Your youngest son is perverse; he does not do right. His heart is in rebellion against God and the truth. He is affected by influences which only make him coarse, rough, and uncourteous. He is a trial to you, and, unless converted, he will be a great tax upon your patience. But harshness and overbearing severity will not reform him. You must seek to do what you can for him in the spirit of Christ, not in your own spirit, not under the influence of passion. You must control yourself in the management of your children. You must remember that Justice has a twin sister, Mercy. When you would exercise justice, show mercy, tenderness, and love, and you will not labor in vain.

Your son has a perverse will, and he needs the most judicious discipline. Consider what have been your children's surroundings, how unfavorable to the formation of good characters. They need pity and love. The youngest is now in the most critical period of his life. The intellect is now taking shape; the affections are receiving their impress. The whole future career of this young man is being determined by the course he now pursues. He is entering upon the path which leads to virtue, or that which leads to vice.

I appeal to the young man to fill his mind with images of truth and purity. It will be no advantage to him to indulge in sin. He may flatter himself that it is very pleasant to sin and to have his own way; but it is a fearful way after all. If he loves the society of those who love sin and love to do evil, his thoughts will run in a low channel, and he will see nothing attractive in purity and holiness. But could he see the end of the transgressor, that the wages of sin is death, he would be overcome with alarm and would cry out: "O my Father, be Thou the guide of my youth."

His success in this life depends very much upon the course he now pursues. The responsibilities of life must be borne by him. He has not been a promising youth. He has been impatient and is wanting in self-control. This is the seed his father is sowing, which will produce a harvest for the sower to reap. "Whatsoever a man soweth, that shall he also reap." With what care should we cast in the seed, knowing that we must reap as we have sown. Jesus still loves this young man. He died for him and invites him to come to His arms and find in Him peace and happiness, quiet and rest. This youth is forming associations which will mold his whole life. He should connect with God and without delay give to Him his unreserved affections. He should not hesitate. Satan will make his fiercest assaults upon him, but he must not be overcome by temptation.

I have been shown the dangers of youth. Their hearts are full of high anticipations, and they see the downward road strewn with tempting pleasures which look very inviting; but death is there. The narrow path to life may appear to them to be destitute of attractions, a path of thorns and briers, but it is not. It is the path which requires a denial of sinful pleasures; it is a narrow path, cast up for the ransomed of the Lord to walk in. None can walk this path and carry with them their burdens of pride, self-will, deceit, falsehood, dishonesty, passion, and the carnal lusts. The path is so narrow that these things will have to be left behind by those who walk in it, but the broad road is wide enough for sinners to travel it with all their sinful propensities.

Young man, if you reject Satan with all his temptations you may walk in the footsteps of your Redeemer and have the peace of heaven, the joys of Christ. You cannot be happy in the indulgence of sin. You may flatter yourself that you are happy, but real happiness you cannot know. The character is becoming deformed by the indulgence of sin. Danger is encountered at every downward step, and those who could help the youth do not see or realize it. The kind and tender interest which should be taken in the young is not manifested. Many might be kept from sinful influences if they were surrounded with good associations and had words of kindness and love spoken to them.

My dear brother, I hope you will not become discouraged because your feelings so often master you when your way or will is crossed. Never despond. Flee to the Stronghold. Watch and pray, and try again. "Resist the devil, and he will flee from you. Draw nigh to God, and He will draw nigh to you."

Upon another point be guarded. You are not at all times as cautious as you should be to abstain from the very appearance of evil. You are in danger of being too familiar with the sisters, of talking with them in a light and foolish way. This will injure your influence. Guard carefully all these points; watch against the first approach of the tempter. You are highly nervous and excitable. Tea has an influence to excite the nerves, and coffee benumbs the brain; both are highly injurious. You should be careful of your diet. Eat the most wholesome, nourishing food, and keep yourself in a calm state of mind, where you will not become so excited and fly into a passion.

You can be of great service in the office, for you can fill a place of importance if you will become transformed; but as you now are you will certainly fail of doing what you might do. I have been shown that you are rough and coarse in your feelings. These need to be softened, refined, elevated. In all your course of action you should discipline yourself to habits of self-control. With the spirit you now possess you can never enter heaven.

"Beloved, now are we the sons of God." Can any human dignity equal this? What higher position can we occupy than to be called the sons of the infinite God? You would be ready to do some great thing for the Master; but the very things which would please Him most, you do not do. Will you not be faithful in overcoming self, that you may have the peace of Christ and an indwelling Saviour?

Your afflicted son needs to be dealt with calmly and tenderly; he needs your compassion. He should not be exposed to your insane temper and unreasonable demands. You must reform in respect to the spirit you manifest. Ungovernable passion will not be subdued in a moment; but your lifework is before you to rid the garden of the heart of the poisonous weeds of impatience, faultfinding, and an overbearing disposition. "The fruit of the Spirit is love, joy, peace, long-suffering, gentleness, goodness, faith, meekness, temperance." They that are Christ's have crucified the flesh, with its affections and lusts; but the brutish part of your nature takes the lines of control and guides the spiritual. This is God's order reversed.

Your faithfulness in labor is praiseworthy. Others in the office would do well to imitate your example of fidelity, diligence, and thoroughness. But you lack the graces of the Spirit of God. You are an intelligent man, but your powers have been abused. Jesus presents to you His grace, patience, and love. Will you accept the gift? Be careful of your words and actions. You are sowing seed in your daily life. Every thought, every word uttered, and every action performed, is seed cast into the soil, which will spring up and bear fruit to life eternal or to misery and corruption. Think, my brother, how the angels of God look upon your sad state when you let passion control you. And then it is written in the books of heaven. As is the seed sown, so will be the harvest. You must reap that which you have sown.

You should control the appetite and in the name of Jesus be a conqueror on this point. Your health may improve with correct habits. Your nervous system is greatly shattered; but the Great Physician can heal your body as well as your soul. Make His power your dependence, His grace your strength, and your physical, moral, and spiritual powers will be greatly improved. You have more to overcome than some others, and therefore will have more severe conflicts; but Jesus will regard your earnest efforts; He knows just how hard you have to work to keep self under the control of His Spirit. Place yourself in the hands of Jesus. Self-culture should be your business, with the object before you of being a blessing to your children and to all with whom you associate. Heaven will look with pleasure upon every victory you gain in the work of overcoming. If you put away anger and passion, and look unto Jesus, who is the Author and Finisher of your faith, you may, through His merits, develop a Christian character. Make a decided change at once, and be determined that you will act a part worthy of the intellect with which God has endowed you.

When I was shown the present condition of man in physical, mental, and moral power, and what he might become through the merits of Christ, I was astonished that he should preserve such a low level. Man may grow up into Christ, his living head. It is not the work of a moment, but that of a lifetime. By growing daily in the divine life, he will not attain to the full stature of a perfect man in Christ until his probation ceases. The growing is a continuous work. Men with fiery passions have a constant conflict with self; but the harder the battle, the more glorious will be the victory and the eternal reward.

You are connected with the office of publication. In this position your peculiar traits of character will be developed. The little courtesies of life should be cherished. A pleasant and amiable temper, blended with a firm principle of justice and honesty, will make you a man of influence. Now is the time to obtain a moral fitness for heaven. The church to which you belong must have the refining, elevating grace of Christ. God requires His followers to be men of good report, as well as to be pure, elevated, and honest; kind, as well as faithful. It is essential to be right in the weightier matters; but this is no excuse for negligence in things apparently of less importance. The principles of the law of God must be developed in the life and character. An amiable temper, combined with firm integrity and faithfulness, will constitute a moral fitness for any position. The apostle Peter exhorts: "Be courteous."

We must be learners in the school of Christ. We cannot imitate His example unless we are pleasing in disposition and condescending in deportment. True Christian politeness should be cultivated. No one else can lessen our influence as we ourselves can lessen it through the indulgence of uncontrollable temper. A naturally petulant man does not know true happiness, and is seldom content. He is ever hoping to get into a more favorable position, or to so change his surroundings that he will have peace and rest of mind. His life seems to be burdened with heavy crosses and trials, when, had he controlled his temper and bridled his tongue, many of these annoyances might have been avoided. It is the "soft answer" which "turneth away wrath." Revenge has never conquered a foe. A well-regulated temper exerts a good influence on all around; but "he that hath no rule over his own spirit is like a city that is broken down, and without walls."

Consider the life of Moses. Meekness in the midst of murmuring, reproach, and provocation constituted the brightest trait in his character. Daniel was of a humble spirit. Although he was surrounded with distrust and suspicion, and his enemies laid a snare for his life, yet he never deviated from principle. He maintained a serene and cheerful trust in God. Above all, let the life of Christ teach you. When reviled, He reviled not again; when He suffered, He threatened not. This lesson you must learn, or you will never enter heaven. Christ must be made your strength. In His name you will be more than conqueror. No enchantment against Jacob, nor divination against Israel, will prevail. If your soul is riveted to the eternal Rock, you are safe. Come joy or come sorrow, nothing can sway you from the right.

You have been afloat in the world, but the eternal truth will prove an anchor to you. You need to guard your faith. Do not move from impulse nor entertain vague theories. Experimental faith in Christ and submission to the law of God are of the highest consequence to you. Be willing to take the advice and counsel of those who have experience. Make no delay in the work of overcoming. Be true to yourself, to your children, and to God. Your afflicted son needs to be tenderly dealt with. As a father you should remember that the nerves that can thrill with pleasure can also thrill with keenest pain. The Lord identifies His interest with that of suffering humanity.

Many parents forget their accountability to God to so educate their children for usefulness and duty that they will be a blessing to themselves and to others. Children are often indulged from their babyhood, and wrong habits become fixed. The parents have been bending the sapling. By their course of training, the character develops, either into deformity or into symmetry and beauty. But while many err upon the side of indulgence, others go to the opposite extreme and rule their children with a rod of iron. Neither of these follow out the Bible directions, but both are doing a fearful work. They are molding the minds of their children and must render an account in the day of God for the manner in which they have done this. Eternity will reveal the results of the work done in this life. "As the twig is bent, the tree's inclined."

Your manner of government is wrong, decidedly wrong. You are not a tender, pitiful father. What an example do you give your children in your insane outbursts of passion! What an account will you have to render to God for your perverse discipline! If you would have the love and respect of your children, you must manifest affection for them. The indulgence of passion is never excusable; it is always blind and perverse.

God calls upon you to change your course of action. You can be a useful and efficient man in the office if you will make determined efforts to overcome. Do not set up your views as a criterion. The Lord connected you with His people that you might be a learner in the school of Christ. Your ideas have been perverted; you must not now lean to your own understanding. You cannot be saved unless your spirit is changed. Notwithstanding the fact that Moses was the meekest man that lived upon the earth, on one occasion he drew the displeasure of God upon himself. He was harassed greatly by the murmuring of the children of Israel for water.

The undeserved reproaches of the people which fell upon him led him for a moment to forget that their murmuring was not against him, but against God; and instead of being grieved because the Spirit of God was insulted, he became irritated, offended, and in a self-willed, impatient manner struck the rock twice saying: "Hear now, ye rebels; must we fetch you water out of this rock?" Moses and Aaron put themselves forward in God's place, as though the miracle had been wrought by them. They did not exalt God, but themselves, before the people. Many will ultimately fail of eternal life because they indulge in a similar course.

Moses revealed great weakness before the people. He showed a marked lack of self-control, a spirit similar to that possessed by the murmurers. He should have been an example of forbearance and patience before that multitude, who were ready to excuse their failures, disaffections, and unreasonable murmurings, on account of this exhibition of wrong on his part. The greatest sin consisted in assuming to take the place of God. The position of honor that Moses had heretofore occupied did not lessen his guilt, but greatly magnified it. Here was a man hitherto blameless, now fallen. Many in a similar position would reason that their sin would be overlooked because of their long life of unwavering fidelity.

But no; it was a more serious matter for a man who had been honored of God to show weakness of character in the exhibition of passion than if he had occupied a less responsible position. Moses was a representative of Christ, but how sadly was the figure marred! Moses had sinned, and his past fidelity could not atone for the present sin. The whole company of Israel was making history for future generations. This history the unerring pen of inspiration must trace with exact fidelity. Men of all future time must see the God of heaven is a firm ruler, in no case justifying sin. Moses and Aaron must die without entering Canaan, subjected to the same punishment that fell upon those in a more lowly position. They bowed in submission, though with anguish of heart that was inexpressible; but their love for and confidence in God was unshaken. Their example is a lesson that many pass over without learning from it as they should. Sin does not appear sinful. Self-exaltation does not appear to them grievous.

But few realize the sinfulness of sin; they flatter themselves that God is too good to punish the offender. The cases of Moses and Aaron, of David, and numerous others, show that it is not a safe thing to sin in word or thought or deed. God is a Being of infinite love and compassion. In the parting address which Moses gave to the children of Israel he said: "For the Lord thy God is a consuming fire, even a jealous God." The touching plea made by Moses that he might be privileged to enter Canaan was steadfastly refused. The transgression at Kadesh had been open and marked; and the more exalted the position of the offender, the more distinguished the man, the firmer was the decree and the more certain the punishment.

Dear brother, be warned. Be true to the light which shines upon your pathway. Said Paul: "I keep under my body, and bring it into subjection: lest that by any means, when I have preached to others, I myself should be a castaway."

317

33. Consecration in Ministers

Three years ago the Lord gave me a view of things past, present, and future. I saw young men preaching the truth, some of whom, at that time, had not yet received it themselves. They have since taken hold of the truth and are trying to lead others to it. I was shown your case, Brother I. Your past life has not been of a character to lead you away from and above yourself. You are naturally selfish and self-sufficient, having all confidence in your own strength. This will prevent you from acquiring the experience necessary to make you a humble, efficient minister of Christ.

There are many in the field who are in a similar condition. They can present the theory of the truth, but are wanting in true godliness. If the ministers now laboring in the gospel field, yourself included, felt the necessity of daily examination of self and daily communion with God, they would then be in a condition to receive the words from God to be given to the people. Your words and daily life will be a savor of life unto life or of death unto death.

You may intelligently believe the truth, but the work is still before you to bring every action of your life and every emotion of your heart into harmony with your faith. The prayer of Christ for His disciples just prior to His crucifixion was: "Sanctify them through Thy truth: Thy word is truth." The influence of the truth should affect not merely the understanding, but the heart and life. Genuine, practical religion will lead its possessor to control his affections. His external conduct should be sanctified through the truth. I assure you before God that you are seriously deficient in practical piety. Ministers should not assume the responsibility of teachers of the people, in imitation of Christ, the great Exemplar, unless they are sanctified to the great work, that they may be ensamples to the flock of God. An unsanctified minister can do incalculable harm. While professing to be the ambassador of Christ, his example will be copied by others; and if he lacks the true characteristics of a Christian, his faults and deficiencies will be reproduced in them.

Men may be able to repeat with fluency the great truths brought out with such thoroughness and perfection in our publications; they may talk fervently and intelligently of the decline of religion in the churches; they may present the gospel standard before the people in a very able manner, while the everyday duties of the Christian life, which require action as well as feeling, are regarded by them as not among the weightier matters. This is your danger. Practical religion asserts its claims alike over the heart, the mind, and the daily life. Our sacred faith does not consist either in feeling or in action merely, but the two must be combined in the Christian life. Practical religion does not exist independent of the operation of the Holy Spirit. You need this agency, my brother, and so do all who enter upon the work of laboring to convince transgressors of their lost condition. This agency of the Spirit of God does not remove from us the necessity of exercising our faculties and talents, but teaches us how to use every power to the glory of God. The human faculties, when under the special direction of the grace of God, are capable of being used to the best purpose on earth, and will be exercised in the future, immortal life.

My brother, I have been shown that you could make a very successful teacher if you would become thoroughly sanctified to the work, but that you would be a very poor laborer if not thus consecrated. You will not, as did the world's Redeemer, accept the servant's capacity, the laborious part of the gospel preacher's duty; and in this particular there are many as deficient as yourself. They accept their wages with scarcely a thought as to whether they have done most to serve themselves or the cause, whether they have given their time and talents entirely to the work of God, or whether they have only spoken in the desk and devoted the balance of their time to their own interests, inclination, or pleasure.

Christ, the Majesty of heaven, laid aside His robes of royalty and came to this world, all seared and marred by the curse, to teach men how to live a life of self-denial and self-sacrifice, and how to carry out practical religion in their daily lives. He came to give a correct example of a gospel minister. He labored constantly for one object; all His powers were employed for the salvation of men, and every act of His life tended to that end. He traveled on foot, teaching His followers as He went. His garments were dusty and travel-stained, and His appearance was uninviting. But the simple, pointed truths which fell from His divine lips soon caused His hearers to forget His appearance, and to be charmed, not with the man, but with the doctrine He taught. After teaching throughout the entire day, He frequently devoted the night to prayer. He made His supplications to His Father with strong crying and tears. He prayed, not for Himself, but for those whom He came to redeem.

Few ministers pray all night, as did our Saviour, or devote hours in the day to prayer that they may be able ministers of the gospel and effectual in bringing men to see the beauties of the truth and to be saved through the merits of Christ. Daniel prayed three times a day, but many who make the most exalted profession do not humble their souls before God in prayer even once a day. Jesus, the dear Saviour, has given marked lessons in humility to all, but especially to the gospel minister. In His humiliation, when His work upon earth was nearly finished and He was about to return to His Father's throne whence He had come, with all power in His hands and all glory upon His head, among His last lessons to His disciples was one upon the importance of humility. While His disciples were contending as to who should be greatest in the promised kingdom, He girded Himself as a servant and washed the feet of those who called Him Lord and Master.

His ministry was nearly completed; He had only a few more lessons to impart. And that they might never forget the humility of the pure and spotless Lamb of God, the great and efficacious Sacrifice for man humbled Himself to wash the feet of His disciples. It will do you good, and our ministers generally, to frequently review the closing scenes in the life of our Redeemer. Here, beset with temptations as He was, we may all learn lessons of the utmost importance to us. It would be well to spend a thoughtful hour each day reviewing the life of Christ from the manger to Calvary. We should take it point by point and let the imagination vividly grasp each scene, especially the closing ones of His earthly life.

By thus contemplating His teachings and sufferings, and the infinite sacrifice made by Him for the redemption of the race, we may strengthen our faith, quicken our love, and become more deeply imbued with the spirit which sustained our Saviour. If we would be saved at last we must all learn the lesson of penitence and faith at the foot of the cross. Christ suffered humiliation to save us from everlasting disgrace. He consented to have scorn, mockery, and abuse fall upon Him in order to shield us. It was our transgression that gathered the veil of darkness about His divine soul and extorted the cry from

Him, as of one smitten and forsaken of God. He bore our sorrows; He was put to grief for our sins. He made Himself an offering for sin, that we might be justified before God through Him. Everything noble and generous in man will respond to the contemplation of Christ upon the cross.

I long to see our ministers dwell more upon the cross of Christ, their own hearts, meanwhile, softened and subdued by the Saviour's matchless love, which prompted that infinite sacrifice. If, in connection with the theory of the truth, our ministers would dwell more upon practical godliness, speaking from a heart imbued with the spirit of truth, we should see many more souls flocking to the standard of truth; their hearts would be touched by the pleadings of the cross of Christ, the infinite generosity and pity of Jesus in suffering for man. These vital subjects, in connection with the doctrinal points of our faith, would effect much good among the people. But the heart of the teacher must be filled with the experimental knowledge of the love of Christ.

The mighty argument of the cross will convict of sin. The divine love of God for sinners, expressed in the gift of His Son to suffer shame and death that they might be ennobled and endowed with everlasting life, is the study of a lifetime. I ask you to study anew the cross of Christ. If all the proud and vainglorious, whose hearts are panting for the applause of men and for distinction above their fellows, could rightly estimate the value of the highest earthly glory in contrast with the value of the Son of God, rejected, despised, spit upon, by the very ones whom He came to redeem, how insignificant would appear all the honor that finite man can bestow.

Dear brother, you feel, in your imperfect accomplishments, that you are qualified for almost any position. But you have not yet been found sufficient to control yourself. You feel competent to dictate to men of experience, when you should be willing to be led and to place yourself in the position of a learner. The less you meditate upon Christ and His matchless love and the less you are assimilated to His image, the better will you appear in your own eyes, and the more self-confidence and self-complacency will you possess. A correct knowledge of Christ, a constant looking unto the Author and Finisher of our faith, will give you such a view of the character of a true Christian that you cannot fail to make a right estimate of your own life and character in contrast with those of the great Exemplar. You will then see your own weakness, your ignorance, your love of ease, and your unwillingness to deny self.

You have but just begun the study of God's Holy Word. You have picked up some gems of truth, which, with much toil and many prayers, have been dug up by others; but the Bible is full of them; make that Book your earnest study and the rule of your life. Your danger will ever be in despising counsel and in placing a higher value on yourself than God places upon you. There are many who are always ready to flatter and praise a minister who can talk. A young minister is ever in danger of being petted and applauded to his own injury, while at the same time he may be deficient in the essentials which God requires of everyone who professes to be a mouthpiece for Him. You have merely entered the school of Christ. The fitting up for your work is a life business, a daily, laborious, hand-to-hand struggle with established habits, inclinations, and hereditary tendencies. It requires a constant, earnest, and vigilant effort to watch and control self, to keep Jesus prominent and self out of sight.

It is necessary for you to watch for the weak points in your character, to restrain wrong tendencies, and to strengthen and develop noble faculties that have not been properly exercised. The world will never know the work secretly going on between the soul and God, nor the inward bitterness of spirit, the self-loathing, and the constant efforts to control self; but many of the world will be able to appreciate the result of these efforts. They will see Christ revealed in your daily life. You will be a living epistle, known and read of all men, and will possess a symmetrical character, nobly developed.

"Learn of Me," said Christ; "for I am meek and lowly in heart: and ye shall find rest unto your souls." He will instruct those who come to Him for knowledge. There are multitudes of false teachers in the world. The apostle declares that in the last days men will "heap to themselves teachers, having itching ears," because they desire to hear smooth things. Against these Christ has warned us: "Beware of false prophets, which come to you in sheep's clothing, but inwardly they are ravening wolves. Ye shall know them by their fruits." The class of religious teachers here described profess to be Christians. They have the form of godliness and appear to be laboring for the good of souls, while they are at heart avaricious, selfish, ease-loving, following the promptings of their own unconsecrated hearts. They are in conflict with Christ and His teachings, and are destitute of His meek and lowly spirit.

The preacher who bears the sacred truth for these last days must be the opposite of all this and, by his life of practical godliness, plainly mark the distinction existing between the false and the true shepherd. The Good Shepherd came to seek and to save that which was lost. He has manifested in His works His love for His sheep.

All the shepherds who work under the Chief Shepherd will possess His characteristics; they will be meek and lowly of heart. Childlike faith brings rest to the soul and also works by love and is ever interested for others. If the Spirit of Christ dwells in them, they will be Christlike and do the works of Christ. Many who profess to be the ministers of Christ have mistaken their master. They claim to be serving Christ and are not aware that it is Satan's banner under which they are rallying. They may be worldly wise and eager for strife and vainglory, making a show of doing a great work; but God has no use for them. The motives which prompt to action give character to the work. Although men may not discern the deficiency, God marks it.

The letter of the truth may convince some souls who will take firm hold of the faith and be saved at last; but the selfish preacher who presented the truth to them will have no credit with God for their conversion. He will be judged for his unfaithfulness while professing to be a watchman on the walls of Zion. Pride of heart is a fearful trait of character.

"Pride goeth before destruction." This is true in the family, the church, and the nation. As when He was upon earth, the Saviour of the world is choosing plain, uneducated men and teaching them to carry His truth, beautiful in its simplicity, to the world and especially to the poor. The Chief Shepherd will collect the undershepherds with Himself. He does not design that these unlearned men should remain ignorant while pursuing their labor, but that they shall receive knowledge from Himself, the Source of all knowledge, light, and power.

It is the absence of the Holy Spirit and of the grace of God that makes the gospel ministry so powerless to convict and convert. After the ascension of Jesus, doctors, lawyers, priests, rulers, scribes, and theologians listened with astonishment to words of wisdom and power from unlearned and humble men. These wise men marveled at the success of the lowly disciples, and finally accounted for it to their own satisfaction from the fact that they had been with Jesus and learned of Him. Their character and the simplicity of their teachings were similar to the character and teachings of Christ. The apostle describes it in these words: "God hath chosen the weak things of the world to confound the things which are mighty; and base things of the world, and things which are despised, hath God chosen, yea, and things which are not, to bring to nought things that are: that no flesh should glory in His presence."

Those who teach unpopular truth today must have power from on high to combine with their doctrine, or their efforts will be of little account. The precious grace of humility is sadly wanting in the ministry and the church. Men who preach the truth think too highly of their own abilities. True humility will lead a man to exalt Christ and the truth, and to realize his utter dependence upon the God of truth. It is painful to learn lessons of humility, yet nothing is more beneficial in the end. The pain attendant upon learning lessons of humility is in consequence of our being elated by a false estimate of ourselves, so that we are unable to see our great need. Vanity and pride fill the hearts of men. God's grace alone can work a reformation.

It is your work, my brother, to humble yourself and not wait for God to humble you. God's hand at times bears heavily upon men to humble them and bring them into a proper position before Him; but how much better it is to keep the heart daily humbled before God. We can abase ourselves, or we can build ourselves up in pride and wait till God abases us. Ministers of the gospel suffer little for the truth's sake today. If they were persecuted, as were the apostles of Christ, and as were holy men of God in later times, there would be a pressing closer to the side of Christ, and this closer connection with the Saviour would make their words a power in the land.

Christ was a man of sorrows and acquainted with grief. He endured the persecutions and contradiction of sinners; He was poor, and suffered hunger and fatigue; He was tempted by the devil, and His works and teachings called forth the bitterest hatred. Of what do we deny ourselves for Christ's sake? Where is our devotion to the truth? We shun the things which do not please us, and avoid care and responsibilities. Can we expect the power of God to work with our efforts when we have so little consecration to the work?

My brother, I was shown that your standard of piety is not high. You need to have a deeper sense of your responsibility to God and to society. Then you will not feel satisfied with yourself, nor will you try to excuse yourself by pointing to the deficiencies of others. You have not so thorough a knowledge of the truth that you should relax your efforts to qualify yourself to instruct others. You need to have a new conversion in order to become an able, devoted minister of the gospel, a man of piety and holiness. If you should devote all your energies to the cause of God, you would give none too much. It is a lame offering at best that any of us can make. If you are continually reaching out after God, and seeking a deeper consecration to Him, you will be gathering new ideas from searching the Scriptures for yourself.

In order to comprehend the truth, you should discipline and train the mind, and seek continually to possess the graces of genuine piety. You scarcely know what this is now. When Christ is in you, you will have something more than a theory of the truth. You will not only be repeating the lessons Christ gave when upon the earth, but you will be educating others by your life of self-denial and devotion to the cause of God. Your life will be a living sermon, possessing greater power than any discourse given in the desk.

You need to cultivate in yourself that unselfish spirit, that self-denying grace and pure devotion, which you wish to see others carry out in their lives. In order to continually increase in spiritual intelligence, and to become more and more efficient, you need to cultivate habits of usefulness in the minor duties lying in your pathway. You must not wait for opportunities to do a great work, but seize the first chance to prove yourself faithful in that which is least, and you may thus work your way up from one position of trust to another.

You will be apt to think you are not deficient in knowledge, and will be inclined to neglect secret prayer, watchfulness, and a careful study of the Scriptures, and will in consequence be overcome by the enemy. Your ways may appear perfect in your own eyes, while in reality you may be very defective. You have no time to parley with the adversary of souls. Now is the time to take your stand and disappoint the enemy. You need to criticize yourself closely and jealously. You will be inclined to set up your opinion as a standard, irrespective of the opinions and judgment of men of experience, whom God has used to advance His cause. Young men in the ministry now know but little of hardships; and many will fail of becoming as useful as they might, for the very reason that things are made too easy for them.

You have responsibilities in your family which you think you understand, but you know little about them as you ought to know. You have many things to unlearn which you have prided yourself on knowing. I was shown that you had gathered up ideas that you take for verity and truth, which are directly opposed to the Bible. Paul had these things to meet and to contend with in young ministers of his day. You have been too ready to accept as light the sayings and positions of men, but be careful how you advance your ideas as Bible truth. Be careful of your steps. I had hoped that such a reformation had taken place in your life that I should never be called upon to write these words.

You have a duty to do at home which you cannot shun and yet be true to God and to your God-given trust. That which I now refer to has not been shown me definitely in your case, but in hundreds of similar cases; therefore when I see you falling into the same error into which many parents in this age of the world are falling I cannot excuse your neglect of duty. You have one child, one soul committed to your trust. But when you show such manifest weakness and lack of wisdom in training this one child, following your ideas rather than the Bible rule, how can you be trusted to teach and manage matters where the eternal interests of many are involved?

I address myself to both yourself and your wife. My position in the cause and work of God demands of me an expression in matters of discipline. Your example in your own domestic affairs will do a great injury to the cause of God. The gospel field is the world. You wish to sow the field with gospel truth, waiting for God to water the seed sown that it may bring forth fruit. You have entrusted to you a little plot of ground, but your own dooryard is left to grow up with brambles and thorns, while you are engaged in weeding others' gardens.

This is not a small work, but one of great moment. You are preaching the gospel to others; practice it yourself at home. You are indulging the whims and passions of a perverse child, and by so doing are cultivating traits of character which God hates and which make the child unhappy. Satan takes advantage of your neglect, and he controls the mind. You have a work to do to show that you understand the duties devolving upon a Christian father in molding the character of your child after the divine Pattern. Had you commenced this work in her infancy, it would be easy now, and the child would be far happier. But under your discipline the will and perversity of the child have all the while been strengthening.

Now it will require greater severity, and more constant, persevering effort, to undo what you have been doing. If you cannot manage one little child that it is your special duty to control, you will be deficient in wisdom in managing the spiritual interests of the church of Christ.

There are errors lying at the very foundation of your experience that must be rooted out, and you must become a learner in the school of Christ. Open your eyes to discern where the difficulty lies, and then make haste to repent of these things and begin to work from a correct standpoint. Labor not in self, but in God. Put away pride, self-exaltation, and vanity, and learn of Christ the sweet lessons of the cross. You must give yourself unreservedly to the work. Be a living sacrifice upon the altar of God.

If the child of a minister manifests passion, and is indulged in nearly all its wants, it has an influence to counteract the testimonies God has given me for parents in regard to the proper management of their children. You are going directly contrary to the light that God has been pleased to give, and are choosing a picked-up theory of your own. But this experiment, so directly in opposition to the instructions of the word of God, must not be carried out to the injury of the very ones whom God would have us instruct in reference to the training of their children.

Your interest should not be swallowed up in your own family to the exclusion of others. If you share the hospitalities of your brethren, they may reasonably expect something in return. Identify your interests with those of parents and children, and seek to instruct and bless. Sanctify yourself to the work of God and be a blessing to those who entertain you, conversing with parents and in no case overlooking the children. Do not feel that your own little one is more precious in the sight of God than other children. You are liable to neglect others while petting and indulging your little one, and this very child gives evidence of your deficient management. She is guilty of acts of disobedience and passion as many times in a day as her will is crossed. What an influence is this to bring to bear upon families whom God is seeking to instruct and to reform from lax ideas in regard to discipline!

In your blind and foolish fondness you have both surrendered to your child. You have allowed her to hold the reins in her tiny fists, and she ruled you both before she was able to walk. What can be expected of the future in view of the past? Let not the example of this indulged and petted child give lessons which will testify against you, and which the judgment will show have resulted in the loss of scores of children. If men and women accept you as a teacher from God, will they not be inclined to follow your pernicious example in the indulgence of their children? Will not the sin of Eli be yours? and will not the retribution that fell on him fall on you? Your child will never see the kingdom of God with her present habits and disposition. And you, her parents, will be the ones who have closed the gates of heaven before her. How, then, will it stand in regard to your own salvation? Remember that you will reap what you sow.

Testimony 29

34. The Judgment

On the morning of October 23, 1879, about two o'clock, the Spirit of the Lord rested upon me, and I beheld scenes in the coming judgment. Language fails me in which to give an adequate description of the things which passed before me and of the effect they had upon my mind.

The great day of the execution of God's judgment seemed to have come. Ten thousand times ten thousand were assembled before a large throne, upon which was seated a person of majestic appearance. Several books were before Him, and upon the covers of each was written in letters of gold, which seemed like a burning flame of fire: "Ledger of Heaven." One of these books, containing the names of those who claim to believe the truth, was then opened. Immediately I lost sight of the countless millions about the throne, and only those who were professedly children of the light and of the truth engaged my attention. As these persons were named, one by one, and their good deeds mentioned, their countenances would light up with a holy joy that was reflected in every direction. But this did not seem to rest upon my mind with the greatest force.

Another book was opened, wherein were recorded the sins of those who profess the truth. Under the general heading of selfishness came every other sin. There were also headings over every column, and underneath these, opposite each name, were recorded, in their respective columns, the lesser sins.

Under covetousness came falsehood, theft, robbery, fraud, and avarice; under ambition came pride and extravagance; jealousy stood at the head of malice, envy, and hatred; and intemperance headed a long list of fearful crimes, such as lasciviousness, adultery, indulgence of animal passions, etc.

As I beheld I was filled with inexpressible anguish and exclaimed: "Who can be saved? who will stand justified before God? whose robes are spotless? who are faultless in the sight of a pure and holy God?"

As the Holy One upon the throne slowly turned the leaves of the ledger, and His eyes rested for a moment upon individuals, His glance seemed to burn into their very souls, and at the same moment every word and action of their lives passed before their minds as clearly as though traced before their vision in letters of fire. Trembling seized them, and their faces turned pale. Their first appearance when around the throne was that of careless indifference. But how changed their appearance now! The feeling of security is gone, and in its place is a nameless terror.

A dread is upon every soul, lest he shall be found among those who are wanting. Every eye is riveted upon the face of the One upon the throne; and as His solemn, searching eye sweeps over that company, there is a quaking of heart; for they are self-condemned without one word being uttered. In anguish of soul each declares his own guilt and with terrible vividness sees that by sinning he has thrown away the precious boon of eternal life.

One class were registered as cumberers of the ground. As the piercing eye of the Judge rested upon these, their sins of neglect were distinctly revealed. With pale, quivering lips they acknowledged that they had been traitors to their holy trust. They had had warnings and privileges, but they had not heeded nor improved them. They could now see that they had presumed too much upon the mercy of God. True, they had not such confessions to make as had the vile and basely corrupt; but, like the fig tree, they were cursed because they bore no fruit, because they had not put to use the talents entrusted to them.

This class had made self-supreme, laboring only for selfish interests. They were not rich toward God, not having responded to His claims upon them. Although professing to be servants of Christ, they brought no souls to Him. Had the cause of God been dependent on their efforts, it would have languished; for they not only withheld the means lent them of God, but they withheld themselves. But these could now see and feel that in occupying an irresponsible position in reference to the work and cause of God they had placed themselves on the left hand. They had had opportunity, but would not do the work that they could and should have done.

The names of all who profess the truth were mentioned. Some were reproved for their unbelief, others for having been slothful servants. They had allowed others to do the work in the Master's vineyard, and to bear the heaviest responsibilities, while they were selfishly serving their own temporal interests. Had they cultivated the abilities God had given them, they could have been reliable burden bearers, working for the interest of the Master.

Said the Judge: "All will be justified by their faith and judged by their works." How vividly then appeared their neglect, and how wise the arrangement of God in giving to every man a work to do to promote the cause and save his fellow men. Each was to demonstrate a living faith in his family and in his neighborhood, by showing kindness to the poor, sympathizing with the afflicted, engaging in missionary labor, and by aiding the cause of God with his means. But, like Meroz, the curse of God rested upon them for what they had not done. They had loved that work which would bring the greatest profit in this life; and opposite their names in the ledger devoted to good works there was a mournful blank.

The words spoken to these were most solemn: "You are weighed in the balances, and found wanting. You have neglected spiritual responsibilities because of busy activity in temporal matters, while your very position of trust made it necessary that you should have more than human wisdom and greater than finite judgment. This you needed in order to perform even the mechanical part of your labor; and when you disconnected God and His glory from your business, you turned from His blessing."

The question was then asked: "Why have you not washed your robes of character and made them white in the blood of the Lamb? God sent His Son into the world, not to condemn the world, but that through Him it might be saved. My love for you has been more self-denying than a mother's love. It was that I might blot out your dark record of iniquity, and put the cup of salvation to your lips, that I suffered the death of the cross, bearing the weight and curse of your guilt. The pangs of death, and the horrors of the darkness of the tomb, I endured, that I might conquer him who had the power of death, unbar the prison house, and open for you the gates of life. I submitted to shame and agony because I loved you with an infinite love, and would bring back my wayward, wandering sheep to the paradise of God, to the tree of life."

"That life of bliss which I purchased for you at such a cost, you have disregarded. Shame, reproach, and ignominy, such as your Master bore for you, you have shunned. The privileges He died to bring within your reach have not been appreciated. You would not be partaker of His sufferings, and you cannot now be partaker with Him of His glory." Then were uttered these solemn words: "He that is unjust, let him be unjust still: and he which is filthy, let him be filthy still: and he that is righteous, let him be righteous still: and he that is holy, let him be holy still." The book then closed, and the mantle fell from the Person on the throne, revealing the terrible glory of the Son of God.

The scene then passed away, and I found myself still upon the earth, inexpressibly grateful that the day of God had not yet come, and that precious probationary time is still granted us in which to prepare for eternity.

35. Our Publications

Some things of grave importance have not been receiving due attention at our offices of publication. Men in responsible positions should have worked up plans whereby our books could be circulated and not lie on the shelves, falling dead from the press. Our people are behind the times and are not following the opening providence of God.

Many of our publications have been thrown into the market at so low a figure that the profits are not sufficient to sustain the office and keep good a fund for continual use. And those of our people who have no special burden of the various branches of the work at Battle Creek and Oakland do not become informed in regard to the wants of the cause and the capital required to keep the business moving. They do not understand the liability to losses and the expense every day occurring to such institutions. They seem to think that everything moves off without much care or outlay of means, and therefore they will urge the necessity of the lowest figures on our publications, thus leaving scarcely any margin.

And after the prices have been reduced to almost ruinous figures, they manifest but a feeble interest in increasing the sales of the very books on which they have asked such low prices. The object gained, their burden ceases, when they ought to have an earnest interest and a real care to press the sale of the publications, thereby sowing the seeds of truth and bringing means into the offices to invest in other publications.

There has been a very great neglect of duty on the part of ministers in not interesting the churches in the localities where they labor, in regard to this matter. When once the prices of books are reduced, it is a very difficult matter to get them again upon a paying basis, as men of narrow minds will cry, Speculation, not discerning that no one man is benefited, and that God's instrumentalities must not be crippled for want of capital. Books that ought to be widely circulated are lying useless in our offices of publication because there is not interest enough manifested to get them circulated.

The press is a power; but if its products fall dead for want of men who will execute plans to widely circulate them, its power is lost. While there has been a quick foresight to discern the necessity of laying out means in facilities to multiply books and tracts, plans to bring back the means invested so as to produce other publications, have been neglected. The power of the press, with all its advantages, is in their hands; and they can use it to the very best account, or they can be half asleep and through inaction lose the advantages which they might gain. By judicious calculation they can extend the light in the sale of books and pamphlets. They can send them into thousands of families that now sit in the darkness of error.

Other publishers have regular systems of introducing into the market books of no vital interest. "The children of this world are in their generation wiser than the children of light." Golden opportunities occur almost daily where the silent messengers of truth might be introduced into families and to individuals; but no advantage is taken of these opportunities by the indolent, thoughtless ones. Living preachers are few. There is only one where there should be a hundred. Many are making a great mistake in not putting their talents to use in seeking to save the souls of their fellow men. Hundreds of men should be engaged in carrying the light all through our cities, villages, and towns. The public mind must be agitated. God says: Let light be sent out into all parts of the field. He designs that men shall be channels of light, bearing it to those who are in darkness.

Missionaries are wanted everywhere. In all parts of the field canvassers should be selected, not from the floating element in society, not from among men and women who are good for nothing else and have made a success of nothing, but from among those who have good address, tact, keen foresight, and ability. Such are needed to make a success as colporteurs, canvassers, and agents.

Men suited to this work undertake it, but some injudicious minister will flatter them that their gift should be employed in the desk instead of simply in the work of the colporteur. Thus this work is belittled. They are influenced to get a license to preach; and the very ones who might have been trained to make good missionaries to visit families at their homes and talk and pray with them are caught up to make poor ministers; and the field where so much labor is needed, and where so much good might be accomplished for the cause, is neglected. The efficient colporteur, as well as the minister, should have a sufficient remuneration for his services if his work is faithfully done.

If there is one work more important than another, it is that of getting our publications before the public, thus leading them to search the Scriptures. Missionary work—introducing our publications into families, conversing, and praying with and for them—is a good work and one which will educate men and women to do pastoral labor.

Everyone is not fitted for this work. Those of the best talent and ability, who will take hold of the work understandingly and systematically, and carry it forward with persevering energy, are the ones who should be selected. There should be a most thoroughly organized plan; and this should be faithfully carried out. Churches in every place should feel the deepest interest in the tract and missionary work.

The volumes of Spirit of Prophecy, and also the Testimonies, should be introduced into every Sabbathkeeping family, and the brethren should know their value and be urged to read them. It was not the wisest plan to place these books at a low figure and have only one set in a church. They should be in the library of every family and read again and again. Let them be kept where they can be read by many, and let them be worn out in being read by all the neighbors.

There should be evening readings, in which one should read aloud to those assembled at the winter fireside. There is but little interest manifested to make the most of the light given of God. Much of it is concerning family duties, and instruction is given to meet almost every case and circumstance.

Money will be expended for tea, coffee, ribbons, ruffles, and trimmings, and much time and labor spent in preparing the apparel, while the inward work of the heart is neglected. God has caused precious light to be brought out in publications, and these should be owned and read by every family. Parents, your children are in danger of going contrary to the light given of heaven, and you should both purchase and read the books, for they will be a blessing to you and yours. You should lend Spirit of Prophecy to your neighbors and prevail upon them to buy copies for themselves. Missionaries for God, you should be earnest, active, vigorous workers.

Many are going directly contrary to the light which God has given to His people, because they do not read the books which contain the light and knowledge in cautions, reproofs, and warnings. The cares of the world, the love of fashion, and the lack of religion have turned the attention from the light God has so graciously given, while books and periodicals containing error are traveling all over the country. Skepticism and infidelity are increasing everywhere. Light so precious, coming from the throne of God, is hid under a bushel. God will make His people responsible for this neglect. An account must be rendered to Him for every ray of light He has let shine upon our pathway, whether it has been improved to our advancement in divine things or rejected because it was more agreeable to follow inclination.

We now have great facilities for spreading the truth; but our people are not coming up to the privileges given them. They do not in every church see and feel the necessity of using their abilities in saving souls. They do not realize their duty to obtain subscribers for our periodicals, including our health journal, and to introduce our books and pamphlets. Men should be at work who are willing to be taught as to the best way of approaching individuals and families. Their dress should be neat, but not foppish, and their manners such as not to disgust the people. There is a great want of true politeness among us as a people. This should be cultivated by all who take hold of the missionary work.

Our publishing houses should show marked prosperity. Our people can sustain them if they will show a decided interest to work our publications into the market. But should as little interest be manifested in the year to come as has been shown in the year past, there will be but a small margin to work upon. The wider the circulation of our publications, the greater will be the demand for books that make plain the Scriptures of truth.

Many are becoming disgusted with the inconsistencies, the errors, and the apostasy of the churches, and with the festivals, fairs, lotteries, and numerous inventions to extort money for church purposes. There are many who are seeking for light in the darkness. If our papers, tracts, and books, expressing the truth in plain Bible language, could be widely circulated, many would find that they are just what they want. But many of our brethren act as though the people were to come to them or send to our offices to obtain publications, when thousands do not know that they exist.

God calls upon His people to act like living men and not to be indolent, sluggish, and indifferent. We must carry the publications to the people and urge them to accept, showing them that they will receive much more than their money's worth. Exalt the value of the books you offer. You cannot regard them too highly.

My soul was agonized as I saw the indifference of our people who make so high a profession. I was shown that the blood of souls will be on the garments of very many who now feel at ease and irresponsible for souls that are perishing around them for want of light and knowledge. They have come in contact with them, but have never warned them, never prayed with or for them, and never made earnest efforts to present the truth to them. I was shown that there has been a wonderful negligence on this point. Ministers are not doing one half what they might do to educate the people for whom they labor upon all points of truth and duty, and, as a consequence, the people are spiritless and inactive. The stake and scaffold are not appointed for this time to test the people of God, and for this very reason the love of many has waxed cold. When trials arise, grace is proportioned for the emergency. We must individually consecrate ourselves on the very spot where God has said He would meet us.

36. Christ's Ambassadors

Ambassadors for Christ have a solemn and important work, which rests upon some altogether too lightly. While Christ is the minister in the sanctuary above, He is also, through His delegates, the minister of His church on earth. He speaks to the people through chosen men, and carries forward His work through them, as when in the days of His humiliation He moved visibly upon the earth.

Although centuries have passed, the lapse of time has not changed His parting promise to His disciples: "Lo, I am with you alway, even unto the end of the world." From Christ's ascension to the present day, men ordained of God, deriving their authority from Him, have become teachers of the faith. Christ, the True Shepherd, superintends His work through the instrumentality of these undershepherds. Thus the position of those who labor in word and doctrine becomes very important. In Christ's stead they beseech the people to be reconciled to God.

The people should not regard their ministers as mere public speakers and orators, but as Christ's ambassadors, receiving their wisdom and power from the great Head of the church. To slight and disregard the word spoken by Christ's representative is not only showing disrespect to the man, but also to the Master who has sent him. He is in Christ's stead; and the voice of the Saviour should be heard in His representative.

Many of our ministers have made a great mistake in giving discourses which were wholly argumentative. There are souls who listen to the theory of the truth and are impressed with the evidences brought out, and then if a portion of the discourse presents Christ as the Saviour of the world, the seed sown may spring up and bear fruit to the glory of God. But in many discourses the cross of Christ is not presented before the people. Some may be listening to the last sermon they will ever hear, and some will never again be so situated that they can have the chain of truth brought before them and a practical application made of it to their hearts. That golden opportunity lost is lost forever. Had Christ and His redeeming love been exalted in connection with the theory of truth, it might have balanced them on His side.

There are more souls longing to understand how they may come to Christ than we imagine. Many listen to popular sermons from the pulpit and know no better than before they listened how to find Jesus and the peace and rest which their souls desire. Ministers who preach the last message of mercy to the world should bear in mind that Christ is to be exalted as the sinner's refuge.

Many ministers think that it is not necessary to preach repentance and faith, with a heart all subdued by the love of God; they take it for granted that their hearers are perfectly acquainted with the gospel, and that matters of a different nature must be presented in order to hold their attention. If their hearers are interested, they take it as evidence of success. The people are more ignorant in regard to the plan of salvation and need more instruction upon this all-important subject than upon any other.

Those who assemble to listen to the truth should expect to be profited, as did Cornelius and his friends: "Now therefore are we all here present before God, to hear all things that are commanded thee of God."

Theoretical discourses are essential, that all may know the form of doctrine and see the chain of truth, link after link, uniting in a perfect whole. But no discourse should ever be delivered without presenting Christ and Him crucified as the foundation of the gospel, making a practical application of the truths set forth, and impressing upon the people the fact that the doctrine of Christ is not Yea and Nay, but Yea and Amen in Christ Jesus.

After the theory of truth has been presented, then comes the laborious part of the work. The people should not be left with out instruction in the practical truths which relate to their everyday life. They must see and feel that they are sinners and need to be converted to God. What Christ said, what He did, and what He taught should be brought before them in the most impressive manner.

The work of the minister is but commenced when the truth is opened to the understanding of the people. Christ is our Mediator and officiating High Priest in the presence of the Father. He was shown to John as a Lamb that had been slain, as in the very act of pouring out His blood in the sinner's behalf. When the law of God is set before the sinner, showing him the depth of his sins, he should then be pointed to the Lamb of God, that taketh away the sin of the world. He should be taught repentance toward God and faith toward our Lord Jesus Christ. Thus will the labor of Christ's representative be in harmony with His work in the heavenly sanctuary.

Ministers would reach many more hearts if they would dwell more upon practical godliness. Frequently, when efforts are made to introduce the truth into new fields, the labor is almost entirely theoretical. The people are unsettled. They see the force of truth and are anxious to obtain a sure foundation. When their feelings are softened is the time, above all others, to urge the religion of Christ home upon the conscience; but too often the course of lectures has been allowed to close without that work being done for the people which they needed. That effort was too much like the offering of Cain; it had not the sacrificial blood to make it acceptable to God. Cain was right in making an offering, but he left out all that made it of any value—the blood of the atonement.

It is a sad fact that the reason why many dwell so much on theory and so little on practical godliness is that Christ is not abiding in their hearts. They do not have a living connection with God. Many souls decide in favor of the truth from the weight of evidence, without being converted. Practical discourses were not given in connection with the doctrinal, that as the hearers should see the beautiful chain of truth they might fall in love with its Author and be sanctified through obedience. The minister's work is not done until he has urged home upon his hearers the necessity of a change of character in accordance with the pure principles of the truth which they have received.

A formal religion is to be dreaded, for in it is no Saviour. Plain, close, searching, practical discourses were given by Christ. His ambassadors should follow His example in every discourse. Christ and His Father were one; in all the Father's requirements Christ cheerfully acquiesced. He had the mind of God. The Redeemer was the perfect Pattern. Jehovah was manifested in Him. Heaven was enshrined in humanity, and humanity enclosed in the bosom of Infinite Love. If ministers will in meekness sit at the feet of Jesus, they will soon obtain right views of God's character and will be able to teach others also. Some enter the ministry without deep love to God or to their fellow men. Selfishness and self-indulgence will be manifested in the lives of such; and while these unconsecrated, unfaithful watchmen are serving themselves instead of feeding the flock and attending to their pastoral duties, the people perish for want of proper instruction.

In every discourse fervent appeals should be made to the people to forsake their sins and turn to Christ. The popular sins and indulgences of our day should be condemned and practical godliness enforced. The minister should be deeply in earnest himself, feeling from the heart the words he utters and unable to repress his feeling of concern for the souls of men and women for whom Christ died. Of the Master it was said: "The zeal of Thine house hath eaten Me up." The same earnestness should be felt by His representatives.

An infinite sacrifice has been made for man, and made in vain for every soul who will not accept of salvation. How important, then that the one who presents the truth shall do so under a full sense of the responsibility resting upon him. How tender, pitiful, and courteous should be all his conduct in dealing with the souls of men, when the Redeemer of the world has shown that He values them so highly. The question is asked by Christ: "Who then is a faithful and wise servant, whom his lord hath made ruler over his household?" Jesus asks, Who? and every minister of the gospel should repeat the question to his own heart. As he views the solemn truths, and his mind beholds the picture drawn of the faithful and wise steward, his soul should be stirred to the very depths.

To every man is given his work; not one is excused. Each has a part to act according to his capacity; and it devolves upon the one who presents the truth to carefully and prayerfully learn the ability of all who accept the truth, and then to instruct them and lead them along, step by step, letting them realize the burden of responsibility resting upon them to do the work that God has for them to do. It should be urged upon them again and again that no one will be able to resist temptation, to answer the purpose of God, and to live the life of a Christian unless he shall take up his work, be it great or small, and do that work with conscientious fidelity. There is some thing for all to do besides going to church and listening to the word of God. They must practice the truth heard, carrying its principles into their everyday life. They must be doing work for Christ constantly, not from selfish motives, but with an eye single to the glory of Him who made every sacrifice to save them from ruin.

Ministers should impress upon those who accept the truth that they must have Christ in their homes; that they need grace and wisdom from Him in guiding and controlling their children. It is a part of the work which God has left for them to do, to educate and discipline these children, bringing them into subjection. Let the kindness and courtesy of the minister be seen in his treatment of children. He should ever bear in mind that they are miniature men and women, younger members of the Lord's family. These may be very near and dear to the Master, and, if properly instructed and disciplined, will do service for Him, even in their youth. Christ is grieved with every harsh, severe, and inconsiderate word spoken to children. Their rights are not always respected, and they are frequently treated as though they had not an individual character which needs to be properly developed, that it may not be warped and the purpose of God in their lives prove a failure.

From a child, Timothy knew the Scriptures, and his knowledge was a safeguard to him against the evil influences surrounding him and the temptation to choose pleasure and selfish gratification before duty. Such a safeguard all our children need, and it should be a part of the work of parents and of Christ's ambassadors to see that the children are properly instructed in the word of God.

If the minister would meet the approval of his Lord, he must labor with fidelity to present every man perfect in Christ. He should not, in his manner of labor, carry the impression that it is of little consequence whether men do or do not accept the truth and practice true godliness; but the faithfulness and self-sacrifice manifested in his life should be such as to convince the sinner that eternal interests are at stake and that his soul is in peril unless he responds to the earnest labor put forth in his behalf. Those who have been brought from error and darkness to truth and light have great changes to make, and unless the necessity of thorough reform is pressed home upon the conscience, they will be like the man who looked into the mirror, the law of God, and discovered the defects in his moral character, but went away and forgot what manner of man he was. The mind must be kept awake to a sense of responsibility or it will settle back into a state of even more careless inattention than before it was aroused.

The work of the ambassadors for Christ is far greater and more responsible than many dream of. They should not be at all satisfied with their success until they can, by their earnest labors and the blessing of God, present to Him serviceable Christians who have a true sense of their responsibility and will do their appointed work. The proper labor and instruction will result in bringing into working order those men and women whose characters are strong and their convictions so firm that nothing of a selfish character is permitted to hinder them in their work, to lessen their faith, or to deter them from duty.

If the minister has properly instructed those under his care, when he leaves for other fields of labor the work left will not ravel out, for it will be bound off so firmly as to be secure. Unless those who receive the truth are thoroughly converted and there is a radical change in their life and character, the soul is not riveted to the eternal Rock; and after the labor of the minister ceases, and the novelty is gone, the impression soon wears away, the truth loses its power to charm, and they exert no holier influence, and are no better for their profession of the truth.

I am astonished that with the examples before us of what man may be, and what he may do, we are not stimulated to greater exertion to emulate the good works of the righteous. All may not occupy a position of prominence; yet all may fill positions of usefulness and trust, and may, by their persevering fidelity, do far more good than they have any idea that they can do. Those who embrace the truth should seek a clear understanding of the Scriptures and an experimental knowledge of a living Saviour. The intellect should be cultivated, the memory taxed. All intellectual laziness is sin, and spiritual lethargy is death.

Oh, that I could command language of sufficient force to make the impression I wish to make upon my fellow laborers in the gospel! My brethren, you are handling the words of life; you are dealing with minds that are capable of the highest development, if directed in the right channel. But there is too much exhibition of self in the discourses given. Christ crucified, Christ ascended into the heavens, Christ coming again, should so soften, gladden, and fill the mind of the minister of the gospel that he will present these truths to the people in love and deep earnestness. The minister will then be lost sight of and Jesus magnified. The people will be so impressed with these all-absorbing subjects that they will talk of them and praise them, instead of praising the minister, the mere instrument. But if the people, while they praise the minister, have little interest in the word preached, he may know that the truth is not sanctifying his own soul. He does not speak to his hearers in such a manner that Jesus is honored and His love magnified.

Said Christ: "Let your light so shine before men, that they may see your good works, and glorify your Father which is in heaven." Let your light so shine that the glory will redound to God instead of to yourselves. If the praise comes to you, well may you tremble and be ashamed, for the great object is defeated; it is not God, but the servant, that is magnified. Let your light so shine; be careful, minister of Christ, in what manner your light shines. If it flashes heavenward, revealing the excellence of Christ, it shines aright. If it is turned upon yourself, if you exhibit yourself, and attract the people to admire you, it would be better for you to hold your peace altogether: for your light shines in the wrong way.

Ministers of Christ, you may be connected with God if you will watch and pray. Let your words be seasoned with salt, and let Christian courtesy and true elevation pervade your demeanor. If the peace of God is ruling within, its power will not only strengthen, but soften your hearts, and you will be living representatives of Christ. The people who profess the truth are backsliding from God. Jesus is soon to come, and they are unready. The minister must reach a higher standard himself, a faith marked with greater firmness, an experience that is living and vivid, not dull and common place, like that of the nominal professors. The word of God sets a high mark before you. Will you, through fasting and prayerful effort, attain to the completeness and consistency of Christian character? You should make straight paths for your feet, lest the lame be turned out of the way. A close connection with God will bring to you in your labor that vital power which arouses the conscience, and convicts the sinner of sin, leading him to cry: "What shall I do to be saved?"

The commission which Christ gave to the disciples just prior to His ascension to heaven was: "Go ye therefore, and teach all nations, baptizing them in the name of the Father, and of the Son, and of the Holy Ghost: teaching them to observe all things whatsoever I have commanded you: and, lo, I am with you alway, even unto the end of the world." "Neither pray I for these alone, but for them also which shall believe on Me through their word." The commission reaches those who shall believe on His word through His disciples. And all who are called of God to stand as ambassadors for Him should take the lessons upon practical godliness given them by Christ in His word and teach them to the people.

Christ opened the Scriptures to His disciples, beginning at Moses and the prophets, and instructed them in all things concerning Himself, and also explained to them the prophecies. The apostles in their preaching went back to Adam's day and brought their hearers down through prophetic history and ended with Christ and Him crucified, calling upon sinners to repent and turn from their sins to God. The representatives of Christ in our day should follow their example and in every discourse magnify Christ as the Exalted One, as all and in all.

Not only is formality taking possession of the nominal churches, but it is increasing to an alarming extent among those who profess to be keeping the commandments of God and looking for the soon appearing of Christ in the clouds of heaven. We should not be narrow in our views and limit our facilities for doing good; yet while we extend our influence and enlarge our plans as Providence opens the way, we should be more earnest to avoid the idolatry of the world. While we make greater efforts to increase our usefulness, we must make corresponding efforts to obtain wisdom from God to carry on all the branches of the work after His own order, and not from a worldly standpoint. We should not pattern after the customs of the world, but make the most of the facilities which God has placed within our reach to get the truth before the people.

When as a people our works correspond with our profession, we shall see very much more accomplished than now. When we have men as devoted as Elijah, and possessing the faith which he possessed, we shall see that God will reveal Himself to us as He did to holy men of old. When we have men who, while they acknowledge their deficiencies, will plead with God in earnest faith as did Jacob, we shall see the same results. Power will come from God to man in answer to the prayer of faith. There is but little faith in the world. There are but few who are living near to God. And how can we expect more power and that God will reveal Himself to men, when His word is handled negligently and when hearts are not sanctified through the truth? Men who are not half converted, who are self-confident and self-sufficient in character, preach the truth to others. But God does not work with them, for they are not holy in heart and life. They do not walk humbly with God. We must have a converted ministry, and then we shall see the light of God and His power aiding all our efforts.

The watchmen anciently placed upon the walls of Jerusalem and other cities occupied a most responsible position. Upon their faithfulness depended the safety of all within those cities. When danger was apprehended, they were not to keep silent day nor night. Every few moments they were required to call to one another to see if all were awake and no harm had come to any. Sentinels were stationed upon some eminence overlooking the important posts to be guarded, and the cry of warning or of good cheer was sounded from them. This was borne from one to another, each repeating the words, till it went the entire rounds of the city.

These watchmen represent the ministry, upon whose fidelity depends the salvation of souls. The stewards of the mysteries of God should stand as watchmen upon the walls of Zion; and if they see the sword coming, they should sound the note of warning. If they are sleepy sentinels, and their spiritual senses are so benumbed that they see and realize no danger, and the people perish, God will require their blood at the watchmen's hands.

"O son of man, I have set thee a watchman unto the house of Israel; therefore thou shalt hear the word at My mouth, and warn them from Me." The watchmen will need to live very near to God, to hear His word and be impressed with His Spirit, that the people may not look to them in vain. "When I say unto the wicked, O wicked man, thou shalt surely die; if thou dost not speak to warn the wicked from his way, that wicked man shall die in his iniquity; but his blood will I require at thine hand. Nevertheless, if thou warn the wicked of his way to turn from it; if he do not turn from his way, he shall die in his iniquity; but thou hast delivered thy soul." Ambassadors of Christ should take heed that they do not, through their unfaithfulness, lose their own souls and the souls of those who hear them.

I was shown the churches in different states that profess to be keeping the commandments of God and looking for the second coming of Christ. There is an alarming amount of indifference, pride, love of the world, and cold formality existing among them. And these are the people who are fast coming to resemble ancient Israel, so far as the want of piety is concerned. Many make high claims to godliness and yet are destitute of self-control. Appetite and passion bear sway; self is made prominent. Many are arbitrary, dictatorial, overbearing, boastful, proud, and unconsecrated. Yet some of these persons are ministers, handling sacred truths. Unless they repent, their candlestick will be removed out of its place. The Saviour's curse pronounced upon the fruitless fig tree is a sermon to all formalists and boasting hypocrites who stand forth to the world in pretentious leaves, but are devoid of fruit. What a rebuke to those who have a form of godliness, while in their unchristian lives they deny the power thereof! He who treated with tenderness the very chief of sinners, He who never spurned true meekness and penitence, however great the guilt, came down with scathing denunciations upon those who made high professions of godliness, but in works denied their faith.

• Manner of Speaking

Some of our most talented ministers are doing themselves great injury by their defective manner of speaking. While teaching the people their duty to obey God's moral law, they should not be found violating the laws of God in regard to health and life. Ministers should stand erect and speak slowly, firmly, and distinctly, taking a full inspiration of air at every sentence and throwing out the words by exercising the abdominal muscles. If they will observe this simple rule, giving attention to the laws of health in other respects, they may preserve their life and usefulness much longer than men in any other profession.

The chest will become broader, and by educating the voice, the speaker need seldom become hoarse, even by constant speaking. Instead of our ministers' becoming consumptives by speaking, they may, by care, overcome all tendency to consumption. I would say to my ministering brethren: Unless you educate yourselves to speak according to physical law, you will sacrifice life, and many will mourn the loss of "those martyrs to the cause of truth," when the facts in the case are that by indulging in wrong habits you did injustice to your selves and to the truth which you represented, and robbed God and the world of the service you might have rendered. God would have been pleased to have you live, but you slowly committed suicide.

The manner in which the truth is presented often has much to do in determining whether it will be accepted or rejected. All who labor in the great cause of reform should study to become efficient workmen, that they may accomplish the greatest possible amount of good and not detract from the force of the truth by their own deficiencies.

Ministers and teachers should discipline themselves to clear and distinct articulation, giving the full sound to every word. Those who talk rapidly, from the throat, jumbling the words together and raising their voices to an unnaturally high pitch, soon become hoarse, and the words spoken lose half the force which they would have if spoken slowly, distinctly, and not so loud. The sympathies of the hearers are awakened for the speaker, for they know that he is doing violence to himself and they fear that he will break down at any moment. It is no evidence that a man has zeal for God because he works himself up into a frenzy of excitement and gesticulation. "Bodily exercise," says the apostle, "profiteth little."

The Saviour of the world would have His colaborers represent Him; and the more closely a man walks with God, the more faultless will be his manner of address, his deportment, his attitude, and his gestures. Coarse and uncouth manners were never seen in our Pattern, Christ Jesus. He was a representative of heaven, and His followers must be like Him.

Some reason that the Lord will by His Spirit qualify a man to speak as He would have him; but the Lord does not propose to do the work which He has given man to do. He has given us reasoning powers and opportunities to educate the mind and manners. And after we have done all we can for ourselves, making the best use of the advantages within our reach, then we may look to God with earnest prayer to do by His Spirit that which we cannot do for ourselves, and we shall ever find in our Saviour power and efficiency.

• Qualifications for the Ministry

A great injury is often done our young men by permitting them to commence to preach when they have not sufficient knowledge of the Scriptures to present our faith in an intelligent manner. Some who enter the field are mere novices in the Scriptures. In other things also they are incompetent and inefficient. They cannot read the Scriptures without hesitating, miscalling words, and jumbling them together in such a manner that the word of God is abused. Those who are not qualified to present the truth in a proper manner need not be perplexed with regard to their duty. Their place is that of learners, not teachers. Young men who wish to prepare for the ministry are greatly benefited by attending our college; but advantages are still needed that they may be qualified to be come acceptable speakers. A teacher should be employed to educate the youth to speak without wearing the vocal organs. The manners also should receive attention.

Some young men who enter the field are not successful in teaching the truth to others because they have not been educated themselves. Those who cannot read correctly should learn, and they should become apt to teach before they attempt to stand before the public. The teachers in our schools are obliged to apply themselves closely to study, that they may be prepared to instruct others. These teachers are not accepted until they have passed a critical examination and their capabilities to teach have been tested by competent judges. No less caution should be used in the examination of ministers; those who are about to enter upon the sacred work of teaching Bible truth to the world should be carefully examined by faithful, experienced persons.

After these have had some experience, there is still another work to be done for them. They should be presented before the Lord in earnest prayer that He would indicate by His Holy Spirit if they are acceptable to Him. The apostle says: "Lay hands suddenly on no man." In the days of the apostles the ministers of God did not dare to rely upon their own judgment in selecting or accepting men to take the solemn and sacred position of mouthpiece for God. They selected the men whom their judgment would accept, and then they placed them before the Lord to see if He would accept them to go forth as His representatives. No less than this should be done now.

In many places we meet men who have been hurried into responsible positions as elders of the church when they are not qualified for such a position. They have not proper government over themselves. Their influence is not good. The church is in trouble continually in consequence of the defective character of the leader. Hands have been laid too suddenly upon these men.

Ministers of God should be of good repute, capable of discreetly managing an interest after they have aroused it. We stand in great need of competent men who will bring honor instead of disgrace upon the cause which they represent. Ministers should be examined especially to see if they have an intelligent understanding of the truth for this time, so that they can give a connected discourse upon the prophecies or upon practical subjects. If they cannot clearly present Bible subjects they need to be hearers and learners still. They should earnestly and prayerfully search the Scriptures, and become conversant with them, in order to be teachers of Bible truth to others. All these things should be carefully and prayerfully considered before men are hurried into the field of labor.

The plan that has been adopted, to have Elder Smith hold Biblical institutes in different states, is approved of God. Great good has been accomplished by these institutes, but all the time is not devoted to this work that would be profitable to our young ministers and to the cause of God. The fruits of the efforts that have already been made can never be fully realized in this life, but will be seen in eternity.

37. Ministers of the Gospel

Brother A: I have been shown that you are not prepared to labor successfully in the ministry. At one time a measure of success attended your efforts; but while this should have inspired you with greater earnestness and zeal, the effect was the opposite. A sense of the goodness of God should have led you to continue to labor in humility and to be distrustful of self. But after your ordination, especially, you began to feel that you were a full-grown minister, capable of presenting the truth in large places; and you became indolent, feeling no burden for souls, and your labor since that time has been of but little value to the cause of God. Possessing physical strength, you do not realize that you are as responsible for the use you make of it as the man of means is for the use of his money. You do not love manual labor; yet you have a constitution which requires severe physical taxation for the preservation of health as well as for the quickening of the mental powers. So far as health is concerned, physical exercise would be of the greatest value to all our ministers; and whenever they can be released from active service in the ministry they should feel it a duty to engage in physical labor for the support of their families.

Brother A, you have idled away time in sleep that instead of being essential to your health has been detrimental to it. The precious hours you have lost, doing no good to yourself or to anyone else, stand against you in the Ledger of Heaven. Your name was shown me under the heading: "Slothful Servants." Your work will not bear the test of the judgment. You have spent so much precious time in sleep that all your powers seem paralyzed. Health may be earned by proper habits of life and may be made to yield interest and compound interest. But this capital, more precious than any bank deposit, may be sacrificed by intemperance in eating and drinking, or by leaving the organs to rust from inaction. Pet indulgences must be given up; laziness must be overcome.

The reason why many of our ministers complain of sickness is that they fail to take sufficient exercise and indulge in overeating. They do not realize that such a course endangers the strongest constitution. Those who, like yourself, are sluggish in temperament, should eat very sparingly and not shun physical taxation. Many of our ministers are digging their graves with their teeth. The system, in taking care of the burden placed upon the digestive organs, suffers, and a severe draft is made upon the brain. For every offense committed against the laws of health, the transgressor must pay the penalty in his own body.

When not actively engaged in preaching, the apostle Paul labored at his trade as a tentmaker. This he was obliged to do on account of having accepted unpopular truth. Before he embraced Christianity he had occupied an elevated position and was not dependent upon his labor for support. Among the Jews it was customary to teach the children some trade, however high the position they were expected to fill, that a reverse of circumstances might not leave them incapable of sustaining themselves. In accordance with this custom Paul was a tentmaker, and when his means had been expended to advance the cause of Christ and for his own support, he resorted to his trade in order to gain a livelihood.

No man ever lived who was a more earnest, energetic, and self-sacrificing disciple of Christ than was Paul. He was one of the world's greatest teachers. He crossed the seas and traveled far and near, until a large portion of the world had learned from his lips the story of the cross of Christ. He possessed a burning desire to bring perishing man to a knowledge of the truth through a Saviour's love. His soul was wrapped up in the work of the ministry, and it was with feelings of pain that he withdrew from this work to toil for his own bodily necessities; but he seated himself to the drudgery of the craftsman that he might not be burdensome to the churches that were pressed with poverty. Although he had planted many churches he refused to be supported by them, fearing that his usefulness and success as a minister of the gospel might be interfered with by suspicions of his motives. He would remove all occasion for his enemies to misrepresent him and thus detract from the force of his message.

Paul appeals to his Corinthian brethren to understand that, as a laborer in the gospel, he might claim his support, instead of sustaining himself; but this right he was willing to forego, fearing that the acceptance of means for his support might possibly stand in the way of his usefulness. Although feeble in health, he labored during the day in serving the cause of Christ, and then toiled a large share of the night, and frequently all night, that he might make provision for his own and others' necessities. The apostle would also give an example to his brethren, thus dignifying and honoring industry. When our ministers feel that they are suffering hardships and privations in the cause of Christ, let them in imagination visit the workshop of the apostle Paul, bearing in mind that while this chosen man of God is fashioning the canvas, he is working for bread which he has justly earned by his labors as an apostle of Jesus Christ. At the call of duty this great apostle would lay aside his business to meet the most violent opponents and stop their proud boasting, and then he would resume his humble employment. His religious industry is a rebuke to the indolence of some of our ministers. When they have opportunity to labor to help sustain themselves they should do so with gladness.

God never designed that man should live in idleness. When Adam was in Eden, means were devised for his employment. Though the race is not always to the swift nor the battle to the strong, yet he that dealeth with a slack hand will become poor. Those who are diligent in business may not always be prospered; but drowsiness and indolence are sure to grieve the Spirit of God and destroy true godliness. A stagnant pool becomes offensive; but a pure, flowing brook spreads health and gladness over the land. A man of persevering industry will be a blessing anywhere. The exercise of man's physical and mental powers is necessary to their full and proper development.

Young ministers should study to make themselves useful wherever they are. When invited to visit persons at their homes, they should not sit idle, making no effort to help the ones whose hospitality they share. Obligations are mutual; if the minister shares the hospitality of his friends, it is his duty to respond to their kindness by being thoughtful and considerate in his conduct toward them. The entertainer may be a man of care and hard labor. By manifesting a disposition not only to wait upon himself but to render timely assistance, the minister may often find access to the heart and open the way for the reception of truth.

God has no use for lazy men in His cause; He wants thoughtful, kind, affectionate, earnest workers. Active exertion will do our preachers good. Indolence is proof of depravity. Every faculty of the mind, every bone in the body, every muscle of the limbs, shows that God designed these faculties to be used, not to remain inactive. Brother A is too indolent to put his energies into the work and engage in persevering labor. Men who will unnecessarily take the precious hours of daylight for sleep have no sense of the value of precious, golden moments. Such men will prove only a curse to the cause of God. Brother A is self-inflated. He is not a close Bible student. He is not what he ought to be, nor what he may become by earnest exertion. He rouses up occasionally to do something; but his laziness, his natural love of ease, leads him to fall back again into the same sluggish channel. Persons who have not acquired habits of close industry and economy of time should have set rules to prompt them to regularity and dispatch.

Washington, the nation's statesman, was enabled to perform a great amount of business because he was thorough in preserving order and regularity. Every paper had its date and its place, and no time was lost in looking up what had been mislaid. Men of God must be diligent in study, earnest in the acquirement of knowledge, never wasting an hour. Through persevering exertion they may rise to almost any degree of eminence as Christians, as men of power and influence.

But many will never attain superior rank in the pulpit or in business because of their unfixedness of purpose and the laxness of habits contracted in their youth. Careless inattention is seen in everything they undertake. A sudden impulse now and then is not sufficient to accomplish a reformation in these ease-loving, indolent ones; this is a work which requires patient continuance in well-doing. Men of business can be truly successful only by having regular hours for rising, for prayer, for meals, and for retirement. If order and regularity are essential in worldly business, how much more so in doing work for God.

The bright morning hours are wasted by many in bed. These precious hours, once lost, are gone never to return; they are lost for time and for eternity. Only one hour lost each day, and what a waste of time in the course of a year! Let the slumberer think of this and pause to consider how he will give an account to God for lost opportunities.

Ministers should devote time to reading, to study, to meditation and prayer. They should store the mind with useful knowledge, committing to memory portions of Scripture, tracing out the fulfillment of the prophecies, and learning the lessons which Christ gave to His disciples. Take a book with you to read when traveling on the cars or waiting in the depot. Employ every spare moment in doing something. In this way an effectual door will be closed against a thousand temptations. Had King David been engaged in some useful employment, he would not have been guilty of the murder of Uriah. Satan is ever ready to employ him who does not employ himself.

The mind which is continually striving to rise to the height of intellectual greatness will find no time for cheap, foolish thoughts, which are the parent of evil actions. There are men of good ability among us, who, by proper cultivation, might become eminently useful; yet they do not love exertion, and, failing to see the crime of neglecting to put to the best use the faculties with which they have been endowed by the Creator, they settle down at their ease, to remain uncultivated in mind. But very few are meeting the mind of God.

Of these slothful servants God will inquire: "What hast thou done with the talents I gave thee?" Many will be found in that day who, having had one talent, bound it in a napkin and hid it in the earth. These unprofitable servants will be cast into outer darkness; while those who had put out their talents to the exchangers and doubled them will receive the plaudit: "Well done, thou good and faithful servant: thou hast been faithful over a few things, I will make thee ruler over many things: enter thou into the joy of thy Lord."

When responsibilities are to be entrusted to an individual, the question is not asked whether he is eloquent or wealthy, but whether he is honest, faithful, and industrious; for whatever may be his accomplishments, without these qualifications he is utterly unfit for any position of trust. Many who have begun life with fair prospects fail of success because they lack industry. Young men who habitually mingle in the little groups gathered in stores or on the street, ever engaging in discussion or gossip, will never grow to the proportions of men of understanding. Continual application will accomplish for man what nothing else can. Those who are never content without the consciousness that they are growing every day will truly make a success of life.

Many have failed, signally failed, where they might have made a success. They have not felt the burden of the work; they have taken things as leisurely as though they had a temporal millennium in which to work for the salvation of souls. Because of this lack of earnestness and zeal, but few would receive the impression that they really meant what they said. The cause of God is not so much in need of preachers as of earnest, persevering workers for the Master. God alone can measure the powers of the human mind.

It was not His design that man should be content to remain in the lowlands of ignorance, but that he should secure all the advantages of an enlightened, cultivated intellect. Every man and every woman should feel that obligations are resting upon them to reach the very height of intellectual greatness. While none should be puffed up because of the knowledge they have acquired, it is the privilege of all to enjoy the satisfaction of knowing that with every advance step they are rendered more capable of honoring and glorifying God. They may draw from an inexhaustible fountain, the Source of all wisdom and knowledge.

Having entered the school of Christ, the student is prepared to engage in the pursuit of knowledge without becoming dizzy from the height to which he is climbing. As he goes on from truth to truth, obtaining clearer and brighter views of the wonderful laws of science and of nature, he becomes enraptured with the amazing exhibitions of God's love to man. He sees with intelligent eyes the perfection, knowledge, and wisdom of God stretching beyond into infinity. As his mind enlarges and expands, pure streams of light pour into his soul. The more he drinks from the fountain of knowledge, the purer and happier his contemplation of God's infinity, and the greater his longing for wisdom sufficient to comprehend the deep things of God.

Mental culture is what we as a people need, and what we must have in order to meet the demands of the time. Poverty, humble origin, and unfavorable surroundings need not prevent the cultivation of the mind. The mental faculties must be kept under the control of the will and the mind not allowed to wander or become distracted with a variety of subjects at a time, being thorough in none. Difficulties will be met in all studies; but never cease through discouragement. Search, study, and pray; face every difficulty manfully and vigorously; call the power of will and the grace of patience to your aid, and then dig more earnestly till the gem of truth lies before you, plain and beautiful, all the more precious because of the difficulties involved in finding it.

Do not, then, continually dwell upon this one point, concentrating all the energies of the mind upon it, constantly urging it upon the attention of others, but take another subject, and carefully examine that. Thus mystery after mystery will be unfolded to your comprehension. Two valuable victories will be gained by this course. You have not only secured useful knowledge, but the exercise of the mind has increased mental strength and power. The key found to unlock one mystery may develop also other precious gems of knowledge heretofore undiscovered.

Many of our ministers can present to the people only a few doctrinal discourses. The same exertion and application which made them familiar with these points will enable them to gain an understanding of others. The prophecies and other doctrinal subjects should be thoroughly understood by them all. But some who have been engaged in preaching for years are content to confine themselves to a few subjects, being too indolent to search the Scriptures diligently and prayerfully that they may become giants in the understanding of Bible doctrines and the practical lessons of Christ. The minds of all should be stored with a knowledge of the truths of God's word, that they may be prepared, at any moment when required, to present from the storehouse things new and old. Minds have been crippled and dwarfed for want of zeal and of earnest, severe taxation. The time has come when God says: "Go forward, and cultivate the abilities I have given you."

The world is teeming with errors and fables. Novelties in the form of sensational dramas are continually arising to engross the mind, and absurd theories abound which are destructive to moral and spiritual advancement. The cause of God needs men of intellect, men of thought, men well versed in the Scriptures, to meet the inflowing tide of opposition. We should give no sanction to arrogance, narrow-mindedness, and inconsistencies, although the garment of professed piety may be thrown over them. Those who have the sanctifying power of the truth upon their hearts will exert a persuasive influence. Knowing that the advocates of error cannot create or destroy truth, they can afford to be calm and considerate.

It is not enough for our ministers to have a superficial knowledge of the truth. Subjects which are handled by men who have perverted their God-given powers to tear down the truth are constantly coming up for investigation. Bigotry must be laid aside. The satanic delusions of the age must be met clearly and intelligently with the sword of the Spirit, which is the word of God. The same unseen Hand that guides the planets in their courses, and upholds the worlds by His power, has made provision for man formed in His image, that he may be little less than the angels of God while in the performance of his duties on earth.

God's purposes have not been answered by men who have been entrusted with the most solemn truth ever given to man. He designs that we should rise higher and higher toward a state of perfection, seeing and realizing at every step the power and glory of God. Man does not know himself. Our responsibilities are exactly proportioned to our light, opportunities, and privileges. We are responsible for the good we might have done, but failed to do because we were too indolent to use the means for improvement which were placed within our reach.

The precious book of God contains rules of life for men of every class and every vocation. Examples are here found which it would be well for all to study and imitate. "The Son of God came not to be ministered unto, but to minister." The true honor and glory of the servant of Christ consists, not in the number of sermons preached, nor in the amount of writing accomplished, but in the work of faithfully ministering to the wants of the people. If he neglects this part of his work he has no right to the name of minister.

Men are needed for this time who can understand the wants of the people and minister to their necessities. The faithful minister of Christ watches at every outpost to warn, to reprove, to counsel, to entreat, and to encourage his fellow men, laboring with the Spirit of God which worketh in him mightily, that he may present every man perfect in Christ. Such a man is acknowledged in heaven as a minister, treading in the footsteps of his great Exemplar. Our preachers are not particular enough in regard to their habits of eating. They partake of too large quantities of food and of too great a variety at one meal.

Some are reformers only in name. They have no rules by which to regulate their diet, but indulge in eating fruit or nuts between their meals, and thus impose too heavy burdens upon the digestive organs. Some eat three meals a day, when two would be more conducive to physical and spiritual health. If the laws which God has made to govern the physical system are violated, the penalty must surely follow.

Because of imprudence in eating, the senses of some seem to be half paralyzed, and they are sluggish and sleepy. These pale-faced ministers who are suffering in consequence of selfish indulgence of the appetite are no recommendation of health reform. When suffering from overwork, it would be much better to drop out a meal occasionally and thus give nature a chance to rally. Our laborers could do more by their example to advance health reform than by preaching it. When elaborate preparations are made for them by well-meaning friends, they are strongly tempted to disregard principle; but by refusing the dainty dishes, the rich condiments, the tea and coffee, they may prove themselves to be practical health reformers. Some are now suffering in consequence of transgressing the laws of life, thus causing a stigma to rest on the cause of health reform.

Excessive indulgence in eating, drinking, sleeping, or seeing, is sin. The harmonious healthy action of all the powers of body and mind results in happiness; and the more elevated and refined the powers, the more pure and unalloyed the happiness. An aimless life is a living death. The powers of the mind should be exercised upon themes relating to our eternal interests. This will be conducive to health of body and mind.

There are many, even among our preachers, who want to rise in the world without effort. They are ambitious to do some great work of usefulness, while they disregard the little everyday duties which would render them helpful and make them ministers after Christ's order. They wish to do the work others are doing, but have no relish for the discipline necessary to fit them for it. This yearning desire by both men and women to do something far in advance of their present capabilities is simply causing them to make decided failures in the outset. They indignantly refuse to climb the ladder, wishing to be elevated by a less laborious process.

38. Our College

The education and training of the youth is an important and solemn work. The great object to be secured should be the proper development of character, that the individual may be fitted rightly to discharge the duties of the present life and to enter at last upon the future, immortal life. Eternity will reveal the manner in which the work has been performed. If ministers and teachers could have a full sense of their responsibility, we should see a different state of things in the world today. But they are too narrow in their views and purposes. They do not realize the importance of their work or its results.

God could not do more for man than He has done in giving His beloved Son, nor could He do less and yet secure the redemption of man and maintain the dignity of the divine law. He poured out in our behalf the whole treasure of heaven; for in giving His Son He threw open to us the golden gates of heaven, making one infinite gift to those who shall accept the sacrifice and return to their allegiance to God. Christ came to our world with love as broad as eternity in His heart, offering to make man heir of all His riches and glory. In this act He unveiled to man the character of His Father, showing to every human being that God can be just and yet the justifier of him that believeth in Jesus.

The Majesty of heaven pleased not Himself. Whatever He did was in reference to the salvation of man. Selfishness in all its forms stood rebuked in His presence. He assumed our nature that He might suffer in our stead, making His soul an offering for sin. He was stricken of God and afflicted to save man from the blow which he deserved because of the transgression of God's law. By the light shining from the cross, Christ proposed to draw all men unto Him. His human heart yearned over the race. His arms were opened to receive them, and He invited all to come to Him. His life on earth was one continued act of self-denial and condescension.

Since man cost heaven so much, the price of God's dear Son, how carefully should ministers, teachers, and parents deal with the souls of those brought under their influence. It is nice work to deal with minds, and it should be entered upon with fear and trembling. The educators of youth should maintain perfect self-control. To destroy one's influence over a human soul through impatience, or in order to maintain undue dignity and supremacy, is a terrible mistake, for it may be the means of losing that soul for Christ.

The minds of youth may become so warped by injudicious management that the injury done may never be entirely overcome. The religion of Christ should have a controlling influence on the education and training of the young. The Saviour's example of self-denial, universal kindness, and long-suffering love is a rebuke to impatient ministers and teachers. He inquires of these impetuous instructors: "Is this the manner in which you treat the souls of those for whom I gave My life? Have you no greater appreciation of the infinite price I paid for their redemption?"

All connected with our college must be men and women who have the fear of God before them and His love in their hearts. They should make their religion attractive to the youth who come within the sphere of their influence. The professors and teachers should constantly feel their dependence upon God. Their work is in this world, but the Source of wisdom and knowledge from which they must continually draw is above. Self must not obtain the mastery. The Spirit of God must control. They must walk humbly with God, and they should feel their responsibility, which is not less than that of the minister. The influence which professors and teachers exert upon the youth in our college will be carried wherever these youth may go. A sacred influence should go forth from that college to meet the moral darkness existing everywhere. When I was shown by the angel of God that an institution should be established for the education of our youth I saw that it would be one of the greatest means ordained of God for the salvation of souls.

Those who would make a success in the education of the youth must take them as they are, not as they ought to be nor as they will be when they come from under their training. With dull scholars they will have a trial, and they must bear patiently with their ignorance. With sensitive, nervous students they must deal tenderly and very kindly, remembering that they are hereafter to meet their students before the judgment seat of Christ. A sense of their own imperfections should constantly lead educators to cherish feelings of tender sympathy and forbearance for those who are struggling with the same difficulties. They may help their students, not by overlooking their defects, but by faithfully correcting wrong in such a manner that the one reproved shall be bound still closer to the teacher's heart.

God has linked old and young together by the law of mutual dependence. The educators of youth should feel an unselfish interest for the lambs of the flock, as Christ has given us an example in His life. There is too little pitying tenderness, and too much of the unbending dignity of the stern judge. Exact and impartial justice should be given to all, for the religion of Christ demands this; but it should ever be remembered that firmness and justice have a sister, which is mercy. To stand aloof from students, to treat them indifferently, to be unapproachable, harsh, and censorious, is contrary to the spirit of Christ.

We need individually to open our hearts to the love of God, to overcome selfishness and harshness, and to let Jesus in to take possession of the soul. The educator of youth will do well to remember that with all his advantages of age, education, and experience he is not yet a perfect overcomer; he is himself erring and makes many failures. As Christ deals with him, he should endeavor to deal with the youth under his care, who have had fewer advantages and less favorable surroundings than he himself has enjoyed. Christ has borne with the erring through all his manifest perversity and rebellion. His love for the sinner does not grow cold, His efforts do not cease, and He does not give him up to the buffeting of Satan. He has stood with open arms to welcome again the erring, the rebellious, and even the apostate. By precept and example, teachers should represent Christ in the education and training of youth; and in the day of judgment they will not be put to shame by meeting their students and the history of their management of them.

Again and again has the educator of youth carried into the schoolroom the shadow of darkness which has been gathering upon his soul. He has been overtaxed and is nervous, or dyspepsia has colored everything a gloomy hue. He enters the schoolroom with quivering nerve and irritated stomach. Nothing seems to be done to please him, he thinks that his scholars are bent upon showing him disrespect, and his sharp criticisms and censures are given on the right hand and on the left.

Perhaps one or more commit errors or are unruly. The case is exaggerated in his mind, and he becomes unjust and is severe and cutting in reproof, even taunting the one whom he considers at fault. This same injustice afterward prevents him from admitting that he has not taken the proper course. To maintain the dignity of his position, he has lost a precious, golden opportunity to manifest the spirit of Christ, perhaps to gain a soul for heaven.

Men and women of experience should understand that this is a time of especial danger for the young. Temptations surround them on every hand; and while it is easy work to float with the current, the strongest effort is required to press against the tide of evil. It is Satan's studied effort to secure the youth in sin, for then he is more sure of the man.

The enemy of souls is filled with intense hatred against every endeavor to influence the youth in the right direction. He hates everything which will give correct views of God and our Saviour, and his efforts are especially directed against all who are placed in a favorable position to receive light from heaven. He knows that any movement on their part to come in connection with God will give them power to resist his devices. Those who are at ease in their sins are safe under his banner. But as soon as efforts are made to break his power, his wrath is aroused, and he commences in earnest his work to thwart the purpose of God if possible.

If the influence in our college is what it should be, the youth who are educated there will be enabled to discern God and glorify Him in all His work; and while engaged in cultivating the faculties which God has given them, they will be preparing to render Him more efficient service. The intellect, sanctified, will unlock the treasures of God's word and gather its precious gems to present to other minds and lead them also to search for the deep things of God. A knowledge of the riches of His grace will ennoble and elevate the human soul, and through connection with Christ it will become a partaker of the divine nature and obtain power to resist the advances of Satan.

Students must be impressed with the fact that knowledge alone may be, in the hands of the enemy of all good, a power to destroy them. It was a very intellectual being, one who occupied a high position among the angelic throng, that finally became a rebel; and many a mind of superior intellectual attainments is now being led captive by his power. The sanctified knowledge which God imparts is of the right quality and will tell to His glory.

The work of the teachers in our college will be laborious. Among those who attend the school there will be some who are nothing less than Satan's agents. They have no respect for the rules of the school, and they demoralize all who associate with them. After the teachers have done all they can do to reform this class, after they have, by personal effort, by entreaties and prayer, endeavored to reach them, and they refuse all the efforts made in their behalf and continue in their course of sin, then it will be necessary to separate them from the school, that others may not be contaminated by their evil influence.

To maintain proper discipline and yet exercise pitying love and tenderness for the souls of those under his care, the teacher needs a constant supply of the wisdom and grace of God. Order must be maintained. But those who love souls, the purchase of the blood of Christ, should do their utmost to save the erring. These poor sinful ones are too frequently left in darkness and deception to pursue their own course, and those who should help them let them alone to go to ruin.

Many excuse their neglect of these careless, wayward ones by referring to the religious privileges at Battle Creek. They say that if these do not call them to repentance, nothing will. The opportunities of attending Sabbath school, and listening to the sermons from the desk, are indeed precious privileges; but they may be passed by all unheeded, while if one with true interest should come close to these souls in sympathy and love, he might succeed in reaching them. I have been shown that personal effort, judiciously put forth, will have a telling influence upon these cases considered so hardened. All may not be so hard at heart as they appear. Our people in Battle Creek should feel a deep interest for the youth whom the providence of God has brought under their influence. We have seen a good work done in the salvation of many who have come to our college, but much more can be accomplished by personal effort.

The selfish love of "me and mine" keeps many from doing their duty to others. Do they think that all the work they have to do is for themselves and their own children? "Inasmuch," says Christ," as ye did it not to one of the least of these, ye did it not to me." Are your own children of more value in the sight of God than the children of your neighbors? God is no respecter of persons.

We are to do all we can to save souls. None should be passed by because they have not the culture and religious training of more favored children. Had these erring, neglected ones enjoyed the same home advantages, they might have shown far more nobility of soul and greater talent for usefulness than many who have been watched over day and night with gentlest care and overflowing love. Angels pity these stray lambs; angels weep, while human eyes are dry, and human hearts are closed against them. If God had not given me another work, I would make it the business of my life to care for those whom others will not take the trouble to save.

In the day of God somebody will be held responsible for the loss of these dear souls. Parents who have neglected their God-given responsibilities must meet that neglect in the judgment. The Lord will then inquire: Where are the children that I gave you to train for Me? Why are they not at My right hand? Many parents will then see that unwise love blinded their eyes to their children's faults and left those children to develop deformed characters, unfit for heaven. Others will see that they did not give their children time and attention, love and tenderness; their own neglect of duty made the children what they are.

Teachers will see where they could have worked for the Master by seeking to save the apparently incorrigible cases that they cast off in the youth of tender years. And the members of the church will see that they might have done good service for the Master in seeking to help those who most needed help. While their interest and love were lavished upon their own families, there were many inexperienced youth who might have been taken to their hearts and homes, and whose precious souls could have been saved by interest and kindly care.

Educators should understand how to guard the health of their students. They should restrain them from taxing their minds with too many studies. If they leave college with a knowledge of the sciences but with shattered constitutions, it would have been better had they not entered the school at all. Some parents feel that their children are being educated at considerable expense, and they urge them forward in their studies. Students are desirous of taking many studies in order to complete their education in as short a time as possible. The professors have allowed some to advance too rapidly.

While some may need urging, others need holding back. Students should ever be diligent, but they ought not to crowd their minds so as to become intellectual dyspeptics. They should not be so pressed with studies as to neglect the culture of the manners; and, above all, they should let nothing interfere with their seasons of prayer, which bring them in connection with Jesus Christ, the best teacher the world has ever known. In no case should they deprive themselves of religious privileges. Many students have made their studies the first great object and have neglected prayer and absented themselves from the Sabbath school and the prayer meeting, and from neglect of religious duties they have returned to their homes backslidden from God.

A most important part of their education has been neglected. That which lies at the foundation of all true knowledge should not have been made a secondary consideration. The fear of the Lord is the beginning of wisdom. "Seek ye first the kingdom of God, and His righteousness." This must not be made last, but first. The student must have opportunities to become conversant with his Bible. He needs time for this. A student who makes God his strength, who is becoming intelligent in the knowledge of God as revealed in His word, is laying the foundation for a thorough education.

God designs that the college at Battle Creek shall reach a higher standard of intellectual and moral culture than any other institution of the kind in our land. The youth should be taught the importance of cultivating their physical, mental, and moral powers, that they may not only reach the highest attainments in science, but, through a knowledge of God, may be educated to glorify Him; that they may develop symmetrical characters, and thus be fully prepared for usefulness in this world and obtain a moral fitness for the immortal life.

I wish I could find language to express the importance of our college. All should feel that it is one of God's instrumentalities to make Himself known to man. The teachers may do a greater work than they have hitherto calculated upon. Minds are to be molded and character is to be developed by interested experiment. In the fear of God, every endeavor to develop the higher faculties, even if it is marked with great imperfection, should be encouraged and strengthened.

The minds of many of the youth are rich in talents which are put to no available use because they have lacked opportunity to develop them. Their physical powers have been strengthened by exercise; but the faculties of the mind lie hidden, because the discernment and God-given tact of the educator have not been exercised in bringing them into use. Aids to self-development must be given to the youth; they must be drawn out, stimulated, encouraged, and urged to action.

Workers are needed all over the world. The truth of God is to be carried to foreign lands, that those in darkness may be enlightened by it. God requires that a zeal be shown in this direction infinitely greater than has hitherto been manifested. As a people, we are almost paralyzed. We are not doing one-twentieth part of the good we might, because selfishness prevails to a large extent among us. Cultivated intellect is now needed in the cause of God, for novices cannot do the work acceptably. God has devised our college as an instrumentality for developing workers of whom He will not be ashamed. The height man may reach by proper culture has not hitherto been realized. We have among us more than an average of men of ability. If their talents were brought into use, we should have twenty ministers where we now have one.

Teachers should not feel that their duty is done when their pupils have been instructed in the sciences. But they should realize that they have the most important missionary field in the world. If the capabilities of all engaged as instructors are used as God would have them, they will be most successful missionaries. It must be remembered that the youth are forming habits which will, in nine cases out of ten, decide their future. The influence of the company they keep, the associations they form, and the principles they adopt will be carried with them through life.

It is a terrible fact, and one which should make the hearts of parents tremble, that the colleges to which the youth of our day are sent for the cultivation of the mind endanger their morals. As innocent youth when placed with hardened criminals learn lessons of crime they never before dreamed of, so pure-minded young people, through association with college companions of corrupt habits, lose their purity of character and become vicious and debased.

Parents should awake to their responsibilities and understand what they are doing in sending their children from home to colleges where they can expect nothing else but that they will become demoralized. The college at

Battle Creek should stand higher in moral tone than any other college in the land, that the safety of the children entrusted to her keeping may not be endangered. If teachers do their work in the fear of God, working with the spirit of Christ for the salvation of the souls of the students, God will crown their efforts with success. God-fearing parents will be more concerned in regard to the characters their children bring home with them from college than in regard to the success and advancement made in their studies.

I was shown that our college was designed of God to accomplish the great work of saving souls. It is only when brought under full control of the Spirit of God that the talents of an individual are rendered useful to the fullest extent. The precepts and principles of religion are the first steps in the acquisition of knowledge, and lie at the very foundation of true education. Knowledge and science must be vitalized by the Spirit of God in order to serve the noblest purposes.

The Christian alone can make the right use of knowledge. Science, in order to be fully appreciated, must be viewed from a religious standpoint. The heart which is ennobled by the grace of God can best comprehend the real value of education. The attributes of God, as seen in His created works, can be appreciated only as we have a knowledge of the Creator. In order to lead the youth to the fountain of truth, to the Lamb of God who taketh away the sins of the world, the teachers must not only be acquainted with the theory of the truth, but must have an experimental knowledge of the way of holiness. Knowledge is power when united with true piety.

• Duty of Parents to the College

Our brethren and sisters abroad should feel it their duty to sustain this institution which God has devised. Some of the students return home with murmuring and complaints, and parents and members of the church give an attentive ear to their exaggerated, one-sided statements. They would do well to consider that there are two sides to the story; but instead, they allow these garbled reports to build up a barrier between them and the college. They then begin to express fears, questionings, and suspicions in regard to the way the college is conducted.

Such an influence does great harm. The words of dissatisfaction spread like a contagious disease, and the impression made upon minds is hard to efface. The story enlarges with every repetition, until it becomes of gigantic proportions, when investigation would reveal the fact that there was no fault with teachers or professors. They were simply doing their duty in enforcing the rules of the school, which must be carried out or the school will become demoralized.

Parents do not always move wisely. Many are very exacting in wishing to bring others to their ideas, and become impatient and overbearing if they cannot do this; but when their own children are required to observe rules and regulations at school, and these children fret under the necessary restraint, too often their parents, who profess to love and fear God, join with the children instead of reproving them and correcting their faults. This often proves the turning point in the character of their children. Rules and order are broken down, and discipline is trampled underfoot.

The children despise restraint and are allowed to speak disparagingly of the institutions at Battle Creek. If parents would only reflect, they would see the evil result of the course they are pursuing. It would indeed be a most wonderful thing if, in a school of four hundred students, managed by men and women subject to the frailties of humanity, every move should be so perfect, so exact, as to challenge criticism.

If parents would place themselves in the position of the teachers and see how difficult it must necessarily be to manage and discipline a school of hundreds of students of every grade and class of minds, they might upon reflection see things differently. They should consider that some children have never been disciplined at home. Having always been indulged and never trained to obedience, it would be greatly for their advantage to be removed from their injudicious parents and placed under as severe regulations and drilling as soldiers in an army. Unless something shall be done for these children who have been so sadly neglected by unfaithful parents, they will never be accepted of Jesus; unless some power of control shall be brought to bear upon them, they will be worthless in this life and will have no part in the future life.

In heaven there is perfect order, perfect obedience, perfect peace and harmony. Those who have had no respect for order or discipline in this life would have no respect for the order which is observed in heaven. They can never be admitted into heaven, for all worthy of an entrance there will love order and respect discipline. The characters formed in this life will determine the future destiny. When Christ shall come, He will not change the character of any individual. Precious, probationary time is given to be improved in washing our robes of character and making them white in the blood of the Lamb.

To remove the stains of sin requires the work of a lifetime. Every day renewed efforts in restraining and denying self are needed. Every day there are new battles to fight and victories to be gained. Every day the soul should be called out in earnest pleading with God for the mighty victories of the cross. Parents should neglect no duty on their part to benefit their children. They should so train them that they may be a blessing to society here and may reap the reward of eternal life hereafter.

39. The Cause in Iowa

I have been shown that the cause in Iowa is in a deplorable condition. Young men have been connected with the different branches of the work who have not been in a condition spiritually to benefit the people. Quite a number of inexperienced and inefficient men have been laboring in the cause who need a great work done for them.

• College Students

The influence of Brother B has not been altogether what it should be. While at the college in Battle Creek he was in many respects an exemplary young man; but he, with other young gentlemen and ladies, in a secretive manner, made an excursion to ——. This was not noble, frank, and just. They all knew that it was a breach of the rules, but they ventured in the path of transgression. These young men, by this act and their attitude since in relation to their wrong course, have cast reflections upon the college that are most unjust.

When the brethren in Iowa accepted the labors of Brother B under these circumstances, they did wrong. If they pursue a similar course in other cases, they will greatly displease God. The fact that he had been a young man of excellent deportment gave him greater influence over others, and his example in standing in defiance of the rules and authority which sustain and control the school influenced others to do as he had done. Laws and regulations will be of no force in conducting the school if such things are sanctioned by our brethren at large. A demoralizing influence is easily introduced into a school. Many will readily partake of the spirit of rebellion and defiance unless prompt and vigilant efforts are continually put forth to maintain the standard of the school by strict rules regulating the conduct of the students.

The labors of Brother B will not be acceptable to God until he shall fully see and acknowledge his wrong in violating the rules of the college and shall endeavor to counteract the influence he has exerted to injure its reputation. Many more students would have come from Iowa had it not been for this unhappy circumstance. Could you, Brother B, see and realize the influence of this one wrong step, and the feelings of passion, of jealousy, and almost hatred that filled your heart because your course was questioned by Professor Brownsberger, you would tremble at the sight of yourself and at the triumph of those who cannot bear restraint and who wage war against rules and regulations which check them from pursuing their own course. Being a professed disciple of the meek and lowly Jesus, your influence and responsibility are greatly increased.

Brother B, I hope you will go over the ground carefully and consider your first temptation to depart from the rules of the college. Study critically the character of the government of our school. The rules which were enforced were none too strict. But anger was cherished; for the time being, reason was dethroned and the heart was made a prey to ungovernable passion. Before you were aware, you had taken a step which a few hours previous you would not have taken under any pressure of temptation. Impulse had overcome reason, and you could not recall the injury done to yourself nor to an institution of God. Our only safety under all circumstances is in being always master of ourselves in the strength of Jesus our Redeemer.

Our college has not that influence of popular opinion to sustain it in exercising government and enforcing its rules, which other colleges have. In one respect it is a denominational school; but, unless guarded, a worldly character and influence will be given to it. Sabbathkeeping students must possess more moral courage than has hitherto been manifested, to preserve the moral and religious influence of the school, or it will differ from the colleges of other denominations only in name. God devised and established this college, designing that it should be molded by high religious interests and that every year unconverted students who are sent to Battle Creek should return to their homes as soldiers of the cross of Christ.

Professors and teachers should reflect upon the best means of maintaining the peculiar character of our college; all should highly esteem the privileges which we enjoy in having such a school and should faithfully sustain it and guard it from any breath of reproach. Selfishness may chill the energies of the students, and the worldly element may gain a prevailing influence over the entire school. This would bring the frown of God upon that institution.

Those students who profess to love God and obey the truth should possess that degree of self-control and strength of religious principle that will enable them to remain unmoved amid temptations and to stand up for Jesus in the college, at their boardinghouses, or wherever they may be. Religion is not to be worn merely as a cloak in the house of God, but religious principle must characterize the entire life. Those who are drinking at the fountain of life will not, like the worldling, manifest a longing desire for change and pleasure. In their deportment and character will be seen the rest and peace and happiness that they have found in Jesus by daily laying their perplexities and burdens at His feet. They will show that there is contentment and even joy in the path of obedience and duty.

Such will exert an influence over their fellow students which will tell upon the entire school. Those who compose this faithful army will refresh and strengthen the teachers and professors in their efforts by discouraging every species of unfaithfulness, of discord, and of neglect to comply with the rules and regulations. Their influence will be saving, and their works will not perish in the great day of God, but will follow them into the future world; and the influence of their life here will tell throughout the ceaseless ages of eternity. One earnest, conscientious, faithful young man in school is an inestimable treasure. Angels of heaven look lovingly upon him. His precious Saviour loves him, and in the Ledger of Heaven will be recorded every work of righteousness, every temptation resisted, every evil overcome. He will thus be laying up a good foundation against the time to come, that he may lay hold on eternal life.

The course pursued at the college by Brother C, in seeking the society of young ladies, was wrong. This was not the object for which he was sent to Battle Creek. Students are not sent here to form attachments, to indulge in flirtation or courting, but to obtain an education. Should they be allowed to follow their own inclinations in this respect, the college would soon become demoralized. Several have used their precious school days in slyly flirting and courting, notwithstanding the vigilance of professors and teachers. When a teacher of any of the branches takes advantage of his position to win the affections of his students with a view to marriage, his course is worthy of severest censure.

The influence of the sons of Brother D and of several others from Iowa, also that of Mr. E of Illinois, has been no benefit to our school. The relatives and friends of these students have sustained them in casting reflections upon the college. The sons of Brother D have ability and aptness, which is a source of gratification to the parents; but when the ability of these young men is exerted to break down the rules and regulations of the college, it is nothing that should excite pleasure in the hearts of any. The paper containing that apt and sharp criticism concerning one who teaches in the college will not be read with such gratification in the day when every man's work shall pass in review before God. Brother and Sister D will then meet a record of the work they did in giving their son poorly concealed justification in this matter. They must then answer for the influence they have exerted against the school, one of God's instrumentalities, and for making the colored statements which have prevented youth from coming to the college, where they might have been brought under the influence of truth.

Some souls will be lost in consequence of this wrong influence. The great day of God's judgment will unfold the influence of the words spoken and the attitude assumed. Brother and Sister D have duties at home which they have neglected. They have been drunken with the cares of this life. Work and hurry and drive are the order of the day, and their intense worldliness has had its molding influence upon their children, upon the church, and upon the world.

It is the example of those who hold the truth in righteousness which will condemn the world.

Upon Christian youth depend in a great measure the preservation and perpetuity of the institutions which God has devised as means by which to advance His work. This grave responsibility rests upon the youth of today who are coming upon the stage of action. Never was there a period when results so important depended upon a generation of men; then how important that the young should be qualified for the great work, that God may use them as His instruments. Their Maker has claims upon them which are paramount to all others.

It is God that has given life and every physical and mental endowment they possess. He has bestowed upon them capabilities for wise improvement, that they may be entrusted with a work which will be as enduring as eternity. In return for His great gifts He claims a due cultivation and exercise of their intellectual and moral faculties. He did not give them these faculties merely for their amusement, or to be abused in working against His will and His providence, but that they might use them to advance the knowledge of truth and holiness in the world. He claims their gratitude, their veneration and love, for His continued kindness and infinite mercies. He justly requires obedience to His laws and to all wise regulations which will restrain and guard the youth from Satan's devices and lead them in paths of peace.

If youth could see that in complying with the laws and regulations of our institutions they are only doing that which will improve their standing in society, elevate the character, ennoble the mind, and increase their happiness, they would not rebel against just rules and wholesome requirements, nor engage in creating suspicion and prejudice against these institutions. Our youth should have a spirit of energy and fidelity to meet the demands upon them, and this will be a guaranty of success. The wild, reckless character of many of the youth in this age of the world is heartsickening. Much of the blame lies upon their parents at home. Without the fear of God no one can be truly happy.

Those students who have chafed under authority, and have returned to their homes to cast reproach upon the college, will have to see their sin and counteract the influence they have cast, before they can have the approval of God. The believers in Iowa have displeased God in their credulity in accepting the reports brought them. They should ever be found on the side of order and discipline, instead of encouraging lax government.

A youth is sent from a distant state to share the benefits of the college at Battle Creek. He goes forth from his home with the blessing of his parents upon his head. He has listened daily to the earnest prayers offered at the family altar, and he is apparently well started in a life of noble resolve and purity. His convictions and purposes when he leaves home are right. In Battle Creek he will meet with associates of all classes. He becomes acquainted with some whose example is a blessing to all who come within the sphere of their influence.

Again, he meets with those who are apparently kind and interesting, and whose intelligence charms him; but they have a low standard of morality and no religious faith. For a time he resists every inducement to yield to temptation; but as he observes that those who profess to be Christians seem to enjoy the company of this irreligious class, his purposes and high resolves begin to waver. He enjoys the lively sallies and jovial spirit of these youth, and he is almost imperceptibly drawn more and more into their company. His stronghold seems to be giving way; his hitherto brave heart is growing weak. He is invited to accompany them for a walk, and they lead him to a saloon.

Oysters or other refreshments are called for, and he is ashamed to draw away and refuse the treat. Having once overstepped the bounds, he goes again and again. A glass of beer is thought to be unobjectionable, and he accepts it; but still, with all, there are sharp twinges of conscience. He does not openly take his stand on the side of God and truth and righteousness; the society of the sly, deceptive class with which he is associated pleases him, and he is led a step further. His tempters urge that it is certainly harmless to play a game of cards and to watch the players in a billiard hall, and he yields repeatedly to the temptation.

Young men attend our college who, unsuspected by parents or guardians, hang about saloons, drink beer, and play cards and games in billiard halls. These things the students try to keep a profound secret among themselves; and professors and teachers are kept in ignorance of the satanic work going on.

hen this young man is enticed to pursue some evil course which must be kept secret, he has a battle with conscience; but inclination triumphs. He meant to be a Christian when he came to Battle Creek, but he is led steadily and surely in the downward road. Evil companions and seducers found among the youth of Sabbathkeeping parents, some of them living in Battle Creek, find that he can be tempted; and they secretly exult in their power and the fact that he is weak and will yield so readily to their seductive influences. They find that he can be shamed and confused by those who have had light and who have hardened their hearts in sin. Just such influences as these will be found wherever youth associate together.

The time will come when that young man who left his father's house pure and true, with noble purposes, will be ruined. He has learned to love the evil and reject the good. He did not realize his danger, not being armed with watchfulness and prayer. He did not place himself at once under the guardian care of the church. He was made to believe that it was manly to be independent, not allowing his liberty to be restricted. He was taught that to ignore rules and defy laws was to enjoy true freedom; that it was slavish to be always fearing and trembling lest he do wrong. He yielded to the influence of ungodly persons who, while carrying a fair exterior, were practicing deception, vileness, and iniquity; and he was despised and derided because he was so easily duped. He went where he could not expect to find the pure and the good. He learned ways of life and habits of speech which were not elevating and ennobling. Many are in danger of being thus lead away imperceptibly until they become degraded in their own estimation. In order to gain the applause of the heartless and ungodly, they are in danger of yielding the purity and nobleness of manhood, and of becoming slaves to Satan.

• Young Ministers

I have been shown that Iowa will be left far behind other states in the standard of pure godliness if young men are permitted to have influence in her conference while it is evident that they are not connected with God. I feel it to be a most solemn duty resting upon me to say that Iowa would be in a better condition today if Brethren F and G had remained silent. Not having experimental godliness themselves, how can they lead the people to that Fountain with which they themselves are unacquainted?

A prevailing skepticism is continually increasing in reference to the Testimonies of the Spirit of God; and these youth encourage questionings and doubts instead of removing them, because they are ignorant of the spirit and power and force of the Testimonies. While thus unsanctified in heart their labor can do the people no good. They may apparently convince souls that we have the truth, but where is the Spirit and power of God to impress the heart and awaken conviction of sin? Where is the power to carry the convicted forward to an experimental knowledge of vital godliness? They have not a knowledge of this themselves; then how can they represent the religion of Christ? If young men would enter the field, in no wise discourage them; but first let them learn the trade.

Brother G might have united his efforts with those of the physicians at the sanitarium, but he could not harmonize with them. He was too self-sufficient to be a learner. He was puffed up and egotistical. He had just as good a prospect as other young men; but while they were willing to receive instruction and to occupy any position where they could be of the greatest service, he would not adapt himself to the situation. He thought he knew too much to occupy a secondary position. He did not commend himself to the patients. He was so overbearing and dictatorial that his influence could not be tolerated in the sanitarium. He was not lacking in ability, and had he been willing to be taught he might have gained a practical knowledge of the work of a physician; had he preserved his spirit in meekness of humility he might have made a success.

But natural defects of character have not been seen and overcome. There has been a disposition on his part to deceive, to prevaricate. This will destroy the usefulness of anyone's life, and would certainly close to him the doors of the ministry. The strictest veracity should be cultivated and all deception shunned as one would shun the leprosy. He has felt embarrassed because of his diminutive stature. This cannot be remedied, but it is within his power to remedy his defective character if he will. Mind and character may, with care, be molded after the divine Pattern.

It is the true elevation of the mind, not an affectation of superiority, that makes the man. The proper cultivation of the mental powers makes man all that he is. These ennobling faculties are given to aid in forming character for the future, immortal life. Man was created for a higher, holier state of enjoyment than this world can afford. He was made in the image of God for high and noble purposes, such as engage the attention of angels.

The youth of today do not generally think deeply or act wisely. Were they aware of the dangers besetting their every step, they would move cautiously and escape many snares that Satan has prepared for their feet. Be careful, my brother, not to appear what you are not. Gilded imitation will be readily distinguished from the pure metal. Examine with the greatest care not only yourself, but the position which each one of your family occupies. Trace the history of each, and meditate as to the result of the course pursued. Consider why it is that some persons are loved and respected by the truly good, while others are despised and shunned. Look upon these things in the light of eternity, and wherein you discover that others have failed, carefully avoid the course that they have pursued.

It will be well to remember that tendencies of character are transmitted from parents to children. Meditate seriously upon these things, and then in the fear of God gird on the armor for a life conflict with hereditary tendencies, imitating none but the divine Pattern. You must work with perseverance, constancy, and zeal if you would succeed. You will have yourself to conquer, which will be the hardest battle of all. Determined opposition to your own ways and your wrong habits will secure for you precious and everlasting victories. But while your strong traits of character are cherished, while you wish to lead instead of being willing to follow, you will make no success. Your feelings are quick, and unless you are guarded you indulge in temper. Upon the young must rest responsibilities and the discharge of important duties; are you qualifying yourself to do your part in the fear of God?

Brother F is not fitted for his work. He has nearly everything to learn. His character is defective. He has not been educated from childhood to be a caretaker, a laborer, a burden bearer. He has not seen and felt the work to be done for himself, and hence is not prepared to appreciate the work to be done for others. He is self-sufficient. He assumes to know more than he really does. When he becomes thoroughly consecrated by the Spirit of God, and fully realizes the solemnity and responsibility of the work of a minister of Christ, he will feel himself entirely insufficient for the task.

He is deficient in many respects; and his deficiencies will be reproduced in others, giving to the world an unfavorable impression of the character of our work and of the ministers who are engaged in it. He must become acquainted with the burdens and duties of practical life before he can be fitted to engage in the most responsible work ever given to mortal man. All young ministers need to be learners before they become teachers. While I would encourage young men to enter the ministry, I would say that I am authorized of God to recommend and urge upon them a fitness for the work in which they are to engage.

The Brethren F are not inclined to be care-takers and burden bearers. Carelessness and imperfection are seen in all they undertake. They are reckless in their conversation and deportment. The solemn, elevating, ennobling influence which should characterize every minister of the gospel cannot be exerted in their lives until they have been transformed and molded after the divine image. Selfishness exists more or less in each of them, though in a much larger degree in some than in others.

There is a spirit of self-sufficiency and self-importance in these young men that unfits them for the work of God. They need to severely discipline themselves before they can be accepted of God as laborers in His cause. There is a natural laziness that must be overcome. They should have a faithful drilling in the temporal affairs of life. They must be learners; and when they show a marked success in the lesser responsibilities, then they will be fitted to be entrusted with greater ones. The different conferences are better off without such inefficient workers. The burden of souls can no more rest upon men in their state of unconsecration than upon babes. They are ignorant of vital godliness and need a most thorough conversion before they can be even Christians.

Brother A F needs a thorough drill in our college. His language is defective. There is a coarseness and want of refinement in his deportment; yet notwithstanding this, he is self-sufficient and entirely deceived in regard to his ability. He has had no real faith in the Testimonies of the Spirit of God. He has not carefully studied them and practiced the truths brought out. While he has so little spirituality he will not understand the value of the Testimonies nor their real object. These young men read the Bible, but they have very little experience in prayerful, earnest, humble searching of the Scriptures, that they may be thoroughly furnished unto all good works.

There is great danger of encouraging a class of men to enter the field who have no genuine burden for souls. They may be able to interest the people and to engage in controversy, while they are by no means men of thought, who will improve their ability and enlarge their capacities. We have a dwarfed and defective ministry. Unless Christ shall abide in the men who preach the truth, they will lower the moral and religious standard wherever they are tolerated. One example is given them, even Christ.

"All Scripture is given by inspiration of God, and is profitable for doctrine, for reproof, for correction, for instruction in righteousness: that the man of God may be perfect, throughly furnished unto all good works." In the Bible we have the unerring counsel of God. Its teachings, practically carried out, will fit men for any position of duty. It is the voice of God speaking every day to the soul. How carefully should the young study the word of God and treasure up its sentiments in the heart, that its precepts may be made to govern the whole conduct. Our young ministers, and those who have been some time preaching, show a marked deficiency in their understanding of the Scriptures. The work of the Holy Spirit is to enlighten the darkened understanding, to melt the selfish, stony heart, to subdue the rebellious transgressor, and save him from the corrupting influences of the world. The prayer of Christ for His disciples was: "Sanctify them through Thy truth: Thy word is truth."

The sword of the Spirit, which is the word of God, pierces the heart of the sinner and cuts it in pieces. When the theory of the truth is repeated without its sacred influence being felt upon the soul of the speaker, it has no force upon the hearers, but is rejected as error, the speaker making himself responsible for the loss of souls. We must be sure that our ministers are converted men, humble, meek, and lowly of heart.

There must be a decided change in the ministry. A more critical examination is necessary in respect to the qualifications of a minister. Moses was directed of God to obtain an experience in care-taking, in thoughtfulness, in tender solicitude for his flock, that he might, as a faithful shepherd, be ready when God should call him to take charge of His people. A similar experience is essential for those who engage in the great work of preaching the truth. In order to lead souls to the life-giving fountain, the preacher must first drink at the fountain himself. He must see the infinite sacrifice made by the Son of God to save fallen men, and his own soul must be imbued with the spirit of undying love. If God appoints us hard labor to perform, we must do it without a murmur. If the path is difficult and dangerous, it is God's plan to have us follow in meekness and cry unto Him for strength.

A lesson is to be learned from the experience of some of our ministers who have known nothing comparatively of difficulties and trials, yet ever look upon themselves as martyrs. They have yet to learn to accept with thankfulness the way of God's choosing, remembering the Author of our salvation. The work of the minister should be pursued with an earnestness, energy, and zeal as much greater than that put forth in business transactions as the labor is more sacred and the result more momentous. Each day's work should tell in the eternal records as "well done;" so that if no other day should be granted in which to labor, the work would be thoroughly finished.

Our ministers, young men especially, should realize the preparation necessary to fit them for their solemn work and to prepare them for the society of pure angels. In order to be at home in heaven, we must have heaven enshrined in our hearts here. If this is not the case with us, it were better that we had no part in the work of God.

The ministry is corrupted by unsanctified ministers. Unless there shall be altogether a higher and more spiritual standard for the ministry, the truth of the gospel will become more and more powerless. The human mind is represented by the rich soil of a garden. Unless it shall receive proper cultivation, it will be overgrown with the weeds and briers of ignorance. The mind and heart need culture daily, and neglect will be productive of evil.

The more natural ability God has bestowed upon an individual, the greater the improvement he is required to make, and the greater his responsibility to use his time and talents for the glory of God. The mind must not remain dormant. If it is not exercised in the acquisition of knowledge, there will be a sinking into ignorance, superstition, and fancy. If the intellectual faculties are not cultivated as they should be to glorify God, they will become strong and powerful aids in leading to perdition.

While young men should guard against being pompous and independent, they should be continually making marked improvement. They should accept every opportunity to cultivate the more noble, generous traits of character. If young men would feel their dependence upon God every moment and cherish a spirit of prayer, a breathing out of the soul to God at all times and in all places, they might better know the will of God.

But I have been shown that Brethren F and G are almost wholly unacquainted with the operations of God's Spirit. They have been working in their own strength and have been so fully wrapped up in themselves that they have not seen and realized their great destitution. They talk flippantly of the Testimonies given of God for the benefit of His people, and pass judgment upon them, giving their opinions and criticizing this and that, when they would better place their hands upon their lips and lie with their faces in the dust; for they know no more of the spirit of the Testimonies than they do of the Spirit of God.

They are novices in the truth and dwarfs in religious experience. The greatest victories which are gained to the cause are not by labored argument, ample facilities, abundance of influence, and plenty of means; but they are those victories which are gained in the audience chamber with God, when earnest, agonizing faith lays hold upon the mighty arm of power. When Jacob found himself utterly prostrate and in a helpless condition, he poured out his soul to God in an agony of earnestness. The angel of God pleaded to be released, but Jacob would not let go his hold. The stricken man, suffering bodily pain, presented his earnest supplication with the boldness which living faith imparts. "I will not let Thee go," he said, "except Thou bless me."

There are deep mysteries in the word of God, which will never be discovered by minds that are unaided by the Spirit of God. There are also unsearchable mysteries in the plan of redemption, which finite minds can never comprehend. Inexperienced youth might better tax their minds and exercise their ability to gain an understanding of matters that are revealed; for unless they possess more spiritual enlightenment than they now have, it would take a lifetime to learn the revealed will of God. When they have cherished the light they already have, and made a practical use of it, they will be able to take a step forward. God's providence is a continual school, in which He is ever leading men to see the true aims of life. None are too young, and none too old, to learn in this school by paying diligent heed to the lessons taught by the divine Teacher. He is the True Shepherd, and He calls His sheep by name. By the wanderers His voice is heard, saying: "This is the way, walk ye in it."

Young men who have never made a success in the temporal duties of life will be equally unprepared to engage in the higher duties. A religious experience is attained only through conflict, through disappointment, through severe discipline of self, through earnest prayer. Living faith must grasp the promises unflinchingly, and then many may come from close communion with God with shining faces, saying, as did Jacob: "I have seen God face to face, and my life is preserved."

The steps upward to heaven must be taken one at a time; every advance step strengthens us for the next. The transforming power of the grace of God upon the human heart is a work which but few comprehend because they are too indolent to make the necessary effort. The lessons which young ministers learn in going about and being waited upon when they have not a fitness for the work have a demoralizing influence upon them. They do not know their place and keep it. They are not balanced by firm principles. They talk knowingly of things they know nothing of, and hence those who accept them as teachers are misled. One such person will inspire more skepticism in minds than several will be able to counteract, do the best they can.

Men of small minds delight to quibble, to criticize, to seek for something to question, thinking this a mark of sharpness; but instead it shows a mind lacking refinement and elevation. How much better to be engaged in seeking to cultivate themselves and to ennoble and elevate their minds. As a flower turns to the sun that the bright rays may aid in perfecting its beauty and symmetry, so should the youth turn to the Sun of Righteousness, that heaven's light may shine upon them, perfecting their characters and giving them a deep and abiding experience in the things of God. Then they may reflect the divine rays of light upon others. Those who choose to gather doubts and unbelief and skepticism will experience no growth in grace or spirituality and are unfitted for the solemn responsibility of bearing the truth to others.

The world is to be warned of its coming doom. The slumbers of those who are lying in sin and error are so deep, so deathlike, that the voice of God through a wide-awake minister is needed to awaken them. Unless the ministers are converted, the people will not be. The cold formalism that is now prevailing among us must give place to the living energy of experimental godliness. There is no fault with the theory of the truth; it is perfectly clear and harmonious. But young ministers may speak the truth fluently, and yet have no real sense of the words they utter. They do not appreciate the value of the truth they present, and little realize what it has cost those, who, with prayers and tears, through trial and opposition, have sought for it as for hid treasures. Every new link in the chain of truth was to them as precious as tried gold. These links are now united in a perfect whole. Truths have been dug out of the rubbish of superstition and error, by earnest prayer for light and knowledge, and have been presented to the people as precious pearls of priceless value.

The gospel is a revelation to man of beams of light and hope from the eternal world. All the light does not burst upon us at once, but it comes as we can bear it. Inquiring minds that hunger for a knowledge of God's will are never satisfied; the deeper they search, the more they realize their ignorance and deplore their blindness. It is beyond the power of man to conceive the high and noble attainments that are within his reach if he will combine human effort with the grace of God, who is the Source of all wisdom and power. And there is an eternal weight of glory beyond. "Eye hath not seen, nor ear heard, neither have entered into the heart of man, the things which God hath prepared for them that love Him."

We have the most solemn message of truth ever borne to the world. This truth is more and more respected by unbelievers because it cannot be controverted. In view of this fact, our young men become self-confident and self-inflated. They take the truths which have been brought out by other minds, and without study or earnest prayer meet opponents and engage in contests, indulging in sharp speeches and witticisms, flattering themselves that this is doing the work of a gospel minister. In order to be fitted for God's work, these men need as thorough a conversion as Paul experienced. Ministers must be living representatives of the truth they preach. They must have greater spiritual life, characterized by greater simplicity. The words must be received from God and given to the people. The attention of the people must be arrested. Our message is a savor of life unto life or of death unto death. The destinies of souls are balancing. "Multitudes are in the valley of decision. A voice should be heard crying: If the Lord be God, follow Him: but if Baal, then follow him."

Prompt, energetic, and earnest action may save an undecided soul. No one can tell how much is lost by attempting to preach without the unction of the Holy Spirit. There are souls in every congregation who are hesitating, almost persuaded to be wholly for God. The decision is being made for time and for eternity; but it is too often the case that the minister has not the spirit and power of the message of truth in his own heart, hence no direct appeals are made to those souls that are trembling in the balance. The result is that impressions are not deepened upon the hearts of the convicted ones, and they leave the meeting feeling less inclined to accept the service of Christ than when they came. They decide to wait for a more favorable opportunity, but it never comes. That godless discourse, like Cain's offering, lacked the Saviour. The golden opportunity is lost, and the cases of these souls are decided. Is not too much at stake to preach in an indifferent manner and without feeling the burden of souls?

In this age of moral darkness it will take something more than dry theory to move souls. Ministers must have a living connection with God. They must preach as though they believed what they said. Living truths, falling from the lips of the man of God, will cause sinners to tremble and the convicted to cry out: "Jehovah is the God; I am resolved to be wholly on the Lord's side." Never should the messenger of God cease his strivings for greater light and power from above. He should toil on, pray on, hope on, amid discouragement and darkness, determined to gain a thorough knowledge of the Scriptures and to come behind in no gift. As long as there is one soul to be benefited, he should press forward with new courage at every effort. There is work, earnest work, to be accomplished. Souls for whom Christ died are in peril. So long as Jesus has said, "I will never leave thee, nor forsake thee," so long as the crown of righteousness is offered to the overcomer, so long as our Advocate pleads in the sinner's behalf, ministers of Christ should labor in hope, with tireless energy and persevering faith.

But while the truth of God is carried by young and inexperienced men whose hearts are scarcely touched by the grace of God, the cause will languish. Brethren F and G are more ready to argue than to pray; they are more ready to contend than to persuade, endeavoring to impress the people with the solemn character of the work for this time. Men who dare to assume the responsibility of receiving the word from the mouth of God and giving it to the people, make themselves accountable for the truth they present and the influence they exert. If they are truly men of God, their hope is not in themselves, but in what He will do for them and through them. They do not go forth self-inflated, calling the attention of the people to their smartness and aptness; they feel their responsibility and work with spiritual energy, treading in the path of self-denial which the Master trod.

Self-sacrifice is seen at every step, and they mourn because of their inability to do more in the cause of God. Their path is one of trial and conflict; but it is marked by the footprints of their Redeemer, the Captain of their salvation, who was made perfect through suffering.

In their labor the undershepherds must closely follow the directions, and manifest the spirit, of the Chief Shepherd. Skepticism and apostasy are met everywhere. God wants men to labor in His cause who have hearts as true as steel and who will stand steadfast in integrity, undaunted by circumstances. Amid trial and gloom they are just what they were when their prospects were brightened by hope and when their outward surroundings were all that they could desire. Daniel in the lions' den is the same Daniel who stood before the king, enshrouded by the light of God. Paul in the dark dungeon, awaiting the sentence which he knew was to come from the cruel Nero, is the same Paul who addressed the court of Areopagus. A man whose heart is stayed upon God in the hour of his most afflicting trials and most discouraging surroundings is just what he was in prosperity, when the light and favor of God seemed to be upon him. Faith reaches to the unseen and grasps eternal things.

There are many in Iowa who are tearing down rather than building up, casting unbelief and darkness rather than light; and the cause of God is languishing when it should be flourishing. Ministers should dare to be true. Paul wrote to Timothy: "Let no man despise thy youth; but be thou an example of the believers, in word, in conversation, in charity, in spirit, in faith, in purity." "Meditate upon these things; give thyself wholly to them; that thy profiting may appear to all. Take heed unto thyself, and unto the doctrine; continue in them: for in doing this thou shalt both save thyself, and them that hear thee."

The word and will of God are expressed in the Scriptures by inspired penmen. We should bind them as frontlets between our eyes and walk according to their precepts; then we shall walk safely. Every chapter and every verse is a communication of God to man. In studying the word, the soul that hungers and thirsts for righteousness will be impressed by the divine utterances. Skepticism can have no power over a soul that with humility searches the Scriptures.

40. Our Publishing Houses

God would have all who are connected with His institutions show aptness, discrimination, and forethought. He would have them become men and women of cultivated intellect, coming behind in no qualification; and as they shall individually feel the necessity of this and shall work to the point, Jesus will aid them in their endeavors. As they work upon the plan of addition in securing the graces of the Spirit, God will work in their behalf upon the plan of multiplication. Connection with God will give the soul expansion, will exalt it, transform it, and make it sensible of its own powers, and will give a clearer sense of the responsibility resting upon each individual to make a wise use of the faculties which God has bestowed.

Everyone should study strict economy in the outlay of means; and he should exercise even greater faithfulness in handling that which belongs to another than in managing his own affairs. But this is seldom done. No individual is personally benefited with the profits of our offices or made to suffer by the losses incurred; but the property belongs to the Lord, and His cause is materially affected by the manner in which the labor is performed. If the cause of God is limited in its resources, important work which might and should be done is neglected.

While economy should always be practiced, it should never degenerate into meanness. All who work in our offices should feel that they are handling God's property, that they are responsible for the increase of the capital invested, and that they will be accountable in the day of God if through lack of diligence and careful thought it decreases in their hands. All are called upon to avoid waste of time and means. The faithfulness or unfaithfulness of the workers to their present trust will determine their fitness to be entrusted with eternal riches. Everyone is required of God to execute the work assigned him with thoroughness and dispatch. The example of each should serve to excite diligence and thoughtfulness on the part of others. By earnest, conscientious faithfulness in everything, earth may be brought nearer heaven, and precious fruit may be borne for both worlds.

The hands employed in the various departments of our offices of publication do not accomplish the amount of work which they would be required to perform in any other office of the kind. Much time is wasted in unnecessary conversation, in visiting away the precious hours, while the work is suffered to lag. In several of the departments, loss is occasioned to the office because of persons engaging in the work who have not exercised care and economy. Were these persons engaged in doing work for themselves, some would accomplish a third more work in a day than they now do. Others would do no more than they now perform.

Business hours should be faithfully employed. To be wasteful of time or material is dishonesty before God. A few moments are squandered here, and a few moments there, which amount in the course of a week to nearly or quite a day, sometimes even exceeding this. "Time is money," and a waste of time is a waste of money to the cause of God. When those who profess the faith are dilatory and reckless of time, showing that they have not a heart interest in the prosperity of the work, unbelievers who are employed will follow their example. If all would use their time to the best account, very much means would be saved to the cause of truth. When the heart is in the work, it will be done with earnestness, energy, and dispatch. All should be awake to see what needs to be done, and apt and quick to execute, working as though under the direct supervision of the great Master, Jesus Christ.

Again, losses occur from lack of thoughtful care in the use of material and machinery. There is a failure to look after all the larger and smaller matters, that nothing be wasted or damaged through neglect. A little squandered here and there amounts to a large sum in the course of a year. Some have never learned to exercise their faculties to save the remnants, notwithstanding the injunction of Christ: "Gather up the fragments that remain, that nothing be lost." Material should not be slashed into to obtain a small piece. A little thoughtful care would lead to the gathering up and using of the little pieces that are now thrown aside and wasted. Attention should be given to saving even so trifling a matter as wastepaper, for it can be turned into money.

By a lack of personal interest many things go to waste which a few moments' thoughtful attention at the right time would save. "I forgot" causes much loss to our offices. And some feel no interest in any work or in anything which does not come under their special branch of the work. This is all wrong. Selfishness would suggest the thought, "It does not belong to me to care for that;" but faithfulness and duty would prompt everyone to care for all that comes under his observation.

The example of the head workers in the bindery is followed by the hands employed; all become careless and reckless; and an amount is wasted equal to their wages. A caretaking person at the head of the work would save hundreds of dollars yearly to the office in that one department.

A principle should exist all through the office to economize. In order to save the dollars, dimes and pennies must be carefully treasured. Men who have been successful in business have always been economical, persevering, and energetic. Let all connected with the work of God begin now to educate themselves thoroughly as care-takers. Even though their work may not be appreciated on earth, they should never degrade themselves in their own eyes by unfaithfulness in anything they undertake. It takes time for a person to become so accustomed to a given course of life as to be happy in pursuing it. We shall be individually, for time and eternity, what our habits make us.

The lives of those who form right habits, and are faithful in the performance of every duty, will be as shining lights, shedding bright beams upon the pathway of others; but if habits of unfaithfulness are indulged, if lax, indolent, neglectful habits are allowed to strengthen, a cloud darker than midnight will settle on the prospects in this life and forever debar the individual from the future life.

One selfish thought indulged, one duty neglected, prepares the way for another. What we venture to do once, we are more apt to do again. Habits of sobriety, of self-control, of economy, of close application, of sound, sensible conversation, of patience and true courtesy, are not gained without diligent, close watching over self. It is much easier to become demoralized and depraved than to conquer defects, keeping self in control and cherishing true virtues. Persevering efforts will be required if the Christian graces are ever perfected in our lives.

Important changes should take place in our offices. To defer work which needs immediate attention until a more convenient time is a mistake and results in loss. The work of repairing sometimes amounts to double what it would had it received attention in season. Many fearful losses and fatal accidents have occurred by putting off matters which should have received immediate attention. The season for action is spent in hesitancy, thinking that tomorrow will do; but tomorrow is frequently found to be too late. Our offices suffer financially every day on account of indecision, dallying, recklessness, indolence, and, on the part of some, downright dishonesty. There are some employed in these offices who pass along as indifferently as though God had given them no mental powers to be exercised in care-taking. Such are unfitted for any post of duty; they can never be depended upon. Men and women who shun duties in which difficulties are involved will remain weak and inefficient.

Those who educate themselves to do their work with dispatch, as well as with economy, will drive their business instead of allowing their business to drive them. They will not be constantly hurried and perplexed because their work is in confusion. Diligence and earnest fidelity are indispensable to success. Every hour's work passes in review before God and is registered for faithfulness or unfaithfulness. The record of wasted moments and unimproved opportunities must be met when the judgment shall sit and the books shall be opened and everyone shall be judged according to the things written in the books. Selfishness, envy, pride, jealousy, idleness, or any other sin which is cherished in the heart, will exclude one from the blessedness of heaven. "To whom ye yield yourselves servants to obey, his servants ye are."

Our offices are suffering for the want of men of stability and firmness. As I was shown from room to room I saw that the work was conducted with indifference. Losses are sustained at every position of trust. The lack of thoroughness is apparent. While some have borne the burdens of care and responsibility, others, instead of sharing these burdens, have pursued a course to increase anxiety and care. Those who have not learned the lesson of economy, and acquired the habit of making the most of their time in childhood and youth will not be prudent and economical in any business in which they engage. It is a sin to neglect to so improve our faculties that they may be used to the glory of God. All have responsibilities to bear; not one can be excused.

There is a variety of minds, and all need more or less cultivation and training. Every movement in connection with the cause of God should be characterized by caution and decision. Without decision, an individual is fickle and unstable as water, and can never be truly successful. All who profess Christ should be workers. There are no drones in the household of faith. Every member of the family has some task assigned him, some portion of the vineyard of the Lord in which to work. The only way to meet the demand of God is to be constantly persevering in our endeavors for higher usefulness. It is but little we can accomplish at best, but every day's effort will increase our ability to labor effectually and to bear fruit to the glory of God.

Some do not exercise control over their appetites, but indulge taste at the expense of health. As the result the brain is clouded, their thoughts are sluggish, and they fail to accomplish what they might if they were self-denying and abstemious. These rob God of the physical and mental strength which might be devoted to His service if temperance were observed in all things. Paul was a health reformer. Said he: "I keep under my body, and bring it into subjection: lest that by any means, when I have preached to others, I myself should be a castaway." He felt that a responsibility rested upon him to preserve all his powers in their strength, that he might use them to the glory of God. If Paul was in danger from intemperance, we are in greater danger, because we do not feel and realize as he did the necessity of glorifying God in our bodies and spirits, which are His. Overeating is the sin of this age.

The word of God places the sin of gluttony in the same catalogue with drunkenness. So offensive was this sin in the sight of God that He gave directions to Moses that a child who would not be restrained on the point of appetite, but would gorge himself with anything his taste might crave, should be brought by his parents before the rulers in Israel and should be stoned to death. The condition of the glutton was considered hopeless. He would be of no use to others and was a curse to himself. No dependence could be placed upon him in anything. His influence would be ever contaminating others, and the world would be better without such a character; for his terrible defects would be perpetuated. None who have a sense of their accountability to God will allow the animal propensities to control reason.

Those who do this are not Christians, whoever they may be and however exalted their profession. The injunction of Christ is: "Be ye therefore perfect, even as your Father which is in heaven is perfect." He here shows us that we may be as perfect in our sphere as God is in His sphere.

Those who are employed in our publishing houses are not improving as God would have them. There is a want of earnest, unselfish interest in the work in which they are engaged. God requires these laborers in His cause to advance in knowledge daily. They should make a wise improvement of the faculties which God has given them, that they may become efficient, thorough workmen and perform their labor without loss to the office.

The wisest of men may learn useful lessons from the ways and habits of the little creatures of the earth. The industrious bee gives to men of intelligence an example that they would do well to imitate. These insects observe perfect order, and no idler is allowed in the hive. They execute their appointed work with an intelligence and activity that are beyond our comprehension.

The ants, which we consider as only pests to be crushed under our feet, are in many respects superior to man; for he does not as wisely improve the gifts of God. The wise man calls our attention to the small things of the earth: "Go to the ant, thou sluggard; consider her ways, and be wise: which having no guide, overseer, or ruler, provideth her meat in the summer, and gathereth her food in the harvest." "The ants are a people not strong, yet they prepare their meat in the summer." We may learn from these little teachers a lesson of faithfulness. Should we improve with the same diligence the faculties which an all-wise Creator has bestowed upon us, how greatly would our capacities for usefulness be increased. God's eye is upon the smallest of His creatures; does He not, then, regard man formed in His image and require of him corresponding returns for all the advantages He has given him?

The offices of publication should be set in order. Those who labor in these institutions should have high aims and a deep and rich experience in the knowledge of God's will. They should ever stand on the side of right and exert a saving influence. Every soul who names the name of Christ should make the most of the privileges enjoyed and faithfully perform the duties assigned him, without murmuring or complaining. The conversation of each should be of an elevated character, calculated to lead other minds in the right channel. The little mention that is made of divine goodness and the love of God shows marked ingratitude and that Christ is not enshrined in the heart.

The offices will never prosper unless there are more disinterested, unselfish workers, who are truly God-fearing men and women, self-denying and conscientiously independent for God and the right. The local editor of the Review and Herald will have occasion to speak with earnestness and firmness. He should stand in defense of the right, exerting all the influence his position grants him. Elder Waggoner has been placed in an unenviable position, but he has not been left alone. God has helped him, and under the circumstances he has done nobly. The Lord has not released him from his position; he must still labor in Oakland and San Francisco.

From those to whom God has entrusted much, He requires much, while those who have but little are required to give accordingly; but all may give themselves and in their actions show their fidelity to the precious cause of Christ. Many can retrench their expenditures and thus increase their liberality for Christ. Self-denial for Christ's sake is the battle before us.

"The love of Christ," said Paul, "constraineth us." It was the actuating principle of his conduct; it was his motive power. If ever his ardor in the path of duty for a moment flagged, one glance at the cross and the amazing love of Christ revealed in His unparalleled sacrifice was enough to cause him to gird up anew the loins of his mind and press forward in the path of self-denial. In his labors for his brethren he relied much upon the exhibition of infinite love in the wonderful condescension of Christ, with all its subduing, constraining power.

How earnest, how touching his appeal: "Ye know the grace of our Lord Jesus Christ, that, though He was rich, yet for your sakes He became poor, that ye through His poverty might be rich." You know the height from which He stooped; you are acquainted with the depth of humiliation to which He descended. His feet entered upon the path of self-denial and self-sacrifice, and turned not aside until He had given His life. There was no rest for Him between the throne in heaven and the cross. His love for man led Him to welcome every indignity and suffer every abuse. "For their sakes I sanctify Myself." I appropriate all My glory, all I am, to the work of man's redemption.

How very little are men moved now to sanctify themselves to the work of God that souls may be saved through them.

Paul admonishes us to "look not every man on his own things, but every man also on the things of others." He bids us imitate the life of the great Exemplar, and exhorts us to possess the mind "which was also in Christ Jesus: who, being in the form of God, thought it not robbery to be equal with God: but made Himself of no reputation, and took upon Him the form of a servant, and was made in the likeness of men: and being found in fashion as a man, he humbled Himself, and became obedient unto death, even the death of the cross." The apostle lingers over point after point, that our minds may grasp and fully comprehend the wonderful condescension of the Saviour in behalf of sinners. He presents Christ before us as He was when equal with God and receiving the adoration of angels, and then traces His descent until He reaches the lowest depths of humiliation, that with His human arm He may reach fallen man and lift him from his degradation to hope, joy, and heaven.

Paul was deeply anxious that the humiliation of Christ should be seen and realized. He was convinced that if the minds of men could be brought to comprehend the amazing sacrifice made by the Majesty of heaven, all selfishness would be banished from their hearts. He directs the mind first to the position which Christ occupied in heaven, in the bosom of His Father; he reveals Him afterward as laying off His glory, voluntarily subjecting Himself to all the humbling conditions of man's nature, assuming the responsibilities of a servant, and becoming obedient unto death, and that death the most ignominious and revolting, the most shameful, the most agonizing—the death of the cross. Can Christians contemplate this wonderful exhibition of the love of God to man without emotions of love and a realizing sense of the fact that we are not our own? Such a Master should not be served from grudging, covetous, selfish motives.

"Ye know," says Peter, "that ye were not redeemed with corruptible things, as silver and gold." Oh, had these been sufficient to purchase the salvation of man, how easily it might have been accomplished by Him who says: "The silver is Mine, and the gold is Mine." But the transgressor of God's holy law could be redeemed only by the precious blood of the Son of God. Those who, failing to appreciate the wonderful sacrifice made for them, withhold their means and their physical, mental, and moral powers from the service of Christ, will perish in their selfishness.

"Whosoever hath not [put to the best use his ability and means], from him shall be taken away even that he hath." Those who are too indolent to realize their responsibilities and exercise their faculties will fail of receiving the blessing of God, and the ability which they had will be taken away and given to the active, zealous workers who increase their talents by constant use. "Seest thou a man diligent in his business? he shall stand before kings; he shall not stand before mean men." A person who diligently labors under the direction of the Spirit of God will possess power and influence, for all may see in him a spirit of untiring devotion to the cause of God in any department where duty calls him.

All the hands in our offices should place themselves in the most favorable condition for the formation of good and correct habits. Several times each day precious, golden moments should be consecrated to prayer and the study of the Scriptures, if it is only to commit a text to memory, that spiritual life may exist in the soul. The varied interests of the cause furnish us with food for reflection and inspiration for our prayers. Communion with God is highly essential for spiritual health, and here only may be obtained that wisdom and correct judgment so necessary in the performance of every duty.

The strength acquired in prayer to God, united with individual effort in training the mind to thoughtfulness and care-taking, prepares the person for daily duties and keeps the spirit in peace under all circumstances, however trying. The temptations to which we are daily exposed make prayer a necessity. In order that we may be kept by the power of God through faith, the desires of the mind should be continually ascending in silent prayer for help, for light, for strength, for knowledge. But thought and prayer cannot take the place of earnest, faithful improvement of the time. Work and prayer are both required in perfecting Christian character.

We must live a twofold life — a life of thought and action, of silent prayer and earnest work. All who have received the light of truth should feel it their duty to shed rays of light upon the pathway of the impenitent. They should be witnesses for Christ in our offices as verily as in the church. God requires us to be living epistles, known and read of all men. The soul that turns to God for its strength, its support, its power, by daily, earnest prayer, will have noble aspirations, clear perceptions of truth and duty, lofty purposes of action, and a continual hungering and thirsting after righteousness. By maintaining a connection with God we shall be enabled to diffuse to others, through our association with them, the light, the peace, the serenity, that rules in our hearts, and set before them an example of unwavering fidelity to the interests of the work in which we are engaged.

With many who are laboring in our offices there is an almost entire absence of the love and fear of God. Self rules, self controls, and God and heaven scarcely enter into the mind. If these persons could see that they are upon the very borders of the eternal world and that their future interests will be determined by their present action, there would be a marked change in every hand employed in these offices.

But many who are engaged in the sacred work of God are paralyzed by Satan's deceptions. They are asleep on the enchanted ground. Days and months are passing, while they remain careless and unconcerned, as though there were no God, no future, no heaven, no punishment for neglect of duty or for shunning responsibilities. But the day is fast approaching when the case of every one will be decided according to his works. Many have a fearfully spotted record in the Ledger of Heaven.

When these workers shall arouse to their own accountability, when they shall lay their polluted souls before God just as they are, and their earnest cry shall take hold on His strength, they will then know for themselves that God does hear and answer prayer. And when they do awake, they will see what they have lost by their indifference and unfaithfulness. They will then find that they have reached only a low standard, when, had the mind and capabilities been cultivated and improved for God, they might have had a rich experience and might have been instrumental in saving their fellow men. And even should they be saved at last, they will realize through all eternity the loss of opportunities wasted in probationary time.

Religious privileges have been too much neglected by those employed in the offices. None should engage in the work of God who treat these privileges with indifference; for all such connect with evil angels and are a cloud of darkness, a hindrance to others. In order to make the work a success, every department in the offices must have the presence of heavenly angels. When the Spirit of God shall work upon the heart, cleansing the soul-temple of its defilement of worldliness and pleasure-loving, all will be seen in the prayer meeting, faithful to do their duty and earnest and anxious to reap all the benefit they can gain. The faithful worker for the Master will improve every opportunity to place himself directly under the rays of light from the throne of God, and this light will be reflected upon others.

And not only should the prayer meeting be faithfully attended, but as often as once each week a praise meeting should be held. Here the goodness and manifold mercies of God should be dwelt upon. Were we as free to give expression to our thankfulness for mercies received as we are to speak of grievances, doubts, and unbelief, we might bring joy to the hearts of others, instead of casting discouragement and gloom upon them. The complainers and murmurers, who are ever seeing the discouragements in the way, and talking of trials and hardships, should contemplate the infinite sacrifice which Christ has made in their behalf. Then can they estimate all their blessings in the light of the cross. While looking upon Jesus, the Author and Finisher of our faith, whom our sins have pierced and our sorrows have burdened, we shall see cause for gratitude and praise, and our thoughts and desires will be brought into submission to the will of Christ.

In the gracious blessings which our heavenly Father has bestowed upon us we may discern innumerable evidences of a love that is infinite, and a tender pity surpassing a mother's yearning sympathy for her wayward child. When we study the divine character in the light of the cross we see mercy, tenderness, and forgiveness blended with equity and justice. In the language of John we exclaim: "Behold, what manner of love the Father hath bestowed upon us, that we should be called the sons of God." We see in the midst of the throne One bearing in hands and feet and side the marks of the suffering endured to reconcile man to God and God to man. Matchless mercy reveals to us a Father, infinite, dwelling in light unapproachable, yet receiving us to Himself through the merits of His Son. The cloud of vengeance which threatened only misery and despair, in the reflected light from the cross reveals the writing of God: Live, sinner, live! ye penitent and believing souls, live! I have paid a ransom.

We must gather about the cross. Christ and Him crucified must be the theme of contemplation, of conversation, and of our most joyful emotion. We should have these special appointments for the purpose of keeping fresh in our thoughts everything which we receive from God, and of expressing our gratitude for His great love, and our willingness to trust everything to the hand that was nailed to the cross for us. We should learn here to talk the language of Canaan, to sing the songs of Zion. By the mystery and glory of the cross we can estimate the value of man, and then we shall see and feel the importance of working for our fellow men, that they may be exalted to the throne of God.

41. Sacredness of Vows

The brief but terrible history of Ananias and Sapphira is traced by the pen of inspiration for the benefit of all who profess to be the followers of Christ. This important lesson has not rested with sufficient weight upon the minds of our people. It will be profitable for all to thoughtfully consider the nature of the grievous offense for which these guilty ones were made an example. This one marked evidence of God's retributive justice is fearful, and should lead all to fear and tremble to repeat sins which brought such a punishment. Selfishness was the great sin which had warped the characters of this guilty couple.

With others, Ananias and his wife Sapphira had the privilege of hearing the gospel preached by the apostles. The power of God attended the word spoken, and deep conviction rested upon all present. The softening influence of the grace of God had the effect upon their hearts to cause them to release their selfish hold upon their earthly possessions. While under the direct influence of the Spirit of God, they made a pledge to give to the Lord certain lands; but when they were no longer under this heavenly influence, the impression was less forcible, and they began to question and draw back from fulfilling the pledge which they had made. They thought that they had been too hasty, and wished to reconsider the matter. Thus a door was opened by which Satan at once entered and gained control of their minds.

This case should be a warning to all to guard against the first approach of Satan. Covetousness was first cherished; then, ashamed to have their brethren know that their selfish souls grudged that which they had solemnly dedicated and pledged to God, deception was practiced. They talked the matter over together and deliberately decided to withhold a part of the price of the land. When convicted of their falsehood, their punishment was instant death. They knew that the Lord, whom they had defrauded, had searched them out; for Peter said: "Why hath Satan filled thine heart to lie to the Holy Ghost, and to keep back part of the price of the land? Whiles it remained, was it not thine own? and after it was sold, was it not in thine own power? why hast thou conceived this thing in thine heart? thou hast not lied unto men, but unto God."

A special example was necessary to guard the young church from becoming demoralized; for their numbers were rapidly increasing. A warning was thus given to all who professed Christ at that time, and to all who should afterward profess His name, that God requires faithfulness in the performance of vows. But notwithstanding this signal punishment of deception and lying, the same sins have often been repeated in the Christian church and are widespread in our day. I have

been shown that God gave this example as a warning to all who should be tempted to act in a similar manner. Selfishness and fraud are practiced daily in the church, in withholding from God that which He claims, thus robbing Him and conflicting with His arrangements to diffuse the light and knowledge of truth throughout the length and breadth of the land.

God in His wise plans has made the advancement of His cause dependent upon the personal efforts of His people and upon their freewill offerings. By accepting the co-operation of man in the great plan of redemption, He has placed a signal honor upon him. The minister cannot preach except he be sent. The work of dispensing light does not rest upon ministers alone. Every person, upon becoming a member of the church, pledges himself to be a representative of Christ by living out the truth he professes. The followers of Christ should carry forward the work which He left for them to do when He ascended into heaven.

Institutions that are God's instruments to carry forward His work on the earth must be sustained. Churches must be erected, schools established, and publishing houses furnished with facilities for doing a great work in the publication of the truth to be sent to all parts of the world. These institutions are ordained of God and should be sustained by tithes and liberal offerings. As the work enlarges, means will be needed to carry it forward in all its branches. Those who have been converted to the truth and been made partakers of His grace may become co-workers with Christ by making voluntary sacrifices and freewill offerings to Him. And when the members of the church wish in their hearts that there would be no more calls for means, they virtually say that they are content that the cause of God shall not progress.

"And Jacob vowed a vow, saying, If God will be with me, and will keep me in this way that I go, and will give me bread to eat, and raiment to put on, so that I come again to my father's house in peace; then shall the Lord be my God: and this stone, which I have set for a pillar, shall be God's house: and of all that Thou shalt give me I will surely give the tenth unto Thee." The circumstances which prompted Jacob to vow to the Lord were similar to those which prompt men and women to vow to the Lord in our time. He had by a sinful act obtained the blessing which he knew had been promised him by the sure word of God. In doing this he showed great lack of faith in God's power to carry out His purposes, however discouraging present appearances might be. Instead of placing himself in the position he coveted, he was obliged to flee for his life from the wrath of Esau. With only his staff in his hand he must travel hundreds of miles through a desolate country. His courage was gone, and he was filled with remorse and timidity, seeking to avoid men, lest he should be traced by his angry brother. He had not the peace of God to comfort him, for he was harassed with the thought that he had forfeited divine protection.

The second day of his journey is drawing to a close. He is weary, hungry, and homeless, and he feels that he is forsaken of God. He knows that he has brought this upon himself by his own wrong course. Dark clouds of despair enclose him, and he feels that he is an outcast. His heart is filled with a nameless terror, and he hardly dares to pray. But he is so utterly lonely that he feels the need of protection from God as he has never felt it before. He weeps and confesses his sin before God, and entreats for some evidence that He has not utterly forsaken him. But his burdened heart finds no relief. He has lost all confidence in himself, and he fears that the God of his fathers has cast him off. But God, the merciful God, pities the desolate, sorrow-stricken man, who gathers the stones for his pillow and has only the canopy of heaven for his covering.

In a vision of the night he sees a mystic ladder, its base resting upon the earth and its top reaching above the starry host to the highest heavens. Angel messengers are ascending and descending this ladder of shining brightness, showing him the pathway of communication between earth and heaven.

A voice is heard by him, renewing the promise of mercy and protection and of future blessings. When Jacob awoke from his dream, he said: "Surely the Lord is in this place; and I knew it not." He looked about him as if expecting to see the heavenly messengers; but only the dim outline of earthly objects, and the heavens above, brilliant with the gems of light, met his earnest, wondering gaze. The ladder and the bright messengers were gone, and the glorious Majesty above it he could see only in imagination.

Jacob was awed with the deep stillness of the night and with the vivid impression that he was in the immediate presence of God. His heart was full of gratitude that he was not destroyed. There was no more sleep for him that night; gratitude deep and fervent, mingled with holy joy, filled his soul. "And Jacob rose up early in the morning, and took the stone that he had put for his pillows, and set it up for a pillar, and poured oil upon the top of it." And here he made his solemn vow to God.

Jacob made his vow while refreshed by the dews of grace and invigorated by the presence and assurance of God. After the divine glory had passed away, he had temptations, like men in our time, but he was faithful to his vow and would not harbor thoughts as to the possibility of being released from the pledge which he had made. He might have reasoned much as men do now, that this revelation was only a dream, that he was unduly excited when he made his vow, and that therefore it need not be kept; but he did not.

Long years intervened before Jacob dared to return to his own country, but when he did he faithfully discharged his debt to his Master. He had become a wealthy man, and a very large amount of property passed from his possessions to the treasury of the Lord.

Many in our day fail where Jacob made a success. Those to whom God has given the greatest amount have the strongest inclination to retain what they have, because they must give a sum proportionate to their property. Jacob gave the tenth of all that he had, and then reckoned the use of the tenth, and gave the Lord the benefit of that which he had used for his own interest during the time he was in a heathen land and could not pay his vow. This was a large amount, but he did not hesitate; that which he had vowed to God he did not regard as his, but as the Lord's.

According to the amount bestowed will be the amount required. The larger the capital entrusted, the more valuable is the gift which God requires to be returned to Him. If a Christian has ten or twenty thousand dollars, God's claims are imperative upon him, not only to give his proportion according to the tithing system, but to present his sin offerings and thank offerings to God. The Levitical dispensation was distinguished in a remarkable manner by the sanctification of property. When we speak of the tithe as the standard of the Jewish contributions to religious purposes, we do not speak understandingly.

The Lord kept His claims paramount, and in almost every article they were reminded of the Giver by being required to make returns to Him. They were required to pay a ransom for their firstborn son, for the first fruits of their flocks, and for the first gathering of the harvest. They were required to leave the corners of their harvest fields for the destitute. Whatever dropped from their hands in reaping was left for the poor, and once in every seven years their lands were allowed to produce spontaneously for the needy. Then there were the sacrificial offerings, the trespass offerings, the sin offerings, and the remission of all debts every seventh year. There were also numerous expenses for hospitalities and gifts to the poor, and there were assessments upon their property.

At stated periods, in order to preserve the integrity of the law, the people were interviewed as to whether they had faithfully performed their vows or not. A conscientious few made returns to God of about one third of all their income for the benefit of religious interests and for the poor. These exactions were not from a particular class of the people, but from all, the requirement being proportioned according to the amount possessed. Besides all these systematic and regular donations there were special objects calling for freewill offerings, such as the tabernacle built in the wilderness and the temple erected at Jerusalem. These drafts were made by God upon the people for their own good, as well as to sustain His service.

There must be an awakening among us as a people upon this matter. There are but few men who feel conscience-stricken if they neglect their duty in beneficence. But few feel remorse of soul because they are daily robbing

God. If a Christian deliberately or accidentally underpays his neighbor, or refuses to cancel an honest debt, his conscience, unless seared, will trouble him; he cannot rest although no one may know but himself. There are many neglected vows and unpaid pledges, and yet how few trouble their minds over the matter; how few feel the guilt of this violation of duty. We must have new and deeper convictions on this subject. The conscience must be aroused, and the matter receive earnest attention; for an account must be rendered to God in the last day, and His claims must be settled.

The responsibilities of the Christian businessman, however large or small his capital, will be in exact proportion to his gifts from God. The deceitfulness of riches has ruined thousands and tens of thousands. These wealthy men forget that they are stewards, and that the day is fast approaching when it shall be said to them: "Give an account of thy stewardship." As shown by the parable of the talents, every man is responsible for the wise use of the gifts bestowed. The poor man in the parable, because he had the least gift, felt the least responsibility and made no use of the talent entrusted to him; therefore he was cast into outer darkness.

Said Christ: "How hardly shall they that have riches enter into the kingdom of God!" And His disciples were astonished at His doctrine. When a minister who has labored successfully in securing souls to Jesus Christ abandons his sacred work in order to secure temporal gain, he is called an apostate, and he will be held accountable to God for the talents that he has misapplied. When men of business, farmers, mechanics, merchants, lawyers, etc., become members of the church, they become servants of Christ; and although their talents may be entirely different, their responsibility to advance the cause of God by personal effort, and with their means, is no less than that which rests upon the minister. The woe which will fall upon the minister if he preach not the gospel, will just as surely fall upon the businessman, if he, with his different talents, will not be a co-worker with Christ in accomplishing the same results. When this is brought home to the individual, some will say, "This is an hard saying;" nevertheless it is true, although continually contradicted by the practice of men who profess to be followers of Christ.

God provided bread for His people in the wilderness by a miracle of mercy, and He could have provided everything necessary for religious service; but He did not, because in His infinite wisdom He saw that the moral discipline of His people depended upon their co-operating with Him, every one of them doing something. As long as the truth is progressive, the claims of God rest upon men to give of that which He has entrusted to them for this very purpose. God, the Creator of man, by instituting the plan of systematic benevolence, has made the work bear equally upon all according to their several abilities. Everyone is to be his own assessor and is left to give as he purposes in his heart.

But there are those who are guilty of the same sin as Ananias and Sapphira, thinking that if they withhold a portion of what God claims in the tithing system the brethren will never know it. Thus thought the guilty couple whose example is given us as a warning. God in this case proves that He searches the heart. The motives and purposes of man cannot be hidden from Him. He has left a perpetual warning to Christians of all ages to beware of the sin to which the hearts of men are continually inclined.

Although no visible marks of God's displeasure follow the repetition of the sin of Ananias and Sapphira now, yet the sin is just as heinous in the sight of God and will as surely be visited upon the transgressor in the day of judgment, and many will feel the curse of God even in this life. When a pledge is made to the cause, it is a vow made to God and should be sacredly kept. In the sight of God it is no better than sacrilege to appropriate to our own use that which has been once pledged to advance His sacred work.

When a verbal or written pledge has been made in the presence of our brethren to give a certain amount, they are the visible witnesses of a contract made between ourselves and God. The pledge is not made to man, but to God, and is as a written note given to a neighbor. No legal bond is more binding upon the Christian for the payment of money than a pledge made to God.

Persons who thus pledge to their fellow men do not generally think of asking to be released from their pledges. A vow made to God, the Giver of all favors, is of still greater importance; then why should we seek to be released from our vows to God? Will man consider his promise less binding because made to God? Because his vow will not be put to trial in courts of justice, is it less valid? Will a man who professes to be saved by the blood of the infinite sacrifice of Jesus Christ, "rob God"? Are not his vows and his actions weighed in the balances of justice in the heavenly courts?

Each of us has a case pending in the court of heaven. Shall our course of conduct balance the evidence against us? The case of Ananias and Sapphira was of the most aggravated character. In keeping back part of the price, they lied to the Holy Ghost. Guilt likewise rests upon every individual in proportion to like offenses. When the hearts of men are softened by the presence of the Spirit of God, they are more susceptible to impressions of the Holy Spirit, and resolves are made to deny self and to sacrifice for the cause of God. It is when divine light shines into the chambers of the mind with unusual clearness and power that the feelings of the natural man are overcome, that selfishness loses its power upon the heart, and that desires are awakened to imitate the Pattern, Jesus Christ, in practicing self-denial and benevolence. The disposition of the naturally selfish man then becomes kind and pitiful toward lost sinners, and he makes a solemn pledge to God, as did Abraham and Jacob. Heavenly angels are present on such occasions. The love of God and love for souls triumphs over selfishness and love of the world. Especially is this the case when the speaker, in the Spirit and power of God, presents the plan of redemption, laid by the Majesty of heaven in the sacrifice of the cross. By the following scriptures we may see how God regards the subject of vows:

"And Moses spake unto the heads of the tribes concerning the children of Israel, saying, This is the thing which the Lord hath commanded. If a man vow a vow unto the Lord, or swear an oath to bind his soul with a bond; he shall not break his word, he shall do according to all that proceedeth out of his mouth." Numbers 30:1, 2. "Suffer not thy mouth to cause thy flesh to sin; neither say thou before the angel, that it was an error: wherefore should God be angry at thy voice, and destroy the work of thine hands?" Ecclesiastes 5:6.

"I will go into Thy house with burnt offerings: I will pay Thee my vows, which my lips have uttered, and my mouth hath spoken, when I was in trouble." Psalm 66:13, 14. "It is a snare to the man who devoureth that which is holy, and after vows to make inquiry." Proverbs 20:25. "When thou shalt vow a vow unto the Lord thy God, thou shalt not slack to pay it: for the Lord thy God will surely require it of thee; and it would be sin in thee. But if thou shalt forbear to vow, it shall be no sin in thee. That which is gone out of thy lips thou shalt keep and perform; even a freewill offering, according as thou hast vowed unto the Lord thy God, which thou hast promised with thy mouth." Deuteronomy 23:21-23.

"Vow, and pay unto the Lord your God: let all that be round about Him bring presents unto Him that ought to be feared." Psalm 76:11. "But ye have profaned it, in that ye say, The table of the Lord is polluted; and the fruit thereof, even His meat, is contemptible. Ye said also, Behold, what a weariness is it! and ye have snuffed at it, saith the Lord of hosts; and ye brought that which was torn, and the lame, and the sick; thus ye brought an offering: should I accept this of your hand? saith the Lord. But cursed be the deceiver, which hath in his flock a male, and voweth, and sacrificeth unto the Lord a corrupt thing: for I am a great King, saith the Lord of hosts, and My name is dreadful among the heathen." Malachi 1:12-14.

"When thou vowest a vow unto God, defer not to pay it; for He hath no pleasure in fools: pay that which thou hast vowed. Better is it that thou shouldest not vow, than that thou shouldest vow and not pay." Ecclesiastes 5:4, 5.

God has given man a part to act in accomplishing the salvation of his fellow men. He can work in connection with Christ by doing acts of mercy and beneficence. But he cannot redeem them, not being able to satisfy the claims of insulted justice. This the Son of God alone can do, by laying aside His honor and glory, clothing His divinity with humanity, and coming to earth to humiliate Himself and shed His blood in behalf of the human race.

In commissioning His disciples to go "into all the world, and preach the gospel to every creature," Christ assigned to men the work of spreading the gospel. But while some go forth to preach, He calls upon others to answer to His claims upon them for tithes and offerings with which to support the ministry and to spread the printed truth all over the land. This is God's means of exalting man. It is just the work which he needs, for it will stir the deepest sympathies of his heart and call into exercise the highest capabilities of the mind.

Every good thing of earth was placed here by the bountiful hand of God as an expression of His love to man. The poor are His, and the cause of religion is His. He has placed means in the hands of men, that His divine gifts may flow through human channels in doing the work appointed us in saving our fellow men. Everyone has his appointed work in the great field; and yet none should receive the idea that God is dependent upon man. He could speak the word, and every son of poverty would be made rich. In a moment of time He could heal the human race of all their diseases. He might dispense with ministers altogether and make angels the ambassadors of His truth. He might have written the truth upon the firmament, or imprinted it upon the leaves of the trees and upon the flowers of the field; or He might with an audible voice have proclaimed it from heaven.

But the all-wise God did not choose any of these ways. He knew that man must have something to do in order that life might be a blessing to him. The gold and silver are the Lord's, and He could rain them from heaven if He chose; but instead of this He has made man His steward, entrusting him with means, not to be hoarded, but to be used in benefiting others. He thus makes man the medium through which to distribute His blessings on earth. God planned the system of beneficence in order that man might become, like his Creator, benevolent and unselfish in character, and finally be a partaker with Him of the eternal, glorious reward.

God works through human instrumentalities; and whoever shall awaken the consciences of men, provoking them to good works and a real interest in the advancement of the cause of truth, does not do it of himself, but by the Spirit of God which worketh in him. Pledges made under these circumstances are of a sacred character, being the fruit of the work of the Spirit of God. When these pledges are canceled, Heaven accepts the offering, and these liberal workers are credited for so much treasure invested in the bank of heaven. Such are laying up a good foundation against the time to come, that they may lay hold on eternal life.

But when the immediate presence of the Spirit of God is not so vividly felt, and the mind becomes exercised in the temporal concerns of life, then they are tempted to question the force of the obligation which they voluntarily assumed; and, yielding to Satan's suggestions, they reason that undue pressure was brought to bear upon them and they acted under the excitement of the occasion; that the demand for means to use in the cause of God was overstated; and that they were induced to pledge under false pretenses, without fully understanding the subject, and therefore they wish to be released. Have ministers the power to accept their excuses and say: "You shall not be holden to your pledge; you are released from your vow"? If they venture to do this, they become partakers of the sin of which the withholder is guilty.

Of all our income we should make the first appropriation to God. In the system of beneficence enjoined upon the Jews they were required either to bring to the Lord the first fruits of all His gifts, whether in the increase of their flocks or herds, or in the produce of their fields, orchards, or vineyards, or they were to redeem it by substituting an equivalent. How changed the order of things in our day! The Lord's requirements and claims, if they receive any attention, are left till the last. Yet our work needs tenfold more means now than was needed by the Jews. The great commission given to the apostles was to go throughout the world and preach the gospel. This shows the extension of the work and the increased responsibility resting upon the followers of Christ in our day. If the law required tithes and offerings thousands of years ago, how much more essential are they now! If the rich and poor were to give a sum proportionate to their property in the Jewish economy, it is doubly essential now.

The majority of professed Christians part with their means with great reluctance. Many of them do not give one twentieth of their income to God, and many give far less than that; while there is a large class who rob God of the little tithe, and others who will give only the tithe. If all the tithes of our people flowed into the treasury of the Lord as they should, such blessings would be received that gifts and offerings for sacred purposes would be multiplied tenfold, and thus the channel between God and man would be kept open. The followers of Christ should not wait for thrilling missionary appeals to arouse them to action. If spiritually awake, they would hear in the income of every week, whether much or little, the voice of God and of conscience with authority demanding the tithes and offerings due the Lord.

Not only are the gifts and labors of Christ's followers desired, but in one sense they are indispensable. All heaven is interested in the salvation of man and waiting for men to become interested in their own salvation and in that of their fellow men. All things are ready, but the church is apparently upon the enchanted ground. When they shall arouse and lay their prayers, their wealth, and all their energies and resources at the feet of Jesus, the cause of truth will triumph. Angels are amazed that Christians do so little when such an example has been given them by Jesus, who even withheld not Himself from death, a shameful death. It is a marvel to them that when professors come in contact with the selfishness of the world they should fall back to their narrow views and selfish motives.

One of the greatest sins in the Christian world of today is dissembling and covetousness in dealing with God. There is an increasing carelessness on the part of many in regard to meeting their pledges to the various institutions and religious enterprises. Many look upon the act of pledging as though it imposed no obligation to pay. If they think that their money will bring them considerable profit by being invested in bank stock or in merchandise, or if there are individuals connected with the institution which they have pledged to help to whom they take exceptions, they feel perfectly free to use their means as they please. This lack of integrity is prevailing to quite an extent among those who profess to be keeping the commandments of God and looking for the soon appearing of their Lord and Saviour.

The plan of systematic benevolence was of God's own arrangement, but the faithful payment of God's claims is often refused or postponed as though solemn promises were of no significance. It is because church members neglect to pay their tithes and meet their pledges that our institutions are not free from embarrassment.

If all, both rich and poor, would bring their tithes into the storehouse, there would be a sufficient supply of means to release the cause from financial embarrassment and to nobly carry forward the missionary work in its various departments. God calls upon those who believe the truth to render to Him the things that are His. Those who have thought that to withhold from God is gain will eventually experience His curse as the result of their robbery of the Lord. Nothing but utter inability to pay can excuse one in neglecting to meet promptly his obligations to the Lord. Indifference in this matter shows that you are in blindness and deception, and are unworthy of the Christian name.

A church is responsible for the pledges of its individual members. If they see that there is a brother who is neglecting to fulfill his vows, they should labor with him kindly but plainly. If he is not in circumstances which render it possible for him to pay his vow, and he is a worthy member and has a willing heart, then let the church compassionately help him. Thus they can bridge over the difficulty and receive a blessing themselves.

God would have the members of His church consider their obligations to Him as binding as their indebtedness to the merchant or the market. Let everyone review his past life and see if any unpaid, unredeemed pledges have been neglected, and then make extra exertions to pay the "uttermost farthing," for we must all meet and abide the final issue of a tribunal where nothing will stand the test but integrity and veracity.

42. Wills and Legacies

"Lay not up for yourselves treasures upon earth, where moth and rust doth corrupt, and where thieves break through and steal: but lay up for yourselves treasures in heaven, where neither moth nor rust doth corrupt, and where thieves do not break through nor steal." Selfishness is a soul-destroying sin. Under this head comes covetousness, which is idolatry. All things belong to God. All the prosperity we enjoy is the result of divine beneficence.

God is the great and bountiful giver. If He requires any portion of the liberal supply He has given us, it is not that He may be enriched by our gifts, for He needs nothing from our hand; but it is that we may have an opportunity to exercise self-denial, love, and sympathy for our fellow men, and thus become highly exalted. In every dispensation, from Adam's time to ours, God has claimed the property of man, saying: I am the rightful owner of the universe; therefore consecrate to Me thy first fruits, bring a tribute of loyalty, surrender to Me My own, thus acknowledging My sovereignty, and you shall be free to retain and enjoy My bounties, and My blessing shall be with you. "Honor the Lord with thy substance, and with the first fruits of all thine increase."

God's requirements come first. We are not doing His will if we consecrate to Him what is left of our income after all our imaginary wants have been supplied. Before any part of our earnings is consumed, we should take out and present to Him that portion which He claims. In the old dispensation an offering of gratitude was kept continually burning upon the altar, thus showing man's endless obligation to God. If we have prosperity in our secular business, it is because God blesses us. A part of this income is to be devoted to the poor, and a large portion to be applied to the cause of God. When that which God claims is rendered to Him, the remainder will be sanctified and blessed to our own use. But when a man robs God by withholding that which He requires, His curse rests upon the whole.

God has made men the channels through which His gifts are to flow to sustain the work which He would have carried forward in the world. He has given them property to be wisely used, not selfishly hoarded or extravagantly expended in luxury and selfish gratification either in dress or in the embellishment of their houses. He has entrusted them with means with which to support His servants in their labor as preachers and missionaries, and to sustain the institutions He has established among us. Those who rejoice in the precious light of truth should feel a burning desire to have it sent everywhere.

There are a few faithful standard-bearers who never flinch from duty or shirk responsibilities. Their hearts and purses are always open to every call for means to advance the cause of God. Indeed, some seem ready to exceed their duty, as though fearful that they will lose an opportunity of investing their portion in the bank of heaven. There are others who will do as little as possible. They hoard their treasure, or lavish means upon themselves, grudgingly doling out a mere pittance to sustain the cause of God. If they make a pledge or a vow to God, they afterward repent of it, and will avoid the payment of it as long as they can, if not altogether. They make their tithe as small as possible, as if afraid that that which they return to God is lost. Our various institutions may be embarrassed for means, but this class act as though it made no difference to them whether they prospered or not. And yet these are God's instrumentalities with which to enlighten the world.

These institutions have not, like other institutions of the kind, received endowments or legacies. And yet God has greatly prospered and blessed them, and made them the means of great good. There are aged ones among us who are nearing the close of their probation; but for the want of wide-awake men to secure to the cause of God the means in their possession, it passes into the hands of those who are serving Satan. This means was only lent them of God to be returned to Him; but in nine cases out of ten these brethren, when passing from the stage of action, appropriate God's property in a way that cannot glorify Him, for not one dollar of it will ever flow into the Lord's treasury.

In some cases these apparently good brethren have had unconsecrated advisers, who counseled from their own standpoint and not according to the mind of God. Property is often bequeathed to children and grandchildren only to their injury. They have no love for God or for the truth, and therefore this means, all of which is the Lord's, passes into Satan's ranks, to be controlled by him. Satan is much more vigilant, keen-sighted, and skillful in devising ways to secure means to himself than our brethren are to secure the Lord's own to His cause. Some wills are made in so loose a manner that they will not stand the test of the law, and thus thousands of dollars have been lost to the cause. Our brethren should feel that a responsibility rests upon them, as faithful servants in the cause of God, to exercise their intellect in regard to this matter, and secure to the Lord His own.

Many manifest a needless delicacy on this point. They feel that they are stepping upon forbidden ground when they introduce the subject of property to the aged or to invalids in order to learn what disposition they design to make of it. But this duty is just as sacred as the duty to preach the word to save souls. Here is a man with God's money or property in his hands. He is about to change his stewardship. Will he place the means which God has lent him to be used in His cause, in the hands of wicked men, just because they are his relatives?

Should not Christian men feel interested and anxious for that man's future good as well as for the interest of God's cause, that he shall make a right disposition of his Lord's money, the talents lent him for wise improvement? Will his brethren stand by and see him losing his hold on this life and at the same time robbing the treasury of God? This would be a fearful loss to himself and to the cause; for, by placing his talent of means in the hands of those who have no regard for the truth of God, he would, to all intents and purposes, be wrapping it in a napkin and hiding it in the earth.

The Lord would have His followers dispense their means while they can do it themselves. Some may inquire: "Must we actually dispossess ourselves of everything which we call our own?" We may not be required to do this now; but we must be willing to do so for Christ's sake. We must acknowledge that our possessions are absolutely His, by using of them freely whenever means is needed to advance His cause. Some close their ears to the calls made for money to be used in sending missionaries to foreign countries and in publishing the truth and scattering it like autumn leaves all over the world.

Such excuse their covetousness by informing you that they have made arrangements to be charitable at death. They have considered the cause of God in their wills. Therefore they live a life of avarice, robbing God in tithes and in offerings, and in their wills return to God but a small portion of that which He has lent them, while a very large proportion is appropriated to relatives who have no interest in the truth. This is the worst kind of robbery. They rob God of His just dues, not only all through life, but also at death.

It is utter folly to defer to make a preparation for the future life until nearly the last hour of the present life. It is also a great mistake to defer to answer the claims of God for liberality to His cause until the time comes when you are to shift your stewardship upon others. Those to whom you entrust your talents of means may not do as well with them as you have done. How dare rich men run so great risks! Those who wait till death before they make a disposition of their property, surrender it to death rather than to God. In so doing many are acting directly contrary to the plan of God plainly stated in His word. If they would do good they must seize the present golden moments and labor with all their might, as if fearful that they may lose the favorable opportunity.

Those who neglect known duty by not answering to God's claims upon them in this life, and who soothe their consciences by calculating on making their bequests at death, will receive no words of commendation from the Master, nor will they receive a reward. They practiced no self-denial, but selfishly retained their means as long as they could, yielding it up only when death claimed them.

That which many propose to defer until they are about to die, if they were Christians indeed they would do while they have a strong hold on life. They would devote themselves and their property to God, and, while acting as His stewards, they would have the satisfaction of doing their duty. By becoming their own executors, they could meet the claims of God themselves, instead of shifting the responsibility upon others. We should regard ourselves as stewards of the Lord's property and God as the supreme proprietor, to whom we are to render His own when He shall require it. When He shall come to receive His own with usury, the covetous will see that instead of multiplying the talents entrusted to them, they have brought upon themselves the doom pronounced upon the unprofitable servant.

The Lord designs that the death of His servants shall be regarded as a loss because of the influence for good which they exerted and the many willing offerings which they bestowed to replenish the treasury of God. Dying legacies are a miserable substitute for living benevolence. The servants of God should be making their wills every day in good works and liberal offerings to God. They should not allow the amount given to God to be disproportionately small when compared with that appropriated to their own use. In making their wills daily, they will remember those objects and friends that hold the largest place in their affections. Their best friend is Jesus. He did not withhold His own life from them, but for their sakes became poor, that through His poverty they might be made rich. He deserves the whole heart, the property, all that they have and are. But many professed Christians put off the claims of Jesus in life and insult Him by giving Him a mere pittance at death.

Let all of this class remember that this robbery of God is not an impulsive action, but a well-considered plan which they preface by saying: "Being in sound mind." After having defrauded the cause of God through life they perpetuate the fraud after death. And this is with the full consent of all the powers of the mind. Such a will many are content to cherish for a dying pillow. Their will is a part of their preparation for death and is prepared so that their possessions shall not disturb their dying hours. Can these dwell with pleasure upon the requirement that will be made of them to give an account of their stewardship?

We must all be rich in good works in this life if we would secure the future, immortal life. When the judgment shall sit and the books shall be opened, every man will be rewarded according to his works. Many names are enrolled on the church book that have robbery recorded against them in the Ledger of Heaven. And unless these repent and work for the Master with disinterested benevolence, they will certainly share in the doom of the unfaithful steward.

It often happens that an active businessman is cut down without a moment's warning and on examination his business is found to be in a most perplexing condition. In the effort to settle his estate the lawyers' fees eat up a large share, if not all, of the property, while his wife and children and the cause of Christ are robbed. Those who are faithful stewards of the Lord's means will know just how their business stands, and, like wise men, they will be prepared for any emergency. Should their probation close suddenly, they would not leave such great perplexity upon those who are called to settle their estate.

Many are not exercised upon the subject of making their wills while they are in apparent health. But this precaution should be taken by our brethren. They should know their financial standing and should not allow their business to become entangled. They should arrange their property in such a manner that they may leave it at any time.

Wills should be made in a manner to stand the test of law. After they are drawn they may remain for years and do no harm, if donations continue to be made from time to time as the cause has need. Death will not come one day sooner, brethren, because you have made your will. In disposing of your property by will to your relatives, be sure that you do not forget God's cause. You are His agents, holding His property; and His claims should have your first consideration. Your wife and children, of course, should not be left destitute; provision should be made for them if they are needy. But do not, simply because it is customary, bring into your will a long line of relatives who are not needy.

Let it ever be kept in mind that the present selfish system of disposing of property is not God's plan, but man's device. Christians should be reformers and break up this present system, giving an entirely new aspect to the formation of wills. Let the idea be ever present that it is the Lord's property which you are handling. The will of God in this matter is law. If man had made you the executor of his property, would you not closely study the will of the testator, that the smallest amount might not be misapplied? Your heavenly Friend has entrusted you with property, and given you His will as to how it should be used. If this will is studied with an unselfish heart, that which belongs to God will not be misapplied. The Lord's cause has been shamefully neglected, when He has provided men with sufficient means to meet every emergency, if they only had grateful, obedient hearts.

Those who make their wills should not feel that when this is done they have no further duty; but they should be constantly at work, using the talents entrusted to them, for the upbuilding of the Lord's cause. God has devised plans that all may work intelligently in the distribution of their means. He does not propose to sustain His work by miracles. He has a few faithful stewards, who are economizing and using their means to advance His cause. Instead of self-denial and benevolence being an exception, they should be the rule. The growing necessities of the cause of God require means. Calls are constantly coming in from men in our own and foreign countries for messengers to come to them with light and truth. This will necessitate more laborers and more means to support them.

Only a small amount of means flows into the Lord's treasury to be appropriated to the saving of souls, and it is with hard labor that even this is obtained. If the eyes of all could be opened to see how prevailing covetousness has hindered the advancement of the work of God, and how much more might have been done had all acted up to God's plan in tithes and offerings, there would be a decided reform on the part of many; for they would not dare to hinder the work of advancing the cause of God as they have done. The church is asleep as to the work it might do if it would give up all for Christ. A true spirit of self-sacrifice would be an argument for the reality and power of the gospel which the world could not misunderstand or gainsay, and abundant blessings would be poured upon the church.

I call upon our brethren to cease their robbery of God. Some are so situated that wills must be made. But in doing this, care should be taken not to give to sons and daughters means which should flow into the treasury of God. These wills often become the subject of quarrels and dissensions. It is recorded to the praise of God's ancient people that He was not ashamed to be called their God; and the reason assigned is that instead of selfishly seeking for and coveting earthly possessions, or seeking their happiness in worldly pleasures, they placed themselves and all that they had in the hands of God. They lived only for His glory, declaring plainly that they sought a better country, even a heavenly. Of such a people God was not ashamed. They did not disgrace Him in the eyes of the world. The Majesty of heaven was not ashamed to call them brethren.

There are many who urge that they cannot do more for God's cause than they now do; but they do not give according to their ability. The Lord sometimes opens the eyes blinded by selfishness by simply reducing their income to the amount they are willing to give. Horses are found dead in the field or stable, houses or barns are destroyed by fire, or crops fail. In many cases God tests man with blessings, and if unfaithfulness is manifested in rendering to Him tithes and offerings, His blessing is withdrawn. "He which soweth sparingly shall reap also sparingly."

By the mercies of Christ and the riches of His goodness, and for the honor of truth and religion, we beseech you who are followers of Christ to dedicate yourselves and your property anew to God. In view of the love and compassion of Christ, which brought Him from the royal courts to suffer self-denial, humiliation, and death, let each ask himself the question, "How much do I owe my Lord?" and then let your grateful offerings be in accordance with your appreciation of the great gift of heaven in God's dear Son.

In determining the proportion to be given to the cause of God, be sure to exceed, rather than fall short, of the requirements of duty. Consider for whom the offering is to be made. This recollection will put covetousness to flight. Only consider the great love wherewith Christ has loved us, and our richest offerings will seem unworthy of His acceptance.

When Christ is the object of our affections, those who have received His pardoning love will not stop to calculate the value of the alabaster box of precious ointment. Covetous Judas could do this; but the receiver of the gift of salvation will only regret that the offering has not a richer perfume and greater value. Christians must look upon themselves only as channels through which mercies and blessings are to flow from the Fountain of all goodness to their fellow men, by whose conversion they may send to heaven waves of glory in praise and offerings from those who thus become partakers with them of the heavenly gift.

43. The Relation of Church Membership

Every man who is striving to overcome will have his own weaknesses to contend with, but it is so much easier for persons to see the faults of their brethren than to see their own that they should be much more diligent and critical with themselves than with others.

All the members of the church, if they are sons and daughters of God, will have to undergo a process of discipline before they can be lights in the world. God will not make men and women channels of light while they are in darkness and are content to remain so, making no special efforts to connect with the Source of light. Those who feel their own need, and arouse themselves to the deepest thought and the most earnest, persevering prayer and action, will receive divine aid. There is much for each to unlearn with respect to himself, as well as much to learn. Old habits and customs must be shaken off, and it is only by earnest struggles to correct these errors, and a full reception of the truth in carrying out its principles, by the grace of God, that the victory can be gained.

I wish I could speak words which would impress us all that our only hope as individuals is to connect with God. Purity of soul must be obtained; and there is much heart searching to be done and much obstinacy and self-love to be overcome, which will require constant, earnest prayer.

Men who are harsh and censorious often excuse or try to justify their lack of Christian politeness because some of the Reformers worked with such a spirit, and they claim that the work for this time requires the same spirit; but this is not so. A spirit which is calm and under perfect control is better in any place, even in the roughest company. A furious zeal does no good to anyone. God did not select the Reformers because they were overbearing, passionate men. He accepted them as they were, notwithstanding these traits of character; but He would have placed tenfold greater responsibilities upon them had they been of humble mind, having their spirits under control of reason. While ministers of Christ must denounce sin and ungodliness, impurity and falsehood, while they are sometimes called to rebuke iniquity among the high as well as the low, showing them that the indignation of God will fall upon the transgressors of His law, yet they should not be overbearing or tyrannical; they should manifest kindness and love, a spirit to save rather than to destroy.

The long-suffering of Jehovah teaches ministers and church members who aspire to be colaborers with Christ, unmistakable lessons of forbearance and love. Christ connected Judas and impulsive Peter with Himself, not because Judas was covetous and Peter passionate, but that they might learn of Him, their great Teacher, and become, like Him, unselfish, meek, and lowly of heart. He saw good material in both these men. Judas possessed financial ability and would have been of value to the church had he taken home to his heart the lessons which Christ was giving by rebuking all selfishness, fraud, and avarice, even in the little matters of life.

These lessons were oft-repeated: "He that is faithful in that which is least is faithful also in much: and he that is unjust in the least is unjust also in much."

Our Saviour sought to impress upon His hearers that a man who would advantage himself by overreaching his neighbor in the smallest item would, if the opportunity were favorable, overreach in larger matters. The least departure from strict rectitude breaks down the barriers and prepares the heart to do greater injustice. Christ, by precept and example, taught that the strictest integrity should govern our actions toward our fellow men. "Whatsoever ye would that men should do to you, do ye even so to them." Christ was continually portraying the defective lives of the Pharisees and reproving them. They professed to be keeping the law of God, yet in their daily acts were practicing iniquity. Many widows and orphans were robbed of their little all to gratify an avaricious desire for gain.

Judas might have been benefited by all these lessons had he possessed a desire to be right at heart; but his acquisitiveness overcame him, and the love of money became a ruling power. He carried the purse containing the means to be used in carrying forward the work of Christ, and little sums were from time to time applied to his own use. His selfish heart grudged the offering made by Mary of the alabaster box of ointment, and he reproved her for her imprudence. Thus, instead of being a learner, he would be a teacher and instruct our Lord in regard to the propriety of her action.

These two men alike had the opportunities and privileges of the continual lessons and example of Christ to correct their sinful traits of character. While they heard His withering rebukes and denunciations against hypocrisy and corruption, they saw that those so terribly denounced were the objects of solicitous and unwearied labor for their reformation. The Saviour wept because of their darkness and error. He yearned over them with unbounded compassion and love, exclaiming to Jerusalem: "How often would I have gathered thy children together, as a hen doth gather her brood under her wings, and ye would not!"

Peter was prompt and zealous in action, bold and uncompromising; and Christ saw in him material that would be of great value to the church. He therefore connected Peter with Himself, that all which was good and valuable might be preserved, and that by His lessons and example He might soften whatever was harsh in his temper and smooth whatever was rugged in his deportment. If the heart were indeed transformed by divine grace, an external change would be seen in true kindness, sympathy, and courteousness. Jesus was never cold and unapproachable. The afflicted often broke in upon His retreat when He needed refreshment and rest, but He had a kind look and an encouraging word for all. He was a pattern of true courtesy. Peter denied his Lord, but afterward repented and was deeply humbled because of his great sin; and Christ showed that He forgave His erring disciple in condescending to mention him by name after His resurrection.

Judas yielded to the temptations of Satan and betrayed his best friend. Peter learned and profited by the lessons of Christ, and carried forward the work of reform which was left to the disciples when their Lord ascended on high. These two men represent the two classes that Christ connects with Himself, giving to them the advantages of His lessons and the example of His unselfish, compassionate life, that they may learn of Him.

The more man views his Saviour and becomes acquainted with Him, the more he will become assimilated to His image and work the works of Christ. The age in which we live calls for reformatory action. The light of truth which shines upon us calls for men of determined action and sterling moral worth to labor diligently and perseveringly to save the souls of all who will hear the invitation of the Spirit of God.

The love which should exist between church members frequently gives place to criticism and censure; and these appear, even in the religious exercises, in reflections and severe personal thrusts. Such things should not be countenanced by ministers, elders, or people. The services of the church should be carried forward with an eye single to the glory of God. When men with their peculiar organizations are brought together in church capacity, unless the truth of God softens and subdues the sharp points in the character, the church will be affected and its peace and harmony sacrificed to indulge these selfish, unsanctified traits. Many, in their close watch to discover the faults of their brethren, neglect the investigation of their own hearts and the purification of their own lives. This brings the displeasure of God. The individual members of the church should be jealous for their own souls, critically watching their own actions, lest they should move from selfish motives and be a cause of stumbling to their weak brethren.

God takes men as they are, with the human element in their character, and then trains them for His service if they will be disciplined and learn of Him. The root of bitterness, envy, distrust, jealousy, and even hatred, which exists in the hearts of some church members, is the work of Satan. Such elements have a poisonous influence upon the church. "A little leaven leaveneth the whole lump." The religious zeal which is manifested in a raid upon brethren is a zeal not according to knowledge. Christ has nothing to do with such testimony.

44. Dishonesty in the Church

"The love of money is the root of all evil." Some who profess the truth do not withstand temptation on this point. Among worldlings in this generation the greatest crimes are perpetrated through the love of money. If wealth cannot be secured by honest industry, men will resort to fraud, deception, and crime in order to obtain it. The cup of iniquity is nearly filled, and the retributive justice of God is about to descend upon the guilty. Widows are robbed of their scanty pittance by lawyers and professedly interested friends, and poor men are made to suffer for the necessaries of life because of the dishonesty which is practiced in order to gratify extravagance. The terrible record of crime in our world is enough to chill the blood and fill the soul with horror; but the fact that even among those who profess to believe the truth the same evils are creeping in, the same sins indulged to a greater or less degree, calls for deep humiliation of soul.

A man who sincerely fears God would rather toil day and night, suffer privation, and eat the bread of poverty than to indulge a passion for gain which would oppress the widow and the fatherless or turn the stranger from his right. The crimes that are committed through love of display and love of money constitute this world a den of thieves and robbers, and cause angels to weep. But Christians are professedly not dwellers upon the earth; they are in a strange country, stopping, as it were, only for a night. Our home is in the mansions which Jesus has gone to prepare for us. This life is but a vapor, which passes away.

The acquisition of property becomes a mania with some. Every time the golden rule is violated, Christ is abused in the person of His saints. Every advantage that is taken of fellow mortals, be they saints or sinners, will stand as fraud in the Ledger of Heaven. God designed that our lives should represent the life of our great Pattern in doing good to others and in acting a holy part in the elevation of man. About this work there hovers a true dignity and a glory which may never be seen and realized in this life, but which will be fully appreciated in the future life. The record of kindly deeds and generous actions will reach into eternity. Just to the extent that man would advantage himself at the disadvantage of his fellow man will his soul become calloused to the influence of the Spirit of God. Gain obtained thus is a fearful loss.

There have been men in important places who have not been guardians of the interests of others. They have been wholly absorbed in their own interests and have neglected to preserve the reputation of the church. They have been selfish and avaricious, not moving with an eye single to the glory of God. The church as a whole is in a degree responsible for the wrongs of its individual members because they countenance the evil in not lifting up their voice against it. The favor of God is not enjoyed for several reasons. His Spirit is grieved by the pride, extravagance, dishonesty, and overreaching which are indulged by some professing godliness. All these things bring the frown of God upon His people.

The unbelief and sins of ancient Israel were presented before me, and I saw that similar wrongs and iniquity exist among modern Israel. The pen of inspiration recorded their crimes for the benefit of those who live in these last days, that we might shun their evil example. Achan coveted and secreted a wedge of gold and a goodly Babylonish garment that were taken as spoil from the enemy. But the Lord had pronounced the city of Jericho accursed and had commanded the people not to take of the spoil of their enemies for their own use. "And ye, in anywise keep yourselves from the accursed thing, lest ye make yourselves accursed, when ye take of the accursed thing, and make the camp of Israel a curse, and trouble it. But all the silver, and gold, and vessels of brass and iron, are consecrated unto the Lord: they shall come into the treasury of the Lord."

But Achan, of the tribe of Judah, took of the accursed thing, and the anger of the Lord was kindled against the children of Israel. When the armies of Israel went out to fight against the enemy, they were repulsed and driven back, and some of them were slain. This brought great discouragement upon the people. Joshua, their leader, was perplexed and confounded. In the greatest humiliation he fell upon his face and prayed: "Alas, O Lord God, wherefore hast Thou at all brought this people over Jordan, to deliver us into the hand of the Amorites, to destroy us? would to God we had been content, and dwelt on the other side Jordan! O Lord, what shall I say, when Israel turneth their backs before their enemies! For the Canaanites and all the inhabitants of the land shall hear of it, and shall environ us round, and cut off our name from the earth: and what wilt Thou do unto Thy great name?"

The answer of the Lord to Joshua was: "Get thee up; wherefore liest thou thus upon thy face? Israel hath sinned, and they have also transgressed My covenant which I commanded them: for they have even taken of the accursed thing, and have also stolen, and dissembled also, and they have put it even among their own stuff." Achan had stolen that which was to be reserved for God and placed in His treasury; he had also dissembled in that when he saw the camp of Israel troubled he did not confess his guilt, for he knew that Joshua had repeated the words of the Lord to the people, that if they should appropriate to themselves that which God had reserved, the camp of Israel would be troubled.

While he is rejoicing in his ill-gotten gain, his security is broken in upon; he hears that an investigation is to be made. This makes him uneasy. He repeats over and over to himself: What does it concern them? I am accountable for my acts. He apparently puts on a brave face and in the most demonstrative manner condemns the one guilty. If he had confessed he might have been saved; but sin hardens the heart, and he continues to assert his innocence. Amid so large a crowd he thinks he will escape detection. Lots are cast to search out the offender; the lot falls upon the tribe of Judah. Achan's heart now begins to throb with guilty fear, for he is one of that tribe; but still he flatters himself that he will escape. The lot is again cast, and the family to which he belongs is taken. Now in his pallid face his guilt is read by Joshua.

The lot cast again singles out the unhappy man. There he stands, pointed out by the finger of God as the guilty one who has caused all this trouble.

If when Achan yielded to temptation he had been asked if he wished to bring defeat and death into the camp of Israel, he would have answered: "No, no! is thy servant a dog that he should do this great wickedness?" But he lingered over the temptation to gratify his own covetousness; and when the opportunity was presented, he went further than he had purposed in his heart. It is exactly in this way that individual members of the church are imperceptibly led on to grieve the Spirit of God, to defraud their neighbors, and to bring the frown of God upon the church.

No man lives to himself. Shame, defeat, and death were brought upon Israel by one man's sin. That protection which had covered their heads in the time of battle was withdrawn. Various sins that are cherished and practiced by professed Christians bring the frown of God upon the church. In the day when the Ledger of Heaven shall be opened, the Judge will not in words express to man his guilt, but will cast one penetrating, convicting glance, and every deed, every transaction of life, will be vividly impressed upon the memory of the wrongdoer. The person will not, as in Joshua's day, need to be hunted out from tribe to family, but his own lips will confess his shame, his selfishness, covetousness, dishonesty, dissembling, and fraud. His sins, hidden from the knowledge of man, will then be proclaimed, as it were, upon the housetop.

The influence most to be feared by the church is not that of open opposers, infidels, and blasphemers, but of inconsistent professors of Christ. These are the ones who keep back the blessing of the God of Israel and bring weakness upon the church, a reproach that is not easily wiped away. While Joshua was lying on his face upon the ground, pouring out his soul to God with agony of spirit and with tears, God's command was a reproof: "Get thee up; wherefore liest thou thus upon thy face?"

The popular churches are filled with men who, while they make a pretense of serving God, are thieves, murderers, adulterers, and fornicators; but those who profess our lowly faith claim a higher standard. They should be Bible Christians, and they must be diligent in the study of the Chart of life. Carefully and prayerfully should they examine the motives which prompt them to action. Those who would put their trust in Christ should begin to study the beauties of the cross now. If they would be living Christians they must begin to fear and obey God now. If they will they can save their souls from ruin and make a success of winning eternal life.

The custom of overreaching in trade, which exists in the world, is no example for Christians. They should not deviate from perfect integrity, even in small matters. To sell an article for more than it is worth, taking advantage of the ignorance of purchasers, is fraud. Unlawful gains, petty tricks of trade, exaggeration, competition, underselling a brother who is seeking to pursue an honest business—these things are corrupting the purity of the church, and are ruinous to her spirituality.

The business world does not lie outside the limits of God's government. Christianity is not to be merely paraded on the Sabbath and displayed in the sanctuary; it is for every day in the week and for every place. Its claims must be recognized and obeyed in the workshop, at home, and in business transactions with brethren and with the world. With many, an absorbing worldliness eclipses the true sense of Christian obligation. The religion of Christ will have such an influence upon the heart that it will control the life. Men possessing the genuine article of true religion will in all their business transactions show as clear a perception of right as when offering their supplications at the throne of grace. The life, with all its capabilities, belongs to God, and should be used to promote His glory, instead of being perverted to the service of Satan in defrauding our fellow men.

Satan has been the adviser of some. He tells them that if they would prosper they must hearken to his counsel: "Do not be overconscientious in regard to honor or honesty; look out sharply for your own interest, and do not be carried away with pity, softness, and generosity. You need not care for the widow and the fatherless. Do not encourage them to look to you and depend on you; leave them to look out for themselves. Do not inquire whether they have food, or if you can bless them with thoughtful, kindly attention. Take care of yourself. Get all into your hands that you can. Rob the widow and the fatherless, and turn away the stranger from his right, and you will have means to supply your various wants." Some have heeded this counsel and despised Him who has said: "Pure religion and undefiled before God and the Father is this, To visit the fatherless and widows in their affliction, and to keep himself unspotted from the world."

Satan offers to men the kingdoms of the world if they will yield to him the supremacy. Many do this and sacrifice heaven. It is better to die than to sin; better to want than to defraud; better to hunger than to lie. Let all who are tempted meet Satan with these words: "Blessed is everyone that feareth the Lord; that walketh in His ways. For thou shalt eat the labor of thine hands: happy shalt thou be, and it shall be well with thee." Here is a condition and a promise which will be unmistakably realized. Happiness and prosperity will be the result of serving the Lord.

45. Importance of Self-Control

Sister H:

I know but little of your life before you professed Christ; but since that time you have not been a truly converted woman; you have not rightly represented Christ, your Master. You accepted the theory of the truth, but have failed to become sanctified through it. You have not practiced self-control, but have gratified your desires and wishes at the expense of health and religion. You are easily irritated, and, instead of putting a strict guard upon your words and actions, you have given loose rein to your passions. The mind is controlled either by Satan or by Jesus; and when you practice no self-control, Satan rules and leads you to do and say things that are wholly satanic. This has been repeated so often that it has become habitual.

Since you have been living with your present husband you have allowed yourself to become exasperated at very trivial matters; and at such times you seem to have a frenzied passion, while Satan stands by and laughs at the misery you are bringing upon yourself and those whom it is your duty to make happy. Your children have had transmitted to them your traits of character, and, besides this, they are daily copying your example of blind, unreasonable passion, impatience, and fretfulness.

In the human heart there is natural selfishness and corruption, which can only be overcome by most thorough discipline and severe restraint; and even then it will require years of patient effort and earnest resistance. God permits us to experience the ills of poverty, and places us in difficult positions, that the defects in our characters may be revealed and their asperities be smoothed away. But after privileges and opportunities have been given of God, after light and truth have been brought home to the understanding, if persons still make excuses for their deformity of character, and continue in their selfishness and jealousy, their hearts become as granite, making it impossible for them to be reformed, except by the chisel, the hammer, and the polishing of the Spirit of God.

I was pointed back to your life and experience when you first came to — —. Your conduct was not consistent; your associations were not right. Your course in visiting the beer gardens with your children did not make a favorable impression upon others in reference to your moral standing. These are sad chapters in your experience. You had light and knowledge, but your inclinations and follies separated you from God.

Many circumstances which occurred while you were living in —— were shown me. Your strong, perverse will led you to disgrace the truth which you professed. Your conduct before the world was not justifiable. The punishment which your daughter received in school for willful disobedience was exaggerated in your mind till it became so heinous an offense as to lead you to seek the protection of the law. The deception you there practiced, your exaggeration of the truth, was a lesson most dangerous to morals.

These things stand registered against you in the books of heaven. You have a stubborn disposition and will not humble your heart to confess a wrong, but will justify your course before men without reference to how it appears in the sight of God. Can you wonder that under such deceptive training your daughter has become what she is? What influence could such a course of training have upon the youthful mind but to make her feel that no one had a right to control her perverse will? The seed sown by your own hand has blossomed and borne fruit which is most bitter.

Love for your soul causes me to write at the present time. I am oppressed with the burden of responsibility which I now take upon myself in writing out these things for you. By your own course you are closing the gates of heaven against yourself and your children, for neither you nor they will ever enter there with your present defective characters. You, my sister, are playing a sad, losing game in life. Holy angels are watching you with sadness; and evil spirits are looking on with triumph as they see you losing, fast losing, the graces that adorn the Christian character, while in their place Satan is implanting his own evil traits.

You have indulged in novel and story reading until you live in an imaginary world. The influence of such reading is injurious to both the mind and the body; it weakens the intellect and brings a fearful tax upon the physical strength. At times your mind is scarcely sane because the imagination has been overexcited and diseased by reading fictitious stories. The mind should be so disciplined that all its powers will be symmetrically developed. A certain course of training may invigorate special faculties and at the same time leave other faculties without improvement so that their usefulness will be crippled. The memory is greatly injured by ill-chosen reading, which has a tendency to unbalance the reasoning powers and to create nervousness, weariness of the brain, and prostration of the entire system. If the imagination is constantly overfed and stimulated by fictitious literature, it soon becomes a tyrant, controlling all the other faculties of the mind and causing the taste to become fitful and the tendencies perverse.

You are a mental dyspeptic. Your mind has been crammed with knowledge of all sorts,—politics, history, theology, and anecdote,—only a part of which can be retained by the abused memory. Much less information, with a mind well disciplined, would be of far greater value. You have neglected to train your mind to vigorous action; therefore your will and inclination have controlled you and been your masters instead of your servants. The result is a loss of physical and mental power.

For years your mind has been like a babbling brook, nearly filled with rocks and weeds, the water running to waste. Were your powers controlled by high purposes, you would not be the invalid that you now are. You fancy you must be indulged in your caprice of appetite and in your excessive reading. I saw the midnight lamp burning in your room while you were poring over some fascinating story, thus stimulating your already overexcited brain. This course has been lessening your hold upon life and enfeebling you physically, mentally, and morally. Irregularity has created disorder in your house, and, if continued, will cause your mind to sink into imbecility. Your God-given probation has been abused, your God-given time wasted.

God bestows upon us talents for wise improvement, not for abuse. Education is but a preparation of the physical, intellectual, and moral powers for the best performance of all the duties of life. Improper reading gives an education that is false. The power of endurance, and the strength and activity of the brain, may be lessened or increased according to the manner in which they are employed. There is a work before you to dispose of your light reading. Remove it from your house. Do not have before you the temptation to pervert your imagination, to unbalance your nervous system, and to ruin your children. By much reading you are unfitting yourself for the duties of a wife and mother, and, in fact, are disqualifying yourself to do good anywhere.

The Bible is not studied as it should be; therefore you do not become wise in the Scriptures and are not thoroughly furnished unto all good works. Light reading fascinates the mind and makes the reading of God's word uninteresting. You seek to make others believe that you are conversant with the Scriptures; but this cannot be, for your mind is filled with rubbish. The Bible requires thought and prayerful research. It is not enough to skim over the surface. While some passages are too plain to be misunderstood, others are more intricate, demanding careful and patient study. Like the precious metal concealed in the hills and mountains, its gems of truth are to be searched out and stored in the mind for future use. Oh, that all would exercise their minds as constantly in searching for celestial gold as for the gold that perishes!

When you search the Scriptures with an earnest desire to learn the truth, God will breathe His Spirit into your heart and impress your mind with the light of His word. The Bible is its own interpreter, one passage explaining another. By comparing scriptures referring to the same subjects, you will see beauty and harmony of which you have never dreamed. There is no other book whose perusal strengthens and enlarges, elevates and ennobles the mind, as does the perusal of this Book of books. Its study imparts new vigor to the mind, which is thus brought in contact with subjects requiring earnest thought, and is drawn out in prayer to God for power to comprehend the truths revealed. If the mind is left to deal with commonplace subjects, instead of deep and difficult problems, it will become narrowed down to the standard of the matter which it contemplates and will finally lose its power of expansion.

That which is the most to be deplored in regard to your course is that your errors and mistakes are being reproduced in your children. I is becoming

427

absorbed in reading; her mental powers are receiving injury, permanent injury, from following your example. She will have no taste or aptitude for study. In early life the mind is impressible. Let the good seed then be sown upon good soil, and it will bear fruit unto eternal life.

The habits formed in youth, although they may in after-life be somewhat modified, are seldom essentially changed. Your entire life has been molded by the legacy of character transmitted to you at birth. Your father's perverse temperament is seen in his children. The grace of God can overcome these wrong tendencies; but what a battle must be fought. Thus it is with your children. You indulge them as you indulge yourself. You have no power to deny the appetite what you desire, and you thus place terrible burdens upon your digestive organs. No woman can have good health and indulge her fancy as you do.

The same is true of your children. Their mother's wrong discipline when she has been able to care for them, and their being left so much of the time without a mother's care, have nearly ruined them. Yet even now a firm, undeviating course will make great improvement in them; they are not beyond control, although it will be most difficult to make them what they might have been had the parents been right. The mother can see the result of the course she has pursued if she wishes, or she can reform and try to counteract the wrong done. The path upon which her children are now entering may lead to virtue or to vice, to honor or to infamy, to heaven or to hell. The influence of a praying, God-fearing mother will last through eternity. She may die, but her work will endure.

Brother and Sister H, neither of you realizes the sad condition of your children. Brother H has neglected to take a decided stand to control them. The little boy, to a great extent, rules the household. The management of your two elder children was entirely wrong. While at times Brother H was too severe and exacting, requiring of them that which he would not have required of his own children, your course, Sister H, was far worse. You took the part of the children in their presence and fired their young hearts with revenge. You gave them lessons of insubordination and talked disrespectfully of your husband before them. This course was just calculated to lead them to despise restraint. An indelible impression was thus made upon their minds.

You are now beginning to see in your elder children the results of this training; yet you are doing the same work, to a great extent, with the children that God has since entrusted to your care. Your inconsistent, uncontrollable spirit is like an insidious poison taken into the system, and its bitter results will appear sooner or later. Its mark is being made, not on sand, but on rock; and in after years it will testify of your work.

My sister, you have not a sensitive conscience. You must consider carefully what habits you are forming, and pray earnestly that your perverse character may be washed from its defilement, in the blood of the Lamb. The conscience must be enlightened, the passions restrained, and the love of truth cherished in the soul before you can see the kingdom of God.

All through your life you have needed fixed and settled principles. Satan is still on your track. Your only hope now is in a thorough conversion to God. Do not be deceived, for God is not mocked. Should your probation close today, I could have no hope of your being saved. Your own health, physical, mental, and moral, depends upon a proper government of your temper. You will doubtless meet with things that will ruffle your spirit and severely test you; but self-control may be yours in the strength of Jesus. Solomon places the one who controls himself above him who conquers in battle: "He that is slow to anger is better than the mighty; and he that ruleth his spirit than he that taketh a city."

By permitting yourself to become unduly excited, you have established a condition of things in your system which will, unless changed, cost you your life. You abuse your husband; you say things to him which no wife should be guilty of saying. You have prevaricated again and again, and have gone so far as to be guilty of deliberate falsehoods to accomplish your ends. A determination to carry out their own will at all hazards is a leading characteristic of your family.

The course of Brother H has not been what it should have been. His likes and dislikes are very strong, and he has not kept his own feelings under the control of reason. Brother H, your health is greatly injured by overeating and eating at improper times. This causes a determination of blood to the brain. The mind becomes confused, and you have not the proper control of yourself. You appear like a man whose mind is unbalanced. You make strong moves, are easily irritated, and view things in an exaggerated and perverted light.

Plenty of exercise in the open air, and an abstemious diet, are essential to your health. You should not eat more than two meals a day. If you feel that you must eat at night, take a drink of cold water, and in the morning you will feel much better for not having eaten.

Your children should not be allowed to eat candies, fruit, nuts, or anything in line of food, between their meals. Two meals a day are better for them than three. If the parents set the example, and move from principle, the children will soon fall into line. Irregularities in eating destroy the healthy tone of the digestive organs, and when your children come to the table they do not relish wholesome food; their appetites crave that which is the most hurtful for them. Many times your children have suffered from fever and ague brought on by improper eating, when their parents were accountable for their sickness. It is the duty of parents to see that their children form habits conducive to health, thereby saving much distress.

Brother H is in danger of apoplexy, and if he continues to disobey the laws of health, his life will be cut short suddenly. As a family you can be happy or miserable. It rests with yourselves. Your own course of action will determine the future. You both need to soften the sharp points of your characters and to speak such words only as you will not be ashamed to meet in the day of God. Make it the rule of your life to go straight forward in the path of duty.

In defiance of numerous temptations which will assail you, be true to a good conscience and to God, and your pathway will be plain to your feet. You may contend about little things that are not worthy of contention, and the result will be trouble. The path of the upright is the path of peace. It is so plain that the humble, God-fearing man can walk in it without stumbling and without making crooked paths. It is a narrow path; but men of different temperaments can walk side by side if they but follow the Captain of their salvation. Those who wish to carry along all their evil traits and selfish habits cannot walk in this path, for it is too straight and narrow.

What pains the Great Shepherd takes to call His sheep by name and invite them to follow in His footsteps. He seeks the wandering. He flashes light from His word to show them their peril. He speaks to them from heaven in warnings and reproofs, and in invitations to return to the right path. He seeks to help the erring by His presence and to lift them when they fall. But many have followed the path of sin so long that they will not hear the voice of Jesus.

They leave all that can give them rest and security, yield themselves up to a false guide, and presumptuously hurry on in blind self-confidence, going further and further from light and peace, from happiness and rest.

I implore you to heed the light which God has given, and reform. The cross of Christ is our only hope. It reveals to us the greatness of our Father's love and the fact that the Majesty of heaven submitted to insult, mockery, humiliation, and suffering for the joy of seeing perishing souls saved in His kingdom. If you love your children, let it be your chief study to prepare them for the future, immortal life. With the unhappy dispositions they now possess, they will never see the paradise of God. Work while it is day; redeem the time, and win the crown of immortal glory. Save yourself and your household, for the salvation of the soul is precious.

46. Unscriptural Marriages

We are living in the last days, when the mania upon the subject of marriage constitutes one of the signs of the near coming of Christ. God is not consulted in these matters. Religion, duty, and principle are sacrificed to carry out the promptings of the unconsecrated heart. There should be no great display and rejoicing over the union of the parties.

There is not one marriage in one hundred that results happily, that bears the sanction of God, and places the parties in a position better to glorify Him. The evil consequences of poor marriages are numberless. They are contracted from impulse. A candid review of the matter is scarcely thought of, and consultation with those of experience is considered old-fashioned.

Impulse and unsanctified passion exist in the place of pure love. Many imperil their own souls, and bring the curse of God upon them, by entering into the marriage relation merely to please the fancy. I have been shown the cases of some who profess to believe the truth, who have made a great mistake by marrying unbelievers. The hope was cherished by them that the unbelieving party would embrace the truth; but after his object is gained, he is further from the truth than before. And then begin the subtle workings, the continued efforts, of the enemy to draw away the believing one from the faith.

Many are now losing their interest and confidence in the truth because they have taken unbelief into close connection with themselves. They breathe the atmosphere of doubt, of questioning, of infidelity. They see and hear unbelief, and finally they cherish it. Some may have the courage to resist these influences, but in many cases their faith is imperceptibly undermined and finally destroyed. Satan has then succeeded in his plans. He has worked through his agents so silently that the barriers of faith and truth have been swept away before the believing ones have had any thought of where they were drifting.

It is a dangerous thing to form a worldly alliance. Satan well knows that the hour that witnesses the marriage of many young men and women closes the history of their religious experience and usefulness. They are lost to Christ. They may for a time make an effort to live a Christian life, but all their strivings are made against a steady influence in the opposite direction. Once it was a privilege and joy to them to speak of their faith and hope; but they become unwilling to mention the subject, knowing that the one with whom they have linked their destiny takes no interest in it. As the result, faith in the precious truth dies out of the heart, and Satan insidiously weaves about them a web of skepticism.

It is carrying that which is lawful to excess that makes it a grievous sin. Those who profess the truth trample on the will of God in marrying unbelievers; they lose His favor and make bitter work for repentance. The unbelieving may possess an excellent moral character; but the fact that he or she has not answered to the claims of God, and has neglected so great salvation, is sufficient reason why such a union should not be consummated. The character of the unbelieving may be similar to that of the young man to whom Jesus addressed the words, "One thing thou lackest;" that was the one thing needful.

The plea is sometimes made that the unbeliever is favorable to religion and is all that could be desired in a companion except in one thing—he is not a Christian. Although the better judgment of the believer may suggest the impropriety of a union for life with an unbeliever, yet, in nine cases out of ten, inclination triumphs. Spiritual declension commences the moment the vow is made at the altar; religious fervor is dampened, and one stronghold after another is broken down, until both stand side by side under the black banner of Satan. Even in the festivities of the wedding, the spirit of the world triumphs against conscience, faith, and truth. In the new home the hour of prayer is not respected. The bride and bridegroom have chosen each other and dismissed Jesus.

At first the unbelieving one may make no show of opposition in the new relation; but when the subject of Bible truth is presented for attention and consideration, the feeling at once arises: "You married me, knowing that I was what I am; I do not wish to be disturbed. From henceforth let it be understood that conversation upon your peculiar views is to be interdicted." If the believer should manifest any special earnestness in regard to his faith, it might seem like unkindness toward the one who has no interest in the Christian experience.

The believing one reasons that in his new relation he must concede somewhat to the companion of his choice. Social, worldly amusements are patronized. At first there is great reluctance of feeling in doing this, but the interest in the truth becomes less and less, and faith is exchanged for doubt and unbelief. No one would have suspected that the once firm, conscientious believer and devoted follower of Christ could ever become the doubting, vacillating person that he now is. Oh, the change wrought by that unwise marriage!

What ought every Christian to do when brought into the trying position which tests the soundness of religious principle? With a firmness worthy of imitation he should say frankly: "I am a conscientious Christian. I believe the seventh day of the week to be the Sabbath of the Bible. Our faith and principles are such that they lead in opposite directions. We cannot be happy together, for if I follow on to gain a more perfect knowledge of the will of God, I shall become more and more unlike the world, and assimilated to the likeness of Christ."

"If you continue to see no loveliness in Christ, no attractions in the truth, you will love the world, which I cannot love, while I shall love the things of God, which you cannot love. Spiritual things are spiritually discerned. Without spiritual discernment you will be unable to see the claims of God upon me, or to realize my obligations to the Master whom I serve; therefore you will feel that I neglect you for religious duties. You will not be happy; you will be jealous on account of the affections which I give to God; and I shall be alone in my religious belief. When your views shall change, when your heart shall respond to the claims of God, and you shall learn to love my Saviour, then our relationship may be renewed."

The believer thus makes a sacrifice for Christ which his conscience approves, and which shows that he values eternal life too highly to run the risk of losing it. He feels that it would be better to remain unmarried than to link his interest for life with one who chooses the world rather than Jesus and who would lead away from the cross of Christ. But the danger of giving the affections to unbelievers is not realized. In the youthful mind, marriage is clothed with romance, and it is difficult to divest it of this feature, with which imagination covers it, and to impress the mind with a sense of the weighty responsibilities involved in the marriage vow. This vow links the destinies of the two individuals with bonds which nought but the hand of death should sever.

Shall one who is seeking for glory, honor, immortality, eternal life, form a union with another who refuses to rank with the soldiers of the cross of Christ? Will you who profess to choose Christ for your master and to be obedient to Him in all things, unite your interests with one who is ruled by the prince of the powers of darkness? "Can two walk together, except they be agreed?" "If two of you shall agree on earth as touching anything that they shall ask, it shall be done for them of My Father which is in heaven." But how strange the sight! While one of those so closely united is engaged in devotion, the other is indifferent and careless; while one is seeking the way to everlasting life, the other is in the broad road to death.

Hundreds have sacrificed Christ and heaven in consequence of marrying unconverted persons. Can it be that the love and fellowship of Christ are of so little value to them that they prefer the companionship of poor mortals? Is heaven so little esteemed that they are willing to risk its enjoyments for one who has no love for the precious Saviour?

The happiness and prosperity of the married life depend upon the unity of the parties. How can the carnal mind harmonize with the mind that is assimilated to the mind of Christ? One is sowing to the flesh, thinking and acting in accordance with the promptings of his own heart; the other is sowing to the Spirit, seeking to repress selfishness, to overcome inclination, and to live in obedience to the Master, whose servant he professes to be. Thus there is a perpetual difference of taste, of inclination, and of purpose. Unless the believer shall, through his steadfast adherence to principle, win the impenitent, he will, as is much more common, become discouraged and sell his religious principles for the poor companionship of one who has no connection with heaven.

God strictly forbade the intermarrying of His ancient people with other nations. The plea is now offered that this prohibition was made in order to prevent the Hebrews from marrying idolaters and forming connections with heathen families. But the heathen were in a more favorable condition than are the impenitent in this age, who, having the light of truth, yet persistently refuse to accept it. The sinner of today is far more guilty than the heathen, because the light of the gospel shines clearly all around him. He violates conscience and is a deliberate enemy of God. The reason which God assigned for forbidding these marriages was: "For they will turn away thy son from following Me." Those among ancient Israel who ventured to disregard the prohibition of God did it at the sacrifice of religious principle. Take the case of Solomon for example. His wives turned away his heart from his God.

47. The Lord's Poor

I was shown that our people living out of Battle Creek do not appreciate the cares and burdens which come upon those at the heart of the work. They allow their church members who are not able to support themselves to come to Battle Creek, thinking that they can obtain work in our institutions. These do not first write and ascertain if there is an opening for them; but crowd themselves upon the church, and find, upon application, that there is already a surplus of hands employed, many of whom are as needy as themselves. They were taken in out of pity, and are still retained, not because they are of the most service to the institutions, but because they are so needy.

There are families residing in Battle Creek who have seen these institutions grow up, and who need and are worthy of positions in them, but who are not able to obtain them because so many from abroad will suffer if not employed. This brings upon the church and these institutions burdens of perplexity to know how to treat all these cases with wisdom, offending none, and showing mercy to all. Our institutions have sustained loss by seeking to help these cases, for frequently the applicants are in poor health and therefore not to be relied upon. Could their places be supplied with able, efficient workers, it would save quite a sum to the cause of God.

It is the duty of every church to feel an interest for its own poor. But many selfish ones have felt gratified to have their poor members move to Battle Creek; for then they would not be required to help support them. The Battle Creek church spend every year from one to five hundred dollars for the support of the poor and sick, whose families must suffer unless they are sustained by charity. God would not be pleased to have this church allow the poor among them to suffer for the necessaries of life; therefore there is a continual draft upon the funds of those at the heart of the work.

Our brethren must retain their poor at home and take those already at Battle Creek off from the hands of the church. They could do very much more than they now do for the poor by furnishing them with work, thus helping them to help themselves. It would be much better to employ these persons in your temporal matters than to send them to the great heart of the work, and let the cause of God be burdened by this inefficient class of workers. Only men and women of culture and of physical and mental strength, caretakers, who have been accustomed to using their own brains rather than the brains of others, are needed at Battle Creek. Would you think it advisable, my brethren, to crowd into responsible positions persons who are incompetent to obtain a livelihood in the common business of life?

There are youth, and men and women, who need to be taught how to employ their ability just where they are.

This is no pleasant duty; but every church is responsible for its individual members, and it should not allow a class who cannot obtain a living where they are in the country, to move to Battle Creek. Brethren in the country have farms and can raise their own supplies. It is therefore much less expensive for the poor to be supported in the country, where provisions are cheap, than to have them come to Battle Creek, where, instead of helping the church and our institutions, means must be continually drawn from the treasury to help them. Those living in the city have to buy nearly all their provisions, and it costs something to take care of the poor.

Brethren in smaller churches, if God has left a work for you to do in caring for His poor, in comforting the desponding, in visiting the sick, in dispensing to the needy, do not be so liberal as to want the Battle Creek church to have all the blessings of this work. You will be justified in coveting the blessings God has promised to those who will care for the poor and sympathize with the suffering.

There must be a charity fund raised to meet the necessities of the poor who are permitted to come to Battle Creek. Each year the sanitarium gives thousands of dollars to charity patients, but who appreciates this great tax upon the institution? None whose names are on the church book should be left to suffer year after year from sickness, when a few months at the sanitarium would give them relief and a valuable experience how to take care of themselves and others when sick. Every church should feel it a Bible duty devolving upon them to care for their own worthy poor and sick.

When a worthy child of God needs the benefit of the sanitarium and can pay but a small amount toward his expenses, let the church act a noble part and make up the sum. Some may not be able to pay anything themselves, but do not let them continue to suffer because of your selfishness. Send them to the sanitarium, and send your pledges and your money with them to pay their expenses. In doing this you will gain a precious blessing. It costs something to run such an institution, and it should not be required to treat the sick for nothing. Could the sum which that institution has expended for charity patients be refunded, it would go a long way toward relieving it of its present embarrassments.

Brethren, do not leave the burden of your poor upon the people and institutions at Battle Creek, but come up nobly to the work and do your duty. Deny yourselves of some things in your houses or in your dress, and lay by in some safe place a sum for the needy poor. Let not your tithes and thank offerings to God be less, but let this be in addition. God does not propose to rain means from heaven with which to sustain the poor, but He has placed His goods in the hands of agents. They are to recognize Christ in the person of His saints. And what they do for His suffering children they do for Him, for He identifies His interest with that of suffering humanity.

God calls upon the young to deny themselves of needless ornaments and articles of dress, even if they cost but a few dimes, and place the amount in the charity box. He also calls upon those of mature age to stop when they are examining a gold watch or chain, or some expensive article of furniture, and ask themselves the question: Would it be right to expend so large an amount for that which we could do without or when a cheaper article would serve our purpose just as well? By denying yourselves and lifting the cross for Jesus, who for your sakes became poor, you can do much toward relieving the suffering of the poor among us; and by thus imitating the example of your Lord and Master, you will receive His approval and blessing.

48. The Cause at Battle Creek

Many who have come to Battle Creek have not come for the purpose of bearing burdens. They have not come because they feel any special anxiety for the prosperity of the cause here, but for their own interest, because they wish to advantage themselves. They hope to secure the benefits to be derived from the institutions located here, without bearing any responsibilities themselves.

Some who have located in Battle Creek in order to have a more favorable opportunity to benefit themselves, are guilty of selfishness and even fraud in dealing with our brethren who have come from abroad. If there are any advantages to be gained, our institutions should receive them, and not those individuals who have done nothing toward building them up and who have only a selfish interest in them. Many who come to Battle Creek are no strength, religiously, to the cause. At heart they are like Korah, Dathan, and Abiram; and if a favorable opportunity were presented, they would follow the example of these wicked men. True, their fraudulent transactions may be concealed from the eyes of their brethren generally; but God marks their course and will finally reward them according to their works.

Some who have been long in Battle Creek, and who ought to be responsible men, are occupying positions of trust in name only. They have been made guardians of our institutions; but their course of action shows that they have no special interest in them nor burden for them. Their thoughts center upon themselves. If we were to judge them by their works we should decide that they consider their own energies too precious to be exercised for these instrumentalities of God, unless they can secure temporal advantages to themselves. These are neglecting to keep the fort, not because they cannot do it, but because they are self-caring, and are content to rock themselves to sleep in the cradle of carnal security.

Men who make it their aim and object in life to please and benefit themselves ought not to remain at this important post. They have no right to be here; for they stand directly in the way of the work of God. Those who neglect the Lord's poor, and who feel no burden for the widow and the fatherless, not making these cases their own and laboring to see justice and equity between man and man, are guilty of neglecting Christ in the person of His saints, because the cause that they know not they do not search out. They have no burdens, and make no effort to sustain the right. If most earnest vigilance is not manifested at the great heart of the work to protect the interests of the cause, the church will become as corrupt as the churches of other denominations.

All who live in Battle Creek will have a fearful account to render to God if they suffer sin upon a brother. It is an alarming fact that indifference, sleepiness, and apathy have characterized men in responsible positions, and that there is a steady increase of pride and an alarming disregard of the warnings of the Spirit of God. The barriers which God's word places about His people are being broken down. Men who are acquainted with the way in which God has led His people in the past, instead of inquiring for the old paths and defending our position as a peculiar people, have linked hands with the world. The most alarming feature in the case is that warning voices have not been heard in remonstrance, entreaties, and warnings. The eyes of God's people seem to be blinded, while the church is fast drifting into the channel of worldliness.

God does not desire wooden men to guard the interests of His institutions and the church, but He wants living, working men,—men who have ability and quick perception,—men who have eyes, and open them that they may see, and hearts that are susceptible to the influences of His Spirit. He holds men to a strict accountability in guarding the interests of His cause at Battle Creek.

There are some in Battle Creek who have never fully submitted to reproof. They have taken a course of their own choosing. They have ever, to a greater or less degree, exerted an influence against those who have stood up to defend the right and reprove the wrong. The influence of these persons upon individuals who come here, and who are brought in contact with them as roomers or boarders, is very bad. They fill the minds of these newcomers with questionings and doubts in regard to the testimonies of the Spirit of God.

They put false constructions upon the Testimonies; and instead of leading persons to become consecrated to God and to listen to the voice of the church, they teach them to be independent and not to mind the opinions and judgment of others. The influence of this class has been secretly at work. Some are unconscious of the harm they are doing; but, unconsecrated, proud, and rebellious themselves, they lead others in the wrong track. A poisonous atmosphere is inhaled from these unconsecrated ones. The blood of souls is in the garments of such, and Christ will say to them in the day of final settlement: "Depart from Me, all ye workers of iniquity." Astonished they will be; but their professedly Christian lives were a deception, a fraud.

If all in Battle Creek stood true to the light God has given them, true to the interests of the church, feeling the worth of souls for whom Christ died, a different influence would be exerted. But here we see acted over to a great extent the experience of the children of Israel. As the people stood before Mount Sinai, listening to the voice of God, they were so forcibly impressed with His sacred presence that they retreated in terror and cried out to Moses: "Speak thou with us, and we will hear: but let not God speak with us, lest we die." There before the mount they made solemn vows of allegiance to God; but scarcely had the thunders and the trumpet and the voice of the Lord ceased, when they were bowed upon their knees before an idol. Their leader had been called away from their sight and was enveloped in a thick cloud, in converse with God.

The fellow laborer of Moses, who was left with the solemn charge of the people in his absence, heard them uttering complaints that Moses had left them, and expressing a desire to return to Egypt; yet, through fear of offending the people, he was silent. He did not stand up boldly for God, but to please the people he made a golden calf. He seemed to be asleep to the beginning of the evil. When the first rebellious word was spoken, Aaron might have checked it; but so fearful was he of offending the people that he apparently united with them and was finally persuaded to make a golden calf for them to worship.

Ministers should be faithful watchmen, seeing the evil and warning the people. Their dangers must be set before them continually and pressed home upon them. The exhortation given to Timothy was: "Reprove, rebuke, exhort with all long-suffering and doctrine."

There have been marriage relations formed in Battle Creek with which God has had nothing to do. Marriages have been ill-assorted in some cases, immature in others. Christ has warned us that this state of things would exist prior to His second appearing. It constitutes one of the signs of the last days. A similar state of things existed before the Flood. The minds of the people were bewitched upon the subject of marriage. When there is so much uncertainty, so great danger, there is no reason why we should make great parade or display, even if the parties were perfectly suited to each other; but that remains to be tested.

When those who profess to be reformers, those in humble life, ape the customs and fashions of the worldly wealthy, it is a reproach to our faith. There are some to whom God gave the word of warning; but did that stop them? No; they did not fear God, for the bewitching power of Satan was upon them. And some in Battle Creek have influenced these poor infatuated ones to follow their own judgment, and by doing this they have crippled their usefulness and incurred the displeasure of God.

God wants men to cultivate force of character. Those who are merely timeservers are not the ones who will receive a rich reward by and by. He wants those who labor in His cause to be men of keen feeling and quick perception. They should be temperate in eating; rich and luxurious food should find no place upon their tables; and when the brain is constantly taxed and there is a lack of physical exercise, they should eat sparingly, even of plain food. Daniel's clearness of mind and firmness of purpose, his strength of intellect in acquiring knowledge, were due in a great degree to the plainness of his diet in connection with his life of prayer.

Eli was a good man, pure in morals; but he was too indulgent. He incurred the displeasure of God because he did not strengthen the weak points in his character. He did not want to hurt the feelings of anyone and had not the moral courage to rebuke and reprove sin. His sons were vile men; yet he did not remove them from their position of trust. These sons profaned the house of God. He knew this, and felt sad in consequence of it, for he loved purity and righteousness; but he had not sufficient moral force to suppress the evil. He loved peace and harmony, and became more and more insensible to impurity and crime. But the great God takes the matter in hand Himself. When the rebuke falls upon him, through the instrumentality of a child, he accepts it, feeling that it is what he deserves. He does not show any resentment toward Samuel, the messenger of God; he loves him as he has done, but condemns himself.

The guilty sons of Eli were slain in battle. He could endure to hear that his sons were slain, but he could not bear the news that the ark of God was taken. He knew that his sin of neglect in failing to stand for the right and restrain wrong had at last deprived Israel of her strength and glory. The pallor of death came upon his face, and he fell backward and died.

What a lesson have we here for parents and guardians of youth, and for those who minister in the service of God. When existing evils are not met and checked, because men have too little courage to reprove wrong, or because they have too little interest or are too indolent to tax their own powers in putting forth earnest efforts to purify the family or the church of God, they are accountable for the evil which may result in consequence of neglect to do their duty. We are just as accountable for evils that we might have checked in others, by reproof, by warning, by exercise of parental or pastoral authority, as if we were guilty of the acts ourselves.

Eli should have first attempted to restrain evil by mild measures; but if that would not avail, he should have subdued the wrong by the sternest measures. God's honor must be sacredly preserved, even if it separates us from the nearest relative. One defect in a man otherwise talented may destroy his usefulness in this life and cause him to hear in the day of God the unwelcome words: "Depart from Me, ye that work iniquity."

Eli was gentle, loving, and kind, and had a true interest in the service of God and the prosperity of His cause. He was a man who had power in prayer. He never rose up in rebellion against the words of God. But he was wanting; he did not have firmness of character to reprove sin and execute justice against the sinner so that God could depend upon him to keep Israel pure. He did not add to his faith the courage and power to say No at the right time and in the right place. Sin is sin; righteousness is righteousness. The trumpet note of warning must be sounded. We are living in a fearfully wicked age. The worship of God will become corrupted unless there are wide-awake men at every post of duty. It is no time now for any to be absorbed in selfish ease. Not one of the words which God has spoken must be allowed to fall to the ground.

While some in Battle Creek have professedly believed the Testimonies, they have been trampling them under their feet. But few have read them with interest; but few have heeded them. The indulgence of self, pride, fashion, and display are mingled with the worship of God. He wants brave men for action, who will not regard the setting up of idols and the coming in of abominations without lifting up the voice like a trumpet, showing the people their transgressions and the house of Jacob their sins.

As soon as Samuel began to judge Israel, even in his youth, he called an assembly of the people for fasting and prayer, and deep humiliation before God. He bore his solemn testimony from the mouth of God. The people then began to learn where their strength was. They entreated Samuel to cease not to cry unto God for them. Their enemies were aroused to meet them in battle, but God heard prayer in their behalf. He wrought for them, and victory turned on the side of Israel.

There is a great work to be done in Battle Creek. Duties have been neglected, important trusts have been betrayed. Men have come here who have added nothing to the strength of the cause, but who are constantly at work to gather the little means possessed by others into their own hands, and thus rob God's treasury. The natural selfishness of their hearts is exhibited wherever a favorable opportunity presents itself to advantage themselves at the disadvantage of others. They have done so until the standard of the worldling is met, and there is but little difference between their manner of dealing and that of the world.

Our people in Battle Creek have greater responsibilities to bear than those in any other place. All who choose to locate here should do so, not merely for their own convenience and benefit, but with an eye single to the glory of God. They should be fully prepared to lift the burdens where and when they need to be lifted; and with self-sacrificing devotion sustain the institutions which God has placed among them. Those who are unwilling to follow this course should go where there are not so heavy burdens to be borne. At this important post, where so much depends upon personal effort, all must act their part unflinchingly; they must be wide awake, that the cause of their Master may not suffer the loss of one soul. Many fail to come up to the gospel standard; they have a selfish regard for their own interest and neglect to see what they can do to be a blessing to their fellow men. Christ wants no idlers in His vineyard. He requires that everyone shall work for time and for eternity.

49. Improvement of Talents

God intends that improvement shall be the lifework of all His followers and that it shall be guided and controlled by correct experience. The true man is one who is willing to sacrifice his own interest for the good of others and who exercises himself in binding up the brokenhearted. The true object of life has scarcely begun to be understood by many, and that which is real and substantial in their life is sacrificed because of cherished errors.

Nero and Caesar were acknowledged by the world as great men, but did God regard them as such? No; they were not connected by living faith to the great Heart of humanity. They were in the world, and ate, and drank, and slept, as men of the world; but they were satanic in their cruelty. Wherever these monsters of humanity went, bloodshed and destruction marked their pathway. They were lauded by the world while they were living; but when they were buried, the world rejoiced. In contrast with the lives of these men is that of Luther. He was not born a prince. He wore no royal crown. From a cloister cell his voice was heard and his influence felt. He had a humane heart, which was exercised for the good of men. He stood bravely for truth and right, and breasted the world's opposition, that he might benefit his fellow men.

Intellect alone does not make the man, according to the divine standard. There is a power in intellect if sanctified and controlled by the Spirit of God. It is superior to riches and to physical power, yet it must be cultivated in order to make the man. The right which one has to claim to be a man is determined by the use made of his intellect. Byron had intellectual conception and depth of thought, but he was not a man according to God's standard. He was an agent of Satan. His passions were fierce and uncontrollable. Through his life he was sowing seed which blossomed into a harvest of corruption. His lifework lowered the standard of virtue. This man was one of the world's distinguished men; still the Lord would not acknowledge him as a man, but only as one who had abused his God-given talents. Gibbon the skeptic, and many others whom God endowed with giant minds, and whom the world called great men, rallied under the banner of Satan and used the gifts of God for the perversion of truth and the destruction of the souls of men. Great intellect, when made a minister of vice, is a curse to the possessor and to all who come within the circle of its influence.

That which will bless humanity is spiritual life. If the man is in harmony with God, he will depend continually upon Him for strength. "Be ye therefore perfect, even as your Father which is in heaven is perfect." It is our lifework to be reaching forward to the perfection of Christian character, striving continually for conformity to the will of God. The efforts begun upon earth will continue through eternity. God's standard of man is elevated to the highest meaning of the term, and if he acts up to his God-given manhood he will promote happiness in this life, which will lead to glory and an eternal reward in the life to come.

The members of the human family are entitled to the name of men and women only when they employ their talents, in every possible way, for the good of others. The life of Christ is before us as a pattern, and it is when ministering, like angels of mercy, to the wants of others that man is closely allied to God. It is the nature of Christianity to make happy families and happy society. Discord, selfishness, and strife will be put away from every man and woman who possesses the true spirit of Christ.

Those who are partakers of Christ's love have no right to think that there is a limit to their influence and work in trying to benefit humanity. Did Christ become weary in His efforts to save fallen man? Our work is to be continuous and persevering. We shall find work to do until the Master shall bid us lay our armor at His feet. God is a moral governor, and we must wait, submissive to His will, ready and willing to spring to our duty whenever work needs to be done.

Angels are engaged night and day in the service of God for the uplifting of man in accordance with the plan of salvation. Man is required to love God supremely, that is, with all his might, mind, and strength, and his neighbor as himself. This he cannot possibly do unless he shall deny himself. Said Christ: "Whosoever will come after Me, let him deny himself, and take up his cross, and follow Me."

Self-denial means to rule the spirit when passion is seeking for the mastery; to resist the temptation to censure and to speak faultfinding words; to have patience with the child that is dull and whose conduct is grievous and trying; to stand at the post of duty when others may fail; to lift responsibilities wherever and whenever you can, not for the purpose of applause, not for policy, but for the sake of the Master, who has given you a work to be done with unwavering fidelity; when you might praise yourself, to keep silent and let other lips praise you. Self-denial is to do good to others where inclination would lead you to serve and please yourself. Although your fellow men may never appreciate your efforts or give you credit for them, yet you are to work on.

Search carefully and see whether the truth which you have accepted has become a firm principle with you. Do you take Christ with you when you leave the closet of prayer? Does your religion stand guard at the door of your lips? Is your heart drawn out in sympathy and love for others outside of your own family? Are you diligently seeking a clearer understanding of Scriptural truth, that you may let your light shine forth to others? These questions you may answer to your own souls. Let your speech be seasoned with grace and your demeanor show Christian elevation.

A new year has commenced. What has been the record of the past year in your Christian life? How stands your record in heaven? I entreat you to make an unreserved surrender to God. Have your hearts been divided? Give them wholly to the Lord now. Make a different life history the coming year from that of the past. Humble your souls before God. "Blessed is the man that endureth temptation: for when he is tried, he shall receive the crown of life, which the Lord hath promised to them that love Him." Put away all pretense and affectation. Act your simple, natural self. Be truthful in every thought and word and deed, and "in lowliness of mind let each esteem other better than themselves." Ever remember that the moral nature needs to be braced with constant watchfulness and prayer. As long as you look to Christ, you are safe; but the moment you think of your sacrifices and difficulties, and begin to sympathize with and pet yourself, you lose your trust in God and are in great peril.

Many limit divine Providence and divorce mercy and love from His character. They urge that the greatness and majesty of God would forbid His interesting Himself in the concerns of the weakest of His creatures. "Are not two sparrows sold for a farthing? and one of them shall not fall on the ground without your Father. But the very hairs of your head are all numbered. Fear ye not therefore, ye are of more value than many sparrows."

It is difficult for human beings to give attention to the lesser matters of life while the mind is engaged in business of vast importance. But should not this union exist? Man formed in the image of his Maker should unite the larger responsibilities with the smaller. He may be engrossed with occupations of overwhelming importance and neglect the instruction which his children need. These duties may be looked upon as the lesser duties of life, when in reality they lie at the very foundation of society. The happiness of families and churches depends upon home influences. Eternal interests depend upon the proper discharge of the duties of this life. The world is not so much in need of great minds as of good men who will be a blessing in their homes.

Testimony 30

50. The Servants of God

God selected Abraham as His messenger through whom to communicate light to the world. The word of God came to him, not with the presentation of flattering prospects in this life of large salary, of great appreciation and worldly honor. "Get thee out of thy country, and from thy kindred, and from thy father's house, unto a land that I will show thee," was the divine message to Abraham. The patriarch obeyed, and "went out, not knowing whither he went," as God's light bearer, to keep His name alive in the earth. He forsook his country, his home, his relatives, and all pleasant associations connected with his early life, to become a pilgrim and a stranger.

It is frequently more essential than many realize, that early associations should be broken up in order that those who are to speak "in Christ's stead" may stand in a position where God can educate and qualify them for His great work. Kindred and friends often have an influence which God sees will greatly interfere with the instructions He designs to give His servants. Suggestions will be made by those who are not in close connection with heaven that will, if heeded, turn aside from their holy work those who should be light bearers to the world.

Before God can use him, Abraham must be separated from his former associations, that he may not be controlled by human influence or rely upon human aid. Now that he has become connected with God, this man must henceforth dwell among strangers. His character must be peculiar, differing from all the world. He could not even explain his course of action so as to be understood by his friends, for they were idolaters. Spiritual things must be spiritually discerned; therefore his motives and his actions were beyond the comprehension of his kindred and friends.

Abraham's unquestioning obedience was one of the most striking instances of faith and reliance upon God to be found in the Sacred Record. With only the naked promise that his descendants should possess Canaan, without the least outward evidence, he followed on where God should lead, fully and sincerely complying with the conditions on his part, and confident that the Lord would faithfully perform His word. The patriarch went wherever God indicated his duty; he passed through wildernesses without terror; he went among idolatrous nations, with the one thought: "God has spoken; I am obeying His voice; He will guide, He will protect me."

Just such faith and confidence as Abraham had the messengers of God need today. But many whom the Lord could use will not move onward, hearing and obeying the one Voice above all others. The connection with kindred and friends, the former habits and associations, too often have so great an influence upon God's servants that He can give them but little instruction, can communicate to them but little knowledge of His purposes; and often after a time He sets them aside and calls others in their place, whom He proves and tests in the same manner. The Lord would do much more for His servants if they were wholly consecrated to Him, esteeming His service above the ties of kindred and all other earthly associations.

Ministers of the gospel have a sacred work. They have a solemn message of warning to bear to the world—a message which will be a savor of life unto life or of death unto death. They are God's messengers to man, and they should never lose sight of their mission or of their responsibilities. They are not like worldlings; they cannot be like them. If they would be true to God they must maintain their separate, holy character. If they cease to connect with heaven they are in greater danger than others and can exert a stronger influence in the wrong direction, for Satan has his eye constantly upon them, waiting for some weakness to be developed whereby he may make a successful attack. And how he triumphs when he succeeds; for when one who is an ambassador for Christ is off his watch, through him the great adversary may secure many souls to himself.

Those who closely connect with God may not be prosperous in the things of this life; they may often be sorely tried and afflicted. Joseph was maligned and persecuted because he preserved his virtue and integrity. David, that chosen messenger of God, was hunted like a beast of prey by his wicked enemies. Daniel was cast into a den of lions because he was true and unyielding in his allegiance to God. Job was deprived of his worldly possessions and so afflicted in body that he was abhorred by his relatives and friends, yet he preserved his integrity and faithfulness to God. Jeremiah would speak the words which God had put into his mouth, and his plain testimony so enraged the king and princes that he was cast into a loathsome pit. Stephen was stoned because he would preach Christ and Him crucified. Paul was imprisoned, beaten with rods, stoned, and finally put to death because he was a faithful messenger to carry the gospel to the Gentiles. The beloved John was banished to the Isle of Patmos "for the word of God, and for the testimony of Jesus Christ."

These examples of human steadfastness, in the might of divine power, are a witness to the world of the faithfulness of God's promises—of His abiding presence and sustaining grace. As the world looks upon these humble men, it cannot discern their moral value with God. It is a work of faith to calmly repose in God in the darkest hour— however severely tried and tempest-tossed, to feel that our Father is at the helm. The eye of faith alone can look beyond the things of time and sense to estimate the worth of eternal riches.

The great military commander conquers nations and shakes the armies of half the world, but he dies of disappointment and in exile. The philosopher who ranges through the universe, everywhere tracing the manifestations of God's power and delighting in their harmony, often fails to behold in these marvelous wonders the Hand that formed them all. "Man that is in honor, and understandeth not, is like the beasts that perish." No hope of glorious immortality lights up the future of the enemies of God. But those heroes of faith have the promise of an inheritance of greater value than any earthly riches—an inheritance that will satisfy the longings of the soul. They may be unknown and unacknowledged of the world, but they are enrolled as citizens in the record books of heaven. An exalted greatness, an enduring, eternal weight of glory, will be the final reward of those whom God has made heirs of all things.

Ministers of the gospel should make the truth of God the theme of study, of meditation, and of conversation. The mind that dwells much on the revealed will of God to man will become strong in the truth. Those who read and study with an earnest desire for divine light, whether they are ministers or not, will soon discover in the Scriptures a beauty and harmony which will captivate their attention, elevate their thoughts, and give them an inspiration and an energy of argument that will be powerful to convict and convert souls.

There is danger that ministers who profess to believe present truth will rest satisfied with presenting the theory only, while their own souls do not feel its sanctifying power. Some have not the love of God in the heart, softening, molding, and ennobling their lives. The psalmist declares of the good man: "His delight is in the law of the Lord, and in His law doth he meditate day and night." He refers to his own experience, and exclaims: "O how love I Thy law! it is my meditation all the day." "Mine eyes prevent the night watches, that I might meditate in Thy word."

No man is qualified to stand in the sacred desk unless he has felt the transforming influence of the truth of God upon his own soul. Then, and not till then, can he by precept and example rightly represent the life of Christ. But many in their labors exalt themselves rather than their Master, and the people are converted to the minister instead of to Christ.

I am pained to know that some who preach the present truth today are really unconverted men. They are not connected with God. They have a head religion, but no conversion of the heart; and these are the very ones who are the most self-confident and self-sufficient; and this self-sufficiency will stand in the way of their gaining that experience which is essential to make them effective workers in the Lord's vineyard. I wish I could arouse those who claim to be watchmen on the walls of Zion to realize their responsibility.

They should awake and take a higher stand for God, for souls are perishing through their neglect. They must have that sincere devotion to God that will lead them to see as God sees and take the words of warning from Him and sound the alarm to those who are in peril. The Lord will not hide His truth from the faithful watchman. Those who do the will of God shall know of His doctrine. "The wise shall understand;" but "the wicked shall do wickedly: and none of the wicked shall understand."

Said Jesus to His disciples: "Learn of Me; for I am meek and lowly in heart." I would plead with those who have accepted the position of teachers, to first become humble learners, and ever to remain as pupils in the school of

Christ to receive from the Master lessons of meekness and lowliness of heart. Humility of spirit, combined with earnest activity, will result in the salvation of souls so dearly purchased by the blood of Christ. The minister may understand and believe the theory of truth, and be able to present it to others; but this is not all that is required of him. "Faith without works is dead." He needs that faith that works by love and purifies the soul. A living faith in Christ will bring every action of the life and every emotion of the soul into harmony with God's truth and righteousness.

Fretfulness, self-exaltation, pride, passion and every other trait of character unlike our holy Pattern must be overcome; and then humility, meekness, and sincere gratitude to Jesus for His great salvation will continually flow out from the pure fountain of the heart. The voice of Jesus should be heard in the message coming from the lips of His ambassador.

We must have a converted ministry. The efficiency and power attending a truly converted minister would make the hypocrites in Zion tremble and sinners afraid. The standard of truth and holiness is trailing in the dust. If those who sound the solemn notes of warning for this time could realize their accountability to God they would see the necessity for fervent prayer. When the cities were hushed in midnight slumber, when every man had gone to his own house, Christ, our Example, would repair to the Mount of Olives, and there, amid the overshadowing trees, would spend the entire night in prayer.

He who was Himself without the taint of sin,—a treasure house of blessing; whose voice was heard in the fourth watch of the night by the terrified disciples upon the stormy sea, in heavenly benediction; and whose word could summon the dead from their graves,—He it was who made supplication with strong crying and tears. He prayed not for Himself, but for those whom He came to save. As He became a suppliant, seeking at the hand of His Father fresh supplies of strength, and coming forth refreshed and invigorated as man's substitute, He identified Himself with suffering humanity and gave them an example of the necessity of prayer.

His nature was without the taint of sin. As the Son of man, He prayed to the Father, showing that human nature requires all the divine support which man can obtain that he may be braced for duty and prepared for trial. As the Prince of life He had power with God and prevailed for His people. This Saviour, who prayed for those that felt no need of prayer, and wept for those that felt no need of tears, is now before the throne, to receive and present to His Father the petitions of those for whom He prayed on earth. The example of Christ is for us to follow. Prayer is a necessity in our labor for the salvation of souls. God alone can give the increase of the seed we sow.

We fail many times because we do not realize that Christ is with us by His Spirit as truly as when, in the days of His humiliation, He moved visibly upon the earth. The lapse of time has wrought no change in His parting promise to His apostles as He was taken up from them into heaven: "Lo, I am with you alway, even unto the end of the world." He has ordained that there should be a succession of men who derive authority from the first teachers of the faith for the continual preaching of Christ and Him crucified. The Great Teacher has delegated power to His servants, who "have this treasure in earthen vessels." Christ will superintend the work of His ambassadors if they wait for His instruction and guidance.

Ministers who are truly Christ's representatives will be men of prayer. With an earnestness and faith that will not be denied, they will plead with God that they may be strengthened and fortified for duty and for trial, and that their lips may be sanctified by a touch of the living coal from off the altar, to speak the words of God to the people. "The Lord God hath given me the tongue of the learned, that I should know how to speak a word in season to him that is weary: He wakeneth morning by morning, He wakeneth mine ear to hear as the learned."

Christ said to Peter: "Simon, Simon, behold, Satan hath desired to have you, that he may sift you as wheat: but I have prayed for thee, that thy faith fail not." Who can estimate the result of the prayers of the world's Redeemer? When Christ shall see of the travail of His soul and shall be satisfied, then will be seen and realized the value of His earnest prayers while His divinity was veiled with humanity.

Jesus pleaded, not for one only, but for all His disciples: "Father, I will that they also whom Thou hast given Me, be with Me where I am." His eye pierced the dark veil of the future and read the life history of every son and daughter of Adam. He felt the burdens and sorrows of every tempest-tossed soul, and that earnest prayer included with His living disciples all His followers to the close of time. "Neither pray I for these alone, but for them also which shall believe on Me through their word." Yes; that prayer of Christ

453

embraces even us. We should be comforted by the thought that we have a great intercessor in the heavens, presenting our petitions before God. "If any man sin, we have an advocate with the Father, Jesus Christ the righteous." In the hour of greatest need, when discouragement would overwhelm the soul, it is then that the watchful eye of Jesus sees that we need His help. The hour of man's necessity is the hour of God's opportunity. When all human support fails, then Jesus comes to our aid, and His presence scatters the darkness and lifts the cloud of gloom.

In their little boat upon the Sea of Galilee, amid the storm and darkness, the disciples toiled hard to reach the shore, but found all their efforts unsuccessful. As despair seized them, Jesus was seen walking upon the foam-capped billows. Even the presence of Christ they did not at first discern, and their terror increased, until His voice, saying, "It is I; be not afraid," dispelled their fears and gave them hope and joy. Then how willingly the poor, wearied disciples ceased their efforts and trusted all to the Master.

This striking incident illustrates the experience of the followers of Christ. How often do we tug at the oars, as though our own strength and wisdom were sufficient, until we find our efforts useless. Then, with trembling hands and failing strength, we give up the work to Jesus and confess we are unable to perform it. Our compassionate Redeemer pities our weakness; and when, in answer to the cry of faith, He takes up the work we ask Him to do, how easily He accomplishes that which seemed to us so difficult.

The history of God's ancient people furnishes us with many encouraging examples of prevailing prayer. When the Amalekites came to attack the camp of Israel in the wilderness, Moses knew that his people were not prepared for the encounter. He sent Joshua with a band of soldiers to meet the enemy, while he himself, with Aaron and Hur, took his position on a hill overlooking the battlefield. There the man of God laid the case before Him who alone was able to give them the victory. With hands outstretched toward heaven, Moses prayed earnestly for the success of the armies of Israel. It was observed that while his hands were reaching upward, Israel prevailed against the foe; but when through fatigue they were allowed to fall, Amalek prevailed. Aaron and Hur stayed up the hands of Moses until victory, full and complete, turned upon the side of Israel and their enemies were driven from the field.

This instance was to be a lesson to all Israel to the close of time that God is the strength of His people. When Israel triumphed, Moses was reaching his hands toward heaven and interceding in their behalf; so when all the Israel of God prevail, it is because the Mighty One undertakes their case and fights their battles for them. Moses did not ask or believe that God would overcome their foes while Israel remained inactive. He marshals all his forces and sends them out as well prepared as their facilities can make them, and then he takes the whole matter to God in prayer. Moses on the mount is pleading with the Lord, while Joshua with his brave followers is below, doing his best to meet and repulse the enemies of Israel and of God.

That prayer which comes forth from an earnest, believing heart is the effectual, fervent prayer that availeth much. God does not always answer our prayers as we expect, for we may not ask what would be for our highest good; but in His infinite love and wisdom He will give us those things which we most need. Happy the minister who has a faithful Aaron and Hur to strengthen his hands when they become weary and to hold them up by faith and prayer. Such a support is a powerful aid to the servant of Christ in his work and will often make the cause of truth to triumph gloriously.

After the transgression of Israel in making the golden calf, Moses again goes to plead with God in behalf of his people. He has some knowledge of those who have been placed under his care; he knows the perversity of the human heart and realizes the difficulties with which he must contend. But he has learned from experience that in order to have an influence with the people he must first have power with God. The Lord reads the sincerity and unselfish purpose of the heart of His servant and condescends to commune with this feeble mortal, face to face, as a man speaks with a friend. Moses casts himself and all his burdens fully upon God and freely pours out his soul before Him. The Lord does not reprove His servant, but stoops to listen to his supplications.

Moses has a deep sense of his unworthiness and his unfitness for the great work to which God has called him. He pleads with intense earnestness that the Lord will go with him. The answer comes: "My presence shall go with thee, and I will give thee rest." But Moses does not feel that he can stop here. He has gained much, but he longs to come still nearer to God, to obtain a stronger assurance of His abiding presence. He has carried the burden of

Israel; he has borne an overwhelming weight of responsibility; when the people sinned, he suffered keen remorse, as though he himself were guilty; and now there presses upon his soul a sense of the terrible results should God leave Israel to hardness and impenitence of heart. They would not hesitate to kill Moses, and through their own rashness and perversity they would soon fall a prey to their enemies and thus dishonor the name of God before the heathen. Moses presses his petition with such earnestness and fervency that the answer comes: "I will do this thing also that thou hast spoken: for thou hast found grace in My sight, and I know thee by name."

Now, indeed, we would expect the prophet to cease pleading; but no, emboldened by his success, he ventures to come still nearer to God, with a holy familiarity which is almost beyond our comprehension. He now makes a request which no human being ever made before: "I beseech Thee, show me Thy glory." What a petition to come from finite, mortal man! But is he repulsed? does God reprove him for presumption? No, we hear the gracious words: "I will make all My goodness pass before thee."

The unveiled glory of God no man could look upon and live; but Moses is assured that he shall behold as much of the divine glory as he can bear in his present, mortal state. That Hand that made the world, that holds the mountains in their places, takes this man of dust—this man of mighty faith—and mercifully covers him in a cleft of the rock, while the glory of God and all His goodness pass before him. Can we marvel that "the excellent glory" reflected from Omnipotence shone in Moses' face with such brightness that the people could not look upon it? The impress of God was upon him, making him appear as one of the shining angels from the throne.

This experience, above all else the assurance that God would hear his prayer and that the divine presence would attend him, was of more value to Moses as a leader than the learning of Egypt or all his attainments in military science. No earthly power or skill or learning can supply the place of God's immediate presence. In the history of Moses we may see what intimate communion with God it is man's privilege to enjoy. To the transgressor it is a fearful thing to fall into the hands of the living God. But Moses was not afraid to be alone with the Author of that law which had been spoken with such awful grandeur from Mount Sinai, for his soul was in harmony with the will of his Maker.

Prayer is the opening of the heart to God as to a friend. The eye of faith will discern God very near, and the suppliant may obtain precious evidence of the divine love and care for him. But why is it that so many prayers are never answered? Says David: "I cried unto Him with my mouth, and He was extolled with my tongue. If I regard iniquity in my heart, the Lord will not hear me." By another prophet the Lord gives us the promise: "Ye shall seek Me, and find Me, when ye shall search for Me with all your heart." Again, he speaks of some who "have not cried unto Me with their heart." Such petitions are prayers of form, lip service only, which the Lord does not accept.

The prayer which Nathanael offered while he was under the fig tree came from a sincere heart, and it was heard and answered by the Master. Christ said of him: "Behold an Israelite indeed, in whom is no guile!" The Lord reads the hearts of all and understands their motives and purposes. "The prayer of the upright is His delight." He will not be slow to hear those who open their hearts to Him, not exalting self, but sincerely feeling their great weakness and unworthiness.

There is need of prayer,—most earnest, fervent, agonizing prayer,—such prayer as David offered when he exclaimed: "As the hart panteth after the water brooks, so panteth my soul after Thee, O God." "I have longed after Thy precepts;" "I have longed for Thy salvation." "My soul longeth, yea, even fainteth for the courts of the Lord: my heart and my flesh crieth out for the living God." "My soul breaketh for the longing that it hath unto Thy judgments." This is the spirit of wrestling prayer, such as was possessed by the royal psalmist.

Daniel prayed to God, not exalting himself or claiming any goodness: "O Lord, hear; O Lord, forgive; O Lord, hearken and do; defer not, for Thine own sake, O my God." This is what James calls the effectual, fervent prayer. Of Christ it is said: "And being in an agony He prayed more earnestly." In what contrast to this intercession by the Majesty of heaven are the feeble, heartless prayers that are offered to God. Many are content with lip service, and but few have a sincere, earnest, affectionate longing after God.

Communion with God imparts to the soul an intimate knowledge of His will. But many who profess the faith know not what true conversion is. They have no experience in communion with the Father through Jesus Christ, and have never felt the power of divine grace to sanctify the heart. Praying and sinning, sinning and praying, their lives are full of malice, deceit, envy, jealousy, and self-love. The prayers of this class are an abomination to God. True prayer engages the energies of the soul and affects the life. He who thus pours out his wants before God feels the emptiness of everything else under heaven. "All my desire is before Thee," said David, "and my groaning is not hid from Thee." "My soul thirsteth for God, for the living God: when shall I come and appear before God?" "When I remember these things, I pour out my soul in me."

As our numbers are increasing, broader plans must be laid to meet the increasing demands of the times; but we see no special increase of fervent piety, of Christian simplicity, and earnest devotion. The church seem content to take only the first steps in conversion. They are more ready for active labor than for humble devotion, more ready to engage in outward religious service than in the inner work of the heart. Meditation and prayer are neglected for bustle and show. Religion must begin with emptying and purifying the heart, and must be nurtured by daily prayer.

The steady progress of our work, and our increased facilities, are filling the hearts and minds of many of our people with satisfaction and pride, which we fear will take the place of the love of God in the soul. Busy activity in the mechanical part of even the work of God may so occupy the mind that prayer shall be neglected, and self-importance and self-sufficiency, so ready to urge their way, shall take the place of true goodness, meekness, and lowliness of heart. The zealous cry may be heard: "The temple of the Lord, The temple of the Lord, are these." "Come with me, and see my zeal for the Lord." But where are the burden bearers? where are the fathers and mothers in Israel? Where are those who carry upon the heart the burden for souls and who come in close sympathy with their fellow men, ready to place themselves in any position to save them from eternal ruin?

"Not by might, nor by power, but by My Spirit, saith the Lord of hosts." "Ye are," says Christ, "the light of the world." What a responsibility! There is need of fasting, humiliation, and prayer over our decaying zeal and languishing spirituality. The love of many is waxing cold. The efforts of many of our preachers are not what they should be. When some who lack the Spirit and power of God enter a new field, they commence denouncing other denominations, thinking that they can convince the people of the truth by presenting the inconsistencies of the popular churches. It may seem necessary on some occasions to speak of these things, but in general it only creates prejudice against our work and closes the ears of many who might otherwise have listened to the truth. If these teachers were connected closely with Christ, they would have divine wisdom to know how to approach the people. They would not so soon forget the darkness and error, the passion and prejudice, which kept themselves from the truth.

Would these teachers work with the spirit of the Master, very different results would follow. With meekness and long-suffering, gentleness and love, yet with decided earnestness, they would seek to direct those erring souls to a crucified and risen Saviour. When this is done, we shall see God moving upon the hearts of men. Says the great apostle: "We are laborers together with God." What a work for poor mortals! We are provided with spiritual weapons to "fight the good fight of faith;" but some seem to have drawn from the armory of heaven only its thunderbolts. How long must these defects exist?

While in the midst of a religious interest, some neglect the most important part of the work. They fail to visit and become acquainted with those who have shown an interest to present themselves night after night to listen to the explanation of the Scriptures. Conversation upon religious subjects, and earnest prayer with such at the right time, might balance many souls in the right direction.

Ministers who neglect their duty in this respect are not true shepherds of the flock. At the very time when they should be most active in visiting, conversing, and praying with these interested ones, some will be employed in writing unnecessarily long letters to persons at a distance. Oh, what are we doing for the Master! When probation shall end, how many will see the opportunities they have neglected to render service to their dear Lord who died for them. And even those who were accounted most faithful will see much more that they might have done, had not their minds been diverted by worldly surroundings.

We entreat the heralds of the gospel of Christ never to become discouraged in the work, never to consider the most hardened sinner beyond the reach of the grace of God. Such may accept the truth in the love of it and become the salt of the earth. He who turns the hearts of men as the rivers of water are turned can bring the most selfish, sin-hardened soul to surrender to

Christ. Is aught too hard for God to do? "My word," He says, "shall not return unto Me void, but it shall accomplish that which I please, and it shall prosper in the thing whereto I sent it."

God will not place His benediction upon those who are negligent, selfish, and ease-loving—who will not lift burdens in His cause. The "Well done" will be pronounced upon those only who have done well. Every man is to be rewarded "according as his work shall be." We want an active ministry —men of prayer who will wrestle with God as did Jacob, saying: "I will not let Thee go, except Thou bless me." If we obtain the victor's crown we must stretch every nerve and exercise every power. We can never be saved in inactivity. To be an idler in the Lord's vineyard is to relinquish all title to the reward of the righteous.

51. Warnings and Admonitions

November 23, 1879, some things were shown me in reference to the institutions among us and the duties and dangers of those who occupy a leading position in connection with them. I saw that these men have been raised up to do a special work as God's instruments, to be led, guided, and controlled by His Spirit. They are to answer the claims of God and never to feel that they are their own property and that they can employ their powers as they shall deem most profitable to themselves. Although it is their purpose to be and to do right, yet they will most surely err unless they are constant learners in the school of Christ. Their only safety is in humbly walking with God.

Dangers beset every path, and he who comes off conqueror will indeed have a triumphant song to sing in the city of God. Some have strong traits of character that will need to be constantly repressed. If kept under the control of the Spirit of God, these traits will be a blessing; but if not, they will prove a curse. If those who are now riding upon the wave of popularity do not become giddy, it will be a miracle of mercy. If they lean to their own wisdom, as so many thus situated have done, their wisdom will prove to be foolishness. But while they shall give themselves unselfishly to the work of God, never swerving in the least from principle, the Lord will throw about them the everlasting arm and will prove to them a mighty helper. "Them that honor Me, I will honor."

This is a dangerous age for any man who has talents which can be of value in the work of God; for Satan is constantly plying his temptations upon such a person, ever trying to fill him with pride and ambition; and when God would use him, it is too often the case that he becomes independent and self-sufficient, and feels capable of standing alone. This will be your danger, brethren, unless you live a life of constant faith and prayer. You may have a deep and abiding sense of eternal things and that love for humanity which Christ has shown in His life. A close connection with heaven will give the right tone to your fidelity and will be the ground of your success. Your feeling of dependence will drive you to prayer, and your sense of duty summon you to effort. Prayer and effort, effort and prayer, will be the business of your life. You must pray as though the efficiency and praise were all due to God, and labor as though duty were all your own. If you want power you may have it; it is waiting your draft upon it. Only believe in God, take Him at His word, act by faith, and blessings will come.

In this matter, genius, logic, and eloquence will not avail. Those who have a humble, trusting, contrite heart, God accepts, and hears their prayer; and when God helps, all obstacles will be overcome. How many men of great natural abilities and high scholarships have failed when placed in positions of responsibility, while those of feebler intellect, with less favorable surroundings, have been wonderfully successful. The secret was: The former trusted to themselves, while the latter united with Him who is wonderful in counsel and mighty in working to accomplish what He will.

Their work being always urgent, it is difficult for some to secure time for meditation and prayer; but this they should not fail to do. The blessing of heaven, obtained by daily supplication, will be as the bread of life to the soul and will cause them to increase in moral and spiritual strength, like a tree planted by the river of waters, whose leaf will be always green and whose fruit will appear in due time.

Some have made a serious mistake in neglecting to attend the public worship of God. The privileges of divine service will be as beneficial to them as to others, and are fully as essential. They may be unable to avail themselves of these privileges as often as do many others. Physicians will frequently be called upon the Sabbath to visit the sick and may be obliged to make it a day of exhausting labor. Such labor to relieve the suffering was pronounced by our Saviour a work of mercy and no violation of the Sabbath. But those who regularly devote their Sabbaths to writing or labor, making no special change, harm their own souls, give to others an example that is not worthy of imitation, and do not honor God.

Some have failed to see the real importance, not only of attending religious meetings, but also of bearing testimony for Christ and the truth. If these brethren do not obtain spiritual strength by the faithful performance of every Christian duty, thus coming into a closer and more sacred relation to their Redeemer, they will become weak in moral power. They will surely wither spiritually unless they change their course in this respect.

The men who have been placed in charge of our institutions occupy important and responsible positions. They cannot well be spared from their post of duty, yet they should not feel that they are indispensable. God could do without them, but they cannot do without God. These men should endeavor to work in harmony. If he fills his position honorably, each must guard the financial interests of the institution committed to his care. But these men should be exceedingly cautious that they look not alone on their own branch of the work and labor for their own department to the injury of other branches of equal importance.

Brethren, you are in danger of making grave mistakes in your business transactions. God warns you to be on your guard lest you indulge a spirit of crowding one another. Be careful not to cultivate the sharper's tact, for this will not stand the test of the day of God. Shrewdness and close calculation are needed, for you have all classes to deal with; you must guard the interests of our institutions, or thousands of dollars will go into the hands of dishonest men. But let not these traits become a ruling power. Under proper control, they are essential elements in the character; and if you keep the fear of God before you, and His love in the heart, you will be safe.

It is far better to yield some advantages that might be gained than to cultivate an avaricious spirit and thus make it a law of nature. Petty sharpness is unworthy of a Christian. We have been separated from the world by the great cleaver of truth. Our wrong traits of character are not always visible to ourselves, although they may be very apparent to others. But time and circumstances will surely prove us and bring to light the gold of character or discover the baser metal. Not one of us is known or read of all men, till the crucible of God tests us. Every base thought, every wrong action, reveals some defect in the character. These rugged traits must be brought under the chisel and hammer in God's great workshop, and the grace of God must smooth and polish before we can be fitted for a place in the glorious temple.

God can make these brethren more precious than fine gold, even the golden wedge of Ophir, if they will yield themselves to His transforming hand. They should be determined to make the noblest use of every faculty and every opportunity. The word of God should be their study and their guide in deciding what is the highest and best in all cases. The one faultless character, the perfect Pattern set before them in the gospel, should be studied with deepest interest. The one lesson most essential for them to learn is that goodness alone gives true greatness. May God deliver us from the philosophy of worldly-wise men. Their only hope is in becoming fools, that they may be wise indeed.

The weakest follower of Christ has entered into alliance with infinite power. In many cases God can do little with men of learning because they feel no need of leaning upon Him who is the Source of all wisdom; therefore, after a trial, He sets them aside for men of inferior talent who have learned to rely upon Him, whose souls are fortified by goodness, truth, and unwavering fidelity, and who will not stoop to anything that will leave a stain upon the conscience.

Brethren, if you connect your souls with God by living faith, He will make you men of power. If you trust to your own strength and wisdom, you will surely fail. It is not pleasing to God that you take so little interest in religious service. You are representative men, and as such, you exert a wider influence than persons in less prominent positions. You should ever seek first the kingdom of God and His righteousness. You should be active, interested workers in the church, cultivating your religious faculties, and keeping your own souls in the love of God. The Lord has claims upon you in this matter that you cannot lightly disregard; you must either grow in grace or be dwarfed and crippled in spiritual things. It is not only your privilege but your duty to bear testimony for Christ when and where you can; and by exercising the mind in this way, you will cultivate a love for sacred things.

We are in danger of regarding Christ's ministers simply as men, not recognizing them as representatives of Him. All personal considerations should be laid aside; we must listen for the word of God through His ambassadors. Christ is ever sending messages to those who listen for His voice. On the night of our Saviour's agony in the Garden of Gethsemane the sleeping disciples heard not the voice of Jesus; they had a dim sense of the angel's presence, but lost the power and glory of the scene by drowsiness and stupor, and thus failed to receive the evidence which would have strengthened their souls for the terrible scenes before them.

Thus the very men who most need divine instruction often fail to receive it because they do not place themselves in communication with heaven. Satan is ever seeking to impress and control the mind, and none of us are safe except as we have a constant connection with God. We must momentarily receive supplies from heaven, and if we would be kept by the power of God we must be obedient to all His requirements.

The condition of your bearing fruit is that you abide in the living Vine. "Abide in Me, and I in you. As the branch cannot bear fruit of itself, except it abide in the vine; no more can ye, except ye abide in Me. I am the Vine, ye are the branches: He that abideth in me, and I in him, the same bringeth forth much fruit: for without Me ye can do nothing. If a man abide not in Me, he is cast forth as a branch, and is withered; and men gather them, and cast them into the fire, and they are burned."

All your good purposes and good intentions will not enable you to withstand the test of temptation. You must be men of prayer. Your petitions must be not faint, occasional, and fitful, but earnest, persevering, and constant. It is not necessary to be alone, or to bow upon your knees, to pray; but in the midst of your labor your souls may be often uplifted to God, taking hold upon His strength; then you will be men of high and holy purpose, of noble integrity, who will not for any consideration be swayed from truth, right, and justice.

You are pressed with urgent cares, burdens, and duties; but the greater the pressure upon you, and the heavier the burdens you have to bear, the greater your need of divine aid. Jesus will be your helper You need constantly the light of life to lighten your own pathway, and then its divine rays will reflect upon others. The work of God is a perfect whole, because perfect in all its parts. It is the conscientious attention to what the world calls little things that makes the great beauty and success of life. Little deeds of charity, little words of kindness, little acts of self-denial, a wise improvement of little opportunities, a diligent cultivation of little talents, make great men in God's sight. If those little things be faithfully attended to, if these graces be in you, and abound, they will make you perfect in every good work.

It is not enough to be willing to give liberally of your means to the cause of God. He calls for an unreserved consecration of all your powers. Withholding yourselves has been the mistake of your life. You may think it very difficult in your position to maintain a close connection with God, but your work will be tenfold harder if you fail to do this. Satan will beset your path with his temptations, and it is only through Christ that you can gain the victory. The same indomitable will that gives success in intellectual pursuits is essential in the Christian course. You must be representatives of Jesus Christ. Your energy and perseverance in perfecting a Christian character should be as much greater than that displayed in any other pursuit as the things of eternity are of more importance than temporal affairs.

If you ever achieve success in the Christian life you must resolve that you will be men after God's own heart. The Lord wants your influence to be exerted in the church and in the world to elevate the standard of Christianity. True Christian character should be marked by firmness of purpose, an indomitable determination, which cannot be molded or subdued by earth or hell. He who is not blind to the attraction of worldly honors, indifferent to threats, and unmoved by allurements will be, all unexpectedly to himself, overthrown by Satan's devices.

God calls for complete and entire consecration, and anything short of this He will not accept. The more difficult your position the more you need Jesus. The love and fear of God kept Joseph pure and untarnished in the king's court. He was exalted to great wealth, to the high honor of being next to the king; and this elevation was as sudden as it was great. It is impossible to stand upon a lofty height without danger. The tempest leaves unharmed the modest flower of the valley, while it wrestles with the lofty tree upon the mountaintop. There are many men whom God could have used with wonderful success when pressed with poverty,— He could have made them useful here, and crowned them with glory hereafter,— but prosperity ruined them; they were dragged down to the pit because they forgot to be humble, forgot that God was their strength, and became independent and self-sufficient.

Joseph bore the test of character in adversity, and the gold was undimmed by prosperity. He showed the same sacred regard for God's will when he stood next the throne as when in a prisoner's cell. Joseph carried his religion everywhere, and this was the secret of his unwavering fidelity. As representative men you must have the all-pervading power of true godliness. I tell you, in the fear of God, your path is beset by dangers which you do not see and do not realize. You must hide in Jesus. You are unsafe unless you hold the hand of Christ. You must guard against everything like presumption and cherish that spirit that would suffer rather than sin. No victory you can gain will be so precious as that gained over self.

52. Moral and Intellectual Culture

In the view given me October 9, 1878, I was shown the position which our sanitarium at Battle Creek should occupy and the character and influence which should be maintained by all connected with it. This important institution has been established by the providence of God, and His blessing is indispensable to its success. The physicians are not quacks nor infidels, but men who understand the human system and the best methods of treating disease — men who fear God and who have an earnest interest for the moral and spiritual welfare of their patients.

This interest for spiritual as well as physical good the managers of the institution should make no effort to conceal. By a life of true Christian integrity they can give to the world an example worthy of imitation, and they should not hesitate to let it be seen that in addition to their skill in treating disease, they are continually gaining wisdom and knowledge from Christ, the greatest Teacher the world has ever known. They must have this connection with the Source of all wisdom, to make their labor successful.

Truth has a power to elevate the receiver. If Bible truth exerts its sanctifying influence upon the heart and character, it will make believers more intelligent. A Christian will understand his responsibilities to God and to his fellow men if he is truly connected with the Lamb of God, who gave His life for the world. Only by a continual improvement of the intellectual as well as the moral powers can we hope to answer the purpose of our Creator.

God is displeased with those who are too careless or indolent to become efficient, well-informed workers. The Christian should possess more intelligence and keener discernment than the worldling. The study of God's word is continually expanding the mind and strengthening the intellect. There is nothing that will so refine and elevate the character, and give vigor to every faculty, as the continual exercise of the mind to grasp and comprehend weighty and important truths.

The human mind becomes dwarfed and enfeebled when dealing with commonplace matters only, never rising above the level of the things of time and sense to grasp the mysteries of the unseen. The understanding is gradually brought to the level of the subjects with which it is constantly familiar. The mind will contract its powers and lose its ability if it is not exercised to acquire additional knowledge and put to the stretch to comprehend the revelations of divine power in nature and in the Sacred Word.

But an acquaintance with facts and theories, however important they may be in themselves, is of little real value unless put to a practical use. There is danger that those who have obtained their education principally from books will fail to realize that they are novices so far as experimental knowledge is concerned. This is especially true of those connected with the sanitarium. This institution needs men of thought and ability. The physicians, superintendent, matron, and helpers should be persons of culture and experience. But some fail to comprehend what is needed at such an establishment, and they plod on, year after year, making no marked improvement. They seem to be stereotyped; each succeeding day is but a repetition of the past one.

The minds and hearts of these mechanical workers are impoverished. Opportunities are before them; if studious, they might obtain an education of the highest value; but they do not appreciate their privileges. None should rest satisfied with their present education. All may be daily qualifying themselves to fill some office of trust.

It is of great importance that the one who is chosen to care for the spiritual interests of patients and helpers be a man of sound judgment and undeviating principle, a man who will have moral influence, who knows how to deal with minds. He should be a person of wisdom and culture, of affection as well as intelligence. He may not be thoroughly efficient in all respects at first, but he should, by earnest thought and the exercise of his abilities, qualify himself for this important work. The greatest wisdom and gentleness are needed to serve in this position acceptably yet with unbending integrity, for prejudice, bigotry, and error of every form and description must be met.

This place should not be filled by a man who has an irritable temper, a sharp combativeness. Care must be taken that the religion of Christ be not made repulsive by harshness or impatience. The servant of God should seek, by meekness, gentleness, and love, rightly to represent our holy faith. While the cross must never be concealed, he should present also the Saviour's matchless love. The worker must be imbued with the spirit of Jesus, and then the treasures of the soul will be presented in words that will find their way to the hearts of those who hear. The religion of Christ, exemplified in the daily life of His followers, will exert a tenfold greater influence than the most eloquent sermons.

Intelligent, God-fearing workers can do a vast amount of good in the way of reforming those who come as invalids to be treated at the sanitarium. These persons are diseased, not only physically, but mentally and morally. The education, the habits, and the entire life of many have been erroneous. They cannot in a few days make the great changes necessary for the adoption of correct habits. They must have time to consider the matter and to learn the right way. If all connected with the sanitarium are correct representatives of the truths of health reform and of our holy faith, they are exerting an influence to mold the minds of their patients. The contrast of erroneous habits with those which are in harmony with the truth of God has a convicting power.

Man is not what he might be and what it is God's will that he should be. The strong power of Satan upon the human race keeps them upon a low level; but this need not be so, else Enoch could not have become so elevated and ennobled as to walk with God. Man need not cease to grow intellectually and spiritually during his lifetime. But the minds of many are so occupied with themselves and their own selfish interests as to leave no room for higher and nobler thoughts. And the standard of intellectual as well as spiritual attainments is far too low. With many, the more responsible the position they occupy, the better pleased are they with themselves; and they cherish the idea that the position gives character to the man. Few realize that they have a constant work before them to develop forbearance, sympathy, charity, conscientiousness, and fidelity—traits of character indispensable to those who occupy positions of responsibility. All connected with the sanitarium should have a sacred regard for the rights of others, which is but obeying the principles of the law of God.

Some at this institution are sadly deficient in the qualities so essential to the happiness of all connected with them. The physicians, and the helpers in the various branches of the work, should carefully guard against a selfish coldness, a distant, unsocial disposition; for this will alienate the affection and confidence of the patients. Many who come to the sanitarium are refined, sensitive people of ready tact and keen discernment. These persons discover such defects at once and comment upon them. Men cannot love God supremely and their neighbor as themselves, and be as cold as icebergs. Not only do they rob God of the love due Him, but they rob their neighbor as well. Love is a plant of heavenly growth, and it must be fostered and nourished. Affectionate hearts, truthful, loving words, will make happy families and exert an elevating influence upon all who come within the sphere of their influence.

Those who make the most of their privileges and opportunities will be, in the Bible sense, talented and educated men; not learned merely, but educated, in mind, in manners, in deportment. They will be refined, tender, pitiful, affectionate. This, I was shown, is what the God of heaven requires in the institutions at Battle Creek. God has given us powers to be used, to be developed and strengthened by education. We should reason and reflect, carefully marking the relation between cause and effect. When this is practiced, there will be, on the part of many, greater thoughtfulness and care in regard to their words and actions, that they may fully answer the purpose of God in their creation.

We should ever bear in mind that we are not only learners but teachers in this world, fitting ourselves and others for a higher sphere of action in the future life. The measure of man's usefulness is in knowing the will of God and doing it. It is within our power to so improve in mind and manners that God will not be ashamed to own us. There must be a high standard at the sanitarium. If there are men of culture, of intellectual and moral power, to be found in our ranks, they must be called to the front, to fill places in our institutions.

The physicians should not be deficient in any respect. A wide field of usefulness is open before them, and if they do not become skillful in their profession they have only themselves to blame. They must be diligent students; and, by close application and faithful attention to details, they should become care-takers. It should be necessary for no one to follow them to see that their work is done without mistakes.

Those who occupy responsible positions should so educate and discipline themselves that all within the sphere of their influence may see what man can be, and what he can do, when connected with the God of wisdom and power. And why should not a man thus privileged become intellectually strong? Again and again have worldlings sneeringly asserted that those who believe present truth are weak-minded, deficient in education, without position or influence. This we know to be untrue, but is there not some reason for these assertions? Many have considered it a mark of humility to be ignorant and uncultivated. Such persons are deceived as to what constitutes true humility and Christian meekness.

53. Duty to the Poor

The managers of the sanitarium should not be governed by the principles which control other institutions of this kind, in which the leaders acting from policy, too often pay deference to the wealthy, while the poor are neglected. The latter are frequently in great need of sympathy and counsel, which they do not always receive, although for moral worth they may stand far higher in the estimation of God than the more wealthy. The apostle James has given definite counsel with regard to the manner in which we should treat the rich and the poor:

"For if there come unto your assembly a man with a gold ring, in goodly apparel, and there come in also a poor man in vile raiment; and ye have respect to him that weareth the gay clothing, and say unto him, Sit thou here in a good place; and say to the poor, Stand thou there, or sit here under my footstool: are ye not then partial in yourselves, and are become judges of evil thoughts? Hearken, my beloved brethren, Hath not God chosen the poor of this world rich in faith, and heirs of the kingdom which He hath promised to them that love Him?"

Although Christ was rich in the heavenly courts, yet He became poor that we through His poverty might be made rich. Jesus honored the poor by sharing their humble condition. From the history of His life we are to learn how to treat the poor. Some carry the duty of beneficence to extremes and really hurt the needy by doing too much for them. The poor do not always exert themselves as they should. While they are not to be neglected and left to suffer, they must be taught to help themselves.

The cause of God should not be overlooked that the poor may receive our first attention. Christ once gave His disciples a very important lesson on this point. When Mary poured the ointment on the head of Jesus, covetous Judas made a plea in behalf of the poor, murmuring at what he considered a waste of money. But Jesus vindicated the act, saying: "Why trouble ye her? she hath wrought a good work on Me." "Wheresoever this gospel shall be preached throughout the whole world, this also that she hath done shall be spoken of for a memorial of her."

By this we are taught that Christ is to be honored in the consecration of the best of our substance. Should our whole attention be directed to relieving the wants of the poor, God's cause would be neglected. Neither will suffer if His stewards do their duty, but the cause of Christ should come first.

The poor should be treated with as much interest and attention as the rich. The practice of honoring the rich and slighting and neglecting the poor is a crime in the sight of God. Those who are surrounded with all the comforts of life, or who are petted and pampered by the world because they are rich, do not feel the need of sympathy and tender consideration as do persons whose lives have been one long struggle with poverty. The latter have but little in this life to make them happy or cheerful, and they will appreciate sympathy and love. Physicians and helpers should in no case neglect this class, for by so doing they may neglect Christ in the person of His saints.

Our sanitarium was erected to benefit suffering humanity, rich and poor, the world over. Many of our churches have but little interest in this institution, notwithstanding they have sufficient evidence that it is one of the instrumentalities designed of God to bring men and women under the influence of truth and to save many souls.

The churches that have the poor among them should not neglect their stewardship and throw the burden of the poor and sick upon the sanitarium. All the members of the several churches are responsible before God for their afflicted ones. They should bear their own burdens. If they have sick persons among them whom they wish to be benefited by treatment, they should, if able, send them to the sanitarium. In doing this, they will not only be patronizing the institution which God has established, but will be helping those who need help, caring for the poor as God requires us to do.

It was not the purpose of God that poverty should ever leave the world. The ranks of society were never to be equalized, for the diversity of condition which characterizes our race is one of the means by which God has designed to prove and develop character. Many have urged with great enthusiasm that all men should have an equal share in the temporal blessings of God, but this was not the purpose of the Creator.

Christ has said that we shall have the poor always with us. The poor, as well as the rich, are the purchase of His blood; and among His professed followers, in most cases, the former serve Him with singleness of purpose, while the latter are constantly fastening their affections on their earthly treasures, and Christ is forgotten. The cares of this life and the greed for riches eclipse the glory of the eternal world. It would be the greatest misfortune that has ever befallen mankind if all were to be placed upon an equality in worldly possessions.

54. Health and Religion

The fear of the Lord will do more for the patrons of the sanitarium than any other means that can be employed for the restoration of health. Religion should in no case be kept in the background, as though detrimental to those who come to be treated. On the contrary, the fact should ever be made prominent that the laws of God, both in nature and revelation, are "life unto those that find them, and health to all their flesh."

Pride and fashion hold men and women in the veriest slavery to customs which are fatal to health and even to life itself. The appetites and passions, clamoring for indulgence, trample reason and conscience underfoot. This is the cruel work of Satan, and he is constantly putting forth the most determined efforts to strengthen the chains by which he has bound his victims. Those who have been all their lives indulging wrong habits do not always realize the necessity of a change.

And many will persist in gratifying their desire for sinful pleasure at any cost. Let the conscience be aroused and much is gained. Nothing but the grace of God can convict and convert the heart; here alone can the slaves of custom obtain power to break the shackles which bind them. The self-indulgent must be led to see and feel that a great moral renovation is necessary if they would meet the claims of the divine law; the soul-temple has been defiled, and God calls upon them to arouse and strive with all their might to win back the God-given manhood which has been sacrificed through sinful indulgence.

Divine truth can make little impression upon the intellect while the customs and habits are opposed to its principles. Those who are willing to inform themselves concerning the effect of sinful indulgence upon the health, and who commence the work of reform, even if it be from selfish motives, in so doing place themselves where the truth of God may find access to their hearts.

And, on the other hand, those who are reached by the presentation of Scripture truth are then in a position where their consciences will be aroused upon the subject of health. They see and feel the necessity of breaking away from the tyrannizing habits and appetites which have ruled them so long.

There are many who would receive the truths of God's word, their judgment having been convinced by the clearest evidence; but the carnal desires, clamoring for gratification, control the intellect, and they reject truth as falsehood, because it comes in collision with their lustful affections.

"The fear of the Lord is the beginning of wisdom." When men of wrong habits and sinful practices yield to the power of divine truth, the entrance of God's word gives light and understanding to the simple. There is an application of truth to the heart; and moral power, which seemed to have been paralyzed, revives. The receiver is possessed of stronger, clearer understanding than before. He has riveted his soul to the eternal Rock. Health improves in the very sense of his security in Christ. Thus religion and the laws of health go hand in hand.

55. Faithful Workers

The management of so large and important an institution as the sanitarium necessarily involves great responsibility, both in temporal and spiritual matters. It is of the highest importance that this asylum for those who are diseased in body and mind shall be such that Jesus, the Mighty Healer, can preside among them, and all that is done may be under the control of His Spirit. All connected with this institution should qualify themselves for the faithful discharge of their God-given responsibilities. They should attend to every little duty with as much fidelity as to matters of great importance. All should study prayerfully how they can themselves become most useful and make this retreat for the sick a grand success.

We do not realize with what anxiety patients with their various diseases come to the sanitarium, all desiring help, but some doubtful and distrusting, while others are more confident that they shall be relieved. Those who have not visited the institution are watching with interest every indication of the principles which are cherished by its managers.

All who profess to be children of God should unceasingly bear in mind that they are missionaries, in their labors brought in connection with all classes of minds. There will be the refined and the coarse, the humble and the proud, the religious and the skeptical, the confiding and the suspicious, the liberal and the avaricious, the pure and the corrupt, the educated and the ignorant, the rich and the poor; in fact, almost every grade of character and condition will be found among the patients at the sanitarium. Those who come to this asylum come because they need help; and thus, whatever their station or condition, they acknowledge that they are not able to help themselves. These varied minds cannot be treated alike; yet all, whether they are rich or poor, high or low, dependent or independent, need kindness, sympathy, and love. By mutual contact our minds should receive polish and refinement. We are dependent upon one another, closely bound together by the ties of human brotherhood.

> Heaven, forming each on other to depend,
> A master, or a servant, or a friend,
> Bids each on other for assistance call,
> Till one man's weakness grows the strength of all.

It is through the social relations that Christianity comes in contact with the world. Every man or woman who has tasted of the love of Christ, and has received into the heart the divine illumination, is required of God to shed light on the dark pathway of those who are unacquainted with the better way. Every worker in that sanitarium should become a witness for Jesus. Social power, sanctified by the Spirit of Christ, must be improved to win souls to the Saviour.

He who has to deal with persons differing so widely in character, disposition, and temperament will have trials, perplexities, and collisions, even when he does his best. He may be disgusted with the ignorance, pride, and independence which he will meet; but this should not discourage him. He should stand where he will sway, rather than be swayed. Firm as a rock to principle, with an intelligent faith, he should stand uncorrupted by surrounding influences. The people of God should not be transformed by the various influences to which they must necessarily be exposed, but they must stand up for Jesus and by the aid of His Spirit exert a transforming power upon minds deformed by false habits and defiled by sin.

Christ is not to be hid away in the heart and locked in as a coveted treasure, sacred and sweet, to be enjoyed solely by the possessor. We are to have Christ in our hearts as a well of water, springing up into everlasting life, refreshing all who come in contact with us. We must confess Christ openly and bravely, exhibiting in our characters His meekness, humility, and love, till men shall be charmed by the beauty of holiness. It is not the best way to preserve our religion as we bottle perfumes lest the fragrance should escape.

The very conflicts and rebuffs we meet are to make us stronger and give stability to our faith. We are not to be swayed, like a reed in the wind, by every passing influence. Our souls, warmed and invigorated by the truths of the gospel, and refreshed by divine grace, are to open and expand, and shed their fragrance upon others. Clad in the whole armor of righteousness, we can meet any influence and our purity remain untarnished.

All should consider that God's claims upon them are paramount to all others. God has given to every person capabilities to improve, that he may reflect glory to the Giver. Everyday some progress should be made. If the workers leave the sanitarium as they entered it, without making decided improvement, gaining in knowledge and spiritual strength, they have met with loss. God designs that Christians shall grow continually, grow up unto the full stature of men and women in Christ. All who do not grow stronger, and become more firmly rooted and grounded in the truth, are continually retrograding.

A special effort should be made to secure the services of conscientious, Christian workers. It is the purpose of God that a health institution should be organized and controlled exclusively by Seventh-day Adventists; and when unbelievers are brought in to occupy responsible positions, an influence is presiding there that will tell with great weight against the sanitarium. God did not intend that this institution should be carried on after the order of any other health institute in the land, but that it should be one of the most effectual instrumentalities in His hands of giving light to the world. It should stand forth with scientific ability, with moral and spiritual power, and as a faithful sentinel of reform in all its bearings; and all who act a part in it should be reformers, having respect to its rules, and heeding the light of health reform now shining upon us as a people.

All can be a blessing to others if they will place themselves where they will correctly represent the religion of Jesus Christ.

But there has been greater anxiety to make the outward appearance in every way presentable that it may meet the minds of worldly patients, than to maintain a living connection with heaven, to watch and pray, that this instrumentality of God may be wholly successful in doing good to the bodies and also to the souls of men.

What can be said, and what can be done, to awaken conviction in the hearts of all connected with this important institution? How can they be led to see and feel the danger of making wrong moves unless they daily have a living experience in the things of God? The physicians are in a position, where, should they exert an influence in accordance with their faith, they would have a molding power upon all connected with the institution. This is one of the best missionary fields in the world, and all in responsible positions should become acquainted with God and ever be receiving light from heaven.

There has never been so important a period in the history of the sanitarium as the present, never a time when so much was at stake. We are surrounded with the perils of the last days. Satan has come down with great power, working with all deceivableness of unrighteousness in them that perish; for he knows that his time is short. The light must now shine forth in our words and deportment with increased brightness on the path of those who are in darkness.

There are some who are not what the Lord would have them to be. They are abrupt and harsh, and need the softening, subduing influence of the Spirit of God. It is never convenient to take up the cross and follow in the path of self-denial, and yet this must be done. God wants all to have His grace and His Spirit to make fragrant their life. Some are too independent, too self-sufficient, and do not counsel with others as they should.

My brethren, we are living in a solemn time. An important work is to be done for our own souls and for the souls of others or we shall meet with an infinite loss. We must be transformed by the grace of God or we shall fail of heaven, and through our influence others will fail with us. Let me assure you that the struggles and conflicts which must be endured in the discharge of duty, the self-denials and sacrifices which must be made if we are faithful to Christ, are not created by Him. They are not imposed by arbitrary or unnecessary command; they do not come from the severity of the life which He requires us to lead in His service. Trials would exist in greater power and number were we to refuse obedience to Christ and become the servants of Satan and the slaves of sin.

Jesus invites us to come to Him and He will lift the weights from our weary shoulders and place upon us His yoke, which is easy, and His burden, which is light. The path in which He invites us to walk would never have cost us a pang had we always walked in it. It is when we stray from the path of duty that the way becomes difficult and thorny. The sacrifices which we must make in following Christ are only so many steps to return to the path of light, of peace and happiness. Doubts and fears grow by indulgence, and the more they are indulged, the harder are they to overcome. It is safe to let go every earthly support and take the hand of Him who lifted up and saved the sinking disciple on the stormy sea.

God calls upon you to mingle the trusting simplicity of the child with the strength and maturity of the man. He would have you develop the true gold of character, and through the merits of Christ you can do this. My soul is burdened for those who do not feel their need of constant connection with heaven in order to do the work devolving upon them as faithful sentinels for God.

Religion is what is needed. We must eat of the bread of life and drink of the water of salvation. We must cherish love, not that which is falsely called charity, which would lead us to love sin and cherish sinners, but Bible charity and Bible wisdom, that is first pure, then peaceable, easy to be entreated, full of mercy and good fruits.

There must be, with all who have any influence in the sanitarium, a conforming to God's will, a humiliation of self, an opening of the heart to the precious influence of the Spirit of Christ. The gold tried in the fire represents love and faith. Many are nearly destitute of love. Self-sufficiency blinds their eyes to their great need. There is a positive necessity for a daily conversion to God, a new, deep, and daily experience in the religious life.

There should be awakened in the hearts of the physicians, especially, a most earnest desire to have that wisdom which God alone can impart; for as soon as they become self-confident they are left to themselves, to follow the impulses of the unsanctified heart. When I see what these physicians may become in connection with Christ, and what they will fail to become if they do not daily connect with Him, I am filled with apprehension that they will be content with reaching a worldly standard, and have no ardent longings, no hungering and thirsting, for the beauty of holiness, the ornament of a meek and quiet spirit, which is in the sight of God of great price.

The peace of Christ, the peace of Christ—money cannot buy it, brilliant talent cannot command it, intellect cannot secure it; it is the gift of God. The religion of Christ—how shall I make all understand their great loss if they fail to carry its holy principles into the daily life? The meekness and lowliness of Christ is the Christian's power. It is indeed more precious than all things which genius can create or wealth can buy. Of all things that are sought, cherished, and cultivated, there is nothing so valuable in the sight of God as a pure heart, a disposition imbued with thankfulness and peace.

If the divine harmony of truth and love exists in the heart, it will shine forth in words and actions. The most careful cultivation of the outward proprieties and courtesies of life has not sufficient power to shut out all fretfulness, harsh judgment, and unbecoming speech. The spirit of genuine benevolence must dwell in the heart. Love imparts to its possessor grace, propriety, and comeliness of deportment. Love illuminates the countenance and subdues the voice; it refines and elevates the entire man. It brings him into harmony with God, for it is a heavenly attribute.

Many are in danger of thinking that in the cares of labor, in writing and practicing as physicians, or performing the duties of the various departments, they are excusable if they lay down prayer, neglect the Sabbath, and neglect religious service. Sacred things are thus brought down to meet their convenience, while duties, denials, and crosses are left untouched. Neither physicians nor helpers should attempt to perform their work without taking time to pray. God would be the helper of all who profess to love Him, if they would come to Him in faith and, with a sense of their own weakness, crave His power.

When they separate from God, their wisdom will be found to be foolishness. When they are small in their own eyes and lean heavily upon their God, then He will be the arm of their power, and success will attend their efforts; but when they allow the mind to be diverted from God, then Satan comes in and controls the thoughts and perverts the judgment.

None are in greater danger than he who feels that his mountain standeth sure. It is then that his feet will begin to slide. Temptations will come, one after another, and so imperceptible will be their influence upon the life and character, that, unless kept by divine power, he will be corrupted by the spirit of the world and will fail to carry out the purpose of God. All that man has, God has given him, and he who improves his abilities to God's glory will be an instrument to do good; but we can no more live a religious life without constant prayer and the performance of religious duties than we can have physical strength without partaking of temporal food. We must daily sit down at God's table. We must receive strength from the living Vine, if we are nourished.

The course which some have pursued, in using worldly policy to accomplish their purposes, is not in harmony with the will of God. They see evils which need correcting, but they do not wish to bring down reproach upon their own heads, and instead of courageously meeting these things, they throw the burden upon another and let him meet the difficulties which they have shunned and in too many cases the one who uses plain speech is made the great offender.

Brethren, I entreat you to move with an eye single to the glory of God. Let His power be your dependence, His grace your strength. By study of the Scriptures and earnest prayer seek to obtain clear conceptions of your duty, and then faithfully perform it. It is essential that you cultivate faithfulness in little things, and in so doing you will acquire habits of integrity in greater responsibilities. The little incidents of everyday life often pass without our notice, but it is these things that shape the character. Every event of life is great for good or for evil. The mind needs to be trained by daily tests, that it may acquire power to stand in any difficult position. In the days of trial and of peril you will need to be fortified to stand firmly for the right, independent of every opposing influence.

God is willing to do much for you, if you will only feel your need of Him. Jesus loves you. Ever seek to walk in the light of God's wisdom, and through all the changing scenes of life do not rest unless you know that your will is in harmony with the will of your Creator. Through faith in Him you may obtain strength to resist every temptation of Satan and thus increase in moral power with every test from God.

You may become men of responsibility and influence if, by the power of your will, united with divine strength, you earnestly engage in the work.

Exercise the mental powers, and in no case neglect the physical. Let not intellectual slothfulness close up your path to greater knowledge. Learn to reflect as well as to study, that your minds may expand, strengthen, and develop. Never think that you have learned enough and that you may now relax your efforts. The cultivated mind is the measure of the man. Your education should continue during your lifetime; every day you should be learning and putting to practical use the knowledge gained.

You are rising in true dignity and moral worth as you practice virtue and cherish uprightness in heart and life. Let not your character be affected by a taint of the leprosy of selfishness. A noble soul, united with a cultivated intellect, will make you men whom God will use in positions of sacred trust.

It should be the first work of all connected with this institution to be right before God themselves, and then to stand in the strength of Christ, unaffected by the wrong influences to which they will be exposed. If they make the broad principles of the word of God the foundation of the character, they may stand wherever the Lord in His providence may call them, surrounded by any deleterious influence, and yet not be swayed from the path of right.

Many fail where they should be successful, because they do not realize how great is the influence of their words and actions. They are affected by circumstances, and seem to think that their lives are their own, and that they may pursue whatever course seems most agreeable to themselves, irrespective of others. Such persons will be found self-sufficient and unreliable. They do not prayerfully consider their position and their responsibilities, and fail to realize that only by a faithful discharge of the duties of the present life can they hope to win the future, immortal life.

If these persons would make the word of God their study and their guide, they would see that no man "liveth to himself." They would learn from the Inspired Record that God has placed a high value upon the human family. The works of His creation upon each successive day were called good; but man, formed in the image of his Creator, was pronounced "very good." No other creature that God has made has called forth such exhibitions of His love. And when all was lost by sin, God gave His dear Son to redeem the fallen race. It was His will that they should not perish in their sins, but live to use their powers in blessing the world and honoring their Creator.

Professed Christians who do not live to benefit others, follow their own perverse will rather than the will of God, and they will be called to account by the Master for their abuse of the blessings which He has given them.

Jesus, heaven's great Commander, left the royal courts to come to a world seared and marred by the curse. He took upon Himself our nature, that with His human arm He might encircle the race, while with His divine arm He grasps Omnipotence, and thus links finite man to the infinite God. Our Redeemer came to the world to show how man should live in order to secure immortal life. Our heavenly Father made an infinite sacrifice in giving His Son to die for fallen man. The price paid for our redemption should give us exalted views of what we may become through Christ.

As John beholds the height, the depth, and the breadth of the Father's love toward our perishing race, he is filled with admiration and reverence. He cannot find suitable language to express this love, but he calls upon the world to behold it: "Behold, what manner of love the Father hath bestowed upon us, that we should be called the sons of God." What a value this places upon man! Through transgression the sons of men became subjects of Satan. Through the infinite sacrifice of Christ, and faith in His name, the sons of Adam become the sons of God. By assuming human nature, Christ elevates humanity. Fallen men are granted another trial and are placed where, through connection with Christ, they may educate, improve, and elevate themselves, that they may indeed become worthy of the name sons of God.

Such love is without a parallel. Jesus requires that those who have been bought by the price of His own life shall make the best use of the talents which He has given them. They are to increase in the knowledge of the divine will, and constantly improve in intellect and morals, until they shall attain to a perfection of character but little lower than that of the angels.

If those who profess to believe present truth were indeed representatives of the truth, living up to all the light which shines upon their pathway, they would constantly exert upon others an influence for good, thus leaving a bright track heavenward for all who are brought in contact with them. But a lack of faithfulness and integrity among its professed friends is a serious hindrance to the prosperity of God's cause. Satan works through men who are under his control. The sanitarium, the church, and other institutions at Battle Creek have less to fear from the infidel and the open blasphemer than from inconsistent professors of Christ. These are the Achans in the camp, who bring shame and defeat. These are the ones who keep back the blessing of God and dishearten the zealous, self-denying workers in the cause of Christ.

In their conduct toward the patients all should be actuated by higher motives than selfish interest. Everyone should feel that this institution is one of God's instrumentalities to relieve the disease of the body and point the sin-sick soul to Him who can heal both soul and body. In addition to the performance of the special duties assigned them, all should have an interest for the welfare of others. Selfishness is contrary to the spirit of Christianity. It is altogether satanic in its nature and development.

In one of His precious lessons to His disciples, our Saviour described God's care for His creatures in these words: "Are not five sparrows sold for two farthings, and not one of them is forgotten before God? But even the very hairs of your head are all numbered." He who stoops to notice even the little birds has a special care for all branches of His work. All who are employed in our institutions are under the eye of the infinite God. He sees whether their duties are performed with strict integrity or in a careless, dishonest manner. Angels are walking unseen through every room of these institutions. Angels are constantly ascending to heaven, bearing up the record with joy or sadness. Every act of fidelity is registered, every act of dishonesty also is recorded, and every person is finally to be rewarded as his works have been.

56. Christian Influence

In their intercourse with others all at the sanitarium who are followers of Christ should seek to elevate the standard of Christianity. I have hesitated to speak of this because some who are ever ready to go to extremes will conclude that it is necessary to discuss with the patients upon points of doctrine and, in the religious meetings held at the sanitarium, to talk as they would if among their brethren in our own house of worship. Some manifest no wisdom in bearing their testimony in these little meetings intended more especially for the benefit of the patients, but rush on in their zeal and talk of the third angel's message, or other peculiar points of our faith, while these sick people understand no more what they are talking about than if they spoke in Greek.

It may be well enough to introduce these subjects in a prayer meeting of believers, but not where the object is to benefit those who know nothing of our faith. We should adapt our prayers and testimonies to the occasion and to the company present. Those who cannot do this are not needed in such meetings. There are themes that Christians may at any time dwell upon with profit, such as the Christian experience, the love of Christ, and the simplicity of faith; and if their own hearts are imbued with the love of Jesus, they will let it shine forth in every prayer and exhortation. Let the fruits of the sanctifying truth be seen in the life, in a godly example, and it will make an impression that no opposing influence can counteract.

It is a shame to the Christian name that so little stability and true godliness are seen in the lives of many who profess Christ. When brought in contact with worldly influences, they become divided in heart. They lean to the world rather than toward Christ. Unless there is a powerful excitement to stir the feelings, one would never think, from their deportment, that they loved the truth or were Christians.

Some will acknowledge the truthfulness of what I have written, but will make no radical change; they cannot discern the deceitful workings of the carnal heart, and because of their spiritual blindness they will be seduced by influences that corrupt and ruin the soul. The spell of temptation will hold under its charm those who see and feel not their danger. At every favorable opportunity the adversary of souls will use them as his agents and will stir every element of depravity which exists in their unsanctified natures. They will manifest a continual tendency toward that which is wrong. Appetite and passion will clamor for indulgence. The habits of years will be revealed under the strong power of Satan's temptations. If this class were many miles from any of our institutions at Battle Creek, the cause of God would be far more prosperous.

Such persons might reform if they would have any true sense of their condition and the pernicious influence which they exert, and would make decided efforts to correct their errors. But they do not meditate or pray or read the Scriptures as they should. They are frivolous and changeable. They are anchored nowhere. Those who would be faithful and exert a saving influence upon others find this class a stumbling block in their path, and their work is tenfold harder than it otherwise would be.

I have been shown that the physicians should come into a closer connection with God and stand and work earnestly in His strength. They have a responsible part to act. Not only the lives of the patients, but their souls also, are at stake. Many who are benefited physically may, at the same time, be greatly helped spiritually. Both the health of the body and the salvation of the soul are in a great degree dependent upon the course of the physicians. It is of the utmost consequence that they are right; that they have not only scientific knowledge, but the knowledge of God's will and ways. Great responsibilities rest upon them.

My brethren, you should see and feel your responsibility and, in view of it, humble your souls before God and plead with Him for wisdom. You have not realized how much the salvation of the souls of those whose bodies you are seeking to relieve from suffering, depends upon your words, your actions and deportment. You are doing work which must bear the test of the judgment. You must guard your own souls from the sins of selfishness, self-sufficiency, and self-confidence.

You should preserve a true Christian dignity, but avoid all affectation. Be strictly honest in heart and life. Let faith, like the palm tree, strike its penetrating roots beneath the things which do appear, and obtain spiritual refreshment from the living springs of God's grace and mercy. There is a well of water which springeth up into everlasting life. You must draw your life from this hidden spring. If you divest yourselves of selfishness, and strengthen your souls by constant communion with God, you may promote the happiness of all with whom you come in contact. You will notice the neglected, inform the ignorant, encourage the oppressed and desponding, and, as far as possible, relieve the suffering. And you will not only point the way to heaven, but will walk in that way yourselves.

Be not satisfied with superficial knowledge. Be not elated by flattery nor depressed by faultfinding. Satan will tempt you to pursue such a course that you may be admired and flattered, but you should turn away from his devices. You are servants of the living God.

Your intercourse with the sick is an exhausting process and would gradually dry up the very springs of life if there were no change, no opportunity for recreation, and if angels of God did not guard and protect you. If you could see the many perils through which you are conducted safely every day by these messengers of heaven, gratitude would spring up in your hearts and find expression from your lips. If you make God your strength, you may, under the most discouraging circumstances, attain a height and breadth of Christian perfection which you hardly think it possible to reach. Your thoughts may be elevated, you may have noble aspirations, clear perceptions of truth, and purposes of action which shall raise you above all sordid motives.

Both thought and action will be necessary if you would attain to perfection of character. While brought in contact with the world, you should be on your guard that you do not seek too ardently for the applause of men and live for their opinion. Walk carefully if you would walk safely; cultivate the grace of humility, and hang your helpless souls upon Christ. You may be, in every sense, men of God. In the midst of confusion and temptation in the worldly crowd you may, with perfect sweetness, keep the independence of the soul.

If you are in daily communion with God you will learn to place His estimate upon men, and the obligations resting upon you to bless suffering humanity will meet with a willing response. You are not your own; your Lord has sacred claims upon your supreme affections and the very highest services of your life. He has a right to use you, in your body and in your spirit, to the fullest extent of your capabilities, for His own honor and glory. Whatever crosses you may be required to bear, whatever labors or sufferings are imposed upon you by His hand, you are to accept without a murmur.

Those for whom you labor are your brethren in distress, suffering from physical disorders and the spiritual leprosy of sin. If you are any better than they, it is to be credited to the cross of Christ. Many are without God and without hope in the world. They are guilty, corrupt, and degraded, enslaved by Satan's devices. Yet these are the ones whom Christ came from heaven to redeem. They are subjects for tenderest pity, sympathy, and tireless effort; for they are on the verge of ruin. They suffer from ungratified desires, disordered passions, and the condemnation of their own consciences; they are miserable in every sense of the word, for they are losing their hold on this life and have no prospect for the life to come.

You have an important field of labor, and you should be active and vigilant, rendering cheerful and unqualified obedience to the Master's calls. Ever bear in mind that your efforts to reform others should be made in the spirit of unwavering kindness. Nothing is ever gained by holding yourselves aloof from those whom you would help. You should keep before the minds of patients the fact that in suggesting reforms of their habits and customs you are presenting before them that which is not to ruin but to save them; that, while yielding up what they have hitherto esteemed and loved, they are to build on a more secure foundation.

While reform must be advocated with firmness and resolution, all appearance of bigotry or an overbearing spirit should be carefully shunned. Christ has given us precious lessons of patience, forbearance, and love. Rudeness is not energy; nor is domineering, heroism. The Son of God was persuasive. He was manifested to draw all men unto Him. His followers must study His life more closely and walk in the light of His example, at whatever sacrifice to self. Reform, continual reform, must be kept before the people; and your example should enforce your teachings.

The case of Daniel was presented before me. Although he was a man of like passions with ourselves, the pen of inspiration presents him as a faultless character. His life is given us as a bright example of what man may become, even in this life, if he will make God his strength and wisely improve the opportunities and privileges within his reach. Daniel was an intellectual giant; yet he was continually seeking for greater knowledge, for higher attainments.

Other young men had the same advantages; but they did not, like him, bend all their energies to seek wisdom—the knowledge of God as revealed in His word and in His works. Although Daniel was one of the world's great men, he was not proud nor self-sufficient. He felt the need of refreshing his soul with prayer, and each day found him in earnest supplication before God. He would not be deprived of this privilege even when a den of lions was opened to receive him if he continued to pray.

Daniel loved, feared, and obeyed God. Yet he did not flee away from the world to avoid its corrupting influence. In the providence of God he was to be in the world yet not of the world. With all the temptations and fascinations of court life surrounding him, he stood in the integrity of his soul, firm as a rock in his adherence to principle. He made God his strength and was not forsaken of Him in his time of greatest need.

Daniel was true, noble, and generous. While he was anxious to be at peace with all men, he would not permit any power to turn him aside from the path of duty. He was willing to obey those who had rule over him, as far as he could do so consistently with truth and righteousness; but kings and decrees could not make him swerve from his allegiance to the King of kings. Daniel was but eighteen years old when brought into a heathen court in service to the king of Babylon, and because of his youth his noble resistance of wrong and his steadfast adherence to the right are the more admirable. His noble example should bring strength to the tried and tempted, even at the present day.

A strict compliance with the Bible requirements will be a blessing, not only to the soul, but to the body. The fruit of the Spirit is not only love, joy, and peace, but temperance also. We are enjoined not to defile our bodies, for they are the temples of the Holy Ghost. The case of Daniel shows us, that, through religious principle, young men may triumph over the lust of the flesh and remain true to God's requirements, even though it cost them a great sacrifice.

What if he had made a compromise with those heathen officers, and had yielded to the pressure of the occasion by eating and drinking as was customary with the Babylonians? That one wrong step would probably have led to others, until, his connection with heaven being severed, he would have been borne away by temptation. But while he clung to God with unwavering trust, the spirit of prophetic power came upon him. While he was instructed of man in the duties of court life, he was taught of God to read the mysteries of future ages.

57. Economy and Self-Denial

Economy in the outlay of means is an excellent branch of Christian wisdom. This matter is not sufficiently considered by those who occupy responsible positions in our institutions. Money is an excellent gift of God. In the hands of His children it is food for the hungry, drink for the thirsty, and raiment for the naked; it is a defense for the oppressed and a means of health to the sick. Means should not be needlessly or lavishly expended for the gratification of pride or ambition.

In order to meet the real wants of the people, the stern motives of religious principle must be a controlling power. When Christians and worldlings are brought together, the Christian element is not to assimilate with the unsanctified. The contrast between the two must be kept sharp and positive. They are servants of two masters. One class strive to keep the humble path of obedience to God's requirements,—the path of simplicity, meekness, and humility,—imitating the Pattern, Christ Jesus.

The other class are in every way the opposite of the first. They are servants of the world, eager and ambitious to follow its fashions in extravagant dress and in the gratification of appetite. This is the field in which Christ has given those connected with the sanitarium their appointed work. We are not to lessen the distance between us and worldlings by coming to their standard, stepping down from the high path cast up for the ransomed of the Lord to walk in. But the charms exhibited in the Christian's life—the principles carried out in our daily work, in holding appetite under the control of reason, maintaining simplicity in dress, and engaging in holy conversation—will be a light continually shining upon the pathway of those whose habits are false.

There are weak and vain ones who have no depth of mind or power of principle, who are foolish enough to be influenced and corrupted from the simplicity of the gospel by the devotees of fashion. If they see that those who profess to be reformers are, as far as their circumstances will admit, indulging the appetite and dressing after the customs of the world, the slaves of self-indulgence will become confirmed in their perverse habits. They conclude that they are not so far out of the way after all, and that no great change need be made by them. The people of God should firmly uphold the standard of right and exert an influence to correct the wrong habits of those who have been worshiping at the shrine of fashion, and break the spell which Satan has had over these poor souls. Worldlings should see a marked contrast between their own extravagance and the simplicity of reformers who are followers of Christ.

The secret of life's success is in a careful, conscientious attention to the little things. God makes the simple leaf, the tiny flower, the blade of grass, with as much care as He creates a world. The symmetrical structure of a strong, beautiful character is built up by individual acts of duty. All should learn to be faithful in the least as well as in the greatest duty. Their work cannot bear the inspection of God unless it is found to include a faithful, diligent, economical care for the little things.

All who are connected with our institutions should have a jealous care that nothing be wasted, even if the matter does not come under the very part of the work assigned them. Everyone can do something toward economizing. All should perform their work, not to win praise of men, but in such a manner that it may bear the scrutiny of God.

Christ once gave His disciples a lesson upon economy which is worthy of careful attention. He wrought a miracle to feed the hungry thousands who had listened to His teachings; yet after all had eaten and were satisfied, He did not permit the fragments to be wasted. He who could, in their necessity, feed the vast multitude by His divine power, bade His disciples gather up the fragments, that nothing might be lost. This lesson was given as much for our benefit as for those living in Christ's day. The Son of God has a care for the necessities of temporal life. He did not neglect the broken fragments after the feast, although He could make such a feast whenever He chose. The workers in our institutions would do well to heed this lesson: "Gather up the fragments that remain, that nothing be lost." This is the duty of all; and those who occupy a leading position should set the example.

Those whose hands are open to respond to the calls for means to sustain the cause of God and to relieve the suffering and the needy are not the ones who are found loose and lax and dilatory in their business management. They are always careful to keep their outgoes within their income. They are economical from principle; they feel it their duty to save, that they may have something to give.

Some of the workers, like the children of Israel, allow perverted appetite and old habits of indulgence to clamor for the victory. They long, as did ancient Israel, for the leeks and onions of Egypt. All connected with these institutions should strictly adhere to the laws of life and health, and thus give no countenance, by their example, to the wrong habits of others.

It is transgression in the little things that first leads the soul away from God. By their one sin in partaking of the forbidden fruit, Adam and Eve opened the floodgates of woe upon the world. Some may regard that transgression as a very little thing, but we see that its consequences were anything but small. The angels in heaven have a wider and more elevated sphere of action than we, but right with them and right with us are one and the same thing.

It is not a mean, penurious spirit that would lead the proper officers to reprove existing wrongs and require from all the workers justice, economy, and self-denial. It is no coming down from proper dignity to guard the interests of our institutions in these matters. Those who are faithful themselves, naturally look for faithfulness in others. Strict integrity should govern the dealings of the managers and should be enforced upon all who labor under their direction.

Men of principle need not the restriction of locks and keys; they do not need to be watched and guarded. They will deal truly and honorably at all times, alone, with no eye upon them, as well as in public. They will not bring a stain upon their souls for any amount of gain or selfish advantage. They scorn a mean act. Although no one else might know it, they would know it themselves, and this would destroy their self-respect. Those who are not conscientious and faithful in little things would not be reformed were there laws and restrictions and penalties upon the point.

Few have moral stamina to resist temptation, especially of the appetite, and to practice self-denial. To some it is a temptation too strong to be resisted to see others eat the third meal; and they imagine they are hungry, when the feeling is not a call of the stomach for food, but a desire of the mind that has not been fortified with firm principle and disciplined to self-denial. The walls of self-control and self-restriction should not in a single instance be weakened and broken down. Paul, the apostle to the Gentiles, says: "I keep under my body, and bring it into subjection: lest that by any means, when I have preached to others, I myself should be a castaway."

Those who do not overcome in little things will have no moral power to withstand greater temptations. All who seek to make honesty the ruling principle in the daily business of life will need to be on their guard that they covet "no man's silver, or gold, or apparel." While they are content with convenient food and clothing, it will be found an easy matter to keep the heart and hands from the defilement of covetousness and dishonesty.

The habits formed in childhood and youth have more influence than any natural endowment in making men and women intellectually great or dwarfed and crippled; for the very best talents may, through wrong habits, become warped and enfeebled. To a great extent the character is determined in early years. Correct, virtuous habits formed in youth will generally mark the course of the individual through life. In most cases those who reverence God and honor the right will be found to have learned this lesson before the world could stamp its images of sin upon the soul. Men and women of mature age are generally as insensible to new impressions as is the hardened rock; but youth is impressible, and a right character may then be easily formed.

Those who are employed in our institutions have, in many respects, the best advantages for the formation of correct habits. None will be placed beyond the reach of temptation, for in every character there are weak points that are in danger when assailed. Those who profess the name of Christ should not, like the self-righteous Pharisee, find great pleasure in recounting their good deeds, but all should feel the necessity of keeping the moral nature braced by constant watchfulness. Like faithful sentinels they should guard the citadel of the soul, never feeling that they may relax their vigilance for a moment. In earnest prayer and living faith is their only safety.

Those who begin to be careless of their steps will find that, before they are aware of it, their feet are entangled in a web from which it is impossible for them to extricate themselves. It should be a fixed principle with all to be truthful and honest. Whether they are rich or poor, whether they have friends or are left alone, come what will, they should resolve in the strength of God that no influence shall lead them to commit the least wrong act. One and all should realize that upon them, individually, depends in a measure the prosperity of the institutions which God has established among us.

58. Position and Work of the Sanitarium

While traveling in the State of Maine, not long since, we became acquainted with Sister A, a lady who accepted the truth while at the sanitarium. Her husband was once a wealthy manufacturer; but reverses came, and he was reduced to poverty. Sister A lost her health and went to our sanitarium for treatment. There she received the present truth, which she adorns by a consistent Christian life. She has four fine, intelligent children, who are thorough health reformers and can tell you why they are so. Such a family can do much good in a community. They exert a strong influence in the right direction.

Many who come to the sanitarium for treatment are brought to the knowledge of the truth, and thus not only are they healed in body, but the darkened chambers of the mind are illuminated with the light of the dear Saviour's love. But how much more good might be accomplished if all connected with that institution were first connected with the God of wisdom and had thus become channels of light to others. The habits and customs of the world, pride of appearance, selfishness, and self-exaltation, too often intrude, and these sins of His professed followers are so offensive to God that He cannot work in power for them or through them.

Those who are unfaithful in temporal affairs will likewise be unfaithful in spiritual things. On the other hand, a neglect of God's claims leads to neglect of the claims of humanity. Unfaithfulness is prevalent in this degenerate age; it is extending in our churches and in our institutions. Its slimy track is seen everywhere. This is one of the condemning sins of this age and will carry thousands and tens of thousands to perdition. If those who profess the truth in our institutions at Battle Creek were living representatives of Christ, a power would go forth from them which would be felt everywhere. Satan well knows this, and he works with all power and deceivableness of unrighteousness in them that perish, that Christ's name may not be magnified in those who profess to be His followers. My heart aches when I see how Jesus is dishonored by the unworthy lives and defective characters of those who might be an ornament and an honor to His cause.

The temptations by which Christ was beset in the wilderness—appetite, love of the world, and presumption—are the three great leading allurements by which men are most frequently overcome. The managers of the sanitarium will often be tempted to depart from the principles which should govern such an institution. But they should not vary from the right course to gratify the inclinations or minister to the depraved appetites of wealthy patients or friends. The influence of such a course is only evil. Deviations from the teachings given in lectures or through the press have a most unfavorable effect upon the influence and morals of the institution, and will, to a great extent, counteract all efforts to instruct and reform the victims of depraved appetites and passions, and to lead them to Christ, the only safe refuge.

The evil will not end here. The influence affects not only the patients, but the workers as well. When the barriers are once broken down, step after step is taken in the wrong direction. Satan presents flattering worldly prospects to those who will depart from principle and sacrifice integrity and Christian honor to gain the approbation of the ungodly. His efforts are too often successful. He gains the victory where he should meet with repulse and defeat.

Christ resisted Satan in our behalf. We have the example of our Saviour to strengthen our weak purposes and resolves; but, notwithstanding this, some will fall by Satan's temptations, and they will not fall alone. Every soul that fails to obtain the victory carries others down through his influence. Those who fail to connect with God, and to receive wisdom and grace to refine and elevate their own lives, will be judged for the good they might have done but failed to perform because they were content with earthliness of mind and friendship with the unsanctified.

All heaven is interested in the salvation of man and is ready to pour upon him her beneficent gifts if he will comply with the conditions Christ has made: "Come out from among them, and be ye separate, saith the Lord, and touch not the unclean."

Those who bear the responsibility at the sanitarium should be exceedingly guarded that the amusements shall not be of a character to lower the standard of Christianity, bringing this institution down upon a level with others and weakening the power of true godliness in the minds of those who are connected with it. Worldly or theatrical entertainments are not essential for the prosperity of the sanitarium or for the health of the patients. The more they have of this kind of amusements, the less will they be pleased unless something of the kind shall be continually carried on. The mind is in a fever of unrest for something new and exciting, the very thing it ought not to have. And if these amusements are once allowed, they are expected again, and the patients lose their relish for any simple arrangement to occupy the time. But repose, rather than excitement, is what many of the patients need.

As soon as these entertainments are introduced, the objections to theatergoing are removed from many minds, and the plea that moral and high-toned scenes are to be acted at the theater breaks down the last barrier. Those who would permit this class of amusements at the sanitarium would better be seeking wisdom from God to lead these poor, hungry, thirsting souls to the Fountain of joy, and peace, and happiness.

When there has been a departure from the right path, it is difficult to return. Barriers have been removed, safeguards broken down. One step in the wrong direction prepares the way for another. A single glass of wine may open the door of temptation which will lead to habits of drunkenness. A single vindictive feeling indulged may open the way to a train of feelings which will end in murder. The least deviation from right and principle will lead to separation from God and may end in apostasy. What we do once, we more readily and naturally do again; and to go forward in a certain path, be it right or wrong, is more easy than to start. It takes less time and labor to corrupt our ways before God than to engraft upon the character habits of righteousness and truth. Whatever a man becomes accustomed to, be its influence good or evil, he finds it difficult to abandon.

The managers of the sanitarium may as well conclude at once that they will never be able to satisfy that class of minds that can find happiness only in something new and exciting.

To many persons this has been the intellectual diet during their lifetime; there are mental as well as physical dyspeptics. Many are suffering from maladies of the soul far more than from diseases of the body, and they will find no relief until they shall come to Christ, the wellspring of life. Complaints of weariness, loneliness, and dissatisfaction will then cease. Satisfying joys will give vigor to the mind and health and vital energy to the body.

If physicians and workers flatter themselves that they are to find a panacea for the varied ills of their patients by supplying them with a round of amusements similar to those which have been the curse of their lives, they will be disappointed. Let not these entertainments be placed in the position which the living Fountain should occupy. The hungry, thirsty soul will continue to hunger and thirst as long as it partakes of these unsatisfying pleasures. But those who drink of the living water will thirst no more for frivolous, sensual, exciting amusements. The ennobling principles of religion will strengthen the mental powers and will destroy a taste for these gratifications.

The burden of sin, with its unrest and unsatisfied desires, lies at the very foundation of a large share of the maladies the sinner suffers. Christ is the mighty healer of the sin-sick soul. These poor afflicted ones need to have a clearer knowledge of Him whom to know aright is life eternal. They need to be patiently and kindly yet earnestly taught how to throw open the windows of the soul and let the sunlight of God's love come in to illuminate the darkened chambers of the mind.

The most exalted spiritual truths may be brought home to the heart by the things of nature. The birds of the air, the flowers of the field in their glowing beauty, the springing grain, the fruitful branches of the vine, the trees putting forth their tender buds, the glorious sunset, the crimson clouds predicting a fair morrow, the recurring seasons—all these may teach us precious lessons of trust and faith. The imagination has here a fruitful field in which to range. The intelligent mind may contemplate with the greatest satisfaction those lessons of divine truth which the world's Redeemer has associated with the things of nature.

Christ sharply reproved the men of His time because they had not learned from nature the spiritual lessons which they might have learned. All things, animate and inanimate, express to man the knowledge of God. The same divine mind that is working upon the things of nature is speaking to the minds and hearts of men, and creating an inexpressible craving for something they have not. The things of the world cannot satisfy their longing. To all these thirsting souls the divine message is addressed: "The Spirit and the bride say, Come. And let him that heareth say, Come. And let him that is athirst come. And whosoever will, let him take the water of life freely."

The Spirit of God is continually impressing the minds of men to seek for those things which alone will give peace and rest—the higher, holier joys of heaven. Christ, the Lord of life and glory, gave His life to redeem man from Satan's power. Our Saviour is constantly at work, through influences seen and unseen, to attract the minds of men from the unsatisfying pleasures of this life to the priceless treasure which may be theirs in the immortal future.

God would have His people, in words and in deportment, declare to the world that no earthly attractions or worldly possessions are of sufficient value to compensate for the loss of the heavenly inheritance. Those who are truly children of the light and of the day will not be vain or frivolous in conversation, in dress, or in deportment, but sober, contemplative, constantly exerting an influence to attract souls to the Redeemer. The love of Christ, reflected from the cross, is pleading in behalf of the sinner, drawing him by cords of infinite love to the peace and happiness found in our Saviour. God enjoins upon all His followers to bear a living testimony in unmistakable language by their conduct, their dress and conversation, in all the pursuits of life, that the power of true godliness is profitable to all in this life and in the life to come; that this alone can satisfy the soul of the receiver.

The glory of God is displayed in His handiwork. Here are mysteries that the mind will become strong in searching out. Minds that have been amused and abused by reading fiction may in nature have an open book, and read truth in the works of God around them. All may find themes for study in the simple leaf of the forest tree, the spires of grass covering the earth with their green velvet carpet, the plants and flowers, the stately trees of the forest, the lofty mountains, the granite rocks, the restless ocean, the precious gems of light studding the heavens to make the night beautiful, the exhaustless riches of the sunlight, the solemn glories of the moon, the winter's cold, the summer's heat, the changing, recurring seasons, in perfect order and harmony, controlled by infinite power; here are subjects which call for deep thought, for the stretch of the imagination.

If the frivolous and pleasure-seeking will allow their minds to dwell upon the real and true, the heart cannot but be filled with reverence, and they will adore the God of nature. The contemplation and study of God's character as revealed in His created works will open a field of thought that will draw the mind away from low, debasing, enervating amusements. The knowledge of

God's works and ways we can only begin to obtain in this world; the study will be continued throughout eternity.

God has provided for man subjects of thought which will bring into activity every faculty of the mind. We may read the character of the Creator in the heavens above and the earth beneath, filling the heart with gratitude and thanksgiving. Every nerve and sense will respond to the expressions of God's love in His marvelous works. Satan invents earthly allurements, that the carnal mind may be placed on those things which cannot elevate and refine and ennoble; its powers are thus dwarfed and crippled, and men and women who might attain to perfection of character become narrow, weak, and defective.

God designed that the sanitarium which He had established should stand forth as a beacon of light, of warning and reproof. He would prove to the world that an institution conducted on religious principles as an asylum for the sick could be sustained without sacrificing its peculiar, holy character; that it could be kept free from the objectionable features that are found in other institutions of the kind. It was to be an instrumentality in His hand to bring about great reforms. Wrong habits of life should be corrected, the morals elevated, the tastes changed, the dress reformed.

Disease of every type is brought upon the body through the unhealthful fashionable style of dress, and the fact should be made prominent that a reform must take place before treatment will effect a cure. The perverted appetite has been pampered until disease has been produced as the sure result. The crippled, dwarfed faculties and organs cannot be strengthened and invigorated without decided reforms. And if those connected with the sanitarium are not in every respect correct representatives of the truths of health reform, decided reformation must make them what they should be, or they must be separated from the institution.

The minds of many take so low a level that God cannot work for them or with them. The current of thought must be changed, the moral sensibilities must be aroused to feel the claims of God. The sum and substance of true religion is to own and continually acknowledge, by words, by dress, by deportment, our relationship to God. Humility should take the place of pride; sobriety, of levity; and devotion, of irreligion and careless indifference.

Those who have had many years of experience in the cause of God should, above all others, put to the highest use the talents entrusted them by the Master. But the example of some has been too much on the side of conformity to the world, rather than of maintaining the distinct and separate character of God's peculiar people. They have had an influence to indulge rather than deny the appetite and the inclination to dress according to the world's standard. This is all in opposition to the work which God and angels are seeking to do for us as a people to bring out, to separate, to distinguish us from the world. We should sanctify ourselves as a people and seek strength from God to meet the demands of this time. When iniquity prevails in the world, God's people should seek to be more closely connected with heaven. The tide of moral evil comes upon us with such power that we shall lose our balance and be swept away with the current unless our feet stand firmly upon the Rock Christ Jesus.

The prosperity of the sanitarium is not dependent alone upon the intelligence and knowledge of its physicians, but upon the favor of God. If it is conducted in a manner that God can bless it will be highly successful and will stand in advance of any other institution of the kind in the world. Great light, great knowledge, and superior privileges have been given. And in accordance with the light which has been received, but has not been improved and therefore is not shining forth upon others, will be the condemnation.

The minds of some are being turned into the channel of unbelief. These persons think they see reason to doubt the word and the work of God, because the course of some professed Christians looks questionable to them. But does this move the foundation? We are not to make the course of others the basis of our faith. We are to imitate Christ, the perfect Pattern.

If any allow their hold on Him to be weakened because men err, because defects are seen in the characters of those who profess the truth, they will ever be on sliding sand. Their eyes must be directed to the Author and Finisher of their faith; they must strengthen their souls with the assurance of the great apostle: "Nevertheless the foundation of God standeth sure, having this seal, The Lord knoweth them that are His." God cannot be deceived. He reads character correctly. He weighs motives. Nothing escapes His all-seeing eye; the thoughts, the intents and purposes of the hearts—all are discerned by Him.

There is no excuse for doubt or skepticism. God has made ample provision to establish the faith of all men, if they will decide from the weight of evidence. But if they wait to have every seeming objection removed before they believe, they will never be settled, rooted, and grounded in the truth. God will never remove all seeming difficulties from our path. Those who wish to doubt may find opportunity; those who wish to believe will find plenty of evidence upon which to base their faith. The position of some is unexplainable, even to themselves. They are drifting without an anchor, beating about in the fog of uncertainty. Satan soon seizes the helm and carries their frail bark wherever he pleases. They become subject to his will. Had these minds not listened to Satan, they would not have been deceived by his sophistry; had they been balanced on the side of God they would not have become confused and bewildered.

God and angels are watching with intense interest the development of character and are weighing moral worth. Those who withstand Satan's devices will come forth as gold tried in the fire. Those who are swept off their feet by the waves of temptation, imagine, as did Eve, that they are becoming wonderfully wise, outgrowing their ignorance and narrow conscientiousness; but, like her, they will find themselves sadly deceived. They have been chasing shadows, exchanging heavenly wisdom for frail human judgment. A little knowledge has made them self-conceited. A more deep and thorough knowledge of themselves and of God would make them again sane and sensible men, and would balance them on the side of truth, of angels, and of God.

The word of God will judge every one of us at the last great day. Young men talk about science and are wise above that which is written; they seek to explain the ways and work of God to meet their finite comprehension; but it is all a miserable failure. True science and Inspiration are in perfect harmony. False science is a something independent of God. It is pretentious ignorance. This deceptive power has captivated and enslaved the minds of many, and they have chosen darkness rather than light. They have taken their position on the side of unbelief, as though it were a virtue and the sign of a great mind to doubt, when it is the sign of a mind too weak and narrow to perceive God in His created works. They could not fathom the mystery of His providence should they study with all their power for a lifetime. And because the works of God cannot be explained by finite minds, Satan brings his sophistry to bear upon them and entangles them in the meshes of unbelief. If these doubting ones will come into close connection with God, He will make His purposes clear to their understanding.

Spiritual things are spiritually discerned. The carnal mind cannot comprehend these mysteries. If questioners and doubters continue to follow the great deceiver, the impressions and convictions of God's Spirit will grow less and less, the promptings of Satan more frequent, until the mind will fully submit to his control. Then that which appears to these bewildered minds as foolishness will be the power of God, and that which God regards as foolishness will be to them the strength of wisdom.

One of the great evils which has attended the quest of knowledge, the investigations of science, is that those who engage in these researches too often lose sight of the divine character of pure and unadulterated religion. The worldly-wise have attempted to explain upon scientific principles the influence of the Spirit of God upon the heart. The least advance in this direction will lead the soul into the mazes of skepticism. The religion of the Bible is simply the mystery of godliness; no human mind can fully understand it, and it is utterly incomprehensible to the unregenerate heart.

The Son of God compared the operations of the Holy Spirit to the wind, which "bloweth where it listeth, and thou hearest the sound thereof, but canst not tell whence it cometh, and whither it goeth." Again, we read in the Sacred Record that the world's Redeemer rejoiced in spirit and said: "I thank Thee, O Father, Lord of heaven and earth, because Thou hast hid these things from the wise and prudent, and hast revealed them unto babes."

The Saviour rejoiced that the plan of salvation is such that those who are wise in their own estimation, who are puffed up by the teachings of vain philosophy, cannot see the beauty, power, and hidden mystery of the gospel. But to all those who are of a humble heart, who have a teachable, honest, childlike desire to know and do the will of their heavenly Father, His word is revealed as the power of God to their salvation. The operation of the Spirit of God is foolishness to the unrenewed man. The apostle Paul says: "But if our gospel be hid, it is hid to them that are lost: in whom the god of this world hath blinded the minds of them which believe not, lest the light of the glorious gospel of Christ, who is the image of God, should shine unto them."

The success of the sanitarium depends upon its maintaining the simplicity of godliness and shunning the world's follies in eating, drinking, dressing, and amusements. It must be reformatory in all its principles. Let nothing be invented to satisfy the wants of the soul and take the room and time which Christ and His service demand; for this will destroy the power of the institution as God's instrumentality to convert poor, sin-sick souls, who, ignorant of the way of life and peace, have sought for happiness in pride and vain folly.

"Standing by a purpose true," should be the position of all connected with the sanitarium. While none should urge our faith upon the patients or engage in religious controversy with them, our papers and publications, carefully selected, should be in sight almost everywhere. The religious element must predominate. This has been and ever will be the power of that institution. Let not our health asylum be perverted to the service of worldliness and fashion. There are hygienic institutions enough in our land that are more like an accommodating hotel than a place where the sick and suffering can obtain relief for their bodily infirmities and the sin-sick soul can find that peace and rest in Jesus to be found nowhere else.

Let religious principles be made prominent and kept so; let pride and popularity be discarded; let simplicity and plainness, kindness and faithfulness, be seen everywhere; then the sanitarium will be just what God intended it should be; then the Lord will favor it.

59. The Influence of Associates

In our institutions, where many are laboring together, the influence of association is very great. It is natural to seek companionship. Everyone will find companions or make them. And just in proportion to the strength of the friendship, will be the amount of influence which friends will exert over one another for good or for evil. All will have associates, and will influence and be influenced in their turn.

The link is a mysterious one which binds human hearts together, so that the feelings, tastes, and principles of two individuals are closely blended. One catches the spirit, and copies the ways and acts, of the other. As wax retains the figure of the seal, so the mind retains the impression produced by intercourse and association. The influence may be unconscious, yet it is no less powerful.

If the youth could be persuaded to associate with the pure, the thoughtful, and the amiable, the effect would be most salutary. If choice is made of companions who fear the Lord, the influence will lead to truth, to duty, and to holiness. A truly Christian life is a power for good. But, on the other hand, those who associate with men and women of questionable morals, of bad principles and practices, will soon be walking in the same path. The tendencies of the natural heart are downward. He who associates with the skeptic will soon become skeptical; he who chooses the companionship of the vile will most assuredly become vile. To walk in the counsel of the ungodly is the first step toward standing in the way of sinners and sitting in the seat of the scornful.

Let all who would form a right character choose associates who are of a serious, thoughtful turn of mind and who are religiously inclined. Those who have counted the cost and wish to build for eternity must put good material into their building. If they accept of rotten timbers, if they are content with deficiencies of character, the building is doomed to ruin. Let all take heed how they build. The storm of temptation will sweep over the building, and unless it is firmly and faithfully constructed it will not stand the test.

A good name is more precious than gold. There is an inclination with the youth to associate with those who are inferior in mind and morals. What real happiness can a young person expect from a voluntary connection with persons who have a low standard of thoughts, feelings, and deportment? Some are debased in taste and depraved in habits, and all who choose such companions will follow their example. We are living in times of peril that should cause the hearts of all to fear. We see the minds of many wandering through the mazes of skepticism. The causes of this are ignorance, pride, and a defective character. Humility is a hard lesson for fallen man to learn. There is something in the human heart which rises in opposition to revealed truth on subjects connected with God and sinners, the transgression of the divine law, and pardon through Christ.

My brethren and sisters, old and young, when you have an hour of leisure, open the Bible and store the mind with its precious truths. When engaged in labor, guard the mind, keep it stayed upon God, talk less, and meditate more. Remember: "Every idle word that men shall speak, they shall give account thereof in the day of judgment." Let your words be select; this will close a door against the adversary of souls. Let your day be entered upon with prayer; work as in God's sight. His angels are ever by your side, making a record of your words, your deportment, and the manner in which your work is done. If you turn from good counsel and choose to associate with those who you have reason to suspect are not religiously inclined, although they profess to be Christians, you will soon become like them. You place yourself in the way of temptation, on Satan's battleground, and will, unless constantly guarded, be overcome by his devices. There are persons who have for some time made a profession of religion, who are, to all intents and purposes, without God and without a sensitive conscience. They are vain and trifling; their conversation is of a low order. Courtship and marriage occupy the mind to the exclusion of higher and nobler thoughts.

The associations chosen by the workers are determining their destiny for this world and the next. Some who were once conscientious and faithful have sadly changed, they have disconnected from God, and Satan has allured them to his side. They are now irreligious and irreverent, and they have an influence upon others who are easily molded. Evil associations are deteriorating character; principle is being undermined. "He that walketh with wise men shall be wise: but a companion of fools shall be destroyed."

The young are in danger; but they are blind to discern the tendencies and result of the course they are pursuing. Many of them are engaged in flirtation. They seem to be infatuated. There is nothing noble, dignified, or sacred in these attachments; as they are prompted by Satan, the influence is such as to please him. Warnings to these persons fall unheeded. They are headstrong, self-willed, defiant. They think the warning, counsel, or reproof does not apply to them. Their course gives them no concern. They are continually separating themselves from the light and love of God. They lose all discernment of sacred and eternal things, and while they may keep up a dry form of Christian duties they have no heart in these religious exercises. All too late these deceived souls will learn that "strait is the gate, and narrow is the way, which leadeth unto life, and few there be that find it."

Words and actions and motives are recorded; but how little do these light, superficial heads and hard hearts realize that an angel of God stands writing down the manner in which their precious moments are employed. God will bring to light every word and every action. He is in every place. His messengers, although unseen, are visitors in the workroom and in the sleeping apartment. The hidden works of darkness will be brought to light. The thoughts, the intents and purposes of the heart, will stand revealed. All things are naked and open to the eyes of Him with whom we have to do.

The workers should take Jesus with them in every department of their labor. Whatever is done should be done with an exactness and thoroughness that will bear inspection. The heart should be in the work. Faithfulness is as essential in life's common duties as in those involving greater responsibility. Some may receive the idea that their work is not ennobling; but this is just as they choose to make it. They alone are capable of degrading or elevating their employment. We wish that every drone might be compelled to toil for his daily bread, for work is a blessing, not a curse. Diligent labor will keep us from many of the snares of Satan, who "finds some mischief still for idle hands to do."

None of us should be ashamed of work, however small and servile it may appear. Labor is ennobling. All who toil with head or hands are workingmen or workingwomen. And all are doing their duty and honoring their religion as much while working at the washtub or washing the dishes as they are in going to meeting. While the hands are engaged in the most common labor, the mind may be elevated and ennobled by pure and holy thoughts. When any of the workers manifest a lack of respect for religious things, they should be separated from the work. Let none feel that the institution is dependent upon them.

Those who have long been employed in our institutions should now be responsible workers, reliable in every place, as faithful to duty as the compass to the pole. Had they rightly improved their opportunities, they might now have symmetrical characters and a deep, living experience in religious things. But some of these workers have separated from God.

Religion is laid aside. It is not an inwrought principle, carefully cherished wherever they go, into whatever society they are thrown, proving as an anchor to the soul. I wish all the workers carefully to consider that success in this life and success in gaining the future life depend largely upon faithfulness in little things. Those who long for higher responsibilities should manifest faithfulness in performing the duties just where God has placed them.

The perfection of God's work is as clearly seen in the tiniest insect as in the king of birds. The soul of the little child that believes in Christ is as precious in His sight as are the angels about His throne. "Be ye therefore perfect, even as your Father which is in heaven is perfect." As God is perfect in His sphere, so man may be perfect in his sphere. Whatever the hand finds to do should be done with thoroughness and dispatch. Faithfulness and integrity in little things, the performance of little duties and little deeds of kindness, will cheer and gladden the pathway of life; and when our work on earth is ended, every one of the little duties performed with fidelity will be treasured as a precious gem before God.

60. The Tract Societies

In my last vision I was pointed back to the rise and progress of the cause of present truth. When our publishing house at Battle Creek was first established, the friends of the cause were few, and our people generally were poor. But when calls for help were made many came nobly forward and aided the cause by taking stock in the publishing work. The Lord was well pleased with the spirit of sacrifice manifested.

Twenty-six years have passed since that time, and in the providence of God the light of truth has been shining everywhere. The beginning was small, and it was necessary that great sacrifices should be made by the early friends of the cause. At every step great obstacles had to be met and overcome.

Our brethren who invested their means in the Review office were doing the very work which the Lord would have them do. He had given them means to be used for the very purpose of advancing His cause.

The lapse of time has brought great changes. Light has increased and has become widespread. While the people who are anxious for truth have been calling, "Watchman, what of the night?" the answer has been given intelligently, "The morning cometh, and also the night." By a thorough investigation of the prophecies we understand where we are in this world's history; and we know for a certainty that the second coming of Christ is near. The result of these investigations must be brought before the world through the press. And as the work has enlarged and increased, greater facilities have been demanded from year to year; improvements have gone steadily forward. It has been a cause of wonder to the world that with this unpopular truth such prosperity should attend the work. But with increased light and confirmed truth, and greater advantages in every way for the advancement of the cause, our works do not correspond with our faith.

If it was right for brethren to take stock in our publishing house when our work was small and our influence narrow, is it not of more consequence today when a much larger work is going forward and a corresponding increase of means is needed? The evidences of our position have been increasing with every year. We have been receiving fresh assurance that we have the truth as revealed in the word of God, that in accepting the third angel's message we have not given heed to fables, but to the "sure word of prophecy." We are now living in the full blaze of the light of Bible truth.

The Lord calls upon His people to arouse and to show their faith by their works. In times past, when our numbers were few, when those who were able felt it their duty to take stock in our publishing house, their prayers and their alms, the fruit of persevering, self-denying effort, came before God as a sweet savor. Our brethren and sisters who have received the precious bread of life brought to them in our publications should be even more willing to give of their means to support the cause than were those who loved the truth in former years.

Brethren, God would bless you in showing your interest in our houses of publication by making them your property. Those who own no stock in these institutions have the privilege of investing their means in this good work. We need your sympathy, your prayers, and your means. We need your hearty co-operation. We hope that all whose hearts the Lord shall make willing will come forward with their means to invest in these institutions. Is it indeed true that we have the last message of mercy to be given to the world? Is it true that our work will soon close? Thus saith the word of God. The end of all things is at hand. Then the warning should be sent to all parts of the earth.

Our houses of publication have become a power in the world. A great change has taken place. With our increased facilities to make the clear light shine forth to those who are in darkness, it is not now so hard as it once was to see and accept the truth. Those who first led out in the work were objects of the combined assaults of evil men and evil angels. The enmity of Satan, working through men as his instruments, was strikingly developed. On the other hand, the believers, though few in number, were earnest and zealous to vindicate the honor of God in exalting His law which had been made void, and to press back the workings of Satan revealed in every form of destructive error.

From the first, Satan has set himself against this work. He has been determined to bring all his power to bear to silence and sweep from the earth those who were laboring for the advancement of light and truth. He has ever had a measure of success. Calumny and the fiercest opposition have been brought to bear to crush out the precious truth by discouraging its advocates. The great adversary has employed his hellish deceptions in various ways, and every effort made has brought to his side one or more of the professed followers of Christ. Those whose hearts are carnal, who are more in harmony with the archdeceiver than with Christ, have after a time developed their true character and gone to their own company.

Satan holds under his control not a few who pass as friends of the truth, and through them he works against its advancement. He employs them to sow tares among the people of God. Thus when danger was not suspected, great evils have existed among us. But while Satan was working with all deceivableness of unrighteousness in them that perish, stanch advocates of truth have stemmed the tide of opposition and held the word uncorrupted amid a deluge of heresies. Although the church has at times been weakened through manifold discouragements and the rebellious element they have had to meet, still the truth has shone brighter with every conflict. The energies of God's people have not been exhausted. The power of His grace has quickened, revived, and ennobled the steadfast and the true.

Again and again was ancient Israel afflicted with rebellious murmurers. These were not always persons of feeble influence. In many cases, men of renown, rulers in Israel, turned against the providential leading of God and fiercely set to work to tear down that which they had once zealously built up. We have seen something of this repeated many times in our experience. It is unsafe for any church to lean upon some favorite minister, to trust in an arm of flesh. God's arm alone is able to uphold all who lean upon it.

Until Christ shall appear in the clouds of heaven with power and great glory, men will become perverse in spirit and turn from the truth to fables. The church will yet see troublous times. She will prophesy in sackcloth. But although she must meet heresies and persecutions, although she must battle with the infidel and the apostate, yet by the help of God she is bruising the head of Satan. The Lord will have a people as true as steel, and with faith as firm as the granite rock. They are to be His witnesses in the world, His instrumentalities to do a special, a glorious work in the day of His preparation.

The gospel message does not win a single soul to Christ, or make its way to a single heart, without wounding the head of Satan. Whenever a captive is wrenched from his grasp, delivered from his oppression, the tyrant is defeated. The publishing houses, the presses, are instrumentalities in God's hand to send out to every tongue and nation the precious light of truth. This light is reaching even to heathen lands, and is constantly making inroads upon superstition and every conceivable error.

Ministers who have preached the truth with all zeal and earnestness may apostatize and join the ranks of our enemies, but does this turn the truth of God into a lie? "Nevertheless," says the apostle, "the foundation of God standeth sure." The faith and feelings of men may change; but the truth of God, never. The third angel's message is sounding; it is infallible.

No man can serve God without uniting against himself evil men and evil angels. Evil spirits will be put upon the track of every soul that seeks to join the ranks of Christ, for Satan wishes to recover the prey taken from his grasp. Evil men will give themselves over to believe strong delusions, that they may be damned. These men will put on the garments of sincerity and deceive, if possible, the very elect.

It is as certain that we have the truth as that God lives; and Satan, with all his arts and hellish power, cannot change the truth of God into a lie. While the great adversary will try his utmost to make of none effect the word of God, truth must go forth as a lamp that burneth.

The Lord has singled us out and made us subjects of His marvelous mercy. Shall we be charmed with the pratings of the apostate? Shall we choose to take our stand with Satan and his host? Shall we join with the transgressors of God's law? Rather let it be our prayer: "Lord, put enmity between me and the serpent." If we are not at enmity with his works of darkness, his powerful folds encircle us, and his sting is ready at any moment to be driven to our hearts. We should count him a deadly foe. We should oppose him in the name of Christ. Our work is still onward. We must battle for every inch of ground. Let all who name the name of Christ clothe themselves with the armor of righteousness.

Brethren and sisters, in behalf of our houses of publication we call upon you to take stock in these institutions. You have nothing to fear; invest your means where it will be doing good; scatter rays of light to the darkest parts of the world. There is no such thing as failure in this work. It is your privilege and duty to do now as your brethren did when there were but few friends of the cause of truth. Take stock in our houses of publication, that you may feel that you have an interest in them.

Many invest their money in worldly speculations, and in doing this are robbed of every dollar. We ask you to show your liberality by making investments in our publishing work. It will do you good. Your money will not be lost, but will be placed at interest to increase your capital stock in heaven. Christ has given all for you; what will you give for Him? He asks your heart; give it to Him, it is His own. He asks your intellect; give it to Him, it is His own. He asks your money; give it to Him, it is His own. "Ye are not your own; for ye are bought with a price." God wants you and yours. Let the words of the royal psalmist express the sentiment of your hearts: "All things come of Thee, and of Thine own have we given Thee."

The time has come when we must know for ourselves why we believe as we do. We must stand for God and for the truth, against a reckless, unbelieving generation. The man who has once known the way of life, and has turned from the convictions of his own heart to the sophistry of Satan, will be more inaccessible and more unimpressible than he who has never tasted the love of Christ. He will be wise to do evil. He has bound himself to Satan, even against light and knowledge. I say to my brethren: Your only hope is in God. We must be clothed with Christ's righteousness if we would withstand the prevailing impiety. We must show our faith by our works. Let us lay up for ourselves a good foundation against the time to come, that we may lay hold on eternal life. We must labor, not in our own strength, but in the strength of our risen Lord. What will we do and dare for Jesus?

Our houses of publication are the property of all our people, and all should work to the point of raising them above embarrassment. In order to circulate our publications, they have been offered at so low a figure that but little profit could come to the office to reproduce the same works. This has been done with the best of motives, but not with experienced and farseeing judgment.

At the low prices of publications the office could not preserve a capital upon which to work. This was not fully seen and critically investigated. These low prices led people to undervalue the works, and it was not fully discerned that when once these publications were placed at a low figure it would be very difficult to bring them up to their proper value.

Our ministers have not had suitable encouragement. They must have means in order to live. There has been a sad lack of foresight in placing the low prices upon our publications, and still another in turning the profits largely into the tract and missionary societies. These matters have been carried to extremes, and there will be a reaction. In order for the tract and missionary societies to flourish, the instrumentalities to make and print books must flourish. Cripple these instrumentalities, burden the publishing houses with debt, and the tract and missionary societies will not prove a success.

There has been wrong management, not designedly, but in zeal and ardor to carry forward the missionary work. In the distribution and wide circulation of papers, tracts, and pamphlets, the instrumentalities to produce these publications have been crippled and embarrassed. There is ever danger of carrying any good work to extremes. Responsible men are in danger of becoming men of one idea, of concentrating their thoughts upon one branch of the work to the neglect of other parts of the great field.

As a people we need to be guarded on every point. There is not the least safety for any unless we seek wisdom of God daily and dare not move in our own strength. Danger is always surrounding us, and great caution should be used that no one branch of the work be made a specialty while other interests are left to suffer.

Mistakes have been made in putting down prices of publications to meet certain difficulties. These efforts must change. Those who made this move were sincere. They thought their liberality would provoke ministers and people to labor to greatly increase the demand for the publications.

Ministers and people should act nobly and liberally in dealing with our publishing houses. Instead of studying and contriving how they can obtain periodicals, tracts, and books at the lowest figure, they should seek to bring the minds of the people to see the true value of the publications. All these pennies taken from thousands of publications have caused a loss of thousands of dollars to our offices, when a few pennies more from each individual would scarcely have been felt.

The Review and Herald and the Signs of the Times are cheap papers at the full price. The Review is a valuable paper; it contains matters of great interest to the church and should be placed in every family of believers. If any are too poor to take it, the church should, by subscription, raise the amount of the full price of the paper and supply the destitute families. How much better would this plan be than throwing the poor upon the mercies of the publishing house or the tract and missionary society.

The same course should be pursued toward the Signs. With slight variations, this paper has been increasing in interest and in moral worth as a pioneer sheet since its establishment. These periodicals are one in interest. They are two instrumentalities in the great field to do their specific work in disseminating light in this day of God's preparation. All should engage just as earnestly to build up the one as the other.

"The eyes of the Lord are upon the righteous, and His ears are open unto their cry." Christ will succor those who flee to Him for wisdom and strength. If they meet duty and trial with humility of soul, depending upon Jesus, His mighty angel will be round about them, and He whom they have trusted will prove an all-sufficient helper in every emergency. Those who occupy responsible positions should daily become more intimately acquainted with the excellency, the faithfulness, and the love of Christ. They should be able to exclaim with assurance: "I know whom I have believed." These men should work as brethren, without one feeling of strife. Each should do his duty, knowing that the eye of God is searching motives and purposes, and reading the inmost feelings of the soul. The work is one. And if leading men do not let their own mind and their own feelings and ideas come in to rule and change the Lord's design, there will be the most perfect harmony between these two branches of the same work.

Our people should make greater efforts to extend the circulation of the Review. If our brethren and sisters would only manifest greater earnestness and put forth more persevering efforts to accomplish this, it would be done. Every family should have this paper. And if they would deny themselves their darling luxuries, tea and coffee, many who do not now have its weekly visits might pay for the messenger of light to come into their household. Almost every family takes one or more secular papers, and these frequently contain love stories and exciting tales of villainy and murder which injure the minds of all who read them. Those who consent to do without the Review and Herald lose much. Through its pages Christ may speak to them in warnings, in reproofs and counsel, which would change the current of their thoughts and be to them as the bread of life.

Our papers should not be filled with long discussions or long doctrinal arguments, which would weary the reader; but they should contain short and interesting doctrinal and practical articles. The price of our papers should not be made so low that no margin is left to work upon. The same interest which has been manifested to circulate the Signs of the Times should be shown in extending the circulation of the Review. If this is done, success will attend the effort.

We are upon the enchanted ground, and Satan is continually at work to rock our people to sleep in the cradle of carnal security. There is an indifference, a lack of zeal, that paralyzes all our efforts. Jesus was a zealous worker; and when His followers shall lean on Him, and work as He worked, they will see and realize corresponding results. An effort must be made to place a proper value on our publications and bring them back gradually to a proper basis. We should not be affected by the cry of speculation, money-making! We should press steadily forward, unmoved by censure, uncorrupted by applause. It will be a greater task to work back upon a proper basis than many suppose, but it must be done in order to save our institutions from embarrassment.

Our brethren should be guarded lest they become stereo-typed in their plans and labors. They may spend time and money in preparing an exact channel, that the work must be done in just such a way or it is not done right.

There is danger of being too particular. There should be greater care to avoid expense in transporting books and persons. The influence is bad upon the cause of God. Brethren, you should move cautiously, economically, and judiciously. A great work is to be done, and our offices are embarrassed. There are men who work faithfully in the office at Battle Creek who do not receive an equivalent for their labor. Justice is not done these men. In other work they could earn double the amount received here, but they conscientiously keep to their business because they feel that God's cause needs their help.

There is a great work to be done in the day of God's preparation in devising and executing plans for the advancement of His cause. Our publications should have a wide circulation, for they are doing a great work. There is much missionary work to be done. But I have been shown that there is danger of having this work too mechanical, so intricate and complicated that less will be accomplished than if it were more simple, direct, plain, and decided. We have neither time nor means to keep all parts of this machinery in harmonious action.

Our brethren who bear responsibilities in devising plans for carrying forward this part of the work must keep in mind that while a certain amount of education and training is essential in order to work intelligently, there is danger of making this too great a matter. By obtaining a most thorough education in all the minutiae, and leaving vital principles out of the question, we become dry and formal workers. The hearts that God has made willing by the operations of His grace are fitted for the work.

God wants heartwork. The unselfish purpose, the pure, elevated principle, the high and holy motive, He will accept. His grace and power will work with these efforts. All who realize that it is the work of God to prepare a people for His coming will find in their disinterested efforts opportunities where they can do tract and missionary labor. But there may be too much means expended and too much time occupied in making matters so exact and minute that the heartwork is neglected and a dry form preserved.

I tell you frankly that Jesus and the power of His grace are being left out of the question. Results will show that mechanical working has taken the place of piety, humility, and holiness of heart and life. The more spiritual, devoted, and humble workers find no place where they can take hold, and therefore they stand back. The young and inexperienced learn the form and do their work mechanically; but true love, the burden for souls, is not felt. Less dwelling upon set forms, less of the mechanical, and more of the power of godliness are essential in this solemn, fearful day of responsibilities.

There is order in heaven; and there should be system and order upon the earth, that the work may move forward without confusion and fanaticism. Our brethren have been working to this end; but while some of our ministers continually bear the burden of souls, and ever seek to bring the people up in spiritual attainments, those who are not so conscientious, and who have not carried the cross of Christ nor felt the value of souls as reflected from Calvary, will, in teaching and educating others in the mechanical working, become formal and powerless themselves, and bring no Saviour to the people.

Satan is ever working to have the service of God degenerate into dull form and become powerless to save souls. While the energy, earnestness, and efficiency of the workers become deadened by the efforts to have everything so systematic, the taxing labor that must be done by our ministers to keep this complicated machinery in motion engrosses so much time that the spiritual work is neglected. And with so many things to run, this work requires so large an amount of means that other branches of the work will wither and die for want of due attention.

While the silent messengers of truth should be scattered like the leaves of autumn, our ministers should not make this work a form and leave devotion and true piety out of the question. Ten truly converted, willing-minded, unselfish workers can do more in the missionary field than one hundred who confine their efforts to set forms and preserve mechanical rules, working without deep love for souls.

Vigilant missionary work must in no case be neglected. It has done much for the salvation of souls. The success of God's work depends very much upon this; but those who do this work are to be those who are spiritual, whose letters will breathe the light and love of Jesus, and who feel the burden of the work. They should be men and women who can pray, who have a close connection with God. The ready mind, the sanctified will, and sound judgment are needed. They will have learned of the heavenly Teacher the most successful manner of appealing to souls. They will have learned their lessons in the school of Christ. They will do their work with an eye single to the glory of God.

Without this education all the teachings received from your instructors in regard to forms and rules, however thorough the lessons may be, will leave you still novices in the work. You must learn of Christ. You should deny self for Christ. You should put your neck under the yoke of Christ. You must carry the burden of Christ. You must feel that you are not your own, but servants of Christ, doing a work that He has enjoined upon you, not for any praise or honor or glory that you shall receive, but for His own dear sake. Into all your work you should weave His grace, His love, His devotion, His zeal, His untiring perseverance, His indomitable energy, that will tell for time and for eternity.

The tract and missionary work is a good work. It is God's work. It should be in no way belittled, but there is continual danger of perverting it from its true object. Canvassers are wanted to labor in the missionary field. Persons of uncouth manners are not fitted for this work. Men and women who possess tact, good address, keen foresight, and discriminating minds, and who feel the value of souls, are the ones who can be successful.

The work of the colporteur is elevated and will prove a success, if he is honest, earnest, and patient, steadily pursuing the work he has undertaken. His heart must be in the work. He must rise early and work industriously, putting to proper use the faculties God has given him. Difficulties must be met. If confronted with unceasing perseverance, they will be overcome. Much is gained by courtesy. The worker may continually be forming a symmetrical character. Great characters are formed by little acts and efforts.

There is danger of not giving sufficient encouragement to our ministers. I was shown some men whom God was calling to the work of the ministry, entering the field as canvassers. This is an excellent preparation if their object is to disseminate light, to bring the truth revealed in God's word, directly to the home circle. In conversation the way will frequently be opened to speak of the religion of the Bible. If the work is taken hold of as it should be, families will be visited, the workers will carry with them tender hearts and love for souls, and will bear, in words and deportment, the fragrance of the grace of Christ, and great good will be the result. This would be an excellent experience for any who have the ministry in view.

But many are attracted into the canvassing field to sell books and pictures that do not express our faith and do not give light to the purchaser. They are induced to do this because the financial prospects are more flattering than can be offered them as licentiates. These persons are obtaining no special fitness for the gospel ministry. They are not gaining that experience which would fit them for the work. They are losing time and opportunities by this kind of labor. They are not learning to bear the burden of souls and daily obtaining a knowledge of the most successful way of winning people to the truth. These men are frequently turned aside from the convictions of the Spirit of God and receive a worldly stamp of character, forgetting how much they owe to the Lord, who gave His life for them. They use their powers for their own selfish interests and refuse to labor in the vineyard of the Lord.

I was alarmed as I saw the various nets of Satan woven about men whom God would use, diverting them from the work of the ministry. There will surely be a dearth of laborers unless there is more encouragement given men to improve their ability with the purpose of becoming ministers of Christ. Satan is constantly and perseveringly presenting financial gain and worldly advantages to engage the minds and powers of men, and keep them from doing the duties essential to give them an experience in the things of God. And when he sees that men will move forward, giving themselves to the work of teaching the truth to those who are in darkness, he will do his utmost to push them to extremes in something that will weaken their influence and cause them to lose the advantage they would gain were they balanced by the Spirit of God.

I was shown that our ministers were doing themselves great injury by carelessness in the use of their vocal organs. Their attention was called to this important matter, and cautions and instructions were given them by the Spirit of God. It was their duty to learn the wisest manner of using these organs. The voice, this gift of heaven, is a powerful faculty for good, and if not perverted, would glorify God. All that was essential was to study and conscientiously follow a few simple rules. But instead of educating themselves, as they might have done by the exercise of a little common sense, they employed a professor of elocution.

As a result, many who were feeling that God had a work for them to do in teaching the truth to others, have become infatuated and crazed with elocution. All that certain ones needed was to have this temptation presented before them. Their interest was attracted by the novelty, and young men and

517

some ministers were carried away with this excitement. They left their fields of labor—everything in the vineyard of the Lord was neglected—and paid their money and gave their precious time to attend a school of elocution. When they came from this drill, devotion and religion had parted company with them, and the burden of souls was laid off, as they would lay aside a garment. They had accepted Satan's suggestions, and he had led them where he chose.

Some set themselves up as teachers of elocution, who had neither discretion nor ability, and they made themselves disgusting to the public, for they did not properly use what knowledge they had gained. Their performances were void of dignity or good sense; and these exploits on their part have closed the door, so far as they are known, to any influence that they may have in future as men to carry the message of truth to the world. This was Satan's device. It was well to make improvement in speaking; but to give time and money to this one branch, and absorb the mind with it, was rushing into extremes and showing great weakness.

Young men who call themselves Sabbathkeepers attach "professor" to their names and abuse the community with that which they do not understand. Many thus pervert the light which God has seen fit to give them. They have not well-balanced minds. Elocution has become a byword. It

has caught up men to engage in a work that they cannot do wisely, and spoiled them for doing a work which, had they been humbly and modestly seeking to accomplish it in the fear of God, they would have made a glorious success. These youth might have been fitting for usefulness in the missionary field as canvassers and colporteurs, or as licentiates proving themselves for ministerial labor, doing work for time and for eternity. But they have been crazed with the thought of becoming teachers of elocution, and Satan stands and laughs that he has caught them in the net which he has laid for them.

God's servants should ever be united. They should repress and control strong traits of character, and day by day they should carefully reflect upon the nature of the life structure they are building. Are they Christian gentlemen in their daily life? Are there seen in their lives noble, upright deeds, which will make their building of character stand forth as a fair temple of God? As one poor timber will sink a ship and one flaw make a chain worthless, so one demoralizing trait of character revealed in words or actions will leave its influence for evil, and if not overcome, will subvert every virtue.

Every faculty in man is a workman that is building for time and for eternity. Day by day the structure is going up, although the possessor is not aware of it. It is a building which must stand either as a beacon of warning because of its deformity or as a structure which God and angels will admire for its harmony with the divine Model. The mental and moral powers which God has given us do not constitute character. They are talents, which we are to improve, and which, if properly improved, will form a right character. A man may have precious seed in his hand, but that seed is not an orchard. The seed must be planted before it can become a tree. The mind is the garden, the character is the fruit. God has given us our faculties to cultivate and develop. Our own course determines our character. In training these powers so that they shall harmonize and form a valuable character, we have a work which no one but ourselves can do.

Those who have sharp, rough traits of character are guilty before God if they do not, by training, repress and root out all the bitterness of their nature. The man who yields to impatience is serving Satan. "To whom ye yield yourselves servants to obey, his servants ye are to whom ye obey." A good character is more precious in God's sight than the gold of Ophir. The Lord would have men act for time and for eternity. We have received good and bad as a legacy, and by cultivation we may make the bad worse or the good better. Shall the bad gain the ascendancy, as with Judas, or shall the evil be purged from our souls and the good predominate?

Principle, right, honesty, should ever be cherished. Honesty will not tarry where policy is harbored. They will never agree; one is of Baal, the other of God. The Master requires His servants to be honorable in motive and action. All greed and avarice must be overcome. Those who choose honesty as their companion will embody it in all their acts. To a large class, these men are not pleasing, but to God they are beautiful.

Satan is working to crowd himself in everywhere. He would put asunder very friends. There are men who are ever talking and gossiping and bearing false witness, who sow the seeds of discord and engender strife. Heaven looks upon this class as Satan's most efficient servants. But the man who is injured is in a far less dangerous position than when fawned upon and extolled for a few of his efforts which appear successful. The commendation of apparent friends is more dangerous than reproach.

Every man who praises himself brushes the luster from his best efforts. A truly noble character will not stoop to resent the false accusations of enemies; every word spoken falls harmless, for it strengthens that which it cannot overthrow. The Lord would have His people closely united with Himself, the God of patience and love. All should manifest in their lives the love of Christ. Let none venture to belittle the reputation or the position of another; this is egotism. It is saying: "I am so much better and more capable than you that God gives me the preference. You are not of much account."

Our ministers in responsible places are men whom God has accepted. No matter what their origin, no matter what their former position, whether they followed the plow, worked at the carpenter's trade, or enjoyed the discipline of a college; if God has accepted them, let every man beware of casting the slightest reflection upon them. Never speak disparagingly of any man, for he may be great in the sight of the Lord, while those who feel great may be lightly esteemed of God because of the perversity of their hearts. Our only safety is to lie low at the foot of the cross, be little in our own eyes, and trust in God; for He alone has power to make us great.

Our ministers are in danger of taking credit to themselves in the work which they do. They think God is favoring them, and they become independent and self-sufficient; then the Lord gives them up to the buffetings of Satan. In order to do God's work with acceptance, we must have the spirit of meekness, of lowliness of mind, each esteeming others better than himself. There is much at stake. The judgment and ability of all are needed now. Every man's work is of sufficient importance to demand that it be performed with care and fidelity. One man cannot do the work of all. Each has his respective place and his special work, and each should realize that the manner in which his work is done must stand the test of the judgment.

The work before us is important and extensive. The day of God is hastening on, and all the workers in the Lord's great field should be men who are striving to become perfect, wanting in nothing, coming behind in no gift, waiting for the appearing of the Son of man in the clouds of heaven. Not one moment of our precious time should be devoted to bringing others to conform to our personal ideas and opinions. God would educate men engaged as colaborers in this great work to the highest exercise of faith and the development of a harmonious character.

Men have varied gifts, and some are better adapted to one branch of the work than another. What one man would fail to do, his brother minister may be strong to accomplish. The work of each in his position is important. One man's mind is not to control another. If one man stands up, feeling that no one shall influence him, that he has judgment and ability to comprehend every branch of the work, that man will fail of the grace of God.

My husband has experience and qualities that are valuable, if these can be sanctified by the grace of Christ. God will make his labors wholly acceptable if he will imitate the Pattern.

God would have Elders Haskell, Butler, Whitney, and White come close to His side. These men may have precious qualities, but unless Christ is revealed in the character, these will be no more acceptable than the offering of Cain. His offering was good in itself, but there was no Saviour in it.

61. Love of the World

Dear Brethren and Sisters at ——: You are in a rich, beautiful country, where the bounties of God's providence have been scattered with a liberal hand; but unless they are wisely improved, these very blessings will prove a curse. Some of you are surfeited with the cares of this life, and some are becoming drunken with the spirit of the world. Your position is one of danger. Especially is this the case with the youth among you. Parents have not closely connected with God so that they could labor intelligently, in His Spirit and power, for the conversion of their children. Continual talk will not convert them. Reproof and restraint are frequently necessary; but these are often carried too far, especially when vital godliness is not exemplified in the life of those who administer the reproof.

Our words and actions constitute the fruit we bear. A consecrated life is a daily, living sermon. But inward piety and true devotion are fast giving place to outward forms. Pure and undefiled religion is the great need of the church at ——. They should make it an individual work to draw near to God. No one can be saved by proxy, but every man and woman must work out their own salvation with fear and trembling. Satan has much more power over some who profess the truth than many realize. Self reigns in the heart, instead of Christ. Self-will, self-interest, envy, and pride shut out the presence of God.

The love of God must pervade the soul, or the fruits of righteousness will not appear. It is not safe to indulge in vanity and pride, or love of power or gain. It is the worst phase of selfishness to fret and censure and complain because you have the power to do this and those whom you abuse in this way cannot prevent you. It is selfishness that causes variance in the family circle and in the church. Unchristian hearts will think they can discern great wrongs in others where none exist and will dwell upon little matters until they appear greatly magnified. The work of adjusting these little matters, which seem so large to some, God has left for His followers themselves to do. Let not those unhappy differences remain till they become a root of bitterness in the church, whereby many will be defiled. When Christ is in the heart it will be so softened and subdued by love for God and man that fretting, faultfinding, and contention will not exist there. The religion of Christ in the heart will gain for its possessor a complete victory over those passions that are seeking for the mastery.

Said Christ: "Seek ye first the kingdom of God, and His righteousness; and all these [needed] things shall be added unto you." This promise will never fail. We cannot enjoy the favor of God unless we comply with the conditions upon which His favor is bestowed. By so doing there will come to us that peace, contentment, and wisdom that the world can neither give nor take away. If you would, as a church, secure the rich blessing of God, you must individually make Him first and last and best in every thought, plan, and work. Obedience to God is the first duty of the Christian. A humble mind and a grateful heart will elevate us above petty trials and real difficulties. The less earnest, energetic, and vigilant we are in the service of the Master, the more will the mind dwell upon self, magnifying molehills into mountains of difficulty. We shall feel that we are abused, when no disrespect even was designed.

The burden of God's work, laid upon Moses, made him a man of power. While keeping, for so many years, the flocks of Jethro, he gained an experience that taught him true humility. But God's call found Moses, as it will find us, inefficient, hesitating, and self-distrustful. The command to deliver Israel seemed overwhelming; but, in the fear of God, Moses accepted the trust. Mark the result: He did not bring the work down to his deficiency; but in the strength of God he put forth the most earnest efforts to elevate and sanctify himself for his sacred mission.

Moses would never have been prepared for his position of trust had he waited for God to do the work for him. Light from heaven will come to those who feel the need of it, and who seek for it as for hidden treasures. But if we sink down into a state of inactivity, willing to be controlled by Satan's power, God will not send His inspiration to us. Unless we exert to the utmost the powers which He has given us, we shall ever remain weak and inefficient. Much prayer and the most vigorous exercise of the mind are necessary if we would be prepared to do the work which God would entrust to us. Many never attain to the position which they might occupy, because they wait for God to do for them that which He has given them power to do for themselves. All who are fitted for usefulness in this life must be trained by the severest mental and moral discipline, and then God will assist them by combining divine power with human effort.

Many in —— will fail because they do not keep up with the advancement of the work, and do not properly represent in their daily life the sanctification of the truth. They do not, like Moses, bring their life up to meet the exalted standard. If they had done this, many more would now be added to their numbers, rejoicing in the truth. It is a fearful thing to lead souls away from Christ by our unsanctified life.

Our religion must be something more than a head religion. It must affect the heart, and then it will have a correcting influence upon the life. Wrong habits are not overcome by a single effort. Only through long and severe struggles is self mastered. This self-training must be taken up by the individual members of the church, and the rubbish which has accumulated around the door of the heart must be removed, ere they can serve God with singleness of purpose, adorning their profession by a well-ordered life and a godly conversation. Then, and not till then, can they teach sinners the truth and win souls to Christ.

There are men in this church who feel that they should teach the truth to others, while they are fretful, impatient, and faultfinding in their own families. Such need that one teach them, until they become patient, God-fearing men at home. They need to learn the first principles of true religion. They should seek God with earnestness of soul, for they have been a scourge in their families and as a desolating hail to depress and destroy their brethren. These men do not deserve the name of husband, "house band;" for they do not bind the family together with the Christian love, sympathy, and true dignity of a godly life and Christlike character.

The solemn, sacred truth—the testing message given us of God to communicate to the world—lays every one of us under the strongest obligation to so transform our daily life and character that the power of the truth may be well represented. We should have a continual sense of the shortness of time and of the fearful events which prophecy has declared must speedily take place. It is because these truths are not made a reality that the life is so inconsistent with the truth which we profess.

Many hide in the earth talents which should be invested where they will be accumulating to be returned to God when He shall say: "Give an account of thy stewardship." Moses became great because he used his talents to do the work of God, and an increase of talents was then given him. He became eloquent, patient, self-reliant, and competent to do the greatest work ever entrusted to mortal man. This is the effect upon character whenever men give themselves to God with the whole soul, and listen for His commands that they may obey them.

Willing obedience to God's requirements gives vital energy and power to the soul. A work enduring as the sun is done for the worker as well as for those for whom he labors. However limited the capacity of the one who engages in this work, the labor which he performs in his humble sphere will be acceptable to God.

"Not everyone that saith unto Me, Lord, Lord, shall enter into the kingdom of heaven; but he that doeth the will of My Father which is in heaven. Many will say to Me in that day, Lord, Lord, have we not prophesied in Thy name? and in Thy name have cast out devils? and in Thy name done many wonderful works? And then will I profess unto them, I never knew you: depart from Me, ye that work iniquity. Therefore whosoever heareth these sayings of Mine, and doeth them, I will liken him unto a wise man, which built his house upon a rock: and the rain descended, and the floods came, and the winds blew, and beat upon that house; and it fell not: for it was founded upon a rock. And everyone that heareth these sayings of Mine, and doeth them not, shall be likened unto a foolish man, which built his house upon the sand: and the rain descended, and the floods came, and the winds blew, and beat upon that house; and it fell: and great was the fall of it."

The reason why our people have not more power is that they profess the truth, but do not practice it. They have but little faith and trust in God. There are but few who bear the burdens connected with His work. The Lord claims the strength of brain, bone, and muscle; but it is too often withheld from Him and given to the world. The service of God is made a secondary matter, while worldly interests receive prompt attention. Thus things of minor consequence are made important, while the requirements of God, things spiritual and eternal, are treated in an indifferent manner, as something which may be taken up at will and let alone at pleasure. If the mind were stayed upon God and the truth exerted a sanctifying influence upon the heart, self would be hid in Christ. If we realize the importance of the truth which we profess to believe we should feel that we have a sacred mission to fulfill, a responsibility involving eternal results. All temporal interests would yield to this.

Brethren in ——, you do not realize your obligation to God and the individual work He has given you to perform for Him. You have the theory of the truth, but do not feel its power in the soul. The barren fig tree flaunted its pretentious branches in the face of heaven; but when the search for fruit was made by the Redeemer, lo, there was nothing but leaves. Unless there is a thorough work wrought for you as individuals and as a church, the curse of God will as surely come upon you as it fell upon that fruitless tree.

The members of the —— church possess talents which would be valuable if put to a right use. The weak man may become strong, the timid may become brave, and the irresolute and undecided may become men of quick and firm decision, when they feel that God considers them of sufficient consequence to accept their labors.

Men in this church must feel that God wishes them to become laborers in His cause in any capacity. Unless they change their course, some will be found in a position similar to that of the Pharisees when Christ addressed them: "The publicans and the harlots go into the kingdom of God before you."

Many feel secure because they profess the truth, while they do not feel its sanctifying influence upon their hearts and do not advance in the divine life.

Brethren, while you as a people profess to have light far in advance of other denominations, your works do not correspond with your profession. Many who have been in the darkness of error gladly accept the truth when it is opened to their understanding. Although they have spent their life in sin, yet when they come to God in penitence and with a sense of their sinfulness they are accepted of Him. Such persons are in a more favorable position for the perfection of Christian character than are those who have had great light and have failed to improve upon it. That which leaves men and women in darkness is their neglect to improve the light and opportunities granted them. Christ hates all vain pretense. When on earth, He ever treated with tenderness the penitent, even though they had been the chief of sinners; but His denunciations fell heavily upon all hypocrisy.

God has given to every man his work, and no one else can do that work for him. Oh, that you individually would apply the eyesalve, that you might see your defects of character and realize how God regards your love of the world, which is crowding out the love of God. Nothing can give you such power, such true self-reliance and nobility of soul, as a sense of the dignity of your work, an assurance that you are co-laborers with God in doing good and saving souls.

The Son of God came to this world to leave an example of a perfect life. He sacrificed Himself for the joy that was set before Him, the joy of seeing souls rescued from Satan's grasp and saved in the kingdom of God. "Follow Me" was Christ's command. Those who follow His example will share in the divine work of doing good and will finally enter into the joy of their Lord.

There is many a man in the humble walks of life today whom the Lord might designate as He did Abraham: "The friend of God." Such men approve that which God approves and condemn that which He condemns. In their presence even the sinner feels a sense of awe, a restraint; for God is with them, and they are living epistles, known and read of all men. There is a softened tenderness, a dignity, a divine propriety, in their deportment, which gives them power over the hearts of their fellow men.

In following Christ, looking unto Him who is the Author and Finisher of your faith, you will feel that you are working under His eye, that you are influenced by His presence, and that He knows your motives. At every step you will humbly inquire: Will this please Jesus? Will it glorify God? Morning and evening your earnest prayers should ascend to God for His blessing and guidance. True prayer takes hold upon Omnipotence and gives us the victory. Upon his knees the Christian obtains strength to resist temptation.

The father who is the "house band" of the family will bind his children to the throne of God by living faith. Distrusting his own strength, he hangs his helpless soul on Jesus and takes hold of the strength of the Most High. Brethren, pray at home, in your family, night and morning; pray earnestly in your closet; and while engaged in your daily labor, lift up the soul to God in prayer. It was thus that Enoch walked with God. The silent, fervent prayer of the soul will rise like holy incense to the throne of grace and will be as acceptable to God as if offered in the sanctuary. To all who thus seek Him, Christ becomes a present help in time of need. They will be strong in the day of trial.

The word of God is a lamp to our feet and a light to our path. "Thy word have I hid in mine heart, that I might not sin against Thee." The heart preoccupied with the word of God is fortified against Satan. Those who make Christ their daily companion and familiar friend will feel that the powers of an unseen world are all around them; and by looking unto Jesus they will become assimilated to His image. By beholding they become changed to the divine pattern; their character is softened, refined, and ennobled for the heavenly kingdom.

When a true, earnest zeal is manifested in your character and works, brethren of the —— church, unbelievers will see by your deportment, and feel in your presence, that you have a peace of which they have no knowledge, a serenity to which they are strangers. They will believe that you are working for God, for your works will be wrought in Him. I was shown that this is the characteristic of a Christian. Satan has destroyed many souls by leading them to place themselves in the way of temptation. He comes to them as he came to Christ, tempting them to love the world. He tells them that they may invest with profit in this or that enterprise, and in good faith they follow his dictation.

Soon they are tempted to swerve from their integrity in order to make as good bargains for themselves as possible. Their course may be perfectly lawful according to the world's standard of right and yet not bear the test of the law of God. Their motives are called in question by their brethren, and they are suspected of over-reaching to serve themselves and thus is sacrificed that precious influence which should have been sacredly guarded for the benefit of the cause of God. That business which might be a financial success in the hands of a sharper who will sell his integrity for worldly gain would be entirely inappropriate for a follower of Christ.

All such speculations are attended with unseen trials and difficulties, and are a fearful ordeal for those who engage in them. Circumstances often occur which naturally cause reflections to be cast upon the motives of these brethren; but although some things may look decidedly wrong, these should not always be considered a true test of character. Yet they often prove to be the turning point in one's experience and destiny. The character becomes transformed by the force of circumstances under which the individual has placed himself.

I was shown that it is a dangerous experiment for our people to engage in speculation. They thereby place themselves on the enemy's ground, subject to great temptations, disappointments, trials, and losses. Then comes a feverish unrest, a longing desire to obtain means more rapidly than present circumstances will admit. Their surroundings are accordingly changed in hope of making more money. But frequently their expectations are not realized, and they become discouraged and go backward rather than forward.

This has been the case with some in ———. They are backsliding from God. Had the Lord prospered some of our dear brethren in their speculations, it would have proved their eternal ruin. God loves His people, and He loves those who have been unfortunate. If they will learn the lessons which He intends to teach them, their defeat will in the end prove a precious victory. The love of the world has crowded out the love of Christ. When the rubbish is cleared away from the door of the heart, and it is thrown open in response to the invitation of Christ, He will come in and take possession of the soul-temple. Had these words of the apostle been more carefully regarded, much trial would have been saved:

"Let your conversation be without covetousness; and be content with such things as ye have: for He hath said, I will never leave thee, nor forsake thee." "But godliness with contentment is great gain. For we brought nothing into this world, and it is certain we can carry nothing out. And having food and raiment let us be therewith content. But they that will be rich fall into temptation and a snare, and into many foolish and hurtful lusts, which drown men in destruction and perdition. For the love of money is the root of all evil: which while some coveted after, they have erred from the faith, and pierced themselves through with many sorrows. But thou, O man of God, flee these things; and follow after righteousness, godliness, faith, love, patience, meekness. Fight the good fight of faith, lay hold on eternal life, whereunto thou art also called, and hast professed a good profession before many witnesses."

The present is our day of trust. To every person is committed some peculiar gift or talent which is to be used to advance the Redeemer's kingdom. All God's responsible agents, from the lowliest and most obscure to those in high positions in the church, are entrusted with the Lord's goods. It is not the minister alone who can work for the salvation of souls. Those who have the smallest gifts are not excused from using the very best gifts they have, and in so doing their talents will be increased. It is not safe to trifle with moral responsibilities nor to despise the day of small things. God's providence proportions His trusts according to the varied capabilities of the people. None should mourn because they cannot glorify God with talents which they never possessed and for which they are not responsible.

One great cause of weakness in the —— church has been that, instead of improving their talents to the glory of God, they have wrapped them in a napkin and buried them in the world. Although some may be restricted to one talent, yet if they will exercise that one, it will increase. God values the service according to what a man has and not according to what he has not. If we perform our daily duties with fidelity and love we shall receive the approval of the Master as if we had performed a greater work. We must cease longing to do great service and to trade on large talents, while we have been made accountable only for small talents and the performance of humble duties. In overlooking the small daily duties, and reaching for higher responsibilities, we utterly fail to do the very work which God has given us.

Oh, that I might impress upon this church the fact that Christ has claims upon their service! My brethren and sisters, have you become servants of Christ? Then if you devote the most of your time to serving yourselves, what answer will you give the Master when He shall bid you render an account of your stewardship? The talents entrusted to us are not ours, be they talents of property, of strength, or of mental ability. If we abuse any or all of these, we shall be justly condemned for our unworthy stewardship. How great are the obligations resting upon us to render to God the things that are His.

Unless this church shall arouse from their lethargy and shake off the spirit of the world, they will mourn when, too late, they find their opportunities and privileges lost, lost forever. The Lord sometimes tests His people with prosperity in temporal things. But He intends that they shall make a right use of His gifts. Their property, their time, their strength, and their opportunities are all of God. For all these blessings they must account to the Giver. While want and destitution are seen among our brethren, and we withhold relief from them when our own necessities are supplied, we neglect a plain duty revealed in the word of God. He gives to us liberally that we may give to others. It is beneficence that overcomes selfishness and ennobles and purifies the soul.

Some abuse the talents given them of God; they close their eyes that they may not see the necessities of His cause and turn away their ears that they may not hear His voice showing them their duty to feed the hungry and clothe the naked. Some who profess to be children of God seem anxious to invest their means in the world lest it shall return to the Giver in gifts and offerings. They forget their divine mission, and if they continue to follow the dictates of their selfish hearts, and expend precious time and means to gratify their pride, God will send reverses, and they will feel pinching want because of their ingratitude. He will entrust His talents to more faithful stewards, who will acknowledge His claims upon them.

Wealth is a power with which to do good or to do evil. If it is rightly used it becomes a source of continual gratitude, because the gifts of God are appreciated and the Giver acknowledged by using them as God intended they should be used. Those who rob God by withholding from His cause and from the suffering poor will meet His retributive justice. Our heavenly Father, who has given us in trust every good gift, pities our ignorance, our frailty, and our hopeless condition. In order to save us from death, He freely gave His beloved Son. He claims from us all that we claim as our own. A neglect of His suffering poor is a neglect of Christ, for He tells us that the poor are His representatives on earth. Pity and benevolence shown to them are accepted of Christ as if shown to Him.

When the Lord's poor are neglected and forgotten or greeted with cold looks and cruel words, let the guilty one bear in mind that he is neglecting Christ in the person of His saints. Our Saviour identifies His interest with that of suffering humanity. As the heart of the parent yearns with pitying tenderness over the suffering one of her little flock, so the heart of our Redeemer sympathizes with the poorest and lowliest of His earthly children. He has placed them among us to awaken in our hearts that love which He feels toward the suffering and oppressed, and He will let His judgments fall upon anyone who wrongs, slights, or abuses them.

Let us consider that Jesus took all the woes and griefs, the poverty and suffering, of man into His own heart and made them a part of His own experience. Although He was the Prince of life, He did not take His position with the great and honorable, but with the lowly, the oppressed, and the suffering. He was the despised Nazarene. He had not where to lay His head. He became poor for our sakes, that we through His poverty might be made rich. He is now the King of glory, and should He come crowned with majesty, millions would do Him homage. All would vie with one another in bestowing honors upon Him; all would plead to be found in His presence. An opportunity is now granted us to receive Christ in the person of His saints. God wants you to appreciate His gifts and use them to His glory. I entreat you to open your hearts to true and disinterested benevolence.

Dear brethren, as a church you have sadly neglected your duty toward the children and youth. While rules and restrictions are laid upon them, great care should be taken to show them the Christlike side of your character and not the satanic side. Children need constant watchcare and tender love. Bind them to your hearts, and keep the love as well as the fear of God before them. Fathers and mothers do not control their own spirit and therefore are not fit to govern others.

To restrain and caution your children is not all that is required. You have yet to learn to do justly and love mercy, as well as to walk humbly with God. Everything leaves its impress upon the youthful mind. The countenance is studied, the voice has its influence, and the deportment is closely imitated by them. Fretful and peevish fathers and mothers are giving their children lessons which at some period in their lives they would give all the world, were it theirs, could they unlearn. Children must see in the lives of their parents that consistency which is in accordance with their faith. By leading a consistent life and exercising self-control, parents may mold the characters of their children.

Too many cares and burdens are brought into our families, and too little of natural simplicity and peace and happiness is cherished. There should be less care for what the outside world will say and more thoughtful attention to the members of the family circle. There should be less display and affectation of worldly politeness, and much more tenderness and love, cheerfulness and Christian courtesy, among the members of the household. Many need to learn how to make home attractive, a place of enjoyment. Thankful hearts and kind looks are more valuable than wealth and luxury, and contentment with simple things will make home happy if love be there.

Jesus, our Redeemer, walked the earth with the dignity of a king; yet He was meek and lowly of heart. He was a light and blessing in every home because He carried cheerfulness, hope, and courage with Him. Oh, that we could be satisfied with less heart longings, less striving for things difficult to obtain wherewith to beautify our homes, while that which God values above jewels, the meek and quiet spirit, is not cherished. The grace of simplicity, meekness, and true affection would make a paradise of the humblest home. It is better to endure cheerfully every inconvenience than to part with peace and contentment.

You greatly need to humble your hearts before God as you see the sad condition of your children, without God and without hope in the world. They do not appreciate and reverence sacred things because common, worldly affairs have been placed on a level with eternal interests. There are youth among you whose service God will accept if they will yield their hearts to Him and connect with Him, as did Daniel and his fellows. But few have a true idea of the peril surrounding the youth of today. It requires a great amount of moral courage, and a constant resistance of temptation, to reach a noble manhood. A character unsullied before God is rare. Many who have not the fear of God before them, and whose feet are in the broad road to death, are waiting to be the companions of your children. I wish I could make the youth see and feel their danger, especially the danger of making unhappy marriages.

A little time spent in sowing your wild oats, dear young friends, will produce a crop that will embitter your whole life; an hour of thoughtlessness, once yielding to temptation, may turn the whole current of your life in the wrong direction. You can have but one youth; make that useful. When once you have passed over the ground you can never return to rectify your mistakes. He who refuses to connect with God, and puts himself in the way of temptation, will surely fall. God is testing every youth. Many have excused their carelessness and irreverence because of the wrong example given them by more experienced professors. But this should not deter any from rightdoing. In the day of final accounts you will plead no such excuses as you plead now. You will be justly condemned because you knew the way but did not choose to walk in it.

Satan, that archdeceiver, transforms himself into an angel of light and comes to the youth with his specious temptations and succeeds in winning them, step by step, from the path of duty. He is described as an accuser, a deceiver, a liar, a tormentor, and a murderer. "He that committeth sin is of the devil." Every transgression brings the soul into condemnation and provokes the divine displeasure. The thoughts of the heart are discerned of God. When impure thoughts are cherished, they need not be expressed by word or act to consummate the sin and bring the soul into condemnation. Its purity is defiled, and the tempter has triumphed.

Every man is tempted when he is drawn away of his own lusts and enticed. He is turned away from the course of virtue and real good by following his own inclinations. If the youth possessed moral integrity, the strongest temptations might be presented in vain. It is Satan's act to tempt you, but your own act to yield. It is not in the power of all the host of Satan to force the tempted to transgress. There is no excuse for sin.

While some of the youth are wasting their powers in vanity and folly, others are disciplining their minds, storing up knowledge, girding on the armor to engage in life's warfare, determined to make it a success. But they cannot make life a success, however high they may attempt to climb, unless they center their affections upon God. If they will turn to the Lord with all the heart, rejecting the flatteries of those who would in the slightest degree weaken their purpose to do right, they will have strength and confidence in God.

Those who love society frequently indulge this trait until it becomes an overruling passion. To dress, to visit places of amusement, to laugh and chat upon subjects altogether lighter than vanity—this is the object of their lives. They cannot endure to read the Bible and contemplate heavenly things. They are miserable unless there is something to excite. They have not within them the power to be happy, but they depend for happiness upon the company of other youth as thoughtless and reckless as themselves. The powers which might be turned to noble purposes they give to folly and mental dissipation.

The youth who finds joy and happiness in reading the word of God and in the hour of prayer is constantly refreshed by drafts from the Fountain of life. He will attain a height of moral excellence and a breadth of thought of which others cannot conceive. Communion with God encourages good thoughts, noble aspirations, clear perceptions of truth, and lofty purposes of action. Those who thus connect their souls with God are acknowledged by Him as His sons and daughters. They are constantly reaching higher and still higher, obtaining clearer views of God and of eternity, until the Lord makes them channels of light and wisdom to the world.

Some of the youth in——are in a hardened state of sin; they are coarse, uncourteous, rough, and rebellious. They have had great light, and have rejected it. If they now choose the way of peace, they must do so from principle rather than from feeling. Sin and holiness can make no compromise. The Bible contains no sanction of ungodliness, no sweet words of forbearance and charity for the persistently impenitent. Jesus came to draw all men unto Himself, and His followers must walk in the light of His glorious example, at whatever sacrifice of ease or reputation, at whatever peril of property or life. In this way only can they fight the good fight of faith.

A pearl of great price is offered to the youth. They may sell all and buy this pearl, or they may refuse it to their own infinite loss. Heaven may be attained by all who will comply with the conditions laid down in the word of God. Our Redeemer was obedient unto death; He gave Himself an offering for sin. Ye are redeemed with the precious blood of Christ, as of a lamb without blemish. "The blood of Jesus Christ His Son cleanseth us from all sin."

Young friends, you may form earnest purposes in your own strength, you may flatter yourselves that you can pursue a straightforward course without yielding the heart to the controlling influence of the Spirit of God; but you are not thus made happy. Your restless spirit needs change and thirsts for pleasure in amusement and hilarity and the society of your young associates. You are hewing out to yourselves broken cisterns which contain no water. A deceptive power controls your mind and actions. Happiness is to be found only in repentance toward God and faith toward our Lord Jesus Christ; for your heart is filled with rebellion; it breathes forth in your words. Your selfish prayers and religious forms may soothe the conscience, but they only increase your peril. Your nature is unrenewed.

The precious blood of Jesus is the fountain prepared to cleanse the soul from the defilement of sin. When you determine to take Him as your friend, a new and enduring light will shine from the cross of Christ. A true sense of the sacrifice and intercession of the dear Saviour will break the heart that has become hardened in sin; and love, thankfulness, and humility will come into the soul. The surrender of the heart to Jesus subdues the rebel into a penitent, and then the language of the obedient soul is: Old things are passed away; behold, all things are become new. This is the true religion of the Bible. Everything short of this is a deception.

The youth have not realized that freedom and light can be retained only through self-denial and constant watchfulness and prayer, with a continual reliance upon the merits of the blood of Christ. When the Holy Spirit is breathing upon the soul, the will and the powers of the man must respond to Its influence. Those who abide in Jesus will be happy, cheerful, and joyful in God. A subdued gentleness will mark the voice, reverence for spiritual and eternal things will be expressed in the actions, and music, joyful music, will echo from the lips; for it is wafted from the throne of God.

This is the mystery of godliness, not easily explained, but nonetheless felt and enjoyed. A stubborn and rebellious heart can close its doors to all the sweet influences of the grace of God and all the joy in the Holy Ghost; but the ways of wisdom are ways of pleasantness, and all her paths are peace. The more closely we are connected with Christ, the more will our words and actions show the subduing, transforming power of His grace.

I appeal to the youth at —— to consider their ways and change their course of action before it shall be too late. Some of you pride yourselves on your capabilities; but the more valuable the talents entrusted to your keeping, the greater will be your condemnation if these gifts of heaven are employed in the service of Satan. God can do without you, but you cannot do without God. It is you who will suffer without Jesus. The commands of God are as briers and thorns to some of the youth in ——. Their knowledge of the truth makes it hard for them to indulge in sinful pleasures, for they cannot altogether put out of the mind the claims of God upon them. There is a feeling of impatience at the restraint which is thus imposed. They try to get away from this admonitory voice; but they find themselves kicking against the pricks, piercing themselves through with many sorrows. Oh, that they would come to the Fountain of living waters before they shall have grieved away the Spirit of God for the last time!

A few words more to the church members. Said Christ: "If any man will come after Me, let him deny himself, and take up his cross, and follow Me." We are not to make crosses for ourselves, by wearing sackcloth, by pinching our bodies, or by denying ourselves wholesome, nourishing food. We are not to shut ourselves in monasteries, away from the world, and do no good to our fellow beings, thinking this is the cross of Christ; neither are we required to expose health and life unnecessarily, nor to go mourning up the hill of Christian life, feeling it a sin to be cheerful, contented, happy, and joyful. These are all self-made crosses, but not the cross of Christ.

To bear the cross of Christ is to control our sinful passions, to practice Christian courtesy even when it is inconvenient to do so, to see the wants of the needy and distressed and deny ourselves in order to relieve them, and to open our hearts and our doors to the homeless orphan, although to do this may tax our means and our patience. Such children are younger members of God's family and are to receive love and care, and to be brought up in the nurture and admonition of the Lord. This is a cross which, if lifted and cheerfully borne for Christ, will prove a diadem of glory in the kingdom of God.

Brethren, for Christ's sake fill up your lives with good works, even though the world does not appreciate your efforts and gives you no credit. This is self-denial. Selfishness is the most galling yoke the members of the church ever placed upon their necks, but there is much of it cherished by those who profess to be Christ's followers. All you have belongs to God. Be guarded, lest you selfishly hoard the bounties He has given you for the widow and the fatherless. Christ left His glory, His honor, His high command, and for our sakes became poor, that we through His poverty might be made rich. Now the question comes home: What will we individually do for Jesus, who gave His life for a ruined world?

62. Simplicity in Dress

In His Sermon on the Mount Christ exhorts His followers not to allow their minds to be absorbed in earthly things. He plainly says: Ye cannot serve God and mammon. Therefore I say unto you, "Take no thought for your life, what ye shall eat, or what ye shall drink; nor yet for your body, what ye shall put on. Is not the life more than meat, and the body than raiment?" "And why take ye thought for raiment? Consider the lilies of the field, how they grow; they toil not, neither do they spin: and yet I say unto you, That even Solomon in all his glory was not arrayed like one of these."

These words are full of meaning. They were applicable in the days of Christ, and they are applicable in our day. Jesus here contrasts the natural simplicity of the flowers of the field with the artificial adorning of raiment. He declares that the glory of Solomon could not bear comparison with one of the flowers in natural loveliness. Here is a lesson for all who desire to know and to do the will of God. Jesus has noticed the care and devotion given to dress, and has cautioned, yea, commanded, us not to bestow too much thought upon it. It is important that we give careful heed to His words.

Solomon was so engrossed with thoughts of outward display that he failed to elevate his mind by a constant connection with the God of wisdom. Perfection and beauty of character were overlooked in his attempt to obtain outward beauty. He sold his honor and integrity of character in seeking to glorify himself before the world, and finally became a despot, supporting his extravagance by a grinding taxation upon the people. He first became corrupt at heart, then he apostatized from God, and finally became a worshiper of idols.

As we see our sisters departing from simplicity in dress, and cultivating a love for the fashions of the world, we feel troubled. By taking steps in this direction they are separating themselves from God and neglecting the inward adorning. They should not feel at liberty to spend their God-given time in the unnecessary ornamentation of their clothing. How much better might it be employed in searching the Scriptures, thus obtaining a thorough knowledge of the prophecies and of the practical lessons of Christ.

As Christians, we ought not to engage in any employment upon which we cannot conscientiously ask the blessing of the Lord. Do you, my sisters, in the needless work you put upon your garments, feel a clear conscience? Can you, while perplexing the mind over ruffles and bows and ribbons, be uplifting the soul to God in prayer that He will bless your efforts? The time spent in this way might be devoted to doing good to others and to cultivating your own minds.

Many of our sisters are persons of good ability, and if their talents were used to the glory of God they would be successful in winning many souls to Christ. Will they not be responsible for the souls they might have saved had not extravagance in dress and the cares of this world so crippled and dwarfed their God-given powers that they felt no burden of the work? Satan invented the fashions in order to keep the minds of women so engrossed with the subject of dress that they could think of but little else.

The duties devolving upon mothers to bring up their children in the nurture and admonition of the Lord cannot be discharged while they continue their present manner of dress. They have no time to pray or to search the Scriptures that they may understand the truth and teach it to their children. It is not only the privilege but the duty of everyone to increase daily in the knowledge of God and the truth. But Satan's object is gained if he can invent anything which shall so attract the mind that this cannot be the case.

The reason why so many are not desirous of attending prayer meeting and of engaging in religious exercises is that their minds are devoted to other things. They are conforming to the world in the matter of dress; and while they are so doing, souls whom they might have helped by letting their light shine in good works are strengthened in their unbelief by the inconsistent course of these professed Christians.

God would be pleased to see our sisters clad in neat, simple apparel and earnestly engaged in the work of the Lord. They are not deficient in ability, and if they would put to a right use the talents they already have, their efficiency would be greatly increased. If the time they now spend in needless work were devoted to searching the word of God and explaining it to others, their own minds would be enriched with gems of truth, and they would be strengthened and ennobled by the effort made to understand the reasons of our faith. Were our sisters conscientious Bible Christians, seeking to improve every opportunity to enlighten others, we should see scores of souls embracing the truth through their self-sacrificing endeavors alone. Sisters, in the day when the accounts of all are balanced, will you feel a pleasure in reviewing your life, or will you feel that the beauty of the outward man was sought, while the inward beauty of the soul was almost entirely neglected?

Have not our sisters sufficient zeal and moral courage to place themselves without excuse upon the Bible platform? The apostle has given most explicit directions on this point: I will therefore . . . that women adorn themselves in modest apparel, with shamefacedness and sobriety; not with broided hair, or gold, or pearls, or costly array; but (which becometh women professing godliness) with good works. Here the Lord, through His apostle, speaks expressly against the wearing of gold. Let those who have had experience see to it that they do not lead others astray on this point by their example. That ring encircling your finger may be very plain, but it is useless, and the wearing of it has a wrong influence upon others.

Especially should the wives of our ministers be careful not to depart from the plain teachings of the Bible on the point of dress. Many look upon these injunctions as too old-fashioned to be worthy of notice; but He who gave them to His disciples understood the dangers from the love of dress in our time and sent to us the note of warning. Will we heed the warning and be wise? Extravagance in dress is continually increasing. The end is not yet. Fashion is constantly changing, and our sisters follow in its wake, regardless of time or expense. There is a great amount of means expended upon dress, when it should be returned to God the giver.

The plain, neat dress of the poorer class often appears in marked contrast with the attire of their more wealthy sisters, and this difference frequently causes a feeling of embarrassment on the part of the poor. Some try to imitate their more wealthy sisters, and frill and ruffle and trim goods of an inferior quality so as to approach as nearly as possible to them in dress. Poor girls, receiving but two dollars a week for their work, will expend every cent to dress like others who are not obliged to earn their own living. These youth have nothing to put into the treasury of God. And their time is so thoroughly occupied in making their dress as fashionable as that of their sisters that they have no time for the improvement of the mind, for the study of God's word, for secret prayer, or for the prayer meeting. The mind is entirely taken up with planning how to appear as well as their sisters. To accomplish this end, physical, mental, and moral health is sacrificed. Happiness and the favor of God are laid upon the altar of fashion.

Many will not attend the service of God upon the Sabbath because their dress would appear so unlike that of their Christian sisters in style and adornment. Will my sisters consider these things as they are, and will they fully realize the weight of their influence upon others? By walking in a forbidden path themselves, they lead others in the same way of disobedience and backsliding. Christian simplicity is sacrificed to outward display. My sisters, how shall we change all this? How shall we recover ourselves from the snare of Satan and break the chains that have bound us in slavery to fashion? How shall we recover our wasted opportunities? how bring our powers into healthful, vigorous action?

There is only one way, and that is to make the Bible our rule of life. All should work earnestly to do good to others, watch unto prayer, take up the long-neglected cross, and heed the warnings and injunctions of Him who has said: "Whosoever will come after Me, let him deny himself, and take up his cross, and follow Me."

My Christian sisters, face the mirror, the law of God, and test your course of action by the first four commandments. These explicitly define our duty to God. He claims the undivided affections; and anything which tends to absorb the mind and divert it from God assumes the form of an idol. The true and living God is crowded out of the thoughts and heart, and the soul-temple is defiled by the worship of other gods before the Lord. "Thou shalt have no other gods before Me," says the commandment. Let us search the heart, compare the life and character with the statutes and precepts of Jehovah, and then seek diligently to correct our errors.

The last six commandments specify the duties of man to his fellow men. Here are brought to view solemn obligations which are trampled upon every day by professed commandment keepers. Those who have been enlightened by the grace of God, who have been adopted into the royal family, ought not always to be children in the work of the Lord. If they wisely improve upon the grace given, their capacity will increase and their knowledge become more extensive, and they will be entrusted with a still greater measure of divine power. In putting forth earnest, well-directed efforts to bring their fellow men to a knowledge of the truth, they will become strong in the Lord; and for working righteousness on the earth, they will receive the reward of eternal life in the kingdom of heaven. This is the privilege of our sisters. And when we see them using God's time and money in needless display of dress we cannot but warn them that they are breaking not only the first four, but the last six commandments. They do not make God the supreme object of their worship, neither do they love their neighbor as themselves.

Christ is our example. We must keep the Pattern continually before us and contemplate the infinite sacrifice which has been made to redeem us from the thralldom of sin. If we find ourselves condemned as we look into the mirror, let us not venture further in transgression, but face rightabout and wash our robes of character in the blood of the Lamb, that they may be spotless. Let us cry, as did David: "Open Thou mine eyes, that I may behold wondrous things out of Thy law." Those to whom God has entrusted time and means that they might be a blessing to humanity, but who have squandered these gifts needlessly upon themselves and their children, will have a fearful account to meet at the bar of God.

"For, behold, the day cometh, that shall burn as an oven; and all the proud, yea, and all that do wickedly, shall be stubble: and the day that cometh shall burn them up, saith the Lord of hosts, that it shall leave them neither root nor branch." The unbelieving world will soon have something to think of besides their dress and appearance; and as their minds are torn from these things by distress and perplexity, they have nothing to turn to. They are not prisoners of hope, and therefore do not turn to the Stronghold. Their hearts will fail them with repining and fear. They have not made God their refuge, and He will not be their consolation. He will laugh at their calamity and mock when their fear cometh.

Those among Sabbathkeepers who have yielded to the influence of the world are to be tested. The perils of the last days are upon us, and a trial is before the professed people of God which many have not anticipated. The genuineness of their faith will be proved. Many have united with worldlings in pride, vanity, and pleasure seeking, flattering themselves that they could do this and still be Christians. But it is such indulgences that separate them from God and make them children of the world. Christ has given us no such example. Those only who deny self, and live a life of sobriety, humility, and holiness, are true followers of Jesus; and such cannot enjoy the society of the lovers of the world.

Many dress like the world in order to have an influence over unbelievers, but here they make a sad mistake. If they would have a true and saving influence, let them live out their profession, show their faith by their righteous works, and make the distinction plain between the Christian and the worldling. The words, the dress, the actions, should tell for God. Then a holy influence will be shed upon all around them, and even unbelievers will take knowledge of them that they have been with Jesus. If any wish to have their influence tell in favor of truth, let them live out their profession and thus imitate the humble Pattern.

Pride, ignorance, and folly are constant companions. The Lord is displeased with the pride manifested among His professed people. He is dishonored by their conformity to the unhealthful, immodest, and expensive fashions of this degenerate age.

Fashion rules the world; and she is a tyrannical mistress, often compelling her devotees to submit to the greatest inconvenience and discomfort. Fashion taxes without reason and collects without mercy. She has a fascinating power, and stands ready to criticize and ridicule the poor if they do not follow in her wake at any cost, even the sacrifice of life itself. Satan triumphs that his devices succeed so well, and Death laughs at the health-destroying folly and blind zeal of the worshipers at Fashion's shrine.

To protect the people of God from the corrupting influence of the world, as well as to promote physical and moral health, the dress reform was introduced among us. It was not intended to be a yoke of bondage, but a blessing; not to increase labor, but to save labor; not to add to the expense of dress, but to save expense. It would distinguish God's people from the world, and thus serve as a barrier against its fashions and follies. He who knows the end from the beginning, who understands our nature and our needs,—our compassionate Redeemer,—saw our dangers and difficulties, and condescended to give us timely warning and instruction concerning our habits of life, even in the proper selection of food and clothing.

Satan is constantly devising some new style of dress that shall prove an injury to physical and moral health; and he exults when he sees professed Christians eagerly accepting the fashions that he has invented. The amount of physical suffering created by unnatural and unhealthful dress cannot be estimated. Many have become lifelong invalids through their compliance with the demands of fashion. Displacements and deformities, cancers and other terrible diseases, are among the evils resulting from fashionable dress.

Many a style of dress that was inappropriate and even ridiculous has been generally adopted because it was the fashion. Among these pernicious fashions were the large hoops, which frequently caused indecent exposure of the person. In contrast with this was presented a neat, modest, becoming dress, which would dispense with the hoops and the trailing skirts, and provide for the proper clothing of the limbs. But dress reform comprised more than shortening the dress and clothing the limbs. It included every article of dress upon the person. It lifted the weights from the hips by suspending the skirts from the shoulders. It removed the tight corsets, which compress the lungs, the stomach, and other internal organs, and induce curvature of the spine and an almost countless train of diseases. Dress reform proper provided for the protection and development of every part of the body.

To those who consistently adopted the reform dress, appreciating its advantages and cheerfully taking their position in opposition to pride and fashion, it proved a blessing. When properly made, it was a becoming and consistent dress, and recommended itself to persons of candid mind, even among those not of our faith.

The question may be asked: "Why has this dress been laid aside, and for what reason has dress reform ceased to be advocated?" The reason for this change I will here briefly state. While many of our sisters accepted this reform from principle, others opposed the simple, healthful style of dress which it advocated. It required much labor to introduce this reform among our people. It was not enough to present before our sisters the advantages of such a dress and to convince them that it would meet the approval of God. Fashion had so strong a hold upon them that they were slow to break away from its control, even to obey the dictates of reason and conscience. And many who professed to accept the reform made no change in their wrong habits of dress, except in shortening the skirts and clothing the limbs.

Nor was this all. Some who adopted the reform were not content to show by example the advantages of the dress, giving, when asked, their reasons for adopting it, and letting the matter rest there. They sought to control others' conscience by their own. If they wore it, others must put it on. They forgot that none were to be compelled to wear the reform dress.

It was not my duty to urge the subject upon my sisters. After presenting it before them as it had been shown me, I left them to their own conscience. Reformatory action is always attended with sacrifice. It demands that love of ease, selfish interest, and the lust of ambition be held in subjection to the principles of right. Whoever has the courage to reform must encounter obstacles. He will be opposed by the conservatism of those whose business or pleasure brings them in contact with the votaries of fashion, and who will lose caste by the change.

Much unhappy feeling was created by those who were constantly urging the reform dress upon their sisters. With extremists, this reform seemed to constitute the sum and substance of their religion. It was the theme of conversation and the burden of their hearts; and their minds were thus diverted from God and the truth. They failed to cherish the spirit of Christ and manifested a great lack of true courtesy. Instead of prizing the dress for its real advantages, they seemed to be proud of its singularity. Perhaps no question has ever come up among us which has caused such development of character as has the dress reform.

While many of the young adopted this dress, some endeavored to shun the cross by indulging in extra trimmings, thus making it a curse rather than a blessing. To those who put it on reluctantly, from a sense of duty, it became a grievous yoke. Still others, who were apparently the most zealous reformers, manifested a sad lack of order and neatness in their dress. It was not made according to the approved pattern. Some would have a variety suit—dress of one material, sack of another, and pants of still another. Others wore the skirt very long, so that only about an inch of the pants could be seen, thus making the dress ill-proportioned and out of taste. These grotesque and untidy costumes disgusted many who would have been pleased with the reform dress proper.

Some were greatly troubled because I did not make the dress a test question, and still others because I advised those who had unbelieving husbands or children not to adopt the reform dress, as it might lead to unhappiness that would counteract all the good to be derived from its use. For years I carried the burden of this work and labor to establish uniformity of dress among our sisters.

In a vision given me at Battle Creek, January 3, 1875, I was shown the state of things which I have here represented, and that the wide diversity in dress was an injury to the cause of truth. That which would have proved a blessing, if uniformly adopted and properly worn, had been made a reproach, and, in some cases, even a disgrace.

Some who wore the dress sighed over it as a heavy burden. The language of their hearts was: "Anything but this. If we felt free to lay off this peculiar style, we would willingly adopt a plain, untrimmed dress of ordinary length. The limbs could be as warmly clothed as before, and we could secure all the physical benefits, with less effort. It requires much labor to prepare the reform dress in a proper manner." Murmuring and complaining were fast destroying vital godliness.

I had no burden of testimony on the subject of dress. I made no reference to it in any way, either to advocate or to condemn. It was the Lord's purpose to prove His professed people and reveal the motives of their hearts. At camp meetings I seldom had anything to say upon the subject. I avoided all questions and answered no letters.

One year ago the subject of dress was again presented before me. I saw that our sisters were departing from the simplicity of the gospel. The very ones who had felt that the reform dress required unnecessary labor, and who claimed that they would not be influenced by the spirit of the world, had now taken up the fashions they once condemned. Their dresses were arranged with all the unnecessary adornments of worldlings in a manner unbecoming to Christians and entirely at variance with our faith.

Thus has been developed the pride of heart indulged by a people that profess to have come out from the world and to be separate. Inspiration declares that the friendship of the world is enmity with God; yet His professed people have expended their God-given time and means upon the altar of fashion.

Our people have been steadily retrograding in the work of reform. Wisdom and judgment have seemed paralyzed. Selfishness and love of display have been corrupting the heart and deteriorating the character. There is a growing disposition to sacrifice health and the favor of God upon the altar of ever-changing, never-satisfying fashion.

There is no style of dress more appropriate to be worn at the sanitarium than the reform dress. The idea entertained by some, that it would detract from the dignity or usefulness of that institution, is a mistake. It is just such a dress as one would expect to find there, and should not have been discarded. In this suit the helpers could perform their work with far less effort than is now required. Such a dress would preach its own sermon to the devotees of fashion. The contrast between their own unhealthful, beruffled, trailing garments and the reform dress, properly represented, suggestive as it is of convenience and ease in using the limbs, would have been most instructive. Many of the patients would have made greater improvement had they accepted the dress reform.

We regret that any influence should have been brought to bear against this neat, modest, healthful dress. The natural heart is ever pleading in favor of worldly customs, and any influence tells with tenfold power when exerted in the wrong direction.

While none were compelled to adopt the reform dress, our people could and should have appreciated its advantages and accepted it as a blessing. The evil results of an opposite course may now be seen. At the sanitarium, physicians and helpers have greatly departed from the Lord's instructions in regard to dress. Simplicity is now rare. Instead of neat, unadorned apparel, which the pen of Inspiration has prescribed, almost every style of fashionable dress may be seen. Here, as elsewhere, the very ones who complained of the labor required to prepare the reform dress have now gone to great extremes in needless adornment.

All this involves so much time and labor that many are obliged to hire their work done at twice what it would have cost had the garments been made in simplicity as becomes women professing godliness. The making of these fashionable dresses frequently costs more than the dress itself. And double the value of the material is often expended for the trimmings. Here pride and vanity are displayed, and a great lack of true principle is seen. If they would be content with plain, simple clothing, many who are dependent on their weekly earnings could do the most of their own sewing. But this is now impossible, and the dressmaker's bill takes from their small wages a considerable sum.

God designed the reform dress as a barrier to prevent the hearts of our sisters from becoming alienated from Him by following the fashions of the world. Those who removed that barrier did not take upon themselves the burden to avert the dangers which must follow. Some in responsible positions have exerted an influence in favor of worldly customs and entirely at variance with the Bible standard. They have done their part in bringing about the present state of worldliness and backsliding.

God has been testing His people. He allowed the testimony concerning dress to become silent, that our sisters might follow their own inclination and thus develop the real pride existing in their hearts. It was to prevent the present state of worldliness that the reform dress was recommended. Many scorned the idea that this dress was necessary to preserve them from following the fashions; but the Lord has permitted them to prove that pride was cherished in their hearts, and that this was just what they would do. It is now shown that they needed the restriction which the reform dress imposed.

If all our sisters would adopt a simple, unadorned dress of modest length, the uniformity thus established would be far more pleasing to God, and would exert a more salutary influence on the world, than the diversity presented four years ago. As our sisters would not generally accept the reform dress as it should be worn, another, less objectionable style is now presented. It is free from needless trimmings, free from the looped-up, tied back overskirts. It consists of a plain sack or loose-fitting basque, and skirt, the latter short enough to avoid the mud and filth of the streets. The material should be free from large plaids and figures, and plain in color. The same attention should be given to the clothing of the limbs as with the short dress.

Will my sisters accept this style of dress and refuse to imitate the fashions that are devised by Satan and continually changing? No one can tell what freak fashion will take next. Worldlings whose only care is, "What shall we eat, and what shall we wear?" should not be our criterion.

Some have said: "After I wear out this dress, I will make the next plainer." Now, if conformity to the fashions of the world is right and pleasing to God, where is the need of making a change at all? But if it is wrong, is it best to continue in the wrong any longer than is positively necessary to make the change? Right here we would remind you of the zeal and earnestness, the skill and perseverance, you manifested in preparing your dress according to the fashion. Would it not be praiseworthy to manifest at least equal earnestness to make it conform to the Bible standard? Precious, God-given time and means were used in fashioning those garments; and now what are you willing to sacrifice to correct the wrong example you have been giving to others?

It is a shame to our sisters to so forget their holy character and their duty to God as to imitate the fashions of the world. There is no excuse for us except the perversity of our own hearts. We do not extend our influence by such a course. It is so inconsistent with our profession of faith that it makes us ridiculous in the eyes of worldlings.

Many a soul who was convinced of the truth has been led to decide against it by the pride and love of the world displayed by our sisters. The doctrine preached seemed clear and harmonious, and the hearers felt that a heavy cross must be lifted by them in taking the truth. When these persons have seen our sisters making so much display in dress, they have said: "This people dress fully as much as we do. They cannot really believe what they profess; and, after all, they must be deceived. If they really thought that Christ was soon coming, and the case of every soul was to be decided for eternal life or death, they could not devote time and money to dress according to the existing fashions." How little did those professedly believing sisters know of the sermon their dress was preaching!

Our words, our actions, and our dress are daily, living preachers, gathering with Christ or scattering abroad. This is no trivial matter to be passed off with a jest. The subject of dress demands serious reflection and much prayer. Many unbelievers have felt that they were not doing right in permitting themselves to be slaves of fashion; but when they see some who make a high profession of godliness dressing as worldlings dress, enjoying frivolous society, they decide that there can be no wrong in such a course.

"We are," said the inspired apostle, "made a spectacle unto the world, and to angels, and to men." All heaven is marking the daily influence which the professed followers of Christ exert upon the world. My sisters, your dress is telling either in favor of Christ and the sacred truth or in favor of the world. Which is it? Remember we must all answer to God for the influence we exert.

We would not by any means encourage carelessness in dress.

Let the attire be appropriate and becoming. Though only a ten-cent calico, it should be kept neat and clean. If there are no ruffles, the wearer cannot only save something by making it herself, but she can save quite a little sum by washing and ironing it herself. Families bind heavy burdens upon themselves by dressing their children in accordance with the fashion. What a waste of time! The little ones would look very inviting in a dress without a ruffle or ornament, but kept sweet and clean. It is such a trifle to wash and iron a dress of this style that the labor is not felt to be a burden.

Why will our sisters rob God of the service due Him, and rob His treasury of money which they should give to His cause, to serve the fashions of this age? The first and best thoughts are given to dress; time is squandered and money wasted. The culture of the mind and heart is neglected. The character is considered of less importance than the dress. The ornament of a meek and quiet spirit is of infinite value, and it is the wickedest of folly to waste in frivolous pursuits our opportunities to secure this precious adorning of the soul.

Sisters, we may do a noble work for God if we will. Woman does not know her power. God did not intend that her capabilities should be all absorbed in questioning: What shall I eat? what shall I drink? and wherewithal shall I be clothed? There is a higher purpose for woman, a grander destiny. She should develop and cultivate her powers, for God can employ them in the great work of saving souls from eternal ruin.

On Sunday the popular churches appear more like a theater than a place for the worship of God. Every style of fashionable dress is displayed there. The poor have not courage to enter those houses of worship. The following remarks were made in my hearing by an attendant at one of those fashionable churches: "It affords such a fine opportunity for studying the fashions. I can see the effect of different styles of dress; and, do you know, I gain great benefit in my business by watching the effect of various dresses on different forms and different complexions. Did you notice that grand trail and that lovely hat? I know just how they were made. I have been taking lessons all day, which I shall put to a practical use."

Not one word was said of Christ or of the sermon preached. How, thought I, can Jesus regard that company, with their display of ornaments and extravagant dress? What dishonor is shown to the house of God! Were Christ upon earth, and should He visit such churches, would He not drive out those desecrators of His Father's house?

But the greatest evil is the influence upon the children and youth. Almost as soon as they come into the world they are subjected to fashion's demands. Little children hear more of dress than of their salvation. They see their mothers more earnestly consulting the fashion plates than the Bible. More visits are made to the dry goods dealer and the milliner than to the church. The outward display of dress is made of greater consequence than the adornment of the character. Sharp reprimands are called forth for soiling the fine clothing, and the mind becomes peevish and irritable under continual restraint.

A deformed character does not disturb the mother so much as a soiled dress. The child hears more of dress than of virtue, for the mother is more familiar with fashion than with her Saviour. Her example too often surrounds the young with a poisonous atmosphere. Vice, disguised in fashion's garb, intrudes itself among the children.

Simplicity of dress will make a sensible woman appear to the best advantage. We judge of a person's character by the style of dress worn. Gaudy apparel betrays vanity and weakness. A modest, godly woman will dress modestly. A refined taste, a cultivated mind, will be revealed in the choice of simple and appropriate attire.

There is an ornament that will never perish, that will promote the happiness of all around us in this life, and will shine with undimmed luster in the immortal future. It is the adorning of a meek and lowly spirit. God has bidden us wear the richest dress upon the soul. By every look into the mirror, the worshipers of fashion should be reminded of the neglected soul. Every hour squandered over the toilet should reprove them for leaving the intellect to lie waste. Then there might be a reformation that would elevate and ennoble all the aims and purposes of life. Instead of seeking golden ornaments for the exterior, an earnest effort would be put forth to secure that wisdom which is of more value than fine gold, yea, which is more precious than rubies.

Those who worship at fashion's altar have but little force of character and but little physical energy. They live for no great purpose, and their lives accomplish no worthy end. We meet everywhere women whose whole mind and heart are absorbed in their love of dress and display. The soul of womanhood is dwarfed and belittled, and her thoughts are centered upon her poor, despicable self. As a fashionably dressed young lady was passing several gentlemen on the street, one of them made some inquiries in regard to her. The answer was: "She makes a pretty ornament in her father's house, but otherwise she is of no use." It is deplorable that those who profess to be Christ's disciples should think it a fine thing to imitate the dress and manners of these useless ornaments.

Peter gives valuable instruction concerning the dress of Christian women: "Whose adorning let it not be that outward adorning of plaiting the hair, and of wearing of gold, or of putting on of apparel; but let it be the hidden man of the heart, in that which is not corruptible, even the ornament of a meek and quiet spirit, which is in the sight of God of great price. For after this manner in the old time the holy women also, who trusted in God, adorned themselves." All that we urge is compliance with the injunctions of God's word. Are we Bible readers and followers of Bible teachings? Will we obey God, or conform to the customs of the world? Will we serve God or mammon? Can we expect to enjoy peace of mind and the approval of God while walking directly contrary to the teachings of His word?

The apostle Paul exhorts Christians not to be conformed to the world, but to be transformed by the renewing of the mind, "that ye may prove what is that good, and acceptable, and perfect, will of God." But many who profess to be children of God feel no scruples against conforming to the customs of the world in the wearing of gold and pearls and costly array. Those who are too conscientious to wear these things are regarded as narrow-minded, superstitious, and even fanatical. But it is God who condescends to give us these instructions; they are the declarations of Infinite Wisdom, and those who disregard them do so at their own peril and loss. Those who cling to the ornaments forbidden in God's word cherish pride and vanity in the heart. They desire to attract attention. Their dress says: Look at me; admire me.

Thus the vanity inherent in human nature is steadily increasing by indulgence. When the mind is fixed upon pleasing God alone, all the needless embellishments of the person disappear.

The apostle places the outward adorning in direct contrast with a meek and quiet spirit and then testifies of the comparative value of the latter: "In the sight of God of great price." There is a decided contradiction between the love of outward adorning and the grace of meekness, the quiet spirit. It is only when we seek in all things to conform to the will of God that peace and joy will reign in the soul.

The love of dress endangers the morals and makes woman the opposite of the Christian lady characterized by modesty and sobriety. Showy, extravagant dress too often encourages lust in the heart of the wearer and awakens base passions in the heart of the beholder. God sees that the ruin of the character is frequently preceded by the indulgence of pride and vanity in dress. He sees that the costly apparel stifles the desire to do good.

The more means persons expend in dress, the less they can have to feed the hungry and clothe the naked; and the streams of beneficence, which should be constantly flowing, are dried up. Every dollar saved by denying one's self of useless ornaments may be given to the needy or may be placed in the Lord's treasury to sustain the gospel, to send missionaries to foreign countries, to multiply publications to carry rays of light to souls in the darkness of error. Every dollar used unnecessarily deprives the spender of a precious opportunity to do good.

My sister, how much time have you spent on needless trimming, time for which you must render an account to God? How much money expended to please your fancy and win the admiration of hearts as vain as your own? It was God's money. How much good you might have done with it! And what a loss have you sustained in this life, and in the future, immortal life, by not doing this! Every soul will be judged according to the deeds done in the body. God reads purposes and motives. Every work and every secret thing is open to His all-seeing eye. No thought, word, or action escapes His notice. He knows whether we love and glorify Him or please and exalt ourselves. He knows whether we set our affections upon things above, where Christ sitteth at the right hand of God, or upon things earthly, sensual, and devilish.

When you place a useless or extravagant article of clothing upon your person, you are withholding from the naked. When you spread your tables with a needless variety of costly food, you are neglecting to feed the hungry. How stands your record, professed Christian? Do not, I beseech you, lay out in foolish and hurtful indulgences that which God requires in His treasury, and the portion which should be given to the poor. Let us not clothe ourselves with costly apparel, but, like women professing godliness, with good works. Let not the cry of the widow and the fatherless go up to heaven against us. Let not the blood of souls be found on our garments. Let not precious probationary time be squandered in cherishing pride of heart. Are there no poor to be visited? no dim eyes for whom you can read the word of God? no desponding, discouraged ones that need your words of comfort and your prayers?

As God has prospered you, has not the indulgence of pride and vanity been steadily increasing? While you are devoting precious time to the study of dress, the inward adorning is neglected; there is no growth in grace. Instead of becoming more heavenly-minded, you are becoming more and more earthly-minded. Foolish and hurtful lusts, groveling appetites, becloud your sense of sacred things. Why will not everyone who professes to love Jesus flee from these soul-destroying indulgences! The world is crazy after show and fashion and pleasure. Licentiousness is steadily and fearfully on the increase. Why will not Christians be true to their high profession!

Christ is ashamed of His professed followers. Wherein do we bear any resemblance to Him? Wherein does our dress conform to the Bible requirements? I do not want the sins of the people upon me, and I will give the trumpet a certain sound. For years I have borne a plain and decided testimony upon this subject, in print and upon the speaker's stand. I have not shunned to declare the whole counsel of God. I must be clear of the blood of all. The fact that worldliness and pride bear almost universal sway is no excuse for one Christian to do as others do. God has said: "Thou shalt not follow a multitude to do evil."

Do not, my sisters, trifle longer with your own souls and with God. I have been shown that the main cause of your backsliding is your love of dress. This leads to the neglect of grave responsibilities, and you find yourselves with scarcely a spark of the love of God in your hearts. Without delay, renounce the cause of your backsliding, because it is sin against your own soul and against God. Be not hardened by the deceitfulness of sin. Fashion is deteriorating the intellect and eating out the spirituality of our people.

Obedience to fashion is pervading our Seventh-day Adventist churches and is doing more than any other power to separate our people from God. I have been shown that our church rules are very deficient. All exhibitions of pride in dress, which is forbidden in the word of God, should be sufficient reason for church discipline. If there is a continuance, in face of warnings and appeals and entreaties, to still follow the perverse will, it may be regarded as proof that the heart is in no way assimilated to Christ. Self, and only self, is the object of adoration, and one such professed Christian will lead many away from God.

There is a terrible sin upon us as a people, that we have permitted our church members to dress in a manner inconsistent with their faith. We must arise at once and close the door against the allurements of fashion. Unless we do this, our churches will become demoralized.

63. Proper Education

Education comprises more than a knowledge of books. Proper education includes not only mental discipline, but that training which will secure sound morals and correct deportment. We have had many fears that those who take students into their houses will not realize their responsibility and will neglect to exert a proper influence over these youth. Thus students will fail to obtain all the benefit which they might receive at the college. The question too often arises: "Am I my brother's keeper?' What care, what burden or responsibility, should I have for the students who occupy rooms in our houses?" I answer: The very same interest that you have for your own children.

Says Christ: "Love one another, as I have loved you." The souls of the youth that are brought under your roof are as precious in the eyes of the Lord as are the souls of your own dear children. When young men and women are separated from the softening, subduing influences of the home circle, it is the duty of those who have the care of them to make home influences for them. They would thus supply a great lack and would be doing a work for God as verily as the minister in the desk. To throw around these students an influence which would preserve them from temptations to immorality, and lead them to Jesus, is a work which heaven would approve.

Grave responsibilities rest upon those who reside at the great center of the work, where are important interests to be sustained. Those who choose their homes at Battle Creek should be men and women of faith, of wisdom, and of prayer.

Hundreds of youth of various dispositions and of different education are associated in the school, and great care as well as much patience is required to balance in the right direction minds that have been warped by bad management. Some have never been disciplined, and others have been governed too much, and have felt, when away from the vigilant hands that held the reins of control, perhaps too tightly, that they were free to do as they pleased. They despise the very thought of restraint. These varying elements brought together in our college bring care, burdens, and weighty responsibility, not only upon teachers, but on the entire church.

The students at our college are exposed to manifold temptations. They will be brought in contact with individuals of almost every stamp of mind and morals. Those who have any religious experience are censurable if they do not place themselves in a position to resist every evil influence. But many choose to follow inclination. They do not consider that they must make or mar their own happiness. It is in their own power to so improve their time and opportunities as to develop a character that will make them happy and useful.

The youth who reside at Battle Creek are in constant danger because they do not connect with heaven. If they would be true to their profession they might be living missionaries for God. By manifesting Christian interest, sympathy, and love, they might greatly benefit the youth who come to Battle Creek from other places. An earnest effort should be made to keep these strangers from choosing superficial, frivolous, pleasure-seeking associates. This class exert a demoralizing influence upon the college, upon the sanitarium, and upon the office of publication. Our numbers are constantly increasing, and vigilance and zeal to keep the fort are steadily decreasing. If they will open their eyes, all may see whither these things are tending.

Many move to Battle Creek to give their children the advantages of the college, and at the same time do not feel their own responsibility in making this move. They do not realize that something more is to be considered than their own selfish interest; that they may be a hindrance instead of a blessing, unless they come with the full purpose to do good as well as to get good. Yet none need lose their spirituality in coming to Battle Creek; if we will follow Christ, it is not in the power of any to lead us astray from the path cast up for the ransomed of the Lord to walk in. No one is compelled to copy the errors of professed Christians. If he sees the mistakes and faults of others, he will be responsible before God and before his fellow men if he does not set a better example. But some make the faults of others an excuse for their own defects of character, and even copy the very objectionable traits which they condemn. Such persons strengthen those of whom they complain as pursuing an unchristian course. With their eyes open they walk into the enemy's snare. Not a few in Battle Creek have pursued this course. Some have come to the place where our institutions are located, with the selfish motive of making money. This class will be no help to the youth either by precept or example.

The dangers of the young are greatly increased as they are thrown into the society of a large number of their own age of varied character and habits of life. Under these circumstances many parents are inclined to relax rather than redouble their own efforts to guard and control their children. Thus they cast a tremendous burden upon those who feel the responsibility. When these parents see that their children are becoming demoralized, they are inclined to find fault with those who have charge of the work at Battle Creek, when the evils have been caused by just such a course as these parents themselves have pursued.

Instead of uniting with those who bear the burdens, to lift up the standard of morals, and working with heart and soul in the fear of God to correct the wrongs in their children, many parents soothe their own consciences by saying: "My children are no worse than others." They seek to conceal the glaring wrongs which God hates, lest their children shall become offended and take some desperate course. If the spirit of rebellion is in their hearts, far better subdue it now than permit it to increase and strengthen by indulgence. If parents would do their duty, we should see a different state of things. Many of these parents have backslidden from God. They do not have wisdom from Him to perceive the devices of Satan and to resist his snares.

In this age of the world, children should have strict watchcare. They should be advised and restrained. Eli was cursed of God because he did not promptly and decidedly restrain his wicked sons. There are parents at Battle Creek who are doing no better than did Eli. They are afraid to control their children. They see them serving Satan with a high hand and pass it by as a disagreeable necessity which must be endured because it cannot be cured.

Every son and daughter should be called to account if absent from home at night. Parents should know what company their children are in and at whose house they spend their evenings. Some children deceive their parents with falsehoods to avoid exposure of their wrong course. There are those who seek the society of corrupt companions and secretly visit saloons and other forbidden places of resort in the city. There are students who visit the billiard rooms, and who engage in card playing, flattering themselves that there is no danger. Since their object is merely amusement, they feel perfectly safe. It is not the lower grade alone who do this. Some who have been carefully reared, and educated to look upon such things with abhorrence, are venturing upon the forbidden ground.

The young should be controlled by firm principle, that they may rightly improve the powers which God has given them. But youth follow impulse so much and so blindly, without reference to principle, that they are constantly in danger. Since they cannot always have the guidance and protection of parents and guardians they need to be trained to self-reliance and self-control. They must be taught to think and act from conscientious principle.

Those who are engaged in study should have relaxation. The mind must not be constantly confined to close thought, for the delicate mental machinery becomes worn. The body as well as the mind must have exercise. But there is great need of temperance in amusements, as in every other pursuit. And the character of these amusements should be carefully and thoroughly considered. Every youth should ask himself: What influence will these amusements have on physical, mental, and moral health? Will my mind become so infatuated as to forget God? shall I cease to have His glory before me?

Card playing should be prohibited. The associations and tendencies are dangerous. The prince of the powers of darkness presides in the gaming room and wherever there is card playing. Evil angels are familiar guests in these places. There is nothing in such amusements beneficial to soul or body. There is nothing to strengthen the intellect, nothing to store it with valuable ideas for future use. The conversation is upon trivial and degrading subjects. There is heard the unseemly jest, the low, vile talk, which lowers and destroys the true dignity of manhood. These games are the most senseless, useless, unprofitable, and dangerous employments the youth can have. Those who engage in card playing become intensely excited and soon lose all relish for useful and elevating occupations. Expertness in handling cards will soon lead to a desire to put this knowledge and tact to some use for personal benefit. A small sum is staked, and then a larger, until a thirst for gaming is acquired, which leads to certain ruin. How many has this pernicious amusement led to every sinful practice, to poverty, to prison, to murder, and to the gallows! And yet many parents do not see the terrible gulf of ruin that is yawning for our youth.

Among the most dangerous resorts for pleasure is the theater. Instead of being a school of morality and virtue, as is so often claimed, it is the very hotbed of immorality. Vicious habits and sinful propensities are strengthened and confirmed by these entertainments. Low songs, lewd gestures, expressions, and attitudes, deprave the imagination and debase the morals. Every youth who habitually attends such exhibitions will be corrupted in principle. There is no influence in our land more powerful to poison the imagination, to destroy religious impressions, and to blunt the relish for the tranquil pleasures and sober realities of life than theatrical amusements. The love for these scenes increases with every indulgence, as the desire for intoxicating drinks strengthens with its use. The only safe course is to shun the theater, the circus, and every other questionable place of amusement.

There are modes of recreation which are highly beneficial to both mind and body. An enlightened, discriminating mind will find abundant means for the entertainment and diversion, from sources not only innocent, but instructive. Recreation in the open air, the contemplation of the works of God in nature, will be of highest benefit.

The great God, whose glory shines from the heavens, and whose divine hand upholds millions of worlds, is our Father. We have only to love Him, trust in Him, as little children in faith and confidence, and He will accept us as His sons and daughters, and we shall be heirs to all the inexpressible glory of the eternal world. All the meek will He guide in judgment, the meek will

He teach His way. If we will walk in obedience to His will, learn cheerfully and diligently the lessons of His providence, by and by He will say: Child, come home to the heavenly mansions I have prepared for you.

64. Accountability to God

We are accountable to God for the wise improvement of every mental faculty and every physical power. Who can measure his responsibility? We must render an account for the influence which we exert. That which seems to us to be a small defect in our character will be reproduced in others in a greater degree, and thus the influence we have exerted for evil may be increased and perpetuated.

Let none venture to speak lightly of the cautions given by those whose duty it is to guard their moral and spiritual welfare. The words may seem to be of little consequence, producing only a momentary impression on the minds of the hearers. But this is not all. In many cases these words find a response in the unsanctified hearts of youth who have never submitted to caution or restraint. The influence of a thoughtless word may affect a soul's eternal destiny. Every person is exerting an influence upon the lives of others.

We must be either as a light to brighten and cheer their path, or as a desolating tempest to destroy. We are either leading our associates upward to happiness and immortal life, or downward to sorrow and eternal ruin. No man will perish alone in his iniquity. However contracted may be one's sphere of influence, it is exerted either for good or for evil. One man upon his deathbed exclaimed: "Gather up my influence, and bury it with me." Could this be done? No, no; like the thistle seed it had been borne everywhere and had taken root and would yield an abundant harvest.

There are few who form evil habits deliberately. By frequent repetition of wrong acts, habits are formed unconsciously and become so firmly established that the most persistent effort is required to effect a change. We should never be slow in breaking up a sinful habit. Unless evil habits are conquered, they will conquer us and destroy our happiness. There are many poor creatures, now miserable, disappointed, and degraded, a curse to all around them, who might have been useful and happy men had they but improved their opportunities. Many youth waste the precious hours of life in idle daydreaming. Such persons have not much force of character or strength of principle. Many drift about, the sport of every changing circumstance.

They are ever looking to others for sympathy, vainly depending upon others for happiness. All who pursue this course will wreck their hopes, both for this life and for the life to come. Young persons who are thrown into one another's society may make their association a blessing or a curse. They may edify, bless, and strengthen one another, improving in deportment, in disposition, in knowledge; or, by permitting themselves to become careless and unfaithful, they may exert only a demoralizing influence.

Jesus will be the helper of all who put their trust in Him. Those who are connected with Christ have happiness at their command. They follow in the path where their Saviour leads, for His sake crucifying self with the affections and lusts. These persons have built their hopes on Christ, and the storms of earth are powerless to sweep them from the sure foundation.

It rests with yourselves, young men and women, whether you will become persons of trust, of integrity and real usefulness. You should be ready and resolute to take your stand for the right, under all circumstances. Our wrong habits cannot be taken to heaven with us, and unless overcome here, they will shut us out of the abode of the righteous. Bad habits, when opposed, will offer the most vigorous resistance; but if the warfare is kept up with energy and perseverance, they may be conquered.

In order to form correct habits, we should seek the company of persons of sound moral and religious influence. We should constantly bear in mind that we may be fitting to inhabit the heavenly courts. The precious hours of probation are granted that we may remove every defect from the character; and we should seek to do this, not only that we may obtain the future life, but that we may be useful here. Young men and women should regard a good character as a capital of more value than gold or silver or stocks. It will be unaffected by panics and failures, and will bring rich returns when earthly possessions shall be swept away.

The youth need a higher, nobler view of the value of Christian character. Sin blinds the eyes and defiles the heart. Integrity, firmness, and perseverance are qualities which all should seek earnestly to cultivate; for they clothe the possessor with a power which is irresistible, a power which makes him strong to do good, strong to resist evil, strong to bear adversity. It is here that true excellence of character shines forth with the greatest luster.

Strength of character consists of two things—power of will and power of self-control. Many youth mistake strong, uncontrolled passion for strength of character; but the truth is that he who is mastered by his passions is a weak man. The real greatness and nobility of the man is measured by the power of the feelings that he subdues, not by the power of the feelings that subdue him. The strongest man is he, who, while sensitive to abuse, will yet restrain passion and forgive his enemies. Such men are true heroes.

Many have such meager ideas of what they may become that they will ever remain dwarfed and narrow, when, if they would improve the powers which God has given them, they might develop a noble character and exert an influence that would win souls to Christ. Knowledge is power; but intellectual ability, without goodness of heart, is a power for evil.

God has given us our intellectual and moral powers, but to a great extent every person is the architect of his own character. Every day the structure is going up. The word of God warns us to take heed how we build, to see that our building is founded upon the eternal Rock. The time is coming when our work will stand revealed just as it is. Now is the time for all to cultivate the powers which God has given them, that they may form characters for usefulness here and for a higher life hereafter.

Every act of life, however unimportant, has its influence in forming the character. A good character is more precious than worldly possessions, and the work of forming it is the noblest in which men can engage.

Characters formed by circumstance are changeable and discordant—a mass of contraries. Their possessors have no high aim or purpose in life. They have no ennobling influence upon the characters of others. They are purposeless and powerless.

The little span of life allotted us here should be wisely improved. God would have His church a living, devoted, working church. But our people, as a body, are far from this now. God calls for strong, brave souls, for active, living Christians, who are following the true Pattern, and who will exert a decided influence for God and the right. The Lord has committed to us, as a sacred trust, most important and solemn truths, and we should show their influence upon our lives and characters.

www.ingramcontent.com/pod-product-compliance
Lightning Source LLC
Chambersburg PA
CBHW070646150426
42811CB00051B/762